.2 on polit. hunting.
Political hunting: large numbers, no material profit: pp. 8–9.

Cavalry's role in prevailing military practices crucial to the political hunt, pp. 15-16. Persia = core area, p. 14.

The Royal Hunt in Eurasian History

ENCOUNTERS WITH ASIA

Victor H. Mair, Series Editor

Encounters with Asia is an interdisciplinary series dedicated to the exploration of all the major regions and cultures of this vast continent. Its time-frame extends from the prehistoric to the contemporary; its geographic scope ranges from the Urals and the Caucasus to the Pacific. A particular focus of the series is the Silk Road in all of its ramifications: religion, art, music, medicine, science, trade, and so forth. Among the disciplines represented in this series are history, archeology, anthropology, ethnography, and linguistics. The series aims particularly to clarify the complex interrelationships among various peoples within Asia, and also with societies beyond Asia.

The Royal Hunt in Eurasian History

Thomas T. Allsen

PENN

University of Pennsylvania Press
Philadelphia

Publication of this volume was assisted by a subvention from the Guggenheim foundation.

Printed in the United States of America on acid-free paper

10 9 8 7 6 5 4 3 2 1

Published by
University of Pennsylvania Press
Philadelphia, Pennsylvania 19104-4112

Library of Congress Cataloging-in-Publication Data

Allsen, Thomas T.
The royal hunt in Eurasian history / Thomas T. Allsen.
p. cm.—(Encounters with Asia)
Includes bibliographical references (p.) and index.
ISBN-13: 978-0-8122-3926-3
ISBN-10: 0-8122-3926-1 (cloth : alk. paper)
1. Hunting—Political aspects—Eurasia—History. 2. Kings and rulers—Eurasia—Social life and customs—History. 3. Animals and civilization—Eurasia—History. I. Title. II. Series
SK21.A46 2006
639'.109—dc22 *2005058583*

For

Opal and Kitkat

the

Black Ears in our Household

Contents

1
Hunting Histories

World Histories and the World of Animals

Almost all peoples have explanations, usually articulated in mythology, for the creation of the world, of life and human culture. In these first grand narratives, beginnings or new departures in the cultural sphere are typically attributed to the intervention of the gods or to the inventions of cultural heros. As wisdom inherited from founders, these narratives, rarely challenged from within, commonly retained their relevancy and currency for long periods of time.

There were, however, "evolutionary" alternatives to these mythologies of bestowal, particularly in the Western intellectual tradition, which has produced a long series of theories that divide human historical development into three successive stages.[1] The most familiar of these, and the first to be based on systematic examination of physical remains, is the "three-age system," which posited sequential stone, bronze, and iron ages. This model, first outlined by Scandinavian naturalists in the late eighteenth century, gave rise to a new kind of grand narrative, one that linked cultural evolution to the human ability to manipulate inanimate materials.[2] But this was not the only three-age system then circulating in Europe; another, far older notion going back at least to Varro in the first century B.C.E., maintained that humans passed through three distinct stages in their history: hunting, herding, and agriculture. These stages, what we would now term subsistence systems, were held to be universal and sequential. Long assumed to be self-evident, this theory survived until the end of the nineteenth century, when the German geographer Eduard Hahn convincingly demonstrated that animals were first domesticated by settled farmers, so that the "herding stage," that is, pastoralism in its varied forms, arose from and followed agriculture.[3]

What is striking about this particular conceptualization of cultural development, whatever its chronological failings, is that in an earlier agrarian age history was seen to turn on the relationship of humans to other animate objects; this, of course, in sharp contrast to the three-age system of the early industrial era, which, true to its own terms of reference, tied historical change to inanimate objects, tools, and materials.

While this oldest of the three-age systems has lost its standing as a viable narrative of culture history, it is nonetheless true that the relationship between humans and animals, so integral to this theory, retains its importance even though the development of this relationship through time cannot be accommodated by simplistic unilineal evolutionary formulas.

For our specific purposes, that of writing a hunting history, one helpful way of conceptualizing this intricate web of human-animal interaction is through David Harris's perceptive typology of animal exploitation. In this schema there are three categories of human-animal ecological relationship: predation, protection, and domestication. Predation, obviously, involves scavenging, fishing, and hunting. Protection entails manipulation of the environment to attract or benefit favored prey, or free-range "herding" of wild species, and limited taming of individual young animals as pets or helpmates. Domestication, on the other hand, involves the creation of breeding populations that are maintained over long periods in genetic isolation from their wild progenitors. What is key here is that as human communities move from predation to protection to domestication, there is a decreasing dependence on wild animals for protein and products, and an increasing dependence on domesticated species.[4]

To Harris's admirable exposition of these transitions, I would only add the following as a corollary: with successful domestication of plants and animals, the economic importance of hunting steadily decreases while its political significance steadily increases. And it is the politics of the hunt that forms one of the central themes of this work. But to properly develop this theme, I must first situate this study in the broader context of the various possible types of hunting histories, some of which have been realized and some of which have not.

Pursuing Protein

Because the hunting-gathering method of resource extraction prevailed throughout most of the history of our species, it has been intensely studied by archeologists and ethnographers in a quest to understand the long-term biological and cultural evolution of hominids.[5] Hunting-gathering societies have also been at the center of many prolonged debates in the social sciences concerning the ecological bases of culture and behavior and the methodological controversies over the use of analogy in historical reconstructions. And most recently, hunter-gatherers have been invoked in weighty theoretical disputes over group versus individual selection.[6]

Indeed, much of the extended history of hunter-gatherers has been hotly contested. This is well exemplified in the changing image of such societies over the past one hundred years. From primitive savages, at the mercy of cruel nature, they were recast as the original "affluent society," enjoying a surprising amount of leisure time as well as a good diet, good health, and a large measure of social equality. Much of this, so the argument runs, was lost with the rise of civilization. In such a perspective agriculture is no longer viewed as progress, an improvement in the human condition.[7]

Interpretations of this earliest stage of our hunting history are so varied because the evidence is scarce and difficult to read. Even such a basic question as the relative role and weight of meat and vegetal matter in the diet of early hominids remains a point of dispute. This is so because the acquisition of meat, whatever its nutritional importance, is a complicated question since this source of energy might be "captured" by active hunting or opportunistic scavenging, or by some combination of the two. While more complex societies tend to view scavenging meat from recent kills as inappropriate, this was hardly the case in foraging societies.[8] Indeed, some specialists now argue that population growth in the Later Paleolithic should be associated with "dietary breadth." This expansion and diversification of the human diet, called the "broad spectrum revolution hypothesis," involved increasing utilization of small animals and scavenging in consequence of growing pressure on available resources.[9]

Although disagreement abounds, there is a strong consensus on at least one crucial point: all agree that there were great variations in the hunting-gathering mode. For some societies predation may be generalized, particularly in temperate climes where gathering is important, or highly specialized, particularly in northern latitudes where people live off species such as reindeer or sea mammals. In the view of many scholars it is the extreme plasticity of this method of resource extraction that explains why humans have been able to occupy and successfully exploit a great variety of ecosystems from the high arctic to tropical rain forests.[10]

But hunting was plastic in yet another important way. The advent of domesticated plants and animals, the so-called Neolithic revolution, did not replace or even displace hunting, as is sometimes implied or imagined by evolutionary models in which new modes of production triumph over and destroy the old. In many places hunting as an economic activity "runs parallel" for millennia with new methods of resource extraction, thus greatly complicating hunting, herding, and agricultural histories.[11] This adaptability is reflected in the striking variations in the hunt found among peoples of very similar ethnic and cultural backgrounds. Among the Tungusic speakers of eastern Siberia and northern Manchuria, for example, some groups followed and hunted wild reindeer as their primary occupation, some combined true pastoral nomadism and hunting, some agriculture and hunting, while still others fished in the summer and trapped fur-bearing animals in the winter; moreover, some Tungus hunted only from horseback and some only on foot.[12]

Such variation, fashioned by environmental conditions, historical contingency, and cultural choice, demonstrates the great flexibility built into human hunting: it mutates, combines comfortably with other means of subsistence, and becomes an auxiliary occupation, supplementing the "new" economy in important ways.

The latter adaptation is particularly evident among the pastoral nomads of the Eurasian steppe who seem to have developed a special "herder-hunter mode of production."[13] Nomads hunted for a number of reasons, including the protection of their herds from predators, but food acquisition was always a powerful motive. The importance of game in their diet is widely reported in ancient and medieval literary sources.[14] Moreover, the accumulating archeological evidence points to the same conclusion. For example, during the Khazar era, from the seventh to the tenth century C.E., wild animal bones account for 20–25 percent of the total recovered from many sites along the Don River. The presence of weapons specialized for the chase further underscores the relevance of the hunt for that economy.[15]

In light of these data it would be mistaken to understand the hunt in nomadic societies as simply a means of procuring "survival food" in times of shortage. Game was in fact part of their normal fare and, moreover, part of the haute cuisine regularly served at the courts of nomadic empires. In the eleventh century, envoys from the Chinese Song dynasty (960–1279) to the Liao (907–1125), founded by the Qitan, were repeatedly treated to such delicacies as marinated pheasant and choice cuts of musk deer meat.[16]

In the era of the Mongolian empire, the thirteenth to the fourteenth century, the same culinary patterns and preferences are noted. Marco Polo relates the prevalence of game birds in the imperial cuisine, which we know from Chinese sources were procured by special hunting households (*liehu*) subordinate to the Bureau of Household Provisions (*Xuanhui yuan*).[17] But commoners, too, were dependent on the hunt. Carpini, in Mongolia in the 1240s, was well aware of the dietary importance of the chase, and Rubruck, a decade later, states unequivocally that the Mongols "obtain a large portion of their food by the chase."[18] The reason for this reliance on game is made abundantly clear by Xu Ting, a Song envoy in Mongolia in the 1230s. He reports that "throughout the entire hunting season [of winter] they constantly eat that which they have taken in the chase and so kill fewer sheep."[19] Hunting, therefore, contributed additional calories and, at the same time, spared herd animals which provide the milk products so central to the nomadic diet.[20] In the Eurasian steppe, herders, for very sound economic reasons, were always skilled and active hunters.

It is perhaps more surprising that throughout premodern times sedentary agriculturalists also relied on the hunt to augment their food supply. Writing in sixth-century northern Europe, Gregory of Tours revealingly remarks that droughts and epidemics not only decimated domestic herds but game animals as well.[21] Such losses are coupled in medieval sources because both categories of animals had economic value to the populace, which ate much game. Thus, land in northern and eastern Europe was routinely evaluated not only in terms of its potential productivity for crops and livestock, but also for its potential harvest of fish and game.[22] This was the case, George Duby argues, because in many parts of early medieval Europe agricultural production was insufficient to feed the population, and consequently hunting and gathering still held a prominent place in the domestic economy of noble and peasant.[23] This means, of course, that knowledge of hunting-gathering techniques never died out in these societies, and that while nominally in an "agricultural mode" they continued to draw upon the time-tested practices of a much earlier mode of production for enrichment and, at times, for survival.

Since early medieval Europe was, arguably, one of the less developed agricultural societies in Eurasia, this continued commitment to hunting may be ascribed to special circumstances and therefore deemed exceptional. What then, of the ancient cradles of agriculture? Had they freed themselves from, progressed beyond, these older methods of resource extraction? The answer is no, hunting still had its place in the nutritional life of the early centers of settled life. To begin in the ancient Near East, stag and gazelle were served at the great banquets of the Assyrian king Ashurnasirpal II (r. 884–860 B.C.E.) and there are biblical references to the consumption of venison in the heyday of King Solomon (1 Kings 4.23–24).[24] In the pre-Islamic empires of Iran, those of the Achaemenids (534–330 B.C.E.), Parthians (247 B.C.E.–227 C.E.), and Sasanids (226–651), court and commoners regularly ate the proceeds of the chase.[25] The same pattern of consumption can be documented in the neighboring region of Transcaucasia in late antiquity and the Middle Ages.[26] In more recent times, according to European travelers, the Mughal court also ate much game, while antelope, hare, peacock, and deer, all killed by local hunters, were readily available "at easie Rates" in the coastal cities of India.[27]

More unexpectedly, this pattern prevailed in China, which by many historians' reckoning had the most sophisticated and productive agrarian economy in the world until the rise of modern scientific farming. During the whole of the imperial era, 221 B.C.E. to 1911, wild rabbit and deer supplemented the rural population's diet, and much game was sold in urban centers such as Hangzhou, one of the major cities of the Song era.[28] In the eighteenth and nineteenth centuries, this was still the case in Beijing and other cities of the north, which received from Manchuria, particularly in wintertime when meat was easier to transport, substantial quantities of deer, boar, and game birds.[29]

Beyond the obvious conclusion that the nutritional contribution of hunting to the human diet did not end with the advent of agriculture, even of the most intensive kind, this brief survey reveals another consequential fact: down to very recent times, there was still much wilderness intact, some of it close to major urban centers and to areas of agriculture. This meant that human encounters with wild animals were commonplace, and these often traumatic confrontations had, as we shall see, serious political ramifications.

Pursuing Profit

Not only did hunting for food continue long after domestication, but the very existence of agricultural societies provided the impetus for the emergence of new types of hunting, one form of which was highly commercialized. This was the specialized hunting for various animal products which were then traded over long distances. In some instances these hunters came from societies, such as ancient Egypt, with a strong economic and ideological commitment to agriculture.[30] Their presence in such environments is evident, too, in the laws of imperial China, which made provision for the regulation and taxation of the professional hunters in their midst.[31]

But what is more intriguing is that even true hunter-gatherers became enmeshed in long-distance commercial networks. One little appreciated example of this phenomenon is the trade in bird-of-paradise plumes; procured in New Guinea, these colorful objects were sent to China, India, West Asia, and into the Pacific for around 2000 years.[32] More familiar is the northern fur trade, in which hunter-gatherers became linked with large-scale, international trading systems through barter arrangements and tributary relationships. Between the ninth and twelfth centuries, for instance, the indigenous peoples of the Volga-Ural region and Western Siberia supplied high-quality furs—sable, ermine, and black fox—to the Bulghars on the middle Volga, who traded them to merchants who then carried the furs to Middle Eastern markets where they commanded high prices.[33]

It is evident from even these few examples that many of the animal products that traveled well were prestige goods from remote and storied lands. In terms of volume and value, fur was probably the most important but tusks and horns also moved great distances. From prehistoric times ivory was in great demand because of its intrinsic qualities, its color, coolness, texture, and durability, as well as its symbolic power.[34] More surprising, perhaps, was the extensive traffic in walrus tusk and narwhal horn, products harvested in the Arctic Ocean and the North Pacific, that in the Middle Ages reached markets from China to the Islamic world.[35]

We need to consider as well the traffic in live animals, a topic to which we will return later. For the moment, a single illustration will suffice to bring home its commercial potential. In the 1680s, according to eyewitness testimony, the king of Siam was continuously engaged in the trapping of wild elephants for the export trade to India. The three to four hundred animals exported annually were, we are told, an important source of income for the royal treasury.[36]

While rarities and exotica dominated this long-distance traffic in animals and animal products, and therefore supplied the incentive for much of the commercial hunting, more mundane commodities are also on record. In the seventeenth and eighteenth centuries, Siam also exported large quantities of deer hides to Japan.[37] There were, then, niches for commercial hunters in most premodern societies; the persistent royal interest in their activities shows it to have been a profitable business, one that is still actively pursued today, and one deserving of more scholarly attention than it has received to date.[38]

Pursuing Power

Since, as previously discussed, most of our history unfolds during the hunting-gathering stage, this method of resource extraction has been subject to intense scrutiny. But once plants and animals are domesticated, hunting loses its privileged status as a key element in a universally recognized mode of production. Scholarly interest in its post-Neolithic history, therefore, drops off precipitously, with the notable exception of the northern fur trade in medieval and early modern times.[39] This relative lack of interest is mistaken on several counts: first, as just argued, hunting continued to have an important economic function, as a source of nutriment and trade goods, and second, hunting, particularly on the elite level, performed in most agrarian and pastoral societies an array of important political functions.

Much of this has been missed, or at least undervalued. Part of the problem is that hunting was so common that it tends to be acknowledged and then ignored. Further, when discussed at all, the history of hunting has been construed too narrowly; for many, the chase is simply an aspect of elite behavior to be included in discussions of everyday life in medieval Europe.[40]

Scholarly writing on the most recent history of hunting continues this approach, concentrating on its recreational aspects in the West and its one-time colonies, and has become enmeshed in contemporary environmental debates.

The hunter's controversial role as conservationist, naturalist, and game manager is, of course, a legitimate and vital part of modern environmental history.[41] But it should also be recognized that these same issues have a much longer history, one closely tied to the royal hunt. To fully uncover these connections, it is necessary to cast a wider thematic, geographical, and chronological net. A start in this direction has been made by students of the medieval Mongols who have recognized that their hunts served a number of purposes in common with other steppe peoples.[42] Still, it seems to me that an even larger context is called for, one that compares political hunting in different cultural and ecological zones of Eurasia over the long term. Only in this way can the multiple functions of the royal hunt be identified and clarified.

This study concentrates on elites and royal persons, and thus on hunting as a predominantly political activity. And while avowedly writing a history from the top down, the general populace and, of equal importance, the animals, will receive their share of attention. So, too, will the environmental and cultural dimensions of the royal hunt; to my mind, the exercise of political authority, the appropriation of nature, and the diffusion of culture are closely entwined in the history of Eurasia.

As my focus is on political hunting, I must distinguish it from the economic variety. First and most important, there is the matter of numbers—as Fernand Braudel has reminded us, numbers do matter. Subsistence hunting can be conducted individually or by collectives of variable but limited size. In agricultural and pastoral societies, however, hunts, or drives, routinely involve far larger numbers, sometimes entire kin groups or settlements and, when conducted on this basis, there is a noticeable increase in ceremonial and political activity. Elaborate feasts are prepared and the organizers of the hunt are recognized and honored, thus according them increased prestige and influence.[43] Large-scale royal hunts involving thousands or tens of thousands of participants were the rule, not the exception, and their magnitude invested this form of hunting with political meaning. Indeed, this is true of any large-scale organizational effort, whether building projects or the production of ceremonies, celebrations, and entertainments. In such cases, the means of production is as important as the product itself. In our case, the royal hunt displays a ruler's ability to marshal and order labor, military manpower, and individuals (both humans and animals) with very special skills. Moreover, by the very nature of the hunt, these abilities were dramatically demonstrated throughout the countryside for the edification of subjects. And a forceful demonstration in one sphere, such as the hunt, strongly implies an equivalent competency in others, such as tax collection or bandit suppression. The royal hunt thus served as an effective reaffirmation of a ruler's capacity to manage large-scale enterprises, that is, to govern.[44]

A second difference between political and economic hunting is also susceptible to quantification, at least in principle. Subsistence hunting was primarily a means of capturing energy and had therefore to be efficient; that is, the energy returns over the long term had to exceed the energy investments. In this sense one can speak of subsistence or commercial hunting as a predominantly economic activity. In contrast, a royal hunt hardly ever returned energy. With their many participants and spectators, their impedimenta, and bag of inedible game—jackals, tigers, and so on—royal hunts typically resulted in a net energy loss. Indeed, such hunts, it is fair to say, were all about the lavish expenditure of energy, and such expenditures are preeminently political acts.[45]

Before proceeding further, I should stress that I do not mean to imply that there were two "pure" types of hunting, the one exclusively for economic ends, the other for political. On the contrary, the motives and objectives for human hunting fall within a continuum, along which there are many fine gradations and unexpected admixtures.

We start at the economic end, where the pursuit of protein is paramount, crucial for survival. But even at the extremes there are no pure types. It is true that in hunting and gathering bands, politics, whether external or internal, is kept at a minimum; indeed, avoidance, departure, and self-segregation are major mechanisms of the political process. Still, it would be mistaken to think of subsistence hunters as completely apolitical. Band societies do have politics, but of a special kind. There is maneuvering over a number of issues, both vital and trivial, that require a collective response: the resolution of social conflict among individual members, questions of relationships with outsiders, and decisions concerning movements to new camping/hunting grounds. The political processes in band societies are therefore informal, typically involving discussions that lead to consensus, and it is in the context of private discussion and public debate that leadership is exercised. Personal power is based, not on coercion, but on individual knowledge, experience, persuasiveness, and force of personality. To use George Silverbauer's apt phrase, in such societies "leadership is authoritative, rather than authoritarian."[46]

In the middle range of the continuum there are those admixtures in which economic and political motivations are more or less evenly balanced. Manchuria can serve as an illustration. Here the subsistence pattern from the Neolithic down to the nineteenth century was a combination of small-scale agriculture, sedentary animal husbandry, craft production, fishing, and hunting—hunting for protein, for profit, and in the quest for political power. Such a combination is particularly well documented in the case of the Jürchen, founders of the Jin dynasty that ruled over North China 1115–1234.[47]

At the opposite end of the continuum, where hunting was pursued primarily for political-ideological ends, its other functions were never entirely submerged. The Qitan, most certainly political hunters, could engage in the chase for quite mundane reasons—for pleasure or for protein—that bore no political significance.[48] Even more revealing, in the Mughal empire (1526–1858), where the royal hunt was a key element in the governance of the realm, a ruler such as Humāyūn (r. 1526–30 and 1555–56), when his political fortunes fell, readily converted his royal hunt into a search for food that was desperately needed for physical survival.[49] Thus, while there are no pure types of hunting, there are nonetheless meaningful distinctions to be made, a point that will be documented and elaborated in succeeding chapters.

This Hunting History

In the course of conducting the research for this work, I slowly came to the realization that the history of hunting cannot be isolated from the study of a much wider range of human-animal interactions that now engage the attention of diverse disciplines, from biology to archaeology and philosophy. Such inquiries can extend from tightly focused investigations of human impact on particular animal populations to fundamental questions about the concept of humanity and animality, that is, about sensitive definitions concerning nature and culture, and the borders that may, or may not, separate these realms.[50]

To understand the royal hunt, we must take into account the myriad ways in which animals, wild and domesticated, are entwined in human cultural history: animals, after all, are foes and friends, symbols and signs; they serve as talismans, as objets d'art, as markers of status, as commodities and presentations, as sources of entertainment, clothing, food, and medicine, and even as sources of wisdom and models of human behavior. The full significance and meaning of human hunting, particularly in its political form, only becomes intelligible when properly situated in this larger tapestry of human-animal interactions. To cite but one obvious example, the special powers attributed to successful hunters derive, in no small measure, from the special powers and properties attributed to the animals they vanquish. Fabulous beasts can only be slain by fabulous humans. This means that we will need to take an interest in the attitudes toward animals and nature held by elites and by the populace at large.

Having delineated my subject thematically, I must now do the same for its temporal and geographical boundaries, at least in a preliminary fashion. Initially, I thought I could "start" with the Achaemenids, the first universal empire, and then work forward in time. I soon discovered, however, that long before the Persians, the royal hunt was a well-established institution in early Egypt,

Mesopotamia, India, and China. I therefore ventured, with considerable trepidation, into these specialized fields of study, in which I have no previous experience or training, in search of antecedents and analogues.

At the other end, one might extend the life of the royal hunt to the mid-twentieth century. In 1940, *Time* featured Hermann Göring on its cover and in the accompanying story noted that the "No. 2 Nazi was Reich Master of Hunt," lived in a 100,000-acre game preserve, imported falcons from Iceland, and expected his guests to play with his pet lion cub, Caesar.[51] In every particular, including the dramatic destruction of his own hunting park at war's end, the Reichsmarshall and Reichsjagdmeister was following age-old practices widely shared by the political elites of Eurasia.[52] More realistically, perhaps, the termination date of the royal hunt should be set in the first half of the nineteenth century, when, under the impact of firearms and new international styles, traditional modes of elite hunting fell into "comparative disuse" in its last bastions, the Middle East and India, although the royal hunt survived in Qājār Iran (1779–1924) almost to the end of the dynasty.[53]

Geographically, there is, I believe, an identifiable core area in which many of the common and distinguishing features of the royal hunting complex were developed. The notion of the core will be elaborated in greater detail in the next chapter, but for now this territory can be defined briefly as Iran, North India, and Turkestan, though, as we shall see, many aspects of this complex show up much farther afield, some reaching the extremities of the Eurasian landmass.

My justifications for covering such a broad sweep of time and space go beyond the search for context or perspective, or the desire to understand the growth of the forest, not just the trees. These are important considerations which I take seriously, but I also have two specific goals in the study that require a history that is both wide and deep. The first is my interest in explaining why the royal hunt became so homogenous across the continent, why certain elements of this complex traveled so far, why courts and cultures with little direct knowledge of one another nonetheless shared a similar hunting style. In short, how can we account for the appearance of "international" standards and styles under premodern conditions of communication? My second goal is to understand why this institution lasted for so long, nearly four millennia. The search for the reasons underlying its extreme longevity leads, naturally, to a consideration of Braudel's notion of "la longue durée." Both issues will be addressed at length in the concluding chapter.

Given the subject matter of this study, it seems advisable to offer the following disclaimer: I am not advancing another grand theory on the decisive role of hunting in human social-cultural evolution. Such a disclaimer is necessary because hunting has often been cast as the engine that drove hominid history. In its extreme form the "hunting hypothesis" asserts that big game hunting explains the basics of early hominid biological, behavioral, and cultural development, that hunting made us truly human. This theory has been justly criticized on a number of grounds. One major line of attack is that early hominid communities were not just hunters but foragers and scavengers engaged in the extraction of a broad range of natural resources. Hunting, therefore, was hardly the predominant element, the source of change; rather it was part of a much larger package of technical, social, and ecological adjustments. Second, the theory's critics have argued that, while less than heroic, scavenging and foraging still require group cohesion, cooperation, and knowledge of nature, all of which encouraged the elaboration of more sophisticated social and communication skills.[54]

These reservations concerning the supposed centrality of hunting in prehistory apply with even greater force to the historic period. The written record affirms, I believe, that the chase was never a dominating factor, never an engine; this record does show, however, that the hunt was fully integrated into the political and cultural life of many of the peoples of premodern Eurasia. Because of this integration, the royal hunt provides a useful window on the past, one that allows exploration of the manifold linkages between nature, culture, and politics, and, at the same time, provides a window that exposes something of the extensive historical connections among the peoples of the Old World.

The royal hunt lends itself to these ends by virtue of its multiple faces and diverse functions, that is, its plasticity, a property which it shares with other types of hunting. As I will try to show, the chase was an ingredient in interstate relations, military preparations, domestic administration, communications networks, and in the search for political legitimacy. But the importance of the royal hunt hardly ends here. It was also closely tied to an issue of critical importance to all societies, that of access to, and preservation of, natural resources. Of equal concern to environmental history, elite hunting was a medium through which images of nature were fashioned and projected, as well as a medium through which actual bits and pieces of living nature were disseminated, sometimes far beyond their home range.

At this time, I can only offer a preliminary reconnaissance of a vast and complex topic. Many individual monographs could and should be written about the royal hunt in particular times and places. Unfortunately, investigations placing elite hunting in its appropriate natural and cultural settings are comparatively rare. This accounts, to some extent, for the uneven coverage of this book. I am painfully aware that important areas such as Korea, Japan, Central Europe, and the Ottoman empire deserve more attention than I could give them. Consequently, new and detailed case studies, once available, will doubtless challenge, modify, and improve upon my findings and portrayals. But if I am not completely off the mark, then perhaps the data and arguments presented here might engender productive revisionism that yields new knowledge, new insights, and new, improved hunting histories. Someday, perhaps, it might even be possible to contemplate a truly planetary perspective that identifies long-term developments across the globe, comparing the relationship between the pursuit of protein and the pursuit of power in the hunting histories of sub-Saharan Africa, pre-Columbian America, Oceania, and Eurasia.

As point of departure for this particular hunting history, we need to answer some very basic questions about elite hunting. Who hunted? Where did they hunt? How frequently did they hunt? How and what did they hunt? Only then can we tackle the central question: why did they hunt?

2

Field and Stream

Who Hunted?

The answer to our first question of who engaged in political hunting has already been proposed: in my view, the vast majority of the royal houses and aristocracies of Eurasia made some use of the chase in the pursuit and maintenance of their social and political power.

This proposition now needs a measure of elaboration and definition. We can begin with a very basic issue in any culture history: geographical distribution. If we treat the centrality of the chase in political life as a cultural trait we find that it was widely but by no means evenly distributed across the continent. There was indeed a core of territories where political hunting was more continuous, concentrated, and intense, and these territories became the centers of innovation and popularization of new styles, techniques, and equipment, and came to serve in historical times as a kind of continental clearinghouse for the latest fads and fashions in elite hunting. These territories include Mesopotamia, Asia Minor, Turkestan, North India, and Transcaucasia, with the Iranian plateau as the hub, the inner core.

The fact that contemporaries and later generations so consistently associate pre-Islamic Iran with the royal hunt is more a matter of self-projection than of foreign stereotyping, since Iranian dynasties always made strenuous efforts to advertise the fabulous exploits of their royal huntsmen in picture and poem.[1] Neighboring courts strove to emulate these practices and the ʿAbbāsid caliphate, the principal successor state of the Sasanids, enthusiastically embraced the royal hunt, which became an important social and political institution throughout the dynasty's long existence (750–1258).[2]

The royal hunt, as previously noted, was found at times well beyond the core. It is in evidence throughout the steppe zone whenever the nomads were politically organized. It surfaces as well in China as an important institution in antiquity and during the imperial era whenever the Middle Kingdom was closely connected to the "Western Region [Xiyu]," or when peoples of Mongolia or Manchuria ruled in China. In fact, it can be argued that North China, where Chinese and nomadic elites to a large extent shared a common environment and a common martial tradition that included the cult of the chase, a fascination with hunting dogs, fine horses, and falconry, became a secondary core and the model for elite hunting in East Asia.[3] Depictions of the hunt in Korean tombs of the fifth and sixth centuries, at least in terms of content, show that Korean elites hunted in much the same fashion as their North Chinese counterparts, or for that matter, the royal hunters of Sasanid Iran.[4] In later times, this convergence can be found at even greater distances. In 1597 Dos Sanctos, a Portuguese missionary, provides a description of a massive "royall hunting" in Ethiopia that could be transferred mechanically, with little or no violence, to Ṣafavid Iran or Manchu China.[5]

While stressing for the moment the tendency toward homogenization, it would be misleading to ignore the exceptions, cultural zones which diverged from the norm. One place where this is most apparent is the Mediterranean and Europe in the classical age. The Greeks hunted, of course, typically small game with hounds and nets.[6] But while important as a social and recreational activity, it never acquired in Greece or Rome the political-military functions exhibited in the core territories. The Roman attitude toward elite hunting is mirrored in the admission of Pliny the Younger that his slaves did most of his hunting, and in the caustic remark of Ammianus that the senatorial class often "hunt by the labors of others."[7] Those who use surrogates in the chase do not cut a heroic figure or accumulate much prestige; still, it is revealing that they felt the need to fabricate a hunting persona.

The reasons for this lack of devotion to the chase are no doubt complex. Environmental differences certainly played some role, but this is easy to overstate. Different political institutions and traditions must also be taken into account. One intriguing factor in the equation was the type of game available. There was no "heroic" prey in Europe as in the Middle East and South Asia, where large carnivores—lions, leopards, and tigers—were still numerous. This difference, whatever its explanatory power, was clearly noticed and commented upon by classical authors over the centuries. Aristotle, for his part, holds that "wild animals are at their wildest in Asia," while Xenophon (d. ca. 355 B.C.E.) pointedly contrasts the prey of the Greeks—hare and deer—with the "big game" pursued by foreign rulers, most especially the lion, which Oppian (third century C.E.) views as the king of beasts, the opponent that best tests "the valiant spirit of the hunters."[8]

A further, and it seems to me, important, element in explaining the restricted role of the hunt in high politics in the Mediterranean is the very different military traditions of classical antiquity. Hunting was probably not a preoccupation of the Roman elite because Romans always valued infantry over cavalry.[9] This preference, rooted in social history and ecology, was modified somewhat when Alexander the Great embraced the Persian-style hunt, and later on the Romans, under the influence of Hellenism and of closer contact with the Near East, adopted selected aspects of the royal hunt. Still, for the Romans, equestrian archers always played a supporting, never a central, role in war and the chase. Thus, in the Far West, royal hunting was a matter of individual choice, not a formalized institution as in the East.[10]

This line of argument is buttressed by the fact that after the disintegration of the Roman empire, when Europe became dominated by its own kind of equestrian warrior, the medieval mounted knights, the royal hunt acquired new significance and elite hunting became commonplace, even mandatory.[11] And once equestrian warriors began to hunt incessantly and in earnest, medieval Europe became increasingly sensitive about foreign norms and receptive to international standards emanating from the core area, a topic addressed in subsequent chapters.

Proofs of the validity of the foregoing arguments cannot be presented now. Here I am still charting my future course, indicating lines of inquiry and introducing arguments. Documentary evidence for specific features of the royal hunting complex appears in following sections that treat venues, animal partners, and so on. Support for more general arguments about a core area, or the vast scale of the royal hunt, is, on the other hand, cumulative in nature and to me convincing in the aggregate.

Where Did They Hunt?

The question of venues will be addressed in the remainder of this chapter and in the next, devoted to hunting parks. Here we will focus on the "field" and the techniques of confronting game on their home ground.

By field, I mean in general the wilderness but I do not wish to imply by that term a natural system unaffected by human influence. Many, indeed most, hunting grounds were both "natural" and "managed," and these venues can be usefully contrasted with the completely built environments represented by hunting parks.

The first thing to be said about wilderness in the world before the rapid population growth of the last two centuries is that there were still vast tracts of original stand forests and jungles almost everywhere. Not unexpectedly, areas such as Manchuria had innumerable fine hunting grounds "full of wild beasts" that were extensively exploited by the Qitan court.[12] But even more populous lands were similarly endowed. In India during the seventeenth century

European travelers were repeatedly struck by the extent of forest and the abundance of game. According to their accounts, both coasts and the interior teemed with game of every description—gazelle, deer, goats, fowl, big cats, bear, and wild boar.[13] What is most arresting is that quality hunting was still found so close to cities. Even in the early nineteenth century one did not have to go far for game in India. There was a "famous sporting jungle" only eight miles from Belaspur, a city near the mouth of the Ganges.[14] Here was a real wilderness a half-day's ride from a substantial urban center.

This situation was by no means unique to India; urban accessible hunting grounds were common elsewhere in Eurasia. In the seventh century there was a luxuriant hunting field called Callicrateia outside the walls of Constantinople; in the period of the twelfth to the fourteenth century there was good hunting in the immediate environs of Yanjing/Beijing and in Liulin, "Willow Forest," just thirty miles to its south; and in the seventeenth century there was a region "aboundinge with wild beasts" only a day's journey from Aleppo.[15]

While accessibility was generally considered an asset, at other times inaccessibility was thought an advantage. Louis the Pious (r. 814–40) hunted in the Vosges, a very remote tract of mountains and wilderness southeast of the Ardennes.[16] Similarly, the Mughal ruler Awrangzīb (r. 1658–1707) undertook a lengthy hunting trip to Kashmir in 1664.[17] The sometime attraction of distance can be explained by a number of factors: the abundance of game, better climate, or simply the desire to get away. More important, perhaps, distant grounds made for exclusivity, and the power to exclude was a vital component of the politics of the royal hunt.

Most monarchs, whether Mongolian qaghans or Mughal emperors, had choices of which wilderness or "fixed hunting place" to visit. And new, interesting locales were constantly being added to their itineraries as courtiers and subjects eagerly informed their sovereigns about little-known and untrammeled hunting spots.[18]

Naturally, rulers often developed an affection for a single site to which they regularly returned. The famous queen of Georgia, Tʿamar (r. 1184–1212), regularly coursed the banks of the Iori River.[19] Similarly, the early rulers of Armenia had a "plain for hunting," called Pʻarakan, that seems to have been in use for several centuries.[20] At about the same time, the subordinate kingdoms that composed Han China in the second century B.C.E. each had their own royal hunting preserves, which were quite vast.[21] And in Kievan Rus, one of its early rulers, Ol'ga (r. 946–64), had hunting grounds (*lovishche*) outside Kiev and throughout the expanses of Novgorod in the north.[22] Here, clearly, political formations at very different levels of complexity adopted the institution of the hunting preserve as a normal feature of court life and established them in very different environments from the taiga of northern Russia to the semitropics of South China.

Hunting preserves were, in fact, a symbol of political authority to be forcefully asserted and jealously guarded. In twelfth-century Mongolia, prior to the Chinggisid unification, ambitious clan leaders staked out hunting grounds, forbidding all others from entering, as an element of the struggle for power in this stateless environment.[23] Further, in a number of early states, conflict over hunting rights and territories mirrored latent princely rivalries. During the reign of Yaropolk (r. 972–80), ruler of Kiev, such a dispute sparked a long and costly struggle among the ruling Riurikid family.[24] In more sophisticated and centralized states princes could confidently monopolize certain attractive hunting grounds as their own.[25] The Mughal emperor Jahāngīr (r. 1605–27) had his favorite hunting ground at Wirngie (Vīr-nāg), near Srinagar, around which he built up appropriate infrastructure, a "pleasure-resort," in the words of the Dutch factor Francisco Pelsaert.[26]

Control over reserves in well-ordered states was assured by various means. Posting and stringent laws against poaching were common, as were patrols by game wardens. Some reserves were even walled in, partially or completely. With the occasional addition of comfortable buildings, an impressive "pleasure-resort" might be fashioned, or more accurately, accreted, over time. At this point of development, such facilities were hardly distinguishable from formal hunting parks.

To make a statement, hunting preserves had to be large. The historical records characterize many as vast or huge, but for a few we have more precise measurements. Odoric of Pordenone, who traveled in China in the 1320s, relates that the Yuan emperor hunted in "a fine forest eight days journey in compass," which the friar locates north of Beijing.[27] In Mughal India, according to an official court source, there was in the time of Akbar (r. 1556–1605) a game preserve in Gujarat along the Narbada River that measured "eight *kos* in length by four in breadth."[28] Since a *kos* was 1.5 to 2 miles, this particular preserve was certainly impressive, between 96 and 128 square miles in area.[29] Even more impressive was a preserve that Ghiyāth al-Dīn, Ghūrid ruler of Afghanistan (r. 1163–1203), laid out between his summer capital Fīrākuh in the mountains of the upper reaches of the Harī Rūd (Herat River) and his winter quarters at Zamīndāvar in the valley of the Hilmand River. Its length was some forty *farsang* (leagues) and at every *farsang* there was erected a mile *(mīl)* marker to post the royal hunting grounds. At Zamīndāvar, Ghiyāth al-Dīn built a large garden full of trees, shrubs, and herbs, and just outside its walls was a huge field, cleared of major vegetation, where game were driven for the convenience of the sultan and his guests.[30] A preserve of this magnitude was more than a symbol of majesty; it was an actual exercise in sovereignty, a demonstration of dominion over land and resources, animals and humans.

Some preserves were highly specialized, such as one devoted to hunting black pheasant near Ṭarāz/Talas in ninth-century Turkestan.[31] But truly regal hunting required diversified game and this entailed diversified environments. This, of course, could be achieved by hunting in different ecological zones and in different seasons. The Georgian king Giorgi III (r. 1156–84) hunted from the Pontic (Black) to the Gurgān (Caspian) Sea in mountains, valleys, and along the shorelines.[32] More desirable, of course, were single preserves that embraced diverse ecologies—plains, forests, and hills—such as the one attributed to the early kings of Armenia, or the one laid out by Ghiyāth al-Dīn in Afghanistan.[33]

At this juncture we take leave of the land, for royal hunters willingly took to the water in the pursuit of different game. Water sport and fowling are mentioned repeatedly in the sources, and it is evident that these pastimes were practiced and popular in all periods and in many climes and cultures. In ancient Egypt, Assyria, Han and Qing China, and Mughal India, water sport typically combined fishing, fowling, and the hunting of aquatic animals. This was done on rivers, lakes, and marshes and was conducted from shore or from boats and barges, often with the aid of decoys.[34]

The principal attraction of this pastime seems to have been the pursuit of waterfowl. Armenian and ʿAbbāsid elites were much enamored with the sport and with the delightful taste of the game.[35] Russian princes of the tenth century had extensive fowling grounds (*perevesishche*) along the Dnepr and its tributary, the Desna.[36] And nomadic elites, products of arid environments, were equally enthusiastic.[37]

Our fullest accounts of fowling on water come from Mughal India, where they did it with decoys, nets, bow and arrow, and birds of prey.[38] Akbar was so taken with the sport that he had an artificial island constructed in a lake near Srinigar, the chief city of Kashmir. Here, from luxurious palaces specially built for the purpose, he and his guests hunted the ducks attracted to the sweet water of the lake.[39]

The impression left by these sources is that water sport was primarily for diversion and pleasure, a search for cool, attractive environments. Nevertheless, the very act of inclusion, the invitation to join the royal party in pleasant, relaxed surroundings, could invest the simple act of duck hunting with political significance.

How Often Did They Hunt?

The frequency and duration of royal hunts are important on two counts: they tell us something about the nexus between hunting and governance, and about the amount of resources invested in the chase. In answering questions about frequency and duration, the historical records are most generous.

One of the earliest indicators of frequency comes from the Shang oracle bone inscriptions, which show that these rulers hunted to some kind of schedule. Their diviners, some apparently specialists in the chase, tried through a form of scapulamancy to determine the success of the hunt and the probability of bad weather and other misfortunes. Judging from the fact that 10 percent of the over 100,000 known divinations concern the chase, the rulers of the late Shang (ca. 1200–1050 B.C.E.), obviously hunted with great frequency.[40] Later, rulers of the Zhou (1122–255) and Han (202 B.C.E.–220 C.E.) hunted as a matter of course, and hunting scenes became one of the more common artistic motifs found on Han-era vessels.[41]

The more precise data from Mughal India indicate the importance of personal preference. Awrangzīb was sometimes restrained, hunting but "once a fortnight," while his ancestor, Jahāngīr, was far more incessant, if not obsessive.[42] By his own testimony and that of contemporaries he hunted almost daily, rain or shine, and stayed out until he had success. Once, he hunted every day for two months and twenty days.[43] This pace is not unlike that of some European monarchs. In the sixth century Guntram, ruler of Burgundy, hunted daily, and in the sixteenth century Louis XIV of France did the same—when he became too old to sit a horse, he followed the chase in an open carriage.[44] In eastern Europe, the twelfth-century prince of Kiev Vladimir Monomakh proudly asserted that even in later life he made it a practice to hunt at least one hundred days a year.[45]

In many of these cases, the monarch was hunting close by the court and could return there for work in the afternoon. Still, there was a current of opinion, found even in the core area, that advocated limits. The second caliph, ʿUmar (r. 634–44), noted for his piety, reprimanded a senior Muslim commander for becoming overly "concerned with hunting."[46] Later on, Kai Kāʾūs, who wrote a mirror for princes in eleventh-century Iran, felt constrained to advise that rulers should restrict their participation in the chase to no more than two days a week, thereby implying that princes, if left to their own devices, would hunt incessantly, to the detriment of the state.[47]

In considering the duration and frequency of royal hunting, the issue of seasonality always comes into play. There were favored hunting seasons in different parts of Eurasia. Two contemporary rulers in the eastern Islamic world, ʿAbdallāh (r. 1583–98), qan of the Uzbeks of Turkestan, and Shāh ʿAbbās (r. 1588–1629), the Ṣafavid, spent the spring months in pursuit of game.[48] In the early medieval West, the Carolingian kings, following the precedent of Charlemagne, held a major hunt in the fall and smaller ones in the spring and summer.[49] In East Asia, winter was often preferred; one Jin ruler, Shizong (r. 1161–90), regularly went out hunting in the first month of the new year and returned to his capital during the second.[50] Some of the reasons for seasonal excursions are obvious: the preservation of game and the desire for diversified hunting experiences. Since, however, these larger expeditions, as will be shown later, were not simply escapes from the press of affairs, but a means of governance, the duration of hunts needs to be explored in more detail.

It is probably safe to assert that there was a close correlation between the length of a hunt and its political content. When, for example, Öljeitü (r. 1304–16), Mongolian ruler of Iran, went out for five days in the foothills near Hamadān, it is likely that he concentrated most of his attention on the chase.[51] When, however, the Qitan emperors went out each winter for sixty days of fishing, fowling, and hunting, ceremonial and political concerns came to the fore and perhaps even dominated the rulers' time.[52] Such lengthy hunting excursions were, of course, quite common among the nomads. Mongolian qans, east and west, regularly took to the field for periods of one to four or five months.[53] While not normally as lengthy, sedentary rulers of China, India, and Turkestan still mounted hunting trips lasting from three weeks to three months or more.[54] What they did in the field during these extended stays is a recurrent theme of this work.

How Did They Hunt?

The chase itself, of course, occupied part of a ruler's time in the field, and we need to know how hunts were conducted and what was hunted. The question of weaponry can serve as a point of departure.

The relationships between weapons of war and those of the chase are complex and rarely clear-cut. Suffice it to say that in the main, missile and projectile weapons were first developed for the hunt and later modified for war, while shock and thrusting weapons—the spear, sword, and mace—were typically specialized for war and had limited use in the hunt.[55] The history of the bow well illustrates the complexities involved. An invention of the Upper Paleolithic, the bow represents a major advance in hunting technology. In the Old World there are two principal types: the composite or reflex bow of eastern Eurasia and the single piece or "self-bow" of northwestern Eurasia. Both were widely employed in hunting and in warfare. Specialization is more often seen in the arrows and arrowheads, some of which were used in the chase and others clearly designed for war, to penetrate armor or to break off in enemy wounds.[56] Thus the bow was an ancient hunting weapon and the common heritage of cultures from China to Africa.

The javelin, a missile weapon, has a similar history but a much more limited range. Restricted to the Mediterranean world, the javelin, with an amentum, or "throwing thong," seems to have been developed for the chase and only later adopted for combat. In the Greek world, it was generally identified as the weapon of commoners.[57] There were, on the other hand, a few missile weapons that had no military applications, such as the harpoons used in ancient Egypt by pharaohs and professional huntsmen to kill hippopotamuses.[58]

For millennia these types of weapons were mainstays of the royal hunt. In time, of course, they were replaced by firearms. In his memoir, the emperor Jahāngīr observes that under his father, Akbar, guns began to enter the royal hunt and that by his own reign had become the "projectile" weapon of choice at the Mughal court, while bows and arrows were increasingly viewed as out of date.[59]

Aside from instruments that killed, there were several that ensnared prey. In ancient Egypt, the ruler, it is claimed, lassoed and captured wild bulls. Whether this is a plausible hunting method or merely royal propaganda, is not known.[60] More certainly, the lasso, the type attached to a long pole, was widely used in the steppe as a tool for herd management, as a weapon of war, and in capturing prey such as stag, reindeer, and the wild ass or onager.[61] Netting of various types was also part of the hunter's arsenal. In the Greek tradition, the hunting net or *dictya* was an invention of the goddess Dictynna/Britomartis and was in common use in the Mediterranean area during the Roman period.[62] In treating nets it is necessary to distinguish between those for downing single animals and the very elaborate net walls used in the massive game drives that so characterize the royal hunt in the core area, a topic discussed shortly.

For small-scale or individual hunting, various ways were used to locate or attract game. Most common, of course, was skilled huntsmen and scouts who brought news of the whereabouts of desirable game.[63] Animals, particularly deer, were also called. There is a very long history of deer calling in North Asia. Under the Qitan, their Jürchen subjects provided, as part of their tribute to the Liao court, experts who imitated the bugling of deer with a horn. In the early eighteenth century, Manchu emperors still had such specialists who, dressed in deer skins and fitted with masks, emulated rutting calls.[64] There was a similar and very ancient tradition in the core area and later in the Far West, where bugles and other devices were used to attract deer by mimicking both rutting calls and the cries of the young.[65]

Besides tracking and calling, the Mughals made wide use of specially trained decoy animals, mainly antelope, to attract and hold their kindred for hunters; this was a subtle form of the chase that had a long history in India.[66]

Not surprisingly, ungulates of various species were standard game animals for most elite hunters. Besides the deer and gazelle, many kinds of wild sheep and goats were hunted.[67] Also abundant were the antelope; the *nilgao* or "blue bull" (*Boselophus tragocamelus*) was frequently hunted in India. At times it is difficult to determine which particular species are meant, since in some languages there is a lack of precision in distinguishing domestic and wild varieties.[68] Another mainstay was the wild boar (*Sus scrofa*), which has been pursued throughout its natural range from the Neolithic down to the present. Somewhat surprisingly, the wild ass (*Equus hemionus*) was a popular prey animal, particularly in the steppe and in Iran.

Royal hunters were strongly attracted to exotic or unusual species. The Achaemenids hunted ostriches and Mughal emperors the rhinoceros of northern India.[69] Large and dangerous game was particularly appealing because it drew attention to the ruler's hunting prowess, bravery, and concern for public safety. In consequence, the most prized, if not the most common prey of princes, was the most "heroic" prey, the great cats, lions and tigers, which were hunted from northern Manchuria to India and Iran.[70]

Modes of the chase varied according to species, time, place, and individual preference and mood. Hunting on foot was not unknown but certainly not common. Xenophon, who knew Iran well, says in his fictionalized biography of Cyrus the Great (r. 549–30) that the Achaemenid court hunted chiefly on horseback.[71] As a statistical truth, it seems safe to assert that most royal hunters went into the field mounted, a form of the chase that was held to produce "intense delight."[72] Indeed, for many elites, hunting was as much a test of horsemanship as it was of hunting skill. In this sense, modern fox hunting is an organic outgrowth of the traditional royal hunt and represents its logical outcome. But while equestrian hunting predominated in late antiquity, the Middle Ages, and well into modern times, there was an equally long period in deep antiquity when elites across Eurasia pursued game from chariots. A closer examination of this phenomenon will help bring out several salient and recurring features of the royal hunt.

Whatever the chronology and place of origin, chariotry began spreading over Eurasia in the course of the second millennium B.C.E. Initially, it appears as a prestige vehicle for rulers, who used it for processions and ceremonial hunts.[73] In the ancient Near East, Egyptian pharaohs and later on Assyrian rulers are depicted hunting ostriches, bulls, and lions from their vehicles.[74] The Achaemenids continued this tradition; a cylinder seal found in Egypt, and inscribed in Old Persian, Elamite, and Babylonian, shows "Darius, Great King" (r. 522–486), slaying lions with bow and arrow from a chariot.[75]

Chariotry arrived in the subcontinent with the Indo-Aryans at the end of the second millennium B.C.E.; although displaced by cavalry in the early centuries

Figure 1. Sayyid Jamal Ali Khan hunting with tethered antelope. Bibliothèque nationale, paris.

C.E., references in the Sanskrit play *Shakuntala* indicate that it was still used for hunting as late as the fifth century.[76] In the Far East, the chariot was introduced to China from the Near East around 1200 B.C.E. As in the West, the chariot in China began as a vehicle of prestige and hunting; only later did its military functions develop, first as a mobile command post and then as a major component of the army, at least down to the immediate pre-Han era, when nomadic cavalry rendered this technology obsolete.[77]

As in other parts of Eurasia, the chariot survived for a while longer as a ceremonial and hunting vehicle. According to references in contemporary prose poems (*fu*), royal charioteers of the Han era continued to pursue tigers, leopards, elk, and deer.[78] There is also brief mention in 74 B.C.E. of a smaller, more maneuverable vehicle called the "pig-sticking chariot [*xizhu che*]." But despite this improvement, the chariot's days were nearing the end, as the Han sources make it clear that on imperial hunts horsemen now greatly outnumbered the charioteers, who gradually fade from the scene.[79]

Sources from the end of the Zhou dynasty, sixth to third centuries B.C.E., repeatedly comment on the fact that the use of the chariot in the chase was fraught with problems.[80] The most obvious, of course, was shooting while directing a moving vehicle. This was overcome in two ways: either the royal archer had a driver to control the horses or, as was the practice in Mesopotamia, the ruler himself guided his steeds by means of reins attached to his waist, thus freeing his hands to wield a bow and arrow.[81] This, however, was only the beginning of the difficulties.

While the wood-bending technology that produced the spoke wheel was a major advance, such wheels were still fragile and liable to break. This meant that the only terrain suitable for chariot hunting had to be open and fairly level. One rather troublesome solution to the problem of terrain, practiced in Armenia in the fourth century C.E., was simply to dismount the vehicle and mount a horse to pursue game that fled into the forest.[82] The more common and permanent solution, however, was to prevent the flight of the game to "inappropriate" environments. Consequently, despite occasional literary references to hunters going singly to the field in a chariot, this was not the normal practice.[83] As Mary Littauer and Joost Crouwel have demonstrated in their careful analysis of hunting scenes on ivory and stone from eighth-century Assyria, successful hunting with a chariot required many attendants to drive game to ground where wheeled vehicles could operate effectively. Further, the king's chariot with his driver was typically accompanied by troops on horseback who followed behind to dispatch and collect game. For lions, as a bas-relief from the time of Ashurnasirpal II (r. 884–860) clearly shows, the king was aided by dismounted soldiers with spears to approach a disabled beast.[84] These foot soldiers can be identified with the "runners" or "skirmishers," armed with shield, spear, and sword, who supported charioteers in battle; they escorted and screened their crew onto the field, finished off disabled enemies, pursued fugitives, and rescued their own comrades.[85] These were all skills transferable to the hunt, which in turn provided excellent preparation for war.

From this survey, it is possible to conclude that in its early, "chariot" phase, a successful royal hunt required: (1) heavy use of the military; (2) extensive logistical support; and (3) careful stage management, particularly of game. All these are characteristics of the later history of the royal hunt, and all will be dealt with at length. For now, we can best introduce these issues by concentrating attention on the circle or ring hunt that so defined royal hunting in the core area and reveals so much about the crucial issue of scale.

Driving of game is, of course, of great antiquity and as a technique has been used in all forms of hunting. Royal hunters in ancient Egypt, Mesopotamia, Iran, China, and medieval Europe regularly used beaters and fire to flush or drive game to more convenient locales where, as Xenophon says, "riding was practicable."[86]

Figure 2. Ashurnasipal II hunting lions. Ninth-century bas-relief, Nimrod. Trustees of the British Museum.

The use of encircling movements to trap large quantities of game is equally ancient and was the centerpiece of princely hunts throughout Eurasia. The technique produced abundant game for sport and at the same time, as a fifth-century Armenian source notes, brought together "groups of princes with their noble sons" in a collective endeavor.[87] The size of such hunts could vary widely. In twelfth-century Syria local nobles organized modest ring hunts, called *al-ḥalqa* in Arabic, while in the Delhi sultanate (1206–1555) and Mughal empire, ring hunts, *qamar-ghāh* in Persian, often assumed much greater proportions.[88]

The largest of the ring hunts, however, are to be found in Inner Asia when the nomads were politically organized. In Turkic several terms were used to describe this method of hunting. The earliest is *saghir* and later on *qumarmīshī*, which appears frequently as a loanword in Persian texts of the Mongolian and Temürid eras.[89] The terminology in Mongolian is a bit more complicated. Zhao Hong, a Song envoy, says in his report of 1221 that the Mongols make a clear distinction between field hunting, *chulie*, literally "to go a-hunting," and great ring hunts, *dawei*, literally "to beat and surround [game]."[90] The modern Mongolian equivalents are *ang*, "hunting in general," and *aba*, "battue," "ring hunt," a word which passed into Manchu with the same meaning.[91] In the imperial era other terms were *qomorgha* (cf. Persian *qamar* and Turkic *qumarmīshī*), and most frequently *jerge* or its unexplained alternative, *nerge*. *Jerge* has the basic meaning of "rank," "order," "row," "column," and is used in that sense in the *Secret History*, the Mongols' own account of the rise of their empire. By extension, however, *jerge* came to mean "battue," "hunting circle," or an "encircling movement" in warfare.[92] Although these indigenous terms were not used by Western travelers in the Mongolian empire, all mention the ring hunt and remark on its size and dramatic, bloody climax when the trapped, frantic animals were slaughtered in great numbers.[93]

We now need to look more closely at the characteristics, organization, and conduct of hunts of this type. The first thing to be noted is that ring hunts are closely associated with the exercise of political authority. This is brought out with great clarity by Maḥmūd Kāshgharī, the eleventh-century lexicographer, who defines the Turkic *saghir* as "a type of hunting of kings with their subjects," and by Rudra Deva, the sixteenth-century rajah of Kumaon, who is at pains to point out that hunts of this type "can be played by kings and noblemen *only*."[94]

As regards technique, the Chinese *dawei*, "beat and surround," nicely captures the essence of the ring hunt.[95] Three examples of the standard ring, all provided by authors personally acquainted with the method, will help us identify other basic features. The first is by Juvaynī, a midlevel bureaucrat in the Mongolian administration of West Asia who traveled through Turkestan to the Mongolian homeland in the 1250s. He relates that under Chinggis Qan (r. 1206–27) the great hunt was held at the beginning of winter and was a massive operation lasting several months. After scouting out concentrations of game, the army formed a vast hunting ring (Persian *nirkah* = Mongolian *nerge*) and drove the game slowly before them, taking great care that none escaped. Military discipline was imposed and, he emphasizes, severe penalties meted out for breaking ranks. Once the ring contracted to a diameter of a league, the troops enclosed the animals in a rope fence on which felt strips were hung. Then, Juvaynī says, the killing began.[96] The second example, by Ibn ʿArabshāh, describes a hunt under Tamerlane or Temür (r. 1370–1405), who used his army and locals, as well as travelers, to form a huge hunting ring; using pipes, drums, and so on, they drove the animals into a circle, at which point the notables started killing animals with assorted weapons.[97] The third description is from the English traveler Ovington, who witnessed a ring hunt in Surat in 1689: "Sometimes a great company of men range the Fields, and walk together into Inclosures, to look after their Game; when once they have espy'd the place where they fancy the Game lies, they inclose the Ground, and Stand in a Ring, with Clubs and Weapons in the Hands, whilst they employ others to beat up the Ground, and raise it for them."[98]

From these accounts, it is clear that beaters were recruited from the army and from the general populace as a kind of corvée. Further, animals of all kinds were forced into the ring, which was defined by some kind of temporary fencing. Last, once animals were penned in, the huntsmen began to select and dispatch them.

Although it is certainly true that the open spaces of Inner Asia and the Middle East lent themselves to this mode of hunting, the ring hunt was quite adaptable, and in fact was deployed in a variety of terrains. Baybars (r. 1260–77), the ruler of the Mamlūks (1250–1519) of Egypt, formed a hunting ring (*al-ḥalqa*) in a forested region; Jahāngīr used it in mountainous regions of India; and Hülegü (r. 1255–65), the first Mongolian ruler of Iran, organized a *jerge* with

Figure 3. Emperor Qianlong in ring hunt. Giuseppe Castiglione, 1757. RMN/Art Resource, NY.

camels in the thickets of the lower Amu Darya to hunt lion![99] And it was flexible in yet another way: sometimes the ring was not fully closed but rather formed with center and two wings into which Qitan emperors entered on a carriage.[100] On other occasions, several complete rings were formed separately and then joined. Chinggis Qan's troops once fashioned two, while Jahāngīr and the Qing emperor Kangxi (r. 1662–1722) had three smaller rings formed in adjoining locales to vary the hunting experience.[101]

At this juncture we can profitably take up the matter of fencing since it leads directly into the question of scale. As already mentioned, netting was an important and ever present piece of equipment in the royal hunt. Armenian kings, Tang princes, Carolingian emperors, and Kievan rulers all took to the field with netting, but its purpose—to encircle game en masse or to capture individual animals—is not always clear.[102]

Chinese sources, as is so often the case, provide early and accurate information that leaves no doubt as to the function of the nets.[103] In 11 B.C.E. the Chengdi emperor (r. 33–7), according to the *Hanshu*, "held a great enclosure [*xiao*] hunt." This was implemented with the aid of 11,000 troops, who surrounded a certain mountain, Nanshan, with a hunting net and once the game was concentrated and penned in, the foreign (Hu) guests of the emperor were allowed their choice of prey.[104] Some 1,250 years later, Peng Daya, a Song envoy, describes the Mongolian version of an enclosure hunt in the following way:

Whenever their ruler goes out on a ring hunt [*dawei*] he must assemble a multitude of people. They remove earth to make holes into which they insert wooden poles as markers. These they tie together using hair rope on which they attach felt "wings." This is just like the Chinese way of netting rabbits. This is continuously connected for one or two hundred Chinese miles [*li*]. Then, when wind causes the "wings" to flutter, all the game is frightened and does not dare to flee. And then they drive [the game] together and seize and strike them.[105]

Courts in the core area also made heavy use of fencing in their hunts. The Mughals constructed various kinds of fenced roads—called *tashqawal* and *nihilam*—to drive and direct game.[106] This was used by Jahāngīr to move concentrations of game from one locale to another for better sport. The fencing in this case was canvas (*sarā-parda*) and at one point enclosed an area of a *kos*, or about two miles.[107] Equally revealing are the comments of Thomas Herbert on the fencing used in royal hunts in Ṣafavid Iran. He records that when game was driven into a desired area "they impale [enfence] it with a huge toil of wire and cords supported by stakes [in the number of] six hundred camels' loads."[108]

The amount of fencing is only one of several indicators of the true magnitude of royal hunts in the core area. The final section takes up other measures.

On What Scale Did They Hunt?

In 1682 the Kangxi emperor, on a great hunting expedition in Manchuria, went off with a small party to hunt in peace away from the din and dust of the main body.[109] That royal hunts, especially the ring variety, were large (and noisy) affairs is beyond dispute. But just how massive were they?

One obvious measure is the number of participants. The *Mu tianzi zhuan*, a semimythical geography compiled sometime between 403 and 350 B.C.E., relates that King Mu of Zhou, who ruled around the beginning of the tenth century, had gone out to hunt with six regiments (*shi*), each nominally 2,500 men strong.[110] In the fourteenth-century Chinese novel *Romance of the Three Kingdoms*, set in the second century C.E., 100,000 men accompany the emperor into the field, where they enclose an area of some two hundred Chinese miles.[111] Given the nature of these works and their distance from the events described, their data are easy to dismiss. But a case can be made that their numbers are not far off the mark: other, more reliable, sources confirm this order of magnitude. The *Hanshu* states that the ruler of the nomadic Xiongnu went out on one occasion with 10,000 troops and on another with 100,000, in what is described as a *pangse* hunt, literally "side [by side] blocking hunt."[112] This is not to say that all hunts were conducted on this scale; more modest figures are noted as well. In

Figure 4. Lion hunt with nets. *Padshahnama*, for 220B. The Royal Collection © 2005. Her Majesty Queen Elizabeth II.

the early third century C.E., the chieftain of the nomadic Tuoba, who later formed the Northern Wei (386–535), mustered "several thousand horsemen" for a hunt, and in later centuries Liao and Jin emperors mobilized comparable numbers.[113] Such figures, however, are at the lower end for a respectable royal hunt. This conclusion certainly finds support in eyewitness testimony of the Jesuit Matteo Ripa, who relates that Kangxi was accompanied by 12,000 troopers on one of his "little hunts" in 1711.[114]

Data from the core show the same range of numbers and fully sustain the conclusions drawn from the East Asian materials. Contemporaries related that Akbar and Shāh Jahān regularly mobilized 4,000–5,000 troopers for their hunts, while Awrangzīb went out with a host of 100,000.[115] The Persian figures are quite compatible. In one case, a Ṣafavid ruler hunted with 12,000 horse and 4,000 foot and, on another, 20,000 beaters were employed.[116] Finally, the German physician Engelbert Kaempfer states that in 1683 the shah, Sulaymān (r. 1660–94), organized a great ring hunt lasting from the beginning of May to July 20 that mobilized 80,000 beaters with staffs and sticks. About half of these, he relates, soon fled their duties because of the scarcity of water, and nearly 500 died miserably.[117]

A second way to get at the question of scale is to look at the amount of space encompassed or covered in royal hunts. There are a number of accounts that address this issue; four will be reproduced in some detail for they convey in striking fashion the immensity of these undertakings.

First, according to the chronicler Jūzjānī, the Ghūrid Ghiyāth al-Dīn organized massive hunts in southern Afghanistan and northern Sīstān. Once a year, he says, the sultan gave orders to draw up a semicircular hunting formation (*barrah* = *parrah*) that extended for more than fifty or sixty leagues (*farsang*). When the semicircle closed after a month of driving game, it contained more than 10,000 beasts of every description.[118]

Second, there is the testimony of Munshī, a court historian under the Ṣafavid Shāh ʿAbbās. He records that in 1598 a huge hunting ring was formed in the plain of Rādikān outside of Mashad; here they organized beaters to drive game toward the plain "within several days' journey on all sides." When the circle was still one league (about three miles) in diameter, the shah and close associates began to hunt.[119]

The third, from Abūʾl Faẓl, a confidant of Akbar, concerns a memorable ring hunt Akbar held near Lahore in 1567. By the emperor's explicit order, all the surrounding districts were temporarily given over to court officials to organize the hunt. Thousands of locals were appointed to drive game and a wide space outside the city was selected "for collecting animals." The beaters, he continues, drove game for one month until they were concentrated in an area about ten

Figure 5. Akbar's ring hunt near Lahore, 1567. *Akbarnāma*, 1950s. Victoria and Albert Museum, London.

miles in circumference. The hunt lasted a total of five days, during which time "various modes of hunting were displayed."[120]

Last, there is the account of the Flemish Jesuit Ferdinand Verbiest, who states that when he accompanied Kangxi to Manchuria in 1683 the imperial party followed "the chase for a length of upwards of nine hundred miles, without a day's intermission."[121]

Taken together, these testimonies, derived from diverse, independent, and often eyewitness sources, affirm that royal hunts were conducted on a monumental scale and were primarily military/political occasions designed to impress. Further evidence for this conclusion will be adduced below in the discussions of conservation measures and the practice of advertising royal hunting prowess.

3
Parks

The Paradise and Its Antecedents

Elites, as portrayed in the sources, pursued game in hills, plains, deserts, forests, and marshes. However labeled, and however natural, such settings were more or less public, often open to observation. The royal hunt with its drama, its pomp and circumstance, was clearly intended as a public spectacle, and such spectacles, if properly staged, helped to promote a sense of awe among subjects. But the quality of majesty, a political asset of great value, is also created by surrounding the royal person with an aura of mystery, which requires privacy and remoteness. The projection of majesty draws perforce on both sources and is most effective when kingly activity is finely calibrated, properly balanced between the two spheres, the public and the private.

In the royal hunt this division of labor is readily apparent: monarchs regularly hunted in two different venues, out in the countryside, a very public arena, and inside secured, artificial environments represented by the paradise of ancients and the hunting parks of the Middle Ages. The latter, of course, were very private abodes, walled, mysterious, and closed to outside scrutiny. This complex and intriguing institution was also widespread, found in some form almost everywhere royal courts mounted royal hunts. They are most closely identified with the ancient Iranians mainly because the Greeks, their long-time adversaries, make frequent mention of these great parks.

In the Greek texts they are called *paradeisos*, which goes back to the Old Persian *paridaida* or the Median *paridaiza*, both of which have the basic meaning of "enclosure" or "domain."[1] This Iranian word is also found in ancient Near Eastern texts, where it appears as *bar-te-tash* in Elamite and as *par-de-su* in Neo-Babylonian.[2] All these sources provide useful information, but the Greek depiction is the most graphic, the one that left a lasting image in the West.

Xenophon, who served as a mercenary under the Achaemenids, is the first to describe these parks in any detail.[3] In 401 B.C.E. he accompanied Cyrus the Younger, brother of the Emperor Artaxerxes II (r. 404–359) and the satrap of Lydia, Phrygia, and Cappodocia, to Celaenae in western Asia Minor, where, he says, Cyrus "had a palace and a large park [*paradeisos*] full of wild animals, which he used to hunt on horseback whenever he wished to give himself and his horses exercise. Through the middle of this park flows the Macander River; its sources are beneath the palace and it flows through the city of Celaenae also."[4] Later Xenophon encountered similar facilities in northern Syria and in Babylonia along the Tigris River; he describes both as beautiful enclosed spaces with many trees.[5]

The presence of paradises in Mesopotamia is confirmed by local, Neo-Babylonian texts. The earliest reference is to the reign of Cyrus the Great (r. 549–530), who ordered a *par-de-su* near Sippar. Another, dating to the reign of his successor, Cambyses (r. 530–22), was constructed near Uruk. Under Artaxerxes I (r. 465–424), an "upper paradise" was built near Nippur in 464.[6] This building program extended to the Iranian homeland; the historians of Alexander and those dependent upon them, record the existence of parks at Pasargadae in southwestern Iran and at Susa, another of their capitals, at the foot of the Zagros Mountains.[7]

The hunting done in these parks was not held in high esteem by classical authors. Xenophon says that such hunting is always successful since it was to a large extent carefully staged. The best that can be said for it, he concludes, is that it builds confidence for the field, where chance plays a greater role.[8] Dio Chrysostom (40–120), writing centuries later, is even more critical of "the Persian chase." To him, killing animals in a park was like killing unarmed prisoners of war and claiming thereby the status of a great warrior.[9]

But whether sporting or not, the park was a key institution in Achaemenid Iran. Nor was it exclusively a royal institution. Many of the *paradeisos* encountered in the sources are in the possession of the satraps, the governor-generals, who were not necessarily members of the royal family. Indeed, according to Xenophon, Cyrus the Great, after his conquest of Mesopotamia, told his newly appointed satraps to build parks and stock them with wild animals.[10] Pharnabazus, satrap of Phrygia, had such a complex at Dascyleium, now identified with ruins found on the shore of Lake Manyas, which Xenophon visited in 395; here he saw an abundance of "winged game" and a collection of wild animals, some in an enclosed park and some "in open spaces."[11]

Near neighbors and successors eagerly embraced the Achaemenid paradise. But before exploring the question of influence we need first to look at the Near Eastern antecedents; this will help us comprehend the formation of the core area and the mechanism by which the ancient Iranian model for the royal hunt was projected across space and back and forth through time.

The strong association between the Achaemenids and the paradise in classical literature did not prevent speculation that hunting parks had even deeper roots. For the Greeks, paradises began in Mesopotamia. Diodorus credits Semiramis, the fabulous queen of Babylon, with constructing such parks in Bagustanis (Behistan) and Media. Later on, he says, the practice was adopted by the Syrians and Persians.[12] Some modern scholarship supports this view, seeing in the royal zoos and gardens of the ancient Near East the prototypes of the paradise.[13]

Analogies and antecedents are found in ancient Egypt. The early pictorial evidence, from around 2350, shows that these were modest affairs, constructed of posts and nets and sometimes ditches. And unlike later paradises, which stocked game, animals were driven into the Egyptian "parks" just prior to the royal hunt. The remains of one such facility, dating from the reign of Amenophis II (ca. 1402–1364) have been found in Soleb, Nubia.[14] The other ingredient, formal and elaborate gardens, date from the Thirteenth Dynasty (1782–1650). These were walled and had pools, flowers, and trees; later on, in the time of Akhenaten (r. 1350–1334), wild animals were included, some caged, such as lions, and some free-ranging.[15]

Closer in time and space are the gardens, parks, and preserves of ancient Mesopotamia. Many believe that the immediate model for the Persian paradise is to be found in the Assyrian *ambassu*, an institution, some argue, which combined the functions of a royal hunting park and botanical garden.[16] Others, however, contest this interpretation, pointing out that the actual functions of the *ambassu* are difficult to assess, that, for example, it is more easily understood as a facility for animal sacrifice than as a hunting park.[17]

What, then, do we make of the paradise? Was it a Persian invention or a borrowing? One possible "compromise" interpretation is to think of this institution as coalescing under the Achaemenids, who drew upon a number of Near Eastern antecedents, none of which was an exact prototype of the paradise, in elaborating their hunting parks. But however murky the question of origins, one thing is certain: it was the ancient Persians who made these parks famous and fashionable.

This brings us back to the question of the Achaemenids' influence and how it was exercised. There are doubtless many reasons for their pronounced imprint on the political culture of West Asia, but one stands out as a major ingredient of their renown: great size. The Achaemenid empire, at least four or five times larger than any of its predecessors, represents a quantum leap in the scale of political organization.[18] Controlling at its zenith the Iranian plateau, the borderlands of northwest India and Central Asia, Mesopotamia, Asia Minor, and Egypt, it must have appeared to contemporaries as the entire world and as a miraculous undertaking. This unprecedented spurt in the growth of state power and range of political action made the Achaemenids, later conflated with pre-Islamic Iran at large, the model for statecraft and kingly government in the core area. Everything associated with their state was consequently imbued with special properties; its very success, in other words, magnified the importance of all Achaemenid institutions and promoted them near and far as essential attributes of sovereignty and majesty, and as necessary ingredients for, and the ultimate measure of, political success. So ingrained was this notion that everything deemed kingly in later times was automatically and retroactively attributed to the Persian kings of yore. As we shall see, paradises are but one expression of this phenomenon.

Hunting Parks at the Core and on the Periphery

Not unexpectedly, client states borrowed much from their Achaemenid masters. The Orontid dynasty of Armenia (ca. 401–200), whose ruling house was of Achaemenid origin, originally administered the territory as satraps and later as independent kings. The last of these, Orontes II (r. ca. 212–200), built a paradise called Genesis on the Akhurean, a northern affluent of the Araxes. Here, in the words of Moses Khorenatsʿi, he "planted a great forest of fir trees on the northern side of the river and secured it with walls to keep inside the swift wild goats, herds of hinds and stags, onagers and boars that they might multiply and fill the forest and give the king joy on the days of the hunt."[19] Succeeding dynasties followed suit. Xosrov (Khusrō), the Arsacid ruler of Armenia (r. ca. 330–38), founded the city of Duin/Dvin on the Arat River southeast of modern-day Erivan, and in its vicinity he had his army plant two large forests of oak that were enclosed with walls. Inside, palaces were built and once the forests matured wild animals were gathered "for the king's hunt, diversion and pleasure." The same source says Xosrov's son and successor, Tiran (r. ca. 338–51), built another hunting park at Mount Masis north of Lake Van.[20] This may well have been a frequent practice; each succeeding king, seeking his own royal identity, added to the number of paradises within the kingdom. For the smaller polities of Transcaucasia and southern Turkestan, regions frequently under the political and cultural sway of Iran, a walled paradise located in or around the royal city was a commonplace.[21]

In tracking the long-term effects of the Old Persian model, what is crucial is that the Sasanids, the historically remembered embodiment of the Achaemenid achievement, also embraced the institution of the paradise. As self-conscious restorers of hallowed Achaemenid traditions, they established hunting parks throughout their vast domains. One that is well described in the sources was located on the Tigris River north of Seleucia and Ctesiphon. Overrun by a Roman army in 363, it was the classic paradise, full of trees, local and exotic game, and luxurious buildings.[22] Near the end of the dynasty, Byzantine forces occupied several other paradises, well stocked with game that Theophanes says belonged to the emperor Khosroe/Khusro II (r. 591–628).[23] The most famous of the Sasanid parks is that at Tāq-i Bustān, near Kirmān, which is depicted in reliefs on the walls of a large grotto. Dating very likely to the reign of Khusro, these reliefs provide a kind of snapshot of kingly hunting in a royal park, which aerial photography shows was rectangular in shape.[24] One notable feature of this park is the provision of microenvironments appropriate to a specific game animal: marsh land for boar and open ground for deer.[25]

The Muslim defeat of the Sasanids in a series of battles fought between 633 and 651 resulted in an Arab occupation of Mesopotamia and the Iranian homeland. In time, and particularly during the formative years of the ʿAbbāsid caliphate, the Arabs took over from the Persians many institutions and emblems of royalty—thrones, crowns, and hunting parks.[26] Arab chronicles and hunting manuals were well aware that the Sasanids had many parks and in some cases connected individual rulers to specific sites.[27] Early caliphs, Hārūn al-Rashīd (r. 786–809) and others, constructed paradises of their own around the capital of Baghdad.[28] That of Mustanjid (r. 1160–70) is described by the Jewish traveler Benjamin of Tudela as "three miles in extent, wherein is a great park with all varieties of trees, fruit-bearing and otherwise, and all manner of animals. The whole is surrounded by a wall, and in the park there is a lake whose waters are fed by the river Hiddekel. Whenever the king desires to indulge in recreation and to rejoice and feast, his servants catch all manner of birds, game, and fish, and he goes to that place with his counselors and princes."[29] Smaller principalities in the region also had their parks. One of the Ispahbad rulers of the eighth century built in Ṭabaristān an extensive hunting park well supplied with deer, wild pigs, hares, wolves, and even leopards.[30] In so doing, he was not necessarily mimicking the ʿAbbāsids, but continuing the Sasanid practice, because Ṭabaristān, south of the Caspian, long preserved its political independence and many Iranian national traditions. The same was true of Turkestan; following local traditions, traceable back to the Sasanids, the ruler of Bukhara in the eleventh century built a hunting park, called Ghūruq, replete with gardens, beautiful buildings, and a diverse collection of game animals.[31] And many centuries later, when the Ṣafavids (1501–1732) ruled over greater Iran, hunting parks were still a visible feature of the landscape, most notably Hazār Jarīb, "A Thousand Acres," near Julfā in Iṣfahān, which is described by several European travelers.[32]

The history of hunting parks in India is similarly long. According to Xuanzang, the Chinese pilgrim who traveled through North India in the 630s, the famous "deer wild [*yelu*]" where the Buddha preached his first sermon to the five mendicants was, in local lore, originally an enclosed hunting grounds.[33] The earliest references to such parks come from classical authors. Quintus Curtius, in his history of Alexander's campaigns, describes an unnamed Indian king in the northwest who was much addicted to hunting, which he says "consists in shooting with arrows animals shut up in a preserve amid the prayers and songs of his concubines."[34] Later on Aelian (ca. 170–230) relates that the Indian kings had large royal parks more grandiose than those of the Persian kings at Susa and Ectabana (Hamadān). These, he continues, were provided with man-made lakes, trees, shrubs, and, of course, birds, fish, and animals, many of which were imported from abroad.[35]

The *Arthaśāstra*, a book of government traditionally ascribed to Kautilya, chief adviser of the founder of the Mauryan empire (321–184, but probably dating in its present form to the fourth century C.E.), recommends for royal hunting an extensive tract of forest, isolated by ditches and a single gate, which should contain fruit trees, lakes, and game animals.[36] The Muslim rulers in India, drawing as well on Persian and Central Asian precedents, continued this older tradition. In the period of the Delhi sultanate (1206–1555) there were several famous hunting parks. Fīrūz Shāh (r. 1351–88) built a large "Palace of Hunting [*kushk-i shikār*]" that was laid out with a sizable hill at its center.[37] An even earlier park of the Khalji sultans of Delhi (1290–1320), noted for the diversity of its game and the pleasure it afforded the ruler and his women, was still well remembered three centuries later in the time of Jahāngīr.[38]

In the Mughal era, parks are numerous and often described by court sources and foreign travelers. One, in Gujarat, a day's ride from Ahmadābād, was about six to eight square miles in size, and full of beautiful buildings and game.[39] Comparable facilities were found in the Hindu-dominated south. Ludovico di Varthema, who visited the capital of Vijayanagar around 1505, states that the city was large and completely walled "with certain very beautiful places for hunting and fowling" that he characterizes, appropriately, as "a second paradise."[40]

The royal hunting park survived in the subcontinent down to the nineteenth century. Godfrey Mundy, traveling in the late 1820s, reports that the "king of Oude [Oudh]," a Muslim ruler, had near Lucknow a park called "Dil Koosha [Dil-kūshah], or Heart's Desire." Within its walls, he continues, there are jungle grasses, trees, and much game—boar, deer, hare, and quail. Later on, Mundy encountered another park near Gwalior, this time belonging to a Hindu prince. It, too, swarmed with "antelope, deer, and other game."[41]

While hunting parks were a standard, continuous, and enduring component of the royal hunt throughout the core area, their history in the Mediterranean basin and Europe is much more intermittent, and the forms they took there differed in some respects from the classic paradise. In the Roman West,

Varro (116–27 B.C.E.) reports that in former times people kept only hares for hunting, but that now, in his day, there are great parks, for "people enclose many acres within walls, so as to keep a number of boars and roes." Further on, he gives many particulars, describing parks, *therotrophium*, up to four square miles, containing well-fed boars, stags, and other beasts. He ascribes this "invention" to the second century B.C.E., when Quintus Hortensius, fabled for his love of luxury, introduced such parks into Latium that soon attracted imitators.[42]

Early Roman emperors, Tiberius (r. 14–37), Nero (r. 54–68), and Domitian (r. 81–96), constructed enclosed animal parks, but these were not exact equivalents of the Persian paradise.[43] They seem rather to be following fashion, playing with selected elements of a foreign model, invoking the paradise without really duplicating it. That garden walls in imperial Rome sometimes had scenes of Persian paradises populated with exotic animals painted on them certainly points in this direction.[44]

The Vandals, by way of contrast, took the Persian originals far more seriously. From the time they established themselves in Libya, about 440, they began, on the testimony of Procopius, to adopt Near Eastern customs, wearing "Medic garments" and hunting and dwelling in parks (*paradeisos*), "which were well supplied with water and trees."[45] The Byzantines, too, placed some value on large hunting parks. When Liudprand, the ambassador of Otto I, arrived in Constantinople, the emperor Nicephorus II Phocas (r. 963–69) asked him if his sovereign had parks and animals. Liudprand replied yes, but the emperor went on to boast of the size of his park and the fact that he had wild asses in it. The park itself, by the ambassador's account, was large and hilly, and possessed abundant game. A little later, an attendant of the emperor told Liudprand that the possession of wild asses would be "no small glory for [Otto]," since it would be a first for a ruler in the West.[46] This exchange is interesting in that it reveals sensitivity to "international" standards; both parties recognized that a decent hunting park was a normal attribute of royalty.

In western Europe, the value placed on hunting parks is expressed in a poem, usually attributed to Einhard, which relates that Charlemagne had a verdant pleasure park "encircled by many walls" not far from his winter capital at Aachen. Within were meadows, streams, woods, and "shady glades" alive with fowl, deer, and "all kinds of wild beasts." In this idyllic setting, we are told,

> Charlemagne, the admirable hero, would often go hunting in grassy field, as he loved to do,
> and give chase to the wild beasts with dogs and whistling arrows,
> laying low multitudes of antlered stags beneath the black trees.[47]

This evocation of Charlemagne's park is certainly reminiscent of classical descriptions of the Iranian paradise. Whatever the accuracy of this poetic depiction, the norm in western Europe was not the full-fledged paradise of old, but the more homely deer park. These appeared in the early medieval period and continued to flourish into the early modern era and beyond.[48] The institution was widespread in England, where they were built by the crown, the nobles, ecclesiastical houses, and aspiring gentry. They typically consisted of woods enclosed by ditches, earthen banks, and palisades. The deer, of course, were stocked. Some parks measured five to six miles in circumference, with the largest up to twenty miles. By 1600, at the height of their popularity, there were about 800 parks in England and 30 more in Wales.[49] One deer park, Lullingstone, created at the beginning of the fifteenth century, enclosed 690 acres; it survived in various forms until 1931 and is now a public space with golf course, nature walks, and other attractions.[50]

While the western European deer park differed in some respects from the paradises in the core with their sumptuous palaces, extensive landscaping, and exotic game, the two institutions nonetheless shared a number of similar economic and social functions. These will be compared and analyzed when we have completed our survey of hunting parks at the eastern end of Eurasia.

Hunting Parks in East Asia

China has a venerable tradition of hunting parks that parallels, to a surprising extent, that of Iran and India, except that its history has more peaks and valleys.

According to Chinese tradition, parks are a very early development. Mencius (ca. 372–289) attributes to King Wen, father of King Wu, the founder of the Zhou dynasty, ca. 1122, a hunting park seventy Chinese miles square, and to his own sovereign, King Xuan of Qi in Shandong, a park of forty square miles.[51] Other sources indicate that "deer parks" were common in the kingdoms of the Spring and Autumn period (722–481), and in the subsequent era of the Warring States (403–221), all the rulers of the dozen rival polities had extensive parks.[52] One was even granted to a neighboring ruler as a diplomatic diversion.[53]

With the unification of China under the Qin (221–206) and Han (206 B.C.E.–222 C.E.), and the inauguration of the imperial period, hunting parks became increasingly visible and extremely well documented. There are a number of these parks, some located in subordinate kingdoms and some at the center that specialized in specific forms of the hunt such as bird netting.[54] But the best known by far was located just outside the capital, Chang'an, the great Shanglin, or "Supreme Forest" park which was first laid out under the Qin and then much expanded during the Former Han.

Its greatest period of growth came during the reign of the famous Martial Emperor, Wudi (r. 148–86 B.C.E.), and, according to the *Hanshu*, generated considerable controversy. This account relates that starting in 138 the emperor organized large hunting excursions outside the capital that lasted up to five days. In time, this chase became more and more elaborate and began to disrupt the agriculture rounds. As one example, the court set up "clothes changing places," twelve in all, and mobilized local peasants to attend the royal party. The emperor soon concluded that the distances traveled were too great and the hunts a burden on the locals. He therefore had a palace official, Wuqiu Shouwang, survey an area southeast of the capital and bought up or sequestered land for a vast hunting park. Plans for the park drew criticism, particularly from an official named Dongfang Shuo, who argued against the huge scale of the hunting grounds, its numerous facilities, extensive walls, and general extravagance. He pointed out that the rich agricultural lands and natural resources important to the court would be lost through the development of the park. Shuo found it quite incredible that the state should encourage forests and wastelands, and extend the range of wild beasts. Last, he warned that such expenditures always ended in disaster and the fall of dynasties. Despite these dire warnings from a respected official, warnings which Wudi, to all appearances, carefully considered, the construction of the park went ahead as originally planned.[55]

The result was a park more than 200 Chinese miles in circumference, which contained within its walls a wide variety of land forms and environments: woods, marshes, hills, valleys, meadows, streams, waterfalls, ponds, islands, and swamps. There was, of course, an extensive list of wild game—boars, geese, and so on—and exotic animals—zebras, yaks, tapirs, wild oxen, water buffaloes, elk, antelope, aurochs, elephants, rhinoceroses, onagers, and camels.[56] No expense was spared to provide Shanglin with sumptuous facilities: there were observation towers, palaces, a zoo, retreats, arcades, verandahs, pavilions, and kitchens, all fitted into a created nature of leveled and terraced hills, deep grottoes, and vantage points for leisurely viewing of the royal hunt. All facilities were furnished with specially made bronze utensils and roof tiles. Interspersed among these "wild" spaces were a wide variety of domesticated plants, both edible and fragrant: citrus, plums, almonds, and grapes, as well as trees of every description.[57] So numerous were the facilities that in the reign of Zhengdi (33–7 B.C.E.) twenty-five palaces and lodges in Shanglin were torn down because they were rarely used.[58]

Shanglin, obviously, was a carefully managed and manipulated environment. Both domesticated animals, dogs and horses, and game, birds and wild boar, were reared there by a large staff of male and female slaves. Underbrush was kept under control for ease of hunting, some of which was still conducted from chariots.[59] The main hunting "season" in the park was late fall and early winter. The emperor led the hunt in a carriage carved from ivory, attended by soldiers, huntsmen, and myriad beaters. The park was so large that scouts had to be sent ahead to locate game. The finale, of course, was a great collective slaughter of the beasts.[60]

Following the collapse of the Later Han in 221 C.E., China entered a four-century period of disunity that saw a series of dynasties of Inner Asian origin dominate the north while indigenous regimes held sway in the south. Those in the north continued the hunting traditions of their ancestors and maintained Chinese-style hunting parks stocked with deer.[61] The Former Qin (359–95), of Tibetan origin, had its own version of Shanglin outside of Chang'an and the Tuoba Wei built a large park called Flowering Forest (Hualin) at its capital, Luoyang. The latter had the usual features—artificial environments, abundant game, and human amenities.[62]

Following the reunification of China by the Sui (581–618) and Tang (618–907), there was a revival and expansion of hunting parks, particularly around the capitals.[63] Tang emperors made frequent use of these parks, although bad times, drought and popular discontent, caused them to curtail the chase.[64]

The Song, a native dynasty (960–1279), showed far less interest in the hunt. The older parks of China, however, provided inspiration and precedent for the mania of pleasure parks (*yuanlin*) that gripped the Song. These facilities, built by the imperial family, officials, and wealthy merchants were no longer used for the chase but many housed zoological collections, particularly of rare and exotic species.[65] The Jürchen Jin dynasty, which pushed the Song out of the north in the early twelfth century, were avid hunters. In Kaifeng, one of the major cities of their realm, the court constructed an imperial hunting park called Shanglin *suo*, literally "Supreme Forest Locale."[66] This was a fitting prelude to a resurgence of interest in hunting parks that accompanied the Mongols' rise to power and the creation under their auspices of the most famous paradise of all, Xanadu.

Most elements of the royal hunting complex were easily grafted onto the Mongols' commitment to the chase. Interest in hunting parks is first expressed by Ögödei (r. 1229–41), Chinggis Qan's third son and successor. In the *Secret History*, Ögödei admits to four major faults, one of which was covetousness, his desire to monopolize game and deprive his kinsmen of the joys of the chase. This he did, he confesses, by having beaten earth fences and walls erected to contain large amounts of prey.[67] Well-informed Persian sources elaborate upon this first attempt at a hunting park. According to them, the facility was built in the region of the Ongqin River, Ögödei's winter quarters, in central Mongolia, well to the south of the imperial capital at Qara Qorum. Its wall, made of wood and clay, is described as "two days in length" with "gates set in it." When hunting, the army formed a huge *jerge* and, slowly collecting game from the surrounding region, drove them into the park. Once inside, the qaghan began hunting and then withdrew to a hill to watch his underlings take their turn. This was such a success that Ögödei's brother, Chaghadai, whose territory was in Turkestan, built a facility between Almaliq and Quyas in the Ili River valley "in the very same manner."[68]

In these hunting parks we see a transitional phase that combines elements of the settled and nomadic tradition. Ögödei's park is the focal point of a gigantic ring hunt, a killing ground, demarcated by walls instead of rope and netting. The next generation of Mongolian parks, however, conforms to sedentary standards and approximates the traditional paradise. One, outside Xian in Shaanxi, belonged to Mangqala (d. 1280), the third son of Qubilai, founder of the Yuan dynasty (1271–1368). As described by Marco Polo, it had high walls five miles around, rivers and lakes, a great palace, and "many wild animals and . . . birds for the chase." These, he adds, "none would dare to hunt . . . except for the Lord [Mangqala]."[69] For the Mongols, such exclusive rights were expressed in the term *qorigh,* from the Turkic *qorugh,* "reserved," or "forbidden precinct," a term that underlies Ghūruq, the name of the paradise built in eleventh-century Bukhara.[70]

Of the Mongolian-built paradises, two stand out. The first was in Dadu, the modern-day Beijing. The construction of the new imperial capital began in 1267, a short distance from the old Jin capital of Yanjing. In 1272 the capital, initially called Zhongtu, was renamed Dadu, which European travelers called Cambaluc, from the Turkic Qan Baliq, "Qan's City." In 1274 Qubilai moved to the new complex, although work on the walls and other facilities continued into the 1280s.[71] When completed, Dadu was divided into two halves, the western part of which contained the hunting park with the by-now familiar artificial hills, lakes, gardens, and wild game, and waterfowl, a delicacy among the Mongols.[72]

The second park, made famous by Coleridge's poem "Kubla Khan," was Shangdu, located about 250 miles north of Beijing, about a ten-day journey by horse. Built in 1256 as a summer residence for Qubilai, then still a prince, the complex was originally called Kaiping Fu. Qubilai's Chinese advisor, Liu Bingzhong, supervised its construction. The city itself had three walls, all of pounded earth, delimiting the outer city, the imperial city, and the innermost palace city. In 1264, after Qubilai became qaghan, the name was changed to Shangdu, "Upper" or "Supreme Capital."[73] The complex was surrounded by a moat and rammed earth walls faced with stone and pierced on all sides with gates and bastions. The hunting park was to the north and west of the city and by recent estimates covered about five square miles. It was enclosed by earthen works and had at its center an artificial hill and lake.[74]

This reconstruction, based on several ground observations over the last century, accords well, discounting some exaggeration, with the depictions found in contemporary sources, those of Marco Polo and Rashīd al-Dīn, the famed historian and statesman of the Mongolian dynasty in Iran. The latter was never in China, but did obtain his data on "Kaimin-fū," as he calls it in Persian, from a Mongolian informant, Bolad Aqa, who had traveled to Shangdu by official post on several occasions. In both accounts the earthen walls, stone facings, wooden palisades, and palaces are noted; Rashīd al-Dīn adds that the chief palace, *qarshī* (Turkic *qarshi*) in his text, was constructed "in the Chinese style," which one would expect from the fact that a Chinese official oversaw construction. Both authors speak, too, of the abundance and diversity of the game animals dwelling within the walls.[75] Here is the standard hunting park, one that gained fame in the Latin West and in the Islamic East, and one that could have passed muster in ancient Iran, Han China, or Mughal India.

The Manchus, another hunting people and founders of the last imperial dynasty in China, the Qing (1644–1911), took a great interest in hunting parks, particularly during the first half of their rule. They had in these years a complex of gardens and hunting parks in the neighborhood of the capital, Beijing, which was administered by officers of the royal household, an organization appropriately called the Shanglin *yuan* [Bureau].[76] A number of these have been described by foreign travelers. The earliest is by Feodor Baikov, a Russian envoy to Kanbali (Qan Baliq) in 1657–58, whose diplomatic report contains the following notice: "And in the kingdom of China, near the imperial court, there is a rounded hill, not too high, and about this hill a planted [*sazhenai*] forest. And in this forest live wild animals—Siberian deer, big-horned sheep, steppe goats [antelope?] but besides these [species, so] the Chinese say, there are no others. And around this rounded hill is a wall of fired bricks."[77] This may, in fact, be the same park John Bell, a Scottish physician in Russian service, visited in 1721. This facility, which he calls Chayza (perhaps Zhaizi, "The Stockade"), also had forests, an artificial hill and lake, and was enclosed with a brick wall. The game within, Bell relates, was driven to the emperor by soldiers formed up in a semicircle.[78] Another park, named Pazhao, according to the Jesuit Ripa, a resident in China from 1710 to 1723, was built by the Kangxi emperor, who visited it for stag hunting once a year.[79] A third, also built by Kangxi, was about six miles west of Beijing. Called Changchun Yuan, "Garden of Joyful Springtime," it was a large facility, surrounded by walls and guarded by "Tartar" troops. It was full of mansions, roads, lakes, rest stops, and game, especially deer.[80] This is the "Chinchiuian" of the Russian accounts, the place where Lev Izmailov and his embassy were lavishly entertained when they presented the gifts of Peter the Great to Kangxi in 1720.[81]

Even more grand was the group of parks at Rehe (Jehol), which takes its name from a local river. This was the Shangdu of the Manchus, their unofficial summer capital, which was in eastern Inner Mongolia, about 120 miles from Beijing. Established by Kangxi in 1681, it was much elaborated by his successors and came to include a small town and several Lamaist temples for the benefit of the local, Mongolian population. The entire complex, called Mulan Weichang, "Enclosed Place," was about 1,300 Chinese miles in circumference, large enough to offer varied topography and environmental conditions needed for its diverse game.[82]

According to Ripa, Kangxi, accompanied by an entourage of 30,000 troops and servants, occupied Rehe from early May to the end of September. Here he and his favored guests lived in comfort amid pavilions, pagodas, bridges, gardens, artificial lakes, and islands, all of which were decorated with works of art.[83] There were two separate hunting parks, one in the east that was reserved for the emperor, his ladies, and eunuchs, and a larger one in the west for guests. George Macartney, the English ambassador to Kangxi, rode about this park for several hours without exhausting the sights, describing it as "wild, woody, mountainous, and rocky, abounding with stags and deer of different species, and most other beasts of chase not dangerous to man." Still, he says, this park, too, had many conveniences, retreats, palaces, and banqueting facilities. Like Shangdu, Rehe would certainly have been recognized for what it was by elites from different times and different cultures. Indeed, Macartney, a man with the classical education typical of his age and station, quite rightly characterizes the entire complex as a "paradise."[84]

The Purposes of Paradise

As a private arena for the pursuit of pleasure and game, hunting parks operated as a symbol of sovereignty throughout Eurasia. Writing in eleventh-century Inner Asia for the ruler of the Qarakhanids (992–1211), an Islamicized Turkic dynasty, Yūsuf Khāṣṣ Ḥājib asserts that building of hunting parks is a major attribute of majesty, like conquest, generosity, and the bestowal of justice. To drive his point home, he associates these activities with the achievements of the storied rulers of the past—Caesar, Khusro, and Alexander.[85] His admonition on this subject was in fact a widely accepted norm. John Mandeville, whose spurious travels were very popular in the late fourteenth century, paints a glowing picture of the Great Qan's hunting park in Camalach (Qan Baliq), its pools, hills, canals, fruit trees, wild fowl, and game.[86] Some three centuries later, Alexander Hamilton, an Englishman on his way to India, relates he heard that the king of Ethiopia, still vaguely associated with Prester John, had a vast, walled park that enclosed palaces, rivers, ponds, gardens, orchards, and "woods for wild game."[87] Here is the common vision of paradise in the West, one that captures all the essential ingredients, and one projected onto any powerful ruler, both real and imagined. In these cases, the rumors well served the cause of enhancing majesty. Like one of Chinggis Qan's tents that attained staggering proportions in popular memory, hunting parks became larger, more fabulous, more magical as their images moved through time and space.[88]

The pursuit of game is, of course, a common feature of this image, but it is certainly not its only, or even its dominant, component. It is now time to examine the full range of services provided by paradises. The malleability of the term "paradise" nicely mirrors the malleability of the institution itself. In some cases the term, like official titles and coinage, drastically depreciated over time. In a Greek sales document from Dura Europus dating from the second century B.C.E., *paradeisos* simply meant a private garden, as did the later Turkic *borduz* and Persian *firdaus*.[89] In other cases, however, the term greatly appreciated. Starting from the very same base, Old Persian *paridaida*, the word in the West acquired through time myriad meanings, many of which, on the surface at least, are quite contradictory. As William McClung has argued, paradise partakes of both the worldly, places of material abundance, and the otherworldly, places of spiritual bliss; they are at one and the same time places of generation and utopian existence and of degeneration, fall, and flight. Lastly, and most important for us, they can be specimens of primordial, pristine nature, untrammeled by humans, or contrarily, they can be elaborate works of artifice in which humans fashion, reorder, and arrange nature.[90]

In the biblical tradition (Gen. 2.8–10 and 19–20), paradise has, quite obviously, powerful cosmological meanings and associations, but as Lars Ringbom points out, the same is true of the Old Iranian tradition, which holds, in his reconstruction, that within their "world empire there lay a holy, kingly city, a place of the center and of origins which is intimately bound up with the idea of the beginnings of all mountains and source of all waters, the original homeland of all plants as well as the primordial hearth of all fire, the original site of kingly authority and the true source of correct belief."[91]

In the later Muslim reformulation of these notions, the Persian garden became for them an earthly counterpart of the Quranic paradise. This earthly paradise, however, is no wilderness; it is well tended, carefully designed for human comfort. Above all, it is full of trees, running water, domesticated plants, and shade.[92]

Given the ideological and religious contexts, the extensive agricultural establishments and responsibilities of hunting parks are only to be expected. In his lengthy discussion of paradises, Xenophon asserts that the Achaemenid royal house "pays as much attention to husbandry as to warfare." To this end, he continues, their kings place paradises, which contain all the good things "the soil will produce," in all districts in which they reside or regularly visit.[93] Such facilities represent the "world garden" and this is why Achaemenid princes ceremonially planted crops there to assure the fertility of the land. This was clearly taken over from earlier, Mesopotamian notions of the "gardener king," fully developed in the Neo-Assyrian and Neo-Babylonian eras (the ninth to the sixth century), when the king was conceived as the Guardian of the Garden of Paradise where he tended the Tree of Life and the Water of Life. Old Persian rulers assumed these sacral functions as cultivator, hunter, and propagator, all of which promoted the fruitfulness of their domains.[94]

To carry out these cosmological duties, particularly in the arid environment of the core area, water was crucial. We have already seen that hunting parks typically had ponds, streams, and lakes. The most striking physical feature of many parks east and west was an artificial hill produced by the excavation of an artificial lake. Hydraulic engineering was integral to their construction, which utilized a variety of irrigation techniques from animal-powered water buckets to well-crafted stone-lined canals and pools controlled by sluice gates.[95]

Agricultural pursuits were by no means unique to the Persian paradise. The royal park of the famous Mauryan ruler of the third century B.C.E., located outside Patna, contained many fruit trees, as did Shanglin and other hunting parks of China.[96] Nor should it be assumed that the agricultural services of parks were mainly ceremonial. The Old Persian paradises were production centers and government granaries.[97] In fact, the ancient paradises might even become purely economic institutions. In Ptolemaic Egypt the *paradeisos* of Persia was transformed into huge, utilitarian, and professionally managed plantations growing fruits, vegetables, and grapes, while those of Dura Europus on the Euphrates operated as large orchards.[98]

One further agricultural service of hunting parks deserves notice. In recent centuries, as is well known, imperial botanical gardens such as Kew in England served as clearing houses for the transfer of plant species across and between continents. Such transfers, it is now recognized, had important ecological and economic consequences. This phenomenon, however, is neither new nor a Western innovation.[99] In the Middle Ages, such botanical gardens are much in evidence, and indeed seem to be intrinsic features of imperial regimes everywhere. In the Muslim world gardens and parks, private and royal, operated as centers for the diffusion of exotic and ornamental plants. Royal parks from

Central Asia to North Africa constituted a long-range network of botanical exchange.[100] But exchanges hardly began with the rise of Islam. Already in the Assyrian era, a public inscription of Ashurnasirpal II asserts that wherever the king went on campaign he collected seeds for new plants and trees, and lists several dozen he cultivated in the royal pleasure gardens.[101] And the same was true of East Asia; as soon as Shanglin was formed in the third century B.C.E., it too was filled with plants of distant origin, especially fruits and trees, a tradition that lasted in China down to the eighteenth century, when Kangxi had specialty crops, such as strawberries, cultivated at Rehe for the enjoyment of his hunting guests.[102]

Another essential function of hunting parks, this one intimately linked to the chase, is forestry. The destruction of forests began quite early in the Near East and in consequence it is not surprising that the Persian paradise was inevitably a timber reserve. Biblical references (Neh. 2.8) allude to this and classical sources are even more explicit. Artaxerxes II had a *paradeisos* full of pine and cypress, which he ordered his soldiers to cut down in time of crisis.[103] Indeed, one destroyed a park, quite literally, by cutting it down.[104] For some later writers, Strabo and Procopius, the term *paradeisos* was synonymous with timber reserves, protected tracts of rare species in largely treeless environments.[105] Growing Greek and Roman interest in trees and forestry was greatly stimulated by the extensive literature on the flora and parks of Iran.[106]

Because royal parks were protected, they constituted convenient and secure storage areas, particularly for foodstuffs. The Achaemenid paradises not only grew crops but also received certain quantities of food supplies—fruit, dates, figs, and substantial amounts of grain.[107] Clearly, the paradise of Achaemenid and Sasanid times was a complex and vital institution that typically included extensive water control and irrigation systems, formal gardens, pleasure houses, ceremonial centers, agricultural lands, orchards, forests, storage facilities, and even peasant villages, all carefully delimited from the outside world, walled and well fortified.[108]

In Pierre Briant's analysis, the ancient paradise had three basic functions: (1) a residence of satraps or kings, an outpost of central authority in the countryside; (2) a model of agricultural prosperity achieved by rational manipulation of nature through irrigation, propagation, and diffusion of useful plants, and the preservation of scarce resources such as timber; and (3) an ideological statement promoting the emperor and his agents as the protectors of the earth and the peasantry, and the guarantors of fertility and prosperity. The contrast between the luxuriance of the paradise and the sparseness of the surrounding countryside demonstrated the king's capacity to dominate nature, his connectedness to the cosmos. This is what Briant calls *vitrine ideologie*, or "showcase ideology."[109]

That these efforts often elicited the desired response is evidenced by the fact that Plutarch, among others, pointedly opposes the Persian king's paradise "in elaborate cultivation" to the surrounding regions so "bare and treeless."[110] Moreover, some millennia and a half later, the Seljuqs (1038–1194), as Scott Redford has recently shown, were still using the very same technique, acting out their cosmic roles in built environments that meaningfully connected horticulture and hunting, fertility and security.[111]

The use of the land for such ends is in fact widespread. In premodern societies, the fashioning of artificial environments that differed markedly from their immediate surroundings was always an act of great ideological import. Monumental landscaping of this sort was a most effective and eye-catching way of imposing political messages on physical locations.[112] Hunting parks were excellent vehicles for this because they document a ruler's control of diverse natural resources—animal, vegetable, and mineral—and, at the same time, recall earlier conquests of nature that fashioned, in Magnus Fiskesjö's apt expression, "predictable wildernesses."[113]

None of this is to argue that hunting parks elsewhere were exact replicas of the Old Persian paradise, but rather that they partook of many (though not all) of its attributes. The parks of Han China, for instance, exhibit a number of shared characteristics. True, their parks were not the hubs of provincial administration, but those in the capital performed similar political and economic functions. This is revealed by the elaborate bureaucracy needed to run these vast establishments. General jurisdiction was in the hands of the Chief Commandant of Waters and Parks (*Shuiheng duwei*) and individual parks were under the direction of a prefect (*ling*) and his subordinates. We are best informed about their duties at Shanglin, where they were responsible for the birds, game, huntsmen, and hunting dogs, for the production and distribution of vegetables, fruits, and timber, for the storage of grain, the supervision of the imperial stud, the fisheries, boatmen, and the many artisans who maintained the park's buildings.[114] Additionally, Shanglin housed the imperial mint, a school for foreign language study, a prison, and provided facilities for criminal executions, animal sacrifices, and sporting events. And, like the paradises of the ancient Near East, this was where the Chinese emperor, at least on occasion, ceremonially plowed the ground in the spring to ensure agricultural fertility.[115]

This has seemingly taken us a long way from hunting, and we can properly close on this theme. While many of the facilities designated as hunting parks abound in fruit trees, cooling ponds, and elegant buildings, others, described in the very same terms, make no mention of game or the chase. They are places dedicated to human pleasure, like the *paradeisos* described by Longus (ca. second century C.E.) in his pastoral romance *Daphnes and Chloe*, or the "orchard" described by Clavijo in his account of Temür's Samarqand in 1405.[116] Some parks appear to be incipient zoos, like the one reported by Masʿūdī in tenth-century Baghdad, or the royal parks of Korea between the tenth and the fourteenth century, which had extensive botanical and zoological collections.[117] To label all such parks hunting parks is of course to prejudice the issue; they were in fact multiuse facilities that sometimes included game for the chase.[118]

This is why hunting parks have such interesting and instructive histories. Hyde Park, Windsor Castle, Versailles, and Tsarskoe Selo all began as royal hunting grounds and subsequently evolved into something else.[119] The secret to their adaptability is that hunting parks always had extremely diverse functions, some of which strengthened over time and some of which atrophied. Consequently, under specific historical circumstances, one of its varied services might come to dominate, and in this way some hunting parks became elaborate gardens while others became royal residences or public places.

To put this somewhat differently, neither hunting nor hunting parks can be easily or meaningfully isolated in these societies, for both were deeply involved in other vital activities, ranging from official travel to military preparation, topics that will be addressed in subsequent chapters.

4
Partners

Animal Assistants

In the long history of human hunting, animal assistants are a comparatively recent development. It is also true that in historical times, societies for which the hunt is a vital source of food or income made very limited use of animal partners, mainly the dog, in the pursuit of game. In contrast, pastoralists and agriculturalists, with their greater experience in modifying animal behavior have trained a wide variety of animals as hunting partners. Here it must be stressed that in most cases the new partners were never domesticated at all, simply reconditioned to hunt under a measure of human control.

This leads to the matter of working definitions necessary for the following discussion of animal assistants. *Domesticated* animals are those whose breeding cycles, territorial organization, and food supply are under human control. This results in social and genetic changes that alter the animals' morphology, coloration, and behavior. In other words, natural selection for long-term survival of the species is replaced under domestication by artificial selection whose goal is to gratify human economic, social, cultural, or aesthetic needs.[1] For the rest, *feral* designates an animal previously domesticated that returns to a wild state, *wild* any animal that has never been domesticated, while *tame,* to use Roger Caras's phrasing, is "an animal still a member of a wild species that has *as an individual* been behaviorally adapted to tolerate the proximity of man."[2]

If we now apply these definitions to human hunting partners, or at least those common to the royal hunt, only two, the dog and the horse, are domesticated. The rest, various species of raptors, hunting cats, and elephants, all fall under the heading of tame. This, in turn, means that the latter must first be captured, that is, hunted, and these quests became a part of the royal hunting culture.[3] We can also categorize animal assistants in another useful way. There are those that directly engage and attack prey—raptors, cats, and dogs—and those who do not—horses and elephants. The latter, as we shall see, were occasionally trained to attack tigers, but like the horse, their primary function was transportation. For our purposes, we can concentrate on the dog among the domesticates and the raptors, hunting cats, and elephants among the tame. We exclude horses because they neither hunt nor are they hunted, and also in the interests of space. We also exclude a few true hunters such as the ferret (*Putorius putorius*), which was domesticated early on, perhaps by 1,000 B.C.E., and was widely used in the West for catching rabbits.[4] This decision is justified on the grounds that the ferret was not thought of as a noble animal and thus not an appropriate partner for a royal hunter.

At this point, it should be acknowledged that in most instances the terms "partner," and even more so "assistant," depreciate the importance of the animals used in the royal hunt because they wrongly imply that the latter mainly found, flushed, or retrieved game for humans. In fact, the situation was typically the reverse: the humans did the tracking and flushing for their animal partners. From the human perspective, therefore, this kind of hunting was to a large extent a matter of logistics, of arranging and witnessing animal combats and competitions.

Viewed in the long term, one of the major trends in the history of royal hunting is the growing preoccupation with animals trained to the chase. Frederick II, Holy Roman Emperor (r. 1212–50) and famed scholar and falconer, divided the chase into three basic types: hunting with inanimate instruments or weapons, hunting with animal partners, and hunting that combines both.[5] There is, of course, no statistical data on which hunting mode was most popular. Anecdotal evidence suggests, however, that hunting with weapons exclusively was rare. Speaking of Tāj al-Dīn, a high official at the court of the Delhi sultan Iltutmish (r. 1211–36), Jūzjānī, a contemporary, says that he hunted only with bow and arrow and that he never "took with him cheetah (*yūz*), hawk (*yāz*), or dog (*sāg*) to any hunting ground."[6] This, evidently, is reported in this manner because his behavior was deemed exceptional. In other cases, royal hunters alternated between hunting with weapons and with animal partners; this, in any event is how Oghuz Qan, mythical progenitor and model ruler of the western, Oghuz Turks, was portrayed in epic tales. "Sometimes," relates one tradition, "he consented to go out hunting with cheetahs (*yūz*) and falcons (*bāz*) . . ." and ". . . sometimes he went to the field to do single combat with wild boars (*gurāz*)."[7] Obviously, there were choices to be made, but going to the field with animal partners was the more normal procedure; indeed, in the core area hunting is often and rightly depicted as the pursuit of wild animals with tame animals.[8] One very good reason for this trend is that hunting is dangerous and the use of animal surrogates provided a measure of safety.[9]

Although the attraction to such animals became well nigh universal in Eurasia, the attraction had a history and a geography that changed over time. Once again, the Mediterranean world of classical antiquity was an exception; it did not share in this fascination with tamed animals of the chase. Xenophon, in his famous hunting manual, *Cynegeticus*, written in the fifth century B.C.E., knew only horses and dogs as helpmates. And this remained the case in the western end of Eurasia until the early Middle Ages, when international standards, emanating from the core, came to exert substantial influence on European elites.

Dogs

A recent examination of the genetic evidence by Charles Vilà and associates confirms that the progenitor of the domesticated dog (*Canis familiaris*) is the wolf (*Canis lupus*). Dogs may have been domesticated several times and recurrent episodes of back breeding with wolves may explain the surprising degree of phenotypic diversity found in dogs. The suggested date of their domestication, based on their analysis of genetic material, is about 100,000 B.P.[10]

While accepting the wolf as the ancestor, paleontologists and archeologists believe domestication came much later. In Juliet Clutton-Brock's reconstruction of canine culture history, the earliest archeological evidence for domestication dates to 14,000 B.P. and is found in Germany. Two thousand years later there is evidence for dogs in Nafutan sites in the Levant, and by 9000 B.P. there are indications that domesticated dogs were common in all human communities in the Old World and the New. From early times, she argues, dogs were used in hunting, particularly in association with long-distance projectile weapons. The first distinguishable breeds appear about four thousand years ago.[11] By Roman times, the basic types—hunting, guard, sheep, and lap dogs—are well defined.[12]

Whatever one may think of the cliché about the dog as man's best friend, it is undeniably true that humans and dogs readily and regularly bond. The Greeks, among others, were well aware that dogs, and most particularly hunting hounds, become extremely attached to their masters, to whom they show great fidelity and a willingness to self-sacrifice.[13] In ancient China, too, dogs saved owners' lives or died sympathetically when the master passed on, thereby exhibiting a sense of righteousness, a capacity for moral judgment.[14]

Many humans, of course, respond to this show of devotion with great affection for their animals. The Egyptian pharaoh Rames IX (r. 1131–1112 B.C.E.) was entombed with a faithful and favorite hound who, of course, had a name.[15] Individualizing and socially recognizing animals by giving them names was widespread, a practice documented in ancient China, classical Greece, medieval Islam, and early modern India.[16] In all these cases the dogs in question were hunters who clearly were judged as worthy partners in a noble enterprise. Such feelings, it will be seen, also characterized the relations of royal hunters with all their tamed animal partners.

The early development of the hunting breeds is best documented in the case of the Egyptian greyhound. While some argue that the greyhound was directly domesticated from wolves, the current view is that the immediate ancestral stock is the pariah dog of Africa and West Asia. Whatever the truth of the matter, something suggesting the greyhound type can be found in rock drawings of the western and eastern deserts in the predynastic period. Much clearer representations of greyhounds and the closely related saluki are common in later Egyptian art. These depictions show changes in this greyhound type from the late predynastic to the dynastic, as the heavier progenitor, with its erect ears, gives way to the more graceful variety we associate with the modern breed.[17]

Although related, the saluki and greyhound are distinct breeds. The confusion arises because both are gazehounds, hunting by sight, and have a similar body type: long legs and deep chests built for speed and endurance in the open terrain of the Middle East. There are, however, recognizable differences in coats and more particularly in the ears: the saluki has long pendulous ears, while the greyhound's are pricked and short.[18] It is almost certain that the saluki and greyhound served as the "basic models" for all subsequent breeds of gazehounds, such as the Afghans and various kinds of wolf hounds.[19]

Depictions of both greyhounds and salukis hunting are increasingly common from the Middle Kingdom (2134–1785) onward. They are often shown in a pack on leashes, accompanying a hunter on foot with bow and arrow or assisting a royal hunter on a chariot in pursuit of foxes, gazelles, hyenas, onagers, and other animals of the desert.[20]

While gazehounds were the hunting dogs par excellence of the core area, they were not alone. Diodorus of Sicily, writing in the first century B.C.E., recognized that the greyhound and its kindred were the most famous of the hunters, but he knew, too, of those who pursued game by scent.[21] Of these, the mastiff, a large, robust sleuthhound with a silky coat and floppy ears was the most prominent. First bred for the protection of herds, mastiffs were later trained to hunt big game in Mesopotamia, where early on they are depicted in art.[22]

In the ancient Near East dogs enjoyed a certain status, particularly in Iran, where dogs of all types were held in high regard, a fact noted by foreign observers and indigenous sources.[23] In the Islamic period, by contrast, the position of the dog, held to be an unclean animal, declined precipitously.[24] But despite their lowly status, dogs were reared for hunting, a fully acceptable and sanctioned activity.[25] In all probability, the reason for this exception was that Muslims recognized in hunting hounds those same qualities of loyalty and bravery so admired by Europeans, Chinese, and others.[26] In any event, the special consideration offered hunting dogs explains why Europeans such as John Chardin, traveling in Iran in the 1670s, records that he saw few dogs except among the court and nobles, the hunting classes.[27] In this stratum of society, however, fine hunting hounds were recognized as symbols of wealth and social status, accepted as a fitting gift among courtiers, and constituted a form of property well protected in the laws of some Muslim societies.[28]

The canine of choice throughout the core area during the Islamic period was the well-established greyhound, an inheritance from deep antiquity. The same was true of India, where Muslim courts made use of the greyhound, the "Persian hound [*sag-i tāzī*]," despite the fact that it did not do particularly well in that climate.[29] The greyhound was also the mainstay of the Christian court of Georgia.[30] Whatever else divided Christian and Muslim elites, hunting and hunting animals were a shared interest, a common passion.

The other gazehound, the saluki, is also much in evidence in the core. The name of this breed first appears in pre-Islamic Arabic poetry. While disputed, the word itself probably derives from Salūqiyyah, the Arabic form of Seleucia.[31] They were widely used under the ʿAbbāsid caliphate, which imported them from a village in Yemen, appropriately called Salūq, that specialized in the rearing of this breed.[32]

For salukis and other hunting hounds, this was done with considerable thought and care. As prized hunting partners, they received special diets and veterinarian treatment for a multitude of injuries and ailments. Bitches were given "maternity leave" after whelping, young dogs were trained and allowed to mature before taken on a hunt, and hounds of any age were usually brought to the field on leashes to prevent premature pursuit and tiring.[33]

In the core area individuals might specialize in hunting with gazehounds. Their usual game was the antelope and gazelle.[34] On occasion, however, fox hunts were organized. In the twelfth century near Hamāh in northern Syria, Usāmah ibn Munqidh witnessed a fox hunt with horse and hound organized by the Zargid ruler of Mosul and Aleppo.[35]

Beyond the core area, most agricultural peoples had their own, home-grown breeds of hunting dogs. In classical Greece, with its broken terrain and heavier vegetation, dogs were bred to hunt by scent, a tradition continued in Byzantium and the medieval West.[36] In fact, from the medieval period onward, Europe, particularly France and England, became the center of the production of new, specialized breeds—trackers, beaters, pointers, setters, and retrievers—a large array of canines that hunted particular prey—deer, wolves, otters, bears, and burrowing animals—singly or in packs.[37]

We are less well informed on the indigenous hunting dogs in ancient India and China, but they are in evidence. In northwest India, Alexander encountered

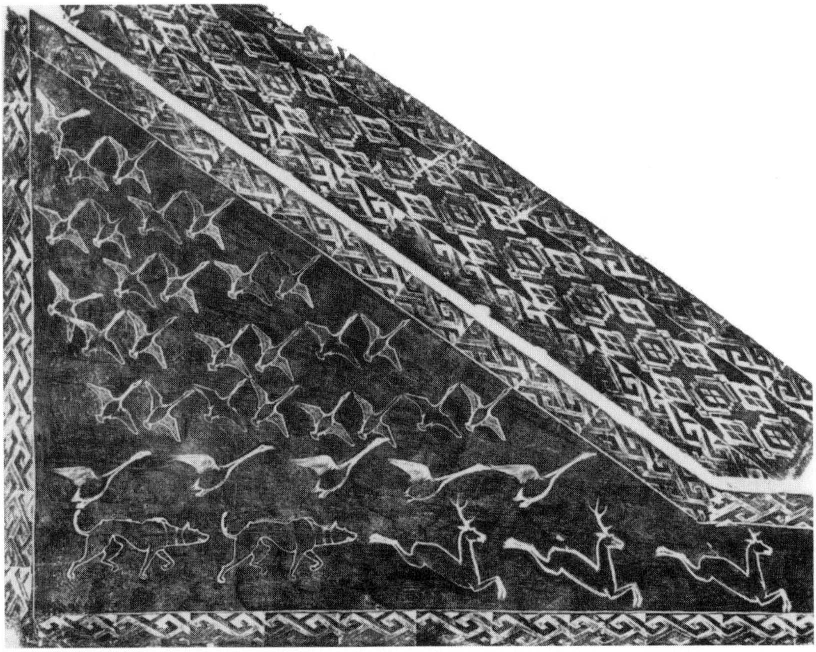

Figure 6. Chinese hunting dogs, Han tomb tile. Royal Ontario Museum.

a breed "famous for hunting" that did not bark in the face of prey and that was capable, in packs, of taking on the Indian lion.[38] The Chinese elite, too, made use of horse and hound in the hunt, and in the post-Shang era had a well established category for "hunting hound [*liegou*]."[39] In the period of the Warring States, the minor kingdom of Han, located south of the middle reaches of the Huanghe, and the kingdom of Yan, in the northeast, were thought to produce the best hounds.[40] There is even pictorial evidence from early Han tomb tiles of large dogs with collars in the typical pointing attitude—the body in a slightly crouching position, neck extended horizontally, and one forepaw bent under and raised several inches above ground—standing before a flock of geese in flight and several running deer.[41] Because of their importance and numbers, there was at Shanglin an "inspector of kennels [*Goujian*]," who oversaw the raising and training of the hunting hounds for the Han court.[42]

This pattern of reliance on locally produced hunting dogs did not, however, prevail for long. By the beginning of the Common Era various breeds of hunting dogs were on the move across Eurasia and by early modern times a massive exchange of canine hunting partners had taken place, a subject taken up later.

Birds

The origins of falconry, like the origins of any complex cultural phenomenon, are typically murky and consequently much debated. Over the last hundred years scholarly arguments have been advanced in favor of the Near East, India, and Inner Asia as the original homeland of the sport.[43]

The early favorite was Egypt. On the basis of both pictorial and textual evidence, several scholars have put forth claims that falconry was practiced by the ancient Egyptians since the time of the Nineteenth Dynasty (1350–1205).[44] Egypt, in fact, seems a likely place to begin. First, because of the falcon deity Horus, falcons were objects of intense interest; they are repeatedly portrayed in art, frequently mummified, held in captivity, and their eggs incubated. Second, fowling was a favorite activity of the early Egyptian elite. They hunted a wide variety of birds using bow and arrow, net, throw-stick, boomerang, and live decoys. They even used the mongoose (*Herpestes nyula*) and genet (genus *Genetta*), a small carnivorous animal related to civets, to assist them. Yet despite this most promising milieu, there is no real evidence that the pharaohs ever hunted with hawks or falcons and, it must be stressed, royal hunts in Egypt are extremely well documented in art historical and literary sources and well studied in recent scholarship.[45]

At present, Mesopotamia is generally held to be the earliest center. Texts associated with the library of Ashurbanipal, a collection that dates to the mid-seventh century B.C.E., attest to the practice of falconry among the rulers of Mesopotamia. Moreover, since much of the material in the library goes back to the Babylonian era, falconry may even be older.[46] Pictorial evidence supports this conclusion. An Assyrian seal dating possibly from the thirteenth century and a bas-relief from the palace of Sargon II (r. 721–705) depict raptors leaving the hunters' arms in pursuit of prey.[47]

The appearance of hawking in other parts of Eurasia is known in general terms but the chronology is uncertain and subject to revision.[48] For India, Aelian reports that various birds of prey—eagles, kites, and others—are caught young and trained to hunt hare and foxes by rewarding them with food; they are turned loose by keepers and return after the kill. Aelian cites as his source Ctesias, a late fifth-century Greek physician at the Achaemenid court whose works on India and Iran are now lost except for fragments preserved in later writers.[49] While compressed and somewhat distorted, the information of Ctesias has the ring of authenticity and leaves the impression that in his day falconry was already a well-established pastime in India.

For East Asia, there are vague references to hawking before the Han era but convincing evidence of the sport comes only in the first two centuries C.E.[50] It is widely assumed that this practice was not native to China and that it was transmitted to the Middle Kingdom from Inner Asia, the area Bertold Laufer thought the original center of falconry.[51] In the immediate post-Han period falconry is mentioned as the hobby of a fourth-century Chinese general, Lu Guang, but only in connection with his tender years, and therefore as a sign of his precociousness; certainly hawking itself was not deemed an unusual activity by this time.[52] By the Tang, Chinese and Korean elites had enthusiastically embraced falconry, sometimes from on horseback in the style of the Western Region.[53] Further to the east, falconry was first introduced into Japan—according to later tradition, in 355 C.E.—when, following the practice of the Koreans, the Japanese successfully trained a native falcon to hunt at the pleasure of the emperor.[54] To all appearances, hawking diffused across the eastern end of Eurasia in a relatively short period.

At roughly the same time, falconry was spreading into the Far West. Aristotle on several occasions mentions a kind of hawking. Men in Thrace, he says, hunted with the aid of hawks. The men first drove small birds into the air by beating the brush; when the prey took off, they were driven back to ground by the hawks, where they were captured. As a reward, the hawks were always left a share.[55] This and similar tales may constitute an incipient form of hawking but there is no indication that the Greeks or Romans hunted with trained raptors, that is, with birds under human control.[56] To be sure, they knew about the sport but did not practice it themselves. Consequently, European falconry was not an inheritance from classical antiquity.[57] The consensus is that falconry diffused from West Asia through the Balkans and was brought into western Europe by the Celts or Goths sometime in the early centuries of the Common Era.[58] In any event, the first secure mention of hawking in western Europe dates from the mid-fifth century. Thereafter, literary and pictorial evidence of falconry in western Europe becomes increasingly abundant.[59] From here falconry spread north, reaching Scandinavia, where it is well attested in archaeology and in literature by the early Viking age.[60]

The greatest period of popularity in Europe comes in the wake of the Crusades, the eleventh to the fourteenth century, when Latin Christians were extensively exposed to the elite fashions of the Muslim world. Thereafter, falconry retained its high status in the West down to the beginning of the eighteenth century, when interest in the sport began to wane.[61]

Falconry flourished as well in Byzantium and eastern Europe. The young Saint Constantine, apostle to the Slavs in the ninth century, was devoted to the sport and to his favorite falcon.[62] Trained falcons (*sokol*) and hawks (*iastreb*) are first noted in Russia during the reign of Vladimir Monomakh (r. 1113–25), and the twelfth-century *Lay of Igor's Host* has several references to falcons flown at swans.[63] This long tradition of Russian falconry reaches its peak under the early Romanovs.[64]

The Arabs, who did so much to stimulate interest in falconry among others, came late to the sport. Some of the basic Arabic terminology, such as *bāz*, "falcon," is of Persian origin, and medieval Arabic sources consistently attribute the "invention" of hawking to the pre-Islamic rulers of Iran.[65] Oddly enough, there is only scanty and indirect information on falconry among the early Persians. A Babylonian source reports that under the Achaemenids there was an official called, literally, "he-who-is-in-charge-of-the-birds-of-the-king." This could be understood as the overseer of the royal poultry, but more likely designates the king's falconer.[66] This interpretation is strengthened by a reference in the Babylonian Talmud to the term *shakārbāzay*, "falconry," which, as B. H. Stricker correctly states, "is clearly of Iranian origin."[67] Additionally, later Arabic and Syriac sources make reference to Middle Persian treatises on falconry and much later Armenian chronicles mention falconry and falconers at the court of the early Armenian kings of the fifth to second centuries B.C.E.[68]

What might perhaps be made of this evidence, however incomplete and indistinct, is that falconry was a minor facet of the royal hunt at the early Persian court, which the Arabs later took over and greatly elaborated. In any event, there is no mention of falconry in pre-Islamic Arabic poetry; this first appears in the verses of the Umayyad era (661–750), a point supported by early coinage, which carry pictures of raptors perched on the arms of handlers, and by Arabic chronicles, which note that caliphs Yazīd (r. 680–83) and Walī (r. 743–44) were avid falconers.[69] By the time of the ʿAbbāsids, hawking was an important part of the courtly royal hunt and a wide range of raptors—falcons, goshawks, sparrow hawks, and even eagles—were flown by caliphs and elites.[70]

This brings us to the question of the birds themselves and the matter of ornithological identifications. Falconry, almost everywhere, used a wide variety of species including, on occasion, owls![71] Sometimes different species, gyrfalcons and hawks, were flown together to confuse prey and maximize the catch.[72] Inevitably, given the plethora of raptors in use, problems of nomenclature arise. To be sure, authors of medieval manuals of falconry made fine and accurate distinctions among hunting birds, and these can be recovered today by careful textual analysis and a knowledge of ornithology. François Viré, for example, has successfully identified the principal raptors mentioned in the Arabic manuals, and since many of the birds and their names came from the Iranian cultural sphere, his work aids our understanding of the Persian terminology.[73] The problem is that much information on elite falconry comes from narrative sources and travel accounts whose terminology is less precise. When these sources use a generic term such as "hawk," it is simply not possible to determine the exact species in question.

The other issue is the equivalence of names across languages. Marco Polo relates that Qubilai Qan hunted regularly with "large eagles," by which he probably meant the golden or common eagle, *Aquila fulva*.[74] What, however, did the Mongols and their many subject peoples call these birds? Very helpful in this regard are the multilanguage lexicons of the Middle Ages. The *Rasulid Hexaglot*, compiled in Yemen in the fourteenth century, provides such equivalents: the Arabic *al-ʿuqāb*, "eagle," is equated with the Persian *ulah*, Turkic *qara qush*, and Mongolian *bürküt*.[75] Thus, despite ambiguities, we know in general what types of birds were popular across time and space, and a great deal about how they were acquired, trained, and deployed.

In looking at the acquisition of raptors, we will limit our investigation at this stage to the initial step, their capture in the wild. Other forms of acquisition—princely presentations, tributes, and purchases—will be taken up later and placed in a somewhat different context.

It was widely recognized by experienced falconers that birds of prey do not readily reproduce in captivity and therefore had to be caught in the wild. The principal question among specialists was whether it was better to capture them as adults or as nestlings.[76] On this there was considerable dispute as well as variation in practice. In the view of Frederick II, raptors taken from the nest were never as strong or robust because he recognized that parents knew better than any falconer what to feed young birds for normal development. Hence the eyass, a nestling in hawking parlance, was not as strong a flyer as the wild-caught adult nor its match in hunting skills.[77] Similar opinions prevailed among Japanese falconers, who realized that between the two there was a series of trade-offs. The wild-caught were already experienced hunters but were likely to have acquired individual tastes and techniques at variance with the desire of the falconer. The eyass, on the other hand, was more easily molded and, of course, developed a closer bond with its master. But they also understood that the eyass needed in consequence more extensive and expensive training and in the end was not as successful a hunter as the wild-caught.[78]

To judge from recent practice, there was never any real consensus on this matter. In Arabia wild-caught adults were generally preferred, particularly for hawks, while in Inner Asia eagles were typically taken as nestlings.[79] Clearly, cultural precedents and the habits of the species sought were the major variables in deciding the age of capture.

For adult birds, the methods of capture varied. Typically they were lured into a confined space with a pigeon or other normal prey and then seized with nets or snares.[80] Some raptors were a valuable commodity. Their breeding grounds were jealously guarded in medieval Europe to prevent disturbance, and sometimes, as in nineteenth-century Mesopotamia, local populations asserted hereditary rights over access to particular nesting sites.[81]

Once captured, the new recruits underwent some rough handling and rigorous training. Fortunately, these practices, fairly uniform throughout Eurasia, are well documented in traditional manuals and in more recent eyewitness accounts. In all cases, the key is what we now call conditioned reflex, a series of punishments and rewards to progressively modify behavior in desired ways.[82]

The first step, always, was "manning," conditioning the bird to tolerate human company, most particularly its handler. For both traditional and contemporary practitioners, this normally involved either hooding or "sealing," that is, temporarily sewing the bird's eyelids shut. Further, the bird's movements were restricted in various ways.[83] The process of manning took months or even a year, during which time the trainer was the sole source of the bird's nourishment.

When sufficiently acclimatized to humans, the handler "retrained" the bird to hunt on command. This technique is described in much the same terms in both European and Muslim sources.[84] First, the handler provided the pupil with freshly killed game and then allowed it to kill live birds presented to it. Finally, the raptor, sometimes on a long leash called a creance, was flown at hobbled birds to ensure a kill. In time, the pupil came to associate a high rate of success and the reward of food with human commands. At this point, the bird, deprived of food, was ready for field trials.

Because birds of prey were so highly prized and because of the heavy investment in their training, they were the recipients of much concern and care. They were carefully cleaned, a kind of preventive medicine, as well as doctored to treat specific health problems. Traditional falconers recognized a wide variety of diseases in their birds and had an equally large repertoire of diagnostic techniques and remedies. Birds had their pulse taken and were dosed with numerous compound medicines and exotic concoctions.[85] No doubt these treatments varied between cultural zones, but since, as we shall see, falconers often moved across such zones, their veterinary skills did as well.

For falconers, both ancient and modern, one of the perennial problems was ensuring the return of a raptor given free flight in the course of a hunt. While tame, once in the air these birds were not readily controlled. A number of means were used, including drums, favored by Russians in the sixteenth century, to recall birds back from the hunt.[86] By far the most common technique was the lure, which served as both a visual signal and a reward to induce a bird to return after it has missed its prey. As explained by Ḥusām al-Dawlah, a nineteenth-century Persian falconer still operating within an ancient, inherited tradition, the lure, usually fresh meat attached to a piece of leather on a long cord, is shown to a young bird in training, who feasts on the small proffered portion. Thereafter, the bird, attached to a creance, is taken farther and farther away from the lure, eventually released, and is thereby conditioned to return to the lure for the expected reward.[87]

Despite this training, birds still flew the coop. Because this was such a recurrent problem, hunts had to be organized to find those so "lost," and individual birds were affixed with special marks (*nīshān*) to prevent mixups and disputes.[88] The Mongols were perhaps the best prepared to cope with these contingencies. As nomads, they were well accustomed to returning stray domestic animals to their rightful owners, and this practice was extended in imperial times to animals of the chase. There was even a special officer at the Yuan court, called a *boralki/buralki*, charged with the return of lost animals, including fugitive falcons.[89]

The other principal means of preventing the defection of raptors was bonding. Handlers bathed their charges, gave them favored foods, and bestowed upon them names, which they called out whenever rewarding their birds.[90] Normally, one handler was in charge of an individual bird from the time of its capture. There is, naturally, no statistical or historical data on how well this worked with the raptors, but the humans most obviously bonded with their birds. In the cycle of Turkic Oghuz epics called the *Book of Dede Korkut*, nightmares include one's falcon dying in one's own hand, and a list of grievances include parting from one's comrades or horse and the loss of one's youth or falcon.[91] Temürid officials and Arab sheiks mourned the loss or passing of their hunting birds; one Arab nobleman even buried his in a coffin after a funeral procession.[92] For some, the relationship with a hunting bird was beyond value. In early twentieth-century Xinjiang, C. P. Skrine met a "Kirghiz" (here a Kazakh) who told him he would not part with his *qara qush*, a hunting eagle with a seven-foot wingspan, for a hundred taels of silver, a very princely sum in that time and place.[93]

Falconry required considerable equipment, most of which was standard across the continent. Besides the lure, there were jesses, leather straps with rings attached to the birds' legs, to which a creance was secured. Bells were used to track a bird that made a kill in covered ground. Hoods, too, became standard to keep the bird calm during transport to the hunting grounds. And, of course, the falconer needed a stout glove to launch (and land) his charge.[94] Some species required specialized equipment. Because the hunting eagle was so large and heavy, it was carried on a forked stand that could be affixed to a saddle, a com-

Figure 7. Mughal Prince with falcon, watercolor, ca. 1600–1605. Los Angeles County Museum of Art, Nasli and Alice Heeramaneck Collection.

mon practice in Inner Asia down to recent times. A tenth-century Arab manual of falconry calls this a *dushākh*, a word that goes back to the Persian *dūshakhah*, "branched" or "bifurcated."[95] Naturally, enthusiasts of the sport developed an extensive vocabulary as well as the specialized equipment.[96]

The deployment of raptors in the field took several forms. Most basically, according to Kai Kāʿūs, the royal hunter could approach the sport in one of two ways; either he could have a specialist fly his birds, thus emphasizing the skill of one's retainers, or the prince could fly his own birds, thereby demonstrating personal attainments.[97] In practice, of course, a prince could have it both ways.

Another choice to be made was the means of conveyance. It is possible to fly raptors on foot, from boats, or, as Qubilai did, from elephants, but for elites across Eurasia the preferred method and the norm was from horseback.[98] The visual evidence from medieval Iran, Russia, and England repeatedly shows falconers, men and women, astride mounts with raptors on their wrists.[99] Consequently, open, unfenced ground was the best terrain for falconry since it benefitted bird, horse, and rider.[100]

The prey most commonly associated with falconry is, of course, other birds. In Yemen in the fourteenth century the Rasūlid royal house flew a variety of falcons and hawks at migrating birds coming south for the winter.[101] This was surely widespread, as was the Mughal practice of putting up prey such as herons by ringing the flock with horsemen and then loosing raptors.[102]

Birds may well have been the normal prey of Eurasia's many royal falconers, but the prestige prey was the larger ground-dwelling animals normally hunted with horse and hound. Indeed, one of the defining characteristics of royal hunting is that animals of the chase were "trained up" to attack game that was far larger than they would tackle in nature. This was done because royal hunters, Mughal emperors, Hindu rajahs, and others, saw in this a more entertaining "sport," one that showed off the "heart and courage" of their birds.[103]

Eagles, the largest of the trained birds of prey, were obvious candidates for this kind of hunting. In nature, the golden eagle typically hunts rabbits and marmots, whose body weight is at best only 20 percent of their own.[104] The transformation of the eagles' normal behavior was accomplished by the usual program of rigorous reconditioning. Chardin, in Persia in the 1670s, says that they start the eagles' training with large birds such as crane, and next move to even larger quarry, antelope and deer. This they do, he continues, "by tying a Bit of flesh to the Head of one of those flea'd [flayed] Beasts and stuff 'd with straw which they lay on four Wheels, and keep moving as the Beast [eagle] is eating, to use him to it." Thereafter the handlers take the birds to the field singly or in pairs to harry the head and eyes of the game, and so slow it or distract it that the hunters can dispatch it. Chardin concludes that this tactic is applied to most game except the wild boar, which he says will turn on and "tear the Bird to Bits."[105] John Ovington, in Surat a decade later, reports the very same training technique, "Meat upon the nose of a counterfeit Antelope," and the same field trials.[106] This practice was followed in Qing China and Inner Asia, where eagles were trained to attack foxes, wolves, deer, and wild goats unaided.[107]

Figure 8. Hunting eagle attacking deer. *Oriental and Western Siberia: A Narrative of Seven Years Explorations and Adventures* (1858), 493.

Smaller birds could also be trained to this end. Muslim manuals give step-by-step instructions for inducing saker falcons (*Falco cherrug*) to harry gazelle or antelope.[108] Once properly prepared, falcons and hawks could assist in the hunt for ungulates; after a kill was made they were rewarded with blood and flesh.[109] Anthony Jenkinson reports that in Bukhara in the 1550s hawks were used to harry "wilde horses," that is, onagers, so that the hunter could catch it and kill it with hand weapons.[110] Sometimes the smaller birds were trained, at least in India, to attack this larger quarry in relays so that, in Ovington's words "one of the Hawkes always mounts as the other stoops [swoops]."[111]

The deployment of hawks and hounds in tandem was also common. This was done not only for the sport or spectacle but because greyhounds, as fast as they are, cannot keep up with gazelles and antelope, so hawks are used to overtake and slow down the prey for the trailing dogs.[112]

To achieve the needed coordination and cooperation, the two species must be trained together from an early age. The procedures are reported by traditional falconers and Western travelers.[113] As a first step, greyhound pups are fed beneath a falcon's perch so that they associate food with the birds and so that the two are acclimatized to one another. In the next stage, a falcon is flown at a lure and the dog released to follow it. When the dog nears the bird, it is halted and given food it particularly enjoys. This is repeated and the distance covered by the dog is progressively increased. Then the two are jointly trained in "controlled hunts" with tethered or crippled prey to insure success and reward. Lastly, hound and bird are taken out for a field test against a wild antelope or gazelle. The greyhound rapidly learns that the falcon is its helpmate and begins to watch its movements with great care. Typically, the falcon will strike the prey three or four times; if the greyhound does not catch up, the bird quits and "sulks." If successful, the dog will hold down the catch, but not kill or shake it to prevent injury to the falcon.

This use of hound and hawk in partnership is certainly very old and widespread. It is extensively documented in the core area and is found as well in early Japan.[114] While the system is also depicted on an eleventh-century rune stone from Scandinavia, and practiced by Frederick II in southern Europe, it does not seem to have achieved the high level of popularity it did in the core, perhaps because it requires open, flat terrain. In Europe, from the Middle Ages onward, dogs were more typically used to flush game, particularly birds, for falcons to take, a practice that was also known and used in Persia.[115]

The success of hunters in modifying the behavior of animals of the chase, and their wide exposure to the habits of animals in natural settings, raise the intriguing question of the social distribution of knowledge of nature in the premodern age. In stark terms, who were the most sophisticated and able naturalists of their day, scholars or hunters? I cannot pretend to answer this very complex question, but I have formed the opinion that huntsmen and falconers possessed an empirical knowledge of animals that was accurate and often unencumbered by hoary literary tradition. This was, to a degree, recognized by huntsmen themselves. A manual from circa 995, written by the anonymous chief falconer of the Fāṭimid caliph of Egypt, argues that hunting was the best way to learn about nature and about animal species, behavior, and anatomy.[116] Furthermore, he practiced what he preached. In his long chapter on the goshawk (*Accipiter gentiles*), Arabic *bāzī*, he begins with the characteristics of the bird's plumage, its size and weight, methods of training, its prey in nature, care and feeding in the mews, and finally, the diagnosis and treatment of a variety of its ills.[117]

Frederick II is justly famous for his many insights into nature and his love of science, a fact that contemporaries widely recognized.[118] His work on falconry, written around 1248, contains extended discussions of avian taxonomy, feeding patterns and preferences, migrations, reproductive behavior, physiology, pathology, plumage and, of course, falcons' capture, training, and care.[119] Modern scholars have repeatedly noted his commitment to observation and his skepticism of ancient authority, including that of Aristotle.[120]

Frederick's work is perhaps best seen as the culmination of the treatises on falconry prepared in the Muslim world and the Latin West. These, too, it deserves stressing, developed in time a bookish tradition in which authors borrowed heavily from predecessors, in part because the study of the chase itself was considered a legitimate branch of scholarship.[121] But despite this tendency, the empirical tradition among huntsmen was never completely submerged. Certainly the Mughal emperor Jahāngīr (r. 1605–27) learned directly from his experiences with raptors, closely examining their physiology, crops, beaks, coloration, sexual markers, feeding habits, and the behavior of their prey.[122] This same habit of mind is found in Ḥusām al-Dawlah, who carefully observed the behavior of newly acquired raptors and then compared it to the inherited wisdom and lore, much of which he dismissed on the basis of direct experience.[123]

This practical and empirical knowledge of selected parts of nature can be compared quite favorably to the purely literary traditions found in many cultures. In China, for example, there was a tradition of "ornithology" that talked about a variety of birds, and even offered crude taxonomic schemata. Generally, however, these discussions were divorced from direct observation and seldom rose above animal lore, using birds as examples of human vice and virtue.[124] And these failings were by no means unique to China. Zoology in the West, in Francis Klingender's assessment, was really unaffected by the scientific revival of the thirteenth century. Except for medicine, there was little fresh observation of nature, which was still the domain of huntsmen, farmers, falconers, and artists.[125] This conclusion is sustained by George Sarton, who argues that throughout the Middle Ages and the Renaissance, "naturalists," with a few notable exceptions, were actually philologists engaged in the translation and editing of ancient and classical texts, and that, as a group, they exhibited little curiosity about animals and plants themselves.[126] In consequence, much basic knowledge of nature was certainly known to huntsmen, foresters, and artisans centuries before it is reported in the scholarly literature.[127] In Europe this situation did not change dramatically until the eighteenth and nineteenth centuries, when fieldwork was slowly legitimized and finally achieved an honorable place in science alongside the more prestigious laboratory work.[128]

The above sketch is only offered as an impression, a "soft" opinion, but I believe that the question itself is valid and vital, and one that should receive a balanced treatment. That is to say, the issue should be approached cross-culturally. Certainly many current opinions on "Western" or "Eastern" attitudes toward nature themselves suffer from a decided bookish bias that needs to be reassessed in light of actual engagement with nature, of which hunting is only one form.

This takes us to a final and related question in the history of falconry, that of its social distribution. To this point, elites have been the focus of attention, but it is evident that of all the modes of royal hunting, hawking was by far the most democratic. Over the last several centuries, hunting with birds was widely popular among the nomads of the steppe, a pastime that has enjoyed a recent revival in Kazakhstan.[129] All this suggests that the techniques used to modify birds' behavior were not monopolized by courts and professional falconers. Moreover, such knowledge goes much farther back in time. We know from old Mongolian sources that the grandfather of Chinggis Qan caught and trained his own falcon (*qarchiqai*) and that he used it to acquire food in bad times, and that Chinggis's father used his for sport.[130] Following the formation of the empire this was still the pattern; according to Rubruck, who traveled in the eastern steppe in the 1250s, gyrfalcons were abundant and used by many, not just princes.[131]

The evidence points as well to popular participation in falconry among the settled populations of Iran, Turkestan, and Afghanistan.[132] Indeed, falconry is said to be the national sport of contemporary Qatar.[133] The great popularity in the core area, and particularly its democratic character, can be explained in part by economic and logistic considerations. Raptors of various types are native to all these areas and can be acquired by means of capture at little expense. Further, once trained, a bird can in some measure feed itself.

But if falconry was so affordable, so popular in the core area, how did it manage to retain its status as a noble pursuit? The answer, of course, is scale. Aristocratic falconry entailed a complex support structure, a certain pomp and pageantry, and the assistance of professional falconers. It also entailed large numbers of birds because to fly the same hawk twice in a row was beneath the dignity of a prince.[134] A noble needed more raptors than a commoner and a ruler more than his retainers. Not surprisingly, those rulers with a mad passion for the sport collected all kinds from all climes, but equally telling, those less enthusiastic still felt the need to retain numerous skilled falconers and to accumulate large collections of hunting birds.[135]

How many was enough? In Mandeville's fanciful travel account, the Great Qan of China is said to have 150,000 falconers and, presumably, the same number of falcons.[136] This, of course, is a fantastic figure, but it does point up the fact that such numbers were one measure of powerful and distant rulers. More realistically, Marco Polo relates that Qubilai traveled with "quite five hundred" trained birds of prey.[137] His account is fully consistent with later descriptions of the royal mews of Ṣafavid Iran, which Chardin says housed 800 birds.[138]

A further criterion of a truly royal mews was the diversity of its holdings. Majesty required that a ruler possess and fly all known types of raptors, a standard recognized across Eurasia, from Mamlūk Egypt and Ṣafavid Iran to Mughal India and Qing China.[139] As Bernier, a physician at the Mughal court, insightfully remarked, the great array of raptors that accompanied Awrangzīb on his travels were "intended both for show and for field sports."[140]

Writing in the late twelfth century, the crusader William of Tyre spoke of the "soaring hawks and falcons with which the nobility is wont to take delight when hunting."[141] In point of fact, there were many reasons for this delight. For one thing, as a form of the chase that made fewer physical demands, it could be pursued into old age. Jahāngīr, among others, became increasingly fascinated with the sport as he grew older.[142] For another, high-quality birds make a wonderful prop at court. Once Rubruck was kept waiting at an audience with the Mongolian qaghan Möngke (r. 1251–59) while His Majesty leisurely inspected a number of his birds.[143] Moreover, a successful bird was something to boast about, as the Mughal founder Bābur (r. 1526–30) did of his favorite hawk.[144] For Frederick II, however, falconry was the most noble form of hunting because it involved great skill and knowledge. In his view, it was not so much the bag but the original training of the birds that made a falconer notable and noble.[145]

Elephants

Although not technically animals of the chase—a term normally reserved for dogs, birds, and cats—elephants are included on three grounds: first, to capture wild elephants, rulers had to organize major expeditions that were to all intents and purposes royal hunts; second, elephants were widely used in part of the core area as mounts to hunt other animals; and third, rulers' apparent dominance over these and other powerful beasts provides a larger and critical context into which the royal hunt must be situated.

Though smaller than the African elephant (*Loxodonta africana*), the Indian variety is called *Elephas maximus*. Both have been tamed but the Indian elephant has been most systematically exploited by humans. Since the time of the Indus Valley civilizations, circa 2000 B.C.E., humans have made use of the Indian elephant in war and, more consequentially, in forest work.[146] Elephants are therefore one of the few animals to take an active part in the modification and reduction of their own natural habitat.

Information on the capture and training of wild elephants circulated quite widely in the ancient world. Aristotle is well aware that elephants are readily tameable and intelligent, and that in India they are captured with the aid of tame animals and then trained.[147] Several centuries later Strabo provides a more extended account of the procedures used. He says that first a deep circular trench is dug, with a narrow bridge as the only entryway. Tame females are then placed in the center to attract their wild cousins. When this succeeds, the entryway is closed and, using tame elephants, trainers secure the wild and lead them to stalls. Here, he continues, they are brought under control with fasting and food. Thereafter, their handlers teach them to obey commands.[148]

His account accords well with much later and more detailed descriptions of methods of capturing elephants contained in travel relations and local sources. Since elephants were so important for warfare, transportation, hunting, and state occasions in Mughal India, the emperor was directly involved in their acquisition. Under Akbar, huntsmen were always on the lookout for wild herds, and when they had located them, a number of techniques were used for capture—camouflaged enclosures, pits or trenches, concealed cages, and even lassoing.[149] In all cases, however, the trapped animals were hemmed in and tethered to the tame for transport to training facilities.[150] A similar range of methods was used in Ceylon and Southeast Asia.[151]

Accounts of training procedures emphasize the importance of food as punishment and reward and the role of already tamed animals in the process, either through free association or by tethering.[152] These same accounts also stress that the time required for taming was not very long. By reputation, the Ceylonese elephant was the easiest to train; this preference is first noted by Pliny and later by European travelers.[153]

From a very early period, elephants were acclaimed for their great intelligence. In the West, this notion goes back to Aristotle and was later picked up by other classical authors.[154] Moreover, this was not just a Western image of a distant and exotic species but one shared with peoples much closer at hand. The Mughal court possessed an intimate knowledge of elephants, their physiology and behavior, and the Muslim rulers freely recognized and utilized the special skills of Hindus in handling and training elephants. Both parties attributed great intelligence to elephants and showed much respect for these animals collectively and individually.[155] Like the stories of dogs' loyalty to their masters, tales of bonding between humans and elephants are very ancient, and circulated in the West as well as in India itself.[156]

Within its natural range, and in some adjacent regions, the Indian elephant was for several millennia considered a strategic commodity. This explains why rulers tried to make their capture a court monopoly and why they often participated personally in these enterprises.[157] So important were these "animals of state" to the Mughals that Akbar had them mustered daily as a check on their numbers, health, and availability.[158]

Supply was a recurrent problem and fresh recruits were always in demand. The reasons for the shortage were various. Mughal rulers were expected to "transfer" elephants to courtiers and officers as a sign of favor and as an emblem of high office.[159] Further, there was considerable attrition among newly captured beasts. In 1630, it was reported that of the 130 elephants captured in Gujarat, only seventy survived the trip to Shāh Jahān's court.[160]

The most serious difficulty, however, was that elephants rarely breed in captivity, and this fact necessitated much expense and extremely complex logistics. In effect, elephants, once captured and trained, had to be returned to the wild to breed in natural environments and then be recaptured.[161] Further, given their needs for food and space, elephants could not be easily concentrated in one place. The solution was to rotate the court's 1,000 or so elephants back and forth between the capital and distant locales that could sustain them in groups ranging from twenty-five to sixty animals.[162]

Rulers in South and Southeast Asia were willing to make huge investments in elephants because they were considered a major military asset and measure of strength. Measures of military might have changed over time. For the ancient Chinese and others, a ruler's military potential was expressed in the number of chariots, and for us in the twenty-first century, the number of aircraft carriers or armored divisions.[163] In South and Southeast Asia the standard from antiquity to early modern times was war elephants. Pliny mentions this in the first century C.E. and so do Chinese Buddhist pilgrims in the sixth and seventh centuries.[164] Starting in the tenth century, Muslim writers make the same point about Hindu kings, and once Muslim rule was consolidated in North India under the Delhi sultanate (1206–1555), Muslims began to measure their own strength by the same yardstick.[165] Finally, when Europeans arrived in Mughal India, they, too, applied the local standard.[166]

Since this measure was so widely accepted, rulers in India and Southeast Asia lost no opportunity to demonstrate their elephant power. They displayed their beasts in endless processions, diplomatic receptions, religious celebrations, entertainments, and rites of passage in the royal family—weddings, coronations, and funerals.[167] Such events were akin to modern May Day parades or naval reviews that advertise military strength to both subjects and foreign observers.

Some neighbors were sufficiently impressed to add war elephants to their arsenals. The Sasanids made extensive use of elephants as a shock weapon against their Roman-Byzantine foes, and later the Ghaznavids (977–1186), drawing on Indian models, made wide use of war elephants in Iran and Central Asia.[168] On the other hand, Chinese interest in the military potential of elephants is best characterized as limited and episodic. There are isolated references to elephants in Chinese warfare in the sixth and tenth centuries, and a final brief revival under the Mongols, who became acquainted with war elephants during their campaigns in Burma.[169]

The elephant's place in the royal hunt was largely confined to its natural range. Indian kings of old certainly hunted in the field on elephants, a practice known in the West from sources going back to Alexander's time.[170] What was generally hunted on elephant back was big game. The Delhi sultans and Mughals successfully pursued rhinoceroses from elephants but their real specialty was the big cats.[171] A few elephants were even trained for direct attack. Niccolao Manucci, in India in the latter half of the seventeenth century, reports that they did this by taking a tiger or lion skin stuffed with straw and moving it by ropes. The driver then encouraged the elephant to attack the dummy with feet and trunk.[172] Most commonly though, a number of elephants, fitted with protective padding, were used to surround prey just as in a ring hunt. Initially, the hunters, from a howdah, shot the lions or tigers with bow and arrow and later on with firearms. This method was so successful that by the early nineteenth century a tiger's only hope was to reach terrain impassable to elephants.[173]

Cats

Felines, widely known for their independence and fierceness, seem most improbable hunting partners. Yet humans have successfully trained two species, the cheetah and caracal, to hunt under their control. To explain why this is possible, we need to examine both the natural and cultural history of these animals.

Cheetahs appear first in the fossil record three and a half to three million years ago in eastern and southern Africa. There was a larger European variety that died out 500,000 B.P.; like other feline species, the cheetah decreased in size over geological time.[174] While regarded as a native of the Old World, cheetahs may be distantly related to the puma (*Felis concolor*) and the two may have a common ancestor in the Miocene of North America.[175]

The family Felidae is usually grouped into three genera. The genus *Felis* includes the large majority—cougars, lynx, domesticated cats, and so on—and the genus *Panthera*, the great cats—lions, tigers, and leopards. The taxonomic status of cheetahs has often been subject to revision, but all extant populations, wild and captive, are now considered members of a single genus, *Acinonyx jubatus*.[176] Even the so-called "king cheetah," with its mane and distinctive coat pattern in which blotches and whorls replace true spots, is only a color variant, owing to a recessive gene, of *Acinonyx jubatus*.[177] So, too, is the white cheetah once presented to Jahāngīr, whose spots "were of blue color." This was likely a mutant cheetah rather than a true albino, and is, in any event, the only known example of its kind.[178]

Conventionally included among the big cats, cheetahs are the size of the larger breeds of dogs. Adults weigh about 100 to 110 pounds, males being slightly larger than females. Their height at the shoulder varies from 2.6 to 2.8 feet, and their length from nose to tail from 6.3 to 7.7 feet.[179] The cheetah is the sole representative of its genus because of a number of unique physical features that also explain its prowess as a hunter. These include eyes adapted for hunting in daylight and for picking out horizontal movement; enlarged nasal openings for rapid inhalation during the chase; an elongated tail used as a counterbalance in high-speed twists and turns; "weakly" retractable claws that function as running spikes for better traction; footpads that are hard and ridged like tire treads; and narrow waists and elongated lower limbs for heightened speed.[180]

Its fame, of course, is its great speed. Here the cheetah's decisive advantage is its extremely supple vertebral column. The cheetah does not run in the narrow sense of the word, but uses a "rotary gallop," in reality a series of bounds, called the "stride," measuring 21 to 26 feet in length. The great speed it achieves is a product of its extraordinary ability to flex and extend its backbone. The flexed length of a cheetah is 67 percent of its fully extended length, whereas the horse, which can reach 44 miles per hour, in the flexed position is about 87 percent of its length in the extended position.[181] This combination of features allows the cheetah to reach a speed of 29 meters per second, or about 64 miles per hour.[182] This speed can be sustained only in short bursts of 300 to 500 yards.

As in the case of falcons, earlier scholars maintained that hunting with cheetahs started in Egypt; the standard formulation argues that the practice then spread to Mesopotamia in Assyrian times, and from there to Iran, India, and Central Asia.[183] This assumption was neither unreasonable nor unexpected, since the Egyptians did in fact keep tame cheetahs. The earliest evidence comes from the famous Punt reliefs at Dayr al-Bahrī, near Thebes, which record in word and picture an expedition sent in the reign of the pharaoh queen Hatshepsut (r. 1473–1458 B.C.E.) to the Land of Punt, somewhere in the Horn of Africa, that brought back local rarities and products. Included are two quite distinctive types of "panthers." The first, a single animal, most clearly the heavier bodied leopard (*Panthera pardus*), is labeled "panther of the south," and the second, a well-executed pair of cheetahs with collars and leashes, is labeled "panther of the north."[184] Other representations from the period leave no doubt that tamed cheetahs were common in Egypt. As depicted, these cats do not appear to be under close restraint like some wild beast, but more like a calm, contented dog out for a walk with its master. There is, however, no evidence that the Egyptians ever trained cheetahs to hunt under human direction.[185]

Other scholars, while accepting Egyptian priority, also argue that cheetahs were used for hunting in ancient Mesopotamia.[186] There is even an opinion that the Sumerians were the first to train the cheetah to hunt, and further, that the Hittites trained the true leopard to the chase.[187] A cylinder seal from the period of Uruk II (ca. 2600–2360 B.C.E.) has long been invoked as evidence of hunting leopards in ancient Mesopotamia. The scene shows men hunting goats in rough terrain; one of the men holds on a leash a large, long-legged animal with pointed, erect ears, an elongated muzzle, and upright tail. The unconvincing claim that this is a cheetah fails on several grounds. First, the morphology of the depicted animal is far more like a large dog, a mastiff; cheetahs, in contrast, have rounded, drooping ears and foreshortened muzzles. Second, cheetahs are hunters of the open plains, not the mountains as represented on the seal.[188]

The classical sources provide some inconclusive and distorted information on hunting leopards. Aelian, in the second century C.E. makes one reference to tame leopards, in another relates that an Indian king has tame panthers, and in a third that India has many lions, the smaller of which can be trained to the tether and directed to hunt deer. These cats, he says, "are clever at tracking by scent."[189] His information is incorrect in part and clearly based on rumor, but it is plausibly an early reference to hunting leopards. India had a native stock of cheetahs and Hindus in later ages were considered the great masters at handling them.

Iran, as well, had a native population of wild cheetahs and a very strong commitment to royal hunting. Moreover, there is the persistent medieval tradition that Persian kings of pre-Islamic times hunted with trained cats. The Iranian national epic, the *Shāhnāmah*, composed by Firdawsī around 1010 on the basis of Middle Persian traditions, has the storied Sasanid emperor Bahrām Gor (r. 421–39) hunting with a cheetah (*yūz*).[190] And a thirteenth-century chronicle based on earlier local tradition has the ruler of Ṭabaristān, a contemporary of the Sasanid emperor Yazdagird (r. 632–51), hunting incessantly with falcons and cheetahs. There is a Middle Persian term for cheetah, *yōz* [*ywc*], but precious little contemporary evidence of the sport in Iran (or anywhere else) in pre-Islamic times.[191]

What suggests itself again is that hunting with cheetahs, like hunting with falcons, had for a long time limited popularity and therefore limited visibility. It made no impress on contemporary minds the way trained elephants did, since they were hard to ignore. All that can safely be concluded from the scant evidence is that cheetahs were tamed very early, in the Horn of Africa, and that at some later point, they were taught to hunt by people living within their natural range. The only other obvious inference is that cheetah hunting became very popular and visible with the advent of Islam. This begins in Umayyad times, and is readily documented from literary and pictorial sources for the ʿAbbāsid period, when its popularity spread to all courts, Muslim and non-Muslim, in the core area.[192]

One of the obvious problems in dealing with the cultural history of cheetahs is the profusion and confusion of names. West Europeans who encountered the cheetah in early modern Asia use a multitude of names for the beast—hunting leopard, tame panther, pard, ounce, and gattu pardie.[193] However, peoples living within the natural range of cheetahs usually distinguish it carefully from the true leopard, which is very dangerous to humans. Arabic, for instance, has *al-namir* for leopard and *al-fahd* for cheetah.[194] Stable terminology is also found in North India, where the Mughal court used the Persian *yūz* or the equally unmistakable Hindi designation, *chītā*.[195] Fortunately, the best information on the capture and training of *Acinonyx jubatus* comes from cultures that did employ a clear nomenclature.

Wild cheetahs were caught by a variety of means: traps, snares, and netting, often set up near the animals' favorite "scratching tree," a marking tree where they leave their spoor.[196] The preference was for adult female cheetahs because they were held to be the better hunters since they had to feed their cubs.[197] The young were ignored, for if they had not learned to provide for themselves in the wild they were deemed useless. Only a mother, it was believed by most, could properly prepare a cheetah for the royal hunt.[198]

The medieval Arabic manuals do not give a time schedule for training, but in the later Indian tradition it was thought to take anywhere from three months to a full year.[199] The preparation of cheetahs for hunting in partnership with humans can be broken into several distinct phases.[200]

The first, to borrow a term from falconry, is "manning." According to the Arabic manuals, the new recruit is fettered, hooded, and deprived of food and sleep. Once rendered submissive by this treatment, the animal is slowly acclimatized to human company, often by tethering it on a busy street or walking it on a leash. In India, this is accomplished by taking the cheetah to a village where local women and children are paid to sit by the secured cat gently talking to it for long periods.

The next phase is training the cheetah to ride a horse. First, the cat, tethered to its trainer, is induced with food to leap onto a pillion affixed on a wooden horse. The height of the horse is slowly increased to that of a real horse and soon the cheetah associates the pillion with food. Next, the cheetah is habituated to riding on a real horse with its handler.

At this point, the cheetah's hunting instincts are reawakened. The handler, who has fed the cheetah since its capture, first slaughters an animal before the cheetah and allows it to lap up the blood.

The cheetah can now be taken to the field. To ensure success, the handlers often single out an animal from the herd and drive it to exhaustion, and then the cheetah is unhooded and loosed. As a final test, the cheetah is allowed to select its own target, which it approaches by stalking and then finishes off in open pursuit.

Cheetahs that survived capture and training and passed field trials led a comfortable existence, particularly at a wealthy court. Like princely hounds and hunting birds, they received veterinarian care for assorted ills and injuries. They also ate well; the thirteenth-century manual of al-Manṣūr, citing a work attributed to the chief huntsman of the ʿAbbāsid caliph Mutawakkil (r. 847–61), says that rations of up to seven pounds of mutton per day were needed to properly "build up" a cheetah.[201] This is generally consistent with the regulations issued by Akbar, according to which a first-class cheetah (*yūz*) received five *ser*, about five pounds, of meat per day, a second-class animal four-and-a-half *ser*, down to two and three-fourths for an eighth-class animal. The system of ranking is not explained but presumably it had something to do with hunting success. Each animal, in any event, had its own personal staff—three or four men for a cheetah that rides horses and two for those who hunted from carts. All of Akbar's 1,000 cheetahs had decorated collars and leashes, and gold brocaded saddle cloths.[202]

The obvious question, of course, is why the world's fastest quadruped, caught in the wild as an adult, can be acclimatized to humans and induced to obey their commands. For traditional huntsmen, the answer was self-evident and conventional: species like the cheetah were trainable because they were intelligent.[203] The issue, of course, is far more complex and not easily answered, especially by a historian. However, since the taming, training, and domestication of animals are largely matters of manipulating and modifying preexisting natural behavioral patterns, we must look for evidence of sociability among cheetahs. Knowledge of their social relations and hunting style in the wild offers, I believe, some clues for answering the question of why they are so tameable and why they can be integrated into human-directed hunts.[204]

Cheetahs have a short courtship because of vulnerability to attack from lions and leopards; therefore, no permanent bonds form between the sexes. As adults, female cheetahs have large home ranges that typically overlap with those of other females. Most males are also territorial, but there are some who wander through other males' territories. In contrast to females, who are always solitary, males frequently form into groups of two to four, called coalitions. While they do not hunt cooperatively because the high-speed chase does not lend itself to this method, a coalition, which may last for years, collectively defends a territory that provides water, cover, and open terrain. Males in such coalitions tend to be healthier and larger and seem to live longer than solitary males.

Other evidence of cheetah sociability can be seen in the behavior of siblings, who continue in association for some time after leaving their mother. Last, and most important, since their hunting technique is difficult to learn, cubs stay with their mother for extended periods, up to twenty months, thereby creating strong bonds.

Thus, while cheetahs lack the cohesion of the lion pride, they are hardly examples of the solitary feline. Their capacity to develop strong social bonds, between mothers and cubs, between siblings, and between members of male coalitions, certainly provides some of the behavioral basis for humans' success in turning the cheetah into a hunting partner.

The cheetah's natural hunting techniques, now well known from field observation in the Serengeti, are also a critical ingredient in this process.[205] A cheetah typically starts by stalking its prey, occasionally freezing into stillness to avoid detection. Once zeroed in on an animal it begins a trot to gain momentum and then breaks into full acceleration. The high-speed chase lasts for three to five hundred yards, at which point the cheetah, if unsuccessful, gives up because it cannot dissipate heat effectively and a longer chase would result in a lethal body temperature. If successful, the cheetah comes abreast of its prey, typically a gazelle, and then knocks it over with the aid of its dewclaw. This is why the cheetah attacks prey small relative to its own body size. Once on the ground the cheetah twists the gazelle's neck back and bites the windpipe, suffocating the prey.

Cubs begin hunting with their mother at about five months. Mothers with cubs actually have a high failure rate, around 73 percent, because of their young's inexperience and because of the need to protect offspring from other predators. Like house cats, cheetah mothers capture prey, such as baby warthogs and gazelles, for their young to practice on. To begin with, the presented prey is ineffectually attacked by the young and is killed by the mother. It may take a year or training or more before a young adult can hunt successfully on its own. Interestingly, premodern huntsmen and observers of human-controlled cheetah hunts in the Middle East and India have noticed and recorded all the basics. It was recognized that cheetahs use stealth as well as speed, and that if they missed, they gave up the chase and, as some put it, became "sulky." When this happened, the cat was consoled by its handler and told it would do better next time.[206] This "sulkiness," of course, was a consequence of the need to lower body temperature. Finally, handlers, such as Jahāngīr, well knew that cheetah kills were not bloody affairs but were in fact "captures," at least in their initial stage.[207]

Bonding between handler and cheetah was a natural by-product of their training, and once tamed, cheetahs by all premodern accounts, Muslim and European, behaved like friendly dogs.[208] Akbar had a cheetah that followed him around "without collar or chain," and in the late eighteenth century Sir Charles Malet, an English official in Cambay, had a cheetah that did likewise; it was only leashed for fear it would attack domesticated animals.[209] In more recent times, Joy Adamson, of *Born Free* fame, raised a cheetah cub which became quite tame and very affectionate; even as a young adult it initiated games with any individual who could be coaxed into play.[210] Because they so readily bond, tame cheetahs, like hounds and hunting birds, are always given names.[211]

Commentators on cheetah behavior, whether early travelers or modern field zoologists, agree that these animals pose no threat to humans. Randall Eaton, a biologist working in the Serengeti, has noted that cheetah attacks on humans are rare and are usually associated with human interference with their kills. In his own field experience he relates that he was occasionally stalked by a cheetah, but only when he was stalking them; that is, when he was in crouching or prone position. As soon as he stood up, the cheetahs always lost interest and he was never attacked. Eaton believes that cheetahs took him for potential prey until he stood up. This behavior is perfectly consistent with their hunting style, since they attack prey whose body weight is about half their own. They are not geared up to attacking larger creatures such as adult humans. As Eaton remarks in another context, the cheetah cannot "kill large prey owing to specializations for speed, which have reduced the cheetah's overall size, power and killing tools, the teeth and claws." They have smallish heads that reduce dentition and their claws, well adapted to running, are more like a dog's than a cat's.[212] It is therefore conceivable that humans simply do not register in cheetah brains as appropriate prey.

At royal courts, cheetahs went to the field in style. In Mughal India, they had their own tent, *chītā-khanah*, in the royal encampment and were sometimes carried in a litter, *palki*, with a canopy for shade.[213] In the field, cheetahs hunted in different ways. Sometimes on foot, either in the open or from ambush, but most often cheetahs were launched from conveyances or from the backs of elephants, camels, and horses.[214]

Despite the recommendation of Kai Kāʿūs that a prince should not ride with a cheetah because it was undignified "to act as a leopard attendant," this was, in fact, the common practice.[215] The basic equipment required was the pillion, a hood, and a leash (*qalādah*, a term used in Persian as a counting noun for both hunting dogs and cats).[216] In pictorial representations from the Islamic world and China, handlers are shown with a baton (somewhat like a shortened golf club) used to train and control their charges.[217]

The best description of a cheetah hunt from horseback comes from Chardin; describing the royal hunt in Iran in the 1670s, he relates that they employ trained cats called "Yourze [*yūz*]" and that "they hunt no man." This hunting cat, he continues, chained and wearing blinders, sits behind its trainer on the rump of the horse. When game is found, the handler pulls off the hood, unchains the cheetah, and turns the cat's

> head toward the Prey; if he sees it, he gives a shriek, leaps down, falls on the Beast, and pulls it down; if he missed it he is commonly discouraged, and stops; the Master goes to him, comforts him, makes much of him, and tells him it is not his Fault, and that he had not been set directly before the Beast. They say he [the cat] understands that Excuse, and is satisfied with it.[218]

Figure 9. Cheetah handler with baton. *Shahnama*, ca. 1444. The Cleveland Museum of Art, John L. Severance Fund.

Although medieval experts realized and remarked upon the great speed of the cheetah, its cunning, its use of cover and concealment, were part of its attraction for humans.[219] These skills were best demonstrated in hunts from two-wheeled carts called "hackeries" (Hindi *chhakra*), which was the common practice in India.[220]

Figure 10. Cheetah on hackerie. Selmar Hess print, New York, ca. 1900. Author's Collection.

The most graphic and detailed descriptions of this method of hunting with cheetahs come from the testimony of European travelers, for whom this style of hunting was a great novelty calling for comment.[221] According to their eyewitness accounts, the cheetah, hooded, tethered, and accompanied by two attendants, was carried on a hackery pulled by two bullocks. The cart and the bullocks, a familiar and nonthreatening sight in the Indian countryside, were able to approach to within 200 yards of an antelope herd, at which point the cheetah was unhooded and released. The cat then dropped to the ground, went into a crouch, and began a stealthy advance on the prey, using whatever cover it could find. As soon as the herd showed alarm, the cheetah was off and running and was on its intended victim in a few bounds. Usually it knocked down the antelope with its paw and then seized it by the throat. At this juncture the handlers rushed to the scene, cut the downed animal's throat and then filled a ladle with blood as an immediate reward for the cat. Later on, a haunch was cut off and given to the cheetah.

From these descriptions, it is evident that the cheetah's natural hunting behavior was extensively exploited by their trainers. What handlers actually did in the field was to bring their charge to the prey, release it, let nature take its course, and then artificially terminate the killing phase. In other words, the cheetah's normal hunting techniques were curtailed rather than augmented.

The only new skills they acquired in the course of their training were to tolerate people, ride on horses and carts, and to give up their catch to a human.

Although the process of turning cheetahs into animals of the hunt is explainable and understood in empirical terms by early trainers, it was nonetheless remarkable and thrilling. Many royal hunters were entranced, if not obsessed, with cheetahs. One, the eldest son of the Khwārazmshāh Tekish (r. 1172–1200), exchanged the governorship of Nīshāpūr for that of Marv because that region offered better hunting grounds for his cats.[222] And Akbar, who hunted with cheetahs from boyhood into old age, always regarded it as "one of God's wonders."[223] Even Ḥusām al-Dawlah, a professional falconer writing as the royal hunt was disappearing, considered hunting with cheetahs the original and real "sport of kings."[224]

Also counted among the hunting cats was the caracal. Always considered less regal than the cheetah, it was nonetheless widely used because of its extended natural range; even today it is found over much of the Old World in a variety of environments, excepting only rain forests. Because of its tufted ears, it has often been called the hunting lynx but is not in fact closely related to the true Eurasian lynx (*Lynx lynx* L.) or its New World kindred, the bobcat (*Lynx rufus*). The caracal is believed by some taxonomists to be the lone member of its own subgenus, *Felis caracal* Schreber, 1776.[225] The English name, caracal, comes from the Turkic *qara qulaq*, meaning "black ear," a word also borrowed into other languages such as Mongolian.[226]

When and where this cat was first trained to the chase is unclear. Called *ʿanāq al-arḍ* in Arabic, the caracal was certainly in use by ʿAbbāsid times to hunt birds because of its great leaping ability.[227] In the Mongolian era, the "hunting lynx" was encountered across the continent from Sicily to North China.[228] The main center of its use in later centuries was India, where it was known by both its Turkic name, caracal, and its Persian name, *siyāh-gush*, also meaning "black ear."[229] Basically a scaled-down version of the cheetah, the caracal rode to the field, hooded and leashed, on a pillion behind its master and hunted large birds such as crane and ground game such as hare, fox, and antelope.[230] Abū'l Faẓl records that Akbar was fond of the *siyāh-gush* and adds, most informatively, that "in former times it would attack hare or a fox, but now it kills black deer."[231] This it did, according to Alexander Hamilton's testimony, by jumping on the fleeing prey's back, where it reaches "forward to the Shoulders, and scratches their Eyes out, and gives the Hunters an easy Prey."[232]

Like the eagle, the caracal was successfully conditioned to attack prey that was larger than that it normally hunted in the wild, another example of training up animals to intensify competition and thereby enhance "sport."

5
Administration

Hunting Establishments

Within the core area hunting was a very serious business and the pursuit of game was rarely left to chance. It required careful organization, a multitude of skilled personnel, and substantial investment of resources. As a matter of state, the chase deserved, and often received, the close attention and continuing concern of the sovereign. Consequently, huntsmen and falconers were not menials but honored retainers and influential officers of the court and army.

Royal hunting establishments are very ancient. The royal hunts of ancient Egypt initially were under the control of "overseers" but in later centuries there was a single master of hunt.[1] The early Sasanids, too, had such a master, called *nakhchīrbed*, an officer associated with the highest officials of the court.[2] After the conversion to Islam, the head of the hunt in Iran was titled *amīr-i shikār*, from the Arabic *amīr*, "commander," and the Persian *shikār*, "hunt." In its shortened form, *mīr-i shikār*, the term was very long-lived, lasting down to Qājār times.[3] At the Mughal court, the chief huntsman bore the title *qarāvul bīg*, from the Mongolian *qara'ul*, "vanguard" or "scout," and the Turkic *beg*, "ruler" or "master."[4]

The master commonly had a number of specialists under his authority. Almost everyone of stature had a master of hounds, an office found from classical Greece to Han China.[5] Handlers of domesticated canines, however, enjoyed less prestige than the trainers of wild animals, whose skills were far more mysterious. Across time and space falconers are the most visible and important. The Arabic title for the office is *al-ṣayyād* and the Persian, *bāzyār*, a term which passed into Georgian.[6] The Turkic is *qushchï* and the Mongolian, *siba'uchi*, a term found in Persian, Chinese, and Korean sources.[7] Cheetah keepers, called *yūzbān* in Persian, *chītabān* in Urdu, *barschï* in Turkic, and *barsuchin* in Mongolian, were also in demand and accorded great respect.[8] It is a measure of the extent of contact and exchange of royal hunting culture that within the core area many of these terms were used interchangeably or found in hybrid forms such as *muqaddam-i bārschiāān*, "chief of cheetah keepers," which combines Arabic, Persian, and Turko-Mongolian elements.[9]

In addition to those offices that specialized in handling a particular animal of the chase, there are a few titles indicating specialists in the pursuit of particular prey. In a Slavic language decree of Mengü Temür, qan of the Golden Horde (r. 1267–80), there is a reference to a *buralozhik* (a hybrid Turkic-Slavic term), an officer charged with hunting of wolves, and further on we will encounter specialists in the pursuit of boars and crane.[10]

Official titles tell us something about duties but certainly not everything. Fortunately, we have an official, contemporary document detailing the varied functions of a chief huntsman under the Khwārazmshāhs (1077–1231). According to this source, the principal duty of the *amīr-i shikār* was to ensure the ruler productive hunts. It goes on to note that the master, through skilled assistants, procured and trained birds, hounds, and cats, and oversaw their care and maintenance in the hunting animal compound (*shikār-khānah*). During the hunt, the master was responsible for sealing off the hunting grounds and ensuring that the appropriate animal of the chase arrived on time and was then removed. The document concludes that such a person must not only know the chase but should also be a close and longtime servitor of the ruler.[11]

Similar duties are reported for European huntsmen, who were also organized into a hierarchy and who oversaw many animals of the chase.[12] In medieval China the royal hunting establishment centered around the Five Cages (*wufang*), an animal compound directed by a commissioner (*shi*), who was responsible for providing the court with hounds and raptors.[13] While animals of the chase were usually procured by presentation and purchase, hunting establishments, particularly in the core area, regularly caught and trained local species.[14]

Another function of the royal hunting establishment was the mobilization of manpower, local officials, gamekeepers, and beaters, needed to form the battue for game drives and ring hunts.[15] Finally, it should not be forgotten that royal hunts everywhere developed codes of conduct and etiquette, and often involved ceremonies, feasts, and entertainments.[16] Thus, a good *Jagdmeister* needed social as well as technical and organizational skills.

The search for appropriate huntsmen was never limited to homegrown talent or restricted to people of the same ethnic or religious background as the ruling house. In Mughal India, the Muslim court preferred Hindu cheetah handlers and brought in a contingent of Kashmiri hunters with their own headman to assist in the chase around the capital.[17] Because huntsmen with the right mix of skills were so highly valued, the office in places such as India and Moscovite Russia often became a hereditary family occupation, and huntsmen, once proven, tended to circulate among elite families, princely establishments, and the royal court.[18]

In reviewing the organizational characteristics of the royal hunt, one feature seems historically consistent: hunting establishments are always associated with, and subordinate to, the royal household, the institution that provides for the care, comfort, and personal needs of the ruler, his family, and intimates. In some cases, the royal household functions simultaneously as the royal government; examples of such patrimonial states include the Merovingians and the early Mongolian empire. In many cases, however, a formal bureaucratic structure grows up around the royal household and takes over the day-to-day administration of the realm. But even in the latter case, many individuals hold dual appointments in the household and in the government.

This connection between hunting and household is of long standing in the core area. In the second century B.C.E. the Arsacid rulers of Armenia included huntsmen and falconers among the bodyguards, valets, commissaries, and keepers of regalia.[19] Over a millennium later, the *mushrif*, head of the Ghaznavid sultan's household, oversaw, among other matters, the royal stables and the care of falcons and hunting hounds.[20] In the Mongolian era, falconers and animal trainers numbered among the "pillars of state" and "great officers," all of whom were members of the imperial guard (*kesig*), which doubled as the household establishment.[21] In Mughal India, the head of the royal mews, the *qūsh bīgī*, "lord of birds," was numbered among the notables of state and the same was true of Ṣafavid Iran, where the *mīr-shikār* was part of the royal household and lined up with the military to the left of the throne on state occasions.[22] And in Bukhara in the seventeenth and the eighteenth century the *qūsh-bīgī kalān*, "grand falconer" and head of the royal hunt, had his station next to the commander of the royal guard, and during audiences stood at the foot of the throne and handed documents to the ruler.[23]

Clearly, in the core area, hunting offices had a visible and honorable place in the court hierarchy. In one manuscript of the *Zafar-nāmah*, a history of the campaigns of Temür, there is an illustration of his enthronement in 1370; in this he is attended, appropriately, by his arms bearer in the front of the throne and his huntsmen with a cheetah and falcon lined up at his side.[24] Even in China, with its elaborate bureaucratic traditions, there was always an "inner court," *neichao* or *neiting*, which was separate from and often in opposition to the *waichao*, or "outer court," the formal governmental machinery. From ancient times, huntsmen and gamekeepers were thus insiders, and often well-respected officers of court.[25] This is clearly documented in the Qing when the royal hunt was closely connected to the *neiwufu*, the imperial household administration, and one of its subordinate units, the Imperial Parks administration (*feng chen yuan*).[26]

Because of this structural feature, a head huntsman was close to the throne and, as a by-product of his duties, in frequent communication with the ruler; of necessity he was a confidant, trusted implicitly by his sovereign.[27]

Success and Safety

A ruler, for reasons of prestige, and therefore of state, had to ensure his guests a productive and safe hunt. In the mid-sixteenth century, ʿAbdullāḥ Khān, the shirvānshāh in Azerbaijan, wanting to impress favorably the English factor Anthony Jenkinson, sent him out hawking with an injunction to his gentlemen of court that he be shown "much game and pastime," which, Jenkinson reports with satisfaction, "was done and many cranes were killed."[28]

In a well-ordered court, little was left to chance. The key was the ability to "produce" game in circumstances that almost precluded failure. In the words of an Armenian chronicle, one had to "make ready" fields and forests to fashion "a hunt worthy of kings."[29] This entailed careful scouting and local knowledge, keepers, warders, and falconers who knew the game of specific regions or preserves.[30] The title of the chief huntsmen of the Mughal rulers, *qarāvul bīg*, "master of scouts," nicely reflects their duties as reporters of game, an activity that was highly systematized in India. Bernier, in the 1660s, writes that when the emperor Awrangzīb took to the field for any reason, gamekeepers along his route were required to prepare reports on the type and number of game locally available. "Sentries" were then stationed along the roads of that district to guard the selected hunting ground, which sometimes extended for four or five leagues. Once this was in place, the emperor and his entourage begin to hunt.[31]

As a matter of convenience or courtesy, game might be driven or lured to a predetermined locale where royal guests awaited its arrival. In Manchuria during the Qitan period, "deer callers" attracted game for royal hunters, and in seventeenth-century Siam beaters drove game into an open plain where foreign guests made many kills and left the field much gratified by their "success."[32] Alternatively, the chief huntsmen might locate and hold game in place by various means until the royal party arrived.[33] Royal hunts, if done properly, were very carefully staged affairs.

Hunts within paradises and parks by their very nature were highly controlled. This is clearly illustrated in the reliefs at Tāq-i Bustān. One panel portrays a deer hunt, clearly the Persian fallow deer (*Dama mesopotamica* Brooke), and the other a boar hunt. The "hunt" was held in a walled park with holding pens from which deer, mainly stags, were released singly and on the run, much like the arrangement for calf roping in an American rodeo. Horsemen directed the running deer toward the emperor, who shot them with bow and arrow while riding a full gallop. The boar hunt was also conducted in a park, with lake or swamp in the middle. Indian elephants drove a large herd of pigs toward the water where the emperor shot them from a boat while female harpists in an accompanying vessel serenaded him.[34] The Sasanid title *warāzbed*, "master of boars," is presumably

Figure 11. Temür and huntsmen at accession, *Zafarnamah*, ca. 1485. The John Work Garrett Library, Johns Hopkins University.

connected with these special pig hunts.[35] In both cases, the dead prey was being hauled off for food by elephants and camels. The whole effect was that of a slaughterhouse, the industrial production of meat, rather than a hunt, the pursuit of game.

Despite the careful stage management, safely was still an issue. The Indian political theorist Kautilya cautions kings to hunt only in areas carefully policed by royal huntsmen so that dangerous animals do not pose a threat.[36] The pursuit of such animals required very special measures and precautions, as the following incident illustrates. In the fall of 1692, Kangxi's retinue came across a bear, forced it from its lair, and then mounted huntsmen drove it to a defile where the emperor shot it with an arrow. The animal fell wounded and Kangxi, with four hunters at his side, finished it off with a pike.[37]

While managed to a large degree, there was still a measure of danger to the royal person. This, however, was virtually eliminated when tackling the big cats. Tiger hunts, under Kangxi, consisted of releasing caged cats, baiting them, and killing them with bows, guns, or lances.[38] Similarly, in seventh-century B.C.E. Mesopotamia captive lions were released at the beginning of a royal hunt.[39] In Mughal India an even safer method was devised, which Bernier, traveling with Awrangzīb, described in the following terms. When a lion is spotted, it is kept in the region with "Judas goats," in this case tethered asses. When the emperor nears the scene of action, a last ass is tethered, which has had large amounts of opium rammed down its throat "to produce," Bernier states, "a soporific effect upon the lion." Then the area is closed off with large nets and the perimeter guarded by pikemen. The king now approaches the trapped and drugged lion on elephantback and fires at it until it is dead.[40]

Whatever the judgment on this kind of hunting, the result was that it was true, in the narrow sense, that the king had killed a bear, a tiger, or a lion. This was very much a political act, and such victories over heroic game, however contrived, were, as we shall later see, widely celebrated and carefully advertised.

Careers

Those who served in the royal hunting establishment had varied opportunities for personal gain and advancement. Many rulers took a direct interest in the hunt and in its preparation. The prince of Kiev, Vladimir Monomakh (r. 1113–25), in his "Admonition [*Pouchenie*]" to his sons, states that "at the hunt I myself took charge of ordering the hunters, grooms, falcons [*sokol*], and hawks [*iastreb*]."[41] And Jesuit letters reveal that Akbar knew the names of thousands of beasts kept at court—horses, deer, elephants, cheetahs, and so on—and carefully monitored their health and fitness. Keepers and handlers were rewarded and fined according to the state of their charges.[42] The hunt, therefore, often afforded an opportunity to demonstrate personal qualities and technical skills before the watchful eyes of a powerful prince. And in these type of regimes, as Mark Whittow says of the Byzantines, "closeness to the emperor was everything."[43]

For the energetic, efficient, and ambitious, a royal hunting establishment was a good place to launch a career. To begin with, there was always a title to which special honorifics might be added.[44] In the hierarchical societies of the core, this was always an asset. Further, there were the more tangible rewards.[45] Most commonly, rulers marked superior service through presentations of food, clothing, or bonuses.[46] In the Yuan court in the fourteenth century, the royal falconer who caught the first snow goose of the year with a gyrfalcon (*haiqing*) received one ingot (*ding*) of silver.[47] Somewhat less typically, in the early Mongolian empire, the qaghan Ögödei (r. 1229–41) once bestowed young maidens on his "master of cheetahs and hunting animals."[48] Of far greater economic value, Mamlūk and Mughal rulers bestowed grants of agricultural land on favored falconers and huntsmen.[49]

Promotion within the service was also possible and lucrative. Advancement might come about because of purely technical skill. In one of Boccaccio's tales, which certainly echoes the tenor of the times, a Christian noble captured in the Crusades gains the attention of Saladin because of his talent for training raptors, and once this is known he becomes the sultan's chief falconer.[50] Skills of this kind were indeed highly valued, and noted falconers were remembered and revered across the generations.[51] And those so promoted, such as Richard de Flor, a falconer of Frederick II, gained wealth and influence and produced noble descendants.[52]

The prestige and elevated status of officers of the hunt is well reflected in the fact that some were recipients of these posts *because* of their birth. Chinggis Qan granted his eldest son, Jochi (d. 1227), the position of master of hunt, and under Tsarina Elizabeth (r. 1741–62) this office was held by Count Razumovskii, a man of noble lineage and an influential figure at court.[53]

High officers of the hunt were political persons and as a matter of course undertook diverse political commissions for their sovereigns, in one instance providing security for the court and in another looking after hostages.[54] But even rank-and-file huntsmen might be thrust into high politics. In 1251 an ordinary animal keeper uncovered a planned countercoup to topple the newly enthroned qaghan, Möngke. The plot failed and the keeper was rewarded with presents and titles.[55] Naturally, there were losers, too. In 1615, a recently promoted *mīr-i shikār* became embroiled in the struggles within the Ṣafavid royal family, backed the wrong faction, and paid with his life.[56]

Huntsmen's exercise of political authority might be informal or routinized. In the Qin kingdom, on the eve of its unification of China, ca. 239 B.C.E., there was a high official, Lao Ai, who controlled palaces, carriages, horses, clothing, parks, and hunting grounds, and who enjoyed a decisive voice in matters of state.[57] His offices certainly gave him contact with the ruler and the opportunity to persuade, but his offices were not "constitutionally" invested with responsibility for policy formulation. Much later on, in the core, the situation was different, more formalized. According to an administrative handbook from the end of the Ṣafavid period, the master of hunt, *amīr-i shikār-bashī*, had as his specific responsibilities the nomination of royal falconers and administering, with another court official, all finances related to the chase. Beneath him was an inspector of the royal mews (*qūsh-khānah*) and huntsmen in the provinces. For his services he drew a huge salary of 800 *tūmān* from the treasury and had other sources of income in the form of special fees. He was, without doubt, the effective head of the royal hunt and by virtue of holding this office, he was also a member of the Council (*Jangī*) of Amīrs, who advised the shah on state matters.[58] His political influence and authority, in other words, was institutionalized, intrinsic to the office of *amīr-i shikār*.

Yusūf Khaṣṣ Ḥājib warns against a career as a bedmaker, cook, or falconer since, he argues, the rewards are few and the work hard.[59] His advice may have been appropriate for his time and place, eleventh-century Turkestan, but for the core area at large, falconers and other huntsmen often made good careers, some of whom were transferred or promoted to varied desirable and remunerative posts outside the royal hunt. This tradition of advancement is clearly articulated by Thomas Artsruni, an Armenian chronicler writing circa 904, who relates that in early Achaemenid times two Mede slaves in the service of the Armenian king Tigran began as falconers and then moved to cupbearers and, finally, achieving noble status, became provincial governors.[60] Whether historical or not, an author of the tenth century finds this progression normal, and more to the point, their reputed feat was actually duplicated in Iran. Under Shāh ʿAbbas, one Yūsuf Khān, a Christian Armenian and slave (*ghulām*), was first employed in the royal mews (*qūsh khānah*) and because of his skill in handling hunting birds and animals, soon became master of hunt. From there he rose to governor of Ustarābad and lastly, military governor of Shirvān in Azerbaijan. Another, Shāhrukh Beg, a Turkic tribesman, began as superintendent (*mushrif*) of the royal mews and ended his career as commander of the imperial guard.[61]

In Central Asia and India similar career patterns can be documented.[62] This is particularly noticeable under the Ghaznavids and the Delhi sultanate, where many slave soldiers who served as cheetah keepers (*yūzbān*) and masters of hunt later became major political players at court.[63] A hunting post, evidently, was a regular way station to higher office, a normal part of a successful career path.

This was not perhaps so frequent farther away from the core regions, but hunting officers could still move on to greater success, as did several *amīr-i shikār* in the Mamlūk kingdom.[64] In Europe, France particularly, falconers were highly prized; between the thirteenth and the seventeenth century the Grand Falconer was a most prestigious and well rewarded office. Louis XIII (r. 1610–43) made his grand falconer, Albert de Luynes, his constable and prime minister.[65] At the other end of Eurasia, huntsmen achieved an even greater coup. The family of Aguda, who founded the Jin dynasty in 1125, were originally highly regarded huntsmen for the last Liao emperors, whose dynasty they toppled.[66] All across the Old World, royal huntsmen were always near to, and sometimes laid hands on, the levers of power.

Costs

The investment of economic and administrative resources in the royal hunt, while not known in detail, was unquestionably substantial. We can gain some sense of the costs by reviewing the extensive and elaborate preparations needed for the Manchus' annual expedition to Mulan, their preserve in Rehe. This involved the following measures:

issuance of imperial edicts announcing the event
organization of logistical support for travel to the preserve
selection of the imperial hunting party
designation and training of participating military units
organization of the imperial progress to Mulan
dispatch of minister of war to the preserve to prepare the hunt
placement and erection of pavilions for use of the imperial party
formation of the battue and organization of the beaters
entrance of the emperor into the hunting circle followed by his guests
recording of each kill and its attribution to individual hunters
dispatch of specialists to mark and isolate tigers for the emperor to shoot
organization of an imperial banquet for all participants following the hunt.[67]

The expenses incurred for an expedition of this magnitude were, of course, only part of the overall costs of a royal hunt. There were a number of fixed costs as well, capital investments in facilities and staffs. Hunting parks had to be built and maintained, huntsmen and wardens paid, and animals of the chase purchased and maintained.

Hunting facilities of various sorts entailed much expense, and in the case of Frederick II were included together with castles and urban parks in his building projects.[68] Substantial sums might sometimes be spent on animal compounds. Writing in the sixteenth century, Rudra Deva recommends that a properly ordered mews should be housed in whitewashed buildings with clean, pleasant surroundings, and that the inmates should be provided with a variety of creature comforts—fans, shade, and netted windows to keep out flies.[69] Some rulers met these standards. In seventeenth-century Iran, the royal hunting birds were kept and put on display in a palatial mews, and many birds of the contemporary Romanov tsars lived in individual rooms decorated with wallpaper and velvet.[70] In India, a ruler's cheetahs were housed in somewhat less grandiose, but still respectable, accommodations.[71] There was as well the specialized equipment needed for a proper royal hunt. In Yuan China, by way of illustration, there was a government office dedicated to the manufacture of leather falcon hoods (*yingmao*).[72]

Maintaining large staffs of handlers was another major demand on the royal purse. In 1331, in consequence of heavy snows, the Yuan court sent aid to over 11,100 households of falconers (*yingfang*) and Mongols (*Menggu*) in Xinghe in southern Mongolia.[73] While not separated out from the Mongols, the very fact that falconers are included points to substantial numbers. The claim of al-ʿUmarī that Muḥammad ibn Tughluq, sultan of Delhi (r. 1325–51), had "10,000 falconers [*bāzdār*] who convey trained birds to the hunt" also says something useful about the great size of hunting establishments.[74] This was true because princes often made a point of having a falconer for each of their birds. The Fāṭimid caliph al-Ḥāfīẓ(r. 1131–49) of Cairo adopted this practice as did the Ṣafavid ruler Sulaymān I (r. 1666–94), who had some 800 falconers.[75] Of course, such visible representatives of the princely household had to be properly turned out in costly attire.[76]

The animals of the chase were expensive to obtain and even more so to maintain, since all were carnivores requiring much meat, that most costly form of food. On this subject we have some precise and suggestive detail. In 1474 the Italian merchant Barbaro saw the Aq Qoyunlu court depart Tabrīz with its troops, pavilions, pack animals, and its hunting animals, which he helpfully enumerates:

leopards to hunt, 100
falcons, 200
greyhounds, 3,000
other hounds, 1,000
goshawks, 50[77]

He gives no figures on their support, but from other sources we can gain some sense of the volume of consumption. We can start with raptors. When in the field, of course, they can be fed on prey they catch themselves or on the kills of hunters.[78] The great cost comes when the birds, which even for a minor princeling might number 700, were in the mews.[79] In Mughal India the birds were fed at least twice a day and in Ṣafavid Iran, on Chardin's testimony, they were "fed with Fowls Flesh all Day long."[80] Such rations required prodigious amounts of meat, taken from societies in which calories were perennially scarce. In medieval France there was a special poultry yard to provide sustenance for the royal raptors, while in seventeenth-century Russia the royal mews consumed daily 100,000 pairs of pigeons; in Siam during the same century, the king had so many falcons that it took "two whole buffaloes to feed his birds each day."[81]

The cats were even more voracious, and a ruler such as Akbar, who had 1,000 cheetahs, was faced with the expense of providing them with something on the order of 4,000 pounds of meat per day.[82] And these requirements pale in comparison with those of court elephants. The informant of al-ʿUmarī rightly states that the 3,000 elephants of the Delhi sultan ate vast amounts of rice, barley, and grass, which represents a huge financial burden, one that only a "great state" could possible bear.[83] These assertions are fully borne out by later observations of Western travelers in Mughal India who provide details on the outlay for their food—grass, and thirty pounds of sugar cane—and for their servants who might number up to ten for a single animal.[84]

Finally, we cannot forget the game animals kept in parks. Akbar issued minute regulations regarding the feeding of the gazelles (*āhū*) in one of his parks, which numbered 12,000. Their diet of grass was supplemented with grain, especially for the females.[85]

Total figures for upkeep of a hunting establishment are rare.[86] There are, however, a few figures from ʿAbbāsid times that say something about their magnitude. In the mid-ninth century, the annual expenditure on hunting staff alone was 500,000 dirhams.[87] This does not count the outlays for animals and their upkeep. A later ʿAbbasid budget from 918, which indicates overall court and government expenditures, includes among the regular line items monies "for feeding of birds, animals, and wild animals," and yearly outlays "for the purchase of predatory animals and birds [and] for the furnishings of animals."[88] Unfortunately, figures for specific expenditures are not given, but again, their inclusion shows them to be major items.

We do, however, have one report, from India, on total expenditures on animals. According to Manucci, Dāʾūd Khān (d. 1715), Awrangzīb's client in the Deccan, spent about 250,000 rupees per annum to maintain his hunting animals and exotic pets.[89] His master's expenditures on animals must have been many times this amount.

The scale of investment in the royal hunt, whatever the exact amounts, raises the further question of finances and methods of payments. In the ʿAbbāsid and in many other cases, funding came directly from the state treasury; under the Delhi sultans, for instance, the royal kennels received regular payments from this source.[90] Much earlier, Elamite tablets dating from 509–499 show that the Achaemenid government provided food rations to royal hounds; in one document sixty-eight animals are mentioned and in another twenty-six.[91] And a great many other Achaemenid royal hounds, according to Herodotus, were farmed out to four large villages in Babylonia who were charged with their care and feeding, in return for which they were exempt from all other obligations to the state.[92]

Tax exemptions were used elsewhere for similar ends. During the Liao, imperial hunts were so immense, requiring so many supplies, that those living within the vicinity of the traveling camp had their taxes remitted to compensate them for their burdens.[93] Special surcharges might also be levied to finance the royal hunt. In 1289, Mstislav, prince of Volynia, imposed an extraordinary "hunter's tax [*lovchee*]" exacted in food and drink from the population of Berestia because of their rebelliousness.[94]

In the Muslim world there were yet other options. In the eighteenth century, the rulers of Bukhara established a *vaqf* (pious foundation) in Balkh, which provided, among other things, special incomes for chief falconers and head huntsmen and for the crane hunters (*ṣāyyadan-i kulang*); these were intended to support the royal hunt with food, shelter, and manpower.[95]

There were, obviously, many methods of funding, and since most involved the transfer of money or scarce resources, there were many opportunities for fraud, corruption, and the abuse of official power on the part of the royal huntsmen and animal handlers. The Mongolian court in Iran was particularly plagued with these problems. In the reign of Ghazan (1296–1304), falconers (*qūshchiān*) and cheetah keepers (*barschiān*), who drew supplies for their charges from an assigned district (*vilāyāt*), used this right as a pretext for endless exactions. They systematically overstated the number of animals in their care and thereby laid illegal claim to large amounts of travel rations (*ūlāgh*) and forage, which became a heavy burden on the regions they lived in or traveled through. Invoking their status as guardians of the Il-qan's hunting animals, they also extorted bribes from anyone who inadvertently approached or trespassed on their precincts, regularly stripping their victims of their money, mounts, and clothing. To put an end to these outrages, the Mongolian court established and circulated ration norms for their 1,000 hunting birds (*jānvar*) and 300 leashes of cheetahs (*yūz*) to prevent huntsmen from making unreasonable demands on their districts. Those who persisted in these practices were subject to severe punishment.[96] These measures, however, did not end the problems, for in 1320 Abū Saʿīd (r. 1316–35), in a Mongolian-language decree, ordered bands of falconers and cheetah keepers to cease causing distress among the populace.[97]

In China, too, such illegal practices were common. Toward the end of the reign of the Tang emperor Dezong (r. 780–805), employees of the Five Cages (*wufang*) used their connections to extort money from the people and to run up unpaid bills at public houses. Such practices continued until his successor, Shunzong, came to the throne.[98] Crimes of this nature were likely widespread in hunting establishments across the continent and constituted an important indirect cost of running a royal hunt.

In the eyes of Chinese scholar officials there was yet another, and far more damaging, indirect cost arising from the royal hunt. Starting with Mencius in the fourth century B.C.E., there was steady criticism of the lavish expenditures on the royal hunt and more particularly with the vast hunting parks and preserves, which had the effect of denying common people access to the resources of the forest, and even worse, withdrawing large tracts of land from agricultural production.[99] Since the fundamental notion of Chinese economic theory was that agriculture was the root (*ben*) of the economy, this loss of land was heavily criticized. In 195 B.C.E., Xiao He, chief minister of the Han emperor, recommended that hunting parks be turned over to the populace for cultivation, and a hundred years later the same recommendation was made by Huan Kuan in his *Discourses on Salt and Iron*, a series of debates on economic policy, in which he points out additionally that such a measure would helpfully expand the tax base.[100] On occasion, such advice was accepted; in 76, 107, and 109 C.E., land in Shanglin and Guangcheng, a hunting park near Luoyang, was distributed to the poor in times of calamity.[101]

In closing this discussion, the Chinese sources provide us with one further indication of the heavy investment in the royal hunt. From Han times onward, government officials repeatedly recommended economizing on the royal hunt and the resources expended on robes, carriages, palaces, parks, dogs, and horses.[102] In their view, court expenditures were a major source of economic strain and the royal hunt a major contributor to rising court costs.

Although anecdotal in nature, the cumulative evidence points to the royal hunt as a large-scale consumer of resources—animal, human, administrative, and financial. As generations of Chinese scholars consistently argued, the royal hunt made little economic sense, and their concerns and criticisms lend credence to our earlier conclusions concerning the impressive scale of royal hunting and the need to investigate its significance from the perspective of politics.

6
Conservation

Killing and Sparing

In traditional societies, and to some extent in modern ones as well, conservation measures are rarely sustained or systematic; rather, they are temporary, piecemeal, sporadic, and arise from divergent motives.[1] And much, in fact, was incidental, as for example, when a ninth-century Tang emperor, in search of a release from a prolonged illness, freed raptors from the royal mews or when an early Mongolian qaghan, to celebrate his accession, pardoned prisoners and decreed a brief halt in the hunting of game animals.[2] Obviously, while such initiatives had the effect of sparing game, they were not primarily directed toward this end.

Efforts that focused consciously and exclusively on conservation came from hunting practice and the desire for future takes. This was an acute issue for royal hunters because their hunting methods resulted in a large number of kills. Within the royal hunt there was an inherent and permanent tension between the desire to amass triumphs over animals and the desire to preserve stocks for further displays of hunting prowess. And since the royal hunt was essentially a political act, often performed in the public eye, it had to be successful and the most obvious, easily comprehended yardstick of success was the bag, the body count.

Literary portrayals of the royal hunt from within the core consistently evoke scenes of vast slaughter. In Niẓāmī's poems of the late twelfth century, Bahrām Gor, with lance and lasso, leaves behind "hillocks" of slain deer and onagers.[3] A contemporary Georgian poet, Rust'haveli, speaks of "fields dyed purple with blood" and slain "wild beasts without measure."[4] Another Georgian work of the age, *Visramiani*, proclaims that the hero, Ramin, "had slain so much game that mountain and plain could not find room for them."[5] Even Chinese literature has such scenes; a prose poem of the second century B.C.E. records that the slaughter was so vast that the emperor's chariot wheels were stained "with blood."[6]

Historical works, as well, speak in general terms about the great quantity of prey killed in ring hunts. Juvaynī reports that among the Mongols a tally was usually kept of kills, but that sometimes the number of dead was so large that they only counted the beasts of prey and onagers, that is, the prestige kills.[7] Marco Polo says much the same thing about Qubilai's hunts, in which lines of game, a day's march in length, are herded to the center of the ring and then slain in profusion.[8]

But what of actual numbers? Was the scale of the carnage so vast? The sources do provide figures that sustain the literary formulas. In the ring hunts of Kangxi in Manchuria, the Jesuit Ferdinand Verbiest counted bags of 300 harts in half a day and for more remote areas, a thousand harts and sixty tigers.[9] Chardin reports that in Iranian ring hunts the animals killed—a mixture of deer, wolves, foxes, and others—commonly reaches 800 but sometimes, he was told, the kill might reach 14,000 beasts.[10] Don Juan, a Persian convert to Christianity, relates a recent historical tradition according to which Ṭahmāsp (r. 1524–76) once organized a huge ring hunt that resulted in killing 30,000 deer and harts in "a day's sport."[11]

All this might be dismissed as a fantasy, a traveler's tale, or the by-product of cultural bias. Indigenous sources, however, tell the same story. According to Niẓām al-Dīn Muḥammad, a contemporary, Akbar in the early winter of 1567 held a gigantic ring hunt near Lahore in which beaters drove together an estimated 15,000 animals—deer, jackals, and so on; the resulting "hunting ground was five *kos* (ten English miles) on every side."[12] No total of kills is given but the numbers were great. And beyond those killed by hunters, we must take into account the effect of the unnatural concentration of large numbers of animals, both predators and prey, in confined spaces for a number of days. Without question, many would have died in consequence of thirst, shock, accident, and animal combats induced by panic and redirected aggression.

To maintain a supply of game for future displays of majesty required some restraint, a body of regulations governing the hunt consciously adopted and enforced by the royal hunters themselves. The purpose of such "rules of the chase," as Mencius recognized, was to make it more difficult to bag game and thereby make the hunt more sporting.[13]

Elementary rules of conservation were widely accepted and applied. The most basic, natural method of protecting game was the concept of the hunting season. Pliny and Abū'l Faẓl, among others, well understood that unlike humans animals have a fixed breeding season.[14] The acceptance of seasonality is well documented in China. As early as the sixth century B.C.E., the kingdoms constituting the Eastern Zhou acknowledged annual cycles of hunting geared to breeding seasons.[15] This is made even more explicit in a Tang dynasty regulation that "all gathering, fishing, and hunting must be done in [the appropriate] season," a law enforced by the Bureau of Forestry (*yubu*) under the Ministry of

Works (*gongbu*).[16] In Qing China, even wild pigs, notoriously rapid breeders, were hunted only in season in the region north of Beijing.[17]

The concept of a hunting season meant, of course, preferential treatment of female and young animals, a very ancient practice. In statistical studies of red deer remains, heavily hunted by Mesolithic cultures of Europe, there is evidence that young males were harvested more frequently than females or older stags since they had the least to do with herd reproduction.[18] This was a widespread prescription among hunters across Eurasia and was even extended to the rapidly multiplying hare in Xenophon's treatise on the chase.[19] In the Iranian world, this wisdom is manifest in a later tradition that has Bahrām Gor ban hunting of onagers under four years of age.[20] Here was sanction for conservation from a storied and heroic royal hunter. The Mongols, while in control of North China, prohibited the killing of any type of wild animal (*qinshou*) "during pregnancy or breeding time," a decree that was imposed as well on the Uighurs of the Tianshan.[21] In Mughal India the general prohibition against hunting females at times included tigers, although Jahāngīr, the author of the policy, violated it on occasion.[22] This defense of the female was imposed at times on hunting partners, at least the cheetah, which Ibn Manglī asserts could be trained to catch only male gazelles![23]

While all these regulations were accepted as norms among elite hunters, they were undercut by the style of hunting. To be sure, an experienced hunter could be selective, sparing female and young, but ring hunts by their very nature were indiscriminate; the solution, therefore, was restraint and quarter. In the Zhou, the net fencing was modified to entrap fewer animals and in the Mongolian empire the ring hunt was terminated, on the pleas of elders, before all the trapped animals were killed.[24] The Manchus followed similar policies, as did the Ṣafavids and Mughals. We even have some numbers: once Shāh ʿAbbās released 2,000–3,000 gazelles from a ring, while Jahāngīr freed about half of the hundred deer in another, and Shāh Jahān on one occasion encircled about 2,000 *nilgao*, but killed only 300.[25] Rulers must be seen as merciful and ruthless. Like gods, it is best if princes are loved *and* feared.

The concept of over hunting was well entrenched; those locales "emptied" of game had to be given time to recover.[26] By contemporary testimony the Byzantine emperor Isaac Comnenus (r. 1057–59) often hunted beasts in the "natural habitat" so as to "avoid reducing the number of animals kept in special reserves."[27] The Yuan court hunted some locales only "every third or fourth year," and Kangxi, a devoted hunter, recognized that some kind of rotation was necessary to give the game time to reproduce, and in consequence he reduced the frequency of ring hunts.[28]

Royal hunters oftentimes protected specific species from molestation, except of course, from themselves: Jahāngīr banned the hunting of antelope in the region of Amānābād, Awrangzīb the hunting of crane around his capital, and in the Liao, only the emperor could shoot stags with antlers."[29] In ancient Mari in Mesopotamia, Yuan China, and Mughal India only the emperor, to use Roe's words, could "meddle with Lions."[30] All big cats were considered kingly game, and hunting them the sole prerogative of the ruler.

But this was not their only motive for protection. In some instances, it might even be a reward for some service an animal species rendered a ruler's subjects. In seventh-century Sīstān, the Umayyad governor ordered weasels and porcupines protected because they regularly killed snakes, a threat to humans.[31] In the Yuan, there was a similar and well-documented case involving cranes. In the fall of 1299 locusts invaded Jiangsu province and were set upon by thousands of bald cranes (*tuchiu*), who killed the insects on the ground and in the air. In return, the central chancellery obtained an imperial decree protecting these birds in Jiangsu. The ban remained in force for over fifty years.[32] In both cases, traditional governments utilized what we would now call "natural controls" to deal with unwanted pests and insect infestations.

Another very common practice to protect game supplies was to restrict hunting rights to the elite, that is, place limits on the number of hunters. The Qitan in 1071 made it illegal for their Chinese subjects to hunt.[33] About the same time, William the Conqueror imposed a broad ban on hunting deer, boar, and hare in England, and several centuries later Qubilai did much the same in North China and Korea. The penalties for violation of these prohibitions were typically severe, blinding or execution.[34] The obvious purpose of these measures was to protect game but it was also often the point of such laws to keep weapons out of the hands of the general populace. As small minorities in their own states, neither the Normans, Qitans, or Mongols had any interest in seeing the subject population gain experience in the use of arms.

This exclusion policy was never completely successful. Beyond the problem of poaching, which was hard to police, royal hunters were compelled from time to time to acknowledge commoners' right to hunt, even in royal forests. Sometimes, as in fourteenth-century France, it was a matter of custom and legal precedent.[35] In others, it was forced by famine; in 1291 Qubilai rescinded his ban on catching animals in China because of widespread hunger and fear of social unrest.[36] And sometimes commoners were permitted to hunt as a sign of royal benevolence; in Mughal India royal hunting preserves were guarded when the ruler was in the vicinity, but when he was not, small game, birds and hares, could be taken with a net.[37] But even in such cases, it should be noted, the elite who used hunting as training for war never encouraged the populace to hunt big game with military-style weapons.

Game Management

Managing a successful royal hunt always entailed the management of nature. A steady supply of game required controls on hunting and longer-term efforts to protect, improve, or fashion environments in which game animals might thrive. Practices designed to achieve these ends took two basic forms in traditional societies, stocking and habitat preservation.

Stocking of areas with desirable game has a long history. Assyrian rulers of the twelfth to the ninth centuries captured wild animals from which, the royal inscriptions proudly announce, they "formed herds." Some animals were sacrificed to the gods, others, especially exotics, were placed on display, but the standard game animals such as deer, gazelle, and ibex, were "placed in the mountains," an obvious reference to stocking.[38] In the early modern age European courts pursued similar policies. French kings of the sixteenth century, all avid hunters, tried to populate their hunting grounds with exotic game—reindeer from Lapland and pheasants from "Tartary."[39] With far greater success, the Anglo-Norman nobility imported the English fallow deer to parts of southern and eastern Ireland.[40] In Inner Asia, the nomads, experts in moving animals, engaged in some very long-range stocking. On Chinggis Qan's order, his eldest son, Jochi, drove a large herd of onagers (*gūr-khar*) from the Qipchaq steppe to the vicinity of Fanākat on the Syr Darya. For a while these animals were used for entertainment, chased down and captured, and when they tired of this, each prince branded those animals he had taken and set them free for future sport.[41]

In the core area, there is much evidence of stocking. Jahāngīr was particularly active. When red antelope became restricted to two locales, he had some captured and sent to other areas as breeding stock. On another occasion, he had 404 head of wild deer captured in a ring hunt near Samanagar taken to Fathpur and let loose on a plain in the region. Later on, 84 additional deer were "tagged" with nose rings and sent to the same area.[42] Even more impressive were the efforts of his contemporary, Shāh ʿAbbās in Iran. In a letter ʿAbbās sent Jahāngīr, circa 1619, he thanks the Mughal ruler for a gift of Indian birds and requests additional species, a horned buffalo and a breeding pair of antelope. He then reports to his fellow sovereign that the forest (*jangal*) he has established in Farāhābād has flourished and that is why he has requested further Indian species.[43] His selection of Farāhābād as the locale for recreating a bit of India in Iran was most appropriate, since it is in Māzandarān near the estuary of the

Tajūn along the coast of the Caspian Sea, which is hot and humid and produces thick scrub and dense forests.

China, too, had its gamekeepers and traditions of stocking, which is very evident in the hunting parks of the Zhou and Han periods.[44] In later centuries, the Manchus kept the marshes north of Beijing well supplied with wild boar for the emperor's pleasure.[45]

Although it is true that if taken together, these varied efforts anticipate some notions of contemporary game management, they were hardly articulated, integrated, or sustained policies in the modern sense; for the most part, they were the consequence of the inclinations of individual rulers. More consistent and far more productive in long-term results were attempts to protect, extend, improve, or create habitats that benefited game animals. Such practices, it should be stressed, were not necessarily intentional but sometimes a by-product of a desire to monopolize or at least partially control natural resources, most especially water and forest products. The mix of motives is well illustrated in the history of elite fowling. Since waterfowl afforded much sport, royal hunters adopted various strategies to secure an adequate supply. Frederick II created a bird sanctuary in a swampy area near Foggio in southeast Italy, while Indian and Persian elites carefully stocked lakes and ponds with fish which attracted and sustained popular game birds such as cranes and herons.[46] Another technique, used by the Qitans and later on by the Mongols was to plant various kinds of grain around bodies of water to attract fowl and to ensure fat, tasty game for later hunts.[47] Beyond protecting and augmenting natural bodies of water, some devoted royal hunters created them. Armenian kings of the fifth century C.E. built artificial watercourses with the express purpose of attracting "an abundance of birds for the delight and sport of the nobility addicted to the hunt."[48] Chinggisid princes, similarly addicted, constructed artificial pools in the arid regions of central Mongolia and Turkestan "for the flocking" of waterfowl.[49] This was still the practice in early nineteenth-century Khiva, where the ruler hunted waterfowl on lakes constructed along irrigation canals.[50]

In the foregoing instances, the primary purpose is to concentrate game by the provision of suitable habitats. This is not so, however, in the case of the "tank," an Indian institution that also attracted waterfowl. The tank, in the sense of a large storage pond, was a ubiquitous feature of the landscape throughout the subcontinent.[51] Such reservoirs are in evidence from prehistoric times and their royal sponsorship is widely heralded in early literature and inscriptions.[52] Later on in the period of the Delhi sultanate and the Mughal empire, both Muslim and Hindu princes refurbished old tanks and built new ones.[53]

Found along communication lines, in the countryside and near cities, tanks were sometimes quite large, two to ten miles in circumference. Often lined with stone to prevent seepage and ringed with trees to limit evaporation, tanks were created by damming and diverting streams.[54] These pleasing, human-built environments naturally drew waterfowl of all types and elite hunters as well.[55] But while an attractive hunting locale, this was by no means the original or the primary purpose of tanks, which, as many European travelers correctly recognized, was water storage and irrigation. Boating, recreation, fish farming, and fowling were derivative, secondary functions.[56]

If the unintended consequence of tank construction in India was good duck hunting, then one can say that the intended consequence of forest preservation in the medieval West was good deer hunting. The German language helpfully distinguishes between *Waldgeschichte*, the history of natural woodlands, and *Forstgeschichte*, the history of forests managed by humans.[57] The word "forest" is itself very revealing in this regard; it is derived from the Latin *foris*, "outside," meaning lands of any description—woodland as well as moorland, pasture, and even agricultural land—that were outside the common law and subject to special laws regulating the royal hunt.[58] In medieval England, the term forest was directly equated with hunting preserves set aside by the king in various counties where there was food for "venison," here meaning the edible flesh of any wild animal.[59] Thus, the very concept of forest originated in the hunt, not natural history. Naturally, the forest was jealously guarded by the court; its "vert and venison," that is, all its beasts and the vegetation needed to provide them with cover and food, was under the direct protection of the king's laws. In this system the forest and the royal park were synonymous; hunting parks were simply enclosed forests. No one, of course, had the right to make use of the wood, pasture, or game in a royal forest without the permission of the king or his agents, the foresters. The latter, of necessity, were gamekeepers as well as law enforcement officials who helped operate a separate court system for violations of forest law, one that generated much royal revenue through fines.

While Anglo-Saxon kings pursued the chase and had game preserves, they had not asserted an exclusive right over large tracts of the countryside, thereby excluding commoners from the resources of the forest. This forest system was imported from France with the Norman conquests. Through "afforestation" William and his sons added much to the royal hunting preserves, often evicting established communities. For their own political and economic reasons, the Norman kings became steadfast defenders and extenders of the "natural" habitats of their realm.

On the continent, *Forstgeschichte* follows a roughly similar path. Early medieval kings such as the Merovingians had preserves and foresters, and jealously guarded their game and forests.[60] But at this early date there was still so much wilderness throughout northern Europe that rulers often encouraged colonization and cultivation of these tracts because it benefited the court financially in the long term.[61] However, as the amount of wilderness began to decline in the late medieval era, rulers tended to guard and monopolize the remaining forests with greater zeal. This in turn led to widespread encroachments on royal forest in the search for vert and venison. In Norman England the poachers came from all ranks of society: the nobility, peasantry, clergy, and outlaw gangs.[62] In response to the poaching of game, wood, or ground cover, royal laws became increasingly harsh and savage, including the death penalty.[63]

For northern Europe, at any rate, royal hunting and conservation were inextricably linked. Medieval nobles were sophisticated and devoted "conservationists" even though their purposes and worldviews differed radically from those of modern environmentalists. Still, they expended much energy preserving habitats for game animals in England and France. And in Germany, with its numerous principalities, there was a multitude of *Forst- und Jagdmeisters* who managed game, organized the royal hunt, and protected forests. In time they even imported new trees and shrubs to enhance the environment for game animals, and slowly the term "afforestation" lost its original meaning of the appropriation of lands for hunting preserves and took on its modern meaning of planting new forests in barren wastes.[64]

In the core area, ecological conditions were substantially different, as were the hunting techniques, which were geared to open country rather than the forest. Nonetheless, royal hunting grounds were still off-limits except at the sufferance of the ruler. In places such as Turkestan and India, these territories were taboo, and those who trespassed were subject to heavy punishment, including enslavement.[65] Within the Iranian political orbit similar efforts were made to preserve habitat. Satraps in Achaemenid service had their foresters and according to later tradition, an Armenian king of Parthian origin, Khosrov III (r. 330–39), planted an oak forest beside the Azal River to encourage game and birds for hunting.[66] Like Shāh ʿAbbās's *jangal* at Farāhābād, it too was created by appropriation and new planting, that is, by afforestation in both senses of the word.

Hunting and forestry were also closely linked in early China. This emerges from discussions of public access to natural resources found in hunting parks and preserves. Mencius endeavored to convince rulers of his day that it was contrary to the principles of the Sage Kings to create large royal hunting grounds that excluded the people and treated those who killed the king's deer as murderers. Rather, he recommended government-controlled preserves that shared the bounty of nature with the populace, particularly firewood and small game. To Mencius, this was not only good government but sound economics as well.[67] The officials charged with maintaining these forests were from the beginning concerned with game management.[68] In pre-Han and Han times, foresters (*shanyu* or *yu*) cut timber, protected preserves, organized game drives, and supplied royal parks with prey.[69]

Later dynasties, politically committed to the chase, followed these precedents. Both the Yuan and the Qing took care to protect their forests, particularly those near the capital, promulgating laws prohibiting hunting in imperial preserves, which were patrolled by gamekeepers and sometimes by members of the imperial guard.[70] The Manchu's major preserve at Mulan survived intact for several decades after the last royal hunt there in 1821; soon thereafter, under the unrelenting pressure of poachers, loggers, and land-hungry peasants, Mulan rapidly declined and by 1906 the forest cover was only 5 percent of its original extent.[71]

It should be noted, however, that the motives for forest preservation varied across the continent. In China, for example, one perennial concern was soil erosion arising from the deforestation of mountains, which by the time of Mencius was already a serious problem.[72] And in contrast to Europe and to some extent China, forestry in premodern Japan was only marginally connected with elite hunting; for the most part, forests were managed as a source of wood for building and fuel, and as a source of plant matter for fertilizing intensive agriculture.[73] But whatever the prime motive for preservation, habitat for game was in some measure protected, even though, as Glacken says, through an "unwitting conservation."[74]

There was yet another type of unintended conservation that periodically helped to reduce the pressure on game: social dislocation that might be catastrophic for human communities was often beneficial for wildlife and their habitat. This could take various forms: drought in the Middle East or plague in Russia that led to depopulation, abandoned lands, and the return of natural habitats suitable for game.[75] Political miscalculation sometimes had similar effects; in one case, reported by Pelsaert, overtaxation in Mughal India caused many peasants to flee and in consequence, he says, "the fields lie empty and unsown, and grow into wilderness."[76]

War, however, was even a greater boon to nature. During the periods of intense warfare, the commitment of the army, as well as the casualties among the elites, reduced the frequency and scale of royal hunts and this encouraged the recovery of game populations.[77] Additionally, war produced a general depopulation that benefited game. During the reign of Giorgi II (1072–89), the Georgians were under incessant Seljuq pressure and suffered many reverses. By about 1080, the Turks' annual summer expedition resulted in the death, flight, or enslavement of the frontier population. In the words of a Georgian chronicle, the situation became so bad that "there was neither sowing nor reaping in those days: the countryside was laid to waste and reverted to forest, and the fields were no longer inhabited by men, but by game and wild beasts."[78] The same happened along the forest-steppe frontier of medieval Russia, where the frequent flight of the sedentary population produced the return of natural cover, what the geographer Aleksandr Voeikov termed *le boisement involontaire.*[79] Such reversions attracted wildlife and in places such as the Middle Don, according to eyewitness testimony from 1389, the only occupants of these former agricultural lands were "elk, bear, and similar animals."[80] To some degree these assertions may be literary topos, but they also reflect an ecological reality, the rapidity with which nature can reconquer untended cultivated lands.

In certain cases, prolonged military conflict might even produce "no man's lands" between the contending parties that were extensive, enduring, and beneficial to wildlife. In the New World, the so-called "war zones," vast tracts separating the territories of rival Amerindian tribes, operated to preserve habitat and game, particularly megafauna such as deer and bison, which were often scarce in lands under permanent tribal control.[81] The modern equivalent is the DMZ, a narrow no man's land across the entire peninsula that now serves as a refuge for plants and animals endangered or extinct elsewhere in Korea.[82]

Warfare not only spared game by creating buffers, diverting soldiers from the hunt, and reducing human population through famine, disease, and flight, but more grimly, the casualties of war provided much nourishment for scavenging and carnivorous animals, a phenomenon frequently noted in ancient texts.[83] Typical is the report of Theophylact, who says that the Byzantine defeat of the Sasanids in 578 left so many unburied Persian dead in the field that there was a ready feast for the passing wild beasts.[84] Further to the east, the long period of warfare attending the fall of the Ming and the rise of the Manchus, population losses in the southern provinces of China produced human carrion and more forest and this led to the growth of the tiger population.[85] The same phenomenon occurred during the Vietnamese War, when tigers in Southeast Asia made a temporary comeback.[86]

As a final example of the complex and sometimes unexpected relationship between war and conservation of game, we can profitably examine the policies of the Delhi sultanate. To begin with, they, like other rulers across Eurasia, had formal hunting preserves and wastelands from which agriculturalists were carefully excluded. But what is most instructive here is how reserves were created in the first instance. In one case, at least, Sultan Fīrūz Shāh (r. 1351–88) systematically ravaged the Hindu region of Katehr "under the guise of hunting," with the consequence, evidently intended, that the locals fled, so that "nothing but game lived there."[87]

None of this is to argue that war was inevitably a blessing for wildlife, but simply that it could be, and often was.

Cultural Constraints

To this point, most of the measures for ensuring future stocks of prey flowed, whether intended or not, from the actions, decisions, and policies of the ruling class, that is, from the royal hunters themselves. But they were not free of wider cultural practices and norms, not of their own making, that placed additional constraints on their hunting behavior.

Most conspicuously, religious convictions, conventions, and institutions placed limits on the chase and protected wildlife, limitations which rulers, even powerful ones, had to consider, if not always obey. Some of these took the form of positive injunctions; in Islamic law, for instance, animals, as God's creatures possessing souls, enjoy the right of access to public water.[88] Many others took the form of prohibitions. In the medieval West, hunting and hawking met with clerical disapproval for practical and theoretical reasons. For one, it was a secular activity in which churchmen should not participate, and second, it was held to be expensive and distracting.[89] This hardly stopped nobles from hunting, but the Church could restrict the chase on its own lands, in effect creating animal and bird sanctuaries.

This occurred even in the core area. A charter issued by the Georgian Giorgi III in 1170 to a monastery north of Tbilisi severely limited access of royal falconers to their lands to very brief periods and to a specific locale.[90] Sanctuaries of this type are quite common and some even more restrictive. The interdiction of hunting around Mecca was absolute. Within the *ḥaram*, the sacred precinct, marked by pillars, nothing could be killed, neither humans or animals. Even the accidental death of the smallest creature was to be avoided, the only exception being self-defense against dangerous animals.[91]

Of the religions of the Near East, only one, Manichaeism, placed a total ban on the chase. Its founder, Mani (216–76), equated hunting with wickedness and sin and purportedly converted several princes he chanced upon while they were out hunting. Modern commentators argue that Mani's rejection of the chase grew out of his respect for life in all its forms and his opposition to the luxurious lifestyle of the elite.[92] Since Manichaeism was a persecuted, minority religion, it was rarely in a position to enforce its beliefs. Far more successful in curbing the killing of animals are religions indigenous to India, most notably Buddhism and Jainism.

For Buddhism, nature had great religious significance and over time its value tended to increase. Certain schools of Chinese and Japanese Buddhism even raised the question of whether nonsentient beings, plants and trees, could attain Buddhahood. While not all believers went this far, all agreed that animals, as sentient beings, were capable of enlightenment, and thereby gained a special moral status among Buddhists, as they did among Jains.[93]

The Buddhist prohibition against killing any living creature is well known. The implementation of such precepts is most closely associated with the name of Aśoka, the great Mauryan ruler (ca. 274–232 B.C.E.). According to tradition, following the defeat of the Kalingas in the southeast, a campaign attended by much bloodshed, Aśoka, in revulsion, embraced dharma, usually understood as a conversion to Buddhism. Thereafter, he had many edicts inscribed throughout his realm in Prākrit, the vernacular, in which he proclaims the end of his hunting tours, replacing them with moral tours of inspection and instruction, and announces his own abstention from most meats as a source of nutrition.[94]

These prohibitions against killing circulated widely in the form of stories. In the *Legend of King Aśoka*, written in the second century C.E., the horrible deaths suffered by elites are typically ascribed to hunting practices in previous lives. Such past sins, it is asserted, could only be overcome by acts in support of Buddhism.[95] Moreover, hermits, esthetes, divines, and Brahmans regularly preached against hunting, particularly to rulers.[96] The Buddha, they could argue, ransomed with a piece of his own flesh a dove attacked by a ruler's hunting hawk.[97] Their beliefs could be enforced on their own lands; monasteries and hermitages, so numerous in India, became animal sanctuaries and this tradition accompanied Buddhism as it spread north and east.[98] Sometimes, too, secular rulers were persuaded to accept these teachings. In the early seventh century, the king of Kanauj in North India, according to Chinese accounts, reinstated Aśoka's prohibitions and banned the killing of all creatures in his realm.[99]

These precepts traveled with Buddhism as it spread to the north and east. The proscription of hunting as an evil deed was promulgated in Inner Asia through Tibetan and Uighur translations of Indian Sanskrit stories.[100] In the eastern Iranian kingdom of Khotan, circa 300 B.C.E. to 1000 C.E., several of its rulers were reportedly avid hunters and warriors until they renounced killing under the inspiration of Buddhism.[101] And an Old Uighur confession counts killing anything a sin, and specifically includes hunters (*tazaqchi*), falconers (*qushchi*), and fowlers (*itärchi*) among the transgressors, a notion that also received wide circulation in Tang China.[102]

All this might well be dismissed as no more than empty, pious pronouncements, but there can be little doubt that Buddhism did exercise influence on rulers' attitudes toward animals and the chase. Xuanzang, while traveling to India, passed through the territory of the western Türk empire in 630, and in a locale between Lake Issyk Kul and the Talas River saw a deer wild where a large number of animals lived, unmolested, under the qan's full protection.[103] Qitan rulers also responded, at least selectively, to Buddhist concerns for animals. The Liao court banned hunting to celebrated Buddhist holidays and several times had all its hunting birds released, halting falconry for brief periods, a practice that occurred sporadically in Korea and Japan.[104]

Another Indian religion, Jainism, went somewhat farther in its abhorrence of bloodletting and concern for the welfare of animals.[105] This is manifest in the animal homes and hospitals (*goshals* and *pinjrapole*) that so astounded foreign travelers. These had their origins in the third century B.C.E. in precedents attributed to Aśoka. Such facilities are found mainly but not exclusively in western India and are closely associated with the Jains.[106] These hostels and hospitals were for both domesticated and wild animals. Most outsiders who encountered these institutions were bemused or full of ridicule, particularly since they even treated noxious insects such as lice and fleas.[107] An exception is the Englishman James Forbes, who inspected a Jain animal hospital at Surat in 1772. Although he thought the institution "remarkable," he provides a clear and precise account of its nature and functions. Within its walls were various wards in which sick and wounded animals recovered and others where the aged spent their last days. This hospital contained both domesticated and wild animals—monkeys, birds, turtles, and others.[108]

Hindus took a more moderate stance than the Jains, but their religious beliefs most certainly affected their attitudes and hunting behavior. This ambivalence is well illustrated by the hunting manual of Rudra Deva, which offers a rather labored defense of the chase by equating it with older, formalized animal sacrifices; if, he contends, one follows the practices of the sages and first anoints the beasts of the forest with water, then the hunt becomes a praiseworthy, religious act, not a sinful slaughter of living creatures.[109] Thus, while rajahs hunted, there were nagging doubts and, in comparison with Muslim princes, many more restrictions on the kind of game that could be killed, especially those such as peacocks that had symbolic and religious meaning for Hindus.[110] Some, moreover, moved well beyond these restrictions. In 1708 Hamilton met in Orixa (Orissa) a local Hindu ruler who placed severe limits on hunting the abundant game and fowl within his domain. The beasts, Hamilton continues, "are all tame, because none dares kill them but the prince, except those he gives written Licences to, and these are but seldom obtained."[111] On occasion, popular sentiments also upheld restrictions of this sort; in 1803 an incident involving the shooting of birds by servants of the Qājār ambassador in Bombay, led to conflict with Hindu soldiers and to the death of a Persian official.[112]

In this environment, even a Muslim ruler and an avid hunter such as Akbar developed qualms about killing and was at times ambivalent about hunting; in the end, however, he authorized and justified killing "in battle and the chase."[113] His son and successor, Jahāngīr, developed similar moral scruples about hunting and took a vow against killing animals that lasted from 1618 to 1622.[114]

Indian religions had a profound effect on China, but there were as well indigenous cultural and ideological currents that militated against the chase and brought forth a measure of sympathy and respect for the animal kingdom. The continuing debate about the advisability of the royal hunt is one expression of this. Taizong (r. 626–49), the second emperor of the Tang, once demoted one of his sons for excessive devotion to the chase and then berated his son's tutor, Quan Wanji, for failing to reform his charge. In response, another court official, Liu Fan, said, "Fang Xuanling serves your majesty yet is unable to persuade you to stop hunting. How can it be that only [Quan] Wanji is guilty?" The emperor, much irritated, then withdrew his critical comments.[115] This exchange is revealing on several levels. First, it is evident that the amount of time spent hunting was a point of dispute at court and that there were ongoing pressures to curtail the chase because of costs. Second, it is very likely that Chinese court officials often decried hunting not necessarily for reasons of protecting nature but of preventing emperors from spending extended periods away from the capital and the influence of the literati, and spending it in the company of "undesirables"—military men, frontier officials, and foreigners.

A further restraint on royal hunters was a convention, operative during the Tang, that the emperor did not kill anything "if the fur and feathers cannot be used for clothing, or if the meat is unfit for sacrifices."[116] In other words, as a norm, prey must have utility, animals cannot be killed solely for "sport."

Another powerful motive for protection was the belief in portents, which could halt certain kinds of hunting. For example, in 63 B.C.E., the Han emperor Xiaodi (r. 74–49) decreed that in the commanderies around Chang'an, the capital, no migrating birds could be killed in spring and summer because he believed that they were supernatural (*shen*) and provided intelligence of the future.[117] This illustrates well how spiritual sanctions could slow but not permanently halt the chase.

Beyond these very specific, sometimes idiosyncratic motives that relieved pressure on game, there were general attitudes that raised the status of animals and provided respectable arguments for their defense. In the early Chinese Buddhist texts, humans and animals are placed in a moral relationship to one another. This precept was further solidified in the contemporary "accounts of anomalies (*zhiguai*)," short descriptions of strange phenomena in which animals endowed with human attributes interact with humans on a basis of reciprocity, implying that both are members of a single moral community.[118] This belief led in time to the practice of *fengshang*, "releasing animals," which combined Buddhist and Chinese notions about transmigration and retribution and the social lessons of liberation. The movement, which peaked in Ming times, focused attention on domesticated animals destined for the butcher and on smaller wild game.[119] Thus, in China as in India, animals had some moral standing in contrast to the situation in the Christian world where they were thought to be without souls. The consequences of these differing precepts for the actual treatment of animals and their implications for more general attitudes toward nature will be considered at the end of this chapter.

Species Endangered

The deeper connections between conservation and the royal hunt can be approached through a close examination of the cultural history of two species, the onager and the cheetah. This will help focus attention on some key questions surrounding the issues of endangerment and extinction.

The onager or Asiatic wild ass, *Equus hemionus*, is composed of six geographical races or subspecies spread across Eurasia from the Middle East to Mongolia. Additionally, there is the more distantly related kiang, *Equus kiang*, of Tibet. Some claims have been made that the onager was at one time domesticated in the ancient Near East for use as a draft animal. This, in the opinion of Clutton-Brock, is extremely unlikely since the onager is irascible and intractable.[120] But it is still possible, as Varro asserts, that it was interbred with horses and donkeys in antiquity.[121]

In premodern times, onagers were common in Asia Minor and found as far as the Egyptian-Nubian frontier in the southwest.[122] The Syrian population, which was numerous in the Middle Ages, became extinct in the course of the eighteenth century.[123] At the eastern end of their range, onagers and kiangs were still encountered in some numbers in the mid-nineteenth century. Now they are extremely rare, on the endangered species list, surviving only in small relic populations in Turkmenistan and India, and in larger herds on nature reserves in Xinjiang and the Jungharian Gobi of Mongolia.[124]

How to account for this long-term decline? For one thing, onagers, like other wild ungulates, were thought a danger to crops, a concern that is very ancient.[125] For another, onagers have long been sources of food. The principal game of the Mesolithic cultures east of the Caspian in the tenth to sixth millennia, as revealed by osteological remains, was gazelle and onager.[126] In historic times, the taste for wild ass is still evident in Turkestan, Iran, and Syria, where its flesh, considered a great delicacy, was consumed with relish into the nineteenth century.[127] Further, in the Middle East, the onager, believed to live for extended periods, was long a source of medicine; its hooves and brains were ingredients in potions and its flesh thought to fortify human health.[128]

Although all these were thought good reasons for killing wild asses, there is no doubt that they were also hunted, and hunted extensively, because they were considered great "sport" by elites across Eurasia. Called *ḥimār al-waḥsh* in Arabic, *gūr-khar* or *khar-gūrah* in Persian, and *qulan* in Turkic and Mongolian, the onager had a widespread reputation for its endurance and speed, characteristics noted by numerous authors from the core area and beyond.[129] Equally important, onagers were held to be fighters and their reputation for an active defense brought them to the hippodrome of Constantinople, where they were pitted against leopards and lions.[130] Moreover, onagers, herd animals, were viewed by elite hunters as loyal and courageous. In the Middle Persian romance about Ardasher (r. 227–40), onagers sacrifice themselves for the family and young, they come unhesitatingly to the protection of their own; they were therefore noble opponents, worthy of a royal hunter.[131]

Because of this image, sources from the core area, Armenian, Georgian, Arabic, and Turkic, all speak of onagers as a favored game of elites, one that only a great huntsman, a Bahrām Gor, or a great beast, a lion, could bring down.[132] In consequence, royal hunters continuously pursued the wild ass over the millennia and across the continent. They were hunted in ancient Mesopotamia and early China, and throughout the Muslim era.[133] In the steppe zone, Strabo reports in the first century C.E. that Sarmatian nomads hunted wild asses and later on the Mongols took up the sport with great enthusiasm.[134]

Methods of hunting them varied. In the late fifth century B.C.E., Xenophon ran down onagers with relays of horses, since they could easily outdistance cavalry mounts.[135] Also common was a technique recommended in Muslim hunting manuals and practiced by Shāh ʿAbbās: the asses were first slowed by arrows and then finished off with spears or swords, shock weapons designed for human foes.[136] Sometimes they were caught in ring hunts; in 1634 in Punjab, Shāh Jahān encircled a herd near their favorite watering hole, where many were captured, presumably for restocking.[137]

There is no question that onagers were heavily hunted. But were they "hunted out" by royal hunters? This is an obvious explanation for their current plight; caution, however is required before reaching this judgment. In the first place, there is no evidence of depletion during the heyday of the royal hunt; observers in the late Middle Ages and in early modern times repeatedly refer to the large number of onagers encountered in Iran, India, and Inner Asia.[138] Chronology and geography are all important in rendering a decision on this matter. It is possible, for instance, that they were hunted out in Syria by the eighteenth century, but that their decline in western China and Xinjiang is primarily the result of habitat fragmentation and reduction. It is also plausible to suggest that the introduction of firearms in more recent times had a pronounced effect, given the great difficulty of killing onagers by more traditional means. Or, it may be the case that onagers lost out in competition for pasture when modernizing regimes, following the Soviet model, began programs to intensify pastoral production in the middle decades of the twentieth century. Only detailed local studies can cast new light on the many uncertainties.

Oddly enough, while royal hunters' responsibility for the decline of onagers, a preferred prey, is unclear, the case for their role in the decline of the cheetah, a favored predator *and* beloved partner, is easier to make. More particularly, there is evidence to show that elite hunters bear primary responsibility for the cheetah's eradication in some parts of its natural range.

At the beginning of the Common Era, cheetahs inhabited the plains of East Africa, now their last major bastion in the wild, and were also found from North Africa through Iran, southern Turkestan, and into northwest India. From medieval to early modern times, cheetahs were systematically trapped in Iraq, Iran, Afghanistan, and Māzandarān, and by the twentieth century were thought extinct throughout the region.[139] Recently, however, a very small relic population of the Asiatic cheetah, numbering thirty to sixty individuals, was found in the area of the Kavir Desert. An international effort to study these animals is now under way.[140] The Indian cheetah population survived well into the nineteenth century, at which point it was still being heavily trapped and trained to the hunt for the indigenous nobility.[141] By the mid-twentieth century, wild cheetahs were no longer found in the subcontinent; the last three were sighted and shot in 1948 by the maharajah of Korwai.[142]

While cheetahs were sometimes hunted for sport and for their skins, this does not provide a convincing reason for their decline within the core area.[143] A better explanation is their incessant capture for the use as hunting partners. We know, for example, that Ghazan, Mongolian ruler of Iran, had 300 cheetahs, and that Akbar, according to his son's testimony, "once collected together 1,000 cheetahs."[144] When one considers that cheetahs, as predators toward the top of the food chain, are thinly spread out over extensive tracts, the capture of this many animals would have a pronounced effect on their population dynamics. Additionally, the fact that cheetahs do not breed well in captivity must be considered in some detail to properly assess the role of human factors in their decline.

Various causes have been advanced to explain the fall in cheetah population. Loss of genetic diversity, recently thought to be a leading contributor to their decline in the wild and poor reproductive performance in captivity, is being challenged along several lines. Low populations of cheetahs in the wild are now attributed to predation of the young by lions and leopards, a fact well known to traditional huntsmen in the core, to habitat loss, and their problems in captivity to improper husbandry practices.[145] The latter point is underscored by the fact that the first captive cheetah birth recorded in the modern zoological literature was in 1956 in the Philadelphia Zoo.[146] The result of these difficulties is that there are still no self-sustaining cheetah populations in captivity.[147]

The solution currently recommended by field-workers familiar with cheetah breeding behavior is that captive animals must have opportunities for natural interaction with potential mates that include male competition for females, thus inducing oestrus, extended courtship chases, and normal diet, not cat food. The problem, then, is not genetic but managerial, and the solution requires the creation of the right physical and social environment for successful breeding.[148] As noted by many zoologists, cheetahs, while easily tamed, fail the first test for domestication: the ability to reproduce in captivity. If this problem had been mastered in earlier times, it is probable that the cheetah today would be a fairly common domesticated animal.[149]

Their reproduction problems in captivity were recognized quite early. Jahāngīr, for one, notes that during his father's day a male cheetah slipped his leash and mated with a female who produced three cubs that survived to adulthood. He recorded this event, he says, "because it appeared strange." Indeed it was, since it appears to be the only known instance of Indian cheetahs breeding in captivity.[150]

If we now combine what is known of cheetah reproductive behavior with elite hunting practices, we have a possible explanation for cheetah decline in India. Accounts of Mughal emperors' quests for captive cheetahs as hunting partners show that they targeted, as elsewhere, adults and particularly females in their extensive programs of trapping.[151] This meant that every cheetah captured and trained was removed permanently from the breeding population. But this was not all the damage. Since females were deemed the best hunters and untrained cubs considered useless, the young left to fend for themselves in the wild must have survived in very small numbers, if at all. To put this another way, elites' treatment of cheetahs ran directly counter to their general policy toward prey, that is, sparing females and young. Further, we must take into account the difficulties of trapping and transporting animals, which surely led to many, if incalculable, casualties. And, if we add to the 1,000 cheetahs at the Mughal court those captured for the use of the innumerable petty princes and noble houses of premodern India, we can reasonably conclude that large numbers of animals were removed from the wild breeding population every year for centuries on end.

Finally, to adequately account for their decline we need to note briefly that great numbers of cheetahs were sent, well beyond their natural range, to China,

Mongolia, and western Europe. In principle, though this might have led to the expansion of the species through the creation of feral breeding populations, this did not happen in the case of cheetahs.[152] On the contrary, foreign interest in cheetahs only worsened their plight, since self-sustaining captive populations could not be established and replacement cats had to be imported from afar, further diminishing the number of cheetahs in the wild. It may be a simplification, ignoring some other factors, but it is at least suggestive that the only viable breeding populations of wild cheetahs left in the world, those in East Africa, are in a region where they were never trained to hunt under human control.

In the narrow sense, it is true that elites in Iran and India did not "hunt out" cheetahs in this part of their natural range, but they did trap and train them in such numbers so as to alter catastrophically cheetah population dynamics and thus alter in fundamental ways cheetah geography and history.

Natural Attitudes

To close out this chapter, we take up some general issues concerning premodern concepts of conservation and attitudes toward nature, at least those that can be usefully viewed through the prism of the royal hunt. One obvious question is who conserved? If we understand conservation as conscious short-term restraint for long-term benefit, then many of the most active conservationists in history were political elites, the royal hunters and the polities they controlled. Through laws, hunting conventions, and ritual, nobles in England and other European lands endeavored to ensure continued good hunting in their domains.[153] This habit of state-enforced conservation measures was later exported to the New World with the expansion of Europe.[154]

These attitudes and practices were not, however, unique, a case of Western particularism. In China conservation was largely a state-sponsored effort and took the form there, as Mark Elvin points out, of government or court monopolies and quasi-monopolies on the products of nature—wood, game, and fish.[155] Clearly, more than love of nature or even enlightened self-interest for sport was at work here; in China and Europe and in the lands between, royal hunting and conservation were vehicles for asserting elite control over economic resources of all kinds. While this may be the case in complex societies based on intensive agriculture, is it true of smaller-scale foraging, agricultural, and pastoral societies? This is a matter of intense debate among social scientists, environmentalists, and development specialists. One point recently emphasized in these discussions is that the wealthier strata, out of narrow self-interest, engage in some forms of conservation and at times coerce others into doing the same.[156] As a general characterization, this observation can be comfortably applied to the royal hunt and its attendant conservation measures.

Any examination of motives for conservation inevitably brings up the matter of ideology and attitudes toward nature at large. Ideology is regularly invoked and often seen as a dominating force in human interaction with nature. Sometime it is used to explain very specific practices, whether harmful or beneficial, and sometimes to explain conjectured fundamental differences in approaches to nature found in the West and those in the rest of the world. In these formulations, the critical differences appear, it is argued, with the spread of Christianity into the West. According to this theory, the belief that humans, created in God's image, had the right, even the obligation, to manipulate nature, itself divinely created to serve human ends, emerged in the late Middle Ages. This led in turn to technological progress and even greater success in altering nature.[157] If true, then Christianity, as an ideology, can be considered a critical engine of global historical change whether for good or evil.

Ideologies, worldviews of various kinds, certainly play a role in mediating human interaction with nature, but in the view of some scholars, political, demographic, and technological factors seem paramount in controlling what happens on the ground and to the ground. For example, Chinese cosmological views on the necessary balance between humans and nature were hardly "operational," that is, they did not serve as a guide to practice in the day-to-day effort to extract energy from natural systems.[158] Yi-fu Tuan, among others, makes the important point that in the interplay "between environmental attitudes and environmental behavior" is never straightforward and that actions are rarely in accord with philosophies of nature.[159] In other words, Daoist precepts about living in harmony with nature, so regularly praised by Western humanists, did not in fact prevent serious environmental problems—deforestation, erosion, and destruction of animal species—any more than Old Testament injunctions giving humans dominion over nature "caused" such problems.[160]

Thus, despite well-articulated ideologies of sympathy for nature, complex societies have repeatedly failed to live within their own guidelines; they systematically transformed nature in substantial ways and with unanticipated, and oftentimes unpleasant if not catastrophic consequences. Examples of the failure of ideology are not hard to find. After all, Buddhist kings regularly hunted for pleasure and profit.[161] And in the West, the Romans, though they claimed to honor and revere the earth, *mater terra*, did much to transform the earth with their engineering skills.[162]

The notion that arose in the West that humans should and could control and manipulate nature was surely a by-product, as Charles Bowlus suggests, of specific historical circumstances, interlocking ecological, economic, demographic, and intellectual shifts that took place in late medieval Europe, and not a consequence of precepts intrinsic to some all-pervasive ideology inherited from antiquity, that is, the "Judeo-Christian tradition."[163] The great appeal of ideology as an explanation, one suspects, is because cosmological precepts are conveniently preserved in bookish traditions, in well-studied and indexed canon, and are thus readily recoverable, whereas information on the actual engagement with nature on the ground is far more diffuse and is harder to come by.

It is also important to recognize that attitudes toward nature from within the same cultural tradition and even within the same literary work are by no means consistent or uniform. Pliny views the human place in nature quite ambiguously, and so of course, does the Old Testament.[164] As Keith Thomas points out, the injunction (Gen. 1.26–30) to rule nature did not generate the behavior of "Westerners," rather, it rationalized it in specific historical contexts. And equally important, the same biblical source (Gen. 2.15) would be drawn upon, when needed, to support an alternative, even diametrically opposed, benevolent, "environmentally friendly" attitude toward the natural world.[165]

This apparent contradiction calls for explanation. In literate societies, classical, canonical texts seem to operate as sources of inspiration and ideology. Certain key passages tend to be repeated and leave the impression of permanence, that a single coherent idea dominates people's minds and behavior through time. This, however, is a distortion, one that inhibits our understanding of historical change. Societies, in fact, contain within themselves at any given moment options, alternative organizational, behavioral, and ideological models. In Philip Salzman's formulation, some alternative models are manifest and some are latent, that is some "are currently operative" while others are held "in reserve." The alternatives are enacted when relevant, when called to mind by specific events. This, he rightly argues, is not necessarily a conscious or cynical invocation of convenient justifications for momentary interests; rather, these options provide flexibility and fluidity, the means of adaptation. They are, in short, mechanisms of change.[166]

Since the rules of engagement with nature, as well as nature itself, are in flux, a uniform, internally consistent, all-encompassing attitude toward nature is hardly possible or even desirable. It may be that the very contradictory ideas about nature carried within any given cultural tradition are an asset, since such "contradictions" do not, as so often asserted, account for the collapse of systems but seem rather to explain their survival and longevity. This ambivalence and inconsistency is clearly evident in the royal hunt, in the horrific slaughter of animals for sport and spectacle on the one hand, and in the very sound and sober conservation practices on the other. These contradictions are conveniently mirrored in the Turkic and Mongolian word *qorugh/qorigh*, a term that could designate the territory around a monastery in which hunting was prohibited or designate a park and preserve where elites killed animals in large numbers.[167]

Finally, we return to the question of the historic role of hunters in the endangerment and extinction of species. To be sure, overkill does occur and can be documented in recent times: a number of sea mammals and terrestrial animals have been hunted to extinction.[168] This attitude, that it is permissible to plunder nature, well conveyed by German *Raubwirtschaft*, has wrought particular devastation on those species that provide products—feathers, furs, and ivory—in demand for purposes of personal adornment.[169] Depredations of this type have been, for the most part, the work of commercial hunters. But subsistence hunters, for quite different ends, also take a heavy toll. Kent Redford's recent study of the Amazon basin shows that in the progressive "defaunization" of the region subsistence hunting accounts for about 57,000,000 animals a year, while commercial hunting adds only several million to this total.[170] Historically, major faunal and avian die-offs are often correlated with the first arrival of human populations into "pristine" ecosystems. This is quite evident throughout the Pacific Ocean, where many bird species, including the giant moa of New Zealand, died out inconsequence of this human invasion.[171] It deserves notice that in these and other cases, the agents of destruction were subsistence, not commercial hunters. In any event, it is not just hunting kills, the quest for food, furs, or trophies, that account for decline in populations. In Jared Diamond's analysis, human agency in animal extinctions takes a number of forms; besides overkill, these include habitat destruction, introduced predators, competitors, diseases, as well as various other secondary effects.[172]

What, then, of the royal hunters? Did they hunt out the now extinct aurochs, the giant wild ox (*Bos primigenius primigenius*) of northern and central Europe, a favorite prey of medieval kings?[173] Specific cases are always hard to answer, since extinction of any species is usually a complex matter. In the case of the forest elephant of Lingnan in South China, its disappearance around 1400 can be explained by either hunting, climatic change, or habitat destruction.[174] Despite these difficulties and complexities, it is nonetheless evident, as a statistical truth, that the principal cause of most historic extinctions is agriculture, not hunters, royal or otherwise.

As Daniel Hillel has argued, agriculture, while certainly not alone, is the major anthropogenic agent of environmental change, and accounts, over the long term, for the reduction of the earth's biological diversity.[175] Cultivators' efforts to control wild nature are phenomena of *la longue durée*, and their success, achieved cumulatively and incrementally in the face of innumerable setbacks, is therefore hardly visible at any given point in time. The elites' attempts to manipulate nature, by contrast, are often publicized and recorded and are more apparent in the short-term historical record. As concrete, datable "historic events" we tend to celebrate or condemn royal confrontations with nature and to ignore or romanticize those of the cultivators, even though the imprint of the peasant agriculturalist on the land was by far the most profound. In measuring these issues, we must always keep in mind that agriculturalists, of whatever type, are in the business of simplifying nature.

The correlation between human demographic expansion, agricultural intensification, and the diminution of wild species was expounded upon by the famed eighteenth-century naturalist Georges Buffon, and mentioned in particular cases by earlier travelers.[176] Thomas Herbert, in Iran between 1627 and 1629, noted that while some tiger hunting still took place, kills were increasingly infrequent because, he explained, their habitat in Hyrcania (Māzandarān) just south of the Caspian had been denuded of its trees by encroaching towns and farmlands and tigers were now rare.[177] At about the same time, the precipitous decline of tigers in Lingnan in South China can also be tied to destruction and fragmentation of their forest habitat through its appropriation by agriculturalists.[178] The same fate befell many prey animals. The Persian deer (*Dama mesopotamica*), long-hunted, had become extremely rare by the nineteenth century, surviving only in isolated pockets in Khuzistān. In the opinion of one recent investigator, this animal is now in danger of complete extinction because of population pressure and land hunger that has greatly disturbed its remaining range.[179]

The hope that some day nations "shall beat their swords into plowshares" (Isa. 2.4) may be eagerly awaited by most humans, but it holds out poor prospects for the animal kingdom. Far more species have been endangered and made extinct by the plow than by the sword.[180]

7

A Measure of Men

Hunting and Hierarchy

Hunting defined people in varying ways. It was a marker that helped to identify the most elevated and, at the same time, the most debased segments of humanity. As a measure of men, hunting was a flexible and subtle criterion in which the style and purposes of the chase were all-important. Such differences helped to create a number of hierarchies; we need to see how these played out in specific cases, to see what different types of hunting communicated about cultural, ethnic, and social identities.

In the Far West, Tacitus, writing in the first century C.E., remarks that people such as the Fenni, who exist entirely by hunting, "live in astonishing barbarism and disgusting misery."[1] Some five centuries later, Procopius, commenting on the Scrithiphini, inhabitants of Thule, the far north, says that their "life is akin to that of beasts" because they hunt exclusively and grow nothing "edible from the earth."[2] In the eastern Islamic world, Gardīzī, in the eleventh century echoes these same sentiments; speaking of the Khūrī (Quri) of southern Siberia, he thinks them a savage people because they ate only meat of game and wore only the skins of wild animals.[3] For these writers, hunting for a living is the prime index of primitiveness; from their perspective, that of the literate strata of complex agrarian societies, one should not live too close to nature. The notion that those who did so were clearly inferior, culturally and morally, was widespread across Eurasia.[4]

It was, therefore, an unmitigated tragedy when those deemed higher on the scale of civilization fell back into the hunting mode. Constantine Porphyrogenitus, in the tenth century, relates that once a district of Serbia was so devastated by the Bulghars that seven years after the event all that was found there were fifty men "supporting themselves by hunting."[5] Equally telling is the portrayal of Chinggis Qan's youth found in the *Secret History*, which relates that following the death of his father, the young Temüjin (the future Chinggis Qan), his mother, and brothers were reduced to shooting birds, fishing, and grubbing roots to survive. Hunting for food was certainly accepted in pastoral societies, but *total dependence* on this method of subsistence was understood as a sign of decline, emblematic of the family's impoverishment and loss of political standing in Mongolian society.[6]

This cultural hierarchy, in which hunting plays such a visible role, readily and regularly merged with conceptions of ethnicity. In the Chinese tradition, repeated frequently in official historiography, the sons of the legendary Yellow Emperor, who dispersed into a "vast wilderness" where "herding and hunting formed the bases of life," became the nomads/barbarians, while the sons who stayed at home took up agriculture and became the Chinese.[7] This equation of hunting = nomadism = foreign was persistent and long-lived in China,[8] and is found in the West as well. Priscus, in the fifth century, says the Huns, the ultimate nomadic barbarians for Westerners, arose from a hunting people.[9]

That hunting was an important criterion for self-identification by the "hunters" themselves is well illustrated by the Manchu case. Bell, in 1720, reports that Kangxi greatly relished the hunt beyond the Great Wall and insisted on living off the land to toughen his people and to "prevent their falling into idleness and effeminacy among the Chinese."[10] In his own writings, Kangxi speaks movingly about the taste of tea made from melted snow, of fresh venison roasted over an open fire, and of the availability of bear's paw, a rarity in China and a dish connected with the ancient bear cults of North Asia.[11] For foreign conquerors of China such as the Manchus, the hunting expeditions north of the wall were a return to an idealized nature and to native cultural roots that could revitalize and reaffirm ethnic identity and solidarity.

The use of hunting as a marker to distinguish strata within a particular community has long been recognized. The close linkage between noble status and the chase in medieval Europe is an obvious case in point.[12] This, of course, was equally true of the core area. In Muslim tradition, didactic stories of early Persian, mainly Sasanid, rulers such as Khusro Anushirvan (r. 531–59) are frequently given hunting settings.[13] This was a proper activity of kings, and it was these kings who provided political models for the 'Abbāsids and their successors. But as a criterion for social distinction, hunting never stood alone. In Boccaccio's formulation, among the virtues of nobility, for both men and women, were beauty, manners, intelligence, and physical skills such as handling horses and falcons.[14] Very similar notions are found in the core. The *Letter of Tansar*, a Middle Persian work that was translated into Arabic in the eighth century and then retranslated into New Persian somewhat later, distinguishes nobles from artisans and merchants by dress, horses, lofty dwellings, and "hunting."[15]

The ready acceptance and application of such normative formulas within the Muslim world is easily documented. In the 1330s the celebrated traveler Ibn Baṭṭuṭah met a nobleman from Herat, a certain Malik Warnā, and pronounced him "an excellent man, who had a natural liking for positions of authority, and for hunting, falcons, horses, slaves, attendants, and royal garments made of rich stuffs." Such a man, he continues, can always gain employment at the courts of India.[16] In this he was quite correct. Bābur, some two centuries later, repeatedly valued men according to such criteria, which ranged from literary abilities, to hawking, to holding one's liquor well.[17] Clearly, this was a habit of mind; to these writers, the vital place of hunting skill in establishing high social status was self-evident.

But hunting was not just a sign of nobility; as Marcelle Thiébaux has pointed out, in the medieval West it was believed that "Hunting had an ennobling effect upon its practitioners."[18] The Arabic world of this age certainly shared this belief. Of course, not all kinds of hunting were considered valorous or ennobling. In early Arabic poetry the heroic hunter was always armed with spear or javelin and always rode a steed; he never used the bow, nor did he surprise game from ambush. The hunt, to be socially elevating, had to be a true chase in which the huntsman confronts quarry at close range.[19] Hunting styles, as styles are wont to do, change over time and space. As falconry spread, it became intimately linked with gentility and aristocratic culture; it is so portrayed in medieval European literature, law, and iconography, and in some cases the falcon was seen as an extension of the knight and a symbol of his quests in love and war.[20] Not surprisingly, falcons and falconers decorated the early coinage and royal seals of Rus princes, and in the Liao, sumptuary laws forbade commoners from possessing falcons.[21] That the right kind of animal assistants were crucial to noble hunting is evident in Qāshānī's assertion that coursing with greyhounds, falconry, and riding swift horses "are the source of joy and fellowship for kings, sultans, notables, and qaghans."[22]

Few elites anywhere in Eurasia would have disputed his pronouncement, or that of an earlier Chinese source, which states that a certain Tang prince "hunted well by nature."[23] Such sentiments are commonplace and, in the core, subject at times to illuminating amplification. Speaking of his own day, the reign of the Sasanid emperor Peroz (459–84), the chronicler Lazar Pʿarpecʿi asserts that the Mamikoneans, an Armenian noble family much despised by rival lines, demonstrated their inherent virtue and value in the field: "At archery," he says, "they were expert and accurate, in hunting they were swift in their movements and first at the kill; they were dextrous with both hands, and in every respect upright and graceful."[24] That is, their inner, natural nobility manifested itself in the chase in a way that no one, not even bitter rivals, could deny.

It follows, too, that upstarts with aristocratic pretensions had, perforce, to take up field sports. This is nicely illustrated in the behavior of the Zhuo family, successful merchants in Sichuan province during the Han period. Once they had acquired sufficient wealth they partook of "the pleasures of field sport, shooting and hunting in direct imitation of men of princely [*jun*] standing."[25]

Hunting was undoubtedly one of the most visible and dramatic ways of communicating one's social pretensions because it allowed an effective display of possessions and noble demeanor. John Fryer, in Iṣfahān circa 1677, says that in the royal parks and preserves near the Ṣafavid court "are seen every Evening all the Gentry of the City Riding to and fro with Hawks on their Fists, managing their Steeds, making matches for Shooting, Hunting, Coursing, or Hawking, Shewing their Gallantry in Apparel and Retinue, as well as Disposition to Sport."[26] Naturally, in such public posing, their birds, too, were most carefully presented, in hoods sumptuously decorated with golden beads, tassels, pearls, and other precious stones.[27]

Equally critical in establishing one's social station was the possession of leisure time. To Engelbart Kaempfer, a German physician in Iran, the reigning shah, Sulaymān I (r. 1666–94), seemed to spend all his time at leisure, sometimes hosting banquets or carousing with intimates or hunting with a large entourage in the countryside.[28] While this apparent devotion to pleasure drew Kaempfer's censure, it is probable that Sulaymān would have been gratified with this result. Royalty and nobility have time for life's enjoyments. The widespread depiction of hunting scenes in the mosaic pavements favored by the provincial landed aristocracy of the late Roman era was very likely a statement of wealth communicated through vivid portrayals of leisure-time activities.[29]

Hunting further ennobled if it was disinterested, if the dangers involved were accepted to aid others. In the Greek tradition, gods and heroes do battle with fabled animal adversaries, fierce lions and enormous boars, as one of their "labors."[30] Hunting, then, can be presented as a public service, such as the English gentry proclaimed the fox hunt in the nineteenth century.[31] They were hardly the first to do so; ancient kings and medieval sultans, as we shall see later on, regularly advanced the same claims.

While hunting could ennoble in a number of ways, hunting for the purpose of economic gain had the opposite effect; this was the essential distinction elites made between hunting that elevated and that which debased. This attitude is pointedly expressed by the Hindu ruler Rudra Deva, when he proclaims that only "low people," those who hunt from need, make use of snares or traps.[32] In the Islamic world formal pronouncements on hunting regularly stress that it was a legitimate activity of rulers when done for the sake of amusement, diversion, and relaxation.[33] More explicitly, the anonymous treatise on hunting prepared by the chief falconer of the Fāṭimid caliph makes the point that there are only two types of hunters, the underclass that hunts for gain and the prince who hunts "for pleasure."[34] In similar fashion, Kai Kā'ūs, asserts that a prince always hunts for "the sport and not the meat."[35] To do otherwise was to invite derision. In indicating the straightened circumstances of an *amīr* in fifteenth-century Central Asia, the historian Mīrzā Ḥaydar tells us that he had to go out "hunting to provide for his wedding feast" and "killed antelopes for the meat." From this, the author concludes sarcastically, "one may judge the rest of the provisions thereby."[36] This is not to say that game could not be served at a royal feast or elite wedding; certain kinds of game, pheasant for example, considered a great delicacy from the Mediterranean world to China, was always acceptable fare.[37] What was crucial in these situations is that a noble must never be seen to hunt out of hardship or necessity.

The vital importance of the chase to social standing is affirmed by yet another body of evidence, that relating to the valuation of land. In describing provinces and locales in Iran, China, and India, Marco Polo regularly includes a thumbnail sketch of populace, products, trade, cities, *and* the quality of the hunting grounds.[38] This incessant concern for the hunting possibilities afforded by any region was hardly new to his age. In Warring States period, the southern kingdom of Chu was deemed especially fortunate because it held the region of Yunmeng, a great wilderness full of rhinoceros, tiger, buffalo, and deer.[39] And, at about the same time, Arsaces (r. 247-ca. 212 B.C.E.), founder of the Parthian dynasty, located one of his major cities, Dara, in a region that was defensible, fertile, well watered, and abounding in game for the chase.[40]

The lands neighboring Turkestan were similarly assessed. According to local tradition, recorded in the Middle Ages, Bukhara was first settled because the region had water, trees, and "plenty of game."[41] In Transcaucasia, land was judged on the same basis. Pʿarpecʿi, writing about eastern Armenia in the late fifth century, offers criteria for a desirable and prosperous kingdom, possessing those "resources necessary for the livelihood, pleasure, and recreation of men." These include well-watered plains, fertile soil, mineral deposits, sweet flowers, medicinal plants, pasture lands, hard-working peasants, skilled artisans, abundant game in the mountains, and canals that attract waterfowl.[42] For nobles of neighboring Georgia, the assessment of properties included pastures, water supplies, vineyards, mills, fields, and hunting grounds. The absence of the latter was considered a serious problem, one well worth fighting over.[43]

In the minds of the Mughals, agricultural productivity and the quality of the hunting and fowling grounds were the principal measures of a locality's worth.[44] These judgments influenced where rulers went and even what lands they might trouble to conquer. This is not at all unlike the situation in China during the late Shang, circa 1200–1050. In David Keightley's analysis, the court conceived of its territory as lands under cultivation and as hunting grounds where the elite could "take to the field." It is most revealing that the graph *tian* is both a noun, "field," and a verb, "to hunt," and that this latter meaning predominates in the oracle bone inscriptions.[45] In such milieus, governing and hunting are hard to distinguish.

Princely Virtues

Hunting, however, was not only a marker of social standing, it was one of the principal ways of taking measure of a monarch, of assessing their individual fitness and their ability to exercise political and military authority. Several comments of Tacitus concerning public expectations of monarchs in the core are most instructive in this regard. In one, he records that the Parthians were deeply suspicious of Vorones I (r. ca. 7–12), a native son, because of his adopted Roman ways and "his rare appearance in the hunting field." In another, he notes Armenians warmly welcomed a foreigner, the Pontic prince Zeno, as their new ruler because of "his affection for the chase."[46] Tacitus, to be sure, was distant from these events, but the general message conveyed here is undeniable: that many peoples intimately associated kingship with physical capacities and feats, and that these were commonly attested by, and projected through, the royal hunt.

Physical criteria for kingship and the attribution of superhuman abilities to kings can be traced back to ancient Egypt, where pharaohs were credited with extraordinary athletic skills, and to Sumer, where monarchs possessed incredible foot speed and, of course, great skills as huntsmen.[47] Millennia later, rulers were still routinely depicted as expert and awesome hunters. Contemporaries of ʿAbdallāh II (r. 1583–98), the Uzbek qan of Turkestan, and the Qājār sovereign Nāṣir al-Dīn (r. 1848–96) praise their unsurpassed skills at the chase.[48] Like Möngke Qaghan, who presided over the vast Mongolian empire at the apex of its power, they were "by temperament" hunters.[49]

In the core area this equation was axiomatic and widely propagated in art, poetry, and in political writings.[50] And it follows, too, that if rulers were inevitably expert hunters, then expert hunters might well become rulers, since the skills and temperament needed for both occupations were similar if not identical. Carpini, among others, accepted this correlation and invokes it in his explanation of the rise of the Mongols; in his recounting, Chinggis Qan, like Nimrod, "became a mighty hunter before the Lord, and learned to steal and take men for prey," and then "went into other territories and any man he could capture and get to join his band he did not let go again."[51] In other words, as a very successful hunter, Chinggis Qan attracted a following and formed a state. The account of the rise of another nomad, Shad, the putative founder of the Kimek, a Turkic confederation of the eleventh century, has a similar story line; first he acquires retainers by his skills at the chase, and then begins his conquests.[52] In a variation on this theme, a legend current in Mughal times claimed that the local Hindu ruling house near Ajmīr descended from a famed hunter whose feats attracted the attention of the local rajah, who made him a trusted minister of state. When the rajah died, the hunter became the new sovereign.[53]

But by far the most famous of these successful hunter stories, one with a very long life span, is that of the rise of Ardashir, founder of the Sasanid dynasty. In early Persian tradition, the signs of his kingly qualities were evident from the beginning: every day Ardashir went on a hunt (*nakhchīr*) and played polo (*chōbēgān*), and with heavens help excelled all others.[54]

For their successor states in the core area, the Sasanids came to embody the Old Persian traditions of statecraft and their rulers became models for later royal hunters. This model was personified by, and projected through, the storied life of Bahrām V Gor (r. 421–39), who, in early Arabic accounts, wins his throne by snatching the royal regalia, which was placed between two fierce lions, killing them both with his mace. With this show of skill and courage, his rival withdraws and the populace willingly accepts his authority.[55] In Iran, his feats and memory were perpetuated in endless stories, legends, and poems that circulated everywhere Persian was the literary language.[56]

While the medieval Muslim world regularly attributed special qualities, particularly great hunting prowess, to kings of yore, this was never the sole attribute.[57] Like elites, princes were judged by criteria that varied somewhat in time and space but nonetheless retained a certain coherence that implies the existence of transcultural expectations and standards. Some of these measures were imposed from without, but some are clearly internal. As an example of an "external review," we can begin with Josephus's critique of Herod the Great, king of Judea (r. 37–4 B.C.E.). Writing after the fact, circa 75–79, Josephus speaks at length of the king's intellectual attainments and then adds:

> Herod's genius was matched by his physical constitution. Always foremost in the chase, in which he distinguished himself above all by his skill in horsemanship, he on one occasion brought down forty wild beasts in a single day; for the country breeds boars and, in greater abundance, stags and wild asses. As a fighter he was irresistible; and at practice spectators were often struck with astonishment at the precision with which he threw the javelin, the unerring aim with which he bent the bow.[58]

Many centuries later, an anonymous chronicler eulogizing Vladimir, prince of Volynia (r. 1268–88), affirms that he was knowledgeable in both religious and secular learning, courageous, honest, generous to the church and poor, and "a skillful hunter."[59] Such expectations are conveniently summed up in the *Visramiani*, which holds a potential ruler should be physically attractive, hirsute (i.e., have a beard), strong, courageous, a good horseman and huntsman, and possess a knowledge of chess, music, and so on; once in power, an ideal king should defend the realm, dispense justice, aid the poor, drink well, distribute gifts, read learned books, and hunt.[60]

Self-evaluations by early kings are rather rare, but we do have Strabo's claim, based on earlier Greek sources, that on the tomb of Darius III (r. 336–330), the last Achaemenid ruler, defeated by Alexander, there was an epitaph that supposedly read: "I was a friend to my friends; as horseman and bowman I proved myself superior to all others; as a hunter I prevailed, I could do everything."[61] The historicity of the inscription is not at issue here; what matters is that such an assertion was plausible and believable in its day; it was the kind of sentiment expected of ancient, particularly Persian, kings.

For a royal self-evaluation whose authenticity is not in doubt, let us look at the epitaph of a Georgian king, Vakhtang VI, ruler of K'art'li (r. 1711–14 and 1719–23), who ended his days as an exile in Astrakhan. This epitaph, prepared at his own direction, lists the following as his principal achievements:

restoration of religious shrines
repair of holy vestments
building a new palace with mirrors
introduction of printing, thereby "multiplying the ink"
extension of irrigation works
stocking a lake with fish
hunting over the hills, slaying deer and wolves
codifying laws
preparing a commentary of *The Man in the Panther's Skin*, the national epic of Georgia
teaching courtly manners to his entourage[62]

This is very representative of what traditional kings were expected to do—build, legislate, encourage religion, enlarge the tax base, and hunt.

We may now find it surprising that someone would place the slaying of deer and introduction of printing technology on the same plane, but it is doubtful that this ever troubled Vakhtang. Hunting was not viewed as something extraneous to governing or to personal development. Intellectual, moral, and physical attainments were interconnected, mutually supporting, part of a package. This can be seen in Xenophon's expectations of a king. For him, hunting, and the dangers it entails, was a major criterion of kingship and the best measure of manliness. And more to the point, he equates skill and courage in the hunt with such virtues as honesty, willingness to learn, self-discipline, and fairness.[63] Intellectual qualities also come into play, since a skillful hunter must read nature and follow its signs in a systematic fashion and this, Dio Chrysostom argues, provides excellent mental exercise and discipline.[64] The Indian rajah Rudra Deva was of the same opinion; in his manual he repeatedly asserts that hunting was an intellectual challenge and that it drew upon the same set of emotional and mental resources used in politics and governance.[65]

Given this *mentalité*, it should occasion no surprise that great kings were often precocious hunters, some extremely so. In the Uighur version of the legend of Oghuz Qan, the hero is hunting a mere forty days after his birth.[66] Somewhat more reasonably, Cyrus the Great as a child could ride, shoot, and slay game like an adult, and the youthful Ghazan amazed everyone with his skills at riding and hawking.[67] Obviously, many attributes of kingship were held to be innate, but these still had to be brought to the surface and perfected by training and experience.

Most certainly princes and nobles were encouraged to hunt from a very early age by fathers. Amenemhet I (r. ca. 1991–1962 B.C.E), in a "teaching" to his son extols hunting and boasts of his achievements in the chase, the capture of lions and crocodiles.[68] Vladimir Monomakh closes his admonition to his sons by enjoining them to fear neither "death . . . nor war, nor wild beast" and to "do a man's work [*muzh'skoe delo*] as God presents it to you."[69] The skills needed for this work were obtained in a variety of ways, sometimes quite informally simply by hunting with adults on one's own initiative. In epic and historical sources this was thought natural, particularly for an ambitious prince preparing himself for the throne.[70]

More formal methods of training are also in evidence and are perhaps the norm. In Egypt, the pharaoh Tutankhamen (r. ca. 1334–1325) was educated in the palace school in which hunting and fowling were part of the established curriculum.[71] In late fourth-century Armenia, tutors and servants taught noble children the arts of hunting and hawking.[72] A century later, Vakhtang Gorgaslan, king of Georgian Iberia (r. ca. 446–510), ordered those entrusted with his sons' upbringing to do so in the town of Ujarma, along the banks of the river Yori, because "he reckoned this locality convenient for hunting and sheep raising."[73] While terse, the meaning is clear: the area had sufficient resources, pasture and sheep, to support a princely establishment, and good "educational opportunities" provided by abundant game.

In the Muslim world, from early ʿAbbāsid times, the sons of royal houses and noble families were trained in *al-furūsīyah al-nabīyah*, "noble chivalry," that is, in skills on horseback—war, archery, polo, and hunting.[74] In most essentials, this same practice is found in Manchu China, where young princes, under the guidance of family members and retainers, spent a good part of their formative years acquiring such skills.[75]

Sometimes young princes were self-taught, at least in legend. In the Assyrian version of the *Epic of Gilgamesh*, the hero undergoes an extended ordeal, a period of preparation, in which he lives in the desert, killing dangerous beasts, eating their flesh, and wearing their skins.[76] According to Justin, Mithridates II, the future king of Pontus (r. 124–88), did much the same thing; while still the heir apparent, he took to the forests, where he quickly learned to hunt and escape dangerous beasts, and it was this "survival training" that produced in him the physical and mental toughness required of a monarch.[77] More creditably, it is reported by contemporaries that it was a common practice among the Mughals of Central Asia for young nobles to voluntarily go to the wilderness to live alone, eating the flesh of antelope and wearing their skins. Such behavior was considered as an "act of manliness and bravery" and was purportedly undertaken by one of their rulers, Sultan Saʿīd Khān (r. 1486–1537).[78] While these accounts may not be strictly historical, it nonetheless is a typical formula and follows ancient Persian prescriptions for preparing the young for military and political leadership.[79]

Because the chase was so central to a princely education, first kills were celebrated, treated as important rites of passage. The first, successful hunt of princes in the Oghuz epic is celebrated with a feast of horse, camel, and mutton, that is, with great lavishness.[80] Chinggis Qan anointed his young grandchildren Qubilai and Hülegü after their first kills by rubbing some of the dead animals' fat upon their thumbs, a common ritual found across Eurasia.[81] Later, the same ritual was performed for Ghazan on the occasion of his first success. This time, a certain Qorchi Buqa, a *mergen*, or marksman, performed the honors, obviously as a means of magically transmitting his archery skills to the young prince.[82]

In some hunting cultures, the first kill is not left to chance. The Carolingian poet Ermoldus Nigellus tells us that Charles the Pious (r. 814–40), the son and successor of Charlemagne, was brought a captured doe and "then taking up arms suited to his tender years, he struck the beast in the back, as it stood, trembling."[83] Hunting, begun in early youth, normally continued into old age. Lothar, the Merovingian king, hunted in the fifty-first year of his reign, and it was an illness that seized him during the chase that caused his death.[84] The same is true of Charlemagne, who hunted until the last year of his life, age seventy-one or so.[85] The Mongolian qaghan Ögödei, despite bad health and advice to the contrary, went to the field in December 1241 and then died celebrating his successes with wine.[86] Two other famed rulers, Shāh ʿAbbās and Kangxi, who had to be carried about in an "open" sedan chair, insisted on hunting despite age and illness.[87]

To some extent this behavior can be explained by their love of the chase, a personal fight against aging that deprives one of life's pleasures; Oghuz Qan's bitter lament on the end of his hunting is an eloquent expression of this feeling of irreplaceable loss:

My heart yearns to hunt
Because of old age I have not the courage.[88]

But there is more to it than this; there was an important political dimension as well. The royal hunt, as Mencius well understood, was a demonstration of the ability to rule, the means of projecting an image of vigor and authority.[89] The hunt was an excellent way of dispelling rumors of ill health, incapacity, or death, rumors that typically provoked political infighting and struggles for succession; it was, in short, a way of looking kingly and in command.

To be creditable, then, a ruler or a pretender needed a hunting establishment. King Xiao of Liang, one of the hereditary kingdoms subordinate to the Han, displayed his political pretensions by creating a large hunting park over 300 Chinese miles square, and further, when he went out to hunt he did so in a manner that "resembled an emperor."[90] In similar fashion, Ibn ʿArabshāh describes an aspirant for the rulership of Sīvās (Sebastia) in Rum as one who loved letters but "walked nevertheless decked in military guise and manner and imitated the life of princes, in riding and hunting."[91] Consequently, rulers who fled their homeland took some of their huntsmen with them in order to form a believable government in exile. When, for instance, Archil, the four-time king of Imeretʿi in western Georgia took refuge in Russia in 1682, he brought a large retinue, including falconers (*sokolniki*), that the Romanov court supported in part.[92]

This association of hunting with kingship was at times so complete that rulers were compelled to hunt regardless of physical disability or disinclination. One of the Qitan emperors, Jingzong (r. 968–83), unable to sit a horse owing to childhood infirmities, nonetheless "intermittently followed the ancient custom" of hunting in each of the four seasons.[93] In the Byzantine empire, especially under the Comneni, emperors were generally devoted to the chase, but one, Michael VII (r. 1071–78), was a most reluctant huntsman who, according to a contemporary witness, always wanted the quarry to escape and averted his eyes whenever game was downed.[94] Clearly, he went to the field under duress, to meet others' expectations and maintain the proper image.

The image of hunting as a masculine activity is widespread and is probably correct in a strictly statistical sense. But historically, women were hunters. Herodotus reports that among the Sauromatae, Iranian nomads of the western steppe, women often hunted on horseback with their husbands and on their own, and Xenophon praises the goodness of both male and female hunters.[95] In many societies aristocratic women were expected to participate in the royal hunt. One of the stories in the Oghuz epics speaks of a *qatun*, "princess," or "consort," who rides, shoots, and hunts well, proving herself worthy of her husband.[96] The wives of Qitan rulers hunted as a matter of course and Jahāngīr's wives and concubines shot deer with guns during ring hunts and downed tigers from elephants.[97] While some highborn women no doubt joined in from expectation, some certainly did so from personal preference. In 1835, near Agra, Fanny Parks, an English traveler, encountered Mulka Bigam, niece of the reigning Mughal emperor, out in the field hunting with cheetahs from a covered carriage drawn by bullocks, thus enjoying the sport while adhering to Muslim rules of propriety.[98]

Female rulers, not surprisingly, typically engaged in the chase. In the time of Akbar, the ruler of Jalalpūr, a woman and a Hindu, was an active and enthusiastic hunter.[99] So, too, was Ol'ga, famed princess of Kiev, 945–69.[100] Later on, the tsarinas Elizabeth (r. 1741–62) and Catherine II (r. 1762–96) regularly hunted even though it entailed some danger, particularly riding at "breakneck" speed through forests.[101] In Catherine's case, she, as a foreigner and a woman, was clearly attempting to conform to Russian social norms and trying to appear vigorous and forceful. Such efforts at controlled masculinization can be detected as well in the portrayal of Queen T'amar of Georgia (r. 1184–1212). In the chronicles of her reign, T'amar is depicted as an avid hunter, and this can be linked with other attempts to associate the sovereign with male virtues, such as frequent depiction of her with warrior saints in church art.[102]

But while hunting was part of the job description for rulers in the core area, there was nonetheless a belief that it could be done to excess, that enthusiasm for the chase at times became a form of obsessive behavior that was self-destructive and a danger to the state.[103] As an antidote, there were cautionary stories told about such rulers. Bahrām Gor was, at the beginning of his reign, so devoted to the hunt that he ignored the affairs of state and, it is said, his realm fell into rapid decline until he changed his ways after receiving wise counsel.[104] Georgian chronicles severely censure two sovereigns, Giorgi II (r. 1072–89) and Giorgi Lasha (r. 1212–23), the son of T'amar, for neglect of their princely duties owing to the distractions of incessant hunting.[105] The same criticism was leveled at assorted Qitan, Mongolian, and Mughal rulers.[106] Even Roman emperors overindulged on occasion. While Constans (r. 337–50), a devoted huntsman, was in the field, his chief military officers successfully conspired at his assassination.[107] Not too surprisingly, rulers were sometimes encouraged to excess by power-hungry retainers. Priscus says the Byzantine emperor Theodosius II (r. 408–50) was urged to pursue "wild-beast hunting" so that his advisers and eunuchs could wield royal authority.[108]

More responsible court and government officials tried, however, to curtail obsessive royal hunters. In medieval China, Il-qan Iran, and Mughal India, they mounted two basic lines of argument: hunting deflected attention from more important matters and the sport was inherently dangerous, exposing the ruler to a variety of threats.[109] Indeed it was a time of danger. In the first place, as will be detailed later, the chase was a favored occasion for intrigue and political murder. The other great danger, of course, arose from the hunt itself, a topic we turn to next.

Courting Danger

Hunting, it was widely recognized, was both a physical and mental challenge. Dio Chrysostom says the hunter must ride and run, meet the charge of game, and endure heat and cold as well as hunger and thirst.[110] To this list, the Indian political thinker Kautilya adds wildfires and becoming lost in wilderness.[111] In the opening lines of the second act of the fifth-century Sanskrit drama *Shakuntala*, the court clown, sighing, exclaims to the audience: "Damn! Damn! Damn! I'm tired of being friends with a sporting king." He continues complaining about the long days in the wilds, uncomfortable nights, hurried meals, and physical exhaustion and ends by imploring his enthusiastic sovereign for a day off from the rigors of the chase.[112]

And beyond all this, there is the possibility of death. Kai Kāʿūs reminds his readers that many a prince has died in the field.[113] Even though carefully stage-managed, the royal hunt regularly led to fatalities. Sicknesses contracted during expeditions account for the deaths of several Byzantine emperors, Russian princes, and Muslim sultans.[114] Errant missiles also took an occasional victim, as did other, unspecified, "accidents" leading to serious injury or death.[115] Perhaps the most persistent danger was falls from horseback. A Türk general in Tang service once warned Taizong (r. 626–49) about the risks of "pursuing rabbits" on horseback, even within the confines of an imperial park.[116] His advice was well directed, for the sources provide an impressive list of equestrian-related deaths and injuries during the chase: a Xianbi chief, a crusading king, a Byzantine general, a Lombard king, a Georgian monarch, a Mongolian qan, a prince of Kashgar, and a Georgian huntsman in Siam; even the famed Bahrām Gor is supposed to have died when his horse fell into a deep pit.[117]

Wild beasts, an obvious source of danger, seemingly took a lesser toll. Stags and elk sometimes inflicted damage on royal hunters, even death, but this was fairly rare.[118] More common were the close calls that one lived (and loved) to tell the next generation. In his admonition to his sons, Vladimir Monomakh extols the virtues of the chase and minimizes the risks, yet he relates that in a lifetime of hunting he was tossed on a bison's horns, gored by a stag, stomped by an elk, attacked by a boar, bitten by a bear, and unhorsed by another unnamed beast.[119]

The trick, of course, was to be, or appear to be, heroic and to survive the experience. In part, hunting bestowed glory because it was recognized that humans, as Pliny says, are "the weakest among all animals."[120] Many beasts are faster, stronger, quicker, and larger than the best human specimens. Moreover, there was the awareness that many animals have far more acute senses than humans, that their powers of sight, hearing, and smell were unequaled.[121] Thus, testing one's self against animals' best qualities and emerging victorious always brought particular renown because no competition with a mere mortal could be as physically challenging. One prince of Ṭabaristān in pre-Islamic times was credited with chasing a stag for forty leagues and then killing the quarry after swimming a river.[122] In so doing, he beat the animal at its own game, pace and endurance, and thereby earned his fame in the eyes of posterity.

But most of all, the chase was a means of certifying a prince's courage. Atys, son of Croesus, king of Lydia, in Herodotus's recounting, was much upset when he learned that his father did not wish him to go on a dangerous hunt. In response, Atys argued that wars and hunting parties were the major sources of glory and the way to prove bravery to friends, family, and subjects. How, he asks his father, could he walk in the agora and look the citizens in the face if he were excused from this enterprise?[123] Many princes must have experienced this kind of pressure and in consequence felt compelled, against all good sense and the instinct for survival, to confront the beast.

One way to do this was to fight captured animals in confinement. This had the "advantage" of an appreciative audience who could later broadcast the deed. Chinese sources report that in Han times one young courtier was lowered into a tiger pit to test his claims of bravery, and foreign travelers report that at the Muscovite court of the late sixteenth century, nobles, armed with pikes, fought bears in a large pit.[124] Success in such a match brought fame, and in one case forgiveness. In Armenian tradition, a certain Smbat, a nobleman who joined a rebellion against the Byzantine emperor Maurice (r. 582–602) was punished by being thrown to wild beasts at the circus; to the amazement of all, he killed a bear, bull, and lion, at which point he was spared for his courage.[125]

More commonly, of course, these confrontations took place in the hunting grounds. In this situation, the young brave sought out the fiercest, most powerful foe available in their world. In Europe this might be the bear or the wild boar, while in Inner Asia wild (or more likely feral) Bactrian camels (*shutur-i ṣaḥrāī*) were held to be a most fitting and formidable opponent for a prince.[126]

Of course, wherever big cats were present, they automatically became the measure of bravery. The Liao emperor Shengzong (r. 983–1031) was much acclaimed for killing two tigers in quick succession with bow and arrow from horseback.[127]

Naturally, in both historical and epic traditions, even more glory accrues to the hunter who confronts his quarry on foot, with hand weapons, in individual combat.[128] Consequently, the supreme test of bravery and strength was in overcoming that most fearsome of all foes, big cats, on the ground, and more or less unaided.

According to chronicle accounts, the ʿAbbāsid caliph al-Amīn (r. 809–13) once killed a lion with a dagger, while Ghiyāth al-Dīn, the Seljuq sultan of Iraq (r. 1134–52), reputedly killed several lions "in such a manner that no creature was his helper or assistant."[129] The accuracy of these reports might well be challenged, but there are later accounts from Mughal India that convincingly show that big cat combats became more or less institutionalized at court. This appears to have begun with Akbar; while still a prince he killed, on foot, a female tiger with one blow of his sword and as emperor, it is claimed, he only hunted tigers on the ground with firearms.[130] Around 1609, at age seventeen, Shāh Jahān killed a lion with a sword in the presence of his father, Jahāngīr, but with the assistance of a Hindu attendant.[131] Lastly, there is the report of Bernier that Awrangzīb commanded his son Maḥmūd to hunt a lion without the customary netting, asserting that he had done so while he was a prince. The prince passed this test of obedience and courage "with the loss of only two or three men" and some "mangled" horses. After this, Bernier remarks, the stern Awrangzīb showed his son increased favor.[132]

These combats, even when conducted with assistance and in a partially controlled environment, can be deemed foolhardy in the extreme. But it must be remembered that this would only have to be done once: if the lion won, there was no prospect of a return bout, but if the prince won, he could live off the moment for the rest of his life. Who would ever question the courage of a man who *once* fought a lion?

Publicizing Prowess

Skill with a bow was a necessary requirement for hunting success, one that is repeatedly invoked in sources from China to the Near East as an attribute of royal hunters. Such claims are made on behalf of Hunnic, Sasanid, Seljuq, and Qara Qitai rulers, all of whom were believed to have a "natural talent" for archery.[133] The skills of some, however, went beyond the natural to the supernatural. In one demonstration of marksmanship Bahrām Gor took up the challenge of piercing the foot and ear of an onager with a single arrow. This he did by throwing a pebble into the animal's ear and when it tried to dislodge it he let fly an arrow that penetrated both appendages, an anecdote that first appears in late ninth-century Arabic works and lived on in Persian literature and art down to the mid-nineteenth century.[134]

Even more widespread is the classic hunter's tale of slaying several animals with one arrow. Bahrām Gor downs an onager and a lion simultaneously; a noble at the court of the Lodi dynasty of India (1451–1526), reputedly killed two wolves with one shot; ʿAbdullāh, an Uzbek qan, did the same with two onagers, and Kangxi, with two mountain goats.[135] The record, however, surely belongs to the Qitan emperor Shengzong, whose arrow, it is claimed, passed through three deer! This astounding feat became the theme of a question in the Liao civil service exams, a truly novel method of publicizing a ruler's hunting skill.[136]

The principal issue here is not the veracity of these claims but the audience for such stories. Most certainly, the highborn concerned themselves with such matters. Even outside the core area, the conversations of nobles usually focused, as Xenophon says, on "youthful days, hunting exploits, horses, and love affairs."[137] And within the core, of course, nobles boasted incessantly of their hunting prowess and argued bitterly over the number of game they downed.[138]

Hunting skills were unquestionably a major component of aristocratic self-image, but to what extent was this shared by the populace at large? Feats recorded in chronicles conveyed one's skills to posterity, but measures taken to broadcast these skills to subjects show a sensitivity to public perception, an indication that the elite believed the populace was interested in their rulers' performance at the chase.

One obvious evidence of performance is the number of kills, the bag. This was the raw statistical data collected to build a case, the data offered in squabbles among elites and that "released" in public relations campaigns. The idea that trophies and tallies certified one's hunting prowess and social position is well documented in the modern West. One English aristocrat, Lord De Grey, by his own detailed "score cards," killed 250,000 pheasants, 150,000 grouse, and 100,000 partridges between 1867 and 1923. His totals were achieved, of course, because armies of beaters drove the game to His Lordship, a kind of ring hunt with birds.[139] For the English elite, this was one means of asserting their dominance over nature, their own lands, and of pressing and legitimizing claims on foreign territories.[140]

This, however, was a very old game, played out in other parts of Eurasia long before Europe had anything resembling a state. One of the earliest indications of this concern with numbers comes from Assyria. For centuries, their rulers took care to tabulate the royal bag, at least for big game; Ashurnasirpal II

(r. 884–860), we are told in a royal inscription, downed 450 lions, 390 wild bulls, and 200 ostriches, the only birds deemed worthy of recording.[141] The bag of the pharaohs—lions, elephants, and wild cattle—was recorded on historical scarabs that were disseminated like commemorative coins of later times.[142] A variant theme is sounded in an inscription from pre-Islamic Hadramawt that proudly announces the joint tally of king and guests, thereby shifting emphasis from the individual skill of the royal hunter to the collective success of the royal hunt, that is, to the ruler's organizational abilities.[143]

Early Chinese rulers exhibited the same preoccupation with tallies and totals. Shang kings carefully recorded their bag of buffalo, pigs, tigers, and deer on oracle bones.[144] The succeeding Zhou dynasty also kept hunting accounts. A later narrative source says that King Mu bagged during one extended hunt 420 wild boars and deer, 2 tigers, and 9 wolves, all plausible figures.[145] Poetic references make clear that following royal hunts in the Han era, extensive records were made of the type of catch, the method of the kill, and totals for the military units and individuals involved.[146] This practice was still in evidence in Yuan and Qing China, where every effort was made to tabulate the number downed and to identify individual kills.[147]

In the core area, rulers went to even greater lengths to properly document their tallies, which were regularly inserted in court chronicles. Jahāngīr tells us how many birds and beasts his father, Akbar, killed with a specific gun, and another source relates Shāh Jahān's bag, including the number of shots taken at a given animal.[148] This was possible because from Akbar onwards the event recorders (*vāqiʿ-navīs*) at court took down, among other things, "the nature of hunting parties" and "the slaying of animals." The result is that we know a great deal about Mughal emperors' hunting scores. For Shāh Jahān, we know what types of animals he brought down in a given period of time, how many shots it took, and what his daily records were for a specific animal.[149]

Data on Jahāngīr's success in the field is even more detailed and quite revealing of the elite hunting *mentalité* in the core area. Like those of other emperors, his accounting methods and categories were extremely varied; sometimes he reports on the totals, divided by species, accumulated by an entire hunting party during an extended expedition, and sometimes the party's take on a specific day.[150] On other occasions he relates his personal numbers for the duration of an expedition or for a single day, again by species and often by method.[151] We also have some long-term figures. Jahāngīr tells us that his "hunt accountants" kept very complete and detailed records from the time he commenced hunting at age twelve until his eleventh year on the throne, that is, between 1580 and 1616, and the results are arresting, to say the least: 28,532 head of game were taken in his presence; 17,167 of these he killed personally. These included

86 tigers
889 *nilgao*
1,670 antelope of various types
miscellaneous numbers of bear, cheetahs, and others
13,464 birds of different species.[152]

There was ample precedent in India, the centerpiece of the British empire, for Lord De Grey's mania.

The Mughal emperors exhibited another characteristic now closely identified with Great White Hunters of the nineteenth and twentieth centuries—concern with the size of animals bagged. Both Jahāngīr and Awrangzīb were preoccupied with the length and weight of their kills, particularly big game, which was always carefully measured and described; the largest specimens sometimes were painted by court artists.[153]

In neighboring Iran, Shāh ʿAbbās, like his contemporary Jahāngīr, had his household officials keep full account of his "total bag."[154] Of even greater interest, pretenders and rebels did the same. According to Munshī, in 1609 "some crazy lost soul decided to pass himself off as the shah" to rural folk in remote areas of Azerbaijan. One of his principal means of deception, Munshī says, was to equip himself with animals "designed to look like a hunter's bag." Appearing thus in small villages, his disguise worked and he was treated as royalty until discovered and executed.[155] Clearly, princely persona and hunting prowess were associated in the minds of the populace.

A chronicler eulogizing Prince Vladimir of Volynia asserts that he was a "good and courageous hunter" who downed wild boar and bear without attendants, and that he was widely known for this "throughout the entire land."[156] If, as seems so evident, royal hunters wished to convey their feats of skill and courage to subjects, how was this accomplished? To begin with, part of the populace saw some of the action and others viewed the triumphal return of the ruler with his bag on display. Also, word of mouth must have played a prominent role in societies with limited literacy. Feats of derring-do circulated in Mughal India, and those who were not witnesses soon heard of it, most likely in a much embroidered form.[157]

In Iran and in neighboring regions where Persian literature flourished, court poetry was an important vehicle of exalting a ruler's virtues, his strength, skill, valor, and sense of justice. In the Islamic era, court poets often likened the skills of their patrons to those of the legendary Rostam, or the mythologized Bahrām Gor who vanquished lions with his bare hands. These celebrations of hunting achievements, communicated both orally and in writing, always closely linked the ruler's success as a warrior and his ability to protect and extend his realm.[158] Political images in the premodern world were every bit as contrived, manufactured, as those in the modern.

Of greater importance was the role of visual communication. As Priscilla Soucek has written, royal hunting parks with their animal motifs were portrayed often in the art of East and West Asia: such themes are found on silverware and textiles, and in paintings, manuscript illumination, reliefs, tiles, and so on. Clearly, much of this art was conceived and executed to convey the ruler's hunting prowess to various audiences.[159] Multimedia presentations were also possible and quite common. Bahrām Gor's hunting achievements were immortalized in the *Shāhnāmah*, the Persian national epic, and represented pictorially on silver and stucco in Iran and neighboring regions over an extended period of time. He became completely identified with hunting and was readily recognized for his specific feats.[160] The core area indeed was saturated with this image of the heroic royal hunter, an image delivered in picture and word.

Many of these pictorial representations have survived or at least are described in contemporary or near contemporary sources. This practice began quite early. Already during the period of the New Kingdom, circa 1550–1070, Egyptian monarchs are shown in reliefs killing big game, most particularly lions, sometimes from chariots with bow and arrow, and sometimes on foot with hand weapons.[161] The effort at publicizing the pharaohs' heroic hunts, particularly of elephants, was evidently successful, for Osiris, famed early Egyptian king in the Greek tradition, was remembered for such feats and for his "inscribed pillars" relating these "campaigns." That the Greek Ptolemies continued these practices in later centuries affirms that this was a most powerful image, one that proved helpful in legitimizing their rule over the native population.[162]

The Greeks remembered, too, the hunting propaganda of ancient Mesopotamia, which they viewed through the life of Semiramis, the semi-mythical Queen of the Land between the Rivers. According to this tradition, she made a special effort to broadcast her hunting exploits by having the walls of her palace decorated with many scenes of the chase, in one of which the queen, on horseback, slays a leopard with a javelin.[163] Indeed, Mesopotamia produced a vast amount of this style of political art; one might even say that they were the early masters of pictorial propaganda presented as a package, a thoroughly coordinated program. In the Neo-Assyrian era, the ninth to the seventh centuries, palace reliefs were employed to narrate, in Irene Winter's analysis, specific events, most importantly wars, but also submissions and tributes, cultic observances, and royal hunts. The first of these reliefs are found in the palace reception hall at the capital of Nimrud. The hunting scenes show the king's mastery of ferocious beasts, almost always lions, and these are presented in "serial episodes," from pursuit to kill, to the final libation over the vanquished beast.

All this was intended to impress visitors to the hall, whether royal guests, foreign envoys, or subjects, that the sovereign was actively engaged in vital events, and that he possessed great physical power and spiritual force.[164]

Such reliefs might also be combined with texts in the form of public inscriptions. Reliefs on the palace walls at Nineveh are accompanied by short epigraphs that label and describe the action. Again, these are mostly scenes of war and hunting in which the king is always triumphant. He overwhelms human foes, plunders their cities, executes their leaders, and most important for us, he spears lions, seizes them by the ears and tail, and smashes their skulls with a mace. One epigraph conveys a political message that is hard to miss: it has the Elamite king being pursued by "raging lions," fleeing to his Assyrian counterpart, Ashurbanipal (r. 668–29), to implore his aid. The Assyrian king intercedes, cuts through a host of lions and saves the cowering Elamite.[165]

This royal pursuit of lions, whether from horseback with a spear or from a chariot with a bow, is pictured repeatedly. In either case, the lion's fate is sealed once pursued by the king. This is conveyed by the fact that one lion lies dying while the king attacks another.[166] On royal seal impressions the monarch dispatches a lion by grasping its head with his left hand while plunging a dagger into the beast's chest with his right hand. Such impressions, found on clay bullae are frequently uncovered in excavations.[167] The aftermath of the hunt, as depicted in reliefs, shows dead lions placed before an altar over which the king makes libations, and the accompanying inscriptions record the numbers killed.[168]

The Iranians took over some of the Mesopotamian imagery and propaganda techniques. A monumental rock sculpture at Sar-Mashad in southern Iran shows a Sasanid ruler, perhaps Bahrām II (r. 276–93), in personal combat with two lions; as in Assyrian reliefs, one is already dead and the other is being killed by a mighty blow of the emperor's sword.[169] Many centuries later, a ruler of the first Bulgarian empire, perhaps Tervel (r. 701–18), had himself depicted spearing a lion in a large-scale relief executed on a cliff face near his capital, Pliska.[170] The fact that by this time lions had been extinct in the Balkans for close to a thousand years only serves to underscore the great power of this image, one long identified with imperial authority.

One new visual medium for the dissemination of this ancient message is metal work, mainly plates, the so-called "Sasanian" silver. Typically, these show various rulers hunting from horseback with bow and arrow—in all cases with dead and dying prey strewn beneath their mounts' hooves. A few plates portray individual combat against big cats, leopards and tigers.[171] The frequency of finds of this silverware in neighboring territories, in Prudence Harper's view, leads to the plausible conjecture that these objects, so often adorned with

Figure 12. Ashurbanipal pouring libation over dead lion, bas-relief at Nineveh. Trustees of the British Museum.

triumphant royal hunting scenes, were sent as official presentations to clients and rivals to communicate the prowess and power of the Sasanid emperors.[172]

Painting also served as a medium for hunting propaganda. Ammianus Marcellenus, an eyewitness, says that in 362 when Roman armies bivouacked in a grove near Seleucia on the Tigris, they found "a pleasant and shady dwelling, displaying in every part of the house, after the custom of that nation, paintings representing the killing of wild beasts in various kinds of hunting; for nothing in their country is painted or sculpted except slaughter in diverse forms and scenes of war."[173] In the Islamic period, travelers encountered similar paintings: a large, public banqueting hall of the Fāṭimids was decorated with hunting scenes, and the audience hall of the Qara Qoyunlu dynasty, 1380–1468, located outside of Tabrīz, had a vast ceiling mural depicting royal hunts and battles.[174]

Qing China made use of paintings to this same end. During the reign of Qianlong (1736–95), and at the emperor's initiative, an extensive program of commemorative art was instituted emphasizing martial values; included were portrayals of troop reviews, rituals for departing and returning armies, and the autumn hunt at Mulan. This was part of a larger, carefully orchestrated propaganda campaign in which visual representations played an important role in the effort to instruct and inspire current and future generations of subjects with appropriate martial virtues.[175]

Trophies are yet another way of documenting hunting success. This is likely a very ancient practice, one connected with the retention of animal teeth, tusks, and bones for use in self-adornment, ritual, and magic.[176] In the modern West, trophy display is most often associated with taxidermy and the collection of horns and antlers.[177] There are, however, clear precedents for all this in the core area. Malik Shāh (r. 1072–92), under whom the Seljuq dynasty reached its apogee, publicized his kills by building towers from the hooves of gazelles and onagers throughout his realm.[178] Shāh Ismāʿīl (r. 1501–24) built in Khui, Azerbaijan, a large palace called Dawlah Khānah which featured, according to an Italian traveler, three turrets eight yards in circumference and fifteen to sixteen feet in height composed of antlers of stags taken by the shah and his lords.[179] On an even grander scale, his successor, Ṭahmāsp, incorporated some thirty thousand deer and hart skulls into the summit of the highest tower in Iṣfahān, the future Ṣafavid capital.[180] And Akbar, his contemporary, placed hundreds of thousands of deer antlers on pillars positioned every couple of miles on the road from Agra to Ajmīr. All these, according to eyewitness testimony, were taken in his majesty's hunts, and were displayed at his order "as a memorial to the world."[181]

These extended, extensive, and expensive efforts at broadcasting hunting success strongly suggest that the populace took interest in the royal hunt and in the prowess of their sovereigns. It is true, of course, that this particular evidence must be read in reverse, since it does not emanate from the subjects themselves, but it is extremely unlikely that rulers across Eurasia would have misread public sentiments for millennia, that the populace was disinterested and, in the end, unmoved. Additional proofs that this reading is valid will be offered in Chapter 9.

8

Political Animals

Power of Animals

Hunting was not simply a matter of a physical challenge faced with skill and courage but was fused with a much larger issue, that of the power exercised over animals, beings, it was widely believed, endowed with spiritual force as well as speed and strength. Hunting, therefore, was an activity suffused with spirituality. Gods and goddesses watched over game animals, sometimes even taking their form; they handed down rules, taboos of various kinds and, of course, rewarded and punished hunters according to their compliance with these rules and their proper spiritual preparation for the chase.[1]

Since, in most traditional societies, whether hunting, pastoral, or agricultural, it was commonly believed that animals were numinous, it is hardly surprising that they are among the most frequently used symbols in the human repertoire. Their physical powers are endlessly invoked as a measure of human capacity; their names and images are used to express political notions; as symbols of solidarity they appear repeatedly on banners, flags, emblems, and heraldry;[2] and their spiritual force is deeply entwined in religious belief, practice, and ceremony.

Animals possess, moreover, yet another and vital attribute, the power to explain and model human behavior. From Aesop's *Fables* to Orwell's *Animal Farm*, animal analogies have been extensively drawn upon to explore and dramatize human relationships. One who understands animals, it follows, understands not just nature but human nature as well.

The most notable collection of these animal fables is the *Pañchatantra*, a cycle of animal fables originating in India sometime before the fourth century C.E. The Sanskrit version was translated into Middle Persian, then Arabic, and subsequently into many of the languages of Europe and Asia, including Mongolian.[3] Something of the wonderment produced by animals and the fables about them is revealed in Abū'l Faẓl's comments about the varied fauna of India, the homeland of so many of these tales: "The astonishing feats which the animals of this country can perform and the beautiful variety of coloring is beyond the power of my inexperience to describe. Former romancers have related stories in abundance of their extraordinary characteristics, but the writer of this work mentions nothing that he himself has not seen or heard from accurate observers."[4]

In both their written and oral forms, and in diverse cultural contexts, animal stories were not only entertaining but edifying, and therefore always had a didactic purpose. The message that animals profitably instruct humans, if humans understand animals, was constantly repeated and affirmed. For Xenophon, the behavior of hawks and wolves has much to teach cavalry officers in matters of raiding, plundering, and retreating; for Procopius, animals' territorial instincts tell us something important concerning human attachments to their motherland.[5] Wisdom is found in wild beasts. The continuer of Thomas Artsruni relates that decorations in Armenian palaces and churches in the early ninth century had many pictures of wild animals, their numerous types and their "struggle for existence," all of which, he asserts, "is very pleasing to wise men."[6]

These seekers after wisdom were always interested in anomalies of size, shape, and behavior, which were recorded in chronicles like other important historical events.[7] The reason for this concern with the irregularities of nature is not hard to discern: animals were a source of information about forthcoming events, omens of good or ill fortune. A pack mule accompanying the armies of Xerxes (486–465 B.C.E.) to Greece dropped a foal with double sex organs, indicating trouble ahead, a portent the emperor ignored to his detriment.[8] Whether historical or not, Herodotus's anecdote illustrates the point that humans have long read into animals knowledge of the future, the most prized and the most elusive knowledge of all.

Animal auguries are endless in variety—the barks of dogs, neighing of horses, the colors of cows, and calls of frogs—and are extremely widespread in time and space. Augury of this type is based upon a presumed connection between animal behavior and future cultural or natural events. This type of divination was not inspired prophecy but a matter of "disclosure" of indistinct connections. And while world religions turned to revelations from the other world for knowledge of future and of final things, popular culture still looked toward nature, particularly animals, for signs of imminent happenings. The diviner's question, repeatedly found in the Shang oracle bones, for example, is what should I do today, not what is the spiritual fate of humankind. Knowledge of natural signs could be vested in specialists, but in many cases it was in the public domain.[9] For our purposes, it is most important to recognize that inasmuch as the signs were quite visible, many could try to read them and that therefore the populace at large associated animals with the possession of useful intelligence and believed that heavenly or cosmic forces resided in them and spoke through them.

One form of animal behavior that was thought particularly auspicious was their propensity to flock and disperse. Aristotle, among others, notes that soothsayers are vitally interested in this phenomenon.[10] In ancient China and in early modern India, the unusual congregation of snakes was taken as a portent, on occasion even a positive one.[11]

For obvious reasons—their identification with the heavens and their flocking behavior—birds were the most popular species for prognostication, a method of divining found everywhere in the Old World. In ancient Greece the gods, who were silent, spoke through birds—their sounds, flight patterns, posture, and activities.[12] The Romans and the ancient Germans divined by birds, and the practice continued in medieval Europe.[13] Muslims and Hindus in South and Southeast Asia also prognosticated by bird flights and more particularly by their cries, a technique followed by the Tibetans.[14] In early China it was the flocking, flights, and plumage patterns of birds that were read as heavenly portents.[15]

These divinations, while practiced by the populace, were by no means a superstition limited to the ignorant masses. Ruling elite also believed in, and had regular recourse to, such divinations. The king of Chu in 489 B.C.E. encountered a large migration of birds and immediately had this read by his historian/diviner. And Alexander the Great, adhering to Athenian belief, followed owls to victory in Egypt.[16] Many others, from ancient Syrian kings to Hunnic chieftains, Sasanid shahs, Rus princes, and Mughal emperors sought the guidance of birds in their conduct of state.[17]

Birds, without doubt, were the favored medium, but any animal might become an omen, an instrument of the gods, or embody and reveal cosmic forces. Changes in the behavior of birds, fish, hedgehogs, and so on, might well foretell changes in the weather or natural disasters such as drought and earthquakes.[18] Animals served, too, as instruments of higher powers. In some cases they brought salvation or victory; wild elephants discovered and placed flowers at a sacred site in northern India, thus making it known to humans, while in early medieval Europe God used wild animals to guide Christian armies to a hidden river ford and then on to victory.[19] In other instances, animals are instruments of justice and retribution. In many traditional and folk cultures animals are seen to have the ability to render decisions about right and wrong, conveying in their behavior some kind of divine intention or heavenly sign.[20] Sometimes trusted domesticated animals, particularly horses, turn on and dispatch their masters, typically evil kings or disloyal officials.[21]

Animals had within them many potent forces helpful to humans. These included the ingredients for medicine and magic, never clearly distinguished by traditional practitioners. In traditional pharmacy, animal ingredients assumed a vital, though never dominant, role. Bezoars, concretions formed in the alimentary canals of various animals, especially ruminants, were thought to have magical properties and were used as rain stones in weather magic. Even more widespread was the belief in the healing properties of bezoars, which led to a lively transcontinental trade in this commodity in the Middle Ages.[22]

But many other, and more readily and locally obtainable animal products entered the medical repertoire. Together with vegetal and mineral ingredients, the classical, Christian, and Muslim medical traditions used endless animal products—liver of hedgehogs, urine of goats, dung of white dogs, dried sea urchins, and so on.[23] Birds also contributed; on the very ancient principle that "like begets like," it was believed that eagle gall mixed with honey, if rubbed in the eyes, produced keen sight.[24] In the Chinese tradition as well, animal ingredients are quite common and in their pharmaceutical literature there were categories, based on "natural origins," for quadrupeds, fowl, and worms/fish.[25]

Two animal products that stand out for their presumed potency are antlers and horn. Stag antlers in velvet were highly prized in Chinese medicine.[26] Even more precious was the "unicorn" horn, which served as an antidote to all forms of poison and a cure for many ills.[27] The idea of unicorn horn, with its special properties, was soon transferred to the rhinoceros, and trade in this product began very early.[28] In China, the horn was, and still is, valued as an aphrodisiac, but in the Indies it remained a sovereign remedy for poison, venom, and sundry diseases.[29]

In the above cases, bits of animal confer great potency if properly prepared and ingested, that is, transferred to human receptacles. But it was also held possible to transfer the entire spiritual essence and physical capacity of animals to humans. Such transfers often, but not inevitably, came about through hunting. In Central and South America, killing a jaguar (*Panthera onca*), the supreme predator of the region, elevated social standing, and eating its flesh transferred the animal's physical and spiritual qualities to the hunter.[30] This appropriation of animal powers by magical means is very widespread. There is a hint of transference of this nature in ancient Egypt, where the pharaohs hunted lions and in battle took on the qualities, if not the appearance, of a "fierce-eyed lion," a claim that was well known to the Greeks.[31]

More familiar are the berserks, a phenomenon, as Michael Speidel has recently shown, that extended well beyond the Scandinavians and Celts, and was found throughout western Eurasia between 1300 B.C.E. and 1300 C.E. One defining feature of this kind of warfare was the close identification of the warrior with fierce animals such as the bear or wolf; berserks were seen as, and no doubt believed themselves to be, shape-shifters who took on animal form as well as behavior.[32] The means of transference varied. In the Celtic world, warriors did their hair up in equine, ursine, or lupine style before combat or, animal-like, went into battle completely naked.[33] Most commonly, berserks went into battle in the skins of ferocious beasts; in the Middle East, those of lions and leopards, and in northern Europe, those of bears. Thus the name *berserkir* or "bear shirt," for an individual who went howling into battle with the ferocity of a crazed and powerful predator, invulnerable to mere humans. This, in the Scandinavian sagas is called the "berserker rage."[34] In this part of the world, the battle rage often involved the use of drugs or alcohol to induce the persona of the predatory beast.[35]

The relationship of humans to animals in many traditional cultures, Mircea Eliade argues, was manifold and very powerful, since animals were links to the cosmos and to the mythic past. For them "donning the skin of an animal was becoming that animal." Such mimicry, he continues, was often a mechanism for an out-of-body experience, a shamanic spiritual quest, or a means of acquiring animal powers for purposes of hunting and making war.[36] Moreover, when humans take on animal form or behavior, the whole becomes greater than the sum of its parts and the creatures so fused thereby all the more powerful, cunning, and dangerous.[37] Belief in such creatures, always represented as some kind of deity or demon possessed of extraordinary powers, was found throughout Eurasia and has a very long history.[38]

In premodern societies, therefore, animals and animal specialists, whether falconers or berserks, had for rulers great political-military potential. The ability to control, or, through specialists, appear to control, certain kinds of animals in specific contexts was a political asset because it demonstrated influence over both natural and spiritual realms, skills not thought evenly distributed among humans. Consequently, rulers were keen to possess and dominate various kinds of political animals and their handlers. The quintessential political animal of South and Southeast Asia, the white elephant, can serve as a case in point.

White animals were widely held to be propitious, bringing good fortune to the possessor. The ancient Iranians, Turks, Qitans, and Mongols all sought beasts of this color for ceremonial or sacrificial use.[39] But the most prized by far were the light-colored elephants. When Europeans arrived in the East, the center of the white elephant cult was Pegu, a kingdom in what is now southern Burma. In the late sixteenth century, according to their accounts, its ruler had four white elephants, which all foreigners residing in the capital were required to view and admire. These were not mere curiosities, but animals of state over which the king maintained a strict monopoly.[40] As central actors in the elaborate political theater that characterized the region, white elephants were in demand throughout Southeast Asia and, on occasion, even became a source of interstate tension and warfare.[41]

The reason for this intense desire for white elephants is to be found in Indian political culture. Elephants of any coloration were important in Indian mythology and cosmology as the all-powerful pillars of the universe. Frequently represented in Hindu and Buddhist iconography, elephants are portrayed as guardians of life, bringers of prosperity, fertility, and health. They are also associated with the primary fluid, the universal milk, and hence white elephants possessed special potency, the ability to attract clouds, the monsoons, rain, and renewal. Elephants, quite naturally, became symbols of kingship and majesty, a guarantor of earthly welfare, a moving throne on which the ruler presents himself to his subjects, and a moving citadel from which he presents himself to enemies.[42]

These ideas about elephants and kingship traveled well beyond the Indian cultural sphere and were known to distant peoples at an early age. By the time of Aelian, reports of Indian kings' quests for white elephants were already circulating in the West, and the Muslim world, too, recognized that white elephants were an attribute of sovereignty in India as well as in Sasanid Iran.[43] In medieval Persian tradition, it was held that white elephants bowed before rulers because they instinctively recognized and accepted true royalty.[44]

The political deployment and public response to white elephants is well documented in the kingdom of Arakan, a state located on the northwestern coast of modern Burma. Here, in the early decades of the seventeenth century, there was a particularly handsome specimen, which was carefully tended and housed, beautifully caparisoned, and presented with much pomp on select occasions.[45] According to contemporary Jesuit letters, this royal white elephant was widely reverenced by the peoples of Burma and its fame, it is claimed, "spread throughout the East." Whenever it was paraded in state, the elephant attracted large throngs and produced great rejoicing, and because of its widespread reputation for spiritual potency it was much coveted by the Mughal emperor Akbar, who wished to "be Lord of the white elephant."[46]

Akbar and other rulers in the core area spent much of their lives in the company of animals that served them as mounts, game, hunting partners, and political props. Hunting, as a means of demonstrating kingly controls over wild, natural forces was an important source of political legitimation, but by itself was incomplete; besides the physical mastery of animals, a true sovereign had to display moral and spiritual ascendency over wild beasts.

Power over Animals

Rulers, as Norbert Elias remarks, must be seen in the company of, and loyally served by, their world's most distinguished personages to effectively communicate their dominance of the human sphere.[47] In my view, it was equally imperative that rulers be seen in the company of, and obediently served by, their world's most impressive beasts to effectively communicate their dominance of the natural sphere.

Control over wild animals is "unnatural" and always indicates special spiritual or magical power, whether used for good or for evil. The latter purpose is best exemplified by the witch and her "familiar." There are, however, many more cases where control is viewed in a positive light, as a signal that the individual directing the beast can render important services to the general populace, those who can only control, through normal means, everyday domesticated animals.

This was so because animals were held to be gifts of the gods or of cultural heroes, who by definition possessed superhuman powers. No one doubted the gods' abilities to tame any beast, no matter how ferocious or strong. In Mesopotamia, for example, goddesses, central figures in popular cults, tamed lions and made them into companions and servants.[48]

Conversing with animals is another manifestation of this control. Humans who have this ability, like animals who speak human languages, cannot be fitted into well-established categories, and this behavior, as Robert Campany says, crosses clearly demarcated boundaries that few can pass.[49] In both Mongolian and Muslim tradition, those who could converse with birds understood portents or enjoyed special access to heavenly messengers.[50] Anomalous behavior of this type dramatizes individual gifts or abilities that can only be explained by the possession of esoteric knowledge, extraordinary powers, or special connections with other worlds, other planes of existence.

Holy men of all persuasions cross boundaries and make connections. In the medieval West, Christian saints were viewed as vehicles through which God exercised his power on earth. They demonstrated this capacity in various kinds of miracles, which typically included healing the sick, telling the future, influencing the weather, and asserting control over powerful domesticated animals—and, in emulation of Daniel in the lion's den, over ferocious beasts as well. Medieval hagiography is full of tales of beasts who obeyed monks, wolves that helped them clear fields, and stags that helped with plowing. These, according to Christian tradition, were "redomesticated beasts" that had fallen into a wild state, become feral, following their expulsion from paradise.[51]

Influence over animals, exemplified by Saint Francis of Assisi (1182–1226), was claimed for many. Wild beasts as the "adoring subjects" of a saint were a topos in hagiography, and such episodes as Saint Jerome's removal of a thorn from a lion's paw were conveyed in legend and in numerous works of medieval art.[52]

The same is true of Eastern Christianity. In Armenian and Syriac traditions saints traveled with lions or bears; in the latter instance, the beast had killed the divine's donkey and was henceforth compelled to act as his new "servant."[53] In Russia, Saint Sergius (1314–92) went to the wilderness to prove himself and there developed such spiritual power that bears came to him and ate from his hand.[54] As a measure of popular belief in such matters, it is most revealing that in traditional Russia, those individuals who trained bears for the purpose of entertainment were held by rural folk to have occult powers. This association of magical powers with domination of wild animals was naturally disputed by the Orthodox establishment, who claimed a monopoly on such powers. Both church officials and secular moralists roundly condemned animal trainers, their black magic, and their hold over the common folk.[55]

Within the Islamic world, religious personages exhibited gifts similar to their Christian counterparts; this is not too surprising, since they drew on the same biblical precedents and pagan prototypes reproduced in animal fables. Typical of these is the experience of Majd al-Dīn, the religious judge of the city of Shiraz. In Ibn Baṭṭuṭah's recounting, he ran afoul of Abū Saʿīd (r. 1316–35) over a matter of doctrine and the sultan, as punishment, had him thrown to the dogs. But when these enormous hounds, specially trained as executioners, reached him "they fawned on him and wagged their tails before him without attacking him in any way." Naturally, Abū Saʿīd, overwhelmed by this display, immediately made obeisance before Majd al-Dīn, lavished presents upon him, and accepted his teaching and spiritual guidance.[56] Most often, such stories of extraordinary power over animals are attributed to Sufi divines, popular saints in the Islamic tradition.[57] Again, this indicates that this equation was widely known and believed.

India was perhaps home to the most sophisticated, even professional, holy men skilled in the art of dominating wild and dangerous creatures. Best known are the snake charmers. Linschoten, in the 1580s, says of these fakirs, whom he calls soothsayers and witches, that they have "about them many live snakes which they do know how to bewitch" and so render them harmless.[58] Several centuries later, Fanny Parks encountered fakirs who carefully "tamed" alligators by regular feeding.[59]

Farther east, the form of animal domination was much closer to the Mediterranean pattern. Alexander Hamilton, who traveled through Malacca, the southern tip of the Malay Peninsula in the early eighteenth century, says that the local religion, a mixture of Islam and paganism, had many "great sorcerers, who by their spells can tame wild tigers, and make them carry them whither they order them, on their backs."[60] The feat of taming wild tigers by spiritual/magical means was by this time very old. In China, a Daoist hermit of the fourth century had made a tiger his servant, and a century later a Buddhist monk "converted" a man-eating tiger, who ceased his depredations and protected the local villagers, who, predictably, embraced Buddhism.[61]

While we lack public opinion polls from these earlier ages, we do have some helpful guidance concerning popular imagination and attitudes, and this points to the conclusion that for both commoners and elites power over wild animals was automatically equated with spiritual potency. And if domination of this kind inevitably indicated spiritual potency, such potency, in its turn, always suggested esoteric knowledge and divine favor, attributes all rulers craved, coveted, and claimed.

Model kings of antiquity, like goddesses and saints, were credited with the power of direct communication with animals. In later traditions, sage kings such as King Solomon or the Yellow Emperor command wild animals to march with their armies and the beasts do so, staying in their appointed stations.[62] In the Persian Alexander romance, God grants the young Alexander power over animals and other natural forces, and in the medieval Persian version of the Oghuz epic, one of their early rulers, Tümen Qan, understands well the languages of all animals and particularly the words of wolves.[63]

The types of animals rulers dominated were diverse and often specific to time and place, for example, reverential fish in fourteenth-century Champa (South Vietnam) and tame, music-loving antelope in eighteenth-century Maratha.[64] But more often, control was imposed over dangerous beasts. Typical is an Arab report of circa 1000 that the ruler of Srīvijaya in western Sumatra rendered docile the local crocodiles so that they posed no threat to his subjects.[65]

Another common theme concerns animal guardians who protect rulers from harm. In one tradition, a loyal bull, horse, and stag watch over the sleeping Mithridates of Pontus (second to first centuries B.C.E.), while in another, scorpions and a house cat turn aside threats to Alexander the Great.[66] The great cats also made a contribution to royal security, or at least to the image of royal invulnerability. Aḥmad II, Sāmānid ruler of Khurāsān and Transoxania (r. 907–14), by later tradition had a trained lion in his bedroom to protect himself from disloyal retainers.[67] Much later, in the 1780s, according to rumor circulating among British residents, Tipoo (Tipu), the sultan of Mysore in southwest India, was guarded while asleep by four tigers.[68] To have lions and tigers as devoted friends was to have, one can only assume, hesitant foes. In any event, many rulers thought so, and surrounded themselves with large, nominally obedient, felines.

The Indian and Buddhist traditions closely associated lions with kingship.[69] In Justin's epitome of Pompeius Trogus, Sandrocottos, that is, Chandragupta (r. 321–297), founder of the Mauryan empire of India, was early on marked for royal dignity by the fact that a lion befriended him and a wild elephant joined his service.[70] This theme reappears in later Indian drama. In the seventh act of the *Shakuntala* the king encounters by chance his unknown son and recognizes the young lad by an imperial birthmark on his back and by his ability to control wild animals. Indeed, the youth is so skilled at this that his foster mothers dub him "All-Tamer," most particularly because he "tamed" a lion cub.[71]

Queen Tʿamar of Georgia (r. 1184–1212) also had a "magnetic attraction" for animals of all types and a very special affinity for lions. On one occasion, a contemporary chronicler relates, the Shirvānshāh sent to her a lion cub, which she reared by herself despite the fact that it was bigger and more ferocious than most of its kind: "When it was brought into the palace it displayed such love and ardor for Tʿamar, divine in splendor, that even in double harness it could not be restrained until it laid its head on her breast and licked her face, as the metaphrasts in the tales of the martyrs of old. When it was restrained or controlled, tears would flow from its eyes like a stream watering the earth."[72] Rulers' power over such beasts assumed many forms. In later tradition, the lions kept at court by the Umayyad caliph ʿAbd al-Malik (r. 685–705) took on the temperament of their master and thus when a courtier out of favor approached, the chained beasts showed their fangs and tried to reach him with their claws.[73] They knew the mind of their master and showed their solidarity with him.

Whatever credence one puts in these tales of kingly control of the king of beasts, there is no doubt that "tamed" lions were found frequently and in great numbers at royal courts in the core area, and sometimes beyond. The practice started early: lions were kept as "court pets" in ancient Egypt and several pharaohs of the thirteenth and twelfth centuries are pictured with tamed lions beside their thrones or running beside their horse or chariot.[74] In later centuries there were lions at the Byzantine, Seljuq, and Ṣafavid courts, sometimes together with tigers and leopards.[75]

To be an effective political statement court cats had to be displayed skillfully in an appropriate setting. When in 917 the Byzantine ambassador arrived in Baghdad for a caliphal audience, he was led through a formation of a hundred lions, fifty on either side, each with keeper, collar, and muzzle. And the Fāṭimid court of Egypt had ten tigers that went in procession with a hundred attendants.[76] Under the Ṣafavids, the two court lions were fastened with gold chains and before each was a large golden basin filled with water.[77] More impressively, at the Yuan court lions were specially trained so that, when brought before the qaghan, they seemed, as Marco Polo says, "to know him for Lord," or as Odoric phrases it, "to salute the Lord with a reverence."[78]

Occasionally, of course, wild beasts escaped their handlers, causing courtiers to flee in terror.[79] Sometimes, however, great cats were purposely allowed to move about the court as a test of courage and obedience. Jahāngīr kept a lion that Roe says allowed people to touch it on the head, and Shāh ʿAbbās had a tame lion, which he himself petted; this, he felt, proved his courage, and he made a point of instructing the Mughal ambassador present to relate this fact to his sovereign.[80]

But there were much sterner tests than this. John Jourdain, an eyewitness, relates that one of Jahāngīr's favorite sports was "to bringe forth a wild lyon and lett him loose amonge the [court] people, to see if there be any soe hardie as to stand against the lion." Those who did won royal praise and favor. While a test of bravery, to be sure, it was something else as well. These confrontations were carefully staged to limit the danger and control the outcome. The human combatant was supplied with a "gluffe [glove] on his hand, and a little trunchion [club] of a foote and a half longe." What is more important is that the "kinge" ended such sport before any serious damage was done. Thus, when Jahāngīr decided "to take up the lion," no doubt with the assistance of handlers, the impression was left that the king lorded over lions as well as humans.[81] A similar test was witnessed at the court of a minor rajah in Mysore in the early nineteenth century. According to the testimony of a British officer, Basil Hall, this ruler kept two "well fed and well bred" royal tigers at his court that were allowed to roam about with their attendants, who held them on leashes. This much worried the European guests but not the locals, and Hall noted that the rajah watched the discomfitted English from the "corner of his eye" and smiled "at the success of his trick."[82]

Obviously, to pull off these theatrics successfully, to look regal without perpetrating carnage that would have defeated the whole point of these exercises, required a supply of tame cats and of handlers "who train lions for the amusement of princes."[83] There were indeed many such specialists at courts and others who trained lions for commercial profit. This was somewhat of a cottage industry in parts of Eurasia. A Chinese envoy to Herat in 1415 records the efforts to train lions, still found along the Amu Darya, which he says were not always successful.[84] In the mid-seventeenth century, Tavernier saw near Sidhpur, a town between Aḥmadābād and Agra, lion taming which he was told took five or six months. The method, as Tavernier describes it, is yet another example of conditioned reflex: four or five lions are tied by their hind legs to firm posts twelve paces apart; another rope is looped around the animals' necks and held by the trainer; people are hired to watch this spectacle and when the lions move toward them, the beasts are instantly pelted with small stones as the handler pulls on the neck ropes; slowly, the lions are accustomed to people, yet conditioned not to approach them too closely.[85] A product of this training regimen, kept well fed and tended by skilled handlers, was ready for presentation at court.

The other major animal of state was, of course, the majestic elephant. As Masʿūdī remarked in the mid-tenth century, the elephant was an appropriate choice because of its size, strength, intelligence, utility, longevity, dignity, nobility, and its refusal to accept base people as its masters.[86] This assessment, made from outside the animals' natural range, was wholly consistent with the views of insiders. Akbar, who was reared in Afghanistan, felt himself greatly empowered by these beasts: "When I came to India I was much attracted by the elephants, and I thought that the use of their extraordinary strength was a prognostication of my universal ascendency."[87] To the Mughals, elephants were a major source of pomp and majesty and an instrument of governance and conquest.[88] Consequently, as animals of state and as symbols of kingship, control over the royal elephants was a normal part of any struggle for power or succession in Indian regimes, whether Hindu or Muslim.[89]

Elephants performed their purely political duties in two main arenas. They bore rulers and high officials around the countryside on inspections and hunts. As Ovington remarks, in India a great man almost always traveled by elephant so as "to maintain the dignity of his post and station."[90] Their most impressive performances were, however, reserved for the imperial court, where the royal elephants were on parade daily. The changing-of-the-guard ceremony was political theater of the first order and required the very best elephants. Fryer, in the late seventeenth century, says that the elephants of Ceylon were the most sought after because they were famed for their "prostrations," in which they placed "their Necks between their Feet submissively."[91] Elephants were judged, therefore, not just by their size or coloration, but by their performing ability.

These displays have a long history in India; classical authors, Aristotle and Pliny, well knew the elephant parades and their political importance in India, knowledge that itself is a good indication of the impact and effectiveness of their performances.[92] Ibn Baṭṭuṭah, who saw one in the 1330s at the Delhi court, nicely captures their essence when he says that their elephants, fifty in number, were "trained to make obeisance to the sultan and incline their heads, and when they did so the chamberlains cry in a loud voice, 'Bismillah'."[93]

Accounts from the Mughal period elaborate upon the details and cast light on the inner workings of these performances. In Tavernier's recounting, there was a regular parade at Awrangzīb's court when the household elephants, long and carefully trained for their particular duties, were inspected. Each animal in turn approached to within fifty paces from the ruler, bowed, placed its trunk on the ground, and then elevated its head three times. Following this, the animal was inspected to see that it was healthy and well fed.[94] The audience for these displays of obedience were always well chosen—ambassadors, officers of state, local rulers, or, on days when Awrangzīb gave a public audience (*durbar*), select subjects and petitioners.[95]

As a theatrical effect, the audience was supposed to be left with the impression that it was the ruler's command, or even his mere presence, that initiated the elephant's act of submission.[96] Further, it left many with the feeling, most certainly intended, that these animals, cleaned and regally caparisoned, turned out on their own volition like well-disciplined troopers reporting for guard duty. This emerges clearly from Jourdain's observations on the elephant parade in 1611 during the reign of Jahāngīr. In describing the operation of the imperial guard at Agra, he relates that court nobles were assigned guard duty on a twenty-four-hour rotation. At five in the afternoon there was a ceremonial changing of the guard, at which time those on watch "doe their dutie to the Kinge, and so departe." He then adds, most helpfully, that

> the King's elaphannts doe also keepe watch, and come as dutie to the Kinge *to doe their dutye as the men*; for when the Kinge beholds them, they all att once putt their trunks over their heads giveinge the salam to the Kinge, then they departe, for they will not be gone before the Kinge looks at them; then they march by degrees with their pages before them and their wives after them. Every Elaphannt riall [royal] hath two or four younge elephannts for their pages, and two wives which followe them, alias shee [female] elaphannts. They are very ritchlie trapped with velvett, cloth of gould and other ritch stuffes.[97]

All this, of course, was very carefully stage-managed to show the ruler dominant over great beasts. The elephant muster replicated the human counterpart in all respects, in behavior, deportment, and in the public acknowledgment of the chain of command. As Aelian well understood, the elephant guard parades and the reverences came about because keepers and trainers relayed royal commands.[98] But even though trade secrets were out, these spectacles were still impressive, and no matter how contrived, they riveted attention, commanded admiration, and produced majesty.

As an adjunct to these ritualized demonstrations, the control Mughal emperors exercised over these great beasts was further certified by frequent stories of their personal confrontations with "disobedient" elephants. These tales, no doubt much embroidered in the retelling, begin in the reign of Akbar and assume over time the forms of literary topoi. In each case, a Mughal emperor must face down a *mast* (rutting) bull elephant at court over which its trainers, the professionals, have lost all control; naturally, the emperor mounts and soon masters the maddened beast.[99] Spiritual authority, moral ascendency, and a commanding presence win the day and discipline and good order are restored in the ranks.

Southeast Asia, with its abundant supply of elephants, also made heavy use of them as an animal of state. Here, as in India, war elephants were a measure of military strength and "tame elephants" a measure of economic well-being.[100] Moreover, they were displayed in much the same way: in royal elephant processions and in loyal elephant guards mounted for the protection of the sovereign.[101] That command over these animals was a vital attribute of kingship in this part of the world is dramatically revealed in an episode witnessed by a Persian embassy to Siam in the 1680s. When one of the king's elephants went berserk, carrying its mahout into the jungle, "breaking its own straight road," the sovereign's outrage was so great that he had both handler and animal put to death.[102] This, obviously, was treated as an unforgivable instance of lèse-majesté; terrible punishment followed this breach of discipline, most of all for shattering, at least temporarily, a carefully cultivated image of order, hierarchy, and dominance.

From time to time, elephants functioned as animals of state in locales beyond their home range, from North China to Rome. Both Caesar and Heraclius celebrated military victories with elephant parades.[103] The Umayyads also had royal elephants, one of which they presented, circa 667, to Juansher, prince of Caucasian Albania (Azerbaijan). When the animal, originally from India, arrived in Albania, it much amazed the locals and, as it was surely trained to do, paid its "homage" to the prince.[104] This tradition was continued at the early ʿAbbāsid court, where elaborately caparisoned and decorated elephants conducted notables to court and participated in victory celebrations.[105] The Ghaznavids, with their Indian connections, made extensive use of the elephant as an animal of state, a practice they transmitted to the Seljuqs.[106]

In East Asia, the Song dynasty had an Office of Elephant Care (*yangxiang suo*) under the Imperial Stud, which was charged with training and maintaining the emperor's tame elephants.[107] The Yuan, as we have seen, had its elephants, and their successors, the Ming and Qing, maintained a stable of several dozen well-trained animals that saluted and trumpeted the emperor and foreign envoys when they arrived at the gates of Beijing.[108] While these demonstrations were certainly regarded as solemn state occasions, it is important to recognize that elephants were never fully integrated into court life in China; they were always a sideshow, never the main attraction as they were in India or Siam.

Animals provided yet another service at royal courts: entertainments featuring animal competitions and combats. These are of considerable antiquity. The circus of Rome and later Byzantium regularly staged fights between various beasts, and of course between humans and animals.[109] While human participation was uncommon in the rest of Eurasia, except in cases of punishment, animal combats were not. In ancient Iran, India, and China, rulers set dogs, lions, tiger, boars, bulls, rams, and elephants against each other in bloody struggles resulting in deaths of one or more of the animals.[110] That was indeed their purpose, and in the absence of death such combats were deemed failures, disappointments.

In later centuries these entertainments retained their popularity and became a normal part of court culture in the core area and in Southeast Asia. One basic type was interspecies competition. Mughal courts staged fights between tigers and bulls, leopards and boars, lions and elephants, elephants and buffaloes, and lions and tigers set against bulls and rams.[111] Sometimes, as in Rome, these spectacles were staged as public entertainments. In the 1830s the king of Oud/Awadh in northeastern India organized fights involving bears, buffaloes, rhinoceroses, and tigers that were witnessed by thousands of the local population.[112]

The other principal competitions involved animals of the same species. These, too, could be bloody, but were not necessarily intended as struggles to the death. The variety of animals used is extensive: the Mughal court featured cock fighting, as well as camel, buffalo, ram, and boar competitions.[113] More popular, at least for a time, were antelope (*āhū*) fights. These involved much betting on winners according to very elaborate rules on gaming established by Akbar, who was deeply entranced with this sport and was once seriously gored "refereeing" a match.[114]

By far the most prominent and permanent of the intraspecies combats were those between elephants. Travelers in India in the seventeenth century repeatedly describe these matches, usually held in the Red Fortress at Agra.[115] According to Manucci, Shāh Jahān was much devoted to all kinds of animal combats, but was especially fond of elephant fights. These were tightly controlled, he says, because the animals were so expensive.[116] But as one might well imagine, such fights were not easily contained; as Mundy puts it, in the heat of battle these elephants "will not be ruled by words," and in these cases fireworks were set off in order to "sever them."[117]

In the minds of those who staged and those who watched, these fights were understood as entertainments that added another measure of pomp and dignity to the court and showed off its endless resources in animals and animal specialists. In one sense, the interspecies fight staged at court was simply the replication inside of their hunting methods outside, in which game animals and animals of the chase were "matched up" in the field for the elites' viewing pleasure. But it was more than this. Some of the competitions, particularly elephant matches, were prestige sports, the true sport of kings over which Mughal rulers claimed a monopoly. Thus, it became a very distinctive marker of sovereignty that few others, even if permitted, could afford. And, of course, it was a display for foreign audiences of the power and ferocity of the native wild beasts that seemed to do the bidding of their master, the king.

As previously discussed, many if not most peoples of premodern Eurasia saw animals as instruments of justice and divine retribution, and kings made use of them for the same ends. The practice of throwing the condemned to animal executioners is, of course, ancient and common. Such deaths, so horrifying, no doubt were thought to be effective deterrents and so were often staged as public spectacles.

In the Western historical memory this punishment is closely associated with Rome, which did execute prisoners in this fashion.[118] So much so, that for generations of martyrs, both Jewish and Christian, being thrown to lions became a standard symbol of religious persecution.[119] Big cats were used elsewhere, but in their natural range the elephant became the executioner of choice. In India, Hindu rulers of Chola, 888–1267, and the Muslim rulers of the Delhi sultanate and Golkanda executed tax evaders, rebels, and enemy soldiers "under the feet of elephants," and in the Mughal era political conspirators and common criminals met the same fate, a practice well known in Southeast Asia at this time.[120]

The reason for this preference is that an elephant, unlike the lion, can be trained to dispatch prisoners in varied ways. In Siam in the early eighteenth century, the condemned were first thrown in the air, then stomped to death, while in the Delhi sultanate the prisoner was first thrown to the ground and then, on the sultan's command cut to pieces "with pointed blades fitted to their tusks."[121] What is key here is that the elephant, actually under the control of a mahout, appears to be responding to the ruler's mood or his commands. This allowed the possibility of a last-minute reprieve, thereby producing a shaken, docile, and thankful, survivor. In Siam elephants were trained to roll the guilty party "about the ground rather slowly so that he is not badly hurt."[122] Akbar, on several occasions, used this technique to chastise "rebels" and then in the end the prisoners, presumably much chastened, were given their lives.[123] This same control also made it possible to conduct a kind of trial by ordeal, in which the condemned rebel, if he managed to fend off the elephant, was released.[124]

In all these cases the image projected goes beyond the power to end life and grant clemency to humans; here again, the emperor is seen presiding over very powerful beasts who always seem to do his bidding. This perhaps is the reason why elephant executions at times enjoyed some popularity outside the animals' natural range, in the Sasanid, Byzantine, and Temürid empires.[125]

To sum up these discussions, animals presented a spiritual as well as a physical challenge to humans. There were endless flows of energy, spiritual force, and information between the human and animal realms, and those who understood these flows, who could tap into them, were "naturally" set apart. Those able to kill, capture, control, and communicate with wild beasts necessarily had within themselves great physical and spiritual powers that raised them above normal humans, that marked them as rulers. And just as the king's physical ascendancy over animals, his hunting prowess, was extensively publicized, so too was his moral and spiritual domination of wild beasts. By these means, rulers proclaimed their ability to exercise control over nature and to appropriate some of its powers.[126]

Such a perception of royal authority clearly emerges from Notker's portrayal of Pepin the Short (r. 747–68), founder of the Carolingians. Writing long after the fact, the early tenth-century, Notker claims that when certain military leaders disparaged Pepin he had a ferocious lion set upon a bull and challenged his officers to drag it off or kill it. All refused, saying it was humanly impossible to do so. Pepin thereupon killed both beasts with one stroke of his mighty sword and all his doubting commanders fell at his feet proclaiming him the rightful ruler "over the whole of mankind," because, Notker adds, "not only was Pepin master of beasts and men, but he fought an incredible battle against the powers of evil."[127] Here then was a ruler superbly equipped to defend his realm against human foes, wild nature, and malevolent spirits, all of which was certified by his mastery of great beasts.

Direct, or seemingly direct, royal control over animals had yet another purpose, that of modeling political authority by dramatizing the existence of natural hierarchies and the king's position at the apex. Modeling took a number of forms and was expressed in a number of ways. If the monarch presided over a hierarchy of humans, the monarch's animals presided over a hierarchy of their own kind. His animals were also the best and, like the ruler himself, must always appear to be dominant and triumphant. The pride, the prestige, is not merely in the possession of the best but in the unerring selection of the best. And this usually meant that animal competitions, like royal hunts, were carefully arranged to ensure the desired outcome.[128]

These animal hierarchies were particularly well articulated under the Mughals and were a model of political authority within the court itself. Among the royal animals there was always an alpha, the leader of its own kind. Elephants had their head, a sort of sergeant of the guard, and so did the cheetahs. At the Mughal court, one of the lead cats was Najan; it achieved this status when, in pursuit of a deer, it leaped across a twenty-five-yard ravine and downed the prey. The courtiers who witnessed this were amazed and cheered the performance. In this cat's honor, a special drum was beaten when it entered court or proceeded to the field.[129] As with their own hunting feats, Mughal emperors advertised the success of their cheetahs in paintings hung in royal tents.[130]

This modeling, however, did more than affirm natural hierarchies, or present the ruler as an unerring judge of animal talent; it also helped to establish his capacity to harmonize the wild and the tame, to mediate and negotiate the relationship between nature and culture. This essential kingly responsibility is well exemplified in the medieval Persian version of the Alexander romance, in which Porus, a mythical ruler of ancient India, orders that "elephants and lions be arrayed" in the central square of his capital.[131] A true king, a model king, can bring wild nature into the very centers of civilization, form it up in ranks, and make it obey. This Awrangzīb did in a somewhat different, but effective, fashion. According to Manucci's eyewitness testimony, the emperor, "As proof of his justness and to advertise his good deeds, sends out every day to walk through the principal square [of the capital] a fierce lion in company of a goat that has been brought up alongside it since birth. This is to show that his decisions are just and equal, without any bias. This is done at court solely that the world may be notified of his justice."[132] While this symbolizes justice and equality before his majesty, it is also a concrete and compelling example of the ruler's power over beasts, since the goat must suppress its instinct to flee and the lion must suppress its true nature in the interests of order and harmony. As Andrews points out, Awrangzīb always traveled with a variety of animals for purposes of show and as a demonstration of his ability to control, like a Solomon of old, both carnivores (*dad*) and herbivores (*dam*).[133] In truth, this was a very old game. When Alexander entered Babylon as conqueror, the local governor came out to submit with gifts of herbivores and carnivores (properly restrained) as an acknowledgment that the Achaemenids' power over the forces of nature had passed to another.[134]

In an even more basic demonstration of this kind, Uzun Ḥasan, ruler (1453–78) of the Aq Qoyunlu Turkmen, had wild wolves on tethers taken to the square of his capital, Tabrīz, and loosened on the spectators; the wolves were prevented from doing major harm by the king's men, who were specially trained and equipped to keep them under control.[135] Here the message conveyed was slightly different: never forget that nature is a threat and needs royal restraint. This, too, was the purpose of the elephant-tiger combats that courts throughout Southeast Asia staged in early modern times. In these, the elephant, tamed and trained, represented order, kingly authority, while the tiger was the symbol of the uncontrollable and the rebellious. The tigers in such contests were always handicapped in some way so that the elephant, the king's *man*, would inevitably emerge victorious. If an elephant did not make a good show of it, the handler was severely punished for having humiliated his sovereign. It was essential that the tiger die.[136]

This royal preoccupation with animals and the manipulation of their behavior is directly linked to notions of cosmic kingship. Forms of cosmic kingship, or divine right monarchy, as it was styled in Europe, were until very recently found everywhere in the world, in Oceania, Eurasia, Africa, and the Americas, wherever and whenever complex societies and states emerged. Indeed, judged by its range and longevity, cosmic kingship in its great diversity is the most successful political-ideological system in global history. It rests upon the conviction that a particular ruler or ruling line holds power as part of a larger cosmic or religious design, and that, conversely, such rulers have communication and influence with these transcendental forces. The question is, how can this supposed influence be exercised and made creditable? Elemental forces of nature, wind, rain, or perturbations of the earth, can only be addressed ritually through prayer, sacrifice, and sympathetic magic. Animals, however, are a different matter: they can be controlled, intimidated, tamed, trained, and killed. Animals, therefore, often stand in for nature at large; they can be used in modeling, displaying, and documenting rulers' cosmic connections, influence, and responsibilities. Paradoxically enough, the animals easiest to control and contain are the largest, the elephants and the lions, the powerful animal assistants and the heroic game; the smaller species, rabbits and insects, not to speak of microbes, do much more damage and are far more difficult to keep in check. No kingdom, or any modern state, has ever succeeded in eliminating rodents, but many have triumphed over large predators, driven them to extinction or held their populations in check.[137]

Traditional kings, like modern politicians, do what they can, make a show of concern, prefer to address problems with short-term answers and to avoid those that are long-term, open-ended, or have no apparent solution. This preference is vividly expressed in a passage found in the Assyrian version of the *Epic of Gilgamesh*:

> Instead of thy bringing on the deluge,
> Would that a lion had risen up to diminish mankind!
> Instead of thy bringing on the deluge,
> Would that a wolf had risen up to diminish mankind![138]

The political lesson to be drawn from this lamentation is self-evident: rains cannot be quelled but troublesome beasts can be hunted down.

9
Legitimation

Animals and Ideology

For our purposes, ideologies of legitimation can be divided into two basic types: systematized political doctrines that are enunciated by priests and scholars and buttressed by appeals to philosophies, theologies, and cosmologies, and a far more diffuse variety that arises from, and is articulated through, popular religion and popular culture. Kings, of course, draw upon formal, official theories in defining and presenting themselves, but at the same time their behavior is also framed and modified by popular expectations of kings. The royal hunt, I believe, reveals much about the dynamic between formal doctrine and popular sentiment.

Although the manifold connections between animals, royal hunting, state formation, and legitimacy are complex and took on distinctive shape and coloration in specific historical contexts, there are still certain common features that surface across time and space. Chief among them is the fact that, as previously discussed, animals of all types were thought to contain spiritual force and/or cosmological significance, and many, as in ancient Egypt, were worshipped, held to be gods themselves or, at the very least, vessels containing heavenly messages and guidance, much of which was political in content.[1] This is well exemplified in the Uighurs' ethnogenetic myth, which relates that when driven from Mongolia in 840, they found their new homeland, Besh Baliq, on the slopes of the Tianshan, by following the cries of domesticated and wild animals.[2]

In many cultures, birds were the favored messengers of heaven and their messages, too, were political. Among the birds, raptors, who Aelian says were especially beloved of the gods, were the most politicized.[3] Across Eurasia, hunting birds are frequent figures in mythologies of ethnic and state formation, where they appear as ancestral totems, community guardians, portents of political success, heralds of heaven, epiphanies of gods, and cultural heroes.[4]

More particularly, in North and Central Asia eagles are invested with special powers and properties. As birds of the sun and the representative of divine authority, eagles were fecund; they gave rise to other powerful beings, from hunting dogs of the highest quality to shamans whose ritual costume of eagle feathers symbolized their spiritual flights.[5] Eagles, quite naturally, had important political functions. For the Turks, the eagle was a cosmic force, in liaison with heaven (*tengri*); one of its names, *bürküt*, may go back to *berk qut*, "sure good fortune," an essential attribute of kingship in the steppe world.[6] Their political role was, however, hardly limited to the steppe. In Achaemenid Iran, early Greece, and Byzantium, eagles served as symbols of imperial power and as portents indicating shifts in political authority and military fortunes.[7] Even in Roman political ritual the apotheosis of the emperor was achieved by releasing an eagle from atop the imperial funeral pyre which carried the ruler to heaven, where he was subsequently worshiped alongside the other gods.[8]

Since animals contained divine force and conveyed divine messages, it is hardly surprising that the hunt was itself viewed as a form of spiritual communication. In traditional societies, hunting always has ideological content. Archaic religions such as Shamanism are inextricably tied to hunting because all nature, and most particularly game, is animated by potent spiritual force. Thus, in the Siberian forest, hunters must "pay back" nature when extracting resources, that is, game is taken on the basis of reciprocity, with carefully negotiated spiritual compensation.[9] In the steppe, similar rules were operative. The Qitan royal couple ceremonially hunted hare to honor the sun god and offered the first-caught swan as a sacrifice to the ancestral temple.[10] And for the Turks and Mongols, hunting, whether individual or collective, was held to be spiritually charged and therefore always entailed much manipulation of the forces of nature exercised through various purification rituals, taboos, sacrifices, invocations, and ceremonies of thanksgiving to mountains, forests, and game.[11]

Such ideological associations are much in evidence in the sedentary world. Because the Assyrian rulers fulfilled their religious obligations successfully, the gods, according to royal inscriptions, gave them "wild beasts" and "commanded" them to hunt.[12] A royal hunt was thus a religiously sanctioned attribute of kingship; indeed, it was a requirement of office. In later centuries the hunting of deer by the king was a ritual act of great significance, involving sacrifices to earth, mountains, and rivers. Such ritual deer hunts are found in Sasanid Iran, the Koguryŏ kingdom of Korea, and in seventh-century Japan.[13] Interestingly, in varied historical contexts from Han China to Mughal India, chasing the elusive deer became a metaphor for the pursuit of royal authority.[14]

While the ideological content of the royal hunt varies in consequence of different physical settings and religious beliefs, the parallels are nonetheless striking. The common denominator in the core area and the steppe is the notion of good fortune; such good fortune was never a matter of "dumb" luck, a throw of the dice, but of a special dispensation, success that was spiritually earned. In all these cultures skilled hunting was viewed both as a matter of technical, physical attainment, and as control over natural forces, a control effected by supernatural, magical means. Therefore, special skill in hunting demonstrated one's possession of particular spiritual power, a charisma that could be transferred to the political arena.[15]

Charisma of this kind is at the very heart of imperial ideology in the ancient Near East and later on among the steppe peoples. It appears there as part of a larger ideological package, which includes universal authority, a heavenly mandate to rule, and the monarch's royal glory, his very special good fortune. In Middle Persian this glory is called *khvarənah*, in Turkic *qut*, and in Mongolian *suu*.[16] The hunt shows the ruler's success, a success ordained by the gods.

This equation has very ancient roots. As Wolfgang Decker observes, "in Egyptian royal dogma, the successful hunter is interchangeable with the unconquerable warrior."[17] The doctrine was further refined and elaborated in Mesopotamia. Here, according to Elena Cassin, kings and gods were long and closely identified with lions.[18] The literary and iconographic sources of the Assyrian period make it clear that rulers of the first millennium B.C.E. not only hunted as a religious-political duty but that the kingly hunter was never more "royal," that is, more charismatic, than when confronting a lion in single combat. This was a kind of test, an ordeal, to determine the sovereign's fitness to rule. Moreover, in his combat with the lion the triumphant king assimilated some of the essential qualities of the vanquished beast and consequently took with himself into battle such leonine qualities as courage, strength, and ferocity. And since the lion is the king of the untamed world, the king's victory enabled him to extend his sovereignty beyond the ordered, civilized realm (*mātu*) to the vast tracts of unorganized, savage wilderness (*erṣetu*). On this basis, Assyrian kings claimed to be "universal" rulers holding dominion over the "four corners of the world."

The king's relationship to lions and wilderness is thus vital, complex, and outwardly contradictory. On the one hand, the wild, the undomesticated, nourishes his kingly powers, providing him with crucial spiritual force to conduct successful military operations; on the other hand, the wild in the form of the lion is a threat to the ordered and domesticated world, a world that needs protection against the malevolent forces of nature and supernature. Hunting lions was consequently the mechanism by which a proper balance was struck between the menace of nature and its essential nurturing function. Because this was a vital spiritual and political matter, royal lion hunting became highly ritualized, that is to say, minutely stage-managed, even to the extent of breeding captive lion populations "like flocks" to ensure a ready supply of feline ideological foils.[19]

Figure 13. Achaemenid cylinder seal. The Morgan Library, New York.

The ancient Iranians took over many of these notions when they conquered Mesopotamia in the sixth century B.C.E. Achaemenid cylinder seals portray, in direct emulation of Assyrian prototypes, royal heroes standing on sphinxes dangling hapless lions by the hind leg, while on Sasanid silverware, as already noted, the ruler-hero is typically pictured in the act of shooting one lion while another lies dead in the foreground.[20] Such scenes show the king as inevitably triumphant, at the height of his powers, displaying his divinely imbued royal glory or fortune in the form of a nimbus or halo; they convey, in a more readily transportable medium, the very same ideological themes developed in the wall reliefs at Tāq-i Bustān and at other locales within Iran.[21]

The concept of the ever-victorious king, blessed with the halo of royal glory, survived for centuries. These ideas were reproduced in Iranian art well into the Islamic period and fully integrated into the political culture of neighboring Armenia and Georgia.[22] Further afield, the concept of royal glory, so closely associated with hunting and animals, is encountered as well in the religious beliefs of the early Iranian nomads and appears to have passed to the Turkic people through the mediation of the Soghdians.[23] These associations survived down to early modern times in places such as Mughal India. As Bernier reports, in Awrangzīb's day the royal lion hunt had to end in success since failure portended "infinite evil to the state." Consequently, on those occasions when a trapped lion escaped, it would be pursued for days until cornered and killed.[24] As ever-triumphant heroes, kings had always to be successful, and this is why their hunting "luck" was carefully manufactured, never left to chance.

Figure 14. Shahjahan hunting with gun and halo. *Padshahnama.* The Royal Collection © 2005. Her Majesty Queen Elizabeth II.

Threat

The search for legitimacy is hardly limited to ideology alone. Politics always has a local and wholly mundane dimension; who sees to it that the potholes on my street are fixed in the spring, or, closer to our theme, who rids my village of troublesome tigers? This is a very basic question of practical politics, of services rendered for taxes paid. We can best approach this issue by exploring the threat, real and imagined, animals pose for traditional societies. This in turn will lead into a discussion of popular attitudes toward nature and the royal hunt.

Wild animals threaten human interests in a variety of ways: as household pests, competitors for forage with domesticated animals, competitors for prey with human hunters, and, most important for us, as crop raiders and predators on livestock and people. The recent history of Malawi in East Africa well illustrates that all these problems remain critical concerns for many modern populations.[25] For the more distant past the information, while far less abundant, presents a very similar picture.

We start with the pests and work up to the more fearsome creatures. Rodents, of course, are a perennial challenge. Bandicoots (*Bandicota benegalensis*), the large rats of India, persistently penetrated food stores and were considered by the populace "a dangerous enemy."[26] Rabbits, at times, can produce local famines by their assaults on standing crops, and when they did so in the Balearic Islands in Roman times or in China under the Mongols, affected populations demanded government aid and action.[27]

Another major pest across large stretches of Eurasia was the jackal (*Canis aureus*), a very social animal that hunts and scavenges in large packs. Found throughout India, Turkestan, Iran, and Transcaucasia, they invaded villages and cities at night for food, killed poultry, damaged crops, dug up fresh graves to devour corpses, and made a horrible din with their communal vocalizing.[28]

Such beasts were a danger to one's livelihood, but not to life or limb; wild pigs, however, were a great danger to both.[29] An early Armenian chronicler complains of their recurrent invasions of fields and vineyards, and notes the recourse to spiritual force that was sometimes used to curtail their depredations and restore the damage.[30] Much later, Hamilton, who traveled the Indies between 1688 and 1723, relates that wild boars represented a serious problem for agriculturalists from Baṣrah at the head of the Persian Gulf to mainland southeast Asia because they uprooted and destroyed so many crops.[31]

The reason why they posed such a problem is that they are voracious and, at the same time, extremely aggressive and unpredictable. The mythical king Moabad in the *Visramiani* is done in by a great boar that rushes from the forest into his tent during open court.[32] In historical accounts, the animal is every bit as ferocious; the Byzantine emperor Maurice, while on a progress was attacked by a wild boar and narrowly escaped serious injury.[33] Their reputation as extremely dangerous game was well earned. Xenophon, in his treatise on hunting, repeatedly describes the extreme risks involved in pursuing boars, and later writers in the Muslim and Christian worlds affirm this view.[34] Consequently, it is not surprising that in ancient traditions boars achieved mythic proportions and that cultivators, whose fields they invaded, greatly feared them.[35]

In attempting to measure the sense of menace and dread produced by wild animals, it must be remembered, as Braudel points out, that prior to the great explosion of the world population around 1800, wilderness of various types was commonly found near all human settlements, towns, and even large cities.[36] These "wastes" contained myriad predatory animals that constituted a very real threat to human safety. This is not to argue that wild animal attacks were so frequent as to be an important source of human mortality, but that incidents were frequent enough to induce a climate of perpetual threat and fear, and thus popular support for measures to control wild beasts.

In the medieval West, one did not have to go to the forests to encounter wolves; from time to time, they invaded towns and entered churches, showing no regard for the startled humans.[37] During winter, ravenous wolves reportedly entered Russian villages, whose inhabitants were forced to flee for their lives.[38] No less an authority than Albertus Magnus assured his readers that once wolves kill a man, they "seek out humans because of the sweetness of their flesh."[39] And even in lands with far bigger threats, wolves were a serious problem: in 912–13, they entered the great city of Baghdad in numbers, and near Agra in 1835 a child was killed by a wolf in a public place.[40] Wolves had the disconcerting and horrifying habit of confronting humans on humans' own turf.

The big cats, of course, are the most fearsome of the predators. True leopards, while not much larger than cheetahs, are particularly dangerous because in the wild they regularly kill game that is larger than themselves and so do not hesitate to attack humans. In twelfth-century Syria a Frankish warrior was killed outside a church; in seventeenth-century India leopards made nightly raids into Rajāpur, a town near the Malabar coast; and in the nineteenth century a leopard killed several donkeys in the stable of a village to the north of Delhi.[41] Like wolves, leopards sometimes entered human spaces in search of a good meal.

For many, the tiger is the man-eater par excellence. Their reputation for ferocity and desire for human flesh spread westward quite early. By the first centuries C.E., the tigers of India are described in classical sources as "nearly twice as large of lions," or as having a deadly sting in their tails; naturally, these animals and those of neighboring Hyrcania were "man-eaters," *martichoras*, usually understood as the Persian *mardkhora*, "man-slayer."[42]

The man-eating behavior of big cats has long been misunderstood. Humans in fact are not normal prey for tigers. Outbreaks of man-eating at unusually high levels are a result of human disturbance of natural predator-prey balances. When tigers have access to their normal prey and sufficient space, they avoid human contact. Man-eaters are not, then, as often represented, older decrepit animals pursuing easier prey. This, Charles McDougal argues, is demonstrated by the geography of man-eating tigers, which were concentrated in recent times in South China, India, and Malaya, all locales experiencing rising human populations and habitat destruction, and not in areas like Siberia, where there is room for big cats.[43]

In southern Eurasia, confrontations began early. In the pre-Han era the Chinese saw tigers as man-eaters with a particular penchant for human flesh, an image that received further elaboration in Tang times.[44] Later on, Marco Polo frequently speaks of the danger from "lions," meaning tigers, in the countryside and near major population centers in South China.[45] Foreign travelers said much the same about India. Aggressive tigers, they state, are encountered on the roads, in small villages, near major cities, along both coastal plains, and particularly in the Ganges River delta. Everywhere they take a toll of the locals and produce a climate of fear.[46]

Beyond this fear of specific animals there was a more general feeling of menace produced by wild animals at large, of wild nature inhibiting the activities and threatening the lives of humans. This comes out most clearly in early travel literature, whatever its source. Chinese Buddhist pilgrims in India speak of the threat posed by savage animals along the Ganges and on the roads between major cities.[47] The famous Arab traveler Ibn Baṭṭuṭah advises traveling in large groups to a religious shrine outside Baṣrah because of "wild beasts," and later on in India relates a run-in with a rhinoceros.[48] The latter confrontation is most revealing, since even though such animals tried to avoid humans they were nonetheless encountered, seen as a danger, and hunted down.

The Ṣafavid embassy to Siam in the 1680s assert in their report that travel within the country is usually by boat because of the terrain and the forests full of dangerous beasts. When on land, guards had to be set and fires tended all night. Even in the rivers there was danger from freshwater crocodiles, who occasionally feasted on the unwary.[49] Accepted at face value, travel through wilderness and between cities took on the appearance of a military operation, and interestingly, this is how matters are portrayed by Europeans in southeast Asia. From Marco Polo to Alfred Wallace, Westerners make reference to fortified encampments, the need for fires, the necessity of always traveling in groups, and of the extreme dangers lurking everywhere in the countryside.[50] In eighteenth-century Pegu, according to Hamilton, criminals were simply banished to the forests for a set time, where they were soon killed by ferocious beasts.[51] Those in transit in many parts of India, with local guides, talk of the necessity of scouting ahead, setting fires, and posting guards to keep dangerous animals at bay. Even then, it was thought advisable to sleep in trees.[52]

The account of Sebastian Manrique, a Portuguese missionary, of his journey through the heavily forested hill country between Bengal and Arakan in the 1630s, provides a detailed account of these precautions. With some thirty armed troops and two elephants supplied by the local Mughal governor in Ramu, they literally fought their way to Arakan. They constantly fired muskets to drive beasts from the roads and tied themselves in trees to sleep each night. Such extreme measures, Manrique adds, were often employed by the local population, which in the dry season built large fires every night to keep wild animals away.[53]

The situation, as portrayed in travel accounts, was somewhat better in Iran, but still there is the usual warning, this from the Ṣafavid period, of the many big cats and bears to be met with in hill and plain and of the need to travel in large groups for safety.[54] But to what extent are these travelers' accounts reliable? How great was the sense of menace of the indigenous population? These are not easily answered questions. To be sure, some accounts are reporting travelers' tales, in the sense that they are simply repeating rumors about more distant regions they themselves have not visited.[55] While such statements can be discounted, it is different with the testimony of those who actually traveled through the regions they described. No doubt, there is exaggeration and misunderstanding and fear induced by alien environments, but even these fears were not created in a vacuum; to a useful degree, they reflect and refract local conditions and concerns. For example, Abbé Carré on his journey to India twice passed through Mesopotamia in the early 1670s, and he relates in detail the many dangers from boars, leopards, and lions along the Tigris and Euphrates and speaks, moreover, of their threat to the local population.[56] The ever-present danger from lions is much emphasized here, and we will use this as a test case to compare indigenous sources, especially as they depict local sentiment and royal hunters' actions, with those conveyed by foreign accounts. To do this properly, we must first consider the royal hunter in yet another role, that of animal control officer.

Animal Control Officer

In this section we again take up rulers' claims of legitimacy. Previously, we considered official, state-sponsored, and propagated ideology; here the issue is approached from another angle, that of rulers acting in conformity with subjects' professed interests, beliefs, and expectations. Such an approach to legitimacy is, admittedly, rather restrictive since it excludes wider considerations of legality and consent. Nonetheless, this narrow focus serves our immediate need, which is to examine the linkage between social classes and their specific functions,

functions which, as Joseph Schumpeter argues, they must "actually discharge as a class."[57] For us, this raises two fundamental questions: was the royal hunt held to be such an obligation by the elite themselves, and did their subjects view the royal hunt as a necessary and desirable public service?

The elite, as in ʿAbbāsid times, could plausibly claim that their hunts bagged animals that were both a pest and a threat.[58] The claim of public service is even more evident in the actions of Achaemenid rulers who sent their troops out to stomp infestations of scorpions between Susa and Media, and in those of a Umayyad governor general who helped "rid" a locale near Mosul of the same danger.[59] Much bigger game was also tackled in the name of public interest. Pharaohs of the Old Kingdom killed hippopotamuses whose appetites led them to damage crop land along the Nile.[60] A later echo of the royal animal control officer can be found in the English elite's pursuit of the fox. This kind of hunting, as enthusiasts have proclaimed since the Middle Ages, was actually a community service since it kept down "vermin" that preyed on the poultry and lambs of small holders.[61]

Tiger hunts, not unexpectedly, were regularly portrayed in similar fashion. A Han general hunted down tigers whenever he heard of one in the vicinity and early Indian rulers did the same.[62] In later times Mughal emperors and local rulers used a wide variety of means—poison, trained buffaloes, elephants, and guns—to keep tiger populations under control.[63]

Royal hunters also mounted campaigns of a more general kind against all "undesirables" in specific regions. Chinese rulers of the Warring States period are credited with ridding districts of dangerous beasts and the Mamlūk sultan Baybars in 1264 cleared the forest of Arsūf (Arsur), north of Jaffa, of all ferocious animals, including lions.[64] Georgian kings even made a public spectacle of these efforts. In the seventeenth century the monarch and his courtiers shot and killed hundreds of penned up foxes, jackals, and wolves outside the royal palace, to the approval of their assembled subjects, as a demonstration of their efforts on behalf of the public good.[65] For Rudra Deva, rulers acquired "religious merit by killing ferocious animals such as wolves and tigers, by the protection of standing crops, [and] by the slaughter of stags and other animals."[66]

There can be no doubt that royal hunters made every effort to portray their hunts in a positive light, as a disinterested service to subjects. To answer the more difficult question of popular attitudes toward their ruler's discharge of this public obligation, we need to examine popular attitudes toward nature at large.

Public opinion polls, of course, are not available, but we have various indications of popular views of nature. The first thing to note is that there was no single, predominant, or monolithic attitude; popular attitudes were surely situational. Still, in many situations there is good evidence of fear and antagonism toward the natural world and, more specifically, toward wild animals.

This is clearly brought out in reports of popular "resistance" movements against noxious beasts. At times, these took the form of generalized counterattacks. The population of early Armenia regularly poisoned boars, bears, wolves, and onagers, and in 1772 the people of Travencore on the southwestern tip of India organized large expeditions, which took the form of ring hunts, to kill off forest beasts deemed dangerous to humans.[67] On other occasions, popular ire was directed against specific species. One district in Italy in the first century C.E. made "war" on locusts three times a year, and similar efforts were made on the island of Lemnos.[68] Down to the nineteenth century, Mongolian herders made constant war on wolves; their deep hatred of these animals is evident from the fact that they did not just kill them but captured them with lassoes and then flayed them alive.[69]

Tigers, too, came in for special attention. At times the motive was simple revenge. Wallace in Java in 1861 reports that when a tiger killed a young boy, the local population organized a massive hunt that ended in the death of the "guilty" beast.[70] At other times, there were more generalized, preventive assaults. There are indications, for example, that by the time of Alexander the Great, Indians tried to control tiger populations with poisons and by killing cubs whenever possible.[71] More certainly, in the early nineteenth century, Indian villagers in the Upper Provinces set traps and snares for tigers on their own and encouraged armed Westerners to kill such predators.[72] And during the seventeenth and eighteenth centuries in Lingnan in South China, there was a prolonged popular war with tigers. They were hunted by the locals and as their habitat was destroyed and fragmented, the tigers, lacking normal prey, turned to people. This set up a dynamic in which fear of forests and tigers was intensified. The final solution was straightforward: no forests, no tigers.[73]

James Forbes, who spent two decades traveling widely in India, speaks of the frequency of human encounters with wild animals, particularly tigers, and the danger they posed to villages, travelers, and anyone toiling on the edges of the wilderness, such as salt pan workers who were the constant prey of these animals. Even straggling soldiers on the march in "close country" often fell victim to tigers. Naturally, this produced a heightened sense of menace among peoples living near forests and jungles, who, Forbes relates, holed up within their walled villages each night as if preparing for an enemy attack.[74]

These fears were articulated in varied ways. Among the mountain peoples of southwest China, there is a folkloric tradition of human sacrifices to propitiate the mountain god, who was personified as a tiger.[75] And, like the belief in werewolves in the Far West, which was ancient and widespread, the notion of weretigers was equally common in China and India.[76] In the early 1330s in the area of Gwalior in North India, Ibn Baṭṭuṭah came across a small town plagued by a tiger that entered each night and carried off people. The locals, he says, all had stories about this tiger that roamed the town despite a wall and closed gates; some, of course, said that it was really a man with the power to change himself into a beast who sought only the blood of his victims.[77] Against such horrifying creatures only magical defenses were truly effective. And magic was used even against real tigers. Fryer in the 1670s says that on the Malabar coast, where "Tigres" abound, the natives had Brahmins cast a spell on them to prevent attacks.[78] Interestingly, the British later held tigers, as distinct from noble lions, as cruel, rapacious, and particularly fond of human flesh, "man-eaters by nature."[79] This, in all likelihood, is a reflection of the British experience in India and of indigenous attitudes toward this cat.

Premodern peoples' views of the wild were clearly variable. Too often, however, the attitude of preindustrial and non-Western peoples is presented as homogenous and as basically benign, when in fact the situation is far more complex. It is true, of course, that most hunter-gatherers do not see themselves as separate from nature; they tend to see nature as "generous" or "giving," a kindly parent or ancestor. But such views are not fully shared by agriculturalists, who often see themselves as outside the forest, which is viewed as a dangerous enemy to be overcome. In short, their relationship to the wild, unlike the hunter-gatherers, is not based solely on reciprocity but contains elements of competition and confrontation.[80] This is hardly surprising since agriculture is nature's most ancient and successful enemy. And it is, quite naturally, agriculture's practitioners—peasants, landlords, farmers, and agronomists—who have fashioned the definitions, indeed, framed the very categories of weeds and vermin, and identified what should be eliminated. Certain species are seen as unwanted competitors for crops and pastures, crows or wild ungulates, and others as threats to life and limb, wolves or big cats. The royal hunt, therefore, can readily be fitted into this agriculturist worldview and at times is fully congruent with the strong desires of the cultivators that certain animal populations be brought under control, if not exterminated. All this is nicely reflected in a tale incorporated into a Muslim hunting manual, in which a Persian peasant petitions his king to rid the neighborhood of a rampaging lion; the unnamed monarch, desirous of doing right, immediately orders his provincial governor "to seek out the lion and kill it."[81]

Evidence of popular expectation that elites were indeed obliged to keep dangerous beasts at bay is found in a variety of sources. According to Herodotus, the subjects of King Croesus of Lydia complained to their sovereign about a gigantic boar disrupting the local economy and obtained his aid in killing it.[82] Mencius reports that in the fourth century B.C.E. a scholar, Feng Fu, adept at killing tigers, was much applauded by the peasantry.[83] Qitan emperors responded to requests from villagers in Rehe to drive off tigers killing cattle and humans.[84] Jahāngīr's motives for hunting big cats are most revealing in this context, and probably provide us with a more balanced view of the activity. Sometimes a hunt was planned well in advance as a sport and the tigers marked by scouts. On other occasions, tigers were simply encountered by chance and became targets of opportunity. Still, there are many other times when the emperor went out explicitly on the request of locals to rid the countryside or roadways of "man-eating" tigers and lions.[85]

Subjects clearly expected the royal court or its agents to take an active role in curbing aggressive nature. Not surprisingly, when European empires replaced home-grown rulers in various parts of Asia, the locals automatically assumed that the new regime would continue to perform the duties of the royal animal control officer. The great white hunters portrayed in such fiction as *Harry Black and the Tiger* had real-life counterparts in individuals such as George Orwell, who, as a police official in British Burma, was once called upon by irate locals to kill a rampaging bull elephant in "must," a task he was loath to perform.[86]

The question naturally arises as to why the populace petitioned elites for these services when they were capable of killing the beasts on their own. There are probably several reasons for this. First, and most obvious, it was very dangerous work. Second, hunts for individual animals or more general drives required much labor and took villagers away from their fields for extended periods. More generally, it may be that in the minds of many agriculturalists, common folk control domesticated beasts while rulers, who proclaimed such mastery, were held responsible for wild beasts.

This, however, represents only part of the story. The royal hunt might well serve the interest of the masses, but it could also become a major burden. The standard image of elite hunters riding through fields trampling down crops and the occasional peasant is also a historical reality. Already in the fifth century B.C.E., Xenophon reminds his fellow hunters to avoid "growing crops" when on cultivated land.[87] Chinese sources from the Han, Liao, and Yuan remark on incidents in which royal hunters interrupt agricultural work and repeatedly record decrees prohibiting such disturbances.[88] On other occasions, as medieval Chinese and Georgian records show, hard feelings arose because commoners were called upon to provide supplies for royal hunts and to serve as beaters.[89] Bernier describes the travail caused by the royal hunt for the subjects of the Mughal empire in the 1660s. He says that while "a pack of dogs will engage their thoughts and affection," they are "indifferent to the sufferings of so many poor people, who, compelled to follow the unfeeling monarch [Awrangzīb] in the pursuit of game, are left to die of hunger, heat, cold, and fatigue."[90]

Subjects had, then, many reasons to resent and fear the royal hunt. What then, do we make of public opinion in this matter, or what Jack Goody in another context called "the weight of popular culture"?[91] The simple class conflict model explains little and leaves too much out. This is because the relations between ruler and ruled are multifaceted and dynamic, containing an array of possibilities from the confrontational to the cooperative. In the sphere of culture, as Redfield has argued, the great tradition and the little traditions that make up any given civilization are interactive and interdependent. Elements of elite culture filter down to the masses, and many folk beliefs and customs are appropriated, reinterpreted, and provided proper intellectual underpinnings by the elite and the literati in their pay.[92] These two poles in reality form a whole that, as Andrews says, "enliven one another through exchange."[93] This dynamism is evident in the political sphere, where there is a lively sense of reciprocity at the core of subordinate classes' concept of justice, their "moral economy," as James Scott terms it. Accordingly, lower-class resistence or rebellion is most often designed to force rulers to meet their obligations, as measured by subordinates' notions of "norms of reciprocity" and "standards of performance," than to destroy or displace them.[94]

Not unexpectedly, any large-scale state- or court-sponsored activity had the potential to impinge upon the subjects' sense of reciprocity and thus activate their moral judgment. The royal hunt was just such an activity, one that inevitably called forth the full gamut of responses. It might produce sullen outrage if it interfered with agricultural rounds, but it is equally true that in other situations a ruler who refused to hunt down a noxious or dangerous beast could elicit the very same response. Clearly, then, this ongoing and intense interaction between elite norms and popular norms produced a set of expectations among the lower orders that in their turn shaped the deportment and actions of the ruling strata.

The attitude of the populace to the royal hunt, like their attitude toward nature at large, seen as both nurturing and threatening, was surely one of considerable ambivalence. The royal hunt was a two-edged sword for local villagers. While it placed extra burdens on them, it also kept down unwanted animal populations. It might even result in special rewards. Macartney relates that he was informed on good authority that when a village in Shandong was damaged by a flood, the Qianlong emperor, who often hunted there, immediately sent special relief to the survivors because he had a personal connection with them.[95]

At this point we need to examine more closely the relationship between official ideology and practical politics in the search for legitimacy. To this end, we can profitably return to royal hunters' pursuit of lions, since this activity was always invested with great ideological significance and was, in consequence, the subject of so much official propaganda.

In antiquity lions were found throughout the core and are regularly portrayed as grave threats to livestock, as man-eaters who invade villages and towns.[96] In ancient Egypt, lions constituted a perennial source of economic disruption as a result of the damage they perpetrated and the menace they presented. In such a perspective, the pharaohs' frequent boasting of their bag of big cats was more than a validation of personal courage, it was a way of demonstrating royal engagement with a pressing "policy" problem.[97] The same is true of Mesopotamia, where leonine ideology was most fully articulated; here, too, lions were felt to be a threat to humans and to the economy. This is reflected in fables, epics, and in law codes, which address the liability of shepherds when animals in their charge are killed by lions; equally revealing, Assyrian royal inscriptions and seal impressions state explicitly that expanding lion populations must be controlled since they represent a continuing threat to shepherds and flocks.[98]

In later centuries, classical authors leave the impression that Mesopotamia is overrun with lions and note the frequent encounters of Greek and Roman armies with them.[99] Indeed, the region's reputation as the center of a deadly lion "infestation" traveled far. In speaking of Mesopotamia (Daqin) in the third century C.E., one Chinese dynastic history reports: "Finally, while no one fears bandits or highwaymen, there are many savage tigers [*hu*] and lions [*shizi*] on the road that intercept and injure travelers, and [unless] they number more than a hundred or are carrying military weaponry, they might suddenly be devoured by those [beasts]."[100] In the following century, another dynastic history repeats the substance of this warning, adding that the country, owing to lion depredations, is impassable except in caravan.[101]

That locals thought this was a real plague is evidenced by the fact that in addition to heroic royal combats, there are frequent references to more practical, economical methods of killing lions. A Babylonian poem alludes to the practice of trapping them in pits, while Xenophon says that in Syria they were systematically poisoned using their favorite food as bait.[102] Further, in the second and third centuries, when Rome occupied the region, among the units stationed at Dura Europas were the *ad leones*, who apparently specialized in hunting lions.[103]

By all accounts, these problems, attitudes, and techniques were closely duplicated in the Muslim era. In twelfth-century Syria lions were often encountered in the vicinity of settlements, where they attacked and killed people, requiring the local elite to hunt them down.[104] The situation in Mesopotamia, especially along the rivers, was much the same. Arabic sources report concentrations of lions on the Euphrates and the feelings of dread these animals provoked in travelers is clearly expressed in historiography and poetry.[105] Later European accounts also depict the situation in grim terms, down to the mid-nineteenth century, when lions finally became extinct in the region.[106]

The means Muslim authorities used to keep lions in check are interesting. Following Roman precedent, the ʿAbbāsid caliph al-Amīn (r. 809–13) had a specially equipped force of troops for the pursuit of lions and a network of observers who spotted and reported their appearance in the area near the capital, Baghdad.[107] Even more intriguing, in Umayyad and early ʿAbbāsid times, the caliphate supported measures to transfer Gypsies (*Zuṭṭ*) of Sind (India) and their water buffalo (*Bubalus bubalus L.*), an early domesticate of South Asia, to Mesopotamia, where they established herds along the frontier with Syria, and in the south at Kaskar to drive off a growing lion population that was deemed increasingly threatening. The horns of the buffaloes were fitted with special covers to assist them in their task.[108] It may even be the case here that besides killing lions, the buffalo were intended to compete with them for habitat along the rivers. If lions can be thought of as "pests," then this constitutes one of the earlier and more inventive experiments in natural or ecological control of an unwanted species.

The lion "problem" in the subcontinent was of a different order. There were fewer lions and, of course, tigers always took center stage. Already in the early sixteenth century lions were said to be increasingly rare.[109] Their numbers were further reduced in the nineteenth century by "the zeal of English sportsmen and the price put on their heads by the Government."[110] Still, the Indian lion (*Panthera leo persica*) has held on; they now number about 250 in the Gir forest of Gujarat and remain in conflict with the local villagers.[111]

During the Mughal era lion hunting was both a royal duty and a royal prerogative. In 1617, while staying at Mandu in western India, Thomas Roe was repeatedly harassed by a lion, which Jahāngīr gave him license to kill.[112] More commonly, however, the Mughal emperors seemed to welcome the opportunity to make a show of hunting down lions that threatened and terrorized the country folk. Their expeditions sometimes ended in bloody confrontations in which the lion was killed with swords.[113]

All this, of course, is reminiscent of royal lion hunting in the ancient Near East, with its staged combats and demonstrations of the king's ability to constrain wild nature.[114] What this suggests is that ideology and practical politics run on parallel tracks, form an integrated package, and that ideological projections that survive for millennia only do so because they effectively tap into popular belief and are sensitive to, and play on, popular expectation.

State and Nature

Contemporary states carefully mediate their citizens' interaction with nature. There are now extensive rules of engagement in the form of laws governing fishing, hunting, logging, land and water use. To moderns, this mediation is exemplified in the environmental impact statement. While the general trend is toward restricting human engagement with nature, the modern state still countenances and promotes large-scale manipulation of nature through the extension of agriculture, hydroelectric systems, and the like. This duality also characterized the attitudes and policies of more traditional states; they, too, preserved and protected, and, at the same time, made strenuous efforts to manipulate and restrict nature. To achieve these goals, premodern states expended great energy and resources mediating that complex web of interrelationships between its human population and the environment, between culture and nature.

This mediation can be categorized and analyzed under three headings. First, there is the ceremonial: state ideology is normally closely linked to ritual efforts to ward off the powers of nature while simultaneously trying to mobilize these selfsame powers. Second, much administrative ingenuity is invested in trying to control access to, and utilization of, natural resources. While it can never exercise a complete monopoly over the gifts of nature, the state always endeavors to maximize its take, even if it later chooses to share out some of the bounty with its subjects. Third, physical means—dams, dykes, drainage projects, terracing, and afforestation—are a major and visible part of this effort.

At times these various forms of mediation are deployed to defend nature against the assaults of humans and at others to protect people from the ravages of nature. The exact motives and means have varied and changed over time, but the responsibility to do so has been a constant preoccupation of archaic, traditional, and modern states. And it is within this larger political framework that we must now try to situate the royal hunt.

These considerations take us back again to attitudes, popular and elite, toward nature. Nature, of course, had a multiple personality, it presented many different faces, but one of its most evident characteristics was its aggressiveness. This is constantly expressed in historical anecdotes and literary topoi about the rapid return of nature whenever culture, that is, human-imposed order, is in retreat or disarray. Commenting on princely strife and inroads of the Qipchaqs in 1093, an anonymous sermon inserted into the *Russian Primary Chronicle* says that, in consequence of political disorder, "all our cities are desolate, as are our villages; we move through fields where herds of horses, sheep, and cattle grazed and all we now see is emptiness; the fields are overgrown and have become the habitation of wild beasts."[115] Writing about 900 years later, the Ukrainian historian Mykhailo Hrushevsky says the same thing about Tatar raids of the late fifteenth century that left the lower Dnieper region "completely vacant, and for several decades [it] was abandoned to wild animals."[116]

Such images are indeed powerful statements about decline and define the ultimate form of defeat. The prophecy of Isaiah (13.21–22) says that when Babylon is destroyed, it will be overrun with nature in the form of wild animals.[117] The fear of destructive animal infestations is in fact a recurring theme, one repeated by chroniclers of later centuries. Describing conditions near Edessa in 504–5, in the aftermath of a Sasanid invasion, the Syriac writer Joshua records that there was a further invasion of beasts, particularly boar, attracted to the many corpses. Increasingly numerous and aggressive, they soon entered the villages, killing children and then adults; in self-defense, the villagers were forced to make war on them with the help of professional hunters.[118] The Armenian chronicler Drasxanakertcʿi has a similar tale to tell. He relates that in his own day, the early tenth century, political discord, war, hard winters, and bad harvests led to widespread famine, banditry, and social disintegration. As chaos and death engulfed the Armenian cities, corpses accumulated, filling the streets and squares, and these soon attracted wild animals, especially wolves, who, with an abundant food supply quickly multiplied and began to devour living humans. No respecters of social rank, "both the venerable and the meek were cut down together by the claws of these beasts."[119]

Equally horrifying, with the breakdown of the social order, even long-domesticated animals could revert to a wild state. According the historian Dionysius, this is just what happened in Syria and Mesopotamia when the great Justinian plague of 541–44 decimated village populations.[120]

These and other stories of earlier infestations and reversions were regularly recycled in literary form and, more important, in many parts of the Middle East, there were constant reminders of Nature's many victories over human-imposed order in the wild beasts that roamed through the ruins of districts that had been depopulated in the past.[121]

The sense that nature, in the absence of stable political authority and security, rapidly reclaims the land is dramatically brought out in a passage from the seventeenth-century Georgian historian Vakhushti Bagrationi: "And after the death of Shāh Ṭahmāsp [I, Ṣafavid ruler, 1524–76], Alexander [II, r. 1574–1604] lived in peace. And in this time Kakhetʿi was so populated that it was difficult to find good hunting. And Alexander, who passionately loved the chase, said 'Would that Kakhetʿi be devastated in order to have a multitude of game.' And so it was in the time of his grandson Tʿeimraz [I, r. 1606–16 and 1623–32], although he never had time to go hunting."[122] Such episodes, whether real, imaginary, or hoped for, live long in historical memories and impart a consistent message: without social order, cultural landscapes quickly revert to nature, and it is the beasts of the forests and deserts who serve as Nature's assault troops.

Although a frequently used literary device, the theme of fall and reversion was also a social and ecological reality. In China, regime changes often created conditions for the rapid expansion of nature. Luoyang, a major metropolis and last capital of the Northern Wei, was suddenly abandoned in 534 when the court moved to Ye; when Yang Xuanzhi visited it thirteen years later he was shocked to find ruins covered with wild vines, streets full of thorny bushes, and wild beasts and birds in abandoned buildings.[123] During another period of dynastic change and political disturbance at the end of the same century, well-developed monastic lands near Hangzhou on the east coast of China rapidly returned to wilderness.[124] Reversions of this type were a regular feature of Chinese environmental history and most people had either experienced such falls or heard tales of the miseries they always entailed.

For the subcontinent, where there is far less documentation, our examples are restricted to more recent centuries. But these, coming from some very astute observers, are quite telling. Forbes reports that in consequence of famine and social disorganization in Gujarat in 1781, packs of wolves began attacking the weakened and floating population. Later the same year, he encountered at Dholka, a town south of Aḥmadabād, an outbreak of banditry so intense and sustained that "cultivation only flourished near the town; the distant plains," he says, "were assuming the appearance of a forest overrun with a variety of game." And at Jaunpur, four years later, another famine provided so many human corpses for the local wolves that they, like their brethren in tenth-century Armenia, multiplied and began to attack the living, including armed sentries sent there to deal with the outbreak.[125] Over a century earlier, Bernier witnessed similar relapses attending the breakdown of government authority. He cites the case of the islands making up the delta of the Ganges, which were once full of thriving villages and productive agriculture but had been recently reclaimed by nature. According to his testimony, this was the result of widespread piracy, emanating from Arakan, that caused the local populace to flee; the islands soon became a "dreary waste" in which antelope and boar flourished, and this, in turn, attracted tigers. These beasts, he relates, swam between the islands preying upon the remnant population, including boatmen in their boats. But as Bernier well understood, despotic government can also drive the populace away, allowing much land to revert to "dreary wilderness" and to "plains overrun with thorns and weeds."[126] The same problem was recognized by Jesuits in early seventeenth-century Pegu, who attributed the advance of jungles and tigers to incompetent and corrupt government.[127]

In all the cases cited above, culture lost out to rampant nature; there was a fall from a higher state to a primitive, uncertain existence. It will be helpful for our ends to determine how this higher state was achieved in the first instance, at least as recounted in the mythologies. What, in other words, were the historical memories and models invoked in the search for solutions when nature challenged culture? The answer is that the available stock of models was surprisingly uniform across Eurasia.

Very typical is the myth of the Yao people of southwestern China, in which Yi the Archer controls natural disasters and frees the people from wild animals, thereby making agriculture possible.[128] Ancient texts, whether historical, mythical, or prescriptive, or some combination of the three, regularly connect the emergence of settled life and the "first" or pristine state, with some kind of heroic assertion of control over nature, and, moreover, consistently view such control as a prerequisite for civilized life.[129]

China provides a clear example of these "state formation tales." For the ancient Chinese, primitive humanity was at the mercy of nature, and the rise of complex society, the state, and high culture, is therefore portrayed as the story of the acquisition of those tools and techniques that allowed humans to defend themselves against the assaults of beasts, floods, and famine. Those chiefly responsible for these gifts were the sage kings of yore, Yao, Yu, and Shun. They made settled life possible by controlling rivers and banishing wild animals dangerous to humans to remote areas. Once these rulers died, however, chaos and bad government ensued and the beasts returned and the duke of Zhou, minister to the first Zhou emperor, had to flush out the tigers, leopards, rhinoceroses, and elephants and again banish them to distant parts so that civilization could flourish anew. By the time of Mencius, fourth century B.C.E., these mythical cultural heroes, Yao, Yu, and Shun, were historicized and accepted as actual rulers while the duke of Zhou became for Confucians the ideal minister.[130]

Thus, for the Chinese, individuals skilled in the management of nature and beasts made possible the first state. So, too, in the ancient Near East, where another animal management specialist, Nimrod, "a mighty hunter before the Lord," that is, "by the will of Yahweh," is depicted in the Old Testament (Gen. 10.8–10) and in later Christian tradition as the first mighty ruler in human history.[131] And, as in the Chinese case, even after a cultural order is imposed, vigilance is needed, for new threats continuously emerge; thus, in the Gilgamesh epic, the hero must defend an existing state by slaying the bull of heaven sent down by an angry goddess to destroy the city of Erech.[132] In the ancient Iranian tradition, found in the *Avesta*, reversion is also a central theme. Here Jamshīd (Yima-xshaeta) is portrayed as presiding over a golden age in which humans and nature are in harmony, but once he has lost his royal glory (*khvarənah*) for impiety, there is loss of control, estrangement, and fall.[133]

The medieval Muslim world drew on all these traditions for their model rulers. In Arabic sources Nimrod (Namrūd) is remembered as the first king of Babylon and the world, and as a "master of eagles" who could harness their powers of flight.[134] They were well acquainted, too, with Solomon, whose vast wisdom extended to nature and wild animals (I Kings 4.33).[135] And they drew extensively on the Persian tradition that attributes to their "sage" rulers, Hoshang and Farīdūn, mastery over animals.[136] These feats were kept very much alive in artistic representation and in royal propaganda. An illustrated *Shāhāmah* manuscript from Topkapi Sarai shows Gayomard, the first king in the Iranian creation myth, seated on his throne surrounded by his retinue and in the foreground an assortment of big cats fawning before him.[137]

It is therefore not surprising that Muslim rulers like Jahāngīr put forward claims of his own domination of nature: "in the time of my own reign wild beasts have abandoned savagery, tigers have become so tame that troops of them without chains or restraint go about amongst the people, and they neither harm men nor have any wildness or alarm."[138] While obviously untrue, his assertion nonetheless evokes an image of the successful monarch with deep roots across the continent. Sasanid monarchs, as we have seen, had themselves repeatedly portrayed in heroic combats with big cats and in ceremonial hunts of deer and boar, who degrade pasture land and damage crops. The king's furious assaults on these beasts, recorded in the reliefs at Tāq-i Bustān, are closely association with notions of the fecundity and fertility of the earth. Thus, the king on the chase is fulfilling an important cosmological function and at the same time acting as protector of agriculturalists and herders.[139] Bahrām Gor's feats of dispatching unwanted beasts were certainly precedents for later rulers, such as a seventh-century ruler of Ṭabaristān who reputedly rid his land of all dangerous animals.[140] What is most crucial here is that many in the medieval world took these stories at face value. Ibn Baṭṭuṭah, for one, repeats and affirms these traditions that kings of yore had special strengths that allowed them to confront and kill large beasts, particularly lions, that mere mortals, even a company of armed troops, could not face.[141]

The common theme running through these traditions and claims is that from the beginning of history model rulers and successful states kept nature in check and wild beasts at bay. It is not too surprising, then, that later states were held responsible by their own subjects for the containment of aggressive nature.

This containment policy, both in terms of mythology and royal propaganda, was focused on "mobile nature," predatory animals and fantastic, oversized beasts.[142] From Marduk to Indra to Saint George, mythology is full of heroes who demonstrate their courage as well as their physical and magical powers by slaying dragons. These synthetic creatures, amalgams of diverse zoological parts, are anomalies representing chaos, and their defeat represents a return to order.[143] Such enhanced creatures, lions with wings, were commonplace in many ancient artistic traditions—the early steppe, ancient Near East, and the late Roman Mediterranean.[144] And when these artistic representations died out in late antiquity, such kingly combats were continued in epics of the Middle Ages. Oghuz Qan makes his name, starts his political career, and forms his state by liberating a people oppressed by a fabulous beast (*kïat*) that he hunts down and vanquishes after much travail.[145]

The long popularity of this theme tells us something about the general import of real and fantastic beasts in these societies and, more particularly, about the centrality of the royal hunter in the defense of culture from the persistent menace of nature. It is understandable, therefore, that throughout the ancient Near East, from Egypt to Urartu in Transcaucasia, the ruler is regularly viewed as a shepherd who protects his flock, his subjects, from evil enemies, anarchy, and dangerous animals.[146] Among the various titles of Mesopotamian, particularly Assyrian, monarchs are "shepherd of all habitations," "faithful shepherd," "shepherd of mankind," "shepherd of the four corners," "marvelous shepherd," and "chief herdsman." And this office, the royal inscriptions make clear, is given the ruler by the dispensation of the gods.[147]

The credibility and popular acceptance of such claims can only be evaluated indirectly, through an examination of the state's role in keeping nature at bay. This, as already argued, was one of the central functions of the state. In ancient India, as Nancy Falk remarks, there was a "complex relationship between wilderness and kingship." Rulers and would-be rulers had to interact with the wilderness to conquer, placate, contain, and appropriate its raw power. It was both a test and a validation of his right to rule. His transactions took many forms—fashioning a royal pleasure park (*ārāma*) in the jungle, which became the ceremonial seat of kingship, and subduing fierce wilderness beings (*yakshas*).[148] Like the royal combats with lions in ancient Mesopotamia, these struggles were held to be critical tasks of Indian kings because the wilderness had a vitality that, when incorporated into a polity, imparts strength to the latter despite the fact that it still continues to disrupt, to present a threat. Thus, the wild, David Shulman argues, has a dual nature that both threatens and nurtures, and it is the king's duty to manage this dialectic between its dual personalities.[149] This, in fact, is a widely held formula. As Mary Helms points out, in traditional societies political leadership is often vested in those who provide linkages between the realm of culture, the tame, the cooked, and the realm of nature, the wild, the raw. These leaders tap into the physical and spiritual resources of the wild and at the same time hold it back, prevent its encroachment on the tame.[150]

Not unexpectedly, animals, the embodiment of the wild, are viewed as a perpetual threat to human interest and safety. Classical writers compiled a lengthy bill of charges against these implacable enemies in the wild kingdom and not only large carnivores were indicted: mosquitoes, scorpions, spiders, moles, rodents, snakes, sparrows, and baboons all assault humans and destroy the sown land, making it uninhabitable. And this they do across the known world, from India to Ethiopia to the Mediterranean.[151] Like human enemies, they are seen to invade and conquer. Shortly after Alexander's death, the Antariatae, neighbors of the Macedonians, abandoned their country to hordes of frogs and mice.[152] In the reign of Khusrau I Anushirvan (r. 531–79), masses of jackals invaded Iran, signaling the empire's weakness and the need for vigilance and reform.[153] Following the Qin conquest of Sichuan circa 316 B.C.E., an albino tiger began killing people, and soon other tigers joined in, claiming 1,200 victims. The new sovereign, the Qin emperor, then intervened "militarily" to defeat this powerful alliance of big cats.[154] In more recent times, Macartney understood the Great Wall of China not only as a defensive work against human enemies, but as a barrier designed "to shut out from the fertile provinces of China the numerous and ferocious beasts of the wilds of Tartary."[155]

These perceptions are consistent with the tendency to bracket together human and animal foes. Thomas Artsruni, writing in the early ninth century, often speaks of areas of extreme danger where brigands and wild beasts, or beasts and enemies, mount attacks and despoil the countryside.[156] Xuanzang, in northwestern India in the mid-seventh century, remarks on "a great forest wild, where savage beasts and bands of robbers inflict injury on travelers."[157] About a millennium later, the Hindu ruler Rudra Deva quotes approvingly older dictums to the effect that: "The operations of kings for killing of animals are said to be the same as those for killing enemies."[158] His Muslim contemporaries, the Mughals, practiced such prescriptions; they viewed the wilderness regions near Delhi as a hotbed of opposition, teeming with bandits, rebels, heretics, and wild beasts, and used the same instrument, the royal hunt, to contain these enemies of the established order.[159] Even in the British period, this attitude was still prevalent. A certain Mr. Shore, a British political officer in Bengal in the 1820s, thought it his duty to bring under control, in the words of a contemporary, "all the brigands and wild beasts that infest his province."[160]

Human enemies are widely dehumanized, that is "animalized," turned into rats, wolves, and tigers; conversely, animal foes are sometimes "humanized," accused of acting in concert and imbued with conscious evil intent. That animals represent a collective threat to humans is perhaps quite old. There is even a "man-the-hunted" thesis that suggests the threat of animal predation and consequent human dread of carnivorous animals was an integral part of hominid evolution.[161] Whatever the merits of this hypothesis, it is evident that once political organization emerged, wild animals, like rebels and foreign foes, became enemies of the state and routinely treated as a problem of government.

This is evidenced by the fact that popular appeals for state intervention regularly accompany outbursts of nature. When Ovington arrived in Surat in 1689, a devastating plague of locusts had just destroyed a field in the vicinity. In consequence, he writes, "The Poor Husbandman bewailed his Loss to the [Mughal] Governor of the City," whom he hoped would be "moved to repair the Damage and relieve the Man."[162]

At times, nonviolent methods, at least in theory, were used to blunt these incursions. In China, the appearance of tigers (*hu*), understood as bandits as well as great cats, was typically equated with bad government, which benevolent rule could overcome. Music, it was thought by some, could be used to exercise control over the natural world, creating there and in the human sphere the proper harmony and hierarchy. Others felt, on the contrary, that tigers of either type could only be controlled by force and guile.[163]

This, to be sure, was the normal solution. Thus, the Achaemenid army's antiscorpion campaigns, and the Roman army's attacks on locusts in Syria.[164] Of a similar character were the more generalized assaults on undesirable species in the Middle East, India, and China, or, to take the practice into modern times, the campaign undertaken in South Africa against all carnivores at the turn of the last century.[165]

Xenophon enthusiastically endorses Socrates's notion that agriculture and hunting were compatible, complementary, and mutually supporting activities; husbandry produces horses and hounds, and the latter help prevent wild animals from injuring crops and herds.[166] It is most likely that, presented to any ruler of premodern Iran, India, or the steppe, this formula would have been accepted as self-evident. No people or state could possibly flourish without checks on nature, and the royal hunt was often seen by populace and elite as the first line of defense.

Pastoralists and farmers, of whatever cultural background, are in the business of restricting nature, that is, trying to dominate or minimize nature within certain fixed boundaries. And once such a simplified domain is established, any unwanted nature, wolves or weeds, that enters, is considered wild, intrusive, and out of bounds. Human conflict with wild nature and wild animals continues into our own day, in both the developed and undeveloped worlds and in urban and rural settings. This entails not only a clash between nature and culture, but a conflict among human populations, and in conjunction these tensions inevitably bring into play political authorities, whether tribal chieftains, medieval kings, nation-states, or international organizations as mediators in these ongoing confrontations.

Quite typically, when the danger and damage, real and imagined, reach certain levels, thresholds of tolerance may be surpassed, and in John Knight's analysis some kind of collective political action follows. This can take the form of a local initiative or an appeal to a higher political or spiritual authority. This is particularly acute when the boundary crossers are predators who pose a threat to human life. In defense against these invasions the full power of the state is brought to bear to protect the "frontiers."[167]

For our purposes, it is critical to recognize that in premodern societies of all kinds, nature was seen as strong, robust, and endless. Among classical writers, for example, the displacement of wild animals by domesticated was a benefit, a desirable goal.[168] There was no thought or concern about extinction since wild animals were generally regarded as enemies and in any event, their numbers were beyond calculation. And, equally important, any weakness in the social order allowed a rapid return of aggressive nature. Both Pliny and Strabo comment on how a lack of human solidarity led to the loss of fertile lands to invasive "wild animals" and "wild beasts."[169]

This brings us to one of the decisive differences between traditional and contemporary views of the natural world. In contrast to modern intellectuals who worry much about the fragility of nature, their counterparts in premodern societies fretted greatly over the fragility of culture. To this earlier generation of scholars, churchmen, and bureaucrats, the wild seemed strong and aggressive while the tame seemed weak and vulnerable. And surely the lower orders of society, herders and peasants, who daily battled weather, wolves, and weeds, shared their view. For them, nature could take punishment and often needed it.

To some extent, local populations could mount their own defense, but given the great powers of nature, the state was an essential buffer and backup. In this regard, it is interesting that classical authors often invoke the threat of wild beasts as the principal stimulus toward state formation. This is brought out clearly in the works of Diodorus of Sicily, writing in the first century B.C.E. He begins with the premise that in their original unorganized state, humans were extremely vulnerable to animals: "Then, since they were attacked by wild beasts, they came to each others aid, being instructed by expediency, and when gathered together in this way by reason of their fear, they gradually came to recognize their mutual characteristics." That is, competition with animals produced human identity and an organized human society. Later on, he argues that with the rise of the state, the balance of power began to turn in humans' favor. Osiris, a mythical early Egyptian ruler, he says, was instrumental in this victory, when copper was discovered and people at his court fashioned weapons to kill beasts and tools to cultivate. Here again, control of wild animals is a prerequisite for agriculture. Further on in his formulation, Heracles is made to continue this work over the wider world by clearing wild beasts from the land and presenting it to peasants.[170] This recounting of the emergence of the state and civilization is, obviously, in full accord with Chinese and Indian notions: sage kings, model rulers, and cultural heroes hold nature and animals in check and allow the land to be cultivated and agriculture to flourish. For all complex agricultural societies, "Western" and "Eastern," nature and culture were separate realms that had to be kept quite distinct. Nature's powers were drawn upon but they should not be allowed to get out of hand or to cross forbidden boundaries.

Archaic, traditional, and modern states share a set of essential functions; they regulate interactions among their own subjects, negotiate contacts with outsiders, and mediate relations between nature and culture. And whatever the exact role of environment in the emergence of early states, there is every reason to believe that once formed, statist solutions to problems posed by natural forces are commonplace. Such an argument, it seems to me, is not deterministic, since controlling nature through domestication, or limiting and restraining the wild through physical or ritual means, always requires effective control over humans.[171]

The process of state formation is certainly complex and we may never arrive at a precise formula, only a useful recipe. Current models of the process are largely cast in terms of conflict resolution or of social integration.[172] Our earliest models, however, see humans organizing against nature, not against other humans. While it may be objected that this resolves nothing about the conditions surrounding the origins of pristine states, and only speaks to the *mentalité* of the historical periods in which these texts, whether scholarly or mythological, were created and reproduced, there can be no doubt that early states were very much in the business of confronting and transforming nature. Fiskesjö's recent study of the emergence of the Shang state emphasizes that one of the principal activities of their kings was the conversion of wilderness into cultural landscapes, a project in which hunting the abundant wildlife of North China figures most prominently.[173]

To sum up, given the concerns about the aggressiveness of nature, particularly in times of political disorder, subjects accepted the state as a necessary buffer between the wild and the tame, and viewed the royal hunter as a normal and expected attribute of that state. Through the medium of the royal hunt rulers acted out cosmic roles and, at the same time, performed very specific, tangible, and expected services at the local level. In the quest for legitimacy, the royal hunt made its contribution, but did so as one element in a larger ideological-political package.

10

Circulation

On the Road

We now turn to the royal hunt, the movement of the sovereign through the countryside, as a means of controlling humans. As a preface, it needs to be recognized that premodern rulers were on the move for a variety of reasons. These are not always easy to isolate because their motives tend to be interlocking, rather than mutually exclusive. However, as Charles Melville argues, the following are often in play.[1] In some cases, this was simply the continuance of a nomadic heritage of the ruling elite, and therefore a reaffirmation of cultural and ethnic identity, a way of distinguishing rulers from subject populations. In realms with low productive capacity, it was largely a matter of resources. Early Frankish rulers, unable to live off the resources of any one locale for long, were, of necessity, itinerant, regularly moving people to supplies.[2] But even when this was not necessary, kings nonetheless moved about to preside over state ceremonies, conduct inspections, identify and solve problems—that is, to administer the realm.[3] This often entailed visiting and renewing personal ties with assorted dependants, clients, nobles, tribal chieftains, local officials, and march wardens who might otherwise withhold resources or drift into rebellion. Rulers therefore went out on a progress or hunt to remind all who was king and to reaffirm their sovereign rights. A large-scale royal hunt conducted in the open countryside well served these ends as a dramatic and visible reenactment of the conquest/occupation/war that established the kingdom in the first instance.

Since progresses were an important element in the governance of the realm, kings took their government, or at least part of it, on the road. This is very apparent and readily documented in the case of nomadic empires. We know that Qubilai, Mongolian conqueror of South China, spent much time on the road, traveling with a huge retinue, in essence a slimmed-down version of the imperial court/government composed of officials, guardsmen, huntsmen, commissaries, advisors, soothsayers, and so on.[4] The same was true of the Mongolian regime in Iran, where the high officials were constantly on the move, hunting and traveling between the capital and various seasonal camps.[5] Such mobility, to be sure, was intrinsic to their basic way of life; as a Song envoy said of the early Chinggisid state, "when the Mongolian ruler changes his tent site to go on a ring hunt [*xiaolie*], all the so-called officials go along. They simply say: 'break camp!' "[6]

While governments formed by sedentary peoples may have moved less frequently and with greater difficulty, they did move. In Arab tradition, going back to Sasanid precedent, the king on his progresses was expected to take with him guards, advisors, entertainers, and part of the treasury.[7] The Mughals most certainly adhered to these prescriptions. When Awrangzīb went to Kashmir in 1662 to inspect this important holding and enjoy its healthful climate and fine hunting grounds, he was accompanied by most of his court, a vast establishment of officials, servants, wives, troops, horses, elephants, and animals of the chase.[8]

Movements of this magnitude required good logistics and substantial infrastructure. Food requirements, only partly met by hunting, and some of the water had to be transported.[9] So too did the elaborate tentage needed to house the royal party. In Turkish and Mongolian states, a special officer, called a *yurtchi*, was in charge of the royal tents and equipment on all journeys.[10] Little if any distinction was made between the preparations for a hunting trip, imperial progress, or military expedition.

The preferred method of royal travel was the advanced camp, Persian *pishkhānah*, in which the ruler is accompanied by two identical camps, one of which is always sent ahead so that at the end of the day a comfortable household is ready to receive the royal person.[11] While providing royal comforts, the system greatly complicated logistics, since each camp included large pavilions, carpets, lighting, and provisions. In Akbar's day, each of these elaborate establishments required 100 elephants, 500 camels, 400 carts, 100 bearers, 500 troopers, and a staff of 1,830.[12] By Awrangzīb's reign, these heavy demands had been reduced somewhat, but each camp still required 60 elephants, 200 camels, 100 mules, and 100 porters for its conveyance.[13]

The origin of this system is not known, but the use of alternating camps was already well known to the Byzantine emperors of the eighth century.[14] Whatever its age, this system was made possible in sedentary states by a substantial investment in the infrastructure of travel, much of it closely tied to the royal hunt.

In early Iran there were multiple capitals and the emperors, as the Greeks well understood, traveled constantly between them.[15] They were also aware that in Achaemenid Mesopotamia paradises were sited regularly along the main communications routes.[16] One of the main functions of such parks, certainly, was to provide support for official travel, that is, housing, security, remounts, and food supplies.[17] In later centuries, hunting facilities continued to perform

Figure 15. Hunting camp of Qianlong. Giuseppe Castiglione, 1757. RMN/Art Resource NY.

the very same services in Iran and its hinterlands. Under Ashak III, the Arsacid ruler of Armenia (r. 380–89), royal encampments were often located near a "walled hunting park" that was well supplied with feasting halls and other creature comforts.[18] In Islamic times, chroniclers portray Khurshīd (d. 761), ruler of Ṭabaristān, and Mughīth al-Dīn, a twelfth-century Seljuq ruler of Iraq, as constantly on the move through their realms, staying at various hunting grounds and lodges where rations were stockpiled.[19]

In the time of Shāh ʿAbbās, Herbert records that from Iṣfahān to the Caspian there were royal lodges (*mahāl* or "rest stops") about every twelve miles and that some of these were situated for hawking and hunting. The shah used this route, Herbert says, to "see the extent of his empire and likewise have a prospect of the better parts of Persia."[20] We know, too, that the shah connected his hunting grounds at Farāhābād with other cities of the region by building, over time, stone bridges and causeways across the marshy ground of the Caspian shore.[21] Facilities that rulers initially created because they were well situated for hunting, could later be incorporated into wider communication networks.[22]

The pattern of official travel in Mughal India was comparable. Rulers moved from one hunting facility to another in making their rounds. Jahāngīr had a number of "fixed hunting places" in northern India that are also described as halting places.[23] As late as 1829, Godfrey Mundy, a British officer on an official inspection tour with the commander of the military forces in the

Upper Provinces, was allotted camping grounds in the Rumnah (Hindi *rumnā*) or "royal preserved park" of a Hindu prince located outside Lucknow.[24]

The situation in the Far West was quite different, at least initially. In contrast to the core area where hunting facilities were fully integrated into the infrastructure of official travel, the famous road system of Rome was dedicated from the outset to the movement of foot soldiers and administrators. But with the fall of the Roman order in the West, Europe's infrastructure for official travel took on a new form, one that resembled that of the core area. Since the rulers could not live off local resources for long, they left their nominal capitals on annual circuits that required moves from one royal estate to another, that is, between villas commonly built near favored hunting grounds.[25] As previously noted, these hunting grounds were important economic resources for Frankish kings and many became exclusive preserves progressively enclosed and guarded to monopolize the rich resources of the forest that the itinerant court intensively exploited for short periods each year. The royal hunt was, therefore, an integral part of the political economy of the Frankish kingdoms and fully integrated with the royal court travel and with annual political events such as the grand assembly of nobles.[26]

Royal hunting can also be understood as a form of exploration, a means of familiarizing a ruler with his realm, and of discovering assets, problems, and possibilities.[27] The frequency with which the sources associate royal hunts with discovery argues that this expectation was common wisdom. This is evident in tales of hunters who "discover" their brilliant political futures in the field. Several classical sources relate that Hunnic "statehood" and its subsequent military expansion grew out of a hunt that led a party in pursuit of a deer in Scythian territory, thus launching the Huns on the course of empire.[28] This same theme reappears in the Oghuz legend in which the sons of Oghuz Qan go out hunting one day and "by good fortune" find three silver arrows and a golden bow, age-old symbols of rulership in the nomadic world.[29] This notion was still very much alive in the eighteenth century, when Nādir Shāh, the Turkmen conqueror of Iran (r. 1736–47), reputedly found, while out on a hunting expedition, the famed treasure of Temür (Tamerlane) and an inscription that foretold of its discoverer's rise to great power.[30]

Among the more concrete finds attributed to hunting excursions were discoveries of choice locales. Chinggis Qan, in Mongolian tradition, came across an auspicious locale marked by a single flourishing tree, which he decreed would become his burial ground.[31] Two rulers, a thirteenth-century prince of Volynia and a fifteenth-century sultan of Gujarat reportedly found the sites of their future capitals while on hunting expeditions.[32] Others, a Sasanid emperor and an Oghuz ruler, went out hunting and found, at least in legend, beautiful

Figure 16. Qianlong entering village near Mulan. Giuseppe Castiglione, 1757. RMN/Art Resource NY.

young maidens who became their consorts.[33] Again, the message, repeated in many forms, is that royal hunting was a profitable voyage of discovery. No wonder, then, that the hunt, chance discovery, special good fortune, and political power were consistently equated in the core area and in the steppe world.

Rulers, of course, also find problems on these tours. The Liao emperor Xingzong (r. 1031–55) encountered royal tombs that had fallen into disrepair and the Jin emperor Shizong (r. 1161–90) an incompetent magistrate.[34] Delhi sultan Fīrūz Shāh (r. 1351–88) is portrayed as learning much from hunting excursions. On one he discovers the need to construct a new palace, on another the need for a large canal, and on a third he encounters, by chance, a commoner who explains to him the deficiencies of the current methods of tax assessment and collection.[35]

Encounters of royal hunters with the populace are a very common theme in works of history and poetry; Sasanid emperors and ʿAbbāsid caliphs out on hunts meet and learn from their subjects.[36] This, to be sure, was a frequent literary device, like the prince going among his people in disguise; but such encounters did occur and these occasions could provide a prudent prince with useful information. Kangxi, while on a hunt, did in fact meet a subject wronged by his own officials and corrected the situation.[37] The hunt thus provided a plausible stage upon which ruler and commoner could meet and talk, where the king could show justice, kindness, humanity, and forgiveness. This was behavior expected of kings, and kings sometimes met expectations.[38]

In the above instances, one particular use of the hunt is highlighted by the source, most often for didactic purposes. On the ground, however, a royal hunt was never so restricted in its aims or functions; any hunting trip could easily accommodate political activity and, conversely, any trip, whatever its expressed purpose, could easily accommodate the chase. The Mamlūk sultan Nāṣir al-Dīn (r. 1309–40) hunted on his way to Mecca, as did Akbar when he visited holy sites in North India, and the Uzbek ruler ʿAbdallāh II (r. 1583–98) moved continuously and wherever he went he hunted.[39] Thus, in many instances it is difficult, perhaps meaningless, to distinguish a hunting expedition from an administrative round. They were, in point of fact, combined operations.

This is well documented in the Liao case. Qitan emperors had annual rounds that combined hunting trips with tours of inspection. Each of the four seasons saw the emperor hunting in a different region of his realm where he had camps, *nabo* in Chinese transcription. In the spring, the court was near the Sungari taking swans with raptors, following which there was a great feast. In summer he moved to Rehe, where he hunted ground game. In the fall he moved to another area of Rehe for the "tiger" season. In the winter, the royal hunt was combined with military practice. In all these movements the emperor was accompanied by officials of the state and accommodated in an elaborate and mobile encampment.[40] During these annual rounds, we know from the chronological table of imperial progresses in the Liao dynastic history, the Qitan rulers observed Chinese and native rites, attended animal combats and polo matches, inspected smelting and lumbering operations, visited markets, and watched grain harvesting and tree planting. While concentrated in the fall months, royal hunts took place throughout the entire year, interspersed with political, economic, and ceremonial activities.[41]

The Mongols, another nomadic people, conformed to this pattern in spirit if not in detail. Their rulers, from China to Iran, regularly conducted state business while hunting in the field; they made military decisions, received intelligence, dispatched messengers, rewarded princes, and then went back to the chase.[42] Since they traveled with such large staffs, they too had to separate themselves from their traveling camps (*ordo*) to hunt; the commotion caused by their following scared game away.[43]

While such governance systems might be expected of nomadic regimes, they are found among sedentary people as well. In a passage of his "Admonition" Vladimir Monomakh, prince of Kiev, says, "And now I relate to you, my children, my exertions as I toiled in travels and in hunts." What then follows is a lengthy catalog of his military and administrative activities as a prince.[44] For him, hunting and governance were inseparable. This well describes the situation in ancient China. Recent study of oracle bone inscriptions indicates that Shang rulers spent most of their time in annual rounds, hunting, and inspecting (*tianxing*).[45] In China, the institution of inspection tour/royal hunt, later called *xunshou* and *xunlie*, lasted for millennia and was most evident among dynasties of frontier or foreign origin.[46]

In the core area, too, this was the common practice, one attributed to model kings and followed by real princes. The *Visramiani* on one occasion has Moabad, mythical king of pre-Islamic Iran, say, "I am going to Zaul to hunt and attend the affairs of state," and later, relates that when Ramin succeeded his brother Moabad he "began to travel in all directions in his lands, to inquire into the affairs of state, to hunt and to tilt."[47] This is how historical chronicles later describe the rounds of Armenian and Georgian rulers who sally forth to hunt and inspect or to hunt and attend to local affairs.[48]

The political benefits of itinerancy were varied and substantial. Farrukhān, ruler of Ṭabaristān at the turn of the eighth century, used the hunt to visit his march wardens (*marzubān*) and to reestablish personal ties with local officials, while Lothair I (r. 840–55) went hunting to deprive vassals of their benefice for vacillation during his struggle for the Carolingian throne.[49] But royal hunts could serve more benign purposes as well. Mongolian qans sometimes used the occasion to pay social calls on high officials and courtesy calls on important constituents such as religious leaders, who exercised influence over their communities.[50]

The royal hunt, in truth, was an extremely flexible political tool. Our best picture of the operation of these hunting/inspection tours and their underlying political uses comes from Turkestan and India.[51]

The ruler of Khiva, Muḥammad Raḥīm (r. 1806–25), we know from Nikolai Muraviev's eyewitness testimony, was perpetually on the move, nominally hunting; with his large entourage he moved between "fortified country houses" in the desert visiting Turkmen tribes with whom he regularly exchanged "presents."[52] Most certainly, these hunting rounds were used as a pretext to reassert or, more accurately, renegotiate his tenuous sovereignty over his turbulent tribal subjects. The hunting guise was crucial because the ruler, if confronted with resistance or recalcitrance, could simply move on, ostensibly seeking out better "hunting" possibilities, without any loss of face.

In the subcontinent, Mughal rulers were also constantly on the move. Indeed, such progresses were central to their strategy of rule. Stephen Blake has established that between 1556 and 1734 the Mughal court was on tour almost 40 percent of the time. And when they went out they did so in force, traveling with an official and unofficial entourage numbering somewhere between 150,000 and 200,000 individuals of every description, occupation, and station. Not surprisingly, as Blake has further shown, when the emperor was on a progress, the population of the capital dropped precipitously.[53]

Consequently, when the Dutch factor van den Broecke says that Jahāngīr spent "a year in Gujarat in hunting," we should understand that he was on an inspection tour.[54] The pace of these tours was typically slow because there was much to engage the attention of the ruler, some of it involving humans and some involving cheetahs.[55] The general pattern of circulation among major cities of the realm was always punctuated by many side trips connected with hunting opportunities and government business.[56]

Abū'l Faẓl, in his works on Akbar, makes very explicit connections between the hunt and governance, ideas that he attributes to his master. In his handbook, the *Āʿīn-i Akbarī*, he says that Akbar "always makes hunting a means of increasing his knowledge, and besides, uses hunting parties as occasions to inquire, without having first given notice of his coming, into the condition of the people and the army." More specifically, the emperor used the hunt to examine questions of taxation, landholding, and official corruption. "Short-sighted and shallow observers," Abū'l Faẓl concludes, "think that his majesty has no other object in view but hunting, but the wise and experienced know that he pursues higher aims."[57] In his biography of Akbar, the *Akbharnāmah*, Abū'l Faẓl elaborates on this theme. In one entry he says that while Akbar's camp was set up in a hunting mode, "yet he constantly engaged in state affairs, in the conquering of countries, in promoting and exalting the loyal, and in casting down the evil minded and the insincere and in testing everyone's merits." He adds that Akbar's "true intent in miscellaneous matters, such as hunting, etc., is to acquaint himself with the condition of the people without the intermediary of interested persons and hypocrites, and to take proper measures for the protection of mankind."[58]

Akbar, despite Abū'l Faẓl's claims, had no monopoly on this insight; many other rulers in India understood these possibilities.[59] Indeed, in the core area and beyond, the royal hunt was a vital instrument of governance and, as we shall now see, a circuit court in the full sense of these words.

Pursuing Pleasures

Hunting merged with varied governmental functions, but some political benefits emerged directly from the chase itself. The provision of pleasure and entertainment was an essential duty of royal courts and hunting was a major attraction. And while elite hunting in premodern times may have been much more than a simple recreation, a recreation it was. Most certainly, hunting was for the elite a passion, an escape and relaxation.[60] As such, the opportunity to hunt became itself a dispensable commodity, one that had to be earned like any other reward.

The deep personal attraction many felt for the chase is repeatedly proclaimed by rulers, poets, and chroniclers across the continent.[61] As Chaowang Yuanji, son of the Tang founder, phrased it: "I would rather not eat for three days than not hunt for one."[62] In Europe, elite hunting was treated in literature as a sublime earthly pleasure, a metaphor for the pursuit of love.[63] It was a high-intensity experience and, as Plutarch realized, it was habit-forming, even addictive, and princes so inclined pursued this pleasure obsessively, at times to the exclusion of everything else.[64]

Although the dangers of overindulgence were recognized, it was also held that hunting was a helpful and healthful diversion for rulers and others bearing heavy burdens. Niẓām al-Mulk says that the chase is a relaxation, a recreation that relieves the anxieties of kingship, part of a well-balanced life along with charitable and religious pursuits.[65] Frederick II conveys the very same message: hunting and hawking are necessary for those preoccupied with affairs of state, and he further enjoins rulers "to find relief in the pleasures of the chase."[66] Or, as Rust'haveli frames the matter, kings from time to time must be "careless of Fate."[67] Such prescriptions were unhesitatingly accepted by elites who saw in hunting a principal means of diversion, and a legitimate source of relaxation.[68]

There were, additionally, mundane reasons for mounting a hunt. Shāh Jahān once took to the countryside because his residence at the time, Akbarabād, exhibited signs of pestilence, while Jahāngīr fled to the field to escape the palace during preparations for the New Year (Nawruz) celebrations and, on another occasion, went hunting to avoid irritating petitioners.[69] But whatever the motives, a royal hunt was normally intended to be a pleasurable experience for sovereign and guests, and this required not only "good shooting" but appropriate, pleasant surroundings.

Hunting locales were sometimes chosen because of climate.[70] And once in the field, whatever the weather, comfort and elegance were still considerations. In fiction, thoughtful kings provided guests with pavilions, couches, attendants, and the like.[71] In history they did as well. When a Persian embassy reached Siam in the late seventeenth century, they were taken on several hunts, rode the king's elephants, given "ringside" seats, housed in sumptuous quarters, and always well looked after.[72]

In some cases these facilities were temporary and transportable. Qubilai hunted in great style, in brocade-lined pavilions and tents conveniently spaced as rest stops; even the animal keepers and their animals were so accommodated.[73]

When the Delhi sultan Muḥammad ibn Tughluq went to the field, according to an informant of al-ʿUmarī, a fourteenth-century Arab encyclopedist, he was accompanied by 100,000 horsemen and 200 elephants, and he took with him "four wooden palaces [*quṣūr khashab*]" carried by 800 camels. These were, he says, collapsible buildings, two stories in height and richly decorated, that could be assembled in the field for the comfort of the ruler and his party.[74] Later on, the Mughals hunted tigers in comfort and security from a well-appointed tent on a mobile platform.[75]

James Forbes rightly describes the royal hunts of the Mughals as dazzling affairs: "Their encampments . . . were extensive and magnificent, there they entertained their friends in a sumptuous manner during the continuance of the hunt, which sometimes lasted several weeks. Such [he continues] probably has been the custom in Persia and Arabia, from the time of Nimrod to the present day."[76] And hunts like these required not only tents and furniture but also fencing, enclosures, gates, and separate quarters for the harem.[77] While the equipment and transport used in moving a royal hunting party was less costly than the permanent establishments, it was nonetheless a major expense. We know from van den Broecke's testimony that the treasure bequeathed by Akbar as "given in the royal account books" included the category "Articles used for traveling: tents, *shamianus* [awnings], *kanaits* [cloth enclosures] of gold and silver cloth, embroidered velvets, etc." These were valued at 99 *lack*, nominally 100,000 rupees, slightly more than the valuation of 83 *lack* placed on the total of his weaponry, both traditional and gunpowder.[78]

Beyond the transportable facilities, of course, there were the many permanent hunting parks and lodges. Gagik, an Armenian princeling, had built circa 900 a complex of pleasure palaces overlooking the Araxes River, where deer, boar, and onagers were "all ready for the pleasures of the chase."[79] A water feature seems to have been mandatory for a proper pleasure dome. In 1237 the Mongolian qaghan Ögödei had a hunting villa, called Gegen Chaghan, "Bright and White" in Mongolian (Qiejian chahan, in Chinese transcription), built about seventy Chinese miles north of the capital, Qara Qorum, which early emperors visited with some regularity.[80] From Persian sources, we know that this "pleasure ground [*mutanazzah*]" was located along a series of lakes. The centerpiece was a villa (*kusht*) furnished with embroideries and carpets and with a banqueting hall full of elegant vases and utensils. In front of this facility were the pools used for hawking and fowling.[81] The Mughals, too, had such a pleasure ground on a lake located just outside the city of Ajmīr, which they used as a base for hunting of all kinds. This is the famous Dawlah Bāgh, "Garden of Fortune," that Roe calls a "Garden of Pleasure."[82] With such facilities, courts moved easily between city and country.

The hunting lodges of later European history exemplify this concern for comfort. No longer essential infrastructure for travel and administration, these lodges became another form of display, and over time achieved vast proportions that required heavy investment. Monumentality came to dominate; for instance, Francis I of France (r. 1515–47), a keen huntsman, built a "lodge" along the Loire of 440 rooms, which itself was enclosed within a walled forest some twenty miles in circumference, the early modern European equivalent of the ancient paradise. Such establishments, designed to impress, afforded ample opportunity to fashion large gardens and to furnish and decorate accommodations with expensive wares from goblets to paintings.[83] The king's guests could hunt in well-stocked forests and on artificially created water courses and could do so in fancy dress, with elaborate hunting equipment, and in the expectation of success. A well-presented royal hunt should be comfortable and comforting, and should, as Munshī repeatedly states, offer the guests a taste of the good life.[84]

Such a life naturally demanded good food and drink. Poetic references to the hunt from across Eurasia assume that the chase and the party were synonymous: eat, drink, hunt, and make merry is the uniform theme.[85] This is particularly true of the core area, where Sasanid and Muslim art closely associate the notion of paradise, whether in this life or the next, with hunting and banqueting.[86] These expectations of lavish hospitality were often met. Persian kings, before and after Islam, provided hunting feasts, as did Mongolian qans, Hindu rajahs, Manchu emperors, and Romanov tsars.[87]

Communal, and sometimes very heavy, consumption of alcohol was also a norm. Niẓām al-Mulk, advisor to the Seljuqs, speaks of Sasanid monarchs' penchant for combining the chase with womanizing and drinking, and warns that too much of the latter can bring ruin to the state.[88] But despite these concerns, and Islamic restrictions on alcohol, Muslim courts, the Ghaznavids and others, went to the field well supplied with wine.[89] This was such a frequent occurrence that the royal hunt became identified with good times, even wild times, and viewed as a large, outdoor floating party.[90] From some this drew censure, but for others such stories only added to the allure of the royal hunt.

In this environment, other forms of entertainment were expected and provided. The chase, itself an amusement, could readily be combined with others. Music, of course, was a standard accompaniment. Mencius speaks of "rounds" of entertainment in which the chase, drinking, and music were featured.[91] By Han times royal hunts were routinely followed by a kind of dinner theater, an elaborate banquet at which musicians, dancing girls, actors, and dwarfs performed.[92] In medieval Georgia, where the chase was a prime index of pleasure and a way to celebrate other joyful events, music was an essential adjunct.[93]

Music and hunting were easily combined with refined, sedate intellectual pursuits. ʿAbbāsid caliphs played board games (*nard*) to music while in the field, and in the Heian era (794–1185), hawking expeditions of the Japanese court were conducted at designated, prepared sites and became occasions for poetry readings, music, dancing, and the display of fancy dress.[94] For the more robust and active, the chase, as it was pursued by the Mongols in Iran, was an occasion for polo games, horse racing, and javelin-throwing contests.[95] For elites, hunting was an entertainment that operated on many levels; it was something to do, and something to talk about, at times quite incessantly.[96] Furthermore, we should not forget that the chase was a spectator sport. Audiences were welcomed and oftentimes encouraged and comfortably accommodated. Mencius remarks, disapprovingly, that in his day elite hunting expeditions might have "a thousand carriages in attendance."[97] This was because the great hunts were, in the words of the historian Ban Gu, "the world's greatest spectacle and ultimate sight."[98] Accordingly, as a Chinese prose poem of the second century B.C.E. says, "lovely maidens and fair princesses" always accompanied the royal hunt and provided an appreciative audience for the heroic huntsmen.[99] In later centuries, Manchu and Mughal emperors set up pavilions and platforms so that spectators, especially court ladies, could better view the climax of their ring hunts. The audience was close enough to watch the proceedings and knowledgeable enough to acknowledge individual feats of skill and daring.[100] Many early modern European monarchs, Francis I, for instance, encouraged spectators at royal hunts. Like their counterparts in the rest of Eurasia, these hunts were elaborately stage-managed to ensure success and to impress and entertain onlookers, who were often provided with seating, some in the form of grandstands, from which they could view and admire the "hunt."[101] Access to such facilities was the equivalent of box seat tickets to a World Cup final or to a gala opera premiere, a statement of connections, of participation in the pleasures of the good life.

Favors

The dispensation of royal favor was an essential tool in the political culture of Eurasia, and the royal hunt was one of the major methods of doing so. This could take many forms, but the distribution of the king's bag was perhaps most common. To some extent, this might be seen as a perpetuation of very ancient practices among hunting cultures, in which the harvest of animals was shared out to the participants in the chase, a practice that survived in the steppe until recent times. The Turkic epic tradition expects such behavior and treats fighting over kills as the signal of a break between comrades.[102] In medieval Mongolia, the ancient custom of *sirolγa* required each hunter to share his catch with others, even strangers who chance by.[103]

In complex, politically organized societies, monarchs often behaved in like fashion. Such largesse sometimes took the form of a collective reward in which many benefited. Cyrus the Great, in Xenophon's biography, divides his bag of game among his followers as a demonstration of generosity, an attribute ascribed to superior men everywhere.[104] In the Mamlūk era, game taken by notables was regularly redistributed to underlings as a sign of approval and favor.[105] Great princes, of course, could do no less. Shāh ʿAbbās allotted shares of game killed in large ring hunts to participating troopers, and Awrangzīb sent shares to all his officers of state.[106] These acts might even become institutionalized; the Manchu emperors in the early eighteenth century annually sent the Jesuit missionaries in their employ a plentiful supply of game as a New Year's gift.[107]

Presentations of this kind could also be personalized, sent as a special favor to a particular individual. Al-Nāṣir Muḥammad, the Mamlūk sultan, saw fit in 1320 to honor his client Abū'l Fidā with a gift of gazelles caught with falcons, and a governor of Shirvān in 1568 sent a wild boar as a presentation to a factor of the English Moscovy Company.[108] Even more honor was attached to gifts of game personally killed by a prince; Jahāngīr, a minor Hindu princeling in eighteenth-century Orissa, and Catherine the Great all made gifts of such game to friends, family, and foreign dignitaries, and all took pains to inform the recipients that it was downed by the royal hand.[109]

Honors of this nature were subject to considerable refinement to show degrees of favor. The game presented might be the first kill of the hunt, suitably slaughtered and dressed, signaling great esteem, or most highly prized and individualized, joints of cooked meat could be sent from the king's own table to a favored few.[110] These were gestures understood and recognized across Eurasia and across time, signs of respect that transcended religious and cultural boundaries. It was an international language regularly used by royal hunters to communicate intentions to retainers, foreign dignitaries, and their own subjects.

The royal hunt also produced opportunities for charity, another attribute of sovereignty and majesty. Princes used the proceeds of the chase to show concern for their largest constituency, the general populace, and more commonly, the poorest among them. This could be done in a variety of ways. The Seljuq sultan Malik Shāh had the custom of giving a dinar as alms for every animal downed with his bow.[111] Among the nomads, a ruler might organize a ring hunt to provide winter food supplies for his poorer followers.[112] Elites sometimes used market mechanisms for the distribution: in early Armenia, it was the custom of nobles to trade game for fish from the children of commoners and to do so on very generous terms, and Mughal emperors sometimes sold their edible game on the open market and gave the money to the poor.[113] More common, however, were direct presentations of the game itself. These offerings typically involved a certain amount of staging to show off the ruler and his retainers in a public and positive light. On several occasions Jahāngīr donated his catch to the needy; this was undertaken by his own court officials, who once fed some 200 people.[114] Shāh Jahān, on the other hand, directed that all the game he killed during a certain hunt be cooked with rice in a "huge copper cauldron . . . and served to the poor." To ensure visibility, this was done at the tomb of a Muslim saint.[115]

Rulers used the hunt to dispense favor and food but it was also a vehicle for dispensing opportunity. It was a stage upon which to display one's skills and therefore one's potential value to the royal person. Many times this chance to be seen and to shine was directly linked to the hunt itself. Most obviously, the royal hunt provided an occasion for underlings and guests to impress a prince with their hunting skills. This not only involved making dazzling shots or bringing down much game, but also demonstrating ability in handling men and animals.[116] In the Oghuz epics, "unknowns" who displayed such skills regularly became accepted members of the qan's retinue.[117]

History, too, records such success stories. During the Han royal hunts, the emperor routinely rewarded the successful with "gold and silk" or favorable notice that was particularly helpful in advancing military careers.[118] Better yet, one might even save the life of the monarch. According to Diodorus of Sicily, Tiribazus, a lowly servitor, killed two lions that were attacking the Achaemenid emperor Artaxerxes II, and was elevated to the status of "friend" of the shah, launching him on a career of power and influence.[119]

Other talents could be revealed on the hunt. Körgüz, the powerful Mongolian governor of Khurāsān in the 1240s, began his career as a stirrup holder for a low-level official attached to the retinue of Jochi, Chinggis Qan's eldest son. While on a hunt, Körgüz, suddenly called upon to perform certain secretarial tasks, excelled in their execution, greatly pleasing his prince, who became his sponsor.[120] In patrimonial regimes, in which personal ties are all-important, recognition is the first essential step in social or political advancement. And for the prince, the opportunity to manipulate such ambitions and aspirations was the way to acquire a following and reinforce loyalties, that is, to forge and define his "political party."

To do this successfully, his party needed collective experiences that built up collective identities. Hunts themselves provided this in a number of ways, most obviously the comradeship engendered by shared danger and success. This same end could also be attained through celebrations of military or political victories through which the ruler communicates the message that "we won, we were successful." Cyrus the Great; Saladin; Queen Tʿamar; ʿAlā al-Dīn, the Delhi sultan (r. 1296–1316); Shāh Ismāʿīl, the Ṣafavid founder (r. 1501–24); and Jahāngīr all celebrated military triumphs with chases, sometimes lasting a month or longer.[121] Here was an opportunity to recall and share personal experiences, elaborate, and commemorate a collective achievement and to impress a uniform and satisfying version of events into the minds of all participants.

Like the granting of robes, badges, and titles, inclusion in royal hunting activities was a gesture of approval and trust, an overture, a recognition of one's utility and a call upon one's loyalty.[122] Such a gesture might not even involve going to the field, but could be conveyed by an invitation to inspect a ruler's hunting establishments, a statement of pride and of hospitality.[123]

Most often, of course, the ruler's invitation was for participation in a hunt. This was always considered a very high honor and an indication of personal and political favor. For example, when Abū'l Fidā's father was invited to Cairo by the Mamlūk sultan for the hunting season, he was overcome with joy and gratitude.[124] This was so because such invitations always signaled a measure of intimacy with the seat of power. A Han official with free access to Shanglin park was someone to be reckoned with, and a Mughal retainer built up his prestige by recalling that he had eaten with Humāyūn after a memorable hunt.[125] This intimacy, however contrived and controlled, was consciously cultivated by rulers, who realized that friendly competition with servitors in chess, or polo, or hunting, a kind of temporary, provisional equality, did not diminish royal prestige but enhanced kingly reputations for benevolence. This, in any event, was wisdom Arab writers attributed to model Sasanid emperors.[126]

And beyond forging the all-important personal political ties, the hunt celebrated and cemented the formation of wider political alliances. Once Tʿamar and her consort David Soslan concluded a military agreement with a minor Muslim prince, the principals repaired to the countryside, where they spent a week "feasting and carousing, exchanging presents, hunting and watching games."[127] The royal hunt was often employed as a means of coopting rivals or soothing ruffled feathers. Lazar Pʿarpecʿi, writing in the late fifth century, imputes to Yazdagird I (r. 399–421) the hope that the nobility of eastern Armenia, recently and reluctantly incorporated into the Sasanid elite, "will become accustomed and attached to our religion [Zoroastrianism] by continuous mutual discourse and friendly acquaintance in the pleasures of the hunt and in games that will take place between them."[128] By starting with the chase and games, the shah intended to show the Armenians that there was already much common ground between them and their Iranian masters. On a more modest scale, Bahadūr Shāh, Mughal emperor (r. 1707–12), made a point of hunting with the sons of a defeated rival to ease tensions and to reintegrate the opposition.[129]

Sometimes this technique was forced and unproductive. In 1598, ʿAbdullāh Khān, ruler of the Uzbeks, had a reconciliation with his son on a hunting expedition. In this instance it did not last, but as a public relations gesture it can certainly be viewed as the premodern equivalent of the forced handshake in front of the camera and the obligatory pledge of future cooperation.[130]

The royal hunt was constantly used in this manner. In medieval Europe the chase followed the resolution of political crises and therefore served as a pointed lesson in what Janet Nelson calls "the virtues of collaboration." Thus, in Carolingian times, the royal hunt was mounted after the annual assembly of nobles, always a scene of aristocratic friction and posturing.[131] The Georgian nobility, equally fractious, held such reconciliation hunts often to solemnize and advertise political concord among rival Georgian princely houses.[132] This was the case because the royal hunt was an effective way of showing trust and a good test of professed amity; here former enemies interacted while carrying lethal weapons and accompanied by armed retainers.

If access to the royal hunt was a way of signaling favor and the desire for concord or reconciliation, then exclusion was an unmistakable sign of disfavor, in some cases tantamount to a breaking off of relations, whether personal or diplomatic. To be excluded was a very serious business for it meant denial of rewards: access to entertainments, opportunity to network to improve upon a career, and lastly, and often overlooked, the economic support of the state. This is so because while on a royal hunt, those on the guest list were receiving rations and quarters, sometimes at levels much higher than many could afford on their own.[133] For anyone entertained by the king on an extended hunt, this represented a great savings. In most premodern regimes "pay" was not usually or exclusively in the form of a regular or stipulated salary, but in a series of grants, gifts, and banquets, and the royal hunt, a mobile court, a floating party, was a major vehicle for delivering such rewards. Thus, for those excluded, this was a cut in pay, to say nothing of a loss of face and favor. It was by such means that kings courted support and penalized opposition.

The Court Out-of-Doors

Court life, East and West, North and South, was a series of theatricals and spectacles, some private and some public. Though variable in character, this unending round of banquets, state receptions, entertainments, tournaments, religious observances, executions, and hunts had the same essential purpose: to display the virtues of a prince, his piety, wealth, generosity, skill, intelligence, daring, his firmness and ruthlessness as well as his kindness and mercy.[134] As starring vehicles

Figure 17. Qianlong receiving Tartar horses during hunt at Mulan. Giuseppe Castiglione, 1757. RMN/Art Resource NY.

for princely performers, these spectacles were carefully crafted to ensure dramatic effect and a proper, that is to say, an inevitable outcome: the prince always succeeds, he always rewards the deserving, punishes the guilty, helps the needy, and brings down the game. His inevitable success is his good fortune, his charisma, the centerpiece of his majesty, and the foundation of his legitimacy.

The royal court and the royal hunt are both examples of political theater, and the show was taken on the road for the enjoyment of the provinces. The stationary indoor court and the mobile outdoor court were complementary in many respects. The former placed emphasis on the display of the products of culture while the latter focused on the wonders of nature.[135] But in other respects their functions were identical. Both were seats of government, both sources of entertainment, both sites of celebration, both means of fashioning solidarity, and both prime measures of the good life. Accordingly, princely control of access to either theater was essential.

One striking commonality was the recurrent role of processions. The scale differed, as did the audience, but the purpose was the same. As Braudel rightfully remarks, for people of means there are only "two ways of living and facing the world: display or discretion."[136] Wealthy merchants in premodern societies might opt for discretion, but for ruling elites display was a crucial part of politics. The chase was an appropriate royal activity, Cummins argues, because of the "possibility it offers of the visual magnificence by which kingly and aristocratic dignity may be demonstrated." They may be set apart from common folk by divine wisdom, but "their superiority must be made clear by pomp, pageant, ceremony, procession and other physical glories."[137]

That the royal hunt was such a procession emerges clearly from Kaempfer's descriptions of cavalcades under the Ṣafavids. According to the German physician there were three types of royal processions conducted out-of-doors: brief rides the shah took with his entourage about the capital, grander progresses between major cities, and an intermediate form used when he went out to hunt or to receive foreign envoys.[138] Then as now, such diplomatic receptions were always solemn state occasions closely associated with processions, precedence, and ceremony.

The royal hunt was effective in this regard because it was attractive to a wide audience and, like the purpose of processions indoors, those outdoors functioned as a theatrical spotlight that carefully and subtly focused attention on the star, the royal hunter. It was a great and glittering parade accompanied by considerable fanfare, which had great spectator appeal in premodern Europe.[139] But it was not only Renaissance courts that went to the field in finery; when the Türk qaghan Tong Yabghu went hunting north of Kucha, circa 630, he did so with thousands of troopers, all sporting elaborate hairdos and uniforms of satin, brocade, and fur.[140]

Animals occupied a central place in these proceedings. The Siamese king in the 1680s toured and hunted with a procession of elephants, an honor guard, and a band.[141] Proper mounts were all-important. Fine horses predominated in most of Eurasia, but in their home range to ride in state or to the hunt meant to ride on elephants suitably caparisoned and decorated.[142] Equally visible in these parades were the animals of the chase. Kings required quantity and quality in everything, be it dress, musicians, or hunting hounds. Rust'haveli appropriately populates the hunts of his fictional rulers with uncountable numbers of hawks and hounds.[143] John Sanderson, in Constantinople in the late sixteenth century, describes the spectacle when the "Great Turk" left the city with his "doggs well manned and in their best apparrell . . . and . . . his hawkes by horsemen carried in great number."[144] Ṣafavid shahs also displayed their huntsmen, hawks, and hounds on progresses, and European nobles did the same.[145]

While most elites possessed falcons and hunting dogs as markers of status, only the most powerful could afford menageries and zoos full of exotic animals. These were generally housed at court or at least in the capital for the edification and entertainment of guests. This method of creating majesty is very ancient. Pharaohs had large zoological collections that contained local as well as exotic species from Africa and the East—bears, snakes, elephants, rhinoceroses, and so on.[146] Later on, these menageries were normally kept in hunting parks and paradises from Han China to Sasanid Iran.

The practice, despite occasional pious assaults on the extravagance of zoos, was continued under the ʿAbbāsid caliphate.[147] The Byzantine embassy that visited the caliphal palace in 917 first passed through special quarters where various exotic animals, well trained, ate from their hands.[148] The Fāṭimids and Ṣafavids had extensive collections of strange beasts and exotic birds which they, too, eagerly showed to distinguished visitors.[149] Even the Moscovite tsar Boris Godunov (r. 1598–1605) had a menagerie that included a large lion.[150] Perhaps the best royal zoo in early modern times was found in the Ottoman capital, Istanbul, which contained "many beasts and fowles of Affrica and India."[151]

Such beasts were valuable political capital because they documented a ruler's reach, his contacts with distant, storied lands, and his ability to attract gifts and goods from far-off princes. This constituted tangible evidence that such a ruler was a major player on a very great stage. And, of course, these menageries, fixtures at the court and capital, could also be taken on the road during hunts and tours to generate spectators and enhance majesty.

Strabo was aware that in India kings held processions with many elephants, four-horse chariots, troops, "and tame bison [aurochs], leopards and lions and numbers of variegated and sweet-voiced birds."[152] In later centuries, Seljuq, Ottoman, and Mughal rulers all traveled with tamed wild beasts "for parade," as Bernier terms the practice.[153] Frederick II typically traveled in state with a menagerie of elephants, camels, giraffes, apes, lions, leopards, bears, and birds. On one occasion in 1241 he arrived at a monastery, surely to the consternation of the monks, with an animal entourage of one elephant, twenty-four camels, and five leopards.[154] Naturally, and as intended, these strange beasts, gifts from the Egyptian Ayyūbids, excited great attention in southern Italy, attracting crowds like the circus coming to town.

Processions and parades, whether indoors or out, require order and rules of precedence. The royal hunt, like the court indoors, functioned as a training ground, a place where behavior was modified and courtly manners inculcated. All participants, even servitors, were expected to deport themselves properly at court and during a hunting expedition.[155] Furthermore, invitations to royal hunts, like those to royal courts, were generally not polite queries of interest but command performances. Under Shāh ʿAbbās, invitations were frequently tests of loyalty, and the failure to appear considered as an open break and treated accordingly.[156]

During the hunt itself, and most particularly the ring hunt, the ruler occupied center stage. In the early Mongolian empire, a strict order of precedence was followed once the ring was formed and fenced: first, of course, was the qaghan and his party, followed by the princes, military commanders, ministers of state, and finally the common soldiers.[157] Later, in Yuan times, the emperor entered the ring on an elephant and shot the first arrow; this was the signal that others might begin.[158] The same procedure was followed in Manchu hunts. Kangxi entered the ring, initiated the killing, and indicated who should join in. At the end, a horn sounded on his signal and all killing was halted.[159] The practice in India and Iran was identical. The emperor and his party remained some distance away until the ring was properly formed, and when all was ready the sovereign entered with a select company and began to shoot, followed by high dignitaries according to rank and standing, and lastly the common soldiers.[160]

As a particular favor to an honored guest, a king might defer to another. The Ṣafavid Ṭahmāsp did this for the Mughal ruler Humāyūn when he was in Iran in 1530.[161] But such deference was purely a kingly prerogative; thus, a falconer in a ring is never to release his hawk without the king's command, even if the quarry is near. To a royal hunter like Rudra Deva, this was a matter of high consequence, a rule of propriety that could "never be broken."[162] It was, in short, neither nice, nor wise, to upstage the king.

The hunt thus reflected court hierarchies and precedence, whether indoors or out-of-doors, defined the elite in a public and quite unmistakable manner; this provided guidance on who was moving up and who down and therefore guidance on how best to please the monarch.

While heads of state always had a certain latitude in their behavior and conduct, courts and hunts for the most part operated according to protocol and precedent. In the Turko-Mongolian world these precedents were usually ascribed to Chinggis Qan. In Central Asia as well as Mughal India, the Mongolian ruler's protocols were invoked on all matters relating to the hunt, from entrance into ring to the sharing of the bag. Any violation of these procedures was severely punished, again according to practices ascribed to Chinggis Qan.[163] There is, in fact, a very revealing episode in Rashīd al-Dīn treating such matters: when Odchigin Noyan, Chinggis Qan's youngest brother, disobeyed protocol and "did not go straight to the hunting circle [*jerge*]" as ordered, "he was not permitted in the *ordo* [of Chinggis Qan] for seven days."[164] Here the equation is unmistakable: if you do not behave properly in the court out-of-doors, you will not be admitted to the court indoors.

For the Muslim courts of the Middle Ages, the protocols proper to the royal hunt were attributed to the ancient Persians, protocols that were embraced and transmitted by the caliphate. These governed the deportment of the king and his interaction with his retinue, servants, and court ladies, precedence for the hunters and beasts of prey, access to the prey and the division of the spoils.[165] The point here, as in the case of Chinggis Qan's precedents, is not the historicity of the transmission, but the more important fact that the royal hunt in the Middle East, as elsewhere in Eurasia, was ordered by an elaborate set of norms, rituals, and usages, and that violations of protocols were severely punished and long remembered.[166]

Over time, there was a tendency toward elaboration and greater complexity. In the medieval West, elite hunting became increasingly encased in procedure, ceremony, and etiquette. As reflected in the many manuals of the hunt produced during this period, these entailed the provision of food, drink, and creature comforts for both hunters and spectators, strict rules of engagement that broke the chase down into distinct stages, the development of special circumlocutions and vocabulary that enabled participants to discuss results politely, that is, without discomfiting those less successful and, finally, elaborate regulations for slaughtering, distributing, preparing, and consuming the catch, particularly the stag, Europe's most prized game.[167]

But the royal hunt, with its protocols and rules of precedence, was not solely about formal procedures. Both at court and at the chase manners and etiquette also came into play; in some cases it was about "exceeding" established norms in shows of graciousness and deference. In Mughal India, when invited into the ring, it was considered extremely polite to enter the enclosure with only a few arrows, thereby implying one's willingness to let others claim most of the game. As a high honor, Jahāngīr once gave such a self-effacing hunter fifty arrows out of his own quiver.[168] These gestures, deemed worthy of permanent record, allowed both parties to display their innate generosity of spirit.

Acts such as these were not, however, spontaneous but carefully nurtured by court cultures across the continent. Royal courts, wherever they were situated—feudal Europe, bureaucratic China, or imperial Mongolia—always imposed standards of behavior on courtiers-*cum*-government officials. Adherence to these codes was encouraged by very similar methods of conditioning: repeated censure and praise, punishment and rewards, inclusion and exclusion.[169] In premodern societies the virtues of "good breeding" were instilled in elites by various means and in various settings. These ranged from the discipline of the drill field, to the deportment required by ceremony, to the proper manner of eating at the king's table. The royal hunt as the court out-of-doors played an integral part in this effort.[170] It, too, entailed military discipline, ritual activity, orders of precedence, and "sportsmanship," codes of behavior that guided relationships among gentlemen and gentlewomen; and it, too, provided, like the court indoors, a mechanism for inculcating the habits of obedience in all the king's men.

None of this, of course, precluded factionalism, intrigue, and infighting at court, either for the king's favor or directed against his interests. This brings us to the final proof offered in support of the argument that the royal hunt was simply the court out-of-doors, for the hunt, too, was an arena of intense political struggle.

High politics and elite hunting interacted on many different levels. In some instances, rulers sought solitude in hunting as a means of escape from pressures and as a time for reflection, a time for making important decisions.[171] Since it was hard to deny a ruler his right to hunt, this search for solitude was a standard excuse for isolating oneself for whatever reason, personal or state. In the Umayyad and ʿAbbāsid caliphates, and in the Byzantine and Mughal empires, rulers, their heirs, and rivals undertook lengthy, and timely, hunting excursions as a means of escaping court intrigues and dangers.[172] On several occasions, Mughal emperors went on hunts to provide themselves with alibis while their agents dispatched opponents within their own family.[173]

Court politics, obviously, spilled over into the royal hunt. The young Catherine II, in the years before her accession, soon apprehended that high politics were conducted outside as well as inside and that the chase, which she did not particularly enjoy, provided an excellent occasion to gather political intelligence.[174] The hunt was informative and it was dangerous, the scene of very high-stakes politics where enemies could be eliminated and rulers toppled.

Hunting and political conspiracy are frequently linked. In one Oghuz epic, a son's unauthorized pursuit of game is equated with plotting patricide.[175] Rivals of Herod, king of Judea, planted a rumor that two of his sons planned to kill him on a hunt, a rumor the king believed.[176] The hunt was a time of vulnerability, a good time to strike at a sovereign, and Jahāngīr, for one, was well aware of this.[177] Indeed, conspiracies, blood purges, and assassinations were a recurrent feature of the royal hunt, as the following brief survey reveals.

In Inner Asian history, one of the most famous of these episodes occurred in 209 B.C.E., when Maodun killed his father during a hunt, seized power within the Xiongnu confederation, and established himself as their first *shanyu* or emperor.[178] Somewhat more opaque is the Chinese report that in 168 C.E. the ruler of Sule or Kashgar, a Han client state, was killed by his uncle with an arrow shot during a hunt. The uncle, the text laconically concludes, "made himself king."[179] More certainly, the Qarluq ruler of Almaliq, on the Ili River, while occupied with the chase, was surprised and murdered by rivals in the early thirteenth century.[180] Kings went down, but so did their enemies. A Tibetan king of the seventh century and a Khivan ruler of the early nineteenth century both used royal hunts to isolate and kill opponents.[181]

Similar patterns prevailed elsewhere. Assassination attempts were twice made against the Delhi sultan ʿAlā al-Dīn while he was out hunting and both failed.[182] The hunt also served as a locale for settling disputes among officials. Near the Indus River in the early 1330s, Ibn Baṭṭuṭah relates that one official of the Delhi sultanate assassinated another, his bitter rival, by luring him out to the countryside and then, sounding the alarm for a lion attack, caught him off guard and easily dispatched him.[183] Further west, a Parthian ruler, several Georgian kings, and a number of high-ranking Armenian officials were eliminated during the chase.[184] In the Muslim world, an unsuccessful attempt was made on the life of the Seljuq sultan Sanjar (r. 1118–57) in his hunting grounds, while in the thirteenth century, the attempts against the ruler of Māzandarān and a Mamlūk sultan successfully struck home.[185]

In Europe, particularly in the Middle Ages, the hunt was the scene of violent political clashes. In Merovingian times several kings were assassinated while others rid themselves of plotting family members on hunting excursions.[186] William II (r. 1087–1100), son of William the Conqueror, was killed on the hunt by an arrow shot by one of his own men.[187] Whether this was an accident or an assassination is not clear. Nor is the death of the Byzantine emperor John II (r. 1118–43); the "official" version of events ascribes his death to wounds suffered on a boar hunt in Cilicia, Lesser Armenia, but other sources and modern scholarship assert his death was at the hands of political foes.[188]

This, of course, points up one of the distinct advantages of the hunt for acts of political murder: it could plausibly be disguised as an accident, one of those tragedies so closely associated with the chase. For another, hunting grounds were the one place where almost everyone in the company of the ruler went about armed. Inside a palace, wielding a bow would raise immediate alarm. But there is an even more fundamental reason why the hunt was the scene of so much political violence: the royal hunt was a political prize well worth seizing, for one could not be a creditable prince without such an establishment. In any event, since rulers usually hunted with their advisers, allies, and guardsmen, the royal hunt would have to be dealt with sooner or later. Consequently, in the core area, the seizure of the royal hunt had a psychological effect similar to that in modern politics of seizing the capital city. In short, whether convened indoors or taken out-of-doors for the chase, the royal court was an obvious and natural site for a coup d'état.

11

Intimidation

Initiating Warriors

In a Parthian account of Mani's last days, the Sasanid ruler Bahrām I (r. 273–76) assails him thus: "Eh, what are you good for since you go neither fighting nor hunting?"[1] Obviously, for Bahrām, both activities are of the highest value and constitute proper measures of men. Of equal importance, war and the hunt are bracketed together, implying that they were inextricably linked in the minds of the Sasanid ruling elite. In this, they were hardly alone. The equation of hunting and war, the belief that they were complementary activities that merged into one another, has had many advocates across the millennia. In the classical tradition, it was Hyperbius, the son of Mars, the god of war, who first killed an animal.[2] Here a warrior initiates the hunt. In a recent scholarly formulation, this argument is reversed. In the view of Lawrence Keeley, "War represents a method, derived directly from hunting, for getting from one group what another lacks and cannot peacefully obtain."[3] In this case, hunting is seen as a prerequisite, a preparation for war.

The habit of coupling military and hunting skills is found across the continent and in widely divergent literary forms and cultural-historical contexts. In a letter to a friend, the Byzantine emperor Manual II (r. 1391–1415) automatically equates "arms, spoils, and war, [and] shooting at wild beasts," while a Buddhist document from Khotan speaks of those who "will become hunter and fighter."[4] More explicitly, the anonymous author of a tenth-century Fāṭimid hunting manual argues that the chase follow the principles of war in all essentials.[5] For these writers, and a host of others, the affinity between hunting and warring was both natural and self-evident.[6]

We can start our exploration of this relationship by analyzing several maxims attributed to Chinggis Qan: in one, he decrees that "a wife must, when her husband rides out to hunt or war, keep his household in good order and condition"; in another, he states, "we go out to hunt and down many mountain bulls. We go to war and destroy many enemies. When the Almighty Lord shows the way and makes things easy, people forget and think otherwise."[7] Three points emerge from these maxims. First, participation in the chase, as in war, is mandatory, a call to duty. Second, the collective hunt constitutes a transitional stage between peace and war, a means of mobilizing military manpower. Third, success on the battlefield is produced by hard work and success on the hunting grounds.

A close examination of military methods and training in the core area and beyond shows that the above precepts were in fact operational. One line of evidence is the prominent place of huntsmen in the military establishments of both sedentary and nomadic states.[8] In most cases they were real soldiers; under Alexius I (r. 1081–1118), the chief falconer served in wartime as the Byzantine emperor's personal messenger and the chief huntsmen of Saladin and Shāh ʿAbbās were both killed in action.[9] Others held responsible field grade positions. Elchidei, the falconer of Gheikhatu, Mongolian ruler of Iran (r. 1291–95), was a commander of a *tümen*, a unit of 10,000 troops, and the chief huntsman of Jahāngīr commanded 750 household troops.[10]

From Tang China we have records of special hunting units formed from regular soldiers, and later the Qing court formed a force called the Tiger Hunting Brigade (*huchiang ying*), 600 men strong, from elite units of the Manchu army.[11] Conversely, in the Yuan era, thousands of falconers served as garrison troops and as regulars in the imperial guard.[12]

It is not surprising that hunters were often attracted to military careers, that is, they were self-selected because they were personality types who courted danger or sought adventure. But the matter goes much deeper than this. Everyone recognized that soldiers required physical fitness and it was widely believed that hunting was an excellent form of exercise. Even in the classical West, which held athletics and calisthenics as the main means of conditioning and preparation for war, there was a strong body of opinion that argued hunting also produced sound minds and bodies, increased stamina and mental toughness.[13] Classical writers attribute to the ancient Iranians the notion that hunting was a principal form of exercise and sources from within the core area confirm this.[14] In India, political writings make this point, as does the Sanskrit play *Shakuntala*, in which a general extols "the hunter's form [which] grows sinewy, strong and light."[15] Centuries later in the Mughal era, both Muslim and Hindu authors directly link hunting with exercise and good health.[16] By the Middle Ages, European elites fully subscribed to this international norm.[17]

For some, hunting was even a cure; a wounded prince in one of the Oghuz epics recovers through hunting, and Shāh Jahān, following an illness, finishes the healing process on a leisurely hunt.[18] In China, hunting was not only a cure for ill health and excellent exercise, it was also a general restorative, second only to moral philosophy, that concentrated the mind and produced vigor.[19] Cao Cao, the famed general of the Later Han and founder of the Wei dynasty, 220–64, one of the Three Kingdoms (Sanguo), took a "sick leave" early in his career to avoid enemies at court and to prepare himself for future struggles by a program of reading in autumn and summer and hunting in winter and spring.[20] In the Georgian romance *Visramiani*, the hero, Ramin, does much the same thing; he leaves court, hunts with his hounds and hawks, restores his vigor, and returns to his military and civil duties.[21] In Turkic epics and Latin chronicles, political leaders follow these prescriptions, compelling their followers to hunt lest they lose their physical edge and fall into idleness.[22]

Hunting, then, was widely seen as means of physical conditioning and of psychological renewal, and, of equal value, a liberation from competing and distracting desires. For Hindus, Muslims, and Latin Christians, the chase was thought to suppress carnal desires and thus became a surrogate for sex.[23]

Understandably, hunting was held to be good preparation for war because it taught courage. Plutarch argued that "bravery is an innate characteristic of beasts," but not so of humans. Consequently, he believed that hunting instills in humans the courage that Nature fails to provide.[24] This specific formula may be unique to this author but it is likely that if put to an Iranian, Mughal, or Manchu ruler, they would have agreed without demur.

In addition to these benefits, the hunt taught basic military skills. Again, this view was universal, one classical authors repeatedly emphasized in their discussions of armies in the ancient Near East and Iran.[25] The crucial skills developed were, of course, riding and shooting. Hunting on horseback was the best way to improve equestrian techniques, at least those used in war.[26] In the Middle East and Inner Asia, the marksmanship equestrian archers acquired in hunting was held to be transferable to war because their targets in the chase, like human opponents, were always on the move or in flight. In this view, nothing besides war itself could provide better training.[27] The conviction that hunting is a rehearsal for war is reflected in scenes of the chase found on Sasanid silver that show the mounted monarchs armed with military weapons, sword and dagger, and wearing breastplates and helmets. While the royal hunters carry bows for game, these depictions nonetheless have a distinctively military aspect.[28] This militarized approach to hunting is captured in Bābur's boast that he once nearly decapitated a fleeing onager with a single saber blow.[29] This perhaps accounts for the "favor" shown wild asses by royal hunters; they were useful foils for the practice of equestrian swordsmanship.

Hunting, naturally, was regularly invoked to explain the military prowess of the nomads. In Chinese eyes, Xiongnu skill on the battlefield was a direct result of regular hunting which started in youth.[30] As formulated by the military thinker Li Jing (571–649), the theory maintains that while there was no distinction between Han and barbarian in the beginning, over time the nomads learned to survive in an arid, hostile environment by relying on archery and hunting, and consequently, he concludes, "they are constantly practicing fighting and warfare."[31]

The vast Mongolian conquests are also explained in this manner. According to both Chinese and European observers, Mongolian females, in conformity with Chinggis Qan's precepts, tended the households and flocks while the males did little else but hunt, thereby acquiring their skill at equestrian archery.[32] Moreover, these skills were acquired at a very early age. Peng Daya, who visited the Mongols in the 1230s, reports that "from their fourth or fifth year they carry under their arm a small bow and short arrows and at their majority they spend all four seasons learning the craft of hunting in the field."[33]

The notion is widespread that "martial races" were fashioned by systematic exposure of young males to the chase; it is a notion often favored by outsiders to explain the military attainments of nomads or any other "warlike" tribe.[34] And, it deserves stressing, this widely held stereotype is fully congruent with the self-image of warlike tribes; in the Oghuz epics, fathers take young sons out hunting prior to their first raid against human foes, and the Qitan emperors believed that the chase produced the formidable warriors who were the key ingredient in their success.[35]

This "natural soldier" argument, which is very old, has a certain appeal, but in my view calls for refinement as well as extension. First of all, there is a question of definitions. If organized hunts were designed to teach and test military skills and discipline, how "natural" is the by-product? From my perspective, trained soldiers were not an unintended consequence of the process but rather one of its conscious purposes. But leaving aside the issue of semantics, the concept of the natural soldier, however labeled, has been too restrictive in its application; nomads have been at center stage but other hunting societies have produced excellent soldiers and need to be brought into the analysis. This is important, not only to better understand the preparation of trained, disciplined soldiers, but to grasp broader issues of the shifting balance of military power in Eurasian history.

In comparing the military potential of steppe peoples and their sedentary rivals, it is important to recognize that the nomads, because of the importance of hunting, were a "nation armed," whereas the latter, and more particularly the common folk, were, by the decision of their own rulers, a nation disarmed. The Mongols, for example, were a society in which all the population could make, acquire, and bear arms; once, however, they brought China under control, they tried to restrict possession of weapons, particularly bows and arrows, to the military, the police and, of course, to hunting households.[36]

Nomads, however, were not the only nation in arms. Manchuria, while largely inhabited by small-scale agriculturalists, retained its hunting traditions from antiquity and, like the steppe zone, it also had a population at arms. The chase was one of the primary occupations of the Jürchen, who used the ring hunt (*weilie*), in the words of the Jin emperor Shizong, "to exhibit and practice the [arts] of war" and "to train themselves in mounted archery."[37] The label "nation at arms" can be applied to another people of the northern forests, the early Germans; they, too, had a mixed economy that combined agriculture, animal husbandry, and hunting, and, like the Manchurians, they, too, made their own weapons and went about armed on their daily rounds.[38]

The principal conclusion to be drawn from these considerations is that any *pastoral or agricultural* people for whom hunting was still an important form of energy extraction possessed military potential far greater than their population base might suggest. To use Stanislav Andreski's useful concept, these societies had a high "military participation ratio," a situation, he argues, that typically obtains in tribal societies in which individuals make their own arms and stratification is not well advanced.[39] In consequence of these factors, the great demographic disparity between China and its northern neighbors was somewhat of a mirage, at least in terms of their respective abilities to mobilize military manpower. And this in part helps to explain why Inner Asian peoples were so often militarily dominant down to early modern times.

In the Far West, the connection between hunting and warfare was widely recognized.[40] In British India down to the last century, hunting was still considered to be an appropriate pastime for a soldier, a "natural" adjunct to a military career.[41] But while European rulers, generals, and writers on chivalry, politics, and military affairs all recognize the chase as a preparation for war and as a way to keep fit and test one's nerve and skill with weapons, these were still basically recommendations that individual soldiers should hunt during the "off-season" to stay in shape.[42] This differs from the practice of the core area and the steppe, where the importance of hunting to warfare was by no means restricted to the acquisition of individual skills or fitness. Here the royal hunt was a form of unit training, a method of fostering unit solidarity, a means of developing skills in command, control, and logistics. Hunts for them were large-scale military maneuvers, an imitation of war.

Imitating War

The question of unit training takes us to the very heart of the natural soldier concept. It is, of course, not surprising that royal hunts drew on the military for manpower. Medieval poetry and romances regularly depict soldiers driving game for their sovereign, as do narrative histories and hunting manuals.[43] The exception, again, is the Far West in classical antiquity. Roman armies were neither trained by means of the hunt nor used extensively for that purpose. Tiberius (r. 14–37) once degraded a legion commander for using a few troops in a hunt.[44]

But what was an exceptional procedure in Rome was conventional in the rest of Eurasia. In Han China, Rome's contemporary, subordinate rulers regularly hunted with their troops, who were drawn up into formations by unit, each in its proper place, while their sovereign, the Han emperor, arrayed units under their commanders for game drives. In the latter case, it is explicitly stated that this was done to "practice maneuvers," in conformity with early Chinese military manuals that recommended the army be taken out to hunt in peacetime so that "they do not forget warfare."[45]

After the Han, Chinese armies continued to use the chase as a means of unit training. Li Yuan, founder of the Tang, had some of his troops trained as light cavalry in emulation of their Türk enemies. The regimen of these troopers included Türk food and lodging, as well as Türk-style horsemanship, archery, and hunting.[46] While hunting was depreciated by Chinese scholar-officials, the battue was still used to train troops during the Tang and Song, a practice that could draw upon well-established precedent from ancient China.[47] It is possible that under homegrown dynasties the ring hunt, like polo, survived mainly as a military exercise.[48] The early Ming also followed suit, in this instance more likely under Mongolian influence. In any event, the dynastic founders' "Ancestral Instructions" of 1373 specify that the imperial princes, each of whom had his own guard detachment, were to schedule annual hunting expeditions combined with military maneuvers.[49]

In the core area, as one would expect, the army was deeply involved in the hunt. Ṣafavid armies, from eyewitness testimony, hunted as units during peacetime, and their Georgian auxiliaries even hunted on campaign to stay fit between engagements.[50] The Mughal army under Akbar commonly hunted during campaigns, and Awrangzīb, according to Bernier, hunted with his field army, a force that the writer says numbered 100,000 or more.[51] Such figures are rare, and perhaps suspect, but there is every reason to believe that standing armies, in whole or in part, went to the field to hunt. This practice has ancient roots; according to a commemorative scarab of Amenhotep III (r. 1391–1353), the pharaoh hunted wild cattle with "his whole army . . . behind him."[52] And some twenty-eight hundred years later, another Egyptian ruler, a Mamlūk sultan, allowed one of his commanders to go hunting with a third of the army.[53]

The highest level of military participation in the chase, however, is found in Inner Asia, where the rulers' hunters and soldiers are virtually identified in the epic tradition.[54] As the ninth-century Turkic *Book of Omens* simply states, "The army of the Qanate went out for hunting."[55] That Türk qaghans actually did so is affirmed by the Chinese pilgrim Xuanzong, who saw Tong Yabghu hunting with 200 officers and countless numbers of troops.[56]

There is in fact abundant and unequivocal evidence, some already noted, that the hunt was considered by contemporaries, including royal hunters, as a military operation, a rehearsal for war, and more specifically, as the only practicable method for instilling and maintaining unit cohesion and coordination. This, more than anything else, explains why the hunt became so thoroughly militarized in the core area and across the steppe.

Chinggis Qan, among others, understood that hunting was the proper business of commanders and their troops because it entails scouting, reconnaissance, riding, handling of weapons, physical exertion, and the coordination of individuals and units.[57] The success of a great ring hunt, like success in a military confrontation, depended on discipline, an effective chain of command, and the ability to deploy and control armed formations. The linkage between the two activities is brought out in Bābur's observations on the Mughals of Central Asia, the nomadic successors of the Chagadai Qanate, in the early sixteenth century. He says that their army was still organized exactly as it had been under Chinggis Qan, with a left, right, and center. The bravest warriors were given pride of place on the wings, and whenever a dispute arose over which unit should have the honor, the matter was settled, he states, by giving one wing the prized position in war and the other the position in the ring hunt.[58]

Though sedentaries, the Manchus closely adhered to these same methods and strictures. Chinggis Qan would find nothing to criticize in Kangxi's pronouncements on the subject. For the Qing emperor, hunting was not only "good exercise" that taught basic military skills, riding, shooting, and maintaining formation; it was, he asserts, "training for war, a test of discipline and organization. The squads of hunters [he continues], have to be organized on military principles, not according to convenience on the march or family preferences."[59] According to the Jesuit Verbiest, the purpose of the regular hunting expeditions in times of peace was to keep the troops fit and prepared for the hardships of war. Toward this end, Kangxi planned several expeditions a year in which 60,000 troops, levied from each province, participated. To Verbiest, these were much more like military operations than "a party of pleasure."[60] Unfortunately, there is no extant manual of drill available, but the extensive and specialized terminology in Manchu relating to the formation and structure of the battue, methods of signaling, and placement of troops in the hunting line, says something of the intricacy of the maneuvers and the strict discipline required of military formations assigned to the hunt.[61] Even more revealing, in the *Chingwen jian*, a Manchu, Chinese, Mongolian, Tibetan, and Turki lexicon of the early eighteenth century, the entry for "hunting," *aba*, is defined in Manchu, the control language, as follows: "Training for military proficiency whereby one, with a body of men, either on foot or horse, downs beast and bird with an arrow. From olden times, [this] has enjoyed the highest esteem. Between the standards [*turun*] men march forth with small flags [*kiru*] attached to the back [of their uniforms]."[62] Here the hunt is described in its fully militarized form—an esteemed tradition of yore, the proper training for war, and a picture of men and formations, flags flying, on the march and eager to come to grips with the opposition, animal or human.

The next and very obvious question is to what extent were formations and maneuvers used on the hunting field transferred to the battlefield? We can start with Achaemenid tactics. In describing Darius's operations on the Aegean Islands, Herodotus relates: "Whenever they became masters of an island, the barbarians, in every single instance, netted the inhabitants. Now the mode in which they practice this netting is the following. Men join hands, so as to form a line across from the north coast to the south, and then march through the island from end to end and hunt out the inhabitants."[63] As Karl Meuli has pointed out, the continuity between the Old Persian tactics and those of the later Turks and Mongols reported in the Islamic and Chinese sources, is, to use his word, "striking."[64]

Whatever the ultimate origin of this enveloping maneuver, and it must be very ancient, it was widely used for an extended period of time by various hunting peoples, particularly the nomads. Carpini remarks that the Mongols managed opposing armies like they controlled game in the course of a circle hunt: "If " he says, "it happens that the enemy fight well, the Tartars make a way of escape for them; then as soon as they begin to take flight and are separated from each another, they [the Tartars] fall upon them and more are slaughtered in flight than could be killed in battle."[65] The Persian sources, some of which rest on now lost Mongolian records, report their use of very similar tactics against both sedentary and nomadic foes.[66] Indeed, the nexus of hunting, war, and politics is nicely exemplified in the Mongolian word *jerge/nerge*, "battue." Juvaynī, a contemporary well versed in Mongolian tradition and terminology, uses *nerge* (Persian *nirkah*) to describe Mongolian military maneuvers against the Qipchaqs in 1237 and the Ismāʿīlīs in 1256, to describe a ring hunt for lions along the Amu Darya in 1254 and, finally, to describe a vast manhunt following the contested enthronement of Möngke Qaghan in 1251. In this latter case, the partisans of the victorious Möngke formed a series of interconnected *nerge* extending from Qara Qorum in central Mongolia to the Ili River valley of Turkestan to track down the disloyal opposition, a truly "international" dragnet for political dissidents.[67]

The Mughal founder, Bābur, experienced this turning or encircling movement at the hands of his rivals, the nomadic Uzbeks, during a confrontation in Ferghana in 1501. He found this maneuver "one of the great merits of Uzbek fighting," adding that "no battle of theirs is ever without it." Bābur himself used the same tactic with success against an Indian foe.[68] A common tactic of the steppe, this was called *tolghama/tolghuma* in Turkic, a term derived from the versatile verb *tolghamaq*, to "surround," "encircle," "turn," "spin," "wind," "seize," and "drive back."[69]

This interconnection between hunting techniques and military tactics and organization, at least as it evolved in the steppe, has been most carefully analyzed by the Kazakh scholar Aleksandr Kadyrbaev. He argues that the triune military structure of the nomads, that is, the division into right, left, and center, emerges directly from the organization of the group or battue hunt among the steppe peoples. For him, the collective hunt, in combination with nomadism, stimulated the creation of the traditional military organization, training, tactics, and command structure of the Turkic and Mongolian peoples. And it also explains why the conduct of war by the nomads was always characterized by extensive maneuver and the need for operating space. The forms and methods of nomadic military operations, he concludes, were first worked out and tested in the battue hunt and then applied on the battlefield.[70]

While Kadyrbaev's sequential schema perhaps simplifies a more complex, dynamic relationship between hunting and nomadic warfare, his essential point that their style of warfare is incomprehensible without reference to the hunt is beyond dispute. This, of course, applies as well to other hunting peoples and to those sedentary societies with close steppe connections. The famous banner system, the organizing principle of the Manchu military machine, is intimately linked to the *aba* or hunting battue.[71] Such connection is seen as well among the Mamlūks of Egypt, whose army in the main was recruited from Qipchaq Turkic nomads; here the *ḥalqah*, Arabic "ring," was both the term for a battue formed by thousands of troops and the name of a military unit.[72] And in Russian, *oblava/ablava*, "hunting battue," a term of Turkic origin, also meant a bow-shaped formation that Cossacks, themselves the product of the steppe frontier, used in attack.[73]

The question of whether hunting maneuvers were duplicated exactly on the battlefield is perhaps a secondary consideration; what is crucial is that large bodies of troops were conditioned to operate as cohesive units that interacted efficiently with other such units under stressful conditions. After all, modern armies still use marching and drill as a means of creating unit solidarity and the habits of obedience, but never, of course, employ such formations or movements in combat. Consequently, we need to explore further the role of the chase in fostering discipline, unit identity, and bonding among officers and men.

King Moabad in the romance *Visramiani* rejoices at the coming of spring and the beginning of the hunting season; for him, it was a matter of Nature renewed, and the reassembly of courtiers and elites for the chase, a matter of social renewal.[74] Rust'haveli maintains that in the midst of the chase and in the heat of battle king and courtier are for the moment equals, locked in a common struggle, and that this is what produces true comradeship.[75] There is little doubt that he is right. Jahāngīr recognized that it was by traveling and hunting together that a prince secured the loyalty of courtiers.[76]

But the chase did more than fashion solidarity among the officer corps; equally critical was the forging of strong bonds between commanders and troops. Xenophon says that under Cyrus, young troopers, in rotation, went to hunt with the king. A similar practice, Quintus Curtius relates, was found among the Macedonians.[77] This technique was very long-lived. Niẓām al-Mulk, the Seljuq vazir, commends Sebüktegin, the founder of the Ghaznavids, for achieving a high level of identification with his troops by following the precepts of his patron, Alptegin, who regularly ate, drank, and hunted with his men and treated them "as brothers."[78]

This testing of loyalty on the hunt had important carryover effects since it provided a shared experience and in many cases underscored a shared passion and shared danger.[79] This provides reasons to trust and to feel strong attachments to others, the creation of a sense of brotherhood. The sources of the Mongolian era repeatedly speak to this point in words attributed to Chinggis Qan, who in varying ways asserts that if someone is a good partner in the hunt, he will be a good companion in arms.[80]

In the core area and beyond, unit solidarity was the expected by-product of the collective hunt. This explains why Qitan military formations were named after hunting grounds, and why, in the Warring States and Han eras, units in the field hunting were always identified by their banners and pennants.[81] No doubt friendly rivalries were encouraged to bolster competitive spirit and build morale. At the same time, however, such hunts were an opportunity to widen one's sense of identity and to develop ties to other formations and to the higher levels of command. In the Mongolian case, these vast collective hunts brought together different units and tribes who then had contact with the ruler, with whom they exchanged gifts, as well as sharing the excitement and danger of the hunt, which, in its turn, facilitated bonding within *and* between units. All this was further reinforced by a long period of feasting and drinking, after which the units returned to their individual stations and territories.[82]

The use of the chase to manufacture collective identities is, of course, only one of a number of mechanisms used by armies to achieve these ends, and needs to be evaluated in a wider perspective. In military contexts the most obvious of these mechanisms is drill and marching. This kind of "muscular bonding," as William McNeill calls it, encourages individuals to lose themselves in a larger group, that is, it produces cohesion and coordination and collective obedience.[83] But so, too, does dance. In Judith Hanna's extended analysis, the war dance in precolonial Africa was a status marker, a rite of passage, and a measure of manhood; a physical preparation for war, a series of exercises that improved reflexes and conditioning; a means of increasing group coordination; a morale builder and an incitement to action; a bonding mechanism that enhanced group solidarity and discipline; a form of psychological and physical mobilization; a religious ritual, a mobilization of spiritual forces; and an affirmation of political commitments and loyalty to a designated leader.[84]

The same can be said of the royal hunt in the core and the steppe, which was both militarized and ritualized. And because it was a collectively performed ritual, following prescribed rules, it was truly shared, with each participant carrying out similar acts. Moreover, the activity itself was inherently intense, a matter of life and death, and there was consequently a build up, as Randall Collins phrases it, of "contagious emotion."[85] Such shared emotion, it should be emphasized, can, after the fact, be recalled, enhanced, and recycled, that is, it has a corporate existence, a long life that can be drawn upon to relive and reinforce feelings of group solidarity.

The war dance and the hunt can therefore be considered as full dress rehearsals for war. Nor were the two methods mutually exclusive. This is quite apparent from pictorial evidence. In the pre-Han era, Sichuan was controlled by the Ba people, famed for their warlike spirit. A bronze jar, recovered at Chengdu and dating to the fourth century B.C.E., has most revealing scenes in this regard: one register shows a group of Ba warriors dancing to music while another hunts, and a second register depicts them in battles on land and water.[86]

This is a welcome reminder that sedentary, agricultural peoples, such as the Ba, made heavy use of the hunt for political-military purposes. Georgian, Persian, and Manchu armies were "trained up" to war through the chase, just like the armies of the Turks and Mongols. This means that their armies consisted of disciplined and coherent military formations over which a measure of command and control could be exercised on the battlefield. In other words, sophisticated tactics, strategy, and generalship were possible in these circumstances. This is in sharp contrast to the situation that obtained on the periphery of Eurasia. The Vikings, for example, while certainly famed and feared warriors, had little by way of structure and stratagems. Their tactics, as Peter Foote and David Wilson put it, "were simple and elemental, consisting largely of bashing hell out of the opposing side."[87] Naturally, those in closer proximity to the hunter-soldier tradition had to counter their threat by adopting their methods. The Russians, accordingly, regularly recruited nomadic auxiliaries and built their own army around the defense of their southern frontier. Thus, as Richard Hellie comments, while Moscovy used gunpowder as early as the 1380s, at the end of the sixteenth century her basic military posture "was still toward steppe warfare, with horsemen and bows and arrows."[88]

The foregoing analysis is not to be taken as a final pronouncement on the military ethnography of premodern Eurasia, but is intended to underscore the need to place national military histories in a much wider context, one that compares technologies, organization, tactics, recruitment, and training methods. For, as we have seen, the hunt was central to military preparation among peoples from the northern forest, the steppe zone, and the subtropics.

The contribution of the royal hunt to military preparedness does not, however, end here. Successful war machines require infrastructure and supplies, and the chase contributed to both. Hunting parks offered considerable assistance in this regard. Bābur used parks as camping grounds, for mustering troops, and preparing ambushes.[89] During Jahāngīr's time, Allahabad was both a "pleasure resort" and a strategic fort that commanded the conjunction of three major rivers, the Ganges, Jumna, and Saraswati.[90] In China we see a similar pattern of use. Han and Tang emperors frequently used parks to practice maneuvers, or as military encampments.[91]

The nomads, for their part, employed royal hunting grounds for the same ends. One of the epics has Oghuz Qan preparing for hostilities by collecting his followers and kin on his hunting ground (*shikār-gāh*), where his troops were mustered and ordered for battle.[92] The historical Türgesh qan Kül Chur did much the same thing in 737; he repaired to his hunting preserve with his troops to accumulate supplies, make arrows, and pasture their horses before a campaign.[93]

In the Mongolian era, the Il-qan Ghazan used Alātāgh, a hunting preserve in Armenia, as a base from which to launch a counterstroke against a rebellious general.[94] And in China the Yuan rulers used hunting parks in the same way, as the history of Shangdu/Kaiping illustrates. When Nayan, a cousin of Qubilai, raised a revolt in Manchuria, the Yuan forces used Shangdu as their base of operations; the punitive campaign mounted there, which Qubilai led in person, soon quelled the uprising.[95] In the next century, as the Yuan began to disintegrate, Shangdu again became the scene of fighting against various rebel armies. In 1357 Shangdu was attacked and in the following year some of its buildings were destroyed. It remained, however, in Mongolian hands to the end of the dynasty. In fact, the last Yuan emperor, Toghan Temür (r. 1332–68), held out there, launching counterattacks southward, until September of 1369, when Ming pressure forced him and his followers to flee to Mongolia. Thereafter, Shangdu was transformed into a Ming frontier garrison, where Mongolian and Chinese armies clashed in 1413 and again in 1424.[96]

The classical and Byzantine sources, which provide basic data on the pre-Islamic Persian paradise, almost always mention these parks in connection with military operations; they are defended, abandoned, overrun, and destroyed. This was not by chance, since they were important, legitimate military targets. Diodorus tells us that in 351 B.C.E., when the Phoenicians of Sidon (Saida in modern Lebanon) rebelled against their Achaemenid overlords, their "first hostile act was the cutting down and destroying of the royal park (*paradeisos*) in which the Persian kings were wont to take their recreation."[97] In light of what we know of the functions of these parks, this was more than a dramatic gesture of defiance or a declaration of war; it was a wise tactical move, a strike at a vital military, communication, and supply facility.

The royal hunt made a contribution to the problem of supply in yet another way. Because of limited means of transportation, premodern armies tended to live off the land, requisitioning and plundering supplies from local inhabitants, whether friend or foe. Under these circumstances, chance encounters with game animals were eagerly exploited; the Roman army took deer for food while operating in Mesopotamia in the mid-fourth century, and Russian armies killed boars while on campaign in the mid-thirteenth century.[98] These were targets of opportunity, but more systematic efforts are in evidence. During Cyrus the Younger's attempt to unseat Artaxerxes, the armies of the usurper supported themselves in part by organized hunting, as did Sasanid armies in sixth-century Armenia when faced with the burnt-earth policy of the locals.[99] Even armies on the run sometimes did so; Jalāl al-Dīn, the last Khwārazmshāh, pursued by the Mongols in the 1220s, went hunting to feed his troops.[100]

In describing the military operations of Sviatoslav (r. 962–72), the *Russian Primary Chronicle* says the prince lived off horsemeat, beef, and game (*zverina*) roasted over an open fire.[101] These were typical nomadic campaign rations that Sviatoslav presumably adopted in consequence of his successful operations against the steppe power of the day, the Khazars. This makes perfect sense because in the steppe, where there are far fewer fields or granaries to seize, meat and hunting assumed a greater role in military supply. Even in peacetime nomadic armies harvested game on their own or received it as proceeds from the royal hunt.[102] Such meat might be consumed on the spot, or preserved for later use. Nomads had a number of ways of doing this: drying, jerking, smoking, and freezing. This, very likely, is the true explanation of the "raw" meat Ammianus Marcellinus says Huns kept on their saddles.[103]

When we reach the Mongolian epoch, we gain a clearer picture of the place of hunting in nomadic military supply. Early in his career, Chinggis Qan engaged in a hunt to provision 2,600 of his troops. Later, in sending his famous general Sübedei on a distant campaign into the western steppe, he instructed his commander to hunt selectively to relieve anticipated supply problems but cautions him not to get caught up in the chase and exhaust his mounts.[104] Zhao Hong, the Song ambassador, helpfully adds that "when [the Mongols] go out on campaign against the Middle Kingdom and consume all their sheep, they then shoot hare, deer, and wild pigs for food."[105] Hunting obviously supplements the food supply, but is not necessarily the principal source. The fullest picture comes from the Armenian prince, Het'um, an ally of the Mongols of Iran in the late thirteenth century. He states that Mongolian armies received no rations from their masters and had to live off the chase and the land; he also points out, however, that they take strings of horses with them and that they utilize their milk *and meat*, which they greatly esteem and enjoy.[106] The conclusion that can be reached from this data is that Mongolian campaign rations came from a combination of pillage, domesticated animals brought for the purpose, and the chase; no doubt the proportions contributed by each varied greatly depending on local conditions, the size of the force, and the objectives of the operation.[107]

A final contribution of the hunt to war was the practice it afforded military supply operations. Amir Sayyid ʿAlī, a Mughal governor of Kashghar in the mid-fifteenth century, spent three months every year hunting with his soldiers, during which time they were supplied in the field just like an army in campaign.[108] Kangxi also embraced the practice, arguing that hunting expeditions were good training for the mastery of the "details of transport and supply." Since many troops died of starvation and fatigue in time of war, it is important, he held, while hunting or fighting to have sufficient supplies of liquids, food, tentage, clothing, and remounts.[109]

The large-scale royal hunt, so common to the core and the steppe, was a rehearsal for war, a realistic exercise in military logistics and, as we shall now see, a means of communicating, and concealing, political-military intentions.

Intimating War

Because hunting was a common and legitimate activity, princes could go to the field with large bodies of armed men without necessarily attracting attention or suspicion. But once in the field, away from observation, quite different purposes might be pursued. Thus, the chase was an excellent cover, much used by political elites across the continent, sometimes for quite personal reasons. For one thing, the chase provided an opportunity to disguise preparations for escapes and political defections, flights from domestic or foreign foes.[110]

Naturally, too, hunting was a frequent stratagem in wartime. To be sure, the chase was sometimes a simple recreation, a release from the boredom of a long campaign.[111] More often, however, it had a serious and sinister purpose. The Achaemenids used individual hunters as intelligence agents, but most commonly hunting was a cover for reconnaissance operations. The Umayyad guard corps (*shākiriyyah*) and Mongolian formations (*cherig*) in Iran used the chase to probe the opposition, to ascertain their intentions and capacity.[112] In the wars between China and Tibet at the end of the seventh century, hunting was used by the Tibetans as a cover for offensive military operations, and with equal facility it was used by Byzantine and Khwārazmian armies to disguise redeployments, withdrawals, and full retreats.[113] While a useful stratagem on the battlefield, it could sometimes lead to serious problems by deflecting attention from the main task or, as a Muslim manual of war cautions, by giving away positions, particularly when setting up an ambush.[114]

Given its potential for deception and delay, the hunt had obvious diplomatic applications. In the 1190s T'amar diverted a Muslim princeling with the chase while she decided what to do with him; and in the 1680s the Siamese king, wishing to sort out the purpose of a Ṣafavid embassy, went out hunting and was "unavailable" while his assistants queried the Persians.[115] Hunts in these circumstances were a diplomatic convenience, a genteel means of deceiving. But the hunt, always flexible, also served to impart clear messages in interstate relations.

At the death of Germanicus, adopted son of Tiberius, the Parthian court suspended the royal hunt, thereby signaling its good will.[116] A court might even allow a foreign ruler to mount a hunt within its own frontiers, a privilege the Sui dynasty (581–618) granted a Türk chieftain in 587 as a special sign of favor and trust.[117] One could show respect for foreign envoys by including them in a royal hunt or one could curtail the chase to meet an embassy and thereby communicate interest and respect. When Macartney reached Beijing in 1793, he was informed that Qianlong had ended the autumn hunt so as to meet with the British at the earliest possible date. This show of concern for their time schedule, as Macartney realized, was a diplomatic way of saying that the embassy was not to tarry in China and that they should return home in due course.[118] This was a very subtle exchange that entailed no pointed words or embarrassment for persons or states.

The chase was easily manipulated to convey changing political moods and readily calibrated to fit changing circumstances. This is brought out in the relations between the Sasanids and their client kingdom of Armenia. A representative of the Sasanid emperor sent to the Armenian king Tigranes V (r. 338–51) was perforce entertained by a royal hunt and a feast. But "because of the ill-will, envy, malignity, and deceit of the Persian race," it was decided, according to an Armenian chronicle, that "there was no need for him [the representative] to see the places of extensive hunting . . . but rather to show him some places of sparse hunting [and] to entertain him solely with them." It was further agreed that they would not make any major kills and would carry out their hunt "for the sake of form on account of the perverse bitterness of that evil race."[119] Decades later, in the reign of Yazdagird I (399–421), when the Sasanids tried to place a son of the emperor on the Armenian throne, the local princes showed their disapproval by refusing to "honor him in royal fashion in the hunt or at sport."[120] In both instances subject people sent a clear message to their overlord without engaging in open rebellion.

By its very nature, the hunt allowed courts to flex their military muscle and show their colors; as an exercise this sent powerful messages that could warn off neighbors and rivals or influence their behavior. The very fact that foreign envoys were frequent, even mandatory guests at royal hunts, is one good evidence of this.[121] In early China, this was a common ploy; one prose poem of circa 150 B.C.E. relates that the king of Qi "mobilized all of his soldiers in his realm and provided a multitude of chariots and horsemen" for the benefit of a rival kingdom's envoy.[122] Rulers were always sensitive about the size, success, and magnificence of their hunt in comparison with that of their neighbors. Around 10 B.C.E., another prose poem speaks of a great ring hunt mounted for representatives of the Hu, a generic name for the nomadic peoples to China's north and west. This entailed stocking, driving, and fencing, and climaxed in a massive slaughter of beasts presided over by the Son of Heaven.[123] Notker relates that when the embassy of the ʿAbbāsid caliph Hārūn al-Rashīd arrived in Charlemagne's court, the emperor took them hunting, and when they saw the immense bison and wild oxen "they were filled with mighty dread and they turned and ran." Charlemagne, of course, knew no fear and brought the great beasts down.[124]

The hunt, then, was held to reveal much about a state's power and its leader's character. Niẓām al-Mulk reminds his sovereign that ambassadors are intelligence agents and should take every opportunity to inform themselves about a rival kingdom's topography, economy, army, and its ruler, his character, table, and hunt.[125] These concerns are still much in evidence centuries later when a Manchu envoy was sent to the Qalmaq Mongols on the Lower Volga in 1712; it is most revealing that his imperial instructions state that he should expect Russian inquiries on the governance of the Qing realm, its products, weaponry, and its royal hunt. He was further instructed that, if asked about the latter, he should reply that it was regularly conducted, well ordered, and well provisioned. And, in the event, he was so queried by the Russians, who, naturally, took him on one of their hunts.[126]

If a royal hunt was sufficiently impressive, its fame might spread abroad without the help of envoys. The military treatise of Li Jing states that in the late Zhou era, as the dynasty began to weaken, dependent kingdoms used hunting expeditions as a pretext "to overawe the irreverent," that is, to assert their political authority and de facto independence from the center.[127] A similar strategy was adopted by the Delhi sultan Balaban (r. 1266–87), who hunted regularly during the winter months with a large contingent of troops. Reports of this activity, according to one chronicler, were carried to the Mongolian rulers of Iran, who came to believe that the sultanate was ready for war.[128]

Hunting was a convenient and conventional way of sending rivals pointed signals about military intentions and the ability to carry them out. During his campaign against Edessa in 506, the Sasanid commander, Pharazman, mounted a large expedition in the surrounding countryside and brought a huge bag of animals before the beleaguered and starving city, "as a demonstration of his hunting prowess."[129] A short while later, this kind of psychological warfare was turned against the Persians. Confronting Sasanid armies along the Euphrates in 542 during a period of uneasy peace, the Byzantine general Belisarius sent out 6,000 of his fittest, most imposing troops to hunt some distance from his base camp to show and magnify his strength to Persian officers arriving for further negotiations.[130] Soldiers deployed in this fashion provided a menace without violating the terms of a tense truce.

The hunt was a useful way of talking about and measuring military potential and international status. In one dramatic example from 1444, on the eve of a confrontation with the Ottomans, Vlad Dracul, the Wallachian prince, counseled Władysław, king of Poland and Hungary, to retreat, since, he said, the sultan's hunting entourage was larger than their own army.[131] While rhetorical, the message is unmistakably and depressingly clear: the enemy's reconnaissance force can defeat our field army.

This connection between hunting prowess and international standing is nicely encapsulated in two medieval tales that, even though they do not speak to historical events, do speak eloquently to the place of images and norms in interstate relations of the era. The first, from the Middle East, treats an episode in the reign of Bahrām Gor. According to this tradition, passed down among Muslim authors, when ministers drew Bahrām's attention to the fact that one of his frontiers was being menaced by an enemy, he showed little concern, responding that he would take care of the matter in his own way. He did so by the following device. First, he disguised himself as a lowly page and went to the threatened frontier and placed himself in the enemy's line of march. He then began killing birds and game in vast numbers with bow and arrow. The invader's advanced scouts soon reached him and marveled at his bag. They took the "page" to their ruler. When interrogated, Bahrām claimed to have killed all the animals by himself; he then told the amazed ruler that he had been sent out by his own sovereign as fair warning to the invaders, adding that behind him were a hundred archers much better than he. Appalled by the prospect of facing such men, the ruler of the invading force retreated immediately. Bahrām thereupon returned to his court and informed his worried ministers that all was well.[132]

The second tale, from Notker, has Charlemagne, the model king of medieval Europe, sending Spanish horses and mules to the "Persians," as well as "some dogs specially chosen for their nimbleness and ferocity," which the caliph Hārūn al-Rashīd had requested "for hunting and warding off lions and tigers." Predictably, when the Carolingian envoys arrived, the hounds were soon put to the test. The "German dogs" quickly overtook a rampaging lion and the Carolingian envoys dispatched the beast "with their swords of northern metal." In light of this demonstration, Notker asserts that "Harun, the most powerful of all rulers, who inherited that name, recognized from such minute indications the superior might of Charlemagne and began to praise him in the following words: 'Now I realize that what I have heard of my brother Charles is true. By going hunting so frequently, and by exercising his mind and body with such unremitting zeal, he has acquired the habit of conquering everything under heaven'."[133] From this passage, it is evident that western Europe had developed a certain sensitivity to pan-Eurasian standards in measuring military and political power.

Organizing a royal hunt was, then, a means of displaying martial prowess, understood by rulers, generals, and the wider populace.[134] It was analogous and antecedent to the modern naval demonstration, that "glint of steel," so beloved by statesmen such as Churchill and the two Roosevelts. In modern interstate relations displays of military might are common methods of communicating power and intentions. These methods include well-publicized parades and maneuvers on home ground, dispatch of naval forces to "trouble spots," call-up of reserves, and most extreme, total mobilization. As Hans Morganthau argues, such measures are designed to enhance a state's prestige, its "reputation for power," and at the same time serve "both as a deterrent to, and as a preparation for, war."[135] In the core area at least, this well describes one of the principal functions of the royal hunt.

The royal hunt, however, was not just a demonstration of manpower and weaponry, but of logistics, the capacity to project power at a distance. As Peter Andrews says of Akbar's hunting progresses: "To move such a mass of humanity about the land, at a time when communications were poor, was to make an unforgettable show of strength which frequently rendered war itself unnecessary."[136] This is why early Korean rulers of the Koguryŏ and Silla dynasties marked conquests and new frontiers with "hunting" monuments. These stated simply that the ruler inspected the frontiers, hunted, and returned.[137] This was shorthand for a very compelling formula: I can hunt here, I can make war here, I can project my power this far, this is my territory.

Several enlightening examples of the use of the hunt as an instrument in interstate relations can be cited. In the fourth century B.C.E., the ruler of Shu in Sichuan mounted a large hunting expedition in the Han River valley, a buffer zone between his territory and that of the Qin. Since thousands of troops were involved, the king of Qin came out "hunting" to meet him. In this instance negotiations began and a diplomatic exchange followed.[138] Here, the royal hunt served effectively as a reconnaissance in force and as a diplomatic stimulus. Moreover, the hunt was an effective cover and provided, in this case, as in many others, "deniability," to use a modern neologism.

Some 2,000 years later and about 4,000 miles to the west, there was another and even more illuminating international "hunting incident," between Mughals and Ṣafavids in the early 1620s. It began with the Mughals' occupation of Qandahār in the frontier province of Sīstān. In response, Shāh ʿAbbās cautiously mounted a campaign for its return, which he hoped to accomplish without a major confrontation with Jahāngīr. He therefore intended to approach the city hunting, enjoy the hospitality of the Mughal officers, and then retire; the voluntary return of Qandahār to his control would appear as an act of friendship on Jahāngīr's part. ʿAbbās carried out his plan, hunting and chastising rebels in the region. The local Mughal commanders did not, however, play their expected role and a conflict ensued; after a short siege Qandahār fell to the Ṣafavids. Thereupon, the shah sent two letters to Jahāngīr in the summer of 1622, in which he claimed that he had approached the city only for hunting but when the commanders of the fort failed to respond to his friendly overtures, he besieged and temporarily occupied the city. The whole incident is passed off as a minor misunderstanding arising out of this innocent hunting expedition, and the shah concludes with the hope that Jahāngīr will continue his warm, brotherly relations with his court.[139]

On his part, Jahāngīr accepted, for his own reasons, that this was a case of "misunderstanding." He did, however, remind his brother sovereign that there was no "necessity for visiting one another's countries for spectacle [*sair*] and hunting [*shikār*]."[140] Jahāngīr, of course, well understood this game and had played it himself. On one occasion he made his own "hunting tour of Kabul" to consider possible military action in that direction; in the event, he decided that the time was inopportune for a full-scale campaign into Ṣafavid Khurāsān and called it off.[141] This he could easily do without any loss of face, since officially, and to the world at large, he was only "out hunting."

The royal hunt had a great variety of uses in relations between states. And when signals were misread and diplomacy failed, the royal hunt also served as a way of mobilizing troops, deploying forces, and initiating hostilities. In other words, it was a triggering mechanism for the transition from peace to war and in some instances from war to peace.

Initiating War

For elites across Eurasia, hunting and war were interdependent, complementary, and intertwined in various and unexpected ways. Hunters were warriors and warriors hunted even during periods of conflict. Dāʿūd Khān (d. 1715), a leading Mughal commander and governor of Deccan, went to war with all his hunting establishment and hunted along the way.[142] In legend at least, the animal hunting partners were direct participants in combat. Once, so the story goes, when Ismāʿīl (r. 1501–24) met a rival in battle near the Tigris, a number of aggressive greyhounds emerged from the Ṣafavid lines and confronted those accompanying the enemy. The Ṣafavid canine champions were victorious, and when the human battle was joined, so, too, were the Ṣafavid troops.[143]

This connection between hunting and the initiation of war is seen as well in the Chinese military manual *Methods of Sima*, a text of the fourth century C.E. incorporating earlier material. Its author recommends that in entering enemy territory the army should be restrained so as not to provoke intense resistance; among other things, the troops should treat civilians kindly and should not hunt the local ruler's "wild animals."[144] The assumption here is that an invading army is sometimes in a hunting mode, that wars sometimes begin as hunts.

In the Oghuz epic tradition, hunting expeditions are treated in just this way, as a natural, transitional step toward war.[145] The chase was, in fact, a call to the colors, an act of mobilizing and ordering manpower. The Tanguts, who formed the Daxia dynasty, 1038–1227, in the Gansu Corridor, followed this practice. According to a Chinese account of the procedure, "Every time they mobilized troops, all tribal chiefs were required to take part in a hunt. If they caught something then they dismounted, sat in a circle, drank, cut up their catch, and ate. Everyone reported what they had seen and [then] they selected their commanders [for the campaign]."[146]

The Mongols did much the same thing. In the winter of 1203–4, Chinggis Qan, bent on destroying Ong Qan, his principal rival in the eastern steppe, undertook a great hunt, where "he issued his pronouncements, called out his orders, and roused his troops to victory."[147] Here, the hunt served as a muster and as an occasion for morale building. This precedent was regularly followed by his successors, who used hunts to ready campaigns against the Chinese.[148]

In the post-Mongolian era this method of mobilization is still very much in evidence. Shāh Rukh (r. 1405–47), the son of Temür, organized a ring hunt prior to launching an attack on one of his rivals for power, and so did Sultan Saʿīd Khān as the first step in his military operations in East Turkestan in 1516.[149] The importance of the hunt in emotional mobilization is particularly apparent in the following instance reported by Abū'l Faẓl. While in exile in eastern Iran, Humāyūn, we are told, built up a following in preparation for a return to India and the reclaiming of the Mughal throne. In 1554, on the eve of his successful campaign, he held a large hunt: "And for the sake of the state and for the delight of hearts, he had a *qamar-ghāh* hunt in the neighborhood of Shūrāndam [some distance from Qandahār]. This pleased the officers and His Majesty took an omen from it for the capture of his desires."[150] In other words, the rehearsal went well and the entire cast expected a great success.

In the initiation of hostilities, the royal hunt provided effective cover. The king of Chu held a winter hunt to camouflage his approach to the capital of the rival kingdom of Xu in 530 B.C.E.[151] This was such a common ploy in the Zhou era that it could be misread, as, for example, a few centuries later, when the king of Zhao went out on a great hunt and the ruler of Wei mistakenly thought it an invasion.[152] And as a disguise, the hunt sometimes failed to fool the enemy; in 595 the Byzantines launched a campaign into the Balkans against the Avars, which its commander, Priscus, claimed was a hunting expedition but which the Avar qaghan rightly saw as an offensive operation.[153]

But despite failures, the hunt continued to be used as a cover for opening military operations down to early modern times. This was the regular practice of Delhi sultans in the assaults on Hindu territories, and much used by Mughal emperors against Hindu "rebels" as well as dynastic rivals.[154] Its continued utility rested on the fact that one could never be sure of the true purpose of a foe's hunting expedition. A royal hunter with his army at his side had a very plausible, built-in explanation for this activity, however threatening it might appear. Equally important, a ruler in these circumstances had options, and therefore during the early stages of the "hunt," his intentions were in truth unknowable.

Such a hunting expedition was in reality a "fishing expedition," in the sense that the ruler was probing, looking for opportunities, and thereby positioning himself to take advantage of any opening that presented itself. In the *Visramiani*, Ramin is informed that his elder brother Moabad, the king, "proposes to go tomorrow towards Armenia to hunt; there it may happen that there will be war with the enemy and fighting."[155] The Xiongnu, we know from the Chinese sources, used this very tactic. Chao Cuo, in a memorial to the Han emperor Yen (r. 180–157) on frontier defense, says that even as he writes the Xiongnu are "herding in several places and hunting [*lie*] on the frontier at Yandai, Shangjun, Beidi, and Longxi [there] waiting and preparing an intrusion if the troops at the frontier garrisons are too few."[156] In 68 B.C.E., 10,000 Xiongnu horsemen "hunted" along the Chinese frontier intending to cross over for a raid, but were spotted and withdrew, as did an even larger "hunt" of 100,000 led by their *shanyu* in 62 B.C.E.[157] At the other end of the steppe, in the fourth century C.E., Ammianus Marcellinus, in describing the Halani/Alans, says that "in their plundering and hunting expeditions they roam here and there as far as the Maeotic Sea [Azov] and the Cimmerian Bosporus, and also to Armenia and Media."[158] Both peoples were searching for targets of opportunity, whether a herd of deer or a porous frontier.

The same tactic was readily adapted to defense. In the Persian-Arab tradition, Bahrām Gor, when warned of an impending attack by the Türk qaghan (a historical anachronism), organized a "hunt" by his guard that reconnoitered the enemy position, resulting in the death of their leader and the conquest of their country.[159] Historically, for the armies of Georgian monarchs in the twelfth century, hunting and reconnoitering the lowlands for movements of their Seljuq enemies were inextricably joined.[160] And we can interpret the actions of a European ruler, Louis the German, in the same way. In 865, anticipating a further Viking incursion in the region of the Oise River, he called up his men and went hunting.[161] This was not dereliction of duty but a search for the enemy, an active defense against an imminent external threat.

This heavy reliance on the hunt in the preliminary stages of warfare is graphically illustrated by a confrontation in northern Iran in 1102. In that year, the Qarakhanid ruler Quṭur/Qadir Khān with a large hunting party invaded Khurāsān; while he was engaged in probing the Seljuq defenses near Tirmidh, the sultan Sanjar sent his own hunting party out to intercept the enemy forces which they did. Quṭur was captured, taken to Sanjar's camp and beheaded, bringing an end to the invasion.[162] In this instance, the confrontation was initiated, and decided, by hunting parties, not by field armies.

Ever flexible, the royal hunt served rulers equally well against both foreign and domestic foes. The famous usurper Wang Mang, founder of the short-lived Xin dynasty (19–23 C.E.), once mounted an expedition in the Chinese countryside to hunt heroic game—leopards, tigers, and other savage beasts—and did so with a large army supplied with "armor, rams, tower[-carts], shields, halberds, flags, and banners." This expedition, we are told, was undertaken "to make manifest [emperor's] majesty and military prowess," that is, to assert Wang Mang's control over an increasingly restive countryside.[163] Centuries later, the Ming emperor Zhengde (r. 1506–21) did much the same thing, conducting mock battles and mounting a series of hunting excursions that extended from the Ordos to Nanjing, this time to display his martial skills to subjects and foreigners alike.[164]

The reasons for such exercises were fully understood by the missionary Verbiest. In speaking of the annual hunting expeditions undertaken by Kangxi, the Jesuit asserts that their real purpose was that "he might on the pretext of the chase and of practicing his soldiers in the pursuit of stags, wild boars and tigers, *procure an image and representation of war with human enemies and rebels*, and a rehearsal of conflict which might thereafter ensue." Shortly thereafter, Verbiest adds perceptively that "another motive for the expedition was, the political object of keeping these Western Tartars [Mongols] in obedience, and checking the plots and intrigues of their councils. This was one reason [he concludes], for the magnitude of the force, and the imperial pomp with which the emperor penetrated their county. For this he conveyed also thither some pieces of cannon."[165] This explains why Inner Asian nobles, Mongols and others, had mandatory "turns" at Mulan scheduled by the Court of Colonial Affairs (*lifan yuan*), and why the park's facilities were extensively decorated with paintings of imperial progresses and of the ever-triumphant Manchu emperor downing game.[166]

When intimidation of this sort failed to sway potential adversaries, the hunt could be converted rapidly, almost instantaneously, into a pacification campaign, or such a campaign could be disguised as a hunt.[167] The flexibility and utility inherent in the royal hunt as an instrument of coercion and control were regularly exploited by rulers like Shāh ʿAbbās and Akbar. Their varied uses of the hunt can best be presented in tabular form.

First, the Ṣafavid ruler:

1590. ʿAbbās, wanting to curb the rebellious tendencies of an underling, sets out on a hunt and invites the suspect official to join him. This is certainly understood as the start of a punitive campaign and the upstart comes to terms.

1598–99. The shah, wishing to reconquer Khurāsān from the Uzbeks, begins his campaign as a series of hunts and meanwhile assembles the whole of his army.

1600. ʿAbbās approaches the fort of a disloyal subordinate with a hunting party; this quickly turns into a siege, at which point reinforcements are called in and the stronghold is overwhelmed.

1602. While rebels, shut up in Shirvān, tensely await ʿAbbās, he leisurely hunts; the rebels realize, of course, that this is the opening of a military campaign directed against them.[168]

Next, the Mughal emperor:

1560. Akbar launches a preemptive strike against his senior minister Bayrām Khān, whom he suspects of plotting treason. The emperor and his party leave Agra hunting, and by the time they reach Delhi the party has become a field army. The unanticipated arrival of *force majeure* compels Bayrām to flee to Punjab, where he is finally "hunted down."

1562. Eight villages outside of Agra are held to be centers of banditry and rebellion. Akbar organizes a hunt in that direction, and as he approaches enemy territory his huntsmen scout out the terrain and gather political intelligence from friendly locals; he then launches an attack that routs the fleeing opposition.

1564. Akbar campaigns against rebels in Mālwa. This operation begins as an elephant hunt and culminates in the capitulation of the opposition forces without a fight, and then, coming full circle, ends with a return to elephant hunting.

1568. Akbar approaches a rebel fortress in the Rajput country with a ring hunt, thereby isolating the fort from the surrounding countryside and forcing its surrender.[169]

Here we see the hunt transmuted into war and then dissolving back into hunting. In part, this return to the hunt after a campaign was a celebration of victory and a form of rest and recreation. But it was also a kind of limited demobilization, a temporary standing down that left the message to friend and foe that the royal hunter could respond successfully to any threat at home or on the frontiers.

12

Internationalization

Traffic in Animals

In using "internationalization" as the chapter title, I do not imply the existence of nation-states in the premodern era; here it is used as a convenient label, one that has the added advantage of conveying the idea that many royal hunting practices became common across Eurasia and that this tendency toward homogenization was often transmitted through interstate relations and conventions.

In pursuing this line of inquiry, we focus initial attention on the movement of animals, which offers a window on the transcontinental connections of the royal hunt and a useful index of the historical integration of the Eurasian landmass in the premodern era. This is so because in tracing the diffusion of cultural traits, convergence and independent invention are always a possibility. But the movement of plants and animals beyond their natural range is a different matter; in almost all cases, independent invention is precluded.[1] Thus, while the relationship between Chinese and western European printing remains clouded, we can assert with absolute certainty that neither "invented" their own hunting leopards, and that consequently cheetahs were diffused over great distances by human agency.

From ancient times polities eagerly acquired foreign animals, wild and domestic, and did so by a variety of means. Shalmaneser I, ruler of Assyria (r. 1274–1245 B.C.E.) brought back from his campaigns defeated rivals' "wild animals in captivity."[2] The Sasanids did the same; when Khusro seized Antioch, Jerusalem, and Alexandria from the Byzantines in the 620s, he took as booty "many quadrupeds and birds the very names of which were quite unknown to the lands of the east."[3] Booty was also a source of early China's zoological collections. Lu Guang, a general of the Former Qin (351–94), returned home in 385 from his expedition against Kucha with many treasures and "exotic birds and bizarre animals."[4]

Such animals were also obtainable through commercial channels. In antiquity, the Ptolemies and Romans imported animals from India, and throughout the Middle Ages the Muslims received zoological specimens from tropical Asia and Africa.[5]

The most common method of acquisition, or at least the best documented, is tribute and princely presentation. Assyrian rulers received "sea creatures" as gifts of rulers around the Mediterranean, and primates and crocodiles from Egypt.[6] Animal tributes were well publicized under the Achaemenids. The stairways leading to the audience hall (*apadana*) of Darius and Xerxes at Persepolis were covered with reliefs depicting processions of tribute bearers, the famous "March of Nations," in which envoys from Soghdia to Ethiopia present the Achaemenids with animals—broad-tailed sheep or okapi—that are closely identified with their homeland.[7]

Following this ancient tradition, Muslim rulers exchanged a wide variety of animals among themselves and with neighboring Christian courts.[8] Indian rulers sent native animals including exotic talking birds and rhinoceroses to the Aq Qoyunlu and Ṣafavids.[9] Farther afield, the Mughals and others made many presentations of animals to Western courts that amazed and intrigued the European public throughout the sixteenth century.[10]

The reasons for these zoological transactions varied in time and space, but the common denominators were curiosity, the attraction of the exotic, and the acquisition of political prestige. The sender demonstrated generosity and command over Nature, and the recipient's status was elevated by a convincing display of distant connections. This is easily documented in the case of China. From early times Chinese rulers were keen on obtaining unusual animals. During the Han era Shanglin park was populated by Central Asian horses, Indian rhinoceroses, and West Asian ostriches. The subordinate kingdom of Qi also gathered "rare beasts and odd birds" to enhance its prestige.[11] This desire became well known in surrounding regions, and states wishing to initiate or renew relations with Chinese courts typically sent missions bearing local products and animals.[12] When China was in an expansive mode, they actively sought such beasts for transport to the Middle Kingdom. Zheng He, during his maritime expeditions (1403–33), brought home to China lions, leopards, ostriches, and zebras from Aden and Arabia.[13] The close connection in Chinese minds between foreign embassies and strange animals is fully revealed in the reception accorded the Macartney mission. Shortly after his arrival in Beijing in September 1793, rumors began circulating among the public that he had brought as gifts to the Qianlong emperor "an elephant not larger than a cat, and a horse the size of a mouse [and] a singing bird as big as a hen."[14]

This expectation of strange creatures from faraway realms made perfect sense; after all, English clothing, appearance, technology, and ships were exotic, so why not their animals? And, of course, this *mentalité* was hardly unique to the Chinese, but one that was universal in the premodern world. This was a time when the earth was populated with many fabled and rarely represented animals. A giraffe to a medieval European was more than a rarity, it was a wonder. Consequently, as Mary Helms has argued, nothing better demonstrated on home ground a ruler's great reach, knowledge of distant places, and his far-flung fame than a zoological garden full of strange, foreign animals. Moreover, since such beasts were, by virtue of distant origins, imbued with mystery, they revealed a ruler's spiritual resources as well as his earthly powers.[15] This notion is explicitly expressed in the 1680s when the king of Siam offered elephants to the Ṣafavid shah. In accepting, his envoy says: "Our King's possessions and property are not simply intended for practical uses but it is a requisite of his power of state and world rule that every kind of God's creatures be contained within the royal estates."[16] In exchanging unusual animals, rulers quite consciously, I think, helped to solidify each other's regimes through a kind of professional courtesy. They exchanged many species, but two, the lion and the giraffe, are particularly helpful in exploring the range, motives, and mechanisms of this traffic.

In antiquity and the Middle Ages, wild lion populations were far more widespread than they are today; besides the African variety, there were lions in the Balkans, Mesopotamia, Persia, and southern Turkestan, now all extinct, and in western India, where there is still a small relic population in Gujarat. Many were killed by royal hunters but some were trapped and sent to fellow sovereigns.

In a few instances we know something of their source and routing. A small state in Turkestan, possibly Balkh, sent lion cubs to Gandhāra in northern India in the early sixth century, and Fryer, in the late 1670s, encountered an Indian lion in transit to Iṣfahān, a gift of Awrangzīb to Sulaymān I (r. 1666–94).[17] As late as 1833 the sultan of Morocco gave the American legation in Tangier a lion for President Jackson, a gift that was with difficulty refused.[18] In many other cases, however, matters are far less certain. The origin of the pair of lions Queen Elizabeth sent to Ivan IV of Moscow is not indicated.[19] The gift does, however, tell us of their wide circulation, since, obviously, these lions were "recycled" gifts that the English obtained in some earlier transaction.

The cultural history of lions is in fact quite complex. I cannot claim that I understand all the cultural contexts that conditioned the way peoples from North Africa to North China viewed lions and gave them symbolic meaning, but the essential point is that lions have such contexts and images across the whole of the Old World. Of course, other powerful predators, such as the jaguar of the Americas, have great importance to many people, but mainly those within its natural range, while the lion, by contrast, had meanings and well-articulated cultural niches far beyond its home range. There are two reasons for this wide distribution. First, the symbolic meanings attached to lions were diffused through varied cultural media—art, literature, and religion—and second, lions themselves were transported throughout the continent as part of a long-term and long-distance traffic in wild animals.

We are best informed about this traffic to China. The Chinese, from the linguistic evidence, learned of lions through Indo-European intermediaries. The Chinese *shizi*, "lion," in all probability represents the Tocharian B *ṣecake*, "lion," which in turn goes back to some Iranian form.[20] Lions enter Chinese consciousness during the Warring States period as artistic representations, usually figurines based on West Asian prototypes. These representations soon became fairly common in tombs and temples, where they served as guardian or felicitous spirits.[21] The first living lions came to China in the early centuries of the Common Era from the "Western Region," a term with very wide application.[22] In one case, the ruler of Kashghar (Sule) in 133 C.E. submitted to the Han court "tributes of lions [*shizi*] and zebus [*fengniu*]."[23] The pairing of lions with zebus (*Bos indicus*) may indicate an Indian origin, but other possibilities, Parthia for example, cannot be excluded.

This traffic in lions continued after the fall of the Han. Persia (Posi) exported lions to the Northern Wei (386–535) and the Tang, while India (Tianzhu) exported them to the Song.[24] The Mongolian rulers of China received lions and tigers from their ally, the Mongolian court of Iran.[25] Their successors, the Ming, also received lions as tribute presentations from the Western Region, principally Samarqand, and through commercial channels.[26] ʿAlī Akbar Khiṭā'ī, a Persian merchant who wrote an invaluable book on China in 1516–17, says that Muslim traders traveling overland often brought lions (*shīr*) and other cats to China, where they fetched a good price.[27]

The lion in China, far from the natural range, had from the beginning great symbolic power. The two large guardian lions standing in front of the tomb of the famous Empress Wu (r. 683–705) might be read in different ways. For some, they symbolize the power and majesty of Buddha, but others could have read them as a successful assertion of the ruler's authority over wild Nature. Again, the point is that to all who saw them lions were symbols, whether in the flesh or in art, of physical and spiritual power.[28]

Giraffes (*Girafa camelo pardus*), our second example, are surely one of Nature's most arresting creations. From their natural range, the open county of South and Central Africa, giraffes were early on the move. Already in the middle of the second millennia B.C.E., Punt sent several specimens as tribute to Egypt.[29] In later centuries, Islamic Egypt became the principal redistribution center; some came as tribute from Nubia and some came north as part of the commercial

Figure 18. Tribute giraffes, Tomb of Rekhmire, Egypt, late fifteenth century B.C.E. Werner Forman/Art Resource.

traffic in exotic animals.[30] Once in Egypt, the giraffe (Arabic *zarāfah*) was reexported or offered as royal presentations to caliphs and other Muslim rulers.[31] In the thirteenth and fourteenth centuries, giraffes from Egypt reached courts from Sicily to Central Asia.[32] The Chinese knew about the giraffe, called *qilin* or *zala* (from the Arabic), by the twelfth century, but they first appeared in the flesh, via the Indian ocean routes, in the early Ming.[33]

Thus, by the Middle Ages, there were in the Old World well-established networks specializing in the transcontinental movement of animals, including, of course, those trained to the chase. The means of acquisition were basically the same for animals of all kinds—wild, tamed, and domesticated. The Mongols obtained some of their hunting partners as booty and some as tributes levied on subject peoples, and the Ṣafavid rulers sent agents abroad to purchase "hunting animals" of various sorts.[34] Like the wild beasts, many of the elites' animal partners came as gift from countrymen or neighboring courts.[35]

Neither religious differences nor a history of hostility prevented these exchanges. One such presentation between rivals, the Byzantine emperor Nicephorus and Hārūn al-Rashīd in 806, provides a listing of the royal gifts that was fairly standard. The Byzantine ruler received a slave girl, a royal tent with all the fittings, perfume, exotic food, and drugs, and sent to the caliph gold coins, sumptuous brocade robes, horses, falcons, and hunting hounds.[36] The beasts of prey, certainly, were not the most valuable part of this exchange, but such gifts were always welcome and, as we shall see, a most common feature of interstate relations in the premodern era.

These exchanges, like the royal hunt at large, were thoroughly embedded in other activities, military, commercial, and diplomatic, and the end result was a noticeable trend toward the homogenization of elite hunting practices on a continental scale. This is first evident in the later Middle Ages and becomes quite apparent in the immediate post-Mongolian era. In the twelfth-century romance *Visramiani*, the hero, Ramin, rejoices that he can hunt continually with his cheetahs, hawks, and hounds, while in sixteenth-century Gujarat, its Muslim prince hunted with falcons, greyhounds, bloodhounds, and "ounces," that is, caracals and cheetahs.[37] A standard repertoire of coursing animals was now firmly established throughout the core and in most of the periphery. At the courts of the Italian city-states of the Renaissance, elites hunted local game with nets and temporary fences of strong cloth to direct animal drives and corral game. They hunted on horseback and did so with the assistance of raptors, hunting leopards, and a multitude of dogs. Both men and women hunted, typically in preserves, jealously guarded against poaching, and periodically repaired to villas for rest, refreshment, and entertainment. And in pursuit of the most noble sport of falconry, they used the standard set of birds, the same kind of equipment, and the same means of training and deployment found elsewhere in Eurasia.[38]

How this homogenization of royal hunting culture came about is best approached by documenting the transcontinental diffusion of the principal animals of the chase and their handlers.

Dogs

The range and intensity of the traffic in canines are accurately reflected in the nomenclature of guard and hunting breeds which regularly denote their real and putative homelands. In English we have Russian wolfhound, Irish setter,

Great Dane, spaniel, Scottish terrier, Siberian husky, German shepherd, Afghan, Komandor (Qumandur), and the Alan, a French wolfhound. This list could be greatly expanded but the larger point is that canine breeds, for the most part those employed as hunting assistants, have traveled widely, a movement that began in early historic times and continues to the present.

The first on the move were the greyhound and saluki. From their centers in Egypt and Mesopotamia they soon diffused into the Mediterranean area during the Minoan age, and thereafter into southern Europe in Greco-Roman times.[39] In later centuries, these imports, called *leporarius* or *veltres* in the Latin West, were extensively and successfully modified and bred; the whippets and wolfhounds of Europe are the direct descendants of West Asian gazehounds.[40]

In Iran and Afghanistan, the greyhound was widely popular, the preeminent hunting dog of the region. Here they were called "Arabian [*tāzī*] hounds," and were thought of as worthy princely gifts.[41] The Iranian variety probably gave rise to the Russian borzoi, which is simply an enlarged greyhound with a heavier coat to withstand the harsh winters of the north. The name, first mentioned in the Russian sources in 1613, comes from the Old Slavonic, *br'z'*, "quick" or "swift."[42]

The nomads of the Eurasian steppe had from early times their own dogs, sometimes used in the hunt, but the primary function of these ferocious beasts was to protect herds and camps from wild beasts and human intruders.[43] Breeds of dogs specialized in the chase had to be imported from neighboring sedentary societies; the most popular in the open terrain of the steppe, not surprisingly, were the gazehounds of Iran and Afghanistan. Greyhounds, only slightly modified from the original stock, were still found among the local Kazakh nomads in twentieth-century Jungharia.[44] That these Inner Asian greyhounds were not recent imports is apparent from the linguistic evidence. The hunting hound is *tayghan* in Middle Turkic, *tayig-a* in Mongolian, and *taiha* in Manchu; all those go back to the Middle Persian *tāchik*, "Arab," a word that in time was transferred to the settled, Persian-speaking Muslims.[45] Thus, for the peoples of Inner Asia, specialized hunting hounds were imports from, and closely identified with, West Asia and later with the Muslim world.

The first evidence of greyhounds in China goes back to the Han. They are often depicted on pottery and in bas reliefs, sometimes with great accuracy, engaged in hunting hare and deer.[46] They retained their popularity as hunting dogs and as subjects of artistic representation into the Tang and beyond.[47]

The greyhound became a standard or near-standard breed across the continent and over the millennia. By today's measures, canine fashions changed in slow motion but change they did. A number of regional, short-term fads for foreign imports can be documented. One of the very earliest is a Sumerian reference, circa 2000 B.C.E., to "princely dogs, the Elamite dogs."[48] In Achaemenid times, large "Indian hounds" excellent for hunting deer and boar gained popularity which subsequently spread westward in Hellenistic times.[49]

The mastiff also experienced periods of favor and traveled widely. Closely associated with mountainous regions like Tibet, the mastiff found acceptance in early China and may also have reached Assyria.[50] Another period of popularity came in the late Middle Ages. Marco Polo records that the Tibetans "have the very largest hairy mastiff dogs in the world," which, he says, can catch and dispatch all manner of beasts.[51] The merchant ʿAli Akbar Khiṭā'ī tells us something of their range and renown in the early sixteenth century: "Tibetan dogs are very shaggy and very imposing and [its] face is endowed with a dignity equal to that of a lion. And in the exalted courts of the [Muslim] rulers toward the land of the Sultan of Rūm [the Ottomans], there are such dogs which the Rūmīs call the "Sasanid dog" but [which] by origin is the Tibetan dog. And these Tibetan dogs are found in the mountains of China and it is from there that one acquires these dogs."[52] About a century and a half later, the English version of this dog became famous and attracted the attention of the Mughal emperors, whose domains, of course, bordered on Tibet, a nice illustration of how distance adds to luster.[53]

The western Europeans of the Middle Ages accepted and modified foreign breeds and produced, as we have seen, an impressive array of indigenous sleuthhounds that tracked, flushed, and pursued by scent and sound. While hunting dogs that retrieved and pointed were not entirely unique to the West, it is still true that no other region bred so many specialized hunters, each dedicated to a specific type of terrain or prey. These first began to move east in Carolingian times as princely presentations to Muslim rulers.[54] The next wave came in the twelfth century in consequence of the Crusades, when European bird dogs were introduced into the Holy Lands. Called *zaghārī* in Arabic, perhaps from the German *zeiger*, "pointer," these canines must have aroused considerable interest among the Middle Eastern hunting set.[55] In the succeeding Mongolian era, European bird dogs, possibly retrievers (*da paisa*), reached China.[56] The post-Mongolian period saw Western sleuthhounds firmly established in the courts of the core, often as presentations from European commercial interests.[57]

While a certain number of foreign hunting dogs always came as gifts to a powerful court, many rulers were not content to sit and wait; some actively sought out new breeds from distant lands. Jahāngīr was particularly interested in Western hounds. He once asked Shāh ʿAbbās for "large European hunting dogs," likely mastiffs, of which the Ṣafavid ruler procured and sent nine.[58] Later Jahāngīr continually pestered Roe, the English envoy, about hunting dogs. On one occasion he mentioned specific breeds, mastiffs, Irish greyhounds "and such other Dogges as hunt in your Lands."[59] By the end of the seventeenth century, Ovington noted the growing interest in European dogs during his stay in Surat. Great value was placed on spaniels for waterfowl and Irish wolfhounds and mastiffs were equally coveted. Indeed, two Mughal nobles became embroiled in a heated dispute over ownership of such a dog.[60] These imported varieties, however, never supplanted the local greyhounds, and were always expensive and in short supply because they did not fare well in the new environment; climate, disease, and unfamiliar native fauna took a heavy toll of the dogs imported to the subcontinent.[61]

The operation of this canine exchange network is well exemplified by the experience of sixteenth-century Russia, whose rulers, in return for their gifts of raptors, regularly received hunting dogs from lands as far afield as Persia, Georgia, and England.[62] The Russians, however, gave as well as received. In the latter part of the seventeenth century we know that the Mughals acquired "fine sporting dogs from Usbec [Uzbeks] of every kind."[63] But since, as already noted, the nomads did not develop their own hunting breeds, these animals almost certainly came from even farther to the north, the Russian lands. Such a conclusion is supported by the fact that in 1675, the Romanov court, on the advice of Indian merchants in Moscow, deemed it best to open trade negotiations with the Mughal court with a presentation of gyrfalcons (*krechet*), borzois, and mastiffs. Such a gift, the merchants argued, would be particularly welcome because the Indian rulers obtained these dogs in Iran at high prices, and the Ṣafavids, in their turn, obtained the coveted canines from Moscow![64]

Russians also had a hand in the provision of foreign hunting dogs to the Qing dynasty. The Izmailov embassy of 1720 brought as part of its presents to the Manchu court twelve greyhounds (borzois) and twelve French buckhounds (*gonchie frantsuzkie*). Some were for the prime minister, but the bulk went to the emperor. Each animal, Bell tells us, was duly "catalogued," its name and distinguishing features entered into the records, and a yellow silk collar placed on it to indicate imperial status.[65]

This kind of gift exchange and tribute, so well documented in the early modern age, was hardly new; such exchanges, clearly the major mechanism for the dispersal of specialized breeds across Eurasia, had been going on for a millennium or more and resulted in the accumulation of a great diversity of canine types at major courts. The experience of Tang China affords a good illustration of this phenomenon; court records show that they received presentation canines from Kucha, Samarqand, Ferghana, and the Eastern Roman Empire (Fulin).[66] Most were hunting hounds but some were miniature lap dogs from the Mediterranean trained to do various tricks, presented by the oasis state of Turfan.[67]

This long-term interest in, and insatiable desire for, other people's dogs was fueled in large measure by the expectation that distant canines would possess special properties and by the endless stories of bigger and better breeds in some far corner of the world. At various times and places, the Canary Islands,

Transcaucasian Albania, and Afghanistan were thought to be populated with unexcelled hunting dogs, some so large and strong that they could dispatch lions.[68] The fact that such beliefs persisted for so long, from antiquity through the early modern age, says something of elite hunters' enduring fascination with foreign breeds and the prestige associated with their possession.

To some extent, canine imports could be reproduced locally. Dogs are extremely adaptable, and self-sustaining breeding populations were established for some varieties—greyhounds and mastiffs—across the continent. Only the truly domesticated animal hunting assistants, canines, horses, and ferrets, have managed this.[69] In the case of trained wild species, hunting cats, raptors, and elephants, their cultural range was often increased, sometimes dramatically so, by human agency, but not their natural range. This, of course, has some rather obvious economic implications for the traffic in these animals.

Birds

While many species of trained birds of prey traveled widely, this is not to say that local species were disdained. The Ṣafavid shah Sulaymān, for example, made every effort to capture native birds for his mews.[70] And in the core area, as well as in medieval Europe and Russia, rulers regularly exchanged locally caught raptors with their officials and clients.[71] But as previously argued, falconry was made truly aristocratic only by pageantry, the assistance of professional trainers, and by the accumulation of diverse birds from distant climes. Status and prestige could not long be sustained by local birds alone.

Acquisition of foreign raptors follows the normal pattern. Tax receipts from the early ʿAbbāsid period, circa 785, show that Baghdad received tribute falcons from Armenia and Jīlān/Gīlān in northern Iran.[72] Korea sent a variety of raptors to China during the late Silla period and again in the thirteenth century, when both were under Mongolian rule. Down to early modern times, Korea was also the chief source of wild-caught goshawks for Japan.[73]

Commercial channels were also important; their range is revealed by ornithological knowledge contained in medieval geographies, bestiaries, and travel accounts. From these we learn of the kinds of birds exported from Turkestan, the middle Volga, and the Caspian coast. These birds are treated as just another local product available in the international market.[74] The sources tell us, too, about the high demand for raptors; the Persian embassy to Siam in the 1680s heard that Japan was at that time a hotbed of the sport.[75] Clearly, the qualities of the major species of hunting birds were a subject of "international" attention and opinion. Marco Polo discusses and renders judgments on the goshawks of Georgia, the falcons of Kirmān in Iran, the sakers of Badakhshān, the lanner or heron falcons of the Tangut land, and the goshawks of eastern India.[76] The ornithological horizons of Frederick II were equally wide; his writings reveal that he was well acquainted with the characteristics and behavior of raptor species from East Asia, India, the Middle East, and the high Arctic, and with methods of falconry from England to Arabia.[77]

Naturally, merchants tried to exploit this avid interest in foreign birds. International markets formed, and devoted falconers such as Usāmah's father, a twelfth-century Syrian noble, sent his personal agents to Byzantium to procure the highest quality falcons.[78] Oftentimes, traveling merchants, in fact and in fiction, made presentations of fine birds of prey to rulers as a means of getting their foot in the door.[79] Given the passion for hawking in the Middle Ages, this was a good gambit.

While quality birds were always welcome, whatever the source, it is evident that it was particularly gratifying and advantageous to receive rare species from fabled rulers on the far horizon. In the Persian tradition, Bahrām Gor obtains his favorite goshawk from the emperor of China, and in the Oghuz epic, the prestige of the hero is much enhanced by the receipt of a falcon from the "infidel king of Trebizond."[80]

The historical reality is that rulers constantly exchanged raptors with neighbors near and far. Throughout the Muslim Middle Ages, caliphs and sultans presented each other with raptors of every kind, as one of the items required of royalty.[81] They did the same with Byzantine emperors and later with the Crusaders, which did much to stimulate further interest in falconry in Europe.[82] Rulers in East Europe and in East Asia followed suit, sending various raptors across political and cultural frontiers to their fellow sovereigns.[83]

Many of these exchanges were regional in nature, but there was a truly transcontinental market for raptors. One of the long-term trends detectable in this market was the growing fondness for birds of the far north. Initially, in the tenth and eleventh centuries, this preference was general, attaching to falcons, goshawks, and other species from the north.[84] The reason for this predilection is most clearly articulated by Frederick II, who held that because of the cold climatic conditions, "all rapacious birds born in the seventh climate zone and still further north are larger, stronger, more fearless, more beautiful and swifter than southern species."[85] This opinion was widely and strongly held in the core area, where Persian notables in the seventeenth century paid "great prices" for the "hawks of Moscovy, which they believed far superior to the domestic varieties.[86]

During the twelfth and thirteenth centuries, one particular northern species, the gyrfalcon (*Falco rusticolus*), gradually became the raptor of choice across the continent. The largest and fastest of the falcons, their natural range is the taiga, the subarctic zone of both hemispheres. Their coloring ranges from black, through various shades of gray and brown, to white. Though in nature they seem to prefer small ground game, this was deemed insufficiently sporting, so captured birds were trained up and flown at more appropriate prey, namely geese, swans, herons, and crane.[87]

In the western half of Eurasia, gyrfalcons are occasionally noted in the eleventh century as presents in exchanges between Muslim rulers.[88] Their continental popularity, however, is not fully established until the thirteenth century, the period of Mongolian expansion. We have a number of indications that these birds were much favored by the Chinggisids. In describing the Mongolian elites' selection of proffered royal rewards in the 1240s, a Chinese source relates that a popular choice were gyrfalcons.[89] There is even a public opinion poll of sorts; according to a maxim of Chinggis Qan, recorded in Rashīd al-Dīn's history, when the Mongolian leader asks his followers what is the greatest pleasure of man, they all answer that hunting with falcons and gyrfalcons is the supreme joy.[90]

This preference for gyrfalcons remained with the Mongols throughout the imperial era and beyond.[91] Their passion for this bird was shared by many others, including Frederick II. In his treatise on falconry, gyrfalcons are given pride of place "out of respect for their size, strength, audacity, and swiftness," a judgment still fully accepted by a Persian falconer in the mid-nineteenth century.[92] The true extent and duration of this popularity is afforded by an incident related in the travels of Tulishen, the Manchu envoy to the Qalmaq qan Ayuki. In 1713 he had an audience with Gagarin, the Russian governor-general of Siberia in the city of Tobolsk. After formalities, the conversation turned to hunting and the two soon discovered that the favorite hunting bird of their respective lands was the gyrfalcon. They learned further that neither reared these birds from the nest but rather acquired them wild-caught from the far north.[93]

Linguistic data are also helpful in measuring and tracking this popularity. In the south, beyond their natural range, the term for gyrfalcon is widely shared: *sungqur* in Turkic, *shonqar/singqor* in Mongolian, *shimuko* in Jürchen, *shonkon* in Manchu, *shongkhe* in Korean, and *sunqūr* in Persian and Arabic.[94] Northerners, closer to the birds' habitat, had their own names for this species, Old Norse *geirfálki* and Russian *krechet.*

Among the gyrfalcons, there was a decided preference for those birds white in color. This, too, evolved over time. In both Muslim and Chinese sources of the ninth and tenth centuries, there are occasional references to white falcons in contexts that indicate their rarity and desirability.[95] Masʿūdī, who is well aware that falconry is a truly international pastime much favored by royalty, emphasizes most particularly the supreme qualities of white falcons from snowy climes, Khazaria and the Caucasus.[96] This growing interest in birds of this color was finalized in the Mongolian period, when white gyrfalcons became the most

Figure 19. Qubilai and huntsman with white gryfalcon. Liu Kuan-tao, Yuan Dynasty. National Palace Museum, Republic of China.

prestigious, most coveted raptor. For the Mongols this was a natural choice, since white in their culture was propitious, thought to engender good fortune, and good fortune was an integral element in their imperial ideology.[97]

Once again, this is a transcontinental phenomenon. For Frederick II, who well knows the color range in gyrfalcons, "the white varieties from remote regions are the most valued."[98] And in later centuries, so too did English factors in Moscovy, who quickly realized that the preferred color for "Jarfawkons" was white.[99]

In reconstructing the cultural history of gyrfalcons in Eurasia, several points stand out.

First, gyrfalcons were not trained to hunt under human control within their native range; the hunting-gathering and reindeer herding peoples of the taiga were not falconers. The skills required to modify the birds' behavior resided in the more complex agricultural and nomadic societies to the south.

Second, the demand for these birds was generated by cultural forces at work in these southerly climes, which are not hard to discern. Since almost all the locally available species of raptors in the south had been trained, demonstrated, and exchanged, the only exotics, the only distant and therefore prestigious birds left were to be found in the far north.

Third, the fact that these birds came from "the Land of Darkness," an alien and mysterious clime with extreme conditions of temperature and light, "naturally" endowed gyrfalcons with very special properties in the minds of southern falconers.

Fourth, the very distance from the source of supply meant that gyrfalcons would be expensive, out of reach of the masses who could and did capture and train local species for their own pleasure; thus, by virtue of elevated costs, a gyrfalcon became a most fitting bird for a great prince.

Fifth, the great distances involved also meant that special measures would have to be employed to extract these prized raptors from a region over which no major power in the south, the center of the demand, exercised effective political authority.

Sixth, the passion for gyrfalcons of all colorations, as we shall see in the discussion of their procurement, begins in the east, spreads westward, and is confirmed and consolidated by the formation of the Mongols' transcontinental imperium.

Systematic, government-sponsored quests for northern raptors begins, apparently, with the Qitan. Even in the predynastic period, they showed a sustained interest in the birds of the North Pacific and pressured, and may have created, tribes in the region of the Amur to capture for them eagles, hawks, and falcons, including the "east-of-the-sea grays [*haidong qing*]," the gyrfalcons.[100]

The Qitan also traded with tribes of northeastern Manchuria, such as the Malgal (Mohe), to obtain the desired birds.[101] It is interesting that by the late tenth century, the Qitan demand created an expectation among northern tribes that everyone to their south desired gyrfalcons. Thus, in 992 the Song court was offered a tribute of east-of-the-sea grays which they declined.[102]

Over time, the Qitan elaborated a system of "relay tribute" to ensure a steady supply of gyrfalcons. The Liao court imposed upon their neighbors to the north, the Jürchen, the obligation of levying tribute upon the Jürchens' neighbors to the northeast, the so-called Five Nations (Wuguo), who lived on the lower Amur, to capture east-of-the-sea grays, most particularly the white variety.[103] In order to accomplish this, the Jürchen had to mount major military campaigns to the northeast, sometimes involving 1,000 horsemen. This annual effort was controlled by Liao officials of the well-named *Waiyingfang*, or "Falconry for the Outer Regions." It was this onerous demand on the Jürchens that sparked their rebellion and overthrow of the Liao in 1125.[104]

The Mongols of the Yuan instituted a very similar system, which Marco Polo describes at length. He relates that forty-days march east of the plain of Bargu, the frontier between northern Mongolia and Manchuria, is the "Ocean Sea," the Pacific, and on islands offshore are found the gyrfalcons that the "great Kaan," Qubilai, extracts as tribute from the locals.[105] This system, we know from the Chinese records, required for prompt delivery to the capital a series of twenty-four postal relay stations supplied with horses, fodder, and food (mutton) for the captured birds. The posts, called "gyrfalcon stations [*haiqing zhan*]," were first established in 1260 and subsequently reformed in 1295 and 1308.[106] The northern terminus of these stations was the town of Nuergan (Nurgan/Nurgal) on the lower Amur.[107] Here the local population trapped the east-of-the-sea grays with nets as their tribute.[108] And, as was the case in Liao times, the incessant demands for tribute birds led to a rebellion; in 1346, according to court records, the Yuan authorities charged with procuring gyrfalcons "provoked the wild Wuzhe people and the Water Tatars, all of whom rebelled."[109]

The Ming, once they had consolidated their hold on China, in 1411 sent an expedition to Nuergan and there established a *wei*, or commandery, recruited from the local Jürchen population. The latter acknowledged Ming sovereignty by delivering annual tributes of gyrfalcons and other local products.[110] The Qing as well, at least to the early eighteenth century, still obtained their east-of-the-sea grays from the Amur and places farther to the north.[111]

While China-based dynasties exploited the North Pacific's avian resources for nearly a thousand years, this was not their only source of gyrfalcons. When Chinggis Qan sent forces to southern Siberia and the Yenisei in 1207 to subdue the "forest people," they recognized their new masters with presentations of white gyrfalcons and eagles.[112] The area just to the east of Lake Baikal became so identified as a source of raptors that it was called "the land of falconers [*vilāyāt-i shibāʿūchī*]" in the Persian texts of the era.[113] Further west, the Yenisei region also provided birds; during Qubilai's reign merchants operating in the region brought white gyrfalcons to court, and in the early fourteenth century Yuan officials were sent to the Qirghiz to levy a tribute of "birds of prey [*yingyao*]."[114] These same sources were still available in the early Ming. The Uriyangqadai, a forest tribe, sent falcons to Beijing, and the Oyirad Mongols presented gyrfalcons, in return for which they received high-value satin stuffs.[115]

In the latter instance, some kind of relay tribute was operative, since the Jungharian basin, the home ground of the Oyirad, is far from the taiga. Information on the nomads' interaction with the peoples of central Siberia is unfortunately scant, but we do know that in the Mongolian era the rulers of the Ulus of Orda, descendants of Jochi's eldest son, who held sway over modern-day Kazakhstan and contiguous parts of Siberia, organized an elaborate postal relay system, serviced by horses and dog sleds, to extract northern products.[116] While not specifically mentioned, it is unlikely that the highly valued gyrfalcon was ignored in this tributary trade. More certainly, it is known that the notables of the Siberian qanate, one of the successors of the eastern wing of the Golden Horde, were eager falconers, and that in 1596, as this qanate disintegrated under Russian pressure, ʿAbdullāh II, the ruler of Bukhara, sent an envoy to the Siberian qan, Kuchum, with valuable presents asking for precious furs and gyrfalcons.[117] Clearly, he expected Kuchum to compel his forest friends to procure the desired goods from the taiga.

At this juncture, it will be convenient to survey the traffic in gyrfalcons from the North Atlantic and then again move inland to Moscovy, which became a major source of supply in the post-Mongolian age.

In treating this trade, it must be remembered that since raptors frequently died or flew the coop, there was a constant demand for replacements. Consequently, in medieval Europe, as elsewhere in Eurasia, there was a well-organized and large-scale trade in birds of prey. Starting in the early eleventh century raptors from Iceland and Norway came south to England, and by the thirteenth century these birds regularly reached the Mediterranean.[118] While northern courts tried to monopolize the traffic, private commercial interests soon came to dominate; the Dutch, for example, controlled the trade in trained Scandinavian gyrfalcons, which fetched high prices at European courts.[119]

The price of gyrfalcons, of course, was greatly influenced by the high transportation costs. As Frederick II well knew, the favored breeding grounds of gyrfalcons were the sea cliffs of Norway, Iceland, and Greenland.[120] These locales were known as well in the Muslim world. Abū'l Fidā says that beyond Ireland there is the "Island of Gyrfalcons [Jazīrah al-sanāqir]" and he quotes an earlier geographer, Ibn Saʿīd, who, writing circa 1270, relates that in his day the Mamlūk sultans paid upwards of 1,000 gold dinars for the white variety.[121] Elevated prices such as these attracted many to this trade. Raymon Llull, in his prose novel *Felix* (ca. 1288–89), makes mention of the "many men with gyrfalcons, which they had brought from one end of the world [the Arctic] and were now taking to the Tartars to make money."[122] These birds did in fact reach "Tartar" princes in this age; the Mongolian ruler of Iran, Öljeitü, had, in the words of a contemporary chronicler, "an intense passion for Frankish gyrfalcons [*sunqūr-i farankī*]," and in 1403 the Spanish court sent a presentation of gyrfalcons to Temür that were much coveted by the conqueror's grandson.[123]

The Russians' assumption of a pivotal role in supplying this seemingly insatiable demand for gyrfalcons is a by-product of Moscovy's access to breeding grounds in the north. Their princes were the first falconers to exercise effective and, in time, permanent authority over the taiga and its rich avian treasures.

The Rus princes of the Kievan era imposed heavy fines for stealing hawks and falcons in unattended hunting nets, clearly indicating that birds of prey had already become a valuable, domestic commodity.[124] But it was the growing demand for gyrfalcons in the thirteenth century that brought Russia to the attention of the international market. Marco Polo, as usual, is well informed on their source. He reports that north of "Rosie" in the Sea of Tramontaine, the Arctic Ocean, there are "certain islands" on which "many gyrfalcons are bred" and that these birds are captured and then sent "to different provinces and to many places of the world."[125] At the time of his observations, the Russian principalities were still under the control of the Golden Horde, who, naturally, had an important say in the distribution of these birds, presenting many to the Mamlūks, their principal ally in the Middle East.[126]

By the next century, however, Moscovy had achieved a measure of independence and was now in a position to assert its claims on the lands of Perm and Pechora and thereby control trade in fur and other northern products, including hunting birds.[127] This is evident from a treaty Moscow and Novgorod concluded with Tver in 1319, which stipulates that "whosoever seizes in Vologda [260 miles northeast of Moscow] gyrfalcons [*krechet*] or silver or squirrel skins" must be sent "back for judicial inquiry."[128] The fact that gyrfalcons are bracketed with silver and squirrel skins indicates the high value attached to these birds, and indicates that by this time Russian political authorities were trying to monopolize these particular raptors. This concern is further confirmed by a document from the reign of the Moscovite prince Ivan Danilovich, who, sometime between 1328 and 1341, "made a bestowal on the falconers of Pechora [*sokol'nikov pecherskikh*]" and granted them immunity from various taxes and local legal jurisdictions, "because," he explains, "these people are important to me."[129]

With their conquest of Novgorod in the late fifteenth century, Moscow's market position was greatly enhanced; the grand princes now enjoyed direct access to the breeding grounds of gyrfalcons and other raptors. By the sixteenth century, procurement of gyrfalcons had become carefully organized and very much the concern of the state and its sovereigns. Acquisition and transportation of these birds from their home territory in the north was charged to a corporation of specialists called *pomtsy/pomychniki*.[130] In return for delivering a hundred gyrfalcons annually, they enjoyed considerable privilege; like the earlier falconers of Pechora, they paid no taxes nor any other service to the state, and were immune from local legal interference except in the case of highway robbery and murder. Additionally, when they presented their catch of live birds to the court, they received supplementary recompense in the form of money and textiles.

Organized into groups of about forty, called *vataga*,[131] "artel" or "cooperative," headed by an *ataman*, "chief," they conducted their business in great secrecy, concealing the locales where gyrfalcons could be caught. Once in hand, the birds' transport to Moscow was elaborately arranged and minutely regulated. The activities of the *pomychniki* were later extended to Siberia and the corporation survived in one form or another down to 1827.[132]

In consequence of these efforts, the richness and diversity of Moscow's avian resources became internationally recognized. Almost all foreign travelers in the Moscovite realm comment on the raptors available there, and most particularly the white gyrfalcons found in the vicinity of the Pechora Peninsula.[133] To bring the best prices on the foreign market, the birds exported were usually captured as adults and then trained to the chase. The training of falcons in Russia, which followed locally produced manuals, was achieved by a strict regimen of conditioned behavior and differed little from contemporary practice elsewhere in Eurasia.[134] The training was under the control of the Falconry Department, "*Sokol'nichii put*" in Russian. Between the thirteenth and the seventeenth century, there were a number of such departments that oversaw various branches of the princely establishment or economy—stable, table, hunt, and so on. The heads, called *putnik*, reported directly to the prince. Like the others, the Falconry Department was financed by retaining part of the profits it generated, a practice known as *kormlenie*, or "feeding."[135]

The Falconry Department was also involved in the transportation of birds from Russia to lands farther to the south. Placed in the immediate care of special handlers, *krechatniki*, the birds were carried in padded boxes lined with sheepskin to prevent injury. Additionally, careful provision was made for their food.[136] But even with these precautions, there was a high mortality rate among birds in transit to distant lands such as Georgia and Persia.[137] This is not too surprising since trips from Moscow to Persia at this time took well over one hundred days of hard travel by boat and caravan.[138]

Because white gyrfalcons were so valuable, their export was in effect a monopoly of the state, which used them extensively as presentations to rulers throughout Eurasia.[139] Prized raptors flowed south to nomadic chieftains in the steppe, westward to Renaissance courts in Italy, and to Queen Elizabeth of England, who received from Ivan IV "a large and faire white Jerfawcan for the wilde Swanne, Crane, Goose and other great Fowles."[140] The numbers involved were at times impressive; the ambassador of the Shirvānshāh, according to Afanasii Nikitin, returned home in 1466 from his embassy to Ivan III (r. 1462–1505) with ninety gyrfalcons.[141] So desirable were these birds that in 1515 an Ottoman governor of Caffa in the Crimea requested, and was granted, permission to send a commercial agent to purchase gyrfalcons (*krechet*) in the capital.[142]

Because of the growing importance of these birds in diplomatic relations, Russian rulers of the sixteenth and seventeenth century placed raptors, particularly gyrfalcons, on the list of "prohibited goods [*zapovednye tovary*]." Such goods could not be exported or even transported within the realm on pain of death. As Audrey Burton has pointed out, exceptions could be made to show favor to a particular court, embassy, or group of merchants in expectation of some concession on their part. And, indeed, the Russians often played their "*krechet* card" in the course of their contentious relationships with states to their south—Iran, India, Bukhara, and Georgia—and even in their initial attempt to establish relations with the Qing, a court which had its own supply.[143]

Yet another measure of their value as an international political currency is that Russian gyrfalcons were recycled in further diplomatic exchanges. Ṣafavid Iran, which received their gift gyrfalcons in annual installments, sent some on to other courts. In 1617, when the Russian ambassador arrived with the birds, one was subsequently given to an Indian envoy for delivery to the Mughal court. Indeed, a contemporary diplomatic document records that around 1619 the Persian ruler Shāh ʿAbbās sent the Mughal emperor Jahāngīr a piebald gyrfalcon (*shungār-i ablaq*) that the Ṣafavid had received in the first instance from the Russian tsar Mikhail (r. 1613–45), the first Romanov.[144] This was truly a well-traveled bird, one that began life in the subarctic and ended it in the subcontinent.

To this point, we have concentrated on the north-south movement of these birds. This is misleading, for as David Christian has argued, north-south exchanges between ecological zones and the east-west exchanges between civilizations in fact formed one large interactive network.[145] This is well demonstrated by the movement of gyrfalcons. Once more, Marco Polo is our best guide: he states that the great qan sends some of the falcons taken from the Ocean Sea, the Pacific "to Argon and those other lords of the Levant who are near to the Armenians and Comain [Qumans/Qipchâqs]," that is, to the Yuan emperor's allies in the West such as Arghun, the Mongolian ruler of Iran (r. 1284–91).[146] This westward movement of Pacific gyrfalcons is fully substantiated by Persian and Chinese sources. Qāshānī, a contemporary, relates that the Yuan court twice sent gyrfalcons (*sunqūr*) to Öljeitü.[147] This means, of course, that the mews of Öljeitü contained both "Frankish" gyrfalcons from the North Atlantic and "Chinese" gyrfalcons from the North Pacific.

The same can be said of the Temürids, who received their gyrfalcons from the Spanish court and from the Ming dynasty. The Yongle emperor (r. 1403–25) presented Shāh Rukh's embassy in China, 1419–21, with gyrfalcons on several occasions.[148] The source of Ming gyrfalcons is helpfully spelled out on another diplomatic occasion. In the Persian translation of Yongle's Chinese letter delivered to Shāh Rukh in 1419, the Ming emperor declares that the seven gyrfalcons (*sūnqūrān*) he sends to his fellow prince have all been flown from his "own hand" and then adds that these birds were not native to China (Chīn) but were brought to court as tribute "from the shores of the sea [*atraf-i daryā*]."[149] Here, clearly, is a reference to the *haidong qing*, the "east-of-the-sea grays."

The demand for these birds in the Western Region continued into later centuries. In 1469 the ruler of Turfan (Tulufan), Sultan ʿAlī (Sutan A-li), petitioned the Ming emperor requesting gyrfalcons (*haiqing*) and was told that they were on the list of goods prohibited for export.[150] This brings us full circle: the Ming dynasty, like its contemporary, Moscovite Russia, thought of gyrfalcons as a diplomatic tool, to be monopolized and utilized for political ends.

Elephants

Elephants were exchanged and recycled like other animal partners, albeit on a more limited scale. In the long history of this traffic, the preference was for the Ceylonese variety.[151]

The courts of India were major consumers and the Mughals' demand for elephants seems open-ended. They captured and trained the indigenous animals and imported hundreds from neighboring regions. During the seventeenth century, Aceh in western Sumatra exported elephants to the Mughals, and the Hindu kingdom of Golkanda in central India paid tribute to their Mughal overlords in elephants purchased from Pegu, Ceylon, and Siam.[152] It is also suggestive in this regard that the Afshārid ruler of Iran, Nādir Shāh, toward the end of his reign (1736–47), sent one hundred elephants, originally obtained in the subcontinent, back to India in an apparent attempt to obtain money from the Mughal court.[153]

The necessary skills and infrastructure needed for the traffic in elephants were obviously developed in the first instance for exchanges within the animals' natural range. Most certainly, the vast majority of interstate elephant transactions took place between countries with their own wild stocks. Still, from an early date, elephants found themselves in distant and unfamiliar lands; through tributary and trade relations, Assyrian kings and the Egyptian Ptolemies acquired foreign elephants for show and warfare.[154] In the Mongolian era, elephants from India (Yindu) reached Samarqand, while the Ṣafavids obtained them from Ceylon and Siam.[155]

From the Han dynasty onward, the elephants of China came from various states in Southeast Asia.[156] While China had a native stock in the southern, subtropical regions of the empire, they do not appear to have developed the skill of training elephants, and so relied on outsiders to supply animals that were already tamed and educated for their varied roles.

In large part, the extension of elephants' cultural range far beyond its natural range was a by-product of the recycling of princely gift exchanges that started in India or Southeast Asia. In a few cases the entire chain of presentation is fairly evident: in 864 the ʿAbbāsid caliph received two elephants from the Ṭāhirid rulers of Khurāsān, who obtained them in Kabul, and in 1655/56 Shāh ʿAbbās II sent the Ottoman sultan Muḥammad IV (r. 1648–87) an elephant obtained during successful campaigns in Hindustan.[157] In most cases, however, we simply do not know how Sasanid, Byzantine, or Mamlūk rulers came by the elephants they presented to neighboring courts.[158]

This is true of Hārūn al-Rashīd's gift of an elephant named Abū'l Abaz to Charlemagne in 801. This, the most celebrated princely animal presentation in medieval European history, raises a number of interesting issues about this traffic.[159] First, since Einhard tells us Charlemagne requested the beast from the caliph, it is a fair assumption that besides curiosity the Frankish ruler had some inkling that elephants were considered proper animals of state by his peers to the east. Second, the same episode points up the difficulties encountered in adopting such standards. The elephant died in 810 and was not replaced. One reason, of course, is that elephants are extremely costly to maintain. Indeed, tamed elephants are everywhere an economic drain unless they earn their keep clearing forests for more agricultural land. Recalling that the Carolingians were generally on the move to find resources to sustain their court, it is not too surprising that they could not afford many elephants. The other problem, one intrinsic to this traffic, is that elephants rarely breed in captivity, so they have to be replaced continually. Moreover, those sent to areas beyond their natural range are inevitably subjected to the stress of lengthy travel, which results in increased mortality rates and further drives up replacement costs. These latter considerations apply with equal force to another tame animal partner, the cheetah.

Cats

Through human agency cheetahs moved far beyond their natural range, which originally extended from Morocco to India, and in the south to East Africa. Under human control cheetahs hunted in North Africa, Ethiopia, Arabia, Asia Minor, Transcaucasia, Iran, India, Turkestan, Mongolia, North China, and Europe.[160] Like other animals of the chase, cheetahs were routinely exchanged within their natural range among Hindu, Muslim, and Christian rulers, and in later centuries bestowed upon European officials stationed in the East.[161]

Peoples living within the cheetah's home range developed a precise terminology for these animals, carefully distinguishing them from other feline species. More distant peoples, of course, did not. English is a case in point: cheetahs were most commonly called "hunting leopards" until the early twentieth century when their Hindi name, *chītā*, came into currency. Like English, many other languages of Eurasia tend to lump together under a single name all felines that are not lions, tigers, or domesticated cats. Interestingly, the term used for this broad category of cats is one shared across a broad linguistic spectrum. It is quite possible that the English pard/panther, Greek *pardos*, German, French, and Russian *gepard*, Soghdian *pwrd̄nk*, Persian *pars* and *palank*, and Turkic-Mongolian *bars*, all meaning "leopard" go back to a common source.[162] One might add to this list the Arabic *fahd*, the Chinese *bao*, and perhaps the Georgian *avaza*.[163] In Michael Witzel's opinion, *pard/pandh* is an ancient word meaning spotted wild animal, more particularly snakes and cats, that may have originated in Iran among the non-Indo-European substrate population.[164]

In consequence of this inexactitude, it is not always possible to identify different species of felines in premodern sources, or even to distinguish between the two principal species of cats hunting under human control, the cheetah and the caracal, often, and mistakenly, called the "hunting lynx." Still, it is possible to trace in broad outline the circulation of cheetahs beyond their natural range. The first radiation, to the east, coincides with the expansion of Islam and the establishment of the Tang dynasty, and the second, to both the east and west, coincides with the creation of the Mongolian empire.

While cheetah skins were exported eastward as early as the fifth or fourth century B.C.E., the live animal was not.[165] Han period sources make reference to leopards (*bao*) in Shanglin park, but there is no hint that they were cheetahs trained to the chase.[166] William White, on the basis of art historical evidence, suggests that in Qin-Han times spotted leopards and striped tigers were used in the hunt. Such animals do appear on hunting scenes on tomb tiles, but in contexts that make it impossible to determine if they are partners or prey. True, one of the tigers wears a collar, but hunting with big cats is problematical.[167]

The first incontrovertible evidence for hunting with cheetahs in China comes from mural paintings in Tang tombs of the last half of the seventh century. In one, that of Li Xian (651–84), the heir-apparent prince of Yung, a cheetah and a caracal with exaggerated, tufted ears, sit on fringed pillions behind the saddles of their handlers, to whom they are tethered. In the other, the tomb of Li Zhongrun (682–701), there is a fair rendering of a cheetah tethered to a hunter on foot.[168] Thereafter, artistic representations of hunting cats become common, especially in the form of glazed pottery tomb figurines that depict both cheetahs and caracals on horseback.[169]

Literary references to tribute "leopards [*bao*]" begin in the early eighth century; the first to arrive came in 717, a gift of the ruler of Khotan. This was soon followed by presentations of leopards from the rulers of Bukhara, Kesh, Ferghana, and Maimurgh, a small principality near Samarqand.[170] While all these references are simply to *bao*, Edward Schafer is quite right in arguing that many of these "leopards" were in fact cheetahs.[171] This is evident from several passages in the dynastic history, one of which states that in 762 the Tang emperor placed a "ban on the offering of tribute hawks, sparrow hawks, dogs and leopards." Another records that the Court of State Ceremonial (*Honglu si*), charged with the reception of foreign tribute, had regulations regarding the valuation placed on hawks, falcons, dogs, and leopards.[172]

In time, the Chinese sources began to use more precise terminology that helps identify *bao* as hunting cats and, at the same time, discriminates between the two types. In one case the "striped leopards [*wenbao*]" of Kesh are recorded and, in another, the "red leopards [*chibao*]" of Khottal, a district on the Amu Darya.[173] The qualifier "striped" denotes the cheetah's most arresting visual characteristic, the lachrymose stripe that runs from the corner of its eyes along its muzzle, called in Arabic the "tear streaks [*al-madmaʿān*]." The "red" leopard is the caracal, which has a reddish brown coat and was commonly called the "red lynx" by the English in India.[174]

The popularity of hunting cats lasted through the Tang and then declined, except in the Liao realm. A Song envoy at the Qitan court in 1020 saw three tame "leopards" riding with their handlers out on a hunt.[175] While the source of these particular cats is not indicated, we know that in later decades the Uighurs (Huihu), deeply involved in long-distance trade, made presentations of cheetahs (*wenbao*) to the Liao court.[176]

The next great wave of cats came east in the thirteenth century under Mongolian auspices. The first recorded presentation of cheetahs to the Mongols came in 1220 with the surrender of Bukhara.[177] We do not know if Chinggis Qan was attracted to the sport, but his successors certainly were. One indication of their interest comes from a decree issued in 1234 about tethering horses at a forthcoming diet of notables (*quriltai*): "Common people's horses ought not to be tethered within the [restricted] dismounting area. [If so,] the [horses] will immediately be confiscated and given over to those who tend tigers and leopards [*chuhubaoren*]."[178] The message is clear: illegally parked horses become cat food. By all accounts, there were a great many to feed. In Qubilai's reign Marco Polo talks about the cats stationed at Shangdu as well as the "very large lions," actually tigers, and the many tame leopards and hunting lynxes that always travel with the qaghan in their own cages on carts.[179]

The origins of these hunting cats can be traced in some detail. Substantial numbers came as gifts. When Rubruck was in Qara Qorum in 1254, he encountered envoys of an Indian ruler who "brought eight leopards and ten greyhounds which had been trained to sit on a horse's back just like leopards do."[180] The Yuan dynasty's ally in the West, the Il-qan court of Iran, certainly made contributions. In the 1320s Abū Saʿīd annually sent shipments of lions, tigers, and leopards to the Yuan court.[181] As a matter of pure speculation, it is possible that some of the cheetahs sent to the Yuan court may have come originally from a certain Muhannā ibn ʿIsā, a Syrian Arab tribal leader who went over to the Il-qans in 1321 with "a number of cheetahs."[182] In any event, we must now add political defection to the mechanisms by which trained cheetahs were dispersed across the continent.

One princely presentation of cheetahs to the Yuan court deserves special consideration. In 1326, Özbek, the qan of the Golden Horde (r. 1313–41), sent cheetahs (*wenbao*) to the qaghan, who responded with grants of gold, silver, cash, and silks.[183] Since the Golden Horde had no domestic supply of cheetahs, the question of their origin arises again. The closest source, Iran, was under the control of rivals so the most likely candidate are the Mamlūks, a close ally of the Golden Horde. That the hunt and hunting animals were involved in their ongoing relations is evidenced by the fact that Özbek on several occasions sent raptors to Egypt and on another sent his master of hunt (*amīr shikār*).[184]

Commercial channels also delivered hunting cats to the East. In the early fourteenth century Muslim merchants using the Indian Ocean routes brought leopards (*bao*) and other animals for presentation to the Yuan court, and used this as a pretext for traveling on the official post at government expense. The fact that such illegal access to the postal system was repeatedly banned indicates that cheetahs were in great demand in Mongolian China and that they well served the merchants as a loss-leader.[185] The result was that the Yuan court, like the Tang, was inundated with free hunting cats. And a steady supply of "cheetahs from the Western Region [Xiyu *wenbao*]" was needed because Yuan emperors bestowed them freely on favored officials.[186]

In the Far West, interest in hunting cats begins in Spain. A Hispano-Islamic textile dating from the mid-eleventh century shows a rider with a chained feline, most likely a caracal, sitting on a pillion.[187] However, it took several more centuries and further external stimuli before the sport gained much of a following elsewhere in Europe. This is borne out by the fact that while Albertus Magnus (d. 1280), the leading zoologist of the late medieval period, has heard of cheetahs, his ideas about them are vague and consistently garbled. In one place he speaks of the long-legged "tall hunting dogs of India" that "are generated from bitches and tigers," an understandable allusion to the cheetah's canine attributes. In another, he refers to the Alfech, Arabic, *al-fahd*, the "cheetah," saying that it is the by-product of the lion and leopard, that is, a leo and a pard. Further, in other passages Albertus Magnus conflates information about the true leopard with that of the cheetah.[188]

But at the very time Albertus Magnus was misinforming his readers on the subject, European interest in, and knowledge of, cheetahs was spreading rapidly. The primary catalyst behind this upsurge of interest was undoubtedly Frederick II, who was familiar with hunting leopards and lynxes and kept a number in southern Italy and Sicily. Some cheetahs may have been presentations from Muslim princes, but others were purchased in North Africa through his agents in Malta. This may well be the source of the three "leopards" Frederick sent Henry III of England (r. 1216–72) as a princely gift.[189] Additional stimulus, and cats, came from the Mongols; in 1291 an embassy of the English king Edward I (r. 1272–1307) brought gyrfalcons to the Il-qans in Iran, and the Mongols sent back a "leopard" the following year.[190]

By these varied routes cheetahs soon began to appear in European art with considerable regularity; like their frequent depiction in Islamic art, this provides a useful index of cheetahs' growing popularity and visibility.[191] Moreover, in these depictions cheetahs are clearly distinguished from true leopards and betray none of the confusion found in the writings of Albertus Magnus. For example, an illustrated psalter produced in England in the 1280s has a well-rendered cheetah as a decorative device on the margin.[192] But even more arresting is the cheetah of Pisanello (ca. 1395–1455). His drawing is very naturalistic, the product of an artist who believed that Nature had to be understood to be depicted properly. Most certainly he knew and studied cheetahs at first hand; his cat has the long, sleek lines of *Acinonyx jubatus*, the tell-tale lachrymal or tear stripe on the face, and the appropriate kind of spots, small and solid.[193] Further, Pisanello's cheetah has a "working" rather than a decorative collar around its neck; this animal, obviously, is someone's pet and probably a hunting partner as well.[194]

Italy, not surprisingly, was at the center of Europe's newfound enthusiasm for hunting cats. The late fourteenth-century sketchbook of Biovannino de Grassi shows a tethered cheetah, with solid spots, in the midst of a larger chase scene.[195] Next, the French monarchs of the fifteenth and early sixteenth centuries took up

Figure 20. Cheetah. Drawing by Pisanello, first half of fifteenth century. Louvre. RMN/Art Resource NY.

the sport with imported cheetahs. Like their counterparts elsewhere in Eurasia, these kings went out to the field with a tethered cheetah on a pillion behind their saddle. When game was started, the cat was loosed, and after it downed its prey, it was quickly rewarded with blood and raw meat and so lured back to its perch.[196]

While certainly a visible part of the royal hunt in Europe, cheetahs never achieved the importance they enjoyed in the core area; they remained exotic, never part of the mainstream.[197] And compared to other parts of the continent, their popularity in Europe was short-lived.

At about this same time, hunting cats had their last period of popularity in China. The maritime expeditions of Zheng He (1403–33) returned caracals from Arabia and Hurmuz to Ming China. The record of his voyages correctly says that their Persian name was *xiya guoshi*, *siyāh gūsh*, or "black ear," that it has tufted ears, a mild disposition, and that they are readily tamed.[198] For the most part, however, hunting cats came by land; throughout the fifteenth century, cheetahs (*wenbao*) and caracals (*hala hula* = *qara qulaq*) reached Beijing as presents from various rulers of Iran and Turkestan.[199] ʿAli Akbar Khiṭāʾī, in the early sixteenth century reports that Muslims going overland to China typically bring cheetahs and caracals with them because, he says, these cats are highly valued and can be exchanged for precious cloth. He also knows that there was a

Figure 21. Cheetah on horseback in France, sixteenth century. Paul Lacroix. France in the Middle Ages (1874, reprint 1963).

special part of the imperial palace in Beijing devoted to cats, a "place of lions [*shirān*], tigers [*babrān*], leopards [*palangān*], cheetahs [*yūz*], and caracals [*siyāh gūsh*]."[200] This was the Leopard Quarter, *baofang*, in Chinese, built by the emperor Zhengde (r. 1501–21), who was determined to revive the Ming military through an active program of hunting that entailed cats trained to the chase. The quarter survived, amid growing criticism of its cost, until the very end of the dynasty, when its animals were killed or released.[201]

The enthusiasm for the sport continued unabated for several more centuries in India and Iran, both of which had indigenous supplies, but declined at either end of the continent. Like the elephant, cheetahs did not reproduce in captivity; thus, no self-sustaining breeding populations were established outside their home ground.

The reasons offered for this failure in premodern times are quite revealing. Albertus Magnus's belief that cheetahs were by-products of dogs and tigers or leopards and lions lies at the heart of the medieval understanding of the problem. His views, however, are not his own; they can be traced back to Muslim beliefs that cheetahs are the offspring of leopards and lions or tigers and lions and, as the products of miscegenation, are sterile like mules and other hybrids.[202] Although wrong, this explanation is nonetheless rational and, more crucial for our purposes, was widespread. It was not, therefore, only animals that moved across political, cultural, and ecological frontiers, but also animal lore and animal images, as well as zoological information and misinformation. This is hardly surprising, for as we shall now see, trainers and handlers often accompanied animals of the chase on their long, one-way journeys.

Traffic in Trainers

Artisans, artists, entertainers, and other specialists circulated widely in the premodern world, a phenomenon that can be traced back to deep antiquity.[203] By the Mongolian era, if not before, bird trainers and falconers were among the most well-traveled professionals of the day, and together with their royal patrons constituted an informal ornithological international. One indication that falconry was self-consciously international in outlook is that falconers were much aware of their counterparts in other kingdoms and cultural zones. The Persian Ḥusām al-Dawlah, active at the very end of this long tradition, writes frequently of the techniques, terminology, and "style" of his fellow falconers, past and present, in Turkestan, India, and Iraq. There is great interest in how others conduct the sport, much respect for their skills, and the strong desire for fabled species from distant lands.[204] Falconers lived and worked in a very wide world.

Evidence of the early movement of animal specialists is largely pictorial and mainly from China. By Tang times, the many foreigners in their midst were represented artistically in a series of well-articulated stereotypes. Men of the Western Region were regularly depicted with elongated noses, rounded eyes, lush beards, and pointed felt hats. Individuals so portrayed appear in a variety of artistic contexts, but most regularly in hunting scenes with "western" animals such as greyhounds.[205] They are also depicted in tomb murals and in figurines with raptors and hunting cats on horseback.[206]

For the Chinese, their neighbors to the north and west possessed special abilities in handling animals. This, of course, was particularly true of those who trained "leopards." A painted pottery figurine from the early eighth century dramatically exemplifies this cultural stereotype; it depicts a mounted Westerner, with a distinctive hat and full beard, trying to calm an agitated hunting cat, most likely a caracal, on the rump of his horse.[207] At this point in time, when the Chinese were just adopting the sport, foreign specialists were an absolute necessity: after all, who knew how to deal with recalcitrant caracals or train horses to allow large cats on their backs? The answer, of course, is a very small pool of specialists, mainly Arabs, Persians, and Indians, from the homelands of the sport and the animal. While unstated, the many cheetahs sent to the Tang came "complete" with instructions, that is, with instructors.

With the advent of the Mongolian empire, literary references to the circulation of animal specialists throughout Eurasia start to surface. The Chinggisids themselves impressed many handlers into their service. Juvaynī relates that when Fanākat, near Tashkent, fell to the Mongols in 1220, the population was put to the sword except for "artisans, craftsmen, and masters of hunting animals [*aṣhab-i javārih*]," and that following the conquest of Khurāsān and Turkestan in 1222, "animal keepers [*jānvar-dāri*]" were resettled in "the farthest countries of the east," that is, China.[208] These forcibly transported populations show up in the Chinese sources in various guises. One, certainly, is the reference to troops raised in 1263 from the "Muslim Falcon Quarter [Huihui *yingfang*]."[209] It is also likely that the rights held by the Il-qans of Iran to several thousand hunters, falconers, and artisans in North China down to the fourteenth century included animal specialists and their descendants deported from the eastern Muslim world in the 1220s.[210]

This method of coopting needed trainers and handlers, was, in conscious imitation of Chinggis Qan, followed by Temür, who transported captive falconers from Baghdad to Samarqand in 1401.[211] Impressment, however, was not the only means of acquiring animal specialists or their knowledge. Royal huntsmen often traveled at the behest of their sovereigns. Jalāl al-Dīn, the last Khwārazmshāh (d. 1231), used his chief huntsman (*amīr shikār*) as an envoy to the Seljuqs; the Uzbeks sent their chief falconer on a mission to Shāh ʿAbbās, and the latter sent his own falconer to the Ottomans.[212]

More commonly, however, animal specialists were junior members of embassies. The Golden Horde sent its chief huntsmen to Egypt, and the English sent three falconers to the Il-qans in Iran.[213] In the post-Mongolian period this practice is still much in evidence. Typically, these officials were charged with the delivery to a foreign court of presentations of hunting animals. To this end,

Balkh and various other states of Turkestan sent chief huntsmen or falconers to the Mughals, as did the Ṣafavids, who, in turn, received falconers from eastern Europe.[214] In the latter case, Kaempfer, around 1683, witnessed a reception of ambassadors in which Sulaymān I received six raptors from the Russian court, each presented by a similar number of falconers, and then the Polish court presented five, each conveyed by its own handler.[215] Further, when the Russians delivered gyrfalcons to Alexander II (r. 1574–1604), king of Kakhetʿi in eastern Georgia, the monarch made plain his desire to retain the services of the Russian falconer who accompanied the birds. After much negotiation, the Georgian ruler finally withdrew his demand, hinting pointedly that he was sure the tsar would soon send him more "falcons and a falconer."[216]

In meetings such as this, information was naturally exchanged. We know that Alexander II carefully queried the Russian falconer on the characteristics of the birds presented.[217] Moreover, since diplomatic receptions so often included invitations to the chase, visiting hunters and huntsmen continually observed and participated in royal hunts of their foreign hosts and then returned home. Comparison and borrowing are inevitable in these circumstances.

Several cases can be cited to illustrate this kind of circulation. In one, an eleventh-century Norman noble and military officer, famed for his skill in doctoring hunting birds and horses, served in Constantinople for several years and then went back home.[218] The other involves an Iranian official who fled to India, where he became head of the royal falconers and in 1593, after years in the subcontinent, returned to the Ṣafavid court as a foreign envoy![219] These men, and hundreds like them, were primary catalysts in a long-term, long-range process of cross-fertilization.

The movement of personnel, while important in this information flow, was not the only means of transferring elite hunting culture across time and space. Foreign literature also contributed to the homogenization of the royal hunt. Most often the two worked in tandem. Between the ninth and the seventeenth centuries, Korean and Chinese falconers, together with their hunting manuals, went to Japan.[220] Openness to foreign wisdom also characterizes the medieval Islamic world. Al-Manṣūr, who compiled his hunting treatise in North Africa around 1247, states in the introduction that he obtained his information from previous Arabic manuals and "from various writings by Indians, Turks, Persians, and learned men concerned with this matter among the people of Islam and the people of vision *of all mankind*." [221]

In their turn, the Muslims contributed to the European literature on falconry. Under the auspices of Frederick II Latin and French translations were made of a treatise on falconry attributed to a certain Moamyn, which in actuality is not a single work, but a compilation. The first part consists of portions of the treatise of Adham ibn Muḥriz and that of the Syriac Christian Gitrīf ibn Qudama (Gatrip in Latin), who themselves drew upon a variety of Arab and non-Arab sources. The second part consists of extracts from another earlier work, that of al-Bāzyār, "The Falconer," which draws upon the Persian tradition.[222] Thus, European literature on falconry had, from its inception, deep and diverse Eurasian roots.

The observable convergence of royal hunting styles across the continent came about because of this regular circulation of animals, huntsmen, and literature. As we have seen, this circulation was a persistent feature of court life in the core area, but by no means limited to it. On several occasions, there were large-scale infusions of core hunting animals and their trainers into North China and the eastern steppe, which brought the royal hunts of the Tang and Yuan into close alignment with those of Iran and India.

The same phenomenon is detectable in other parts of the continent. One of the best documented is the flow of Muslim influence into southern Europe under Frederick II. This was quite extensive and long-lasting. First of all, many of the animals in Frederick's famed menagerie, including the hunting cats, were attended by Muslim handlers. On one occasion the emperor spoke Arabic with his leopard keeper while on a royal progress. Further, in a letter to his "Saracen masters," he speaks of the "keepers of lynxes and hunting leopards" in his service, and in another makes reference to a certain "Rainaldin of Palermo," who was in overall charge of the hunting cats. This officer, we know from Frederick's own testimony, was responsible for selecting, training, and transporting cheetahs and directing their handlers. At one point, the emperor queries him on his cheetahs' progress in horsemanship.[223]

Frederick, of course, was far more committed to falconry and learned much from Muslim experts. Again by his own words, he says he summoned the best falconers from the four corners of the earth and then supported these experts in his own lands, "seeking their opinions, weighing the importance of their knowledge and endeavoring to retain in memory the more valuable of the words and deeds." Where the experts came from is not mentioned here, but later on he remarks in passing that some came from Egypt. In any case, his "Saracen falconers" are noted in other sources and there can be no doubt about Muslim influence on Frederick and subsequently on European falconry at large.[224]

This emerges most dramatically in Frederick's discussion of hooding in his treatise. Introducing this topic, he says:

> The falcon's hood is a discovery of Oriental peoples, the Arabs having, so far as we know, first introduced it into active practice. We, ourselves, when we sailed across the seas, saw it used by them and made a study of their manner of manipulating this head covering. The Arabian chiefs not only presented us with many kinds of falcons but sent with them

falconers expert in the use of the hood. In addition to these sources of knowledge . . . we have imported, partly from Arabia, partly from other countries, both birds and men skilled in the art, from whom we have acquired a knowledge of all their accomplishments. As the practice of hooding was one of the most valuable features of their methods, and as we perceived its great utility in taming falcons, we adopted it in manning our own birds and have given it our approval, *so that our contemporaries have learned its use from us*; nor should it be neglected by our descendants.[225]

Here we have an explicit example of the part played by direct observation and itinerant animal specialists in the homogenization of royal hunting practices. But more than that, this remarkable passage presents, clearly and concisely, a rare if not unique account of an episode of cross-cultural diffusion in medieval times as told to us by the principal agent of that diffusion.

This brings us to a final case study of this trend toward homogenization, the penetration of core area usages into Southeast Asia. As is well known, from the thirteenth century onward there was a progressive Persianization of elite Muslim culture in northern India. Many Persians went to the subcontinent to make their fortune and brought with them new literary and artistic models as well as social norms.[226] In the era of the Ṣafavids, some of their servitors and household slaves (*ghulām*) joined this migration. For example, Malik Ayaz, a Georgian slave who became governor of Diu in the early sixteenth century, first gained the notice of his sovereign, Maḥmūd Bigarh, sultan of Gujarat (r. 1458–1511), by his skill at bird hunting.[227] In Awrangzīb's reign, another Georgian convert, Ibrahim Malik, was, in the words of Manucci, "in charge of the hawks, falcons, and the royal hunting establishment."[228] Converts or not, Georgians had very deep connections with the royal hunting traditions of Iran, and some, we know, moved even farther east, ending up in Siam. One of the more notable members of that king's court was a Georgian attendant, at least until he was accidently killed during a royal hunt. And he was not the only source of core influence there: the Siamese king turned over locally captured hawks and falcons to his Persian servitors "for he knew," according to Ṣafavid envoys at his court, "that the Iranians are always interested in hunting and wished that they train these birds and return them to court."[229] Small wonder, then, that in their report of their mission, the Ṣafavid embassy, in comparing the court of Siam with that of Paigū (Pegu) in lower Burma, assert that while the king of Pegu has no royal processions, the king of Siam in court procedure as well as in riding and regular hunting, "has become accustomed to the manner and style of the Mughals."[230]

So, even as the great age of the royal hunt was drawing to a close, hunting fashions generated in the core area were still being exported, still finding acceptance, and still expanding into new territory.

13

Conclusions

History Wide

In studying culture in time and space, scholars have typically started with the dichotomy between high culture, sometimes called the great tradition or civilization, and popular culture, also called the little tradition or folk culture. The latter is seen as local and limited, particular and stable. High culture, which is always superimposed over a number of popular cultures, is far more diffuse geographically but at the same time more coherent internally, more systematic or orthodox. And generally speaking, we tend to measure change in great traditions across time and change in little traditions across space. The difference in approaches to the two is revealed, partly, in the fact that historians usually study the great traditions and ethnographers the little.

More recently, under the impact of globalization, an emergent international culture has been identified, some elements of which, mathematics, are totally denationalized and some, music, still bear the imprint of their ethnic or cultural origins. Thus, we now have a multilayer cultural cake composed of the local, the regional, the ethnic or national, the civilizational, and the international or global.

Chronologically, high and popular cultures can be found coexisting in deep antiquity, presumably from the very inception of complex urban-based societies in the Near East, India, China, and Central Mexico. But when did we begin to acquire the outer, international layer? For most historians, the answer, I suspect, is quite recently. Many would probably agree with Graham Wallas, an English social scientist writing on the eve of World War I, who saw incipient globalization, which he termed "a general change in the social scale," as a phenomenon of the nineteenth century, produced by new technologies of transportation and communication.[1] Others might push back the date of globalization several centuries to the well-named "Columbian exchange," which saw the rapid and planetary-wide dissemination of assorted technologies, ideologies, commodities, biologies, and pathologies. Obviously, if a strictly global criterion is imposed, then by definition this international layer must come after the European voyages of discovery. If, however, we limit our gaze to the Old World, we can discover some of the initial (and unconscious) steps toward "globalization" at a much earlier period.

The emergence of an international culture, which certainly dates to the rise of the Silk Road in the centuries just prior to the Common Era, if not before, is manifest in a number of institutions, social practices, entertainments, and fashions drawn from the high cultures and folk traditions of many distant and different regions, that in time achieved a continental currency. Among these were sewn, fitted jackets with sleeves which by the early Middle Ages were in vogue from China to Europe.[2] Equally visible and even more pervasive was the institution of robing and investiture, one of the mainstays of the political and religious lives of people from Japan to England.[3] On the level of popular culture, picture recitation, which began in India, had a similar reach and range.[4] We can also include polo, the first international sport, played by both elites and commoners from Korea to the Mediterranean.[5] And, of course, the royal hunt is another international institution that ranged across the continent.

At this point, we need to indicate some of the defining characteristics of this international culture. How do we know when a cultural trait, either a practice or object, has become internationalized? This is not an easy task. While much attention has been paid to the cultural life and values of great civilizations and those of local and regional communities, a similar effort has yet to be made in charting the cultural life shared by larger-scale international communities. Still, it is possible to set forth in preliminary fashion some signposts that help to identify and analyze the components of this international culture of premodern Eurasia.

First, and most obviously, such a cultural trait must have wide distribution; its popularity, moreover, must be roughly contemporaneous over a large section of the globe, or in our case, the continent.

Second, in many cases there is recognition that the trait is not ours alone, but is found in other courts, cultures, countries, civilizations, or empires.

Third, a trait typically becomes desirable precisely because of its wide, international currency. Within one's own culture, its prestige may be enhanced by its foreign origin or popularity.

Fourth, many components of this internationalized culture play some role in interstate relations; they accompany, facilitate, mark, or celebrate other types of long-distance, cross-cultural transactions.

Fifth, many components can be used as a means of cross-cultural communication. Certain activities, products, and procedures send clear messages, whether of encouragement or warning, without the need of translation or explanation.

The foregoing implies, of course, that cultural traits move, that they diffuse. This brings us to the heart of the more general and long-running debate on the nature and role of cultural diffusion in history, particularly on a continental or global scale.

Growing recognition in the eighteenth and the nineteenth century that there were many similarities, sometimes striking parallels, among diverse and distant cultures led to a vigorous debate in Europe that gave rise to the comparative method and stimulated the production of new theories to explain the uniformities. For some, these were by-products of the psychic unity of humankind; others propounded evolutionary schemes in which all human cultures passed through similar, if not identical, historical stages; finally, another school held that the uniformities resulted from extensive contact and exchange over long periods of time and across vast tracts of space.[6]

As is well known, some of the early diffusionists adopted rigid positions; they insisted that the human species was singularly uninventive and that cultural change was therefore a consequence of the spread of new traits from a limited number of centers of innovation. In its most extreme formulation, this doctrine posited a single center of origin, most often Egypt, for all the basic elements of early civilization, which subsequently diffused across the globe, giving rise to the early complex societies in Europe, Asia, the Pacific, and the New World.[7] This extremist position quickly came under attack and was systematically and effectively refuted on both methodological and evidentiary grounds.[8] More recently, these older claims have been revived in the guise of Afro-centric theories of history that again derive all important human cultural achievements from Egypt and assert intercontinental and transoceanic diffusion of these traits. This, too, has come under withering criticism but continues to have its adherents.[9]

Because of the glaring weakness of the extreme interpretations, diffusion studies fell into disrepute and decline in the latter half of the twentieth century. The strident claims of a single center of innovation rightly raised deep skepticism, but wrongly diminished, even tarnished, investigations into contact and exchange as a source of cultural change. Furthermore, in reacting to spurious claims there was an unproductive tendency to view with suspicion any exposition of human culture history on the large scale.

Rejection of the grand narrative and of diffusionism, a suspicion of long-term and large-scale problems, precludes a history that is both wide and deep. This is unfortunate, Andrew Sherratt argues, since the long-term perspective is required for identifying change, critical transformations, increases in complexity, or, indeed, periods of stability. He notes further that the tendency to look exclusively at local conditions for explanations of local developments has come to dominate. But local or regional histories are hardly autonomous, that is, local change cannot be explained solely by local conditions and must be placed in wider contexts. In contrast to the "autonomist" perspective, Sherratt offers an "interactionist" approach that looks at transitions and change as the result of the contagious spread of ideas and things between societies. This requires refocusing attention from modes of production to regimes of consumption, to the social meaning of goods and the creation of "intercultural validity," the sharing of international standards that are legitimate and compelling because they are so widespread, seemingly universal.[10]

While it is possible that some critical innovations, human speech or the recent electronics revolution, may have "initially occurred in a single exceptional locality," and then radiated outward into new regions, this is not the norm.[11] The great advantage of Sherratt's perspective is that it does not rely on *a center* but on interaction *between centers*. To put this differently, in an interactionist paradigm, multidirectionality is far more important than unidirectionality, the obsession and fatal flaw of the old-style diffusionism.

The relationships fashioned by these extended networks of interchange are diverse; some are unequal, often called core-periphery, and some equal, in which politically autonomous centers interact culturally and economically. The latter type, called "peer polity interaction," has been elaborated in large part by archeologists. As formulated by Colin Renfrew, this "designates the full range of interchanges taking place (including imitation and emulation, competition, warfare, and the exchange of material goods and information) between autonomous (i.e., self-governing and in that sense politically independent) socio-political units which are situated beside or close to each other in a single geographical region, or in some cases more widely." Such interaction between peer polities over time often results in "structural homologies," particularly between "polities of equivalent scale and status."[12]

The peer polity concept thus attempts to focus on the dynamic relationship of exogenous and endogenous change, most commonly among a cluster of interacting units within a region. Consequently, multiple external stimuli are characteristic of this interaction and the chief source of intensification and change. The mechanisms of mutual stimulation include, among others, competitive emulation that encourages displays of wealth and power to enhance status within a network of polities. This mechanism, most relevant to our inquiry, can express itself in "positive reciprocity," demonstrations of largesse in gift exchange or in the construction of ever larger monuments, such as hunting parks, to outdo rival polities. There is, then, a consciousness about this emulation, and efforts at competitive display tend to be mutually reinforcing. The tendency toward cultural homogenization is not, therefore, a result of "imposition," but more often of "appropriation," the gradual acceptance of behavioral patterns and practices that become conventional; these are adhered to voluntarily because no single center can impose its will on the others.

This process is most easily seen in the interactions of small-scale polities, chieftainships or city-states operating in restricted regions such as ancient Mesopotamia, where the lively interaction of elites from separate principalities resulted in the formation of what Samuel Noah Kramer called "an international aristocratic caste."[13] The same phenomena can be detected in South India; here in the course of the fourteenth and fifteenth centuries Vijayanagar, a conservative Hindu state, adopted the court dress and titulature of neighboring Muslim polities despite the intense anti-Islamic attitudes of its elite. The internationalization of its court culture improved Vijayanagar's political standing and authority and facilitated its participation in, and access to, the resources of a larger system of commercial and cultural exchange.[14]

These larger systems, by-products of interaction between a number of regional spheres, are also common. Duby notes that in the eleventh and the twelfth centuries Christian courts in the Mediterranean, northwestern Europe, and the Slavic world began to emulate one another and their Muslim contemporaries to the south and east.[15] But this, in my view, is by no means the maximum size of interaction spheres in premodern times. Even in antiquity such spheres sometimes spanned the continent; chariotry and certain metal technologies circulated throughout Eurasia and did so without benefit of a dominant cultural or political center.[16]

For our specific purposes, the first issue is how polities distantly separated from one another came to know about each others' hunting practices and styles; in short, how did international standards for the royal hunt come into being? Since the channels conveying these external stimuli have already been examined in detail, they need only be briefly restated here: (1) the international traffic in animals of the chase through commercial exchange and princely presentation; (2) the frequent movement of animal specialists between royal courts by means of attraction, coercion, and diplomatic missions; (3) the regular, often mandatory, participation of foreign guests and envoys in royal hunts; and (4) the many visual representations of foreign royal hunts, the Iranian in particular, that traveled great distances through various artistic media—metal ware, textiles and figurines—reaching the Latin West, China, Korea, and Japan.[17]

In turning from the issue of mechanisms to that of the motives, the reasons for the acceptance of international standards, we can start with the phenomenon of cultural focus, the tendency of people to exhibit greater interest in certain elements of their cultural repertoire than in others. This manifests itself in elaboration, variation, connoisseurship, and in the enthusiastic debate over minutiae which encourages the multiplication of specialized vocabulary.[18] Most importantly for our analysis, this produces a willingness to interrogate and examine in detail similar foci encountered in foreign cultures, a receptivity to outside influence in a particular sphere.[19]

For our elite hunters, there are various lines of evidence that document their pronounced and abiding fascination with the chase, both their own and that of neighbors near and far. First and foremost, they talked about hunting incessantly and did so readily with foreign visitors. Hunting served as a cross-cultural bridge; any foreign notable arriving at court was automatically assumed to be an avid huntsman interested in the topic. Sometimes, as with Roe's conversations with Jahāngīr, hunting was a socially safe topic selected to avoid temporary unpleasantness, and at other times, as in Izmailov's talks with the Manchu prime minister in 1720, the latter simply preferred the chase to discussions of "politicks."[20]

The great attraction of this topic is also a manifestation of the belief among elites that distant, foreign courts were a source of vital information on hunting that should be tapped, a curiosity that did not necessarily extend to other cultural spheres. In his extensive inquiries of the Jesuit fathers, Sultan Murad, the son of Akbar, concentrated on the wild animals of Portugal and the use of raptors in hunting.[21] This same preoccupation with foreign hunting fashions is conveyed in a story about Frederick II. A contemporary source relates that when he received an order of submission from the Mongols, Frederick jokingly remarked that if he submitted he would become a falconer since he knew so much about birds.[22] While never put to the test, the incident shows an accurate understanding of distant court tastes and preferences, and highlights the automatic assumption that any powerful prince would be delighted to obtain the services and the knowledge of a skilled falconer from afar.

Arcane connoisseurship is another common symptom of cultural focus and its attendant interest in foreign variants. The *Cynegetica*, attributed to Oppian, circa the third century C.E., already lists eighteen different "tribes" of hunting dogs bred from Egypt to the Celtic lands to the western steppe. Moreover, Oppian describes at length their attributes and characteristics and speaks of how these "most excellent [hounds] greatly possess the mind of hunters."[23] In later centuries, this was certainly true of Ibn Kushājim, the author of a tenth-century hunting manual, who lays out detailed criteria for judging hunting dogs—color, behavior, shape of head, length of neck, proportions, and so on.[24] And Catherine II speaks with disdain and disgust of her husband, Peter III, who, together with his cronies, continually argued about the relative merits of a wide variety of foreign hounds and staged competitions between different packs to resolve disputes.[25]

Hunting birds, as one might expect, were similarly treated. There was a desire for diverse birds from distant parts, and an extensive, specialized vocabulary developed for the incessant discussions of raptors' behavior, diseases, physical characteristics, and abilities.[26] Connoisseurship always involves making fine distinctions, hopefully ones that others cannot make, to identify slight but "vital" variations, both real and imagined.[27] In his treatise on falconry, Ḥusām al-Dawlah distinguishes three types of goshawks and no less that fourteen types of saker falcons. For each, he details their hunting characteristics and personalities, whether they are "sweet," "noble," or "docile." Naturally, it is these slight, subtle, and often nonexistent differences about which specialists like to argue and debate. For example, Ḥusām al-Dawlah offers the opinion that in judging peregrine falcons (*baḥrī*), one should always count the scales on the middle toe; normally, he tells us, there are seventeen or eighteen but birds with twenty-one are by far the best.[28]

Finally, the most striking evidence of this preoccupation with the hunt is the endless elaboration, the openness to the new, the foreign, and the bizarre. Akbar, by all accounts, was always prepared to try new techniques—hunting deer at night by moonlight, or hunting deer in the narrow defiles of mountainous Badakhshān, which entailed catching the prey by hand.[29] Further, he was quite excited by the prospect of new prey; his first onager hunt, for example. His son Jahāngīr also made immediate and special arrangements to hunt jungle fowl when first introduced to these birds.[30]

There was, of course, a similar attraction to new and novel animal assistants. Cormorants (*Phalacrocorax carbo*) are easily tamed and trained to catch and return fish to their master. In China, the cormorant, domesticated around the tenth century, was used extensively in commercial fishing. In the Far West, however, cormorants were wild-caught and taught to return fish to elite hunters in Italy, Holland, and England. Here, as in Japan, cormorant fishing was exclusively a courtly entertainment and spectator sport.[31]

Moving toward the fringes, we have Marco Polo's claim that Qubilai hunted with "lions," here, clearly meaning tigers. Such a claim is only creditable if understood as caged tigers loosed on prey. How these cats were then induced to return to their cages he does not say.[32] If historical, then its purpose was surely demonstrative, to show that such a thing could be done. In any event, his notice points up the urge to experimentation so often found among royal hunters.

This drive to push existing limits, to explore new possibilities, however strange, is particularly noticeable at the early Mughal court. For one thing, there was a great fascination for hunting with tame *āhū*, deer or antelope, that were trained to capture their wild kindred by the use of special netting attached to their horns, a sport that involved much betting.[33] But most incredibly, the Mughal court trained large frogs to catch sparrows! This amazing feat Abū'l Faẓl discusses in all seriousness.[34] And while the northern Indian "bird frog" did not travel far, the northern European bird dog, as already documented, certainly did.

How then did such transfers play out on the ground in specific instances? The dynamics of peer polity interactions are variable. First, there is the outsiders' appropriation of foreign cultural institutions and objects to enhance international stature and domestic prestige. Second, there is the insiders' penchant for projecting their cultural norms on distant ruling elites. Rulers, like everyone else, assume that certain of their own practices are universal, shared by every other court, no matter how distant. Consequently, cultural practices widespread in, and central to, one's own part of the world are projected on the rest of that world, and such projections become, of course, one of the means by which the practice is demonstrated and diffused still farther afield.

To illustrate the operation of this cultural dialectic, we can profitably examine the transfer of the cheetah to China in the early decades of the eighth century. This was a time of intense Arab military pressure on the non-Muslim rulers of Turkestan, who, in response, appealed to Tang China for support.[35] This took the form of a series of diplomatic/tribute missions that presented, among other items, hunting cats to the Tang court on the assumption that the court would be delighted to receive them and thereby look more favorably on requests for military aid. In this connection, it is important to remember that these transfers involved not only tangible commodities (cheetahs), but also information (in the form of cheetah keepers), and it is this combination that facilitates and encourages uniformity in material culture.[36]

While it is evident that the petty rulers of Turkestan projected their own hunting styles and preferences upon the Tang, why did the Chinese elite accept them so enthusiastically? The answer is twofold. First, the North Chinese elite was already devoted to the hunt and cheetahs represented a new and exciting variation. Second, during the eighth century the Tang court was quite literally inundated with tribute cheetahs from various states in the Western Region, and this barrage of felines produced the perception in China that *all* courts of stature hunted with cats, that this was an accepted international standard.

The episode is instructive in one other respect; while none of the city-states of Turkestan were peers of China (many in fact were clients), they still interacted productively. In this case, and perhaps more frequently than is usually acknowledged, it is the more open and often more innovative periphery that exerts influence on the core.

The phenomena of peer emulation and competitive display are found repeatedly in the history of the royal hunt. Marco Polo's statement that the Mongolian court in China had "the best falcons *in the world*, and likewise dogs" would surely have been music to Qubilai's ears.[37] And this was certainly the response hoped for in Abū'l Faẓl's boast that under the patronage of Akbar "animals of all kinds from Persia, Turkestan and Kashmir, whether game or other, have been brought together to the wonderment of beholders."[38] The goal, of course, was to assemble a package that set a ruler apart from the pack. In the 1320s, when Odoric of Pordenone visited Yuan China, he witnessed just such a demonstration. The emperor, he reports, traveled in a carriage drawn by four elephants and carried with him twelve gyrfalcons, which he flew at any passing birds.[39] This was a most impressive display of reach and resources—hunting in the North China plain with raptors from the subarctic while being hauled about by elephants from the subtropics.

About three centuries later, van den Broecke says in passing that Jahāngīr regularly hunted on horseback and on elephants and did so with "trained leopards," hawks, dogs, and guns.[40] Here we have another ruler, also keen on excelling his peers, using the full panoply of hunting animals, techniques, and technologies, both ancient and modern. And, paradoxically enough, this desire for the new, the conscious quest for the distinctive and foreign to set one's self apart, led directly to frequent borrowing, emulation and, ultimately, to the homogenization of the royal hunt over large parts of Eurasia.

History Deep

We now turn to the question of longevity, why the royal hunt survived for so long. This requires consideration of Braudel's notion of *la longue durée*. For the great French historian, there are three types of historical time: first, the very short-term history of discrete events that appear to be rapidly changing; second, the mid-range history of cyclical change, typically economic trends that may last for decades; third, *la longue durée*, the history of structures that change very slowly over centuries or millennia. While such structures last generation after generation, their rate of "erosion" is so slow that change is imperceptible to any given generation. These structures, Braudel maintained, are often tied to fundamental facts of geology and biology and to human efforts to tap into natural energy cycles. For this reason, they are extremely difficult to transcend or even modify.[41]

Life spans for phenomena of this sort can be most impressive. For example, as David Christian notes, the drier and less densely populated heartlands of Eurasia, despite ethnic and ecological diversity, share one crucial cultural feature: they comprise a region inhabited "by communities that exploited animals more than plants," a specialization, he says, that "can be traced back 6,000 years for pastoralists and perhaps 40,000 for hunter-gatherers."[42] Even longer-lived are basic technologies, such as human manipulation of fire, that were at the center of the interactions between culture and nature over thousands of generations.[43]

This persistence and structural coherence can also find expression in the spatial continuity of some cultures that survive for centuries with roughly the same frontiers.[44] Habits of mind may also enjoy long life spans—the Ptolemaic system of astronomy, for instance. But whatever form they take, these structures, in Braudel's view, are of central importance, dominating the "events," which are not only ephemeral but provisional and usually deceptive, thus distracting historians from the far slower yet more essential changes of *la longue durée.*[45]

There are, naturally, dangers in this approach. Eric Jones, himself a proponent of large-scale history, points out that we are sometimes guilty of "overlabeling," the application of the same name to evolving institutions or values over great lengths of time that creates an illusion of permanence or continuity that is not really there.[46] This is true and must be guarded against, but the advantages of a longer time frame outweigh the disadvantages. For one thing, it assaults traditional temporal units of history, thought to be "natural" fields of study, which are in fact quite arbitrary and artificial, conventions of convenience that are seldom questioned and rarely overturned.[47]

The royal hunt, by its very longevity and wide dispersal, clearly defies the conventional fields and time frames and must be treated on its own terms. But first there is the question about this time frame and whether the institution I have called the royal hunt is not simply an illusion of my labeling.

As regards longevity, continuities with earlier subsistence hunting point to a very early date for the emergence of the royal hunt. In the Near East and Mediterranean world, and indeed throughout Eurasia, the pursuit of protein merged with, and gave rise to, the pursuit of pleasure and political power.[48] The ring hunt, so common in the core area and the steppe, is one evidence of this merger. Many specialists now argue that the collective hunt using weapons, battue, drive lines, and surrounds dates to about 20,000 B.P. in the Old World.[49] Even the hunting park seems to have had an early prototype; the close husbanding of deer, it has been suggested, gave rise in the Neolithic to a system not too dissimilar from the medieval deer park.[50] What we know of the history of such parks suggests that they had deep, local antecedents among all the early centers of civilization in Eurasia.

It is not, therefore, surprising that within the core area there was a very strong sense of the continuity and antiquity of the royal hunt. Even though the ancient Persians, as Herodotus well understood, borrowed much from others, for later generations they became originators and exemplars.[51] In particular, later Muslim authors credited them with many "inventions" and "firsts," from kingship to archery techniques.[52] Thus, almost all facets of the royal hunt were held to be Iranian in origin. This meant that when a new style of hunting became popular, falconry for example, it was automatically ascribed, whatever its actual origin, to the Persian kings of yore. And, like the role of apocryphal literature in religions, these false attributions served to affirm the antiquity and orthodoxy of such practices and to disguise innovation. This left the comforting but mistaken impression of a long unbroken tradition.

But while modes of hunting changed frequently, the essential organizational features and functions of the royal hunt were extremely stable. This is readily apparent from the following enumeration of the basic characteristics of the royal hunt in its ancient, Assyrian phase:

hunting was viewed as a test of the king's courage and skill
his bag of kills is carefully tallied
hunting triumphs are well publicized in royal propaganda
hunting has a ritual character that was intended to legitimize authority
hunting parks, which also functioned as test gardens, were built and facilities created for the comfort of the royal party
feasting and entertainments were integral parts of the chase
hunts were well-organized, staged affairs to insure safety and success
the hunt was equated with war, made extensive use of troops, and had a place in interstate relations[53]

All of this describes with great accuracy the royal hunts of the much later and far distant polities, the Mughals and Manchus. The only things missing are some of the hunting partners, cats and raptors, that later became so popular.

The same conclusions concerning continuity and longevity can be affirmed by looking at the legacy of the royal hunt in the modern age. Europeans most certainly continued the tradition of elite hunting in their overseas colonies. Like the elites they coopted and supplanted, they used hunting expeditions to demonstrate their power over nature, their ability to tame the wild and extend civilization; they hunted to display their capacity to identify, mobilize, and organize resources and thus publicize their superior administrative skills in the countryside; and, finally, the hunt served as an open-air theater in which bravery could be tested, attested, and appreciated.[54]

In sum, the idea that the successful hunter dominates nature and thereby humans was still very much alive in places like British India down to the nineteenth century. But this was hardly a European invention or an accidental by-product of European intervention in Asia; rather, it was a matter of European acceptance and adaptation of an indigenous structure of *la longue durée*.

The final question is why did the royal hunt have such staying power or, more generally, why are there structures of *la longue durée* at all? Do they survive through historic time and prosper across cultural space because they are rigid, resistant to erosion by external forces, or because they are pliable, adaptive to their changing environments, both natural and cultural? And if the latter, why do they not change to such a degree that they lose their original form and become unrecognizable over time? To my mind, the best explanation for their durability is their versatility, an attribute Braudel invokes to explain the long-term success of capitalism.[55]

In treating the history of the royal hunt, it is this characteristic above all that is the source of its impressive life span. It had many purposes, all useful and essential for ruling strata, and all were operational in many diverse cultural, political, and ecological settings. As we have seen, the royal hunt provided recreation, a means of restoring health and escaping unpleasant social situations; it was a measure of men, a marker of social status, a vehicle for political reward and punishment and for modifying behavior; it supplied the infrastructure for travel and a pretext for inspections; it was extensively used for military preparation, for showing the flag, and sending diplomatic signals; it was an instrument for suppressing bandits, protecting people, and checking errant nature; lastly, it was a means of creating myths and images and of projecting ideological concepts and claims of legitimacy.[56]

Like communal dancing and other long-lived and widespread social institutions, the royal hunt is readily described as versatile or flexible, that is, it provides an array of services and can add new ones without necessitating major structural change.[57] This, in fact, is the same kind of "flexibility" so often recognized in human hunting, a property, as Clive Gamble rightly remarks, that can more accurately be characterized as the realization in different settings of the manifold and latent possibilities of this form of resource extraction.[58]

This quality explains why the royal hunt became so interwoven into the very fabric of premodern states in Eurasia and why there was a "political" imperative to hunt long after there was no economic necessity to do so. It is doubtful that those who made the most frequent use of the royal hunt ever classified or enumerated its many features; rather, they just used it, found it satisfactory and satisfying, and could not imagine a world without it.

The royal hunt, to use Polyani's characterization of ancient markets, was embedded in society at large.[59] And this embeddedness explains its final demise. Although its content was modified over the centuries, its basic functions persisted until, in the course of the nineteenth century, the utility of the royal hunt was fatally eroded by the emergence of new standards in the conduct of interstate relations and war. Its essential political matrix was destroyed by a new type of state that was based on drastically different methods of organization and communication, and that possessed, of course, dramatically new ways of checking the onslaughts of wild nature.

Notes

Chapter 1. Hunting Histories

1. For others, see Gellner 1988, 19–20. Citations with dates are in the "Modern Scholarship" section of the bibliography; those without dates are in the "Abbreviations and Primary Sources" section.

2. Daniel 1967, 79–98.

3. Kramer 1967, 73–89.

4. Harris 1996, 447–51.

5. For a sampling of the literature, see Bird-David 1992, 25–47.

6. Wilson 1998, 73–97, with invited commentary.

7. Cohen 1989, 2–6.

8. See Hill 1982, 521–44 and Potts 1984, 129–66.

9. Stiner, Munro, and Surovell 2000, 39–73, with invited commentary.

10. Linton 1955, 150; Coon 1971, 71–73; Legge 1972, 119–24; Fagan 1987, 74; and Simmons 1989, 43–47.

11. Legge and Rowley-Conwy 1987, 88–95 and Balter 1998, 1444–45.

12. Vasilevich 1968, 129–41.

13. Wittfogel and Feng 1949, 126; *LS*, ch. 68, 1037; and *H-ʿĀ*, 97. On the place of hunting in the ancient steppe, see Novgorodova 1974, 70–73.

14. Pliny, VI.161; *H-ʿĀ*, 100; and Pachymérès, II, 446. For further comment and additional source references, see Sinor 1968, 119–21.

15. Noonan 1995, 270–71.

16. *AR*, 30–31, 44, 60, 75, and 85.

17. Marco Polo, 184–85 and 220; and *YS*, ch. 5, 89 and 98, and ch. 87, 2004–5.

18. *MM*, 17 and 100, and Rubruck, 85.

19. Peng and Xu, 475 and 478.

20. Shakanova 1989, 113–14.

21. Gregory of Tours, 592–93.

22. Einhard, 52, and Helmold, 277. On the importance of fish and game in the diet of commoners in western and eastern Europe, see Almond 2003, 90–114, and Kovalev 1999, 21–22.

23. Duby 1974, 17, 20, 23, and 44.

24. *ANE*, II, 103.

25. Herodotus, I.73; Justin, XLI.3; and Zosimus, III.27.

26. Pʿarpecʿi, 164; *H-ʿĀ*, 66; and *TTP*, 36. For archaeological evidence, see Braund 1994, 197.

27. Varthema, 175; Hamilton, I, 209; Forbes, III, 83; and Ovington, 160, for quote.

28. *HS*, ch. 96B, 3914; *HS*/H, 173; Wang 1982, 58; Ebrey 1986, 620; Marco Polo, 328; and Gernet 1962, 137.

29. Ripa, 61–62 and Huc and Gabet, I, 19–20.

30. Clagett 1992, 251.

31. *HS*, ch. 24B, 1180–81; *HS*/D, III, 495–96; and *QC*, 282. For the lively market in domestic Chinese furs, beaver, and otter, see Song Yingxing, 80 and *PRDK*, 133.

32. Swadling 1996, 49–70.

33. Martin 1980, 85–97.

34. Clark 1986, 13–20. On the early trade and procurement of ivory in the Mediterranean, see Hayward 1990, 103–9; and *ARE*, II, 235.

35. Laufer 1913, 315–64.

36. *SOS*, 150–51. Cf. the comments of Rudra Deva, 86 (no. 44).

37. Hamilton, II, 102 and *SOS*, 152.

38. On contemporary wildlife trade and commercial hunting in Asia, see the series of articles introduced by Knight 1999, 8–14.

39. On the possibilities of a comprehensive and comparative history of fur trapping and trade, see Tracy 2001, 403–09.

40. Thompson and Johnson 1965, 315–16.

41. Altherr and Reiger 1995, 39–56.

42. Spuler 1965, 387; Spuler 1985, 346–48; Jagchid and Hyer 1979, 23–37; and Jagchid and Bawden 1968, 90–102.

43. Bunzel 1938, 374–75.

44. These arguments are based on the discussion of P. Wilson 1988, 79–91 and 117–34.

45. Trigger 1990, 119–32 and Smil 1994, 232.

46. Silverbauer 1982, 29. See also Woodburn 1979, 244–64.

47. Guo 1995, 29, 50 and 52 and Shavkunov 1990, 89–128.

48. Cheng Zhuo, 178.

49. Bigam, 66–67, Persian text, and 165–67, English translation.

50. Ingold 1994, 1–16. For notions of humanity and animality in medieval Georgia, see Beynen 1990, 33–42.

51. *Time*, April 1, 1940, 27.

52. On the park's destruction, see Schama 1995, 68–73.

53. Lane 1987, 183 and Hasan-i Fasā'i, 419.

54. For representative critiques of the hunting hypothesis, see Simon 1987, 91–99; Cartmill 1993, 1–27; and Stange 1997, 23–47.

Chapter 2. Field and Stream

1. Gignoux 1983, 101–18 and Tacitus, *Ann.*, II.lvi.

2. Ahsan 1979, 202–5.

3. On elite hunting in antiquity, see Fiskesjö 2001, 130–32; on the Middle Ages, see Wright 1979, 52–53.

4. W. Kim 1986, 43, pl. 3.

5. Purchas, IX, 292.
6. Dio Chrysostom, 70.2. For a detailed discussion, see Anderson 1985, 31–55.
7. Pliny the Younger, I.xi and Ammianus, XXVIII.4.8.
8. Aristotle, *HA*, VIII.28; Xenophon, *Cyn.*, XI.; and Oppian, III.7–62 and IV.77–214. See also Anderson 1985, 1–16.
9. Machiavelli, 338–42 (*Discourses*, ch. XVIII). Cf. Bivar 1972, 273ff. and Ostrogorsky 1969, 101.
10. Anderson 1985, 78–100 and Hyland 1990, 243–46.
11. On the chronology of change to cavalry, see L. White 1966, 3ff.; Bachrach 1983, 1–20; and Genito 1995–97, 78–80.
12. *AR*, 54, and Wittfogel and Feng 1949, 63, 64 and 180.
13. Carré, II, 358 and III, 767; *RG*, 85; Varthema, 122 and 172; and Forbes, II, 488.
14. G. Mundy, 35–36.
15. Theophylact, VIII.8.3–4; *JS*, ch. 6, 133, 137, and 146, ch. 7, 158, and ch. 8, 196 and 198; Quan Heng, 38; Tan 1982, VII, map 7–8, inset of Dada *lu*; and P. Mundy, I, 19.
16. *CC*, 103, 109, and 118.
17. Bernier, 375 and 396.
18. *YS*, ch. 2, 32, 34, 35, and 39; Jahāngīr, I, 90, 202, 248, and 252; and ʿInāyat Khān, 159.
19. *GC*, 15 and 75 and *ZT*, 38 and 39.
20. Agathangelos, 217 and Khorenatsʿi, 363.
21. *CRP*, 31–32.
22. *PSRL*, I, 60; *PVL*, 29, Old Russian text, and 172, modern Russian translation; and *RPC*, 90.
23. *SH*, I, 2 and *SH/I*, 14.
24. *PSRL*, I, 74; *PVL*, 35, Old Russian text, and 172, modern Russian translation; and *RPC*, 90.
25. For examples, see Jūzjānī/L, 159; Jūzjānī/R, I, 577; and Ibn Baṭṭuṭah, III, 560.
26. Pelsaert, 33.
27. *CWT*, II, 235.
28. Abū'l Faẓl, *AA*, II, 250 and III, 448.
29. On *kos*, Anglo-Indian *coss*, see Yule and Burnell 1903, 261–62.
30. Jūzjānī/L, 80–81 and Jūzjānī/R, I, 385–86.
31. Ibn Khurdādhbih, 28, Arabic text, and 20, French translation.
32. *GC*, 109.
33. Khorenatsʿi, 135.
34. Decker 1992, 158–67; *ANE*, II, 67; *CRP*, 35; Ripa, 73; and Jahāngīr, I, 360.
35. Pʿarpecʿi, 43, and Ahsan 1979, 220.
36. *PSRL*, I, 60; *PVL*, 29, Old Russian text and 165, modern Russian translation; and *RPC*, 82. On the term *perevesishche*, see *Slovar* 1975–, XIV, 217.
37. Juvaynī/Q, I, 111; Juvaynī/B, I, 140; and Rūzbihān, 48.
38. Abū'l Faẓl, *AN*, I, 415 and 492–93, and II, 117; Abū'l Faẓl, *AA*, I, 307–8; and ʿInāyat Khān, 445.
39. du Jarric, 76.
40. Fiskesjö 2001, 53. See also Keightley 1978, 30n10, 32n19, 34, 44 and 62.
41. *ZZ*/W, 19; *HS*, ch. 54, 2439; *HS*/W, 12–13; and Laufer 1909, 149 ff.
42. Tavernier, I, 312.

43. Jahāngīr, I, 234; Pelsaert, 51; and Broecke, 34, 46, 47, 53 and 91.

44. Gregory of Tours, 438, and W. H. Lewis 1957, 52.

45. *PSRL*, I. 251; *PVL*, 104, Old Russian text and 242, modern Russian translation; and *RPC*, 214.

46. Ṭabarī, XIII, 192.

47. Kai Kāʿūs, 83–84.

48. Ḥāfīẓ-i Tanīsh, II, 203b, Persian text, and 180, Russian translation; and Munshī, II, 1081, 1179, 1215, and 1297.

49. *CC*, 84, 109, 113, 117, 118, 120, and 125; *ASB*, 33, 34, 35, 40, 162, 170, 171, and 180; and Einhard, 59.

50. *JS*, ch. 7, 170, 172, 174, and 179, and ch. 8, 183, 186, 188, 191, 197, and 200.

51. Qāshānī, 73.

52. Ye Longli, ch. 23, 226.

53. Peng and Xu, 478; *YS*, ch. 2, 37, and ch. 3, 47; and *NC*, III, 106.

54. d'Orléans, 110; Ḥāfīẓ-i Abrū/M, 99–110; *HC*, 180–83; *HI*, *V*, 93; ʿInāyat Khān, 211 and 413; and Muraviev, 63.

55. Keeley 1996, 50 and 52.

56. McEwen, Miller, and Bergman 1991, 76–82.

57. Gardiner 1907, 249–73, esp. 255 and 257, and Drews 1993, 181.

58. el-Habashi 1992, 33–34, 56, 81–82, and 145–46, and Clagett 1992, 251.

59. Jahāngīr, I, 35, 45, 109, and 111, and II, 236–37.

60. el-Habashi 1992, 31 and 53, and Decker 1992, 154.

61. Martynov 1991, 84; Golden 2002, 151; and Niẓāmī, 12.24–25.

62. Diodorus, V.76.3, and Lavin 1963, figs. 71, 79, 81, 110, 122, and 123, all following 286.

63. See, for example, Jahāngīr, I, 362, 371, and 401.

64. Ye Longli, ch. 23, 226; *SCBM*, 147; Wittfogel and Feng 1949, 353; Ripa, 90–91; and Haenisch 1935, 75, entry no. 27.

65. Lawergren 2003, 88–105, and Albertus Magnus, I, 684.

66. Koch 1998, 17–26.

67. This is true of ancient China, Fiskesjö 2001, 12–23, and of the Muslim Middle Ages, al-Manṣūr, 60–61 and 63–69.

68. On the many meanings of *keyik* in Turkic, see Bābur, 6, 8, 10, 224, 296, and 491; Nadeliaev 1969, 194–95; and Bazin 1957, 28–32.

69. Parrot 1961, 185, figs. 236 and 203, fig. 252; Jahāngīr, I, 102; and Rudra Deva, 85–86 (para. 36–40).

70. Manucci, I, 184 and Ripa, 89–90.

71. Xenophon, *Cyr.*, I.iv.7–9.

72. Rudra Deva, 82 (para. 17).

73. Piggot 1992, 45–68.

74. el-Habashi 1992, 142 and 152; Decker 1992, 153–54; Houlihan 1996, 11; *ARI*, II, 50, 55, 91, 150, and 175; Parrot 1961, 269–73 and fig. 345.

75. Porada 1969, 177–78.

76. Sharma 1970, 176, and Kalidasa, 5.

77. Shaughnessy 1988, 189–237, esp. 216–17. On the demise of military chariots in China, see the comments of the late Ming scholar, Song Yingxing, 262.

78. *CATCL*, 420–21.

79. *HS*, ch. 8, 238, and ch. 9, 293; *HS*/D, II, 205 and 329; *HHS* ch. 29, 3646; and *CRP*, 30–31.

80. *ZZ*/W, 162; *SMCC*, 206; and Mencius, 3.38.

81. Amiet 1969, 6–8.

82. Buzand, 128.

83. *ANE*, I, 250.

84. Littauer and Crouwel 1973, 27–33, and *ANE*, I, pl. 40, following 284.

85. Drews 1993, 106, 119–26, and 141–47; *ANE*, I, pl. 40, following 284; Decker 1992, 153; and Parrot 1961, 55–56 and fig. 64.

86. *ARE*, II, 345–46; Xenophon, *Cyr.*, I.iv.13–16 and II.iv.20; Fiskesjö 2001, 103–4 and 113–20; and Gregory of Tours, 243.

87. Pʿarpecʿi, 43.

88. Usāmah, 223, and Dozy 1991, I, 317; *HI*, III, 172; Bābur, 114, 325, and 424; and Jahāngīr, II, 120, 181–82, and 229.

89. *IB*, 27, and Nadeliaev, et al. 1969, 481.

90. Zhao Hong, 456.

91. Lessing 1973, 2 and 43, and Rozycki 1994, 9.

92. *SH/I*, 70, 73, and 153; *SH*, I, 74, 78, and 188; Lessing 1973, 1045; and Doerfer 1963–75, I, 291–93 and 411–14.

93. Rubruck, 85; *MM*, 100–1; Marco Polo, 226 and 229–34; and *CWT*, II, 235.

94. Kāshgharī, I, 281, and Rudra Deva, 88 (para. 51–52), my italics.

95. Ye Longli, ch. 24, 231, and Tao 1976, 8–9.

96. Juvaynī/Q, I, 19–20, and Juvaynī/B, I, 27–28.

97. Ibn ʿArabshāh, 308–9.

98. Ovington, 162.

99. Ibn al-Furāt, I, 85, Arabic text, and II, 69, English translation; Jahāngīr, I, 103 and 120; and Rashīd/K, II, 689.

100. Wittfogel and Feng 1949, 284.

101. Rashīd/K, I, 245; Doerfer 1963–75, I, 162; *SWQZL*, 31; Pelliot and Hambis 1951, 139–41 and 143–44; Jahāngīr, II, 181–82; and Ripa, 86–89.

102. Agathangelos, 217; *JTS*, ch. 64, 2420; *PCR*, 207; *PSRL*, I, 219; *PVL*, 91, Old Russian text, and 229, modern Russian translation; *RPC*, 173.

103. This evidence goes back to the Shang era, on which, see Fiskesjö 2001, 118.

104. *HS*, ch. 10, 327, and ch. 87b, 3558, and *HS*/D, II, 412.

105. Peng and Xu, 478.

106. Beveridge 1900, 137–38, and Bābur, 45.

107. Jahāngīr, I, 203–4 and II, 83–84.

108. Herbert, 81.

109. d'Orléans, 72 and 107.

110. *MTZZ*, ch. 3, 2a–b, Chinese text, and 50–51, French translation.

111. Luo Guanzhong, I, 209.

112. *HS*, ch. 94a, 3788–89.

113. *WS*/H, 53; Wittfogel and Feng 1949, 129; and *JS*, ch. 6, 132.

114. Ripa, 86–89.

115. du Jarric, 10–11; ʿInāyat Khān, 124; and Bernier, 374–75.

116. Don Juan, 40 and 47.

117. Kaempfer, 73.

118. Jūzjānī/L, 81, and Jūzjānī/R, I, 386.
119. Munshī, II, 764. See also 668–69 and 1165 for other large drives.
120. Abū'l Fazl, *AN*, II, 416–17. See also I, 439–40 and 442–43, for another large drive.
121. d'Orléans, 110.

Chapter 3. Parks

1. Frye 1983, 78.
2. Hinz 1970, 425–26; Hinz 1975, 179; Kent 1931, 228–29; and Benveniste 1954, 309.
3. See, for example, Xenophon, *Cyr.*, VIII.i.38.
4. Xenophon, *Ana.*, I.ii.7.
5. Xenophon, *Ana.*, I.iv.9–11 and II.iv.14.
6. Dandamaev 1984, 113–17, and Dandamaev 1992, 20. The best general survey of the Achaemenid paradise, its physical features, facilities, functions, and geographical distribution, is in Tuplin 1996, 93–131.
7. Arrian, *Ana.*, VI.29.4–5; Strabo, XV.iii.7; and Dio Chrysostom, 79.6.
8. Xenophon, *Cyr.*, I.iv.5,11.
9. Dio Chrysostom, 3.137–38.
10. Xenophon, *Cyr.*, VIII.vi.12. See also Briant 1982, 451–52.
11. Xenophon, *Hell.*, IV.i.15–16, and Akurgul 1956, 20–24.
12. Diodorus, II.10.1–2 and 13.1–4.
13. See, for example, Stronach 1994, 3–4, and Foster 1999, 64–71, for a brief pictorial history.
14. Leclant 1981, 727–38, and Houlihan 1996, 42–44.
15. Wilkinson 1990, 204–5.
16. *AS*, 113–14, viii, 17–21; Oppenheim, ed. 1968, 44; Oppenheim 1965, 333; and Soden 1959, 426.
17. See the discussion of Tuplin 1996, 80–88.
18. Taagepera 1978, 108–27, esp. 116, 121–22, and 126.
19. Khorenatsʿi, 182–83.
20. Buzand, 75 and 96.
21. Dasxurancʿi, 143; Quintus Curtius, VIII.i.19; and Arrian, *Ana.*, IV.61.
22. Ammianus, XXIV.4.2; Zosimus, III.23; and Klein 1914, 109–12.
23. Theophanes, 25 and 26.
24. Schmidt 1940, 80, pl. 96.
25. Christensen 1944, 469–72; Herzfeld 1988, 326–38; and Shepard 1983, 1085–89.
26. Shaked 1986, 75–91.
27. *KB*/V, 10, and Masʿūdī, II, 169.
28. Bar Hebraeus, 118.
29. Benjamin of Tudela, 96.
30. Ibn Isfandiyār, 115.
31. Narshakhī, 29.
32. Herbert, 127 and 132–33, and Fryer, II, 245.
33. Xuanzang, II, 45, 51 and 55.
34. Quintus Curtius, VIII.ix.28. Cf. Strabo, XV.i.55.

35. Aelian, XIII.18.
36. Kautilya, 48.
37. *HI*, III, 303, 350, 353, 354, and 366.
38. Jahāngīr, I, 366–67.
39. Abū'l Faẓl, *AA*, II, 248; du Jarric, 200; and Forbes, II, 481–82 and III, 136–37.
40. Varthema, 126.
41. G. Mundy, 13 and 209.
42. Varro, III.iii.8–9, xii.1–3, and xiii.1–3. Cf. Pliny VIII.211.
43. Suetonius, *Tiberius*, LX, *Nero*, XXXI.1–3, and *Domitian*, XIX.
44. Conan 1986, 353.
45. Procopius, *HW*, IV.vi.6–10.
46. Liudprand, 194–95. See also Van Milligen 1899, 75–76.
47. *PCR*, 205.
48. For an overview, see Cummins 1988, 57–67.
49. *ASC*, 188; Cantor and Hatherly 1979, 71–85; and Emery 1973, 274–75.
50. Pittman 1983, 30–77.
51. Mencius, 1.3.
52. *ZZ*/W, 69–70. For the parks of this era, see Hsu 1980, 11–12; Schafer 1968, 320–25; and Hargett 1988–89, 2–3.
53. *ZGC*, 61–62.
54. *WX*, II, 53–71; Sima Guang/C, I, 43; and Bielenstein 1976, 18 and 81.
55. *HS*, ch. 65, 2847–51, and *HS*/W, 83–87.
56. *HS*, ch. 54, 2455; *HS*/W, 40; *CRP*, 37–41; and *WX*, II, 73–89, 113, 207, 209, and 211. For additional data, see Wang 1982, 1 and 8–9; Hervouet 1964, 222–42; and Schafer 1968, 325–31.
57. *HS*, ch. 96b, 3928; *HS*/H, 173; *SJ*, ch. 28, 1384, and ch. 102, 2752; *SJH*, I, 468, and II, 25; *CRP*, 41–44; *WX*, I, 113, 137, 139, 445, and 447, and II, 89–95 and 115–17; and Wang 1982, 101, 102, and 149.
58. *HS*, ch. 9, 285, and ch. 10, 304, and *HS*/D, II, 314 and 377–78.
59. *SJ*, ch. 30, 1428 and 1436; ch. 58, 2084; ch. 87, 2502; ch. 122, 3132; *SJQ*, 204; *SJH*, I, 383, and II, 70, 78, and 380.
60. *SJ*, ch. 125, 3194; *SJH*, II, 422; *CRP*, 44–47; and *WX*, I, 137 and 139, and II, 97–105.
61. Schafer 1956, 259–60.
62. Fu Jian, 166; Yang Xuanzhi, 60–65; and Jenner 1981, 173–75.
63. On this revival, see Schafer 1968, 334–41; Hargett 1988–89, 4–5; and Benn 2002, 68–69 and 95.
64. *VRTE*, 40.
65. Hargett 1989, 61–78, and Hargett 1988–89, 5–43.
66. Fan Chengda, 150.
67. *SH*, I, 218, and *SH/I*, 173–74.
68. Juvaynī/Q, I, 21; Juvaynī/B, I, 29; Rashīd/A, II/1, 147–48; Rashīd/B, 64–65; and Boyle 1972, 125–31.
69. Marco Polo, 264.
70. *MP*, 227–28; Nadeliaev 1969, 460; and De Weese 1994, 179–89.
71. Pelliot 1959–61, I, 140–43, and II, 843–45.
72. Marco Polo, 210–11; *CWT*, II, 218–19; *SH*, I, 41; *SH/I*, 45–46; and Steinhardt 1983, 138.

73. Steinhardt 1990a, 150–54; Steinhardt 1990b, 62–65; Pelliot 1959–61, I, 238–40 and 256–57; and Chan 1967, 126–27.

74. Bushell 1873, 329–38; Impey 1925, 584–604; and Atkinson 1993, 29–35.

75. Rashīd/K, I, 641; Rashīd/B, 277; and Marco Polo, 185–67 and 201.

76. Brunnert and Hagelstrom 1912, 20 and 517–18.

77. *PRDK*, 136.

78. Bell, 166 and 168–72.

79. Ripa, 96.

80. Ripa, 74–75, and Bell, 132–33. See also Malone 1934, 21–43, and 219 for more detail and diagrams.

81. *RKO*, I, 228–29.

82. For general accounts, see Gilbert 1934, 369–73; Elliot 2001, 182–87; Menzies 1994, 55–56; and Hou and Pirazzoli 1979, 15–24, and 37–41.

83. Ripa, 78, 84–85, and 128, and Hedin 1933, 13, 129–32, and 155–60.

84. Macartney, 106–17, 122, 124–27, 132–34, and 144.

85. Yūsuf, 256.

86. Mandeville, 141–42.

87. Hamilton, I, 26.

88. On Chinggis Qan's fabulous tent, see Shaw, 239–40.

89. Welles, Fink, and Gilliam 1959, 89, no. 15a; Kashgarī, I, 343; Nadeliaev 1969, 125; and *FZ*/B, 95, Persian text, and 98, Russian translation.

90. McClung 1983, 17ff.

91. Ringbom 1951, 310.

92. See the important discussions of Moynihan 1979, 38–45, and Reinhart 1991, 15–23.

93. Xenophon, *Oec.*, IV.4–5, 8, 12–14, and 20–25. See also, Aelian, I.59.

94. These concepts are discussed at length by Fauth 1979, 1–53; Widengren 1951, 5–19; and Stronach 1990, 171–80.

95. Aelian, VII.1; Nylander 1970, 114–15; and Stronach 1990, 107–12.

96. *LKA*, 208 and 210, and *HHS*, ch. 4, 175, and ch. 83, 2765.

97. Dandamaev and Lukonin 1989, 143–44.

98. Carroll-Spillecke 1992, 91.

99. Brockway 1983, 31–36.

100. Watson 1983, 117–19; Subtelny 1995, 19–59; and Subtelny 1997, 110–28. For an example of exchange between Central Asia and India, see Bābur, 686.

101. *ANE*, II, 101.

102. Laufer 1967, 262–63, and Ripa, 101.

103. Plutarch, *Artaxerxes*, XXV.1–2.

104. Xenophon, *Hell.*, IV.i.33.

105. Strabo, XV.i.58, XVI.i.11 and ii.41, and Procopius, *B*,VI.vii.2–5.

106. Meiggs 1982, 270–78.

107. *PFT*, 15, 113–16, 497, and 742.

108. Gentelle 1981, 80–96 and esp. 85, and Gignoux 1983, 104–7.

109. Briant 1982, 451–56.

110. Plutarch, *Artaxerxes*, XXV.12. Cf. the comments of Diodorus, II.10.1–6 and 13.1–4, XIV.79.2, and XIX.21.3. and of Ripa, 84, on the contrasts between the park at Rehe and its immediate environs.

111. S. Redford 2000, 313–24.

112. Cf. the comments of J. Fox 1996, 483, and Barber 1996, 868–80.

113. Lewis 1990, 152, and Fiskesjö 2001, 161–63.

114. Bielenstein 1980, 68 and 82–83.

115. *SJ*, ch. 30, 1434–35 and 1936; *SJH*, II, 77 and 78; *HS*, ch. 6, 198, ch. 7, 223, ch. 10, 303, ch. 63, 2743, ch. 68, 2940 and ch. 96b, 3905; *HS*/D, II, 98, 160 and 376; *HS*/W, 49 and 133; and *HS*/H, 153.

116. Longus, IV.1–8, and Clavijo, 215–16.

117. Masʿūdī, VIII, 269, and Henthorn 1971, 60 and 112.

118. Cf. Schafer 1968, 333.

119. For Tsarskoe Selo, see Bardovskaya 2002, 160–63.

Chapter 4. Partners

1. Clutton-Brock 1989, 21–33.

2. Caras 1996, 20–21.

3. The capture of elephants is discussed in some hunting manuals. See Rudra Deva, 86 (para. 44).

4. Pliny, VIII.218, and Zeuner 1963, 401–3.

5. Frederick II, 5.

6. Jūzjānī/L, 258 and Jūzjānī/R, II, 756.

7. Ḥāfiẓ-i Tanīsh, I, 14a, Persian text, and 55, Russian translation.

8. See, for example, Yūsuf, 214–15.

9. Cf. the advise of Kai Kāʿūs, 84.

10. Vilà et al. 1997, 1687–89.

11. A recent DNA study suggests the oldest breeds are those of northeast Asia, the husky, Akita, chow chow, and so on. See Parker et al. 2004, 1160–64.

12. Clutton-Brock 1995, 7–20.

13. Dio Chrysostom, 1.19–20. Cf. also Pliny, VIII.142–45.

14. Campany 1996, 244 and 388, and Gernet 1985, 148.

15. *ARE*, IV, 255.

16. *MTZZ*, 46, Chinese text and 24, French translation; Xenophon, *Cyn.*, VII.5; al-Manṣūr, 17 and 32; and Abū'l Fazl, *AA*, I, 301.

17. Brewer, Redford, and Redford 1994, 114–17; Osborn and Osbornova 1998, 57–68; and Epstein 1971, I, 147–71, are the best guides.

18. Allen and Smith 1975, 120–25, and Epstein 1971, I, 58–71.

19. Houlihan 1996, 76–77, and Fiennes and Fiennes 1970, 101–9.

20. el-Habashi 1992, 31–32 and 142–44; Altenmüller 1967, 13–16 and illus. on 14; *ANE*, I, pl. 41, following 284.

21. Diodorus, V.3.2.

22. Fiennes and Fiennes 1970, 32, 36–38, and 111–16, and Parrot 1961, 64, fig. 68.

23. Herodotus, I.140, and *ZA*, *Vendidād*, IX.

24. For an example of this attitude, see *SOS*, 37.

25. *BF*, 144–46.

26. Ahsan 1979, 211–13. For an example of such admiration, see Usāmah, 137–38.

27. Chardin, 182.

28. Bar Hebraeus, 119; Usāmah, 230 and 241; Herbert, 81 and 243; Jahāngīr, I, 289; and Riasanovsky 1965a, 11.

29. P. Mundy, II, 112; Fryer, I, 280, and II, 305; Jahāngīr, I, 126; and Ovington, 160.

30. *Vis.* 68 and 105.

31. G. Smith 1980, 459–65, and Viré 1973, 231–36.

32. Ahsan 1979, 211–13, and *KB*/P, 47.

33. al-Manṣūr, 28–29, 31, and 33–48.

34. Munshī, II, 1321.

35. Usāmah, 227. Cf. G. Mundy, 274.

36. Xenophon, *Cyr.*, V.1–7; Psellos, 376; Ambrose, *H*, VI.23; and Hicks 1993, 154, 175, 207–8, 212, 213, 237, and 267.

37. Fiennes and Fiennes 1970, 18–22; Thurston 1996, 75–79; Walch 1997, 72–103; and Cummins 1988, 12–30.

38. Quintus Curtius, IX.i.31–34.

39. *CATCL*, 420; *SJ*, ch. 53, 2015; and *SJH*, I, 93. On hunting dogs in the Shang, see Fiskesjö 2001, 109 and 120.

40. *HS*, ch. 99c, 4176; *HS*/D, III, 430; and *ZGC*, 282.

41. W. White 1939, 51, pls. 7, 9, 11, 16, 18–21, and 153.

42. Bielenstein 1980, 83.

43. Keller 1963, II, 23–26.

44. Capart 1930, 222, and Keimer 1950, 52.

45. Houlihan 1986, 46–49, and 140; Houlihan 1996, 112, 138, 144, and 160–61; Brewer, Redford, and Redford 1994, 120–21; el-Habashi 1992, 34–35, 56–59, 82–83, 140–41, and 151; and Decker 1992, 163–67.

46. Meissner 1902, 418–22.

47. Brentjes 1965, 79–81, and Parrot 1961, 62, fig. 66 and 63, fig. 67.

48. Despite its age, the best general guide is still Epstein 1942–43, 497–508.

49. Aelian, IV.26.

50. Erkes 1943, 19; Eberhard 1942, 66–67; and W. White 1939, 59, and pls. 28, 108, and 109.

51. Laufer 1909, 231–34.

52. *JShu*/M, 28.

53. Shaanxi Sheng Bowuguan 1974a, pt. 9; Schafer 1959, 297–99; Benn 2002, 171–72; and Ennin, 401.

54. *NG*, XI.27–28 (pt. 1, 293–94).

55. Aristotle, *HA*, IX.36, and Aristotle, *MTH*, 118.

56. Pliny, X.17–18.23, and Aelian, II, 40 and 42.

57. Pollard 1977, 108–9.

58. Kronasser 1953, 67–79. Cf. Anderson 1985, 151–53, who notes that falconry spread into Roman North Africa at an earlier date.

59. Lindner 1973, 118–56, and Åkerstöm-Hougen 1981, 263–67.

60. Åkerström-Haugen 1981, 267–93, and Hoffman 1957–58, 116–39.

61. Niesters 1997, 162–93, and Nicolai 1809, 7 and note 1. I owe the latter reference to Judith Pfeiffer.

62. Duichev 1985, 51.

63. *PSRL*, I, 251; *PVL*, 105, Old Russian text, and 243, modern Russian translation; *RPC*, 215; and *SPI*, 27–28 and 119, n. 42.

64. Tulishen, 94.
65. al-Ṭabarī, I, 345, and Masʿūdī, II, 279–81.
66. Gelb et al. 1985, XII, 214, and Oppenheim 1985, 579–80.
67. Stricker 1963–64, 317.
68. Möller 1965, 105–6; Artsruni, 101; Khorenatsʿi, 138; Drasxanakertcʿi/D, 55; and Drasxanakertcʿi/M, 73.
69. Stetkevych, 1999, 121–23; Oddy 1991, 59–66; Masʿūdī, V, 156; and al-Ṭabarī, XXVI, 117.
70. Ahsan 1979, 216–20, and al-Ṭabarī, XXXIII, 79–80.
71. Cummins 1988, 190–94, and Albertus Magnus, I, 704.
72. Usāmah, 222–25.
73. Viré 1977, 138–49.
74. Marco Polo, 228.
75. *Hex.*, 227 (200H23). For other examples, see Qazvīnī, *NQ*, 111–12, Persian text, and 78–79, English translation; and Ligeti 1965, 286–87.
76. Husām al-Dawlah, 14, 21, 57–58, and 75–76.
77. Frederick II, 128–35 and 350–51.
78. Jameson 1962, 39–40.
79. Allen and Smith 1975, 117–18, and Lattimore, 107 and 118.
80. Usāmah, 229, and Lansdell, II, 326.
81. Cummins 1988, 195–96, and Layard, 332–33.
82. For accounts of training different species from diverse parts of Eurasia, see *KB*/V, 94–100; al-Raziq 1970, 109–21, with plates; al-Timimi 1987, 78–80; Dementieff 1945, 27–29 and 34–35; and Jameson 1962, 49–65.
83. Rudra Deva, 95 (para. 6–10); Allen and Smith 1975, 118–20; and Shaw, 157–58.
84. Cf. Albertus Magnus, II, 1591–95 and 1616–18, and Ḥusām al-Dawlah, 153–85.
85. Albertus Magnus, II, 1595–1621; Cummins 1988, 208–9; Rudra Deva, 110–19 (para. 26–77); Ḥusām al-Dawlah, 153–85; and Schafer 1959, 335–36.
86. Hakluyt, VI, 365–66.
87. Ḥusām al-Dawlah, 18–19. Cf. Rudra Deva, 96 (para. 11–15).
88. Ibn Shaddād, 146; Ḥāfiẓ-i Abrū/M, 96; *HC*, 150 and 180; and Jahāngīr, II, 53.
89. Meserve 2001a, 121–24; Pelliot 1959–61, I, 112–14; and *YDZ*, ch. 56, 3a.
90. Ḥusām al-Dawlah, 38 and 98.
91. *BDK*, 27, 34, 156–57.
92. Bābur, 270, and Layard, 264–65, 298–99, and 332.
93. Skrine, 232–33. Cf. Lattimore, 107.
94. Cummins 1988, 200–203, and von Gabain 1973, Tafel 11, no. 26 and 29, no. 70.
95. Atkinson, 492–94; *KB*/V, 107–10; and Dozy 1991, I, 475.
96. For the Manchu's vocabulary, see Haenisch 1935, 85, entries 120, 121, 125, 126, 127, 128; and 86, entries 129, 130, 133.
97. Kai Kāʿūs, 85.
98. G. Mundy, 33, and Marco Polo, 231.
99. D. T. Rice 1965, 51–52, illus. 43; Klingender 1971, 423; and Ianin 1970, II, 161 and 168 and *tabitsa* 3 (390, 392, 393), 7 (430), 51 (390), 52 (392, 393), and 58 (430).
100. G. Mundy, 202.
101. *AYS*, 27, 39, 138–42, and 144–45.
102. ʿInāyat Khān, 148–49.

103. Bernier, 377; Jahāngīr, II, 60; and Rudra Deva, 125–26 (para. 35–38).
104. Zhao 1990, 150–52.
105. Chardin, 180–81.
106. Ovington, 161–62.
107. Ripa, 88; Atkinson, 492–94; Muraviev, 109; and Lattimore, 106–7.
108. al-Manṣūr, 110–13, and Ḥusām al-Dawlah, 99–110.
109. Forbes, II, 479–80.
110. *EVTRP*, I, 73.
111. Ovington, 161–62.
112. Ḥusām al-Dawlah, 91.
113. Frederick II, 267–70; Ḥusām al-Dawlah, 70–71, 80, 83, and 84; and Layard, 481–83.
114. al-Manṣūr, 14 and 64; Usāman, 231 and 253; Rust'haveli, 79; Ipsiroglu 1967, 91 and 107; Steinhardt 1990–91, 202–5 and figs. 8, 9, and 11; Jameson 1962, 2, 69, 74, and 87; *TTP*, 12 and 19; d'Albuquerque, I, 84; Fryer, III, 5; Haussig 1992, 316–17 and illus. 541; Teixeira, 220; Carré, I, 124; Bābur, 224; Burton, II, 104–5; and Lattimore, 107.
115. Åkerström-Hougen 1981, 276, fig. 11; Gregory of Tours, 270–71; Cummins 1988, 211–13; Thurston 1996, 69; and Ḥusām al-Dawlah, 84.
116. *KB*/V, 9–10.
117. *KB*/V, 54–88.
118. Albertus Magnus, II, 1608 and 1611; *KF*, 230, 233, and 264; and Abū'l Fidā, *M*, 31.
119. See Frederick II, translator's preface, 105–6.
120. On his skepticism, see Frederick II, 4–5. For modern assessments, see Glacken 1990, 224–26, and Stresemann 1975, 9–12.
121. On this literature, see al-Nadim, II, 739; Hofmann 1968, 77–89; Möller 1965, 20–25 and 107–8; Haskins 1922, 18–27; and Ergert 1997, 102–31. For the hunt as a subject of intellectual inquiry, see Xenophon, I.5.
122. Jahāngīr, II, 292.
123. Ḥusām al-Dawlah, 41.
124. Taylor 1986, 1–22.
125. Klingender 1971, 381.
126. Sarton 1961, 54–63, esp. 60.
127. See the comments on tree rings of Menzies 1996, 631.
128. McCook 1996, 177–97.
129. Simakov 1989a, 129–33; Simakov 1989b, 30–48; and Gouraud 1990, 126–34.
130. *SH*, I, 5 and 11, and *SH/I*, 17–18 and 22. For other examples of hawking in the pre-imperial period, see Rashīd/A, I/1, 298, and *YS*, ch. 1, 1–2.
131. Rubruck, 85, and *MM*, 100.
132. Kaempfer, 58; Burnes, I, 104; and Lansdell, II, 326.
133. al-Timimi 1987, 12.
134. Kai Kāūs, 85.
135. Nīshāpūrī, 99, and du Jarric, 10.
136. Mandeville, 152–53.
137. Marco Polo, 229–30.
138. Chardin, 179–80.
139. Levanoni 1995, 59; Herbert, 243; Abū'l Faẓl, *AA*, I, 304–5; and *RKO*, 233.
140. Bernier, 262 and 364.

141. William of Tyre, I, 174.

142. Jahāngīr, II, 50, 53, 54, 60, 112, 125–26, 284, and 287.

143. Rubruck, 179, and *MM*, 154.

144. Bābur, 399.

145. Frederick II, 5–6, and 105–6.

146. Clutton-Brock 1989, 113–20.

147. Aristotle, *HA*, I.1 and IX.1.

148. Strabo, XV.1.42.

149. Abū'l Fażl, *AN*, II, 368, 370–71, and 393–94; Abū'l Fażl, *AA*, I, 295–96; and Tavernier, I, 218–19.

150. Jahāngīr, II, 4–5; P. Mundy, II, 85–86; and Ovington, 117–18.

151. Manucci, III, 73–74; Hakluyt, *PN*, III, 246–48; Purchas, X, 188–89; and *SOS*, 67–68.

152. See, for example, P. Mundy, III, 332, and the sources cited in notes 143 and 144.

153. Pliny, VI.66–67, 81, 91, and VIII.24; Varthema, 189; Hamilton, I, 190; and Bernier, 49.

154. Pliny, VIII.1–15. Cf. Arrian, *Ind.*, 13–14.

155. Abū'l Fażl, *AA*, I, 123–31.

156. Aelian, I.8 and VI.25, and Manucci, III, 79–79.

157. See Strabo, XV.i.41 and 52, and *SOS*, 67–68.

158. Abū'l Fażl, *AA*, I, 223–24.

159. Jahāngīr, I, 128, and II, 24.

160. ʿInāyat Khān, 48.

161. See the comments of Varthema, 129, and Bowrey, 273–75.

162. P. Mundy, II, 52, 55 and 85.

163. On China, see Han Feizi, 85.

164. Pliny, VI.67–68; Yang Xuanzhi, 235–36; and Hui Li, 172.

165. *HI*, I, 3, 5, 13, 88, and 155, and II, 251; Masʿūdī, I, 178, 375, and 379; Marvazī, 46–47 and 51–52; and al-ʿUmarī/S, 13, Arabic text, and 38, German translation.

166. du Jarric, 6–7 and 33. Cf. *RG*, 9.

167. Reid 1989, 25–28.

168. Ambrose, *H*, VI.33; Theophylact, V.10.6; Christensen 1944, 208; and Bosworth 1963, 115–19.

169. Schafer 1957, 289–91, and Marco Polo, 291–92.

170. See Strabo, XV.i.55.

171. Ibn Baṭṭuṭah, III, 596, and Bābur, 451.

172. Manucci, II, 339.

173. Jahāngīr, I, 136 and 375; du Jarric, 79–80; and G. Mundy, 53–57 and 290. Cf. the description in *SOS*, 70–73.

174. Kitchener 1991, 25–27 and 37, and Turner 1997, 25 and 81.

175. D. B. Adams 1979, 1155–58.

176. Eaton 1974, 17.

177. Aarde and van Dyk 1986, 573–78.

178. Jahāngīr, I, 139–40, and Divyabhanusinh 1987, 269–72.

179. Eaton 1974, 19–21.

180. Kitchener 1991, 7, 16, and 18, and Turner 1997, 104, 107, 109, 112, and 131–33.

181. Hildebrand 1959, 481–95, and Hildebrand 1961, 84–91.

182. Sharp 1997, 493–94.

183. Representative of this school, are Keller 1963, I, 30 and 86, and Zeuner 1963, 417–19.

184. Naville 1898, III, 17 and pl. 80; *ARE*, II, 102–22; and Jéquier 1913, 345–63.

185. Houlihan 1996, 69, 93, 199–200, and 203; Osborn and Osbornova 1998, 121–23; and Störk 1972, 530.

186. Bodenheimer 1960, 44 and 100, and Brentjes 1965, 84–85.

187. Friederichs 1933, 31.

188. Van Buren 1939, 13 and pl. 2, illus. 10. Cf. the comments of Heimpel 1980–83, 599–601.

189. Aelian, VI.2, XV.14 and XVII.26.

190. Melikian-Chirvani 1984, 268–70.

191. Mackenzie 1971, 97.

192. al-Ṭabarī, XXXVIII, 58; Masʿūdī, V, 156; Viré 1974, 85–88; and Rust'haveli, 184.

193. See as examples, Purchas, IX, 34; Bernier, 262; du Jarric, 10; Ovington, 161; and Sanderson, 42.

194. Masʿūdī, II, 38, and Usāmah, 141, 293.

195. Abū'l Faẓl, *AN*, II, 186–87.

196. Best data on capture come from Mughal India. See Abū'l Faẓl, *AN*, II, 508–9; Abū'l Faẓl, *AA*, I, 296–97; and Forbes, I, 272.

197. *KB*/P, 49; Usāmah, 236; and Qazvīnī, *NQ*, 47–48, Persian text, and 53, English translation.

198. Forbes, I, 272. For a contrary point of view, see al-Manṣūr, 16.

199. Abū'l Faẓl, *AA*, I, 297–98, and Forbes, I, 272.

200. For the Arab techniques, see al-Manṣūr, 49–50; Ibn Manglī, 92–106; Viré 1965, 740–42; Ahsan 1979, 207–10; and Mercier 1927, 72–76. For the Indian system, see Boyer and Planiol 1948, 176–77, and Sterndale 1982, 202–3.

201. al-Manṣūr, 29 and 51–52.

202. Abū'l Faẓl, *AA*, I, 297–98. On *ser*, see Yule and Burnell 1903, 807–8.

203. al-Manṣūr, 14 and 16.

204. My discussion of cheetah social behavior is drawn from Kitchener 1991, 170–71, 186, and 188; Turner 1997, 151; Eaton 1974, 4, 335, 46, 107, and 133–35; Caro 1994, 7 and 44–46; Caro and Collins 1987a, 56–64; and Caro and Collins 1976b, 89–105.

205. On hunting techniques, see Eaton 1974, 55–87 and 129–33; Caro 1994, 129–41; and Caro 1987, 295–97.

206. P. Mundy, II, 112; G. Mundy, 24; Bernier, 377; and Chardin, 181.

207. Jahāngīr, I, 417, and II, 39, 40, and 109–10.

208. See, for example, al-Manṣūr, 50.

209. Abū'l Faẓl *AA*, I, 297, and Forbes, I, 272. Cf. Pelsaert, 51, and Parks, I, 398–99.

210. Adamson 1969, 3–25.

211. Abū'l Faẓl, I, 630 and II, 528.

212. Eaton 1974, 105 and 125–27.

213. Bernier, 364, and Andrews 1999, II, 904 and 1095, illus. 190.

214. Abū'l Faẓl, *AA*, I, 299–300. For illustrations see Iessen 1960, 90–91.

215. Kai Kāʿūs, 85.

216. Teixeira, 220; Rice 1954, 25, fig. 7, and 29–30, figs. 13–21; Naumann and Naumann 1976, 51–53; and *HI*, V, 269.

217. Rice 1954, 30, fig. 15; Chung 1998–99, 18, 26 and fig. 21; and Mansard 1993, 93–95.

218. Chardin, 181.

219. al-Manṣūr, 50 and Ibn Manglī, 159–60.

220. Yule and Burnell 1903, 407–8; Beach 1997, 87, pl. 34; and Forbes, I, unnumbered plate following 481, entitled "The Conclusion of a Cheeta Hunt at Cambay."

221. Pelsaert, 51; Bernier, 375–77; Fryer, I, 271, and II, 279–80; G. Mundy, 23–25; Forbes, I, 273–76; and Parks, I, 349.

222. Juvaynī/Q, II, 30, and Juvaynī/B, I, 301–2.

223. Abū'l Faẓl, *AN*, I, 629, and II, 122, 133, and 226 for quote.

224. Ḥusām al-Dawlah, 148.

225. Kitchener 1991, 34 and 59–60.

226. Serruys 1974a, 48 and note 107.

227. Ahsan 1979, 210–11, and Boyer and Planiol 1948, 178–81.

228. Frederick II, 5; Qazvīnī, *NQ*, 46, Persian text, and 32, English translation; and Marco Polo, 226.

229. Forbes I, 277; Parks, I, 394; and G. Mundy, 14 and 201.

230. al-Manṣūr, 16 and 52; Manucci, III, 85; and Forbes, I, 270 and IV, 97.

231. Abū'l Faẓl, *AA*, I, 301.

232. Hamilton, I, 76.

Chapter 5. Administration

1. Decker 1992, 162–63, and *ARE*, IV, 266.

2. Back 1978, 236 and 354, and Frye 1984, 373.

3. Anvarī 1976, 20–21.

4. Abū'l Faẓl, *AA*, I, 452, and Jahāngīr, II, 12.

5. Xenophon, *Cyn.*, IX.2; *SJ*, ch. 117, 3002; and *SJH*, II, 261.

6. *Hex.*, 137 (192C9), and *GD*, 49.

7. Rashīd/A, I/1, 219 and 518–19; Qāshānī, 12; Ḥāfiẓ-i Abrū/M, 96; *HC*, 149 and 180; and Pelliot 1930, 262.

8. Usmanov 1979, 215–19; Abū'l Faẓl, *AN*, II, 242; *MDMT*, 30–31 and 81–83; and Doerfer 1963–75, II, 238–39.

9. Rashīd/K, I, 539 and 546, and Rashīd/B, 142 and 151.

10. Usmanov 1979, 218, and *Slovar* 1975–, I, 356.

11. Horst 1964, 19 and 102.

12. Cummins 1988, 172–86 and 217–19.

13. *XTS*, ch. 47, 1218, and Wittfogel and Feng 1949, 481.

14. Ḥusām al-Dawlah, 40.

15. Wittfogel and Feng 1949, 284, and Lee 1970, 44.

16. Bābur, 273, and *SMACC*, 40.

17. Jahāngīr, I, 185 and II, 53.

18. Jahāngīr, II, 24, 27–28, and 60, and *TGPM*, 209.

19. Drasxanakertcʿi/D, 55, and Drasxanakertcʿi/M, 73.

20. Bosworth 1963, 94–95.

21. Juvaynī/Q, III, 88–89; Juvaynī/B, II, 606; Marco Polo, 223; Rashīd/K, I, 657; Rashīd/B, 297; *YS*, ch. 99, 2524, and ch. 100, 2557; and Hsiao 1978, 93.

22. Abū'l Faẓl, *AA*, I, 5; Munshī, I, 228; and Kaempfer, 259–60.

23. Bartol'd 1964, 391, Persian text and 396, Russian translation; Semenov 1948, 148; Akhmedov 1982, 164–65; and Beneveni, 77 and 122–23. See, however, the cautionary remarks of Bregel 2000, 7–12, on the potential for confusing *qosh begi*, "chief of the royal camp," and *qush begi*, "falconer," in the Arabic script.

24. Bahari 1996, 69, fig. 28.

25. On the high status of gamekeepers in the period of the Warring States, see *ZGC*, 353.

26. Torbert 1977, 29, and Brunnert and Hagelstrom 1912, 16.

27. See the comments in Jahāngīr, II, 216.

28. *EVTRP*, I, 134.

29. Khorenatsʿi, 278.

30. *CWT*, II, 235, and Purchas, VIII, 162.

31. Bernier, 375.

32. *SCBM*, 128 and 147, and *SOS*, 69–70.

33. ʿInāyat Khān, 141, and Manucci, I, 184.

34. Ghirshman 1962, 194–98, figs. 236–37, and Reed 1965, 1–14.

35. Back 1978, 367, and Frye 1984, 373.

36. Kautilya, 43.

37. Kangxi, 22–23.

38. Kangxi, 9, and Bell, 171.

39. Parrot, 1961, 65, fig. 69.

40. Bernier, 378–80.

41. *PSRL*, I, 251; *PVL*, 105, Old Russian text, and 243, modern Russian translation; and *RPC*, 215.

42. du Jarric, 206–7.

43. Whittow 1996, 112.

44. Abū'l Faẓl, *AN*, I, 630.

45. See the comments of Ḥusām al-Dawlah, 74–75.

46. Bābur, 637, and Abū'l Faẓl, *AA*, I, 306–7.

47. Yang Yu, 79.

48. Juvaynī/Q, I, 191; Juvaynī/B, I, 235; Rashīd/K, I, 502; and Rashīd/B, 92.

49. Levanoni 1995, 185, and Jahāngīr, II, 182.

50. Boccaccio, X (603).

51. Ḥusām al-Dawlah, 98–99.

52. Multaner, 466ff.

53. Juvaynī/Q, I, 24; Juvaynī/B, I, 40; Bar Hebraeus, 353; and Catherine II, 85, 96, 99, 103, and 159.

54. al-Nasāwī, 379, and Munshī, II, 1095.

55. Juvaynī/Q, III, 39; Juvaynī/B, II, 574; Rashīd/K, I, 586; and Rashīd/B, 207.

56. Munshī, II, 1096.

57. *SJ*, ch. 6, 227, and *SJQ*, 37.

58. *TM*, 44, 51, 75, 88, and 95.

59. Yūsuf, 174–75.

60. Artsruni, 101–2.
61. Munshī, II, 1260–61 and 1295.
62. Manucci, III, 94 and 220, and McChesney 1991, 117.
63. Jūzjānī/L, 122, 1134, 149, 233, 248, and 285, and Jūzjānī/R, I, 490, 504, and 603–4, and II, 725, 745, and 806.
64. Eisenstein 1994, 129–35.
65. Lacroix 1963, 203–4 and 207.
66. Ye Longli, ch. 10, 101.
67. Hedin 1933, 161–67, and Hou and Pirazzoli 1979, 24–33.
68. *KF*, 233.
69. Rudra Deva, 108–9 (para. 17–21).
70. Kaempfer, 158, and Melnikova 2002, 64.
71. Forbes, IV, 96–97.
72. *YS*, ch. 90, 2293.
73. *YS*, ch. 35, 793.
74. al-ʿUmarī/S, 18, Arabic text, and 41, German translation.
75. Usāmah, 224–25, and Kaempfer, 109.
76. Cf. Rudra Deva, 121 (para. 9–10).
77. *TTP*, 66.
78. Jahāngīr, I, 347.
79. Bābur, 40.
80. Abū'l Faẓl, *AA*, I, 305–6, and Chardin, 180.
81. Lacroix 1963, 197–201 and 204; Dementieff 1945, 24–27; and *SOS*, 157.
82. Abū'l Faẓl, *AA*, I, 297–98. Cf. the comments of Forbes, I, 272–73.
83. al-ʿUmarī/S, 28, Arabic text, and 54, German translation.
84. Manucci, II, 339–40, and Tavernier, I, 99 and 224.
85. Abū'l Faẓl, *AA*, I, 231.
86. Cummins 1988, 250–60, appendix 1, has an account of the expenses for the royal hunt in France in 1398 during the reign of Charles VI, 1380–1422.
87. Ahsan 1979, 233–35.
88. al-Ṣābi', 23 and 24.
89. Manucci, IV, 241.
90. *HI*, III, 356.
91. *PFT*, 8 and 360.
92. Herodotus, I, 192.
93. Wittfogel and Feng 1949, 384.
94. *PSRL*, II, 932, and *Hyp*., 114–15. See also *Slovar* 1975–, VIII, 269, for the term *lovchee.*
95. McChesney 1991, 187–88.
96. Rashīd/K, II, 1087 and 1097–1101.
97. *MDMT*, 30–31 and 81–83.
98. *VRTE*, 16–17, and Waley 1949, 36–37.
99. Mencius, 1.3, 1.24, and 3.33; *CRP*, 37 and 49–51; and *WX*, I, 447 and 449.
100. *SJ*, ch. 53, 2018; *SJH*, I, 96; and Huan Kuan, 81–84.
101. *HHS*, ch. 3, 134, ch. 5, 206 and 213.
102. *SJ*, ch. 10, 432–33; *SJH*, II, 305; *HS*, ch. 9, 281; *HS*/D, II, 306; *VRTE*, 40; and Tao 1976, 86.

Chapter 6. Conservation

1. Cf. the comments of Schafer 1962, 279–308.
2. *XTS*, ch. 9, 20; Juvaynī/Q, III, 32; and Juvaynī/B, II, 569.
3. Niẓāmī, 12, 15–22, and 25.2.
4. Rust'haveli, 13–14, 34, 111–12, and 153–54.
5. *Vis.*, 235.
6. *CRP*, 33–35.
7. Juvaynī/Q, I, 20–21, and Juvaynī/B, I, 28.
8. Marco Polo, 229.
9. d'Orléans, 74 and 109.
10. Chardin, 112.
11. Don Juan, 39–40.
12. *HI*, V, 316–17.
13. Mencius, 3.38.
14. Pliny, VII.38, and Abū'l Faẓl, *AA*, III, 346.
15. *ZZ*/W, 94.
16. *JTS*, ch. 43, 1841, and *XTS*, ch. 46, 1202.
17. Bell, 170.
18. Jarman 1972, 125–47, and esp. 132–35.
19. Xenophon, *Cyn.*, V.14.
20. Niẓāmī, 12.24–34.
21. Cheng Zhufu, ch. 5, 4a, and *YS*, ch. 8, 161, ch. 14, 295, and ch.15, 307. For other measures, see Ratchnevsky 1937–85, IV, 372–75 and 379, and Haenisch 1959, 88–93.
22. Jahāngīr, I, 286.
23. Ibn Manglī, 103–4.
24. Böttger 1956, 11–14; Juvaynī/Q, I, 20 and 21; Juvaynī/B, I, 28 and 29; and *CWT*, II, 236.
25. Ripa, 90; Herbert, 81; Munshī, II, 765; Jahāngīr, I, 120; and ʿInāyat Khān, 265.
26. Broecke, 41.
27. Psellus, 321.
28. *YS*, ch. 5, 88 and 100, and ch. 6, 115; *CWT*, II, 235; Kangxi, 113; and Ripa, 91.
29. Jahāngīr, II, 70; Manucci, III, 85; and Wittfogel and Feng 1949, 237 and 337.
30. Moscati 1962, 63; Ratchnevsky 1937–85, IV, 371–72; Pelsaert, 52; and Roe, II, 392.
31. *TS*, 67.
32. *YS*, ch. 20, 428, and Yang Yu, 70.
33. Wittfogel and Feng 1949, 568.
34. *ASC*, 165; Marco Polo, 233–34 and 257; *YS*, ch. 6, 106, and ch. 16, 352.
35. Rey 1965, 142.
36. *YS*, ch. 6, 346.
37. Bernier, 218 and 375.
38. *ARI*, II, 17, 55, 92, 149, and 175, and *ANE*, 103.
39. Lacroix 1963, 188–89.
40. McCormick 1991, 49.
41. Juvaynī/Q, I, 110–11, and Juvaynī/B, I, 139–40.

42. Jahāngīr, I, 129–30, and 209.
43. *CDIPR*, I, 190.
44. *ZGC*, 353, and Mencius, 3.11.
45. Kangxi, 9.
46. *KF*, 233; Bernier, 416; and Herbert, 84.
47. *AR*, 27 and 43, and Marco Polo, 184.
48. Pʿarpecʿi, 43.
49. Juvaynī/Q, I, 193 and 226–27, and Juvaynī/B, I, 237 and 271.
50. Muraviev, 109.
51. On the disputed etymology of this word, see Yule and Burnell 1903, 898–900.
52. Sarma 1989, 302–3. See also Hui Li, 99 and 103.
53. *HI*, I, 268; III, 206 and 383; IV, 8; V, 335; and VIII, 3.
54. Tavernier, I, 58, 71, 121–22, and 124, and Hall, 192.
55. Jahāngīr, I, 254, and II, 17 and 42. See also Carré, I, 141, and II, 357.
56. P. Mundy, II, 31–32, 55, 60, and 241, and Forbes, II, 294–95 and 413–14.
57. Devèze 1966, 347–80, esp. 348–49 and 364.
58. Darby 1976a, 55.
59. My discussion is based in Petit-Dutaillis 1915, 147–78.
60. Gregory of Tours, 558–59.
61. Duby 1974, 201ff.
62. Birrell 1982, 9–25, and Almond 2003, 125–42.
63. Savage 1933, 32–36 and 40, and Norden 1997, 144–46.
64. Winters 1974, 217–18 and 224–25, and Russell 1997, 97–98.
65. al-Ṭabarī, XXV, 132, and Abū'l Faẓl, *AN*, III, 979.
66. *ANE*, II, 193; Khorenatsʿi, 73ff.; and Kirakos, 49.
67. Mencius, 1.3 and 1.24.
68. Menzies 1996, 608–11.
69. *WX*, I, 135, and II, 115, 119, and 137; *HS*, ch. 99b, 4103; and *HS*/D, III, 270.
70. *CWT*, II, 235; Legrand 1976, 48; and Brunnert and Hagelstrom 1912, 22, 336, and 461–62.
71. Huc and Gabet, I, 19–20; Vermeer 1998, 260; and Menzies 1994, 56–57.
72. Menzies 1996, 650–54.
73. Totman 1989, 1–6 and 26.
74. Glacken 1990, 326 and 346–47.
75. al-Ṭabarī, XIII, 152, and Langer 1976, 357–68.
76. Pelsaert, 47.
77. Xenophon, *Cyr.*, I.iv.16, and Ełishē, 247.
78. *GC*, 3.
79. Voeikov 1901, 109–11.
80. *RTC*, 78–79.
81. Martin and Szuter 1999, 36–45, and Hickerson 1965, 43–65.
82. Kim 1997, 242–43, and Kim and Wilson 2002, A31.
83. S. Kramer 1981, 42–43, and Jos., 110.
84. Theophylact, III.7.19.
85. *VMQC*, 159–60, 167, 168, and 170, and Marks 1998, 161–62.
86. Simmons 1989, 316. In the American Civil War, wild hogs often ate the dead and dying on the battlefields. See Caras 1996, 115.

87. *HI*, III, 103 and 353–54, and IV, 14.
88. Wescoat 1998, 259–79.
89. Thiébaux 1967, 263–65.
90. *GD*, 49.
91. al-Tabarī, VII, 19, 146, and 147, and XX, 2; Ibn Khurdādhbih, 132, Arabic text, and 101–2, French translation; Ibn Khaldūn, II, 255–26; Ibn Baṭṭuṭah, I, 208; al-Balādhurī, I, 69; and Gaudefroy-Demombynes 1923, 9–16.
92. *MMT*, 116; *MK*, 23–27; R. Fox 1987, 566–67; and Goody 1993, 86–87.
93. La Fleur 1973, 93–128 and 227–48, and *TDB*, 112.
94. *EA*, 31, 37, 40, 45, 46, 55–56, and 58.
95. *LKA*, 233–34 and 285–86.
96. Kalidasa, 19.
97. Faxian, 30–31 and 43.
98. Kalidasa, 6, and Faxian 34 and 94. On monasteries as animal refuges in Mongolia, see Przhevalskii, I, 156.
99. Hui Li, 83.
100. *HPKP*, 230.
101. *TTK*, 35–39 and 49–51.
102. *TTT*, 438 (A57–58); Nadeliaev, et al. 1969, 215, 471, and 594; and Benn 2002, 286.
103. Xuanzang, I, 28.
104. Wittfogel and Feng 1949, 263, 264, 301, and 305; Henthorn 1971, 58; Kamata 1989, 149; and Jameson 1962, 4–5.
105. See the remarks of Varthema, 108.
106. Lodrick 1981, 13–14 and 57–70.
107. Linschoten, I, 253–54; Tavernier, I, 63–64; and Ripa, 40.
108. Forbes, I, 256–57.
109. Rudra Deva, 80 (para. 7–9).
110. Tavernier, I, 57–58.
111. Hamilton, I, 214.
112. Ḥasan-i Fasā'ī 106.
113. Jahāngīr, I, 61.
114. Findley 1987, 245–56.
115. *JTS*, ch. 77, 2681.
116. *XTS*, ch. 125, 4400.
117. *HS*, ch. 8, 258, and *HS*/D, II, 237.
118. Campany 1996, 384ff.
119. J. Smith 1999, 51–84.
120. Clutton-Brock 1989, 84, 91, 93–94, 95–96, and 98–101.
121. Varro, II.vi.2–4.
122. Varro, II.i.5, and *Ḥ-ʿĀ*, 68–69 and 152–53.
123. Grant 1937, 14.
124. Shaw, 99; Zhao Ji 1990, 31, 38, 192–93, and 215; Academy of Sciences MPR 1990, 46; and Finch 1999, 22–24.
125. *ANE*, II, 162.
126. Masson and Sarianidi 1972, 29.
127. Theophylact, IV.7.2.; Ibn Baṭṭuṭah, I, 116; *EVTRP*, I, 69; and Ferrier, 138 and 481.

128. al-Manṣūr, 61 and 63; Qazvīnī, *NQ*, 32, Persian text, and 22–23, English translation, and *SBM*, 701.

129. *Hex.*, 223 (199c25); Aelian, XIV.10; Thaʿālibī, 61; and *Vis.* 62.

130. Ammianus, XXIII.4, and Benjamin of Tudela, 70–71.

131. *KDA*, 79.

132. Pʿarpecʿi, 43; Drasxanakertcʿi/M, 75; Drasxanakertcʿi/D, 58; Rust'haveli, 13; Yūsuf, 49–50; and *ON*, 33.

133. Parrot 1961, 67 and fig. 72; Usāmah, 248–49; and Teixeira, 36 and 99.

134. Strabo, VII.iv.8; *SH*, I, 196; *SH/I*, 158; Hetʿum/B, 177 and 182; Rubruck, 84 and 142; *MM*, 100 and 134; and Pelliot 1973, 91–92.

135. Xenophon, *Ana.*, I.iv.2–3.

136. al-Manṣūr, 61, and Munshī, II, 764.

137. ʿInāyat Khān, 140–41.

138. See for example, the comments of Marco Polo, 118, 160–61, and 470, and Bābur, 224 and 325.

139. Nīshāpūrī, 99; *ʿA-D*, 519, Persian text, and 223, Russian translation; and Munshī, II, 1165.

140. *New York Times*, January 8, 2000, F5.

141. Sterndale 1982, 201.

142. Hawkins 1986, 103–4 and 135. On plans to clone Persian cheetahs and reintroduce them into India, *New York Times*, February 1, 2003, A3.

143. Gryaznov 1969, 158–59; *ANE*, II, 239; and Jahāngīr, I, 369.

144. Rashīd/K, II, 1099 and 1100, and Jahāngīr, I, 240.

145. On predation, see al-Manṣūr, 49.

146. Thompson and Landreth 1973, 162–67.

147. Caro and Laurensen 1994, 485–86; Mercola 1994, 961–71; and Eaton 1974, 29–33, 37–38, 40, and 157.

148. Caro 1994, 358–63; Kitchener 1991, 230–33; and Caras 1996, 194–95.

149. Hemmer 1990, 37, and Clutton-Brock 1989, 178–80.

150. Jahāngīr, I, 240. See also Divyabhanusinh 1987, 273.

151. Abū'l Faẓl, *AN*, II, 186–87, 509, and 528.

152. While animal introductions are sometimes successful, for example, rabbits in Australia and mongooses in the Caribbean, the great majority fail to gain a foothold. See Russell 1997, 99–103, and Bates 1956, 797–80.

153. Clutton-Brock 1984, 167–71.

154. Simonian 1995, 31–32.

155. Elvin 1993, 16–21.

156. Ruttan and Mulder 1999, 621–52, with invited commentary.

157. See, for example, Mokyr 1990, 199–205.

158. Elvin 1993, 7–46, esp. 11.

159. Tuan 1968, 176–91.

160. Cf. Hughes 1989, 19.

161. *LKA*, 221, and *SOS*, 157.

162. Hillel 1991, 105.

163. Bowlus 1980, 86–99. Cf. the arguments of L. White 1986, 144–47.

164. Pliny, VII.1–5, and Hillel 1991, 11ff.

165. Thomas 1983, 17–25.

166. Salzman 1978, 618–37, and Salzman 1980, 1–19.
167. Serruys 1974a, 76–91.
168. Officer and Page 1993, 133ff.
169. Brunhes 1920, 340–45.
170. K. Redford 1992, 412–22.
171. McNeill 1994, 302–6, and Cassels 1984, 741–67.
172. Diamond 1984, 838–56. Cf. Davis 1987, 99–115.
173. Gregory of Tours, 558. The last known wild aurochs died in Poland in the early seventeenth century. Ersatz aurochs, back-bred from domesticated stock by zoologists in the 1930s still exist today. See Morrison 2000, 9–12.
174. Marks 1998, 44–46.
175. Hillel 1991, 50, 62, and 176.
176. Glacken 1990, 677–78.
177. Herbert, 169 and 319.
178. Marks 1998, 99–100, 331, and 344–45. At best, only thirty tigers survive in the wild in South China. See Tilson 2002, 26–30.
179. Reed 1965, 16–22.
180. Cf. Hillel 1991, 75.

Chapter 7. A Measure of Men

1. Tacitus, 46.
2. Procopius, *HW*, VI.xv.16–23.
3. Gardīzī, 127.
4. See, for example, *FCH*, 375 and 377, and *TYH*, 18.
5. Porphyrogenitus, *AI*, 159.
6. *SH*, I, 18–20, and *SH/I*, 28–30.
7. *WS*/H, 51.
8. See, for example, Li Zhizhang, 268–69, and Li Zhizhang/W, 67.
9. *FCH*, 223 and 225.
10. Bell, 169.
11. Kangxi, 8–9.
12. Thompson and Johnson 1965, 315–16; R. Anderson 1971, 24, and Almond 2003, 27–60.
13. Niẓām al-Mulk, 36, 37, and 41.
14. Boccaccio, II.9.
15. *LT*, 48.
16. Ibn Baṭṭuṭah, III, 580.
17. Bābur, 33–34, 38, and 67.
18. Thiébaux 1967, 260.
19. Stetkevych 1996, 102–18, esp. 105.
20. Cummins 1988, 223–33.
21. Lindberger 2001, 68–82; Ianin 1970, II, 19, 22, 161, and 394–95, *tablitsa* 3 and 52; and Wittfogel and Feng 1949, 236.
22. Qāshānī, 53.

23. *JTS*, ch. 64, 2420.
24. Pʿarpecʿi, 163–64.
25. *SJ*, ch. 129, 3277.
26. Fryer, II, 295, and III, 122 and 134–35. Cf. Chardin, 180 and 222.
27. Layard, 483.
28. Kaempfer, 44.
29. Lavin 1963, 276–77.
30. Diodorus, II.11.3–4, 12.1–2, 333.2–5, and 59.4; Homer, *Il.* IX.528–50; and Dio Chrysostom, 61.11 and 63.6.
31. Colley 1992, 170–73.
32. Rudra Deva, 86 (para. 42–43).
33. al-Rāvandī, 437ff.
34. *KB/V*, 8.
35. Kai Kāʿūs, 85.
36. Mīrzā Ḥaydar, I, 39, and Mīrzā Ḥaydar, II, 35.
37. Ḥāfiẓ-i Tanīsh, I, 13a and 18a, Persian text, and 53 and 62, Russian translation; Braund 1994, 57; Jordanes, III.21 and VI.47; and *WX*, II, 163.
38. Marco Polo, 118, 119, 134, 135, 136, 138, 141, 263, 265–66, 267, 306, 307, 308, 323, 344, 345, 351, 370, and 417.
39. *ZGC*, 229, 282, and 513.
40. Justin, XLI, 4.
41. Narshakhī, 7 and 32.
42. Pʿarpecʿi, 42–43. Cf the comments of Kirakos, 154.
43. *GD*, 86, 136, and 139, and Rust'haveli, 93.
44. Bābur, 8, 10, and 114; Abū'l Faẓl, *AA*, II, 164, 169, 182, 246, 339, 397, and 410; and Manucci, I, 65, and II, 110.
45. Keightley 1978, 73–74 and 180–81, and Keightley 1983, 527 and 541–43.
46. Tacitus, *Ann.*, II.ii and lvi.
47. J. Wilson 1956, 439–42; S. Kramer 1981, 282–88; and *ANE*, II, 133.
48. Ḥāfīẓ-i Tanīsh, I, 56b, Persian text, and 130, Russian translation, and Ḥusām al-Dāwlah, xx–xxi.
49. *YS*, ch. 3, 56.
50. Niẓāmī, 5.33–44, and Yūsuf, 48.
51. *MM*, 19.
52. Gardīzī, 120–21.
53. Abū'l Faẓl, *AA*, II, 274.
54. *KDA*, 67–68. Cf also al-Ṭabarī, V, 4.
55. al-Ṭabarī, V, 91–93.
56. Niẓāmī, 13.1–16, 16.1–12, and 28.37–44. For his image in Mughal India, see Abū'l Faẓl, *AA*, III, 374–75.
57. *TS*, 33.
58. Josephus, I.xxi.13.
59. *PSRL*, II, 921, and *Hyp.*, 109.
60. *Vis.*, 9 and 392.
61. Strabo, XV.iii.8.
62. Lang 1957, 118.
63. Xenophon, *Ana.*, I.ix.1ff.

64. Dio Chrysostom, 7.12a.

65. Rudra Deva, 65 (para. 3), 66 (para. 5) and 104 (para. 50–60).

66. *ON*, 23.

67. Xenophon, *Cyr.*, I.iii.14, and Rashīd/K, 846.

68. *ARE*, I, 232.

69. *PSRL*, I, 252; *PVL*, 105, Old Russian text, and 243, modern Russian translation; and *RPC*, 215.

70. *BDK*, 15, 42 and 44, and Munshī, I, 41.

71. el-Habashi 1992, 131, 134, and 144.

72. Pʿarpecʿi, 43–44.

73. Juansher, 83.

74. al-Sarraf 2004, 144–46. Cf. the remarks of Kai Kāʾūs, 83; Broecke, 13; and Manucci, II, 324.

75. Kangxi, 9–10.

76. *ANE*, I, 65.

77. Justin, XXXV.2.

78. Mīrzā Ḥaydar, I, 140, and Mīrzā Ḥaydar, II, 112.

79. Widengren 1969, 86–87.

80. *BDK*, 15–16 and 77.

81. Rashīd/K, I, 282–83; Boyle 1968, 1–9; and Boyle 1969, 12–16.

82. Rashīd/K, II, 846. On the term *mergen*, see Cleaves 1978, 442 and 446–47; Doerfer 1963–75, I, 496–98; Haenisch 1935, 83, entry no. 101; and Rozycki 1994, 158.

83. *PCR*, 257.

84. Gregory of Tours, 217.

85. Einhard, 59.

86. Su Tianjue, ch. 57, 20b-21a, and *YS*, ch. 2, 37.

87. Munshī, II, 987 and 1300, and Bell, 169.

88. *ON*, 58–59.

89. *Mencius*, 1.4.

90. *SJ*, ch. 58, 2083, and *SJH*, I, 383.

91. Ibn ʿArabshāh, 107–8.

92. *MIRGO*, 163 and 167.

93. Ye Longli, ch. 6, 60.

94. Psellus, 321, 370–71 and 374–75.

95. Herodotus, IV.116, and Xenophon, *Cyn.*, XIII.18.

96. *BDK*, 113.

97. *AR*, 30, and Jahāngīr, I, 130, 204, and 375.

98. Parks, I, 400.

99. Abū'l Faẓl, *AN*, II, 326–27.

100. *NC*, I, 54.

101. Catherine II, 95–96, 112, 127, 129, and 139. See also Markina 2002, 207–12.

102. *GC*, 73 and 75, and Eastmond 1998, 121.

103. For examples, see Ibn Isfandiyār, 158, and *AIM*, 41.

104. Masʿūdī, II, 168–69.

105. *GC*, 5, 97, and 100.

106. Ye Longli, ch. 11, 118, and ch. 19, 182; *LS*, ch. 30, 358; Rashīd/K, I, 522–23; Rashīd/B, 118–19; Broecke, 91; and *HI*, VIII, 73, 104, and 105.

107. *FCH*, 17.

108. *FCH*, 227 and 229.

109. Fu Jian, 132–33; *JS*, ch. 6, 141–42; Tao 1976, 86; Qāshānī, 228; and Abū'l Faẓl, *AN*, II, 240.

110. Dio Chrysostom, 3.135–36.

111. Kautilya, 360.

112. Kalidasa, 17–18.

113. Kai Kāʿūs, 84.

114. *PSRL*, I, 150; *PVL*, 66, Old Russian text, and 203, modern Russian translation; *RPC*, 136; *NC*, I, 45, 53, and 140; Leo the Deacon, II.10; and Abū'l Fidā, 22.

115. Diodorus, IX.27.1–2; *ASB*, 111–12; al-Ṭabarī, XXVI, 81–82; Jūzjānī/L, 398–99; Jūzjānī/R, II, 1148; and al-Ahrī, 149, Persian text, and 51, English translation.

116. Sima Guang, ch. 193, 6088–89.

117. Schreiber 1949–55, 479–80; William of Tyre, II, 134; Procopius, *HW*, II.xxviii.1–2; *CC*, 42; *GC*, 45; *SH*, I, 196; *SH/I*, 158; Mīrzā Ḥaydar, I, 55; Mīrzā Ḥaydar, II, 47; *SOS*, 70; and al-Ṭabarī, V, 97.

118. *ASB*, 120, and *NC*, I, 26.

119. *PSRL*, I, 251; *PVL*, 104, Old Russian text, and 242, modern Russian translation; and *RPC*, 214–15.

120. Pliny, XII.4.

121. Plutarch, *Mor.*, 343, and Albertus Magnus, II, 1411.

122. Ibn Isfandiyār, 43.

123. Herodotus, I, 37.

124. *HS*, ch. 54, 2450; *HS*/W, 23; and Fletcher, 109v–110r.

125. Sebēos, 54–58.

126. Psellus, 376; Albertus Magnus, II, 1453; Mīrzā Ḥaydar, I, 41, and Mīrzā Ḥaydar, II, 36.

127. Ye Longli, ch. 7, 71.

128. *BDK*, 99–100; Psellus, 57; and Kinnamos, 200.

129. Nīshāpūrī, 105, and Masʿūdī, VI, 432–33.

130. *HI*, V, 271–72 and 329, and Abū'l Faẓl, *AN*, II, 482–83.

131. ʿInāyat Khān, 5, and Beach 1997, 76.

132. Bernier, 182–83.

133. Olympiodorus, 183 (para. 19); *KDA*, 68; Nīshāpūrī, 47; and *LS*, ch. 30, 355.

134. Niẓāmī, 25.29–37, and Marzolph 1999, 331–47.

135. al-Ṭabarī, V, 85–86; Niẓāmī, 13.6–16; *HI*, V, 33; Ḥāfīẓ-i Tanīsh, I, 56b, Persian text, and 130, Russian translation; and Kangxi, 10.

136. Ye Longli, ch. 7, 72.

137. Xenophon, *Hell.*, V.iii.20.

138. Rust'haveli, 12–14, 34, and 52.

139. Cannadine 1990, 364–65. For the hunting score cards of the Russian nobility in this same period, see Paltusova 2002b, 317ff.

140. Ritvo 1987, 271–76, and G. Watson 1998, 265–88.

141. *ANE*, II, 102, and *ARI*, II, 49–50, 55, 57, 91–92, 105, 140, 150, and 175.

142. el-Habashi 1992, 90–91 and 96–97, and Decker 1992, 151–52 and 156. Cf. Osborn and Osbornova 1998, 116.

143. *ANE*, II, 239.

144. Chang 1980, 142–43; Li 1957, 23–24; Keightley 2000, 108–9; Lefeuvre 1990–91, 138; J. Hsu 1996, 81; and Fiskesjö 2001, 102–3.

145. *MTZZ*, ch. 5, 2b, Chinese text, and 74, French translation.

146. *CRP*, 47; *WX*, I, 139; and *CATCL*, 422.

147. *CWT*, II, 236, and Kangxi, 9–10.

148. Jahāngīr, I, 45, and Beach 1997, 84.

149. ʿInāyat Khān, 121–22, 145, 211, 247, and 413.

150. Jahāngīr, I, 121, 129, 130, 167, 190–91, 204, 234, 248, 252, 276, 344, 403, and 404, and Jahāngīr, II, 39 and 229.

151. Jahāngīr, I, 45, 83, 163, 155, 202, 256–57, 341, 342, 345, 346, 347, 349, 352, 368, 402, 408–9, and 439, and II, 109.

152. Jahāngīr, I, 369.

153. Jahāngīr, I, 83–84, 111, 122, 402, 444, and II, 284; and Bernier, 379.

154. Munshī, II, 764.

155. Munshī, II, 987–88.

156. *PSRL*, II 905–6, and *Hyp.*, 102.

157. For an example, see Pelsaert, 52–53.

158. Hanaway 1971, 21–27; Gignoux 1983, 116–18; and Niẓāmī, 16.2–3.

159. Soucek 1990, 11–13. Cf. the comments of Esin 1968, 24–76.

160. Ettinghousen 1979, 25–31.

161. Houlihan 1996, 70–73.

162. Diodorus, I.20.1, 48.1, and III.36.3.

163. Diodorus, II.8.6–8.

164. Winter 1981, 2–38.

165. See Gerardi 1988, 14–15 and 25–28, on which I base these comments.

166. Parrot 1961, 54–61, figs. 62–65, and 209, fig. F.

167. Sachs 1953, 167–70.

168. Parrot 1961, 68–69, figs. 74–76; *ARI*, II, 91–92; and Oded 1992, 157.

169. Hertzfeld 1988, 325 and pl. 123, and Bivar 1972, 280 and pl. 17.

170. Beshevliev 1979, 89, illus. 1, following 253.

171. Tanabe 1998, 93–102; Tiratsian 1960, 477–78, 480–81, and 495; Ghirshman 1955, 5–19; and Voshchinina 1953, 188–93.

172. Harper 1978, 26.

173. Ammianus, XXIV.6.3.

174. Nāṣir-i Khusraw, 57 and *NITP*, 175.

175. Waley-Cohen 2002, 405–6 and 431–33, and Hou and Pirazolli 1979, 13–15 and 40–50.

176. Ergert and Martin 1997, 238–41. For examples of such trophies kept by royal hunters in the Shang, see Lefeuvre 1990–91, 132–36, and J. Hsu 1996, 81–82.

177. Linn-Kustermann 1997, 124–25.

178. Nīshāpūrī, 60–61.

179. *NITP*, 165.

180. Don Juan, 39–40.

181. *HI*, V, 511.

Chapter 8. Political Animals

1. Tuite 1998, 452–60.
2. Bivar 1969, 26–27, and Klingender 1971, 450–61.
3. Cowen 1989, 3–6 and 9–11, and Qazvīnī, *TG*, 233–34.
4. Abū'l Falẓ, *AA*, III, 136.
5. Xenophon, *Cav.*, IV.18 and Procopius, *HW*, II.xii.8–19.
6. Artsruni, 357–58 and 360.
7. See, for example, Tacitus, *Hist.*, I.lxxxvi and III.lvi; Theophanes, 7; and *NC*, III, 54 and V, 13.
8. Herodotus, VII.57.
9. My comments are based on the discussion of P. Shepard 1996, 195–204.
10. Aristotle, *HA*, IX.1.
11. *HS*, ch. 6, 207; *HS*/D, 112; and Manucci, I, 219. See also, 243–44, for another reptile portent.
12. Pollard 1977, 116–29, and Dio Chrysostom, 34.4–6.
13. Tacitus, *Hist.*, I.lxii and III.lvi; Tacitus, *Ger.*, 10; Ammianus, XXVIII.1.7; *PCR*, 173; and Albertus Magnus, I, 717.
14. Forbes, II, 95; *HI*, I, 332; Manrique, I, 61 and 141; and Laufer 1914, 3–35.
15. *HS*, ch. 8, 258; *HS*/D, II, 236–37; and Schreiber 1956, 33.
16. *ZZ*/W, 213, and Diodorus, XVII.49.5–6 and XX.11.3–5.
17. *ANE*, II, 97; Jordanes, XLII.220–21; al-Ṭabarī, V, 331; *PSRL*, II, 801–2; *Hyp.*, 55–56; and Abū'l Faẓl, *AN*, I, 525 and 634.
18. Aristotle, *HA*, IX.6; Pliny, VII.203, VIII.102–3, and X.36–38; Aelian, VI.16, VIII.5, and XI.19; Bar Hebraeus, 262; and Officer and Page 1993, 32, 37–38, and 40–41.
19. Hui Li, 96, and Gregory of Tours, 240.
20. Meserve 2000b, 90–97, and Lewis 1990, 198–99.
21. al-Ṭabarī, V, 73, and Theophanes, 50.
22. Molnár 1994, 127–31, and Laufer 1967, 525–28.
23. Pliny, XXVIII; Aelian, XIV.4; and *SBM*, 664, 681, 685, 695, and so on.
24. Aelian, I.42, and Pollard 1977, 130–34.
25. Unschuld 1986, 138–39.
26. Huc and Gabet, I, 19.
27. Aelian, III.41 and IV.52.
28. *HHS*, ch. 88, 2920. In pre-Han times, rhinoceros were still indigenous to South China. See *ZGC*, 240.
29. *IFC*, 13; Linschoten, II, 9–10; Marvazī, 17 and 23; Zhao Rugua, 223; and Bernier, 204.
30. Saunders 1994, 159–65.
31. *ARE*, II, 265, 306, and 336, and Diodorus, III.36.3.
32. Speidel 2002, 253–90. See also Widengren 1969, 150–51.
33. Miller 1998, 43 and 47–48.
34. Herodotus, VII.69, and Sturluson, *Vnglinga Saga*, ch. 6.
35. Foote and Wilson 1979, 285, 323, and 391, and Golden 1997, 91–93.
36. Eliade 1974, 458–61.
37. Cf. the comments of D. White 1991, 15ff.

38. On the antiquity of such creatures, see Aruz 1998, 12–24.

39. Agathangelos, 41; Ełishē, 66; *IB*, 9, 13, and 19; Wittfogel and Feng 1949, 337, and 348; and Chiodo 1992, 125–51.

40. Hakluyt, *PN*, III, 245–46, and Purchas, X, 187–88.

41. Linschoten, I, 97–98 and 102, and II, 1–2.

42. My discussion is based on Zimmer 1963, 59–60, 92, and 102–9.

43. Aelian, III.46, and Masʿūdī, II, 200.

44. *TS*, 42.

45. Manrique, I, 238ff., 272–75, and 283.

46. Guerreiro, 185–86 and 196.

47. Elias 1994, 474.

48. Aelian, XIII.23, and Naveh and Shaked 1987, 201.

49. Campany 1996, 245–48.

50. Boyle 1978, 177–85, and Herbert, 120.

51. Glacken 1990, 214–16.

52. Flint 1991, 196 and 259–60; Klingender 1971, 456–59; and Friedmann 1980, 19–22 and 229ff. Cf. Sansterre 1996, 12–13.

53. Buzand, 206, and Kirakos, 66.

54. *NC*, IV, 60–61, and *PLDR*, 312, Old Russian text, and 313, modern Russian translation.

55. Zguta 1978, 8–9, and *Dom.*, 118.

56. Ibn Baṭṭuṭah, II, 303–4.

57. Aigle 1997, 242–43.

58. Linschoten, I, 225.

59. Parks, II, 88.

60. Hamilton, II, 45.

61. Hammond 1996, 195–97, and Gernet 1995, 114.

62. al-Ṭabarī, III, 152ff., esp. 154, and Lewis 1990, 200–201.

63. *Isk.*, 184, and Rashīd/J, fol. 598r, Persian text, and 52, German translation.

64. *CWT*, II, 164–65, and Forbes, I, 481–83.

65. Tibbets 1979, 47.

66. Aelian, VII, 46, and *Isk.*, 61–62 and 73.

67. Narshakhī, 94, and Jūzjānī/R, I, 33–34.

68. Forbes, IV, 200.

69. *TDB*, 198.

70. Justin, XV.4.

71. Kalidasa, 84–86.

72. *GC*, 126.

73. Masʿūdī, V, 282–83.

74. Houlihan 1996, 91–95; *ARE*, III, 196 and 201, and IV, 27, 67, and 71; and Aelian, V.39.

75. Comnena, 195; Grigor of Akancʿ, 311; and Chardin, 83.

76. Lassner 1970, 89, and Zhao Rugua, 144.

77. Manucci, I, 21–22.

78. Marco Polo, 226, and *CWT*, II, 239. Cf. Mandeville, 152.

79. al-Ṣābiʾ, 43–44.

80. Roe, I, 198, and Manucci, II, 121.

81. Jourdain, 159–60.

82. Hall, 233–34.
83. Bar Hebraeus, 417.
84. Chen Cheng, 55–56.
85. Tavernier, I, 66.
86. Masʿūdī, III, 23.
87. Abū'l Faẓl, *AA*, III, 445.
88. Abū'l Faẓl, *AA*, I, 123–24.
89. *HI*, IV, 20, 36, and 80.
90. Ovington, 136.
91. Fryer, I, 73, 242, and 271.
92. Aristotle, *HA*, IX.46, and Pliny, VIII.3.
93. Ibn Baṭṭuṭah, III, 661–62. Cf. Varthema, 109.
94. Tavernier, I, 307, and II, 248.
95. Bernier, 261–62, and Manucci, I, 89, and II, 339.
96. See the account of Hall, 236–37.
97. Jourdain, 163; my italics.
98. Aelian, XIII.22.
99. Abū'l Faẓl, *AN*, II, 112–16; Jahāngīr, I, 38, and II, 41; and Beach 1997, 72–73. On *mast*, Persian "drunk," and Anglo-Indian *must*, "rutting," see Yule and Burnell 1903, 604.
100. *CWT*, 164, and *Isk.*, 17.
101. Hamilton, II, 94; Manrique, I, 371 and 390; and Bowrey, 312.
102. *SOS*, 49.
103. Suetonius, *Julius*, XXXVII.2, and Nikephoros, 67, sect. 19.
104. Dasxurancʿi, 127 and 129.
105. al-Ṭabarī, XXXIII, 179–80, and XXXVIII, 29.
106. Nīshāpūrī, 37, 82, and 99–100.
107. *SS*, ch. 164, 3894.
108. Ḥāfiẓ-i Abrū/M, 50–51; *HC*, 169; Ripa, 125–26; Bell, 142–43; *PRDK*, 134; *RKO*, 232; and Brunnert and Hagelstrom 1912, 37.
109. Suetonius, *Claudius*, XXI.3.
110. Herodotus, III.32; Aelian, XV.15; *HS*, ch. 68, 2940; and *HS*/W, 133.
111. Jahāngīr, I, 157; Manrique, II, 162 and 270; P. Mundy, II, 50, 121, 128, and 170; Bowrey, 310; Chardin, 87 and 181–82; and Hall, 210–12.
112. Parks, I, 176–78.
113. du Jarric, 9–10 and 67–68.
114. Abū'l Faẓl, *AA*, I, 228–32, and *HI*, VI, 168 and 193.
115. Pelsaert, 3, and Bernier, 276ff.
116. Manucci, I, 184 and 216, and II, 108, 179, and 340.
117. P. Mundy, II, 127–28.
118. Suetonius, *Claudius*, XIV.
119. Jackson 1985, 50.
120. Zhao Rugua, 95; *HI*, III, 148 and 233; *RG*, 57; du Jarric, 12; Manucci, I, 190; and Manrique, II, 62–63.
121. Hamilton, II, 97, and Ibn Baṭṭuṭah, II, 715–16, and IV, 793.
122. *SOS*, 146–47.
123. Abū'l Faẓl, *AA*, I, 340, and Abū'l Faẓl, *AN*, II, 436.
124. Jahāngīr, I, 339–40.

125. al-Ṭabarī, V, 334; Masʿūdī, III, 208; Jāḥiẓ *KT*, 94; Ibn ʿArabshāh, 142; and Theophylact, III.8.8 and IV.14.14.

126. Cf. the comments of P. Shepard 1996, 110 and 191–94.

127. *TLC*, 160.

128. For examples of rigged competitions, see G. Mundy, 13, 14, and 18–20.

129. Abū'l Faẓl, *AN*, II, 528 and 539.

130. Andrews 1999, II, 1069 and 1070, and illus. 178.

131. *Isk.*, 17.

132. Manucci, II, 416.

133. Andrews 1999, II, 1005.

134. Quintus Curtius, V.i.21.

135. *TTP*, 53.

136. Reid 1988, 184–86.

137. Almost all the world's great cats, and some of the smaller ones, are now on the vulnerable or endangered species list. See McCarthy 2004, 44–53.

138. *ANE*, I, 71.

Chapter 9. Legitimation

1. Kuzmina 1987, 729–45.

2. Juvaynī/Q, I, 45, and Juvaynī/B, I, 61. For other examples, see Braund 1994, 22.

3. Aelian, XII.4.

4. *SH*, I, 14; *SH/I*, 25; Ḥāfīẓ-i Tanīsh, I, 60a, Persian text, and 137, Russian translation; Waida 1978, 283–89; Okladnikov 1964, 411–14; and Okladnikov 1990, 88–89.

5. Dankoff 1971, 102–4, and Eliade 1974, 69–71.

6. Bazin 1971, 128–32.

7. Quintus Curtius, III.iii.16; Xenophon, *Cyr.*, VIII.i.4; Aelian, XIII.1; Xenophon, *Ana.*, VI.v.2–3; Theophanes, 69; and *SCWSC*, 219–20.

8. Price 1987, 94–96.

9. Hamayon 1994, 78–79.

10. Wittfogel and Feng 1949, 132 and 284.

11. Galdanova 1981, 153–62; Kara 1966, 102–4; Bauwe 1993, 11–22; *IB*, 11 and 27; Heissig 1980, 51–57, 83, 87, and 93; and Bawden 1968, 104–40.

12. *ARI*, II 49, 55, 77, 91, 150, and 175.

13. Sugiyama 1973, 31–41.

14. Sima Guang/C, I, 170; *SJH*, I, 183; and Abū'l Faẓl, II, 7.

15. Helms 1993, 153–57, and Hendricks 1988, 221.

16. For overviews, see Gnoli 1990, 83–92; Golden 1982, 37–76; and de Rachewiltz 1973, 21–36.

17. Decker 1992, 148.

18. The following discussion is based on Cassin 1981, 355–401.

19. For lion breeding, see *ANE*, II, 103.

20. Parrot 1961, 250, fig. 250; Porada 1969, 176 and 177, and fig. 88; Lukonin 1977, 164 and 166; and Gignoux 1983, 101–3 and 107–11.

21. Harper 1983, 1115–20.

22. Haussig 1992, 82, illus. 21; Garsoian 1981, 46–54; and Braund 1994, 253–54. See Naumann and Naumann 1969, 47–49, and fig. 6 for an Il-qan representation of a haloed, hunting king.

23. See Litvinskii 1972, 266–82, and Azarpay 1981, 70–73 and 110–12.

24. Bernier, 379.

25. Morris 2000, 36–49.

26. Forbes, I, 41, and Yule and Burnell 1903, 58–59.

27. Pliny, III.79, and VIII.217–18, and Marco Polo, 257.

28. Bowrey, 220; Muraviev, 108; Herbert, 47; Chardin, 173; Hakluyt, *V*, II, 120 and 123; and *EVTRP*, II, 424–25 and 440.

29. The comments of Aelian, V.45, are representative of the classical authors.

30. Buzand, 128.

31. Hamilton, I, 52, and II, 109.

32. *Vis.*, 387.

33. Theophylact, V.16.12–14.

34. Xenophon, *Cyn.*, X.8, 12–16, 18, and 21; Theophylact, VII.2.11–12; Haussig 1992, 78–79, illus. 125; and Usāmah, 231 and 252–52. For a modern account of the dangers, see Hurston 1990, 33–37.

35. Procopius, *HW*, V.xv.7–8.

36. Braudel 1985–86, I, 64–70. For examples, see Varthema, 85 and 131; Usāmah, 173–74; Ibn Baṭṭuṭah, I, 68; and *RG*, 68.

37. Gregory of Tours, 350, and *ASB*, 86.

38. Fletcher, 4v.

39. Albertus Magnus, II, 1519.

40. al-Ṭabarī, XXXVIII, 198, and Parks, I, 407.

41. Usāmah, 140; P. Mundy, V, 59 and 63; and Parks, II, 252.

42. Strabo, XV.i.37; Aelian, IV.21; Mela, III.v; and Ammianus, XXII.vi.50–52.

43. McDougal 1987, 435–48.

44. *ZGC*, 95, and Schafer 1967, 195 and 228–29.

45. Marco Polo, 299, 344, 346, and 348.

46. P. Mundy, II, 170; Carré, I, 180 and 198; Fryer, I, 145–46, 147, and 186, II, 98, and III, 5–6; Bowrey, 119, 211, and 219–20; Hamilton, I, 148 and 219, and II, 3, 13–14, 16, and 17; and G. Mundy, 3–4.

47. Hui Li, 128 and 146, and Faxian, 68 and 93.

48. Ibn Baṭṭuṭah, II, 279, and III, 596 and 727.

49. *SOS*, 47, 49, 164–65, and 175.

50. Marco Polo, 373; Floris, 41; Bowrey, 259–60 and 279; and Wallace, 26.

51. Hamilton, II, 24.

52. Tavernier, II, 185 and 205; Manucci, I, 316, II, 81–82 and 86–87, and III, 462–63; and Manrique I, 395 and 398–404.

53. Manrique, I, 96–99, 104, and 338–39.

54. Fryer, III, 5–6. Cf. also Don Juan, 50.

55. For examples, see *PME*, 83; Marco Polo, 268; *EVTRP*, II, 224; and Tavernier, II, 224.

56. Carré, I, 72, and III, 846, 848, 851, 852, 854, 857, and 864.

57. Schumpeter 1951, 179ff.

58. Ahsan 1979, 240–41.

59. Aristotle, *MTH*, 27; Aelian, XV.26; and al-Balādhurī, I, 278–79.

60. Decker 1992, 149–50.

61. Twiti 37.27–28, and Colley 1992, 172.

62. *SJ*, ch. 109, 2872; *SJH*, II, 122; *HS*, ch. 54, 2444; *HS*/W, 17; and Pliny, VI.91 and VIII.66.

63. Abū'l Faẓl, *AA*, I, 293–94, and Abū'l Faẓl, *AN*, II, 222–23, 327, and 539.

64. *SMCAC*, 40, and Ibn al-Furāt, I, 84–85, Arabic text, and II, 68, 69, English translation.

65. Allen 1971, 331.

66. Rudra Deva, 83 (para. 22).

67. Aelian, XVII.3, and Forbes, I, 354.

68. Pliny, XI.103–6.

69. Huc and Gabet, I, 99.

70. Wallace, 82.

71. Robinson 1953, 77, and Aelian, IV.21.

72. G. Mundy, 97, 274, and 301.

73. Marks 1998, 323–26.

74. Forbes, I, 197, 367–68, and 438, II, 282–85, and III, 89–90.

75. Eberhard 1968, 170–71.

76. On werewolves in the Mediterranean, see Pliny, VIII.80–84; on weretigers in China, see Schafer 1967, 228.

77. Ibn Baṭṭuṭah, IV, 788.

78. Fryer, I, 145–46 and 147.

79. Ritvo 1987, 28.

80. Bird-David 1990, 189–91 and 194–95.

81. al-Manṣūr, 72–73.

82. Herodotus, I.36–43.

83. Mencius, 2.12.

84. *LS*, ch. 32, 374–75.

85. Jahāngīr, I, 136, 166, 185–87, 255, 264, 276, 286, 350–51, 362, 371, and 374, and II, 104–5 and 269.

86. Orwell 1956, 3–9.

87. 87. Xenophon, *Cyn.*, V.34.

88. *HS*, ch. 65, 2847; Wittfogel and Feng 1949, 130, 135, 139, and 386; and *YS*, ch. 3, 51.

89. Wittfogel and Feng 1949, 374, 421, and 501, and *GD*, 79 and 106.

90. Bernier, 145.

91. Goody 1993, 423.

92. Redfield 1956, 40–59.

93. Andrews, I, XXXVI.

94. Scott 1976, 157–92.

95. Macartney, 161.

96. Aristotle, *HA*, VI.31, VIII.28, and IX.44; Strabo, XV.i.19 and XVI.iv.20; Pliny, VIII.47; Herodotus, XII.125–26; and Dio Chrysostom, 21.1.

97. *ARE*, II, 346–47, and el-Habashi 1992, 55–56.

98. S. Kramer 1981, 127; *ANE*, I, 48 and 166, para. 266, and II, 36; Barnett 1976, 13; and Parrot 1961, 156 and 158, fig. 192.

99. Quintus Curtius, XIII.i.15; Strabo, XVI.i.1; and Ammianus, XVIII.7.4–5 and XXIII.5.8.

100. *HHS*, ch. 88, 1920.

101. *SGZ*, ch. 30, 861.

102. *ANE*, II, 162, and Xenophon, *Cyn.*, XI.2.

103. Welles, Fink and Gilliam 1959, 41 and 320, no. 100xx, and Rostovtzeff 1952, 47–49.

104. Usāmah, 113–14, 116–17, and 135–39.

105. al-Balādhurī, I, 280, and al-Ṭabarī, XVIII, 112–13.

106. Teixeira, 42; Layard, 566–67; and Grant 1937, 15.

107. Mas'ūdī, VI, 432–33. See also Dozy 1991, II, 519, under "*labādīd.*"

108. al-Balādhurī, I, 259, and II, 109, and Ahsan 1979, 81, n. 35. See Zeuner 1963, 245–51, and Postgate 1992, 164–65, on the first, Akkadian, introduction of water buffalo.

109. Linschoten, I, 305.

110. G. Mundy, 158–59 and 275–76.

111. Saberwal, et al., 1994, 501–7.

112. Roe, II, 392 and 402.

113. Pelsaert, 52, and Bernier, 182.

114. Cf. Koch 1998, 15.

115. *PSRL*, I, 224; *PVL*, 94, Old Russian text, and 232, modern Russian translation; and *RPC*, 178.

116. Hrushevsky 1941, 151.

117. For other examples in antiquity, see *ANE*, II, 222, and Ezekiel 14.15–19.

118. Joshua, 102–3 and 110. For the use of a spiritual defense against animal infestations, see Trombley 1994, II, 189–90.

119. Drasxanakertc'i/D, 186, and Drasxanakertc'i/M, 189.

120. Dionysius, 81.

121. al-Ṭabarī, IV, 45–46, and Don Juan, 50.

122. Bagrationi, 139–40. Cf. The translation of Allen 1971, 150.

123. Yang Xuanzhi, 6, and Jenner 1981, 99–102.

124. Gernet 1995, 118.

125. Forbes, III, 60–61 and 162, and IV, 81–82.

126. Bernier 175, 227, 233, 442–43, and 444.

127. Guerreiro, 196.

128. Eberhard 1968, 80–82.

129. Hughes 1989, 16–17.

130. Mencius, 3.3; Han Feizi, 96; *SJ*, ch. 5, 173; and *SJH*, II, 122.

131. Machinist 1992, 1116–18; Speiser 1964, 64 and 67–68; and Bar Hebraeus, 8.

132. *ANE*, I, 53–56.

133. *ZA*, pt. II, *Yasht*, XIX.30–38; Yarshater 1983, 422–26; and Stricker 1963–64, 310–17.

134. al-Ṭabarī, II, 26 and 49–50, and Mas'ūdī, II, 96.

135. Niẓām al-Mulk, 179.

136. al-Ṭabarī, I, 341, and II, 108–09.

137. Ipsiroglu 1967, 53 and 99.

138. Jahāngīr, I, 240.

139. Tanabe 1983, 103–16.

140. al-Ṭabarī, V, 100–102, and Ibn Isfandiyār, 30–32.

141. Ibn Baṭṭuṭah, II, 928.

142. In the Persian Alexander romance, the hero confronts bees "the size of dogs." See *Isk.*, 32–34.

143. P. Shepard 1996, 177–78.

144. Khazanov 1975, 30ff.; Lavin 1963, 197ff.; Root 1979, 303–8; Boyce 1982, II, 105; Haussig 1992, 20–21, illus. 9; Klochkov 1996, 38–43; and Schmidt 1957, 8, 12–13, and 20–22.

145. *ON*, 24–27 (3.4–6.3).

146. J. Wilson 1948, 78–80, and Zimansky 1985, 51–52.

147. *ARI*, I, 80, 83, 92, 102, 104, 106, 108, 113, 114, 118, and 119, and II, 5, 85, 121–22, 148, 159, and 191; *ANE*, II, 99, 132, and 201; and Oded 1992, 113–16, 149–51, and 167.

148. Falk 1973, 1–15.

149. Shulman 1985, 24–27, 294–95, and 365. Cf. Brancaccio 1999, 105–18, esp. 17, and Lombard 1974, 474–85.

150. Helms 1993, 160–63.

151. Pliny, VIII.104; Aelian, XVIII.40–41; Diodorus, I.33.4, II.40.6 and 50.2, and III.30.4 and 50.3; Dio Chrysostom, 38.17; and Ammianus, XXII.5.4.

152. Justin, XV.2.

153. al-Ṭabarī, V, 264–65.

154. Sage 1992, 138–39.

155. Macartney, 112–13.

156. Artsruni, 186 and 260.

157. Xuanzang, II, 255.

158. Rudra Deva, 79 (para. 5). Cf. the recommendations of Yusūf, 221 to his Qarakhanid sovereign.

159. Gommans 1998, 21–22.

160. G. Mundy, 87.

161. Ehrenreich 1997, 39–45.

162. Ovington, 80.

163. Hammond 1991, 87–100; Schafer 1991, 4–6; and Han Feizi, 18 and 39–40. On music as a means of controlling wild beasts, see Sterckx 2000, 3–8, and Lawergren 2003, 105–7.

164. Pliny, XI.105–6.

165. Sittert 1998, 333–56.

166. Xenophon, *Oec.* V.5–7. See also Xenophon, *Cyn.*, XIII.11–12.

167. Knight 2000a, 1–35, is the best discussion of these issues.

168. Strabo, II.v.26.

169. Pliny, VI.53, and Strabo, XVII.iii.15.

170. Diodorus, I.8.1–4, 15.5, and 24.5–8.

171. Ingold 1994, 1–19.

172. For a survey and evaluation, see Haas 1982, 34–85.

173. Fiskesjö 2001, 92–96, 98–99, and 146–66. On the wildlife of North China in this period, see Keightley 2000, 107–9; Lefeuvre 1990–91, 131–57; and J. Hsu 1996, 69–87. For comment on the early Indian state and its engagement with nature, see Gadgil and Thapar 1990, 214–16.

Chapter 10. Circulation

1. See Melville 1990, 55–70. His study sets Mongolian practice in a broad comparative framework.
2. Elias 1994, 301.
3. On movement for ritual purposes, see Wechsler 1985, 161–69.
4. Ratchnevsky 1970, 426 and 428, and Marco Polo, 229–30, 233, and 234–35.
5. al-ʿUmarī/L, 100, Arabic text, and 158, German translation.
6. Peng and Xu, 473. The phrase "so-called" is used to show the author's contempt for this non-Chinese regime.
7. Jāḥiẓ, *LC*, 100–101.
8. Manucci, II, 61–68 and 100.
9. Munshī, II, 1092.
10. Nakhchivānī, 62–63.
11. See, for example, *TTP*, 133.
12. Abū'l Faẓl, *AA*, I, 47–49 and 231.
13. Bernier, 218 and 359.
14. Porphyrogenitus, *TT*, 105.
15. Dio Chrysostom, 6.1.
16. Diodorus, XIX, 21.3.
17. For food supplies, see *PFT*, 15 and 113–16.
18. Buzand, 141 and 142.
19. Ibn Isfandiyār, 115, and Nīshāpūrī, 100.
20. Herbert, 141–52, esp. 142, 148, and 151. Cf. the data in Munshī, II, 1057.
21. Munshī, I, 537, and II, 1054–61, 1211–12, and 1237.
22. *NITP*, 165.
23. Jahāngīr, I, 90, 202, 248, and 252.
24. G. Mundy, 209, and Yule and Burnell 1903, 774.
25. For examples, see *ASB*, 127, 140, 152, 175, and 185, and *CC*, 125.
26. This characterization is based on my reading of Hennebicque 1980, 35–57, and Ewig 1963, 25–72, esp. 29, 60, 63, and 70–71.
27. Cf. the comments of Koch 1998, 29.
28. *FCH*, 1, and Jordanes, XXIV. 123–25.
29. *ON*, 59–61; Ḥāfiẓ-i Tanīsh, I, 18b, Persian text, and 63, Russian translation. On the symbolism of the Golden Bow, see Harmatta 1951, 107–49.
30. Avery 1991, 10.
31. Rashīd/K, I, 387.
32. *PSRL*, II, 842; *Hyp.*, 75; and Forbes, III, 117.
33. al-Ṭabarī, V, 41, and *ON*, 8.7–10.4.
34. Ye Longli, ch. 8, 76, and *JS*, ch. 6, 147.
35. *HI*, II, 184, III, 317, and IV, 224 and 225.
36. Niẓāmī, 41.13–84; al-Ṭabarī, XXX, 324–25; and Masʿūdī, VI, 227–28.
37. d'Orléans, 49.
38. Jāḥiẓ, *LC*, 125–26.
39. Abū'l Fidā, *M*, 77; *HI*, V, 372; and Ḥāfīẓ-i Tanīsh, II, 194a, 228a, 233a, and 237a, Persian text and 163, 225, 234, and 241, Russian translation.

40. *LS*, ch. 32, 373–75; Wittfogel and Feng 1949, 131–34; Taskin 1973, 101–15; and Haenisch 1935, 64–66.

41. *LS*, ch. 58, 1037–75, and Stein 1940, 81–93.

42. *YS*, ch. 3, p. 47, and Ḥāfīẓ-i Abrū/B, 118.

43. Qāshānī, 31.

44. *PSRL*, I, 247; *PVL*, 102, Old Russian text, and 240, modern Russian translation; and *RPC*, 211.

45. Keightley 1978, 181; Shaughnessy 1989, ii; Fiskesjö 2001, 104–9; and Wittfogel 1940, 126–28.

46. See He 2003, 472–77, for a summary of his extensive study of the subject.

47. *Vis.*, 191 and 226.

48. Dasxuranc'i, 65, and *GC*, 27 and 101.

49. Ibn Isfandiyār, 101, and *CC*, 170.

50. Juvaynī/Q, I, 174; Juvaynī/B, I, 218; and *MKK*, 258–59.

51. For additional examples, see Munshī, II, 607, 633, 668, 765, 854, 987, and 1139, and Ḥasan-i Fasā'ī, 150 and 167.

52. Muraviev, 60, 63, 127, 141, and 150.

53. Blake 1979, 91–92, and Blake 1983, 22–24.

54. Broecke, 47.

55. See the comments of Guerreiro, 46, and Bernier, 215.

56. Roe, II, 339ff., and 'Ināyat Khān, 159, 298–99, 322, 396, 412, and 504.

57. Abū'l Faẓl, *AA*, I, 292–93.

58. Abū'l Faẓl, *AN*, II, 172 and 226.

59. Rudra Deva, 83 (para. 22–23), and Forbes, IV, 194.

60. See, for example, Poole 1958, 616–21.

61. Ye Longli, ch. 3, 39; Waley 1957, 581–82; Abū'l Faẓl, *AN*, II, 516; *HI*, V, 277; Rudra Deva, 85 (para. 33–35); and Lang 1957, 54.

62. *JTS*, ch. 64, 2420.

63. Anson 1970, 594–607. In some Indo-European languages the words for "hunt" and those for "desire" and "love" are closely related. See Bailey 1985, 99.

64. Plutarch, *Mor.*, 319 and 321. For examples, see al-Ṭabarī, XXXVIII, 156; Nīshāpūrī, 105; du Jarric, 57; and Bernier, 218.

65. Niẓām al-Mulk, 251.

66. Frederick II, 4.

67. Rust'haveli, 49.

68. Forbes, II, 27, and Ḥasan-i Fasā'ī, 155 and 419.

69. 'Ināyat Khān, 305 and 306, and Roe, I, 138, and II, 437–38.

70. Munshī, II, 667, 957, 1057, and 1059.

71. Rust'haveli, 112.

72. *SOS*, 65, 74, 77, 78–79, and 84.

73. Marco Polo, 231–33.

74. al-'Umarī/S, 19, Arabic text, and 44–45, German translation.

75. Andrews 1999, II, 1250 and illus. 255.

76. Forbes, II, 488–89.

77. Abū'l Faẓl, *AA*, I, 47–49, and Andrews 1999, II, "Plan of the Ordu," following 884 and 1277–80.

78. Broecke, 154, and Yule and Burnell 1903, 154, 500–501, and 821.

79. Artsruni, 316.
80. *YS*, ch. 2, 35, 36, and 37; ch. 3, 46; and ch. 58, 1382–83.
81. Juvaynī/Q, I, 193; Juvaynī/B, I, 237; Rashīd/A, II/1, 144; and Rashīd/B, 63. For an Il-qan hunting villa with water feature, see Naumann and Naumann 1976, 34–43.
82. Jourdain, 169, and Roe, I, 159, 240, and 250.
83. Weidner-Weiden 1997, 246–77.
84. Munshī, II, 724, 732, and 1179.
85. *CATCL*, 422; Niẓāmī, II, 16.9–10 and 18; and Kashgharī, I, 226.
86. D. Shepard 1979, 79–92.
87. Henning 1939–42, 951; *TS*, 278; Rashīd/K, II, 736; Rudra Deva, 132–33 (para. 5–10); Hedin 1933, 168–73; and Melnikova 2002, 65.
88. Niẓām al-Mulk, 27 and 96.
89. *HI*, II, 76–77, and III, 317.
90. For further examples, see al-Ṭabarī, XXVI, 126–27, and Nīshāpūrī, 121.
91. Mencius, 5.7.
92. *CRP*, 47–48; Mei Chang, 68–71; *WX*, I, 139, 141, and 143, and II, 105–13.
93. *Vis.*, 57, 68, 105, and 129. Cf. the comments of Khorenatsʿi, 204, and Bagrationi, 90 and 129.
94. Masʿūdī, VIII, 16–17, and Jameson 1962, 6.
95. Qāshānī, 53, 142, and 151.
96. Usāmah, 222.
97. Mencius, 5.7.
98. *HS*, ch. 87b, 3558.
99. *CRP*, 34.
100. Ripa, 86–89, and Jahāngīr, II, 4–5 and 115.
101. Lacroix 1963, 190; Sälzle 1997, 132–43; Cummins 1988, 45–46, 58, and 66; and Almond 2003, 143–66.
102. *BDK*, 45 and 148.
103. *SH*, I, 3; *SH/I*, 14–15; Pelliot 1944, 102–13; Eberhard 1948, 220–21; and Mostaert 1949, 470–76.
104. Xenophon, *Cyr.*, I.iv.10–11.
105. al-Maqrīzi, 76.
106. Munshī, II, 765, and Bernier, 377.
107. Ripa, 67.
108. Abū'l Fidā, 78, and Hakluyt, *V*, II, 120.
109. Roe, I, 105, 110, 126, 156, and 250, and II, 366 and 390; Guerreiro, 46–47; Hamilton, I, 214; and Alexander 1989, 233.
110. Usāmah, 223; Theophylact, IV.7.2; and d'Orléans, 87, 116 and 141.
111. Nīshāpūrī, 60–61.
112. Abū'l Ghāzī, 65.
113. Pʿarpecʿi, 44, and Purchas, IV, 47.
114. Jahāngīr, I, 189–90 and 255.
115. ʿInāyat Khān, 304.
116. Ḥusām al-Dawlah, 25–26 and 49.
117. *BDK*, 135ff.
118. *CATCL*, 422; *SJ*, ch. 109, 2867; and *SJH*, II, 117.
119. Diodorus, XV.10.3–4.

120. Juvaynī/Q, II, 227, and Juvaynī/B, II, 491.

121. Xenophon, *Cyr.*, III.iii.5; Ibn Shaddād, 238; *GC*, 122; *HI*, III, 78; *NITP*, 164; and Broecke, 39.

122. Cf. P. Wilson 1988, 120–21.

123. See, for example, Forbes, II, 97, and G. Mundy, 10–11, 13, and 21.

124. Abū'l Fidā, *M*, 21. For further examples, see 84 and 88; and Mīrzā Ḥaydar, I, 224 and 325, and Mīrzā Ḥaydar, II, 174 and 244.

125. *HS*, ch. 65, 2855, and ch. 68, 2950, and *HS*/W, 92 and 141–42.

126. Jāḥiẓ, *LC*, 101–2.

127. *GC*, 128.

128. Pʿarpecʿi, 53.

129. *HI*, VI, 551.

130. Munshī, II, 730–31.

131. Nelson 1987, 169–71, and *CC*, 102–3, 108, 111, and 125.

132. Bagrationi, 159, 166, and 172.

133. See Munshī, II, 1059, and Ripa, 100 for examples.

134. Cf. Zorzi 1986, 128ff.

135. See, for example, *CRP*, 31–32.

136. Braudel 1985–86, II, 491.

137. Cummins 1988, 5.

138. Kaempfer, 236ff., esp. 242.

139. R. Anderson 1971, 25.

140. Hui Li, 42.

141. *SOS*, 66.

142. Guerreiro, 15, and G. Mundy, 213.

143. Rust'haveli, 73–74 and 111–12.

144. Sanderson, 38 and 59–60.

145. Kaempfer, 72 and 243–44, and Lacroix 1963, 195 and 202–3.

146. Houlihan 1996, 195–208.

147. Masʿūdī, VIII, 19, and Bar Hebraeus, 147.

148. Lassner 1970, 86 and 89.

149. William of Tyre, II, 320, and Kaempfer, 158.

150. Don Juan, 257.

151. Sanderson, 57, 69, and 76, and P. Mundy, I, 189, for the quote.

152. Strabo, XV.i.69.

153. Ibn al-Azraq, 135–36; Sandersen, 59–60; and Bernier, 364.

154. *KFB*, 255–57, and *KF*, 310–11 and 404.

155. Niẓām al-Mulk, 105.

156. Munshī, II, 793 and 988. See also Mīrzā Ḥaydar, I, 11, and Mīrzā Ḥaydar, II, 9.

157. Juvaynī/Q, I, 20, and Juvaynī/B, I, 28.

158. *CWT*, II, 235–36.

159. Kangxi, 13; Bell, 169–70; Menzies 1994, 59–61; and Hou and Pirazzoli 1979.

160. Abū'l Faẓl, *AN*, I, 439–40 and 442–43, and II, 416–17.

161. Abū'l Faẓl, *AA*, I, 292–93, and Munshī, I, 164.

162. Rudra Deva, 123 (para. 23).

163. Mīrzā Ḥaydar, I, 33–34, and Mīrzā Ḥaydar, II, 30.

164. Rashīd/K, I, 383.

165. *KB*/V, 12 and 16–17.
166. For examples, see Munshī, I, 165 and 174.
167. Thiébaux 1967, 262–63 and 265–74, and Almond 2003, 75–82.
168. Jahāngīr, II, 115.
169. The importance of manners in European court life is brought out by Elias 1994, 50 and 67.
170. See the characterization of royal hunt under the early Romanovs in Paltusova 2002a, 14–15.
171. Ibn Isfandiyār, 23, and *BDK*, 137.
172. al-Ṭabarī, XXVI, 127, and XXX, 51–52; Masʿūdī, VI, 281–82; Psellus, 40; and Abū'l Faẓl, *AN*, II, 52.
173. Broecke, 53–54, and Manucci, II, 182.
174. Catherine, II, 96, 128, 134, 138, and 145.
175. *BDK*, 14. For an historical example, from Ghaznavid times, see *HI*, II, 103.
176. Josephus, I.xxiv.8.
177. Jahāngīr, I, 122.
178. *SJ*, ch. 110, 2888, and *SJH*, II, 134.
179. *HHS*, ch. 88, 2927.
180. Juvaynī/Q, I, 57, and Juvaynī/B, I, 76.
181. Beckwith 1987, 60, and Muraviev, 121.
182. *HI*, III, 172–73 and 205.
183. Ibn Baṭṭuṭah, III, 599.
184. Tacitus, *Ann.*, XI.x; *LK*, 66–67; Lang 1957, 35; Artsruni, 126; and Buzand, 128.
185. Juvaynī/Q, II, 4 and 73; Juvaynī/B, II, 278–79 and 340; and Abū'l Fidā, *M*, 22.
186. Gregory of Tours, 304 and 379.
187. *ASC*, 176.
188. Kinnamos, 27, 100, 101–2, and Browning 1961, 229–35.

Chapter 11. Intimidation

1. Henning 1939–42, 951.
2. Strabo, VII.209.
3. Keeley 1996, 161.
4. Manuel II, 112, and Bailey 1985, 99.
5. *KB*/V, 16.
6. Jordanes, VII.51–52, VIII.56, and XX.107; *GOT*, 293; *PDPMK*, 27–28; Jūzjānī/L, 258; Jūzjānī/R, I, 118, and II, 756; Niẓāmī, 28.41–58; and *Vis.*, 296.
7. Rashīd/K, I, 436 and 437.
8. Mencius, 3.18 and 3.38; Dasxuranc'i, 167; and Golden 1980, 154–55.
9. Comnena, 238; Ibn Shaddād, 176; and Munshī, II, 757.
10. Orbelian, 260 and 261, and Jahāngīr, II, 17 and 40.
11. *XTS*, ch. 50, 1330–31, and Brunnert and Hagelstrom 1912, 327 and 331.
12. *YS*, ch. 5, 83 and 90, ch. 99, 2509; Hsiao 1978, 74; and al-ʿUmarī/L, 29, Arabic text, and 111, German translation.
13. Xenophon, *Cyn.*, XII.5–6 and XIII.11, and Dio Chrysostom, 3.135–36.

14. See Suetonius, *Caligula*, V, for example.
15. Kautilya, 360, and Kalidasa, 19–20.
16. *HI*, I, 230, and Rudra Deva, 82 (para. 19–21).
17. Einhard, 50; *ASB*, 46 and 47; and Frederick II, 5.
18. *BDK*, 19, and ʿInāyat Khān, 548.
19. Mei Chang, 61–71 and 94–99, and *CATCL*, 421.
20. Sima Guang/C, II, 412. Cf. *CATCL*, 421.
21. *Vis.*, 119. Cf. also 218 and 295.
22. *BDK*, 24 and *TLC*, 165.
23. Rudra Deva, 128–29 (para. 53–56); Koch 1998, 27–28; Thiébaux 1967, 260–61; and *KB*/V, 9 and 12.
24. Plutarch, *Mor.*, 359, 361, and 505.
25. Xenophon, *Lac.*, IV.7, and *Cyn.*, I.17–18 and XII.1–2, 6.8; Dio Chrysostom, 13.24, 29.10, and 15; and Diodorus, I.53.
26. Xenophon, *Lac.*, IV.7, *Eq.*, VIII.10, and Strabo, XI.1.
27. Latham 1970, 97, and Mīrzā Ḥaydar, I, 95, and Mīrzā Ḥaydar II, 77.
28. Harper 1978, 25–26, 33–35 and pl. 3, 38–41; pl. 6 and 7, 48–50; pl. 12 and 58–59, pl. 17 and 17b; Voshchinina 1953, 188–93; and Bivar, 282.
29. Bābur, 325.
30. *SJ*, ch. 110, 2879, and *SJH*, II, 129.
31. *SMCAC*, 337.
32. Zhao Hong, 445; *MM*, 18; and Marco Polo, 169 and 281.
33. Peng and Xu, 498.
34. See, for example, Strabo, XV.iii.18; and Justin, XXIII.
35. *BDK*, 72, and Wittfogel and Feng 1949, 565 and 568.
36. *YS*, ch. 5, 91, and Ratchnevsky 1937–85, I, 266, and IV, 328–33.
37. *YS*, ch. 59, 1440; *SCBM*, 141; and *JS*, ch. 6, 141–42, and ch. 8, 194.
38. Tacitus, *Ger.*, 6–7, 13, 15, 22, and 24.
39. Andreski 1971, 33–36 and 232.
40. Tacitus, *Ger.*, ch. 15; Einhard, 47; and Machiavelli, *Prince*, ch. XIV, and *Discourses*, ch. XXXIX.
41. Ritvo 1987, 271.
42. Cf. the discussions of Cummins 1988, 4 and 101–2, and Anderson 1985, 17–30.
43. Niẓāmī, 25.4–5; Rustʾhaveli, 13, 33–34, 44, and 153–54; Masʿūdī, VI, 227; Quan Heng, 38; and Rudra Deva, 122 (para. 11–14 and 16–18).
44. Suetonius, *Tiberius*, XIX.
45. *CRP*, 33 and 35; *WX*, I, 135, 137, and 139; and *SMCAC*, 126 and 330–31.
46. Graff 2002, 62–64.
47. Franke 1987, 45 and 84.
48. Liu 1985, 203–24.
49. Farmer 1995, 144.
50. Herbert, 242–43, and Bagrationi, 93.
51. du Jarric, 10, and Bernier, 374–75.
52. *ARE*, II, 346.
53. Levanoni 1995, 59. Cf. also al-Maqrīzī, 74.
54. *BDK*, 24.
55. *IB*, 27.

56. Hui Li, 42.

57. Juvaynī/Q, I, 19 and 21; Juvaynī/B, I, 27–28 and 29; and Bar Hebraeus, 354.

58. Bābur, 155–56.

59. Kangxi, 11–13.

60. d'Orléans, 80–81 and 121–22.

61. Haenisch 1935, 75–78, entries no. 18, 22, 32, 34–38, 43–48, and 53. Cf. Riasanovsky 1965b, 95, on the discipline demanded in Oyirad, western Mongolian, hunts.

62. Haenisch 1935, 73.

63. Herodotus, 6.31.

64. Meuli 1954, 63–86, esp. 73.

65. *MM*, 37.

66. Rashīd/A, II/1, 59, 62, 130, and 135, and Rashīd/B, II, 553–54, 583, 585, 613–14, and 621.

67. Juvaynī/Q, III, 10, 51, 53–54, 100, and 111–12, and Juvaynī/B, II, 553–54, 583, 585, 613–14, and 621.

68. Bābur, 140, 473, and 568.

69. Kadyrbaev 1998, 88, and Nadeliaev et al. 1969, 573.

70. Kadyrbaev 1998, 56–58.

71. Elliot 2001, 57–58 and 103.

72. Dozy 1991, I, 317.

73. *Slovar* 1975–, XII, 62; Fasmer 1971, III, 102; and Nadeliaev et al. 1969, 3.

74. *Vis.*, 362–64.

75. Rust'haveli, 50.

76. Jahāngīr, I, 27–28.

77. Xenophon, *Cyr.*, I.ii.9–11 and VIII.i.38, and Quintus Curtius, V.i.42 and VIII.vi.2–6.

78. Niẓām al-Mulk, 108.

79. *Vis.*, 105 and 130.

80. *SH*, I, 49 and 89; *SH/I*, 51 and 77; and Rashīd/K, I, 436 and 440.

81. Wittfogel and Feng 1949, 569; *ZGC*, 229; and *CATCL*, 421.

82. Rashīd/A, II/1, 149, and Rashīd/B, 65.

83. W. McNeill 1995, 1–11.

84. Hanna 1977a, 115–24.

85. Collins 1992, 42.

86. Sage 1992, 76–78.

87. Foote and Wilson 1979, 284–85.

88. Hellie 1977, 165–66.

89. Bābur, 108, 138, 145, 316, 409, and 639–40.

90. Pelsaert, 6.

91. *WX*, I, 135, 137, and 139; *HS*, ch. 94b, 3831; Sima Guang/C, I, 43; and *XTS*, ch. 50, 1332.

92. Rashīd/A, I/1, 100.

93. al-Ṭabarī, XXV, 1132.

94. *MKK*, 233, 34.

95. *YS*, ch. 14, 298.

96. Quan Heng, 77, 79, 87, and 110, and *MS*, ch. 327, 8463, and 8469, and ch. 328, 8498,

97. Diodorus, XVI.41.5. For remarks on this paradise and its Persian artifacts, see Clermont-Ganneau 1921, 106-9.

98. Ammianus, XXIV.1.5; Zosimus, III.4; *PSRL*, II, 830; and *Hyp.*, 69.
99. Xenophon, *ANA.*, I.iv.2–3, and Menander, 167.
100. Juvaynī/Q, II, 149, and Juvaynī/B, II, 417.
101. *PSRL*, I, 64; *PVL*, 31, Old Russian text, and 167–68, modern Russian translation; and *RPC*, 84.
102. *AK*, 36, and Wittfogel and Feng 1949, 128 and 129.
103. Ammianus, XXXI.2.1, and Shakanova 1989, 112–13.
104. *SH*, I, 95 and 127, and *SH/I*, 86 and 110.
105. Zhao Hong, 447.
106. Het῾um, 217.
107. Cf. The comments of J. M. Smith 1984, 223–28, esp. 226–27.
108. Mīrzā Ḥaydar, I, 48–49, and Mīrzā Ḥaydar, II, 41–42.
109. Kangxi, 13 and 16.
110. Tacitus, *Ann.*, II.lxviii; *ASB*, 120; Nīshāpūrī, 94–95; Barthold 1968, 329–30; Held 1985, 156; and Munshī, II, 1095.
111. Theophylact, II.16.1–3 and VI.1.2–6.
112. Herodotus, I.123; al–Ṭabarī, XXIV, 55–56; and Qāshānī, 77.
113. Beckwith 1987, 46; Theophylact, VIII.14.5; Theophanes, 83; Juvaynī/Q, I, 135; and Juvaynī/B, I, 171–72.
114. al-Ansarī, 98. For further examples of problems arising from hunting on campaign, see Schreiber 1949–55, 469, and Ibn Shaddād, 107.
115. *GC*, 116, and *SOS*, 60.
116. Suetonius, *Caligula*, V.
117. Pan 1997, 104. For another example, see Boodberg 1979, 52.
118. Macartney, 85.
119. Buzand, 96.
120. Khorenats῾i, 324. Cf. also Artsruni, 136.
121. For examples from Inner, South, and Southeast Asia, see *AR*, 73; Zhao Hong, 456; Bigam, 69, Persian text, and 169, English translation; and Tavernier, II, 250.
122. *WX*, II, 69. Cf. *CRP*, 30, 31, and 36.
123. *WX*, II, 119–29 and 137–51.
124. *TLC*, 144–45.
125. Niẓām al-Mulk, 99.
126. Tulishen, 13–16, 81–82, 95–97, and 150–51.
127. *SMCAC*, 331.
128. *HI*, III, 103.
129. Joshua, 110.
130. Procopius, *HW*, II.xxi.1–2.
131. Held 1985, 106.
132. al-Ansarī, 62–64.
133. *TLC*, 147–48.
134. See the comments of Luo Guanzhong in his novel, *Romance of the Three Kingdoms*, I, 209.
135. Morganthau 1950, 54–55.
136. Andrews 1999, I, 903.
137. Henthorn 1971, 44 and 73, and *KM*, 257 and 260.
138. Sage 1992, 108–9.

139. Munshī, II, 1193–95, and *CDIPR*, 205 and 209.
140. Jahāngīr, II, 241–43.
141. Jahāngīr, I, 90.
142. Manucci, IV, 241, and G. Mundy, 195.
143. Munshū, I, 52–53.
144. *SMCAC*, 128.
145. Ḥāfīẓ-i Tanīsh, I, 15a, Persian text, and 57, Russian translation.
146. *SS*, ch. 485, 13993.
147. *SWQZL*, 135–36. See also *YS*, ch. 1, 12.
148. *YS*, ch. 2, 30, and ch. 3, 51.
149. al-Salmānī, 109r, Persian text, and 81–82, German translation; Mīrzā Ḥaydar, I, 289, and Mīrzā Ḥaydar, II, 217–18.
150. Abū'l Faẓl, *AN*, I, 611.
151. *ZZ*/W, 164.
152. *SJ*, ch. 77, 2377. Cf. the comments of Lewis 1990, 17–18.
153. Theophylact, VII.7.4.
154. *HI*, III, 106 and 242; Broecke, 13; and ʿInāyat Khān, 28 and 282–83.
155. *Vis.*, 107.
156. *HS*, ch. 49, 2285.
157. *HS*, ch. 94a, 3788–89.
158. Ammianus, XXXI.2.21.
159. al-Ṭabarī, V, 95–96.
160. *GC*, 8.
161. *ASB*, 127.
162. Nīshāpūrī, 83, and Barthold 1968, 318–19.
163. Liu Zhen, ch. 1, 3.
164. Geiss 1988, 415–16, 418–19, 432, and 433.
165. d'Orléans, 121 and 123; my italics.
166. Chia 1993, 66–70; Hou and Pirazzoli 1979, 33; and Macartney 125 and 130.
167. al-Ahrī, 150, Persian text, and 52, English translation.
168. Munshī, II, 609, 748, 794, 809, and 919.
169. Abū'l Faẓl, *AN*, II, 138–86, 251–52, 351–58, and 439–92.

Chapter 12. Internationalization

1. Carter 1988, 4–5.
2. *ARI*, I, 83.
3. Dasxuranc'i, 77.
4. *JShu*/M, 35.
5. Sidebotham 1991, 22, and Jāḥiẓ, *KT*, 159.
6. *ANE*, I, 188, and *ARI*, II, 55, 143, and 149.
7. Porada 1969, 154–56, and Tilia 1972, 308 and pl. 152, fig. 98.
8. Barthold 1968, 283–84; *TLC*, 147; and *GC*, 29.
9. *TTP*, 53–55, and Munshī, II, 1059.
10. Linschoten, II, 10. For a discussion of European reactions, see Lach 1970, 123–85.

11. *CRP*, 36–37, and *WX*, II, 115, 207, 209, 211, and 213.
12. Pelliot 1903, 263.
13. Ma Huan, 155 and 178.
14. Macartney, 114.
15. Helms 1988, 163–71.
16. *SOS*, 82.
17. Yang Xuanzhi, 237, and Fryer, II, 323–24.
18. Broder 1998, 95.
19. Hakluyt, *V*, 366.
20. Pulleyblank 1995, 427–28; D. Adams 1999, 660; and Bailey 1982, 35.
21. Haussig 1983, 14, 37, 85, and 226; Rawson 1998, 24–28; and Powers 1991, 271–73.
22. Laufer 1909, 155–56, 203, and 236–45.
23. *HHS*, ch. 88, 2927.
24. Yang Xuanzhi, 152; Schafer 1963, 84–87; and Zhao Rugua, 111.
25. *YS*, ch. 30, 674, 677, and 678.
26. *MS*, ch. 332, 8600–8601.
27. Khiṭā'ī, 36–37.
28. Cf. Dupree 1979, 37–38.
29. If not otherwise stated, this discussion is based on Laufer 1928, 20ff.
30. al-Balādhurī, I, 381, and *AI*, 26, 28, 229 and 236.
31. al-Ṭabarī, XXXVIII, 3, and Masʿūdī, III, 3–4.
32. Pachymérès, I, 238; Albertus Magnus, II, 1449–50; *SMOIZO*, 178 and 192, Arabic text, and 189 and 194, Russian translation; and Ibn ʿArabshāh, 220
33. Zhao Rugua, 128, and Duyvendak 1938, 397, 400, and 406.
34. Grigor of Akancʿ, 311 and 321, and Munshī, II, 827.
35. Ahsan 1979, 205–6.
36. al-Ṭabarī, XXX, 264.
37. *Vis.*, 218, and Barbosa, I, 124.
38. Martines 1979, 238–39. Cf. the comments of Schafer 1959, 306–16, on the falconry of an earlier era.
39. For an overview of their diffusion, see Epstein 1971, 58–71 and 147–71.
40. Albertus Magnus, I, 578–79.
41. Jahāngīr, II, 200.
42. *Slovar* 1975–, I, 292, and Fasmer 1971, I, 194.
43. Clausen 1968, 16–17, and Okladnikov 1981, 76 and pl. 92, no. 7. On the ferocity of Mongolian dogs, see Gilmore, 3–5 and 262–63, and Haslund, 191 and 309–10.
44. Lattimore, 105–6.
45. Schwarz 2001, 2; Nadeliaev 1969, 528; Lessing 1973, 768; Tsintsius 1975–77, I, 152; Norman 1978, 269; Livshitz 1962, 87–88; and Bartol'd 1968, 46.
46. Laufer 1909, 153, 162, 163, 168–69, and 266–77.
47. Vollmer, Keall, and Nagai-Berthrong 1983, 210.
48. *ANE*, II, 206.
49. Herodotus, I.192; Xenophon, *Cyn.*, IX.1 and X.1; Diodorus XVII.92.1–3; Strabo, XV.i.31; and Dio Chrysostom, 3.130.
50. Laufer 1909, 248–67.
51. Marco Polo, 272.
52. Khiṭā'ī, 80.

53. Fryer, II, 305–6.
54. *TLC*, 147–48.
55. Viré 1973, 236–40.
56. Marco Polo, 228. See also Albertus Magnus, I, 716, and II, 1460, who speaks of dogs trained to flush birds by scent.
57. Sanderson, 227, and Kaempfer, 158.
58. Jahāngīr, I, 283.
59. Roe, I, 182, and II, 288, 385, 388, and 424.
60. Ovington, 160–61.
61. Parks, I, 229, and G. Mundy, 6.
62. Rogozhin 1994, 96.
63. Bernier, 262.
64. *RIO*, 190.
65. *RKO*, 231, and Bell, 129, 137, and 141.
66. *DTO*, "Supplement," 45, 46, and 84.
67. *XTS*, ch. 221a, 6220; *DTO*, 103; and Schafer 1963, 76–78.
68. Pliny, VIII.149–50; Mandeville, 111; and Jūzjānī/L, 47, and Jūzjānī/R, I, 336–37.
69. On the diffusion of the ferret by human agency, see Lever 1985, 59–62.
70. Kaempfer, 128.
71. Bābur, 276; Abū'l Fazl, *AA*, II, 183; Jahāngīr, I, 218, and II, 61 and 107; ʿInāyat Khān, 511 and 531; Manucci, II, 415–16; Layard, 270; Cummins 1988, 196–97; and *NC*, V, 171 and 172.
72. Ibn Khaldūn, I, 364.
73. Henthorn 1971, 65 and 123, and Jameson 1962, 1–8.
74. *ʿA-D*, 500, Persian text, and 195, Russian translation; Rubruck, 111; *MM*, 115–16; and Abu'l Ghāzī, 77–78.
75. *SOS*, 189.
76. Marco Polo, 98, 119, 138, and 392.
77. Frederick II, 58, 59, 227, 243–44, and 321–22.
78. Usāmah, 228.
79. Boccaccio, II.9.
80. Ḥusām al-Dawlah, 1–3, and *BDK*, 156.
81. *TS*, 169; Baihaqī, 495; Abū'l Fidā, 89; and Abū'l Fazl, *AN*, I, 427.
82. *KB/V*, 65; Ibn Shaddād, 215; Bar Hebraeus, 334–35; and Ibn al Furāt, I, 83 and 164, Arabic text, and II, 68 and 129, English translation.
83. Porphyrogenitus, *AI*, 155, and Ye Longli, 204.
84. al-Muqaddasī, 325; Barthold 1968, 235; and Thaʿālibī, 142.
85. Frederick II, 112.
86. Fryer, II, 304. Cf. Herbert, 243.
87. Glasier 1998, 21–23.
88. Barthold 1968, 284.
89. *YS*, ch. 2, 40.
90. Rashīd/K, I, 441.
91. See, for instance, *CWT*, II, 228–29.
92. Frederick II, 111, and Ḥusām al-Dawlah, 36–42.
93. Tulishen, 96–98.
94. Nadeliaev 1969, 508; Doerfer 1963–75, I, 360–62; *SJV*, 227, no. 459; Ramstedt 1949, 242; *Hex.*, 226 (200A19); and Dozy 1991, I, 694.

95. al-Ṭabarī, V, 389; *XTS*, ch. 219, 6178; Schafer 1959, 311; and Hamilton 1955, 76 and 93.

96. Masʿūdī, II, 27–38.

97. *SH*, I, 14 and 164; *SH/I*, 25 and 37; Uray-Köhalmi 1987, 151–52; and Allsen 1997, 58–60.

98. Frederick II, 121.

99. Hakluyt, *V*, 394.

100. Wittfogel and Feng 1949, 89, 92, 348, 352, 353, 360, and 422.

101. Ye Longli, ch. 22, 213.

102. *SS*, ch. 5, 90.

103. Ye Longli, ch. 10, 102, and Stein 1940, 97–98.

104. *SCBM*, 127 and 152–53.

105. Marco Polo, 177–78.

106. *YS*, ch. 18, 394, and ch. 22, 494, and Olbricht 1954, 53.

107. Located approximately at latitude 54 degrees and longitude 140 degrees. See Tan Qixiang 1982, VII, maps 13 and 83.

108. *YS*, ch. 59, 1400, and ch. 103, 2634, and Cleaves 1957, 474–75 and note 168.

109. *YS*, ch. 41, 874.

110. Melikhov 1970, 267–73, and Serruys 1955, 32–33.

111. Bell, 169.

112. *SH*, I, 173; *SH/I*, 136; Rashīd/A, I/1, 348; Rashīd/K, I, 308; and *YS*, ch. 1, 14.

113. Rashīd/K, I, 672, and Rashīd/B, 322. The Persian text reads *shināʿūchī*, clearly a mistake for *shibāʿūchī*, Mongolian *shibaʾūchi*, "falconers."

114. *YS*, ch. 10, 217, and ch. 22, 485; Rashīd/K, I, 654; and Rashīd/B, 293.

115. *HYYY*, I, 9 and 25, and Serruys 1967, 200–203. According to regulations, in 1411 the Ming court returned ten pieces of colored satin with lining for each tribute horse and four pieces for each gyrfalcon; by 1426, the payments for horses and gyrfalcons were about the same. See Farquhar 1957, 62–63.

116. Marco Polo, 470–73.

117. *YCS*, 81 and 228, and Ziiaev 1983, 22.

118. For a survey based on pictorial and literary evidence, see Rolle 1988, 513–18 and 527–29, and Hoffman 1957–58, 139–49.

119. Cummins 1988, 197–99, and Lacroix 1963, 197, and 201–2.

120. Frederick II, 111.

121. Abū'l Fidā, *G*, 266–67. *Sanāqir* is the Arabic plural of *sunqur*.

122. Llull, 893.

123. Qāshānī, 53, and Clavijo, 169–70.

124. *MRL*, 50.

125. Marco Polo, 474.

126. *SMOIZO*, 255, 318, 425, 427, and 445, Arabic text, and 264, 318, 325, 441, and 438, Russian translation.

127. Martin 1986, 90–91.

128. *GVNP*, 26, and *Slovar* 1975-, VIII, 52.

129. *GVNP*, 142, and Sreznevskii 1989, 459.

130. From the Old Russian *pom'chishche*, "hunting grounds." See Fasmer 1971, III, 324, and *Slovar* 1975–, XVII, 38 and 41.

131. On this term, Turkic in origin, see Golden 1998–99, 80–81, and Fasmer 1971, I, 278.

132. Dementieff 1945, 14ff.

133. Herberstein, 96 and 149; Fletcher, 11r; and Purchas, XIII, 253.

134. Dementieff 1945, 27–29 and 34–35.

135. Kliuchevskii 1959, 192–93, and *Slovar* 1975–, XXI, 66–67.

136. Fekhner 1956, 62–63, and *Slovar* 1975–, VIII, 51.

137. Allen 1961, 104–10, for examples.

138. Chenciner and Magomedkhanov 1992, 124.

139. Rogozhin 1994, 96, and Dementieff 1945, 29–32.

140. Olearius 326; Kaempfer, 30; Gukovskii 1963, 653; and Hakluyt, V, 365 for quote.

141. Nikitin, 11, 33–34, 53, and 71. The number *devianosto* is written out in the earliest copies of his relation.

142. *SIRIO*, 227–28.

143. Burton 1993, 47–48, 50, 51, 62, 65, 68, and 71; *REGK*, I, 213–14; and Laufer 1916, 353–54.

144. Munshī, II, 1160, and *CDIPR*, I, 190; see also 216.

145. Christian 2000, 7ff.

146. Marco Polo, 178.

147. Qāshānī, 49 and 205.

148. Ḥāfīẓ-i Abrū, 95–99, and *HC*, 167 and 179–80.

149. Samarqandī, 385.

150. *MS*, ch. 329, 8529–30.

151. Ibn Khurdādhbih, 70, Arabic text, and 51, French translation.

152. P. Mundy, III, 337, and Bernier, 194.

153. *CDIPR*, II, 110–11.

154. *ANE*, II, 103, and Sidebotham 1991, 12 and 15.

155. Li Zhizhang, 328; Li Zhizhang/W, 94; Kaempfer, 255; and *SOS*, 82–83.

156. *HS*, ch. 6, 176; *HS*/D, II, 60; Pelliot 1903, 252–53, 255, and 274; and Wolters 1958, 605–6.

157. al-Ṭabarī, XXXV, 27, and *CDIPR*, II, 334.

158. Theophylact, I.3.8–10; Joshua, 17; and *SMOIZO*, 178 and 182, Arabic text, and 189 and 194, Russian translation.

159. Einhard, 42–43, and *CC*, 82 and 92, provide the basic data on this episode. For its reflection in art, see Haussig 1992, 100, illus. 160.

160. Werth 1954, 91–92 and map 9, for their natural and cultural ranges.

161. Baihaqī, 495; *GC*, 115; *TTP*, 53–54; P. Mundy, II, 112; and du Jarric, 115.

162. Mallory and Adams 1997, 415; Gharib 1995, 330; and Clausen 1972, 368.

163. The Georgian form is found in the couplet *Vep hkhi avaza*, literally "leopard leopard." See Rust'haveli, 184.

164. Witzel 1999, 59.

165. This skin was recovered at Pazyryk I in the Altai. See Gryaznov 1969, 158–59 and 108, pl. 63.

166. *SJ*, ch. 117, 3034, and *SJH*, II, 277.

167. W. White 1939, 49–50 and pls. IV, V, VI, XXIV, XXV, XXVI, XXVIII, XXXIX, and LV.

168. Shaanxi Sheng Bowuguan 1974a, pls. 3, 5, and 9, and Shaanxi Sheng Bowuguan 1974b, pls. 17 and 18.

169. Kentucky Horse Park 2000, 161, illus. 150.

170. *XTS*, ch. 221b, 6245, and *DTO*, 138 and 34, 47, 50, and 84 of the "Notes additionalles."

171. Schafer 1963, 87–88. The most recent account of cheetahs in China is Zhang 2001, 177–82.

172. *XTS*, ch. 6, 165, and ch. 48, 1258.

173. *XTS*, ch. 221b, 6248 and 6255, and *DTO*, 146 and 168.

174. Sterndale 1982, 198–200, and Zhang 2001, 184.

175. *AR*, 62.

176. *LS*, ch. 20, 245, and ch. 70, 1164–65.

177. *YS*, ch. 125, 3063.

178. *YS*, ch. 2, 33.

179. Marco Polo, 185 and 227–28.

180. Rubruck, 247, and *MM*, 202.

181. *CWT*, III, 89, and *YS*, ch. 30, 674, 677, and 678.

182. Abū'l Fidā, 81.

183. *YS*, ch. 30, 675.

184. *SMOIZO*, 259, Arabic text, and 268, Russian translation.

185. *YS*, ch. 22, 505, and ch. 23, 511, and Rockhill 1914, 427–28.

186. *YS*, ch. 40, 870, ch. 138, 3328 and 3331, and ch. 139, 3352.

187. Baer 1967, 37, 41, and 42, figs. 8 and 9.

188. Albertus Magnus, II, 1226, 1449, and 1530–31.

189. Frederick II, xlv and 5; *KFB*, 270–71; and *KF*, 52.

190. Lockhart 1968, 27, and Paviot 2000, 515–6.

191. Friedmann 1980, 202–3. On the cheetah in Islamic art, see D. T. Rice 1965, 90–91 and illus. 90, and Viré 1974, 87, for additional examples.

192. Klingender 1971, 414, illus. 246.

193. On cheetah's spots compared to those of the leopard, see Turner 1997, 93.

194. Klingender 1971, 480, illus. 296a and 482.

195. Zorzi 1986, 173.

196. Lacroix 1963, 189 and 193 for illus.

197. Cummins 1988, 31.

198. Ma Huan, 172 and 176.

199. Samarqandī, 384, and *MS*, ch. 332, 8601, 8610, and 8615.

200. Khiṭā'ī, 36–37, 80, and 144–45.

201. See Geiss 1987, 1–38, esp. 8–12 and 20–21, for a detailed discussion of the Quarter.

202. *KB*/P, 49–50; al-Manṣūr, 49; and Mercier 1927, 70–71.

203. Burkert 1992, 9–40.

204. Ḥusām al-Dawlah, 4, 6, 21, 23, 33, and 37.

205. Mahler 1959, 199 and pl. XXIIa, following 204.

206. Han Baoquan 1997, pls. 77–92, esp. 91, for a cheetah and its handler, and Kentucky Horse Park 2000, 161, illus. 150.

207. Yarshater 1983b, pl. 45 following 530.

208. Juvaynī/Q, I, 19 and 70, and Juvaynī/B, I, 13 and 92.

209. *YS*, ch. 5, 90.

210. *YS*, ch. 85, 2141.

211. Ibn 'Arabshāh, 161.

212. Nasāwī, 318–19, and Munshī, II, 741, 749, and 1093.

213. *SMOIZO*, 259, Arabic text, and 268, Russian translation; Lockhart 1968, 28; and Paviot 2000, 315.

214. ʿInāyat Khān, 148, 151, 244, 257, 268, 275, 276, and 536; Islam 1970, 228; and Jahāngīr, II, 107–08.

215. Kaempfer, 276–77.

216. *REGK*, I, 215–15.

217. *REGK*, I, 88 and 144–45, and II, 373 and 391.

218. Ciggaar 1986, 48–53.

219. Munshī, II, 661.

220. Jameson 1962, 2, 4, 6, and 10.

221. al-Manṣūr, 13; my italics. Cf. the comments of Möller 1965, 107–10 and 118–24, on the foreign sources underlying Arabic literature on falconry.

222. Akasoy 2000–2001, 94–97. Cf. Haskins 1921, 348–50.

223. Kantorowicz 1957, 310–311 and 404, and *KFB*, 270–72.

224. Frederick II, 3 and 53, and *KFB*, 269.

225. Frederick II, 205–6; my italics.

226. The best introduction is Dale 2003, 199–202.

227. Pearson 1976, 67–68.

228. Manucci, III, 94 and 220.

229. *SOS*, 70 and 73.

230. *SOS*, 199–200.

Chapter 13. Conclusions

1. Wallas 1923, 3–19.

2. Knauer 2004, 8–10.

3. Allsen 1997, 85–86.

4. Mair 1988, 111–31.

5. Liu 1985, 203–5, and Bower 1991, 23–45.

6. Teggard 1941, 93–127, nicely dissects these debates.

7. See for example, Perry 1968, 406–27.

8. See Dixon 1928, 241–64, and Lowie 1937, 160–69.

9. For a critique of these claims, see Haslip-Viera, Ortiz de Montellano, and Barbour 1997, 419–41, with invited commentary.

10. Sherratt 1995, 1–32.

11. Bradshaw 1988, 632–33.

12. See Renfrew 1986, 1–18, for this and the following discussion. Quotes on p. 1.

13. S. Kramer 1981, 224.

14. Wagoner 1995, 851–80.

15. Duby 1974, 177–78. Cf. Elias 1994, 96.

16. On metallurgy, see Linduff 1998, 637–38.

17. Haussig 1988, 124; Haussig 1992, 98, illus. 157, and 312–13, illus. 536–37; and Hayashi 1975, 126–28.

18. On the elaborate terminology for game animals in Middle English, see Twiti, 37.31–34 and 38.10–35.

19. A convenient discussion can be found in Herskovits 1951, 542–53, 560, and 581–85.

20. Roe, II, 361–62, and Bell 129 and 141.

21. du Jarric, 55 and 57.

22. Haskins 1921, 355.

23. Oppian, I, 369–538.

24. *KB*/P, 47–48. Cf. al-Manṣūr, 23–27

25. Catherine II, 122, 126–27, and 133.

26. Usāmah, 89–90.

27. Jahāngīr, II, 10–11.

28. Ḥusām al-Dawlah, 3–11, 47–48, and 49–55. Cf. Rudra Deva, 103 (nos. 51–54).

29. Abū'l Faẓl, *AN*, I, 496 and note 3, and II, 513.

30. *HI*, V, 336, and Jahāngīr, II, 226.

31. Knauer 2003, 32–39.

32. Marco Polo, 227–28

33. Abū'l Faẓl, *AA*, I, 301–2; du Jarric, 10; Jahāngīr, I, 90–91, and II, 42–43; and Pelsaert, 51–52.

34. Abū'l Faẓl, *AA*, I, 304.

35. Gibb 1970, 88–98, and Beckwith 1987, 89.

36. Schortman and Urban 1992, 235–55.

37. Marco Polo, 169; my italics.

38. Abū'l Faẓl, *AA*, III, 135.

39. *CWT*, II, 228–29.

40. Broecke, 91.

41. Braudel 1958, 725–53, esp. 727–35 and 751–53. Cf. Stoianovich 1994b, 426–28.

42. Christian 1998, XIX.

43. Goudsblom 1992, 1–13.

44. Stoianovich 1994a, 20–24.

45. See the analyses of S. Clark 1985, 182–87.

46. Jones 1988, 121.

47. See Christian 1991, 223–38, esp. 224–25.

48. Cf. the comments of Sherratt 1986, 4–7.

49. Straus 1986, 147–76, and Ermolov 1989, 105–8.

50. Jarman 1972, 132–33.

51. Herodotus, I.35.

52. Bosworth 1973, 51–62, and Latham 1970, 100.

53. Trümpelman 1980–83, 234–38.

54. For discussions of the European colonial version of the royal hunt, see Storey 1991, 135–75, and Ritvo 1987, 254ff.

55. Braudel 1985–86, III, 621 and 622.

56. See also the inventories of Koch 1998, 11–14; Almond 2003, 13–27; and Fiskesjö 2001, 136–46.

57. Cf. the comments of W. McNeill 1995, 38, and Hanna 1977b, 229.

58. Gamble 1993, 5, 6, 7, 83–84, and 85.

59. Polyani 1957, 67ff.

Abbreviations and Primary Sources

Abū'l Faẓl, *AA*	Abū'l Faẓl. *The Aʿīn-i Akbār-ī.* Trans. H. Blochmann. Reprint Delhi: Atlantic Publishers, 1979. 3 vols.
Abū'l Faẓl, *AN*	Abū'l Faẓl. *Akbar Nama.* Trans. Henry Beveridge. Reprint Delhi: Atlantic Publishers, 1989. 3 vols.
Abū'l Fidā, *G*	Aboul Féda. *Géographie d'Aboul Féda.* Trans. M. Reinard. Paris: L'imprimerie nationale, 1848. 2 vols.
Abū'l Fidā, *M*	Abū'l Fidā. *The Memoirs of a Syrian Prince.* Trans. P. M. Holt. Wiesbaden: Franz Steiner, 1983.
Abū'l Ghāzī	Abu-l-Ghazi. *Rodoslovnaia Turkmen.* Trans. A. N. Kononov. Moscow: Izdatel'stvo akademii nauk SSSR, 1958.
ʿA-D	Smirnova, L. P., trans. *ʿAjā'ib al-dunyā.* Moscow: Nauka, 1993.
Aelian	Aelian. *On the Characteristics of Animals.* Trans. A. F. Scholfield. Loeb Classical Library. Cambridge, Mass.: Harvard University Press, 1959.
Agathangelos	Agathangelos. *History of the Armenians.* Trans. Robert W. Thomson. Albany: State University of New York Press, 1976.
al-Ahrī	al-Ahrī, Abū Bakr. *Taʾrīkh-i Shaikh Uwais: An Important Source for the History of Adharbaījan.* Ed. and trans. H. B. Van Loon. 's-Gravenhage: Mouton, 1954.
AI	Kubbel, L. E. and V. V. Matveev, trans. *Arabskie istochniki VII–X vekov po etnografii i istorii narodov Afriki.* Moscow-Leningrad: Izdatel'stvo akademii nauk SSSR, 1960.
AIM	Galstian, A. G., trans. *Armianskie istochniki o mongolakh.* Moscow: Izdatel'stvo vostochnoi literatury, 1962.
AK	Yang, Ho-chin, trans. *The Annals of Kokonor*, Indiana University Publications, Uralic and Altaic Series 106. Bloomington: Indiana University, Research Institute for Inner Asian Studies, 1969.
Albertus Magnus	Albertus Magnus. *On Animals: A Medieval Summa Zoologica.* Trans. Kenneth F. Mitchell, Jr. and Irven Michael Resnick. Baltimore: Johns Hopkins University Press, 1999. 2 vols.
d'Albuquerque	d'Albuquerque, Affonzo. *The Commentaries of the Great Afonso Dalboquerque.* Trans. W. D. Birch. London: Hakluyt Society, 1875. 2 vols.

Ambrose, *H*	Ambrose, St. *Hexameron, Paradise, and Cain and Abel.* Trans. John Savage. New York: Fathers of the Church, 1961.
Ammianus	*Ammianus Marcellinus.* Trans. John C. Rolf. Loeb Classical Library. Cambridge, Mass.: Harvard University Press, 1958.
ANE	Pritchard, James B., ed., *The Ancient Near East: An Anthology of Texts and Pictures.* Princeton, N.J.: Princeton University Press, 1973. 2 vols.
al-Ansarī	al-Ansarī, ʿUmar ibn Ibrahim al-Awsī. *A Muslim Manual of War, being Tafrīj al-kurūb fī tadhbir al-ḥurūb.* Trans. George T. Scanlon. Cairo: American University in Cairo Press, 1961.
AR	Wright, David Curtis, trans. *The Ambassador's Records: Eleventh Century Reports of Sung Embassies to the Liao.* Papers on Inner Asia 29. Bloomington: Indiana University, Research Institute for Inner Asian Studies, 1998.
ARE	Breasted, James Henry, trans. *Ancient Records of Egypt.* Chicago: University of Chicago Press, 1908. 5 vols.
ARI	Grayson, Albert Kirk. *Assyrian Royal Inscriptions.* Wiesbaden: Otto Harrassowitz, 1972–76. 2 vols.
Aristotle, *CWA*	Aristotle. *The Complete Works of Aristotle.* Ed. Jonathan Barnes. Princeton, N.J.: Princeton University Press, 1984. 2 vols.
Aristotle, *HA*	Aristotle. *History of Animals.* In Aristotle, *CWA*, I.
Aristotle, *MTH*	Aristotle. *On Marvelous Things Heard.* In Aristotle, *CWA*, I.
Arrian, *Ana.*	Arrian. *History of Alexander.* In Arrian, *HAI.*
Arrian, *HAI*	Arrian. *The History of Alexander and Indica.* Trans. P. A. Brunt. Loeb Classical Library. Cambridge, Mass.: Harvard University Press, 1989.
Arrian, *Ind.*	Arrian. *Indica*, in Arrian, *HAI.*
Artsruni	Artsruni, Thomas. *History of the House of the Artsrunikʿ.* Trans. Robert W. Thomson. Detroit: Wayne State University Press, 1985.
AS	Luckenbill, Daniel David, trans. *The Annals of Sennacherib.* Oriental Institute Publications 2. Chicago: University of Chicago Press, 1924.
ASB	Martin, Janet L., trans. *The Annals of St. Bertin.* Manchester: Manchester University Press, 1991.
ASC	Whitelock, Dorothy, trans. *The Anglo-Saxon Chronicle*, New Brunswick, N.J.: Rutgers University Press, 1961.
Atkinson	Atkinson, Thomas W. *Oriental and Western Siberia: A Narrative*

	of Seven Years Explorations and Adventures. 1858. Reprint New York: Praeger, 1970.
AYS	Varisco, Daniel Martin, trans. *Medieval Agriculture and Islamic Science: The Almanac of a Yemeni Sultan.* Seattle: University of Washington Press, 1994.
Bābur	Bābur, Ẓahir al-Dīn. *The Bābur-nāma in English.* Trans. Annette Susannah Beveridge. London: Luzac, 1969.
Bagrationi	Bagrationi, Vakhushti. *Istoriia tsartvo gruzinskogo.* Trans. N. T. Nakashidze. Tbilisi: Izdatel'stvo "Metsniereba," 1976.
Baihaqī	Baihaqī, Abū'l Faẓl. *Ta'rīkh-i Baihaqī.* Ed. Q. Ghanī and A. A. Fayyaẓ. Tehran: Chāpkhānah bānk-i millī, 1946.
al-Balādhurī	al-Balādhurī. *The Origins of the Islamic State.* Trans. Philip Hitti and F. C. Murgotten. New York: Columbia University Press, 1916–24. 2 vols.
Bar Hebraeus	Bar Hebraeus. *The Chronography of Gregory Abū'l Faraj.* Trans. Ernest A. Wallis Budge. London: Oxford University Press, 1932. Vol. I.
Barbosa	Barbosa, Duarte. *The Book of Duarte Barbosa.* Trans. Mansel Longworth Dames. 1918. Reprint Millwood, N.Y.: Kraus Reprint, 1967. 2 vols.
BDK	Sümer, Faruk, Ahmet E. Uysal, and Warren S. Walker, trans. *The Book of Dede Korkut: A Turkish Epic.* Austin: University of Texas Press, 1972.
Bell	Bell, John. *Journey from St. Petersburg to Pekin, 1714–22.* Edinburgh: Edinburgh University Press, 1965.
Beneveni	Beneveni, Florio. *Poslanik Petra I na Vostoke: Posol'stvo Florio Beneveni v Persiiu i Bukharu v 1718–1725.* Moscow: Nauka, 1986.
Benjamin of Tudela	Benjamin of Tudela. *The Itinerary.* Trans. Marcus Nathan Adler. 1907. Reprint Malibu, Calif.: Pangloss Press, 1987.
Bernier	Bernier, François. *Travels in the Mogul Empire, A.D. 1656–1668.* 2nd ed. Oxford: Oxford University Press, 1934
BF	Meisami, Julie Scott, trans. *The Sea of Precious Virtues (Bahr al-Fav'āîd): A Medieval Islamic Mirror for Princes.* Salt Lake City: University of Utah Press, 1991.
Bigam	Gul-Badan Begum. *The History of Humāyūn (Humāyūn-nāma).* Trans. Annette Susannah Beveridge. 1902. Reprint Delhi: Low Price Publications, 1989.
Boccaccio	Boccaccio, Giovanni. *The Decameron.* Trans. Mark Musa and Peter Bondanella. New York: Norton, 1982.

Bowrey	Bowrey, Thomas. *A Geographical Account of Countries Round the Bay of Bengal, 1669–1679*. Ed. Sir Richard Carnac Temple. 1905. Reprint Nendeln: Kraus Reprint, 1967.
Broecke	van den Broecke, Pieter. *A Contemporary Dutch Chronicle of Mughal India*. Trans. and ed. Brij Narain and Sri Ram Sharma. Calcutta: Susil Gupta, 1957.
Burnes	Burnes, Alexander. *Travels into Bokhara, Being an Account of a Journey from India to Cabool, Tartary and Persia*. 1834. Reprint New Delhi: Asian Educational Services, 1992. 3 vols.
Burton	Burton, Sir Richard. *Personal Narrative of a Pilgrimage to al-Madinah and Meccah*. 1893. Reprint New York: Dover, 1963. 2 vols.
Buzand	Garsoian, Nina G., trans. *The Epic Histories Attributed to Pʿawstos Buzand*. Cambridge, Mass.: Harvard University Press, 1989.
Carré	Carré, Abbé. *The Travels of Abbé Carré in India and the Near East, 1672–1674*. Trans. Lady Fawcett and Sir Charles Fawcett. 1947. Reprint Nendeln: Kraus Reprint, 1967. 3 vols.
CATCL	Mair, Victor H., ed. *The Columbia Anthology of Traditional Chinese Literature*. New York: Columbia University Press, 1994.
Catherine II	Catherine II. *Memoirs of Catherine the Great*. New York: Collier, 1961.
CC	Scholtz, Bernhard Walter, trans. *Carolingian Chronicles: Royal Frankish Annals and Nithard's Histories*. Ann Arbor: University of Michigan Press, 1970.
CDIPR	Islam, Riazul, ed. *A Calendar of Documents on Indo-Persian Relations, 1500–1700*. Karachi: Institute of Central and West Asian Studies, 1979. 2 vols.
Chardin	Chardin, John. *Travels in Persia, 1673–77*. 1927. Reprint New York: Dover, 1988.
Chen Cheng	Morris Rossabi, trans. "A Translation of Ch'en Ch'eng's *Hsi-yü Fan-kuo chih*." *Ming Studies* 17 (1983): 49–59.
Cheng Zhufu	Cheng Zhufu. *Cheng xuelou wen ji*. Taibei: Yuandai zhenben wenji, 1970.
Cheng Zhuo	Franke, Herbert, trans. "A Sung Embassy Diary of 1211–1212: The *Shih-chin lu* of Ch'eng Cho." *Bulletin de l'école française d'Extrême-Orient* 69 (1981): 171–207.
Clavijo	Clavijo, Ruy Gonzales de. *Embassy to Tamerlane, 1403–6*. Trans. Guy Le Strange. London: Routledge, 1928.
Comnena	Comnena, Anna. *The Alexiad*. Trans. E. R. A. Sewter. New York: Penguin, 1985.

CRP — Watson, Burton, trans. *Chinese Rhyme-Prose: Poems in the Fu Form from the Han and Six Dynasties Period.* New York: Columbia University Press, 1971.

CWT — Yule, Sir Henry, ed. and trans. *Cathay and the Way Thither, Being a Collection of Medieval Notices of China.* 1866. Reprint Taibei: Ch'eng-wen Publishing, 1966. 4 vols.

Dasxuranc'i — Dasxuranci, Movsēs, *The History of the Caucasian Albanians.* Trans. C. J. F. Dowsett. London: Oxford University Press, 1961.

Dio Chrysostom — Dio Chrysostom. *Discourses.* Trans. H. Lamar Crosby and J. W. Conoon. Loeb Classical Library. Cambridge, Mass.: Harvard University Press, 1932–51.

Diodorus — *Diodorus of Sicily.* Trans. C. H. Oldfather et al. Loeb Classical Library; Cambridge, Mass.: Harvard University Press, 1935–57.

Dionysius — Pseudo-Dionysius of Tel-Mahre. *Chronicle,* part III. Trans. Witold Witakowski. Liverpool: Liverpool University Press, 1990.

Dom. — Pouncy, Carolyn Johnston, trans. *The Domostroi: Rules for Russian Households in the Time of Ivan the Terrible.* Ithaca, N.Y.: Cornell University Press, 1994.

Don Juan — Don Juan of Persia. *Don Juan of Persia, a Shi'a Catholic, 1500–1604.* Trans. Guy Le Strange, London: Routledge, 1926.

Drasxanakertc'i/D — Draskhanakerttsi, Iovannes. *Istoriia Armenii.* Trans. M. O. Dardinian-Melikian. Erevan: Sovetakan Grokh, 1986.

Drasxanakertc'i/M — Drasxanakertc'i, Yovannes, *History of Armenia.* Trans. Krikov H. Maksoudian. Atlanta: Scholars Press, 1987.

DTO — Chavannes, Edouard, trans. *Documents sur les Tou-Kiue (Turcs) occidentaux.* 1903. Reprint Taibei: Ch'eng-wen Publishing, 1969.

EA — Nikam, Narayanrao Appurao and Richard McKeon, trans. *The Edicts of Aśoka.* Chicago: University of Chicago Press, 1959.

Einhard — Einhard. *The Life of Charlemagne.* Trans. Samuel E. Turner, Ann Arbor: University of Michigan Press, 1960.

Ełishē — Ełishē. *History of Vardan and the Armenian War.* Trans. Robert W. Thomson. Cambridge, Mass.: Harvard University Press, 1982.

Ennin — *Ennin's Diary: The Record of a Pilgimage to China in Search of the Law.* Trans. Edwin O. Reischauer. New York: Ronald, 1955.

EVTRP — Morgan, E. Delmar and C. H. Coote, eds. *Early Voyages and Travels to Russia and Persia by Anthony Jenkinson and Other Englishmen.* 1886. Reprint New York: Burt Franklin, 1963. 2 vols.

Fan Chengda — Hargett, James M., trans. *On the Road in Twelfth Century China: The Travel Diaries of Fan Chengda (1126–1193).* Stuttgart: Franz Steiner, 1989.

Faxian	Legge, James, trans. *A Record of Buddhist Kingdoms: Being an Account by the Chinese Monk Fa-Hein of Travels in India and Ceylon.* 1886. Reprint New Delhi: Munshiran Manoharlal, 1991.
FCH	Blockley, R. C., trans. *The Fragmentary Classicising Historians of the Later Roman Empire.* Vol. II, *Text, Translation and Historiographical Notes.* Liverpool: Francis Cairns, 1983.
Ferrier	Ferrier, J. P. *Caravan Journeys and Wanderings in Persia, Afghanistan, Turkestan and Beloochistan.* 2nd ed. London: John Murray, 1857.
Fletcher	Fletcher, Giles. *Of the Russe Commonwealth.* Ed. Richard Pipes and John V. A. Fine, Jr. Cambridge, Mass.: Harvard University Press, 1966.
Floris	Floris, Peter. *Peter Floris, His Voyage to the East Indies in the Globe, 1611–1615.* Ed. W. H. Moreland. 1934. Reprint Nendeln: Kraus Reprint, 1967.
Forbes	Forbes, James. *Oriental Memoirs.* 1813. Reprint Delhi: Gian Publishing, 1988. 4 vols.
Frederick II	Frederick II of Hohenstaufen. *The Art of Falconry, Being the De Arte Venandi cum Avibus.* Trans. Casey A. Wood and F. Marjorie Fyfe. Stanford, Calif.: Stanford University Press, 1961.
Fryer	Fryer, John. *A New Account of East India and Persia, Being Nine Year's Travels, 1672–1681.* Ed. William Crooke. 1909. Reprint Millwood, N.Y.: Kraus Reprint, 1967. 3 vols.
Fu Jian	Rogers, Michael C., trans. *The Chronicle of Fu Chien: A Case of Examplar History.* Berkeley: University of California Press, 1968.
FZ/B	Baevskii, S. I. "'Rumiiski' slova v persidskom tolkovom slovare 'Zafāngūyā'." *Palestinskii sbornik* 21, 84 (1970): 91–99.
FZ/D	Dankoff, Robert, trans. *The Turkic Vocabulary in the Farhang-i Zafāngūyā (8th/14th Century).* Papers on Inner Asia 4. Bloomington: Indiana University, Research Institute for Inner Asian Studies, 1987.
Gardīzī	Martinez, A. P., trans. "Gardīzīʿs Two Chapters on the Turks." *Archivum Eurasiae Medii Aevi* 2 (1980): 109–217.
GC	Vivian, Katherine, trans. *The Georgian Chronicle: The Period of Giorgi Lasha.* Amsterdam: Adolf M. Hakkert, 1991.
GD	Kakabadze, S. S., trans. *Gruzinskie dokumenty IX–XV vv.* Moscow: Nauka, 1982.
Gilmore	Gilmour, James. *Among the Mongols.* 1883. Reprint New York: Praeger, 1970.

GOT	Tekin, Talât. *A Grammar of Orkhon Turkic.* Indiana University Uralic and Altaic Series 69. Bloomington: Indiana University, 1968.
Gregory of Tours	Gregory of Tours. *The History of the Franks.* Trans. Lewis Thorpe. London: Penguin, 1974.
Grigor of Akancʿ	Grigor of Akancʿ. "History of the Nation of Archers (The Mongols)," ed. and trans. Robert P. Blake and Richard N. Frye. *Harvard Journal of Asiatic Studies* 12 (1949): 269–399.
Guerreiro	Guerreiro, Fernão. *Jahangir and the Jesuits, with an Account of the Travels of Benedict Goes and the Mission to Pegu.* Trans. C. H. Payne. London: Routledge, 1930.
GVNP	Valk, S. N. ed. *Gramoty Velikogo Novgoroda i Pskova.* Moscow-Leningrad: Izdatel'stvo akademii nauk SSSR, 1949.
Ḥ-ʿĀ	Minorsky, V., trans. *Ḥudūd al-ʿĀlam.* 2nd ed. London: Luzac, 1970.
Ḥāfiẓ-i Abrū/B	Ḥāfiẓ-i Abrū. *Ẕayl jāmiʿ al-tavārīkh-i Rashīdī.* Ed. Khānbābā Bayānī. Salsatat-i instishārāt-i aṣār millī, 88. Tehran, 1971.
Ḥāfiẓ-i Abrū/M	Maitra, K. M. trans. *A Persian Embassy to China, being an Extract from Zubatu't Tawarikh of Hafiz Abru.* Reprint New York: Paragon, 1970.
Ḥāfiẓ-i Tanīsh	Ḥāfiẓ-i Tanīsh Bukhārī. *Sharaf nāmah-shāhī.* Ed. and trans. M. A. Salakhetdina. Moscow: Nauka, 1987–88. 2 vols.
Hakluyt, *PN*	Hakluyt, Richard, *The Principall Navigations of the English Nation.* London: J.M. Dent, 1907. 8 vols.
Hakluyt, *V*	Hakluyt, Richard. *Voyages*, London: J.M. Dent, 1939. Vol. I.
Hall	Hall, Basil. *Travels in India, Ceylon and Borneo.* Ed. H. G. Rawlinson. London: Routledge and Sons, 1931.
Hamilton	Hamilton, Alexander. *A New Account of the East Indies.* London: Argonaut Press, 1930. 2 vols.
Han Feizi	Han Fei Tzu. *Basic Writings.* Trans. Burton Watson. New York: Columbia University Press, 1964.
Ḥasan-i Fasāʾī	Ḥasan-e Fasāʾī. *History of Persia Under Qājār Rule.* Trans. Heribert Busse. New York: Columbia University Press, 1972.
Haslund	Haslund, Henning. *Tents in Mongolia.* New York: Dutton, 1934.
HC	Bellér-Hann, Ildikó, trans. *A History of Cathay: A Translation and Linguistic Analysis of a Fifteenth-Century Turkic Manuscript.* Indiana University Uralic and Altaic Series 162. Bloomington: Indiana University, 1995.
Helmold	Helmold. *The Chronicle of the Slavs.* 1935. Reprint New York: Octagon, 1966.

Herberstein	Herberstein, Sigismund. *Commentaries on Muscovite Affairs.* Trans. Oswald P. Backus III. Lawrence: Student Union Bookstore, University of Kansas, 1956.
Herbert	Herbert, Sir Thomas. *Travels in Persia, 1627–1629.* Ed. William Foster. 1929. Reprint Freeport, N.Y.: Books for Libraries Press, 1972.
Herodotus	Herodotus. *The Persian Wars.* Trans. George Rawlinson, New York: Modern Library, 1942.
Hetʿum	Hayton, *La flor des estoires de la Terre d'Orient.* Recueil des historiens du Croisades, Documents arméniens. Paris: Imprimerie nationale, 1906. Vol. II.
Hetʿum/B	Boyle, John A., trans. "The Journey of Hetʿum I, King of Lesser Armenia, to the Court of the Grand Khan Möngke." *Central Asiatic Journal* 9 (1964): 175–89.
Hex.	Golden, Peter, ed. *The King's Dictionary: The Rasūlid Hexaglot, Fourteenth Century Vocabularies in Arabic, Persian, Turkic, Greek, Armenian and Mongol.* Leiden: E.J. Brill, 2000.
HHS	Fan Ye. *Hou Hanshu.* Beijing: Zhonghua shuju, 1973.
HI	Elliot, H. M. E. and John Dawson, trans. *The History of India as Told by Its Own Historians: The Muhammadan Period.* 1867. Reprint New York: AMS Press, 1966. 8 vols.
Homer, *Il.*	Homer, *The Iliad.* Trans. A. T. Murray. Loeb Classical Library. New York: Putnam, 1924.
HPKP	Pelliot, Paul, trans. "La version ouigoure de l'histoire des princes Kalyānamkara et Pāpamkara." *T'oung-pao* 15 (1914): 225–72.
HS	Ban Gu. *Hanshu.* Beijing: Zhonghua shuju, 1990.
HS/D	Pan Ku. *The History of the Former Han Dynasty.* Trans. Homer Dubs. Baltimore: Waverly Press, 1938–55. 3 vols.
HS/H	Hulsewé, A. F. P., trans. *China in Central Asia, the Early Stage: An Annotated Translation of Chapters 61 and 96 of the History of the Former Han Dynasty.* Leiden: E.J. Brill, 1979.
HS/W	Watson, Burton, trans. *Courtier and Commoner in Ancient China: Selections from the History of the Former Han by Pan ku.* New York: Columbia University Press, 1974.
Huan Kuan	Huan K'uan. *Discourses on Salt and Iron: A Debate on State Control of Commerce and Industry in Early China.* Trans. Essen M. Gale. Reprint Taibei: Ch'eng-wen Publishing, 1973.
Huc and Gabet	Huc, Abbé and Joseph Gabet. *Travels in Tartary, Thibet and China, 1844–46.* New York: Harper and Brothers, 1928. 2 vols.

Hui Li	Hwui Li. *The Life of Hiuen-tsiang.* Trans. Samuel Beal. London: Kegan Paul, Trench and Trubnor, 1911.
Ḥusām al-Dawlah	Ḥusām al-Dawlah. *Bāznāmah-i Naṣīrī: A Persian Treatise on Falconry.* Trans. D. C. Pillott. London: Bernard Quaritch, 1908.
Hyp.	Perfecky, George, A., trans. *The Hypatian Codex.* Vol. II, *The Galician-Volynia Chronicle.* Munich: Wilhelm Fink, 1973.
HYYY	Mostaert, Antoine, trans. and Igor de Rachewiltz, ed. *Le matériel mongol du Houa i i iu de Houng-ou (1389).* Mélanges chinois et bouddhiques 18 and 27. Brussels: Institut belge des hautes études chinois, 1977–95. 2 vols
IB	Talat Tekin, trans. *Irk Bitig: The Book of Omens.* Wiesbaden: Harrassowitz, 1993.
Ibn ʿArabshāh	Ibn Arabshah, Ahmed, *Tamerlane or Timur the Great Amir.* Trans. J. H. Sanders. Reprint Lahore: Progressive Books, n.d.
Ibn al-Azraq	Hillenbrand, Carole, trans. *A Muslim Principality in Crusader Times: The Early Artuqid State.* Istanbul: Nederlands Historisch-Archaelogisch Institut, 1990.
Ibn Baṭṭuṭah	Ibn Baṭṭuṭah. *The Travels of Ibn Baṭṭuṭa.* Trans. H. A. R. Gibb. Cambridge: University Press for the Hakluyt Society, 1958–94. 4 vols.
Ibn al-Furāt	Ibn al-Furāt. *Ayyubids, Mamlukes and Crusaders: Selections from the Tārīkh al-Duwal waʾl Mulūk.* Trans. U. and M. C. Lyons, with notes by Jonathan S. C. Riley-Smith. Cambridge: W. Hefer and Sons, 1971. 2 vols.
Ibn Isfandiyār	Browne, Edward G., trans. *An Abridged Translation of the History of Ṭabaristān.* Leiden: E.J. Brill and London: Bernard Quaritch, 1905.
Ibn Khaldūn	Ibn Khaldūn, *The Muqaddimah: An Introduction to History.* Trans. Franz Rosenthal. New York: Pantheon, 1958. 3 vols.
Ibn Khurdādhbih	Ibn Khurdādhbih. *Kitāb al-masālik wa al-mamālik.* Ed. M. J. de Goeje. Leiden: E.J. Brill, 1889.
Ibn Manglī	Ibn Manglī. *De la chasse: commerce des grands de ce monde avec bêtes sauvages des déserts sans onde.* Trans. François Viré. Paris: Sindbad, 1984.
Ibn Shaddād	Ibn Shaddād, Bahāʾ al-Dīn. *The Rare and Excellent History of Saladin.* Trans. D. S. Richards. Aldershot: Ashgate, 2002.
IFC	Major, R. H., trans. *India in the Fifteenth Century.* London: Hakluyt Society Publications, 1857.
ʿInāyat Khān	ʿInayat Khan. *The Shah Jahan Nama.* Trans. A. R. Fuller, ed. W. E. Begley and I. A. Desai. Delhi: Oxford University Press, 1990.

Isk.	Southgate, Minoo S., trans. *Iskandarnamah: A Persian Medieval Alexander Romance.* New York: Columbia University Press, 1978.
Jahāngīr	Jahāngīr. *Tūzuk-i Jahāngīrī or Memoirs of Jahāngīr.* Trans. Alexander Rogers, ed. Henry Beveridge. Reprint Delhi: Munshiram Mansharlal, 1978. 2 vols.
Jāḥiẓ, *KT*	Pellat, Charles, trans. "Ǧāḥiẓiana I: Le *Kitab al-tabaṣṣur bi-l Tiǧara* attribué à Ǧāḥiẓ." *Arabica* 2 (1955): 153–65.
Jāḥiẓ, *LC*	Pellat, Charles, trans. *Le livre de la couronne attribué a Ǧaḥiẓ.* Paris: Société d'é ditions Les Belles Lettres, 1954.
du Jarric	du Jarric, Pierre, S.J. *Akbar and the Jesuits: An Account of the Jesuit Mission to the Court of Akbar.* Trans. C. H. Payne. London: Routledge, 1926.
Jordanes	Jordanes, *The Gothic History.* Trans. Christopher Mierow. Reprint New York: Barnes and Noble, 1960.
Josephus	Josephus, *The Jewish War.* Trans. H. St. J. Thackeray. Loeb Classical Library. Cambridge, Mass.: Harvard University Press, 1961.
Joshua	Pseudo-Joshua the Stylite. *The Chronicle of Pseudo-Joshua the Stylite.* Trans. Frank K. Trombley and John W. Watt. Liverpool: Liverpool University Press, 2000.
Jourdain	Jourdain, John. *The Journal of John Jourdain, 1608–1617, Describing his Experiences in Arabia, India and the Malay Archipelago.* Ed William Foster. Reprint Nendeln: Kraus Reprint, 1967.
JS	*Jinshi.* Beijing: Zhonghua shuju, 1975.
Jshu/M	Mather, Richard B., trans. *Biography of Lü Kuang [from the Jinshu].* Berkeley: University of California Press, 1959.
JTS	*Jiu Tangshu.* Beijing: Zhonghua shuju, 1975.
Juansher	Dzhuansher Dzhuansheriani, *Zhizn Vakhtunga Gorgasala.* Trans. G. V. Tsulaia. Tbilisi: Izdatel'stvo "Metsniereba," 1986.
Justin	Watson, John S., trans. *Justin, Cornelius Nepos and Eutropius.* London: Bell and Sons, 1910.
Juvaynī/B	Juvaynī, ʿAtā-Malik. *The History of the World Conqueror.* Trans. John A. Boyle. Cambridge, Mass.: Harvard University Press, 1958. 2 vols.
Juvaynī/Q	Juvaynī, ʿAtā-Malik. *Ta'rīkh-i Jahāngushā.* Ed. Mirzā Muḥammad Qazvīnī. E. J. W. Gibb Memorial Series 26. London: Luzac, 1912–37. 3 vols.
Jūzjānī/L	Jūzjānī, *Ṭabaqāt-i nāṣirī.* Ed. W. Nassau Lees. Bibliotheca Indica 44. Calcutta: College Press, 1864.
Jūzjānī/R	Jūzjānī, *Ṭabaqāt-i nāṣirī.* Trans. H. G. Raverty. Reprint New Delhi: Oriental Book Reprint, 1970. 2 vols.

Kaempfer	Kaempfer, Engelbert. *Am Hofe der persischen Grosskönigs, 1684–1685*. Trans. Walther Hinz. Tübingen and Basil: Erdmann, 1977.
Kai Kāʿūs	Kai Kāʿūs ibn Iskandar. *A Mirror for Princes: The Qabus Name*. Trans. Reuben Levy. London: Cresset Press, 1951.
Kalidasa	Kalidasa. *Shakuntala and Other Writings*. Trans. Arthur W. Ryder. New York: E.P. Dutton, 1959.
Kangxi	Jonathan D. Spence, trans. *Emperor of China: Self Portrait of K'ang-hsi*. New York: Vintage, 1975.
Kashgharī	Maḥmūd al Kašγarī. *Compendium of the Turkic Dialects (Dīwān Luγāt al-Turk)*. Trans. Robert Dankoff. Sources of Oriental Languages and Literature 7. Cambridge, Mass.: Harvard University Printing Office, 1982. 3 vols.
Kautilya	Shamasastry, Rudrapatna, trans. *Kautilya's Arthaśāstra*. Mysore: Mysore Publishing House, 1967.
KB/P	Phillot, D. C. and R. J. Azoo, trans. "Chapters on Hunting Dogs and Cheetas, being an Extract from the *Kitāb al-Bayzarah*." *Journal and Proceedings of the Asiatic Society of Bengal* n.s. 3 (1907): 47–50.
KB/V	Viré, François. *Le tracté de l'art de volerie (Kitab al-Bayzara)*. Leiden: E.J. Brill, 1967.
KDA	Chunakova, O. M., trans. *Kniga Deianii Ardashir syna Papaka*. Moscow: Nauka, 1987.
KF	Heinisch, Klaus, F., ed. and trans. *Kaiser Friedrich II: Sein Leben in zeitgenössischen Berichten*. Munich: Winkler-Verlag, 1969.
KFB	Heinisch, Klaus J., trans. *Kaiser Friedrich II in Briefen und Berichten seiner Zeit*. Darmstadt: Wissenschaftliche Buchgesellschaft, 1968.
Khiṭāʾī	Khiṭāʾī, ʿAlī Akbar. *Khiṭāʾī-nāmah*. Ed. Iraj Afshār. Tehran: Asian Cultural Documentation Center for UNESCO, 1979.
Khorenatsʿi	Khorenatsʿi, Moses. *History of the Armenians*. Trans. Robert W. Thomson. Cambridge, Mass.: Harvard University Press, 1978.
Kinnamos	Kinnamos, John. *Deeds of John and Manuel Comnenus*. Trans. M. Brand. New York: Columbia University Press, 1976.
Kirakos	Kirakos Gandzaketsi. *Istoriia Armenii*. Trans. L. A. Khanlarian. Moscow: Nauka, 1976.
KM	Szczesniak, Boleslaw, trans. "The Kôtaiô Monument." *Monumenta Nipponica* 7 (1952): 242–68.
Lansdell	Lansdell, Henry. *Russian Central Asia, Including Kuldja, Bokhara, Khiva and Merv*. Reprint New York: Arno Press, 1970. 2 vols. in one.

Lattimore	Lattimore, Owen. *High Tartary*. Reprint New York: AMS Press, 1975.
Layard	Layard, Austin. *Discoveries in the Ruins of Nineveh and Babylon*, London: John Murray, 1853.
Leo the Deacon	Lev Diakon. *Istoriia*. Trans. M. M. Kopylenko. Moscow: Nauka, 1988.
Li Zhizhang	Li Zhizhang. *Xiyu ji*, in MGSL.
Li Zhizhang/W	Li Chih-chang. *The Travels of an Alchemist*. Trans. Arthur Waley. London: Routledge and Kegan Paul, 1963.
Linschoten	Linschoten, John Huyghen van. *The Voyage to the East Indies*. Ed. Arthur Coke Burnell and P. A. Tiele. London: Hakluyt Society Publications, 1985. 2 vols.
Liu Zhen	Liu Zhen. *Dong guan Hanji*. Zhongzhou: Zhongzhou guji chubanshe, 1987.
Liudprand	Liudprand of Cremona. *The Embassy to Constantinople and Other Writings*. Trans. F. A. Wright. Rutland, Vt.: Everyman's Library, 1993.
LK	Tsulaia, G. V., trans. *Letopis Kartli*. Tbilisi: Izdatel'stvo "Metsniereba," 1982.
LKA	Strong, John S., trans. *The Legend of King Aśoka*. Princeton, N.J.: Princeton University Press, 1983.
Llull	Llull, Ramon. *Felix, or the Book of Wonders*. In *Selected Works of Ramon Llull*. Ed. and trans. Anthony Bonner. Princeton, N.J.: Princeton University Press, 1985. Vol. II.
Longus	Longus. *Daphnis and Chloe*. Trans. George Thornley. Loeb Classical Library. London: Heinemann, 1916.
LS	*Liaoshi*. Beijing: Zhonghua shuju, 1974.
LT	Boyce, Mary, trans. *The Letter of Tansar*. Rome: Istituto Italiano per il Medio ed Estremo Oriente, 1968.
Luo Guanzhong	Lo Kuan-chung. *Romance of the Three Kingdoms*. Trans. C. H. Brewitt-Taylor. Rutland, Vt.: Tuttle, 1959. Vol. II.
Ma Huan	Ma Huan. *Ying-yai sheng-lan: The Overall Survey of the Oceans Shores*. Trans. J. V. G. Mills. Cambridge: For the Hakluyt Society, 1970.
Macartney	Macartney, George. *An Embassy to China: Being the Journal Kept by Lord Macartney During His Embassy to the Emperor Ch'ien-lung*. Ed. J. L. Cranmer-Byng. London: Longman, 1962.
Machiavelli	Machiavelli, Nicoló. *The Prince and the Discourses*. New York: Modern Library, 1950.
Mandeville	Mandeville, Sir John. *Travels of Sir John Mandeville*. Trans. C. W. R. D. Moseley. New York: Penguin, 1983.

Manrique	Manrique, Sebastian. *Travels of Fray Sebastian Manrique, 1629–1643*. Trans. C. Eckford Luard. Reprint Nendeln: Kraus Reprint, 1967. 2 vols.
al-Manṣūr	*Al-Mansur's Book on Hunting*. Trans. Sir Terence Clark and Muawiya Derhalli. Warminster: Aris & Phillips, 2001.
Manucci	Manucci, Niccolao. *Storia do Mogor or Mugul India, 1653–1708*. Trans. William Irvine. Reprint New Delhi: Oriental Books Reprint, 1981. 4 vols.
Manuel II	Dennis, Georg T., trans. *The Letters of Manuel II Palaeologus*. Washington, D.C.: Dumbarton Oaks, Center for Byzantine Studies, 1977.
al-Maqrīzī	al-Maqrīzī. *Histoire des Sultans Mamluks de l'Egypte*. Trans. M. Quatremére. Paris: Oriental Translation Fund, 1842. Vol. II, part 1.
Marco Polo	Marco Polo. *The Description of the World*. Trans. A. C. Moule and Paul Pelliot. London: Routledge, 1938. Vol. I.
Marvazī	Minorsky, V., trans. *Sharaf al-Zamān Tahir Marvazī on China, the Turks and India*. London: Royal Asiatic Society, 1942.
Masʿūdī	Masūʿdī. *Murūj al-dhabab wa al-maʿādin*. Ed. and trans. Barbier de Meynard. Paris: L'imprimerie nationale, 1861–77. 9 vols.
MDMT	Cleaves, Francis W., trans. "The Mongolian Documents in the Musée de Téhéran." *Harvard Journal of Asiatic Studies* 16 (1953): 1–107.
Mei Cheng	Mair, Victor H, trans. *Mei Cheng's "Seven Stimuli" and Wang Bar's "Pavilion of King Terng": Chinese Poems for Princes*. Queenston, Ontario: Edwin Mellen, 1985.
Mela	Mela, Pomonius. *Géographie*. Trans. M. Bandet. Paris: Panckoucke, 1843.
Menander	Menander. *The History of Menander the Guardsman*. Trans. R. C. Blockley. Liverpool: Francis Cairns Publications, 1985.
Mencius	*Mencius*. Trans. W. A. C. H. Dobson. Toronto: University of Toronto Press, 1963.
MGSL	Wang Guowei. *Menggu shiliao sizhang*. Taibei: Zhenzhong shuju, 1975.
MIRGO	Paichadze, G. G. ed. *Materialy po istorii russko-gruzinskikh otnoshenii*. Tbilisi: Izdatel'stvo "Metsniereba," 1974.
Mīrzā Ḥaydar, I	Mirza Haydar Dughlat. *Tarikh-i Rashidi*. Ed. W. M. Thackston. Cambridge, Mass.: Harvard University, 1996.
Mīrzā Ḥaydar, II	Mirza Haydar Dughlat. *Tarikh-i Rashidi*. Trans. W. M. Thackston. Cambridge, Mass.: Harvard University, 1996.

MK	Heinrichs, A. and L. Koenen, eds. and trans. "Der Kölner Manikodex (P. Colon. Inv. Nr. 4780)." *Zeitschrift für Papyrologie und Epigraphik* 48 (1980): 1–59.
MKK	Budge, Ernest A. Wallis, trans. *The Monks of Kūblāi Khān*. London: Religious Tract Society, 1928.
MM	Dawson, Christopher, ed. *The Mongol Mission: Narratives and Letters of the Franciscan Missionaries in Mongolia and China in the 13th and 14th Centuries*. New York: Sheed and Ward, 1955.
MMT	Sunderman, Werner, ed. and trans. *Mitteliranische manichäische Texte kirchengeschichlichen Inhalt*. Berlin: Akademie Verlag, 1981.
MP	Ligeti, Louis. *Monuments préclassiques, XIIIe et XIVe siècles*. Budapest: Akadémiai Kiadó, 1972.
MRL	Vernadsky, George, trans. *Medieval Russian Laws*. Reprint New York: Octagon Books, 1974.
MS	*Mingshi*. Beijing: Zhonghua shuju, 1974.
MTZZ	Mathieu, Rémi, trans. *Le Mu tianzi zhuan: Translation annotée, étude critique*. Paris: Presses universitaires de France, 1978.
G. Mundy	Mundy, Godfrey Charles. *Pen and Pencil Sketches in India: Journal of a Tour in India*. 3rd ed. London: John Murray, 1858.
P. Mundy	Mundy, Peter. *The Travels of Peter Mundy in Europe and Asia, 1608–1617*. Ed. Sir Richard Carnac Temple. Reprint Nendeln: Kraus Reprint, 1967–72. 5 vols.
Munshī	Munshī, Iskander. *History of Shah ʿAbbas*. Trans. Roger Savory. Boulder, Colo.: Westview Press, 1978. 2 vols.
Muntaner	Muntanern. *The Chronicle of Muntaner*. Trans. Lady Goodenough. Reprint Nendeln: Kraus Reprint, 1967.Vol. II.
al-Muqaddasī	al-Muqaddasī. *Aḥsan al-taqāsīmfī maʿrifat al-āqālīm*. Ed. M. J. de Goeje. Leiden: E.J. Brill, 1906.
Muraviev	Murav'yov, Nikolay. *Journey to Khiva Through the Turkman Country*. London: Oguz Press, 1977.
al-Nadim	al-Nadim. *The Fihrist of al-Nadim: A Tenth Century Survey of Muslim Culture*. Trans. Bayard Dodge. New York: Columbia University Press, 1970. 2 vols.
Nakhchivānī	Nakhchivānī, Muḥammad Ibn Hindushāh. *Dastūr al-kātib fī taʿyin al-marātib*. Ed. A. A. Alizade. Moscow: Nauka, 1976. Vol. II.
Narshakhī	Narshakhī. *The History of Bukhara*. Trans. Richard N. Frye. Cambridge, Mass.: Medieval Academy of America, 1954.
al-Nasāwī	al-Nasāwī, Muḥammad. *Sīrat al-Sulṭan Jalāl al-Din Mankubirtī*. Ed. H. Hamdī. Cairo: Dār al-fakr al-ʿArabī, 1953.

Nāṣir-i Khusraw — Nāṣir-i Khusraw. *Book of Travels (Safarnāma)*. Trans. W. M. Thackston. New York: Bibliotheca Persica, 1986.

NC — Zenkovsky, Serge A. and Betty Jean Zenkovsky, trans. *The Nikonian Chronicle.* Princeton, N.J.: Kingston and Darwin Press, 1984–89. 5 vols.

NG — Aston, W. G., trans. *Nihongi.* Reprint London: Allen and Unwin, 1956.

Nikephoros — Nikephoros, Patriarch of Constantinople. *Short History.* Trans. Cyril Mango, Washington, D.C.: Dumbarton Oaks, 1990.

Nikitin — Nikitin, Afanasii. *Khozhdenie za tri moria.* 2nd ed. Moscow-Leningrad: Izdatel'stvo akademii nauk SSSR, 1958.

Nīshāpūrī — Nīshāpūrī, Ẓahīr al-Dīn. *The History of the Seljuq Turks from the Jāmiʿ al-Tawārīkh: An Ilkhanid Adaptation of the Saljūqnāma of Ẓahīr al-Dīn Nīshāpūrī.* Trans. Kenneth Allin Luther, ed. C. Edmund Bosworth. Richmond, Surrey: Curzon, 2001.

NITP — Grey, C., trans. *A Narrative of Italian Travels in Persia.* London: Hakluyt Society, 1875.

Niẓām al-Mulk — Niẓām al-Mulk. *The Book of Government or Rules for Kings.* Trans. Hubert Darke. London: Routledge and Kegan Paul, 1960.

Niẓāmī — Niẓāmī, Ganjavi. *The Haft Paykar: A Medieval Persian Romance.* Trans. Julie Scott Meisami. Oxford: Oxford University Press, 1995.

Olearius — Olearius, Adam. *The Travels of Olearius in 17th Century Russia.* Trans. Samuel H. Baron. Stanford, Calif.: Stanford University Press, 1967.

Olympiodorus — Olympiodorus. *Testimonium.* In *FCH.*

ON — Shcherbak, A. M., trans. *Oguz-nāme. Makhaddat-nāme.* Moscow: Izdatel'stvo vostochnoi literatury, 1959.

OP — Kent, Roland G. *Old Persian Grammar, Texts, Lexicon.* 2nd ed. rev. New Haven, Conn.: American Oriental Society, 1953.

Oppian — *Oppian, Collathus, Tryphiodorus.* Trans. A. W. Mair. Loeb Classical Library. Cambridge, Mass.: Harvard University Press, 1928.

Orbelian — Orbelian, Stephanos. *Histoire de la Siounie.* Trans. M. Brosset. St. Petersburg: Academie impériale des sciences, 1864.

d'Orléans — d'Orléans, Pierre Joseph. *History of the Two Tartar Conquerors of China.* Trans. Earl of Ellesmere. Reprint New York: Burt Franklin, 1971.

Ovington — Ovington, J. *A Voyage to Surat in the Year 1689.* Ed. H. G. Rawlinson. Oxford: Oxford University Press, 1929.

Pachymérès — Pachymérès, Georges. *Relations historiques.* Trans. V. Laurent. Paris: Société d'éditions Les Belles Lettres, 1984. 2 vols.

Parks — Parks, Fanny. *Wanderings of a Pilgrim in Search of the Picturesque.* Reprint Karachi: Oxford University Press, 1975. 2 vols.

Pʿarpecʿi — Lazar Pʿarpecʿi. *The History of Lazar Pʿarpecʿi.* Trans. Robert W. Thomson. Atlanta: Scholars Press, 1991.

PCR — Godman, Peter. *Poetry of the Carolingian Renaissance.* Norman: University of Oklahoma Press, 1985.

PDPMK — Malov, S. E., ed. and trans. *Pamiatniki drevnetiurskoi pis'mennosti Mongolii i Kirgizii.* Moscow-Leningrad: Izdatel'stvo akademi nauk SSSR, 1959.

Pelsaert — Pelsaert, Francisco. *Jahangir's India: The Remontrantie of Francisco Pelsaert.* Trans. W. H. Moreland and Pieter Geyl. Reprint Delhi: Idarah-i Adabiyat-i Delli, 1972.

Peng and Xu — Peng Daya and Xu Ting. *Heida shilue.* In *MGSL.*

PFT — Hallock, Richard T., trans. *Persepolis Fortification Tablets.* Chicago: University of Chicago Press, 1969.

PLDR — Dmitriev, L. A. and D. S. Likhachev, eds. *Pamiatniki literatury drevnei Rusi, XIV-seredina XV veka.* Moscow: Khudozhestvennaia literatury, 1981.

Pliny — Pliny. *Natural History.* Trans. H. Rockham and W. H. S. Jones. Loeb Classical Library. Cambridge, Mass.: Harvard University Press, 1960–67.

Pliny the Younger — Pliny the Younger. *Letters.* Trans. William Melmoth, New York: Macmillan, 1923.

Plutarch — *Plutarch's Lives.* Trans. Bernadotte Perrin. Loeb Classical Library. Cambridge, Mass.: Harvard University Press, 1954.

Plutarch, *Mor.* — Plutarch. *Moralia.* Trans Harold Cherniss and William C. Helmbold. Loeb Classical Library. Cambridge, Mass.: Harvard University Press, 1927.

PME — Casson, Lionel, trans. *The Periplus Maris Erythraei.* Princeton, N.J.: Princeton University Press, 1989.

Porphyrogenitus, *AI* — Constantine Porphyrogenitus. *De Administrando Imperio.* Ed. Gy. Moravcsik, trans. R. J. H. Jenkins. Washington, D.C.: Dumbarton Oaks and Harvard University, 1967.

Porphyrogenitus, *TT* — Constantine Porphyrogenitus. *Three Treatises on Imperial Military Expeditions.* Trans. John F. Haldon. Vienna: Verlag der Österreichischen Akademie der Wissenschaft, 1990.

PRDK — Demidova, N. F. and V. S. Miasnikov, eds. *Pervye russkie diplomaty v Kitae: "Rospis" I. Petlina i stateiny spisok F. J. Baikova.* Moscow: Nauka, 1966.

Procopius, *B.* — Procopius. *Buildings.* Trans. H. B. Dewing and Glanville Downey. Loeb Classical Library. Cambridge, Mass.: Harvard University Press, 1961.

Procopius, *HW* — Procopius. *History of the Wars.* Trans. H. B. Dewing. Loeb Classical Library. London: Heinemann, 1914.

Przhevalskii — Prejevalsky, N. *Mongolia, the Tangut Country and the Solitudes of Northern Tibet.* Trans. E. Delmar Morgan. Reprint New Delhi: Asian Educational Services, 1991. 2 vols.

Psellus — Psellus, Michael. *Fourteen Byzantine Rulers.* Trans. E. R. A. Sewter. New York: Penguin, 1984.

PSRL — *Polnoe sobranie russkikh letopisei.* Moscow: Iazyki russkoi kul'tury, 1997–2000. 3 vols. to date.

Purchas — Purchas, Samuel. *Hakluytus Posthumus or Purchas, his Pilgrimes.* Reprint New York: AMS Press, 1965. 20 vols.

PVL — *Povest vremennykh let po lavrent'evskoi letopisi.* 2nd ed. trans. and ed. D. S. Likhachev and V. P. Adrianovoi-Peretts. St. Petersburg: Nauka, 1996.

Qāshānī — Qāshānī, Abū al-Qasīm. *Ta'rīkh-i Ūljaytū.* Ed. M. Hambly, Tehran: B.T.N.K., 1969.

Qazvīnī, *NQ* — Qazvīnī, Ḥamd-Allāh Mustawfī. *The Zoological Section of the Nuzhat al-Qulūb.* Trans. J. Stephenson. London: Royal Asiatic Society, 1928.

Qazvīnī, *TG* — Qazvīnī, Ḥamd-Allah Mustawfī. *The Ta'rīkh-i guzīdah or Select History.* Trans. Edward G. Browne. Leiden: E.J. Brill and London: Luzac, 1913.

QC — Jones, William C., trans. *The Great Qing Code.* Oxford: Clarendon Press, 1994.

Quan Heng — Ch'üan Heng. *Das Keng-shen wai-shih: Eine Quelle zur späten Mongolenzeit.* Trans. Helmut Schulte-Uffelage. Berlin: Akademie Verlag, 1963.

Quintus Curtius — Quintus Curtius. *History of Alexander.* Trans. John C. Rolfe. Loeb Classical Library. Cambridge, Mass.: Harvard University Press, 1946.

Rashīd/A — Rashīd al-Dīn. *Jāmiʿ al-tavārīkh.* Ed. A. A. Alizade et al. Moscow: Nauka. Vols. I, II.

Rashīd/B — Rashīd al-Dīn. *The Successors of Genghis Khan.* Trans. John A. Boyle. New York: Columbia University Press.

Rashīd/J	Rashīd al-Dīn. *Die Geschichte der Oguzen.* Ed. and trans. Karl Jahn. Vienna: Herman Böhlaus, 1969.
Rashīd/K	Rashīd al-Dīn. *Jāmiʿ al-tavārīkh.* Ed. Karīmī. Tehran: Eqbal, 1959. 2 vols.
al-Rāvandī	al-Rāvandī, Muḥammad ibn ʿAlī. *Rāḥat al-ṣudūr va āyat al-ṣur ūr.* Ed. Muḥammad Iqbāl. London: Luzac, 1921.
REGK	Allen, W. E. D., ed. *Russian Embassies to the Georgian Kings (1589–1605).* Trans. Anthony Mango. Cambridge: Published for the Hakluyt Society, 1972. 2 vols.
RG	Moreland, W. H., ed. *Relations of Golconda in the Early Seventeenth Century.* Reprint Nendeln: Kraus Reprint, 1967.
RIO	Antonova, K. A. et al., eds. *Russko-Indiiskie otnosheniia v XVII v.: Sbornik dokumenty.* Moscow: Izdatel'stvo vostochnoi literatury, 1958.
Ripa	Ripa, Matteo. *Memoirs of Father Ripa During Thirteen Years Residence at the Court of Peking.* Reprint New York: AMS, 1979.
RKO	Demidova, N. F. and V. S. Miasnikov, eds. *Russko-Kitaiskie otnosheniia v XVIII veke: Materialy i dokumenty.* Moscow: Nauka, 1978. Vol. I.
Roe	Roe, Sir Thomas. *The Embassy of Sir Thomas Roe to the Court of the Great Mogul, 1615–1619.* Ed. William Foster. Reprint Nendeln: Kraus Reprint, 1967. 2 vols.
RPC	Cross, Samuel Hazzard and Olgerd P. Sherbowitz-Wetzor, trans. and eds. *The Russian Primary Chronicle, Laurentian Text.* Cambridge, Mass.: Medieval Academy of America, 1953.
RTC	Majeska, George P., trans. *Russian Travelers to Constantinople in the Fourteenth and Fifteenth Centuries.* Washington, D.C.: Dumbarton Oaks, 1984.
Rubruck	Jackson, Peter, trans. and David Morgan, ed. *The Mission of Friar William of Rubruck.* London: Hakluyt Society, 1990.
Rudra Deva	Rudra Deva. *Śyainika Śātram: The Art of Hunting in Ancient India.* Trans. M. M. Haraprasad Shastri. Delhi: Eastern Book Linkers, 1982.
Rust'haveli	Rust'haveli, Shot'ha. *The Man in the Panther's Skin.* Trans. Marjory Scott Wardrop. London: Luzac, 1966.
Rūzbihān	Minorsky, V., trans. *Persia in A.D. 1478–1490: An Abridged Translation of Fadlullāh b. Rūzbihān Khunjī's Tārīkh-i ʿĀlam-Ārā-yi Amīnī.* London: Royal Asiatic Society, 1957.
al-Ṣābi'	al-Ṣābi', Hilāl. *Rusūm Dār al-Khilāfah: The Rules and Regula-*

tions of the ʿAbbāsid Court. Trans. Elie A. Salem. Beirut: American University of Beirut, 1977.

al-Salmānī — Tāj al-Salmānī. *Šams al-Ḥusn: Eine Chronik vom Tode Timurs bis zum Jahre 1409 von Tağ al Salmānī*. Trans. Hans Robert Romer. Wiesbaden: Franz Steiner, 1956.

Samarqandī — Samarqandī, ʿAbd al-Razzāq. *Matla-ʿi Saʿdayn va Majmaʿ-i baḥrayn*. Ed. Muḥammad Shafī. Lahore: Chāpkhānah-i Gīlānī, 1941. Vol. II, part 1.

Sanderson — Sanderson, John. *The Travels of John Sanderson in the Levant, 1584–1602*. Ed. William Foster. Reprint Nendeln: Kraus Reprint, 1967.

SBM — Budge, Ernest A. Wallis, trans. *The Syriac Book of Medicines: Syrian Anatomy, Pathology and Therapeutics in the Early Middle Ages*. Reprint Amsterdam: APA-Philo Press, 1976. Vol. II.

SCBM — Franke, Herbert, trans. "Chinese Texts on the Jurchen: A Translation of the Jurchen Monograph in the *San-ch'ao pei-meng*." *Zentral-Asiatische Studien* 9 (1975): 119–86.

SCWSC — Palmer, Andrew, ed. and trans. *The Seventh Century in West Syrian Chronicles*. Liverpool: Liverpool University Press, 1993.

Sebēos — Sebēos. *History*. Trans. Robert Bedrosian. New York: Sources of the Armenian Tradition, 1985.

SGZ — *Sanguo zhi*. Beijing: Zhonghua shuju, 1982.

SH — de Rachewiltz, Igor, trans. *The Secret History of the Mongols: A Mongolian Epic Chronicle of the Thirteenth Century*. Leiden: E.J. Brill, 2004. 2 vols.

SH/I — de Rachewiltz, Igor, ed. *Index to the Secret History of the Mongols*. Indiana University Uralic and Altaic Series 121. Bloomington: Indiana University, 1972.

Shaw — Shaw, Robert. *Visits to High Tartary, Yarkand and Kashgar*. Hong Kong: Oxford University Press, 1988.

Sima Guang — Sima Guang. *Zizhi tongjian*. Beijing: Zhonghua shuju, 1956.

Sima Guang/C — de Crespigney, Rafe, trans. *To Establish Peace: Being the Chronicle of the Later Han for the Years 189–220 as Recorded in Chapters 59 to 69 of the Zizhi tongjian of Sima Guang*. Canberra: Faculty of Asian Studies, Australian National University, 1996.

SIRIO — *Sbornik imperatorkago russkago istoricheskago obshchestva*. Vol. 95, *Pamiatniki diplomaticheskie snoshenii moskovskago gosudarstva c Krymom, Nagaiami i Turtsieiu*, part 2, *1508–1521 vv.*, ed. G. O. Karpov and G. O. Shtendman. St. Petersburg, n.d.

SJ	Sima Qian. *Shiji.* Beijing: Zhonghu shuju, 1982.
SJH	Sima Qian. *Records of the Grand Historian: Han Dynasty.* Rev. ed. Trans. Burton Watson, New York: Columbia University Press, 1993. 2 vols.
SJQ	Sima Qian. *Records of the Grand Historian: Qin Dynasty.* Trans. Burton Watson. New York: Columbia University Press, 1993.
SJV	Kane, Daniel. *The Sino-Jurchen Vocabulary of the Bureau of Interpreters.* Indiana University Uralic and Altaic Series 153. Bloomington: Indiana University, 1989.
Skrine	Skrine, C. P. *Chinese Central Asia.* Reprint New York: Barnes and Noble, 1971.
SMCAC	Sawyer, Ralph D., trans. *The Seven Military Classics of Ancient China.* Boulder, Colo.: Westview Press, 1993.
SMOIZO	Tizengauzen, V., trans. *Sbornik materialov otnosiashchikhsia k istorii Zolotoi Ordy.* Vol. I, *Izvlecheniia iz sochinenii arabskikh.* St. Petersburg: Stroganov, 1884.
Song Yingxing	Sung Ying-sing. *Tien-kung-kai-wu: Exploitation of the Works of Nature.* Taibei: China Academy, 1980.
SOS	O'Kane, John, trans. *The Ship of Sulaiman.* New York: Columbia University Press, 1972.
SPI	*Slovo o polku Igoreve: Na russkom i angliiskom iazykakh.* Trans. Irina Petrova and Dmitry Likhachev. Moscow: Progress Publishers, 1981.
SS	*Songshi.* Beijing: Zhonghua shuju, 1977.
Strabo	Strabo. *The Geography of Strabo.* Trans. H. L. Jones. Loeb Classical Library. Cambridge, Mass.: Harvard University Press, 1967.
Sturluson	Sturluson, Snorri. *Heimskvingla: History of the Kings of Norway.* Trans. Lee M. Hollander. Austin: University of Texas Press, 1964.
Su Tianjue	Su Tianjue. *Yuan wenlei.* Taibei: Shijie shuju yingxing, 1967.
Suetonius	Suetonius. *The Lives of the Caesars.* Trans. John R. Rolfe. Loeb Classical Library. Cambridge, Mass.: Harvard University Press, 1935.
SWQZL	*Shengwu qinzheng lu.* In *MGSL.*
al-Ṭabarī	al-Ṭabarī. *The History of al-Ṭabarī.* Trans. various hands. Albany: State University of New York Press, 1985–99. 39 vols.
Tacitus, *Ann.*	Tacitus. *Annals.* Trans. John Jackson. Loeb Classical Library. Cambridge, Mass.: Harvard University Press, 1937.
Tacitus, *Ger.*	Tacitus. *Germania.* Trans. M. Hutton. Loeb Classical Library. Cambridge, Mass.: Harvard University Press, 1914.

Tacitus, *Hist.*	Tacitus. *Histories.* Trans. Clifford Moore. Loeb Classical Library. Cambridge, Mass.: Harvard University Press, 1925–31.
Tavernier	Tavernier, Jean-Baptiste. *Travels in India*, 2nd ed.. Trans. V. Ball. Oxford: Oxford University Press, 1925. 2 vols.
TDB	Poppe, Nicolas, trans. *The Twelve Deeds of Buddha: A Mongolian Version of the Latitavistara.* Seattle: University of Washington Press, 1967.
Teixeira	Teixeira, Pedro. *Travels of Pedro Teixeira.* Trans. William F. Sinclair. London: Printed for the Hakluyt Society, 1902.
TGPM	Howes, Robert Craig, trans. *The Testaments of the Grand Princes of Moscow.* Ithaca, N.Y.: Cornell University Press, 1967.
Thaʿālibī	Thaʿālibī. *The Book of Curious and Entertaining Information: The Latāf al-maʾārif.* Trans. C. E. Bosworth. Edinburgh: University of Edinburgh Press, 1968.
Theophanes	Theophanes. *The Chronicle of Theophanes.* Trans. Harry Turtledove. Philadelphia: University of Pennsylvania Press, 1982.
Theophylact	Theophylact Simocatta. *The History of Theophylact Simocatta.* Trans. Michael Whitby and Mary Whitby. Oxford: Clarendon Press, 1988.
TLC	Thorpe, Lewis, trans. *Two Lives of Charlemagne.* New York: Penguin, 1977.
TM	Minorsky, Vladimir, trans. *Tadhkirat al-Mulūk: A Manual of Safavid Administration.* Cambridge: Cambridge University Press, 1980.
TS	Gold, Milton, trans. *The Tārikh-e Sistan.* Rome: Istituto Italiano per il Medio ed Estremo Oriente, 1976.
TTK	Emmerick, R. E., trans. *Tibetan Texts Concerning Khotan.* London: Oxford University Press, 1967.
TTP	Alderly, Lord Stanley, ed. *Travels to Tana and Persia by Josafa Barbaro and Ambrogio Contarini.* London: Hakluyt Society Publications, 1873.
TTT	Bang, W. and A. von Gabain. "Türkische Turfan Texte," IV, "Ein neues uighurischen Sündenbekenntnis." *Preussische Akademie der Wissenschaften, Phil.-Hist. Klasse* 34 (1930): 432–50.
Tulishen	Tulishen. *Narrative of the Chinese Embassy to the Khan of the Tourgouth Tartars in the Years 1712, 13, 14 and 15.* Trans. George Thomas Staunton. Reprint Arlington, Va.: University Publications of America, 1976.
Twiti	Twiti, William. *The Art of Hunting, 1327.* Trans. Bror Danielsson. Stockholm: Almqvist & Wiksell, 1977.

TYH	Molé, Gabriella, ed. and trans. *The T'u-yü-hun from the Northern Wei to the Time of the Five Dynasties.* Rome: Istituto Italiano per il Medio ed Estremo Oriente, 1970.
al-ʿUmarī/L	al-ʿUmarī, Ibn Faẓl Allāh, *Das mongolische Weltreich: Al-ʿUmarīs Darstellung der Mongolischen Reiche in seinem Werke Masālik al-abṣār fī Mamālik al-amṣār.* Trans. Klaus Lech. Wiesbaden: Otto Harrassowitz, 1968.
al-ʿUmarī/S	al-ʿUmarā, Ibn Faẓl Allāh. *Ibn Faḍlallāh al-ʿOmarīs Bericht über Indien in einem Werke Masālik al-abṣār fī mamālik al-amṣār.* Trans. Otto Spies. Leipzig: Otto Harrassowitz, 1943.
Usāmah	Usāmah Ibn Munqidh. *An Arab-Syrian Gentleman and Warrior in the Period of the Crusades: Memoirs of Usāmah Ibn Munqidh.* Trans. Philip K. Hitti. Princeton University Press, 1987.
Varro	Varro, Marcus Terentius. *On Agriculture.* Trans. William Davis Hooper. Loeb Classical Library. Cambridge, Mass.: Harvard University Press, 1960.
Varthema	Varthema, Ludovico di. *The Travels of Ludovico di Varthema in Egypt, Syria, Arabia Deserta and Arabia Felix, in Persia, India, and Ethiopia, A.D. 1503–1508.* Trans. John Jones. London: Hakluyt Society, 1863.
Vis.	Wardrop, Oliver, trans. *Visramiani: The Story of the Loves of Vis and Ramin.* London: Royal Asiatic Society, 1966.
VMQC	Struve, Lynn A., trans. *Voices from the Ming-Qing Cataclysm.* New Haven, Conn.: Yale University Press, 1993.
VRTE	Solomon, Bernard S., trans. *The Veritable Record of the T'ang Emperor Shun-tsung.* Cambridge, Mass.: Harvard University Press, 1955.
Wallace	Wallace, Alfred Russell. *The Malay Archipelago.* Reprint New York: Dover, 1962.
William of Tyre	William of Tyre. *A History of Deeds Done beyond the Sea.* Trans. Emily Atwater Babcock and A. C. Krey. New York: Columbia University Press, 1943. 2 vols.
WS/H	Holmgren, Jennifer, trans. *The Annals of Tai: Early T'o-pa History according to the First Chapter of the Wei-shu.* Canberra: Australian National University Press, 1982.
WX	Xiao Tong, *Wen xuan or Selections of Refined Literature.* Trans. David Knechtges. Princeton, N.J.: Princeton University Press, 1982–87. 2 vols.
Xenophon, *Ana.*	Xenophon. *Anabasis.* Trans. Carleton L. Brownson. Loeb Classical Library. Cambridge, Mass.: Harvard University Press, 1992.

Xenophon, *Cav.*	Xenophon. *On the Cavalry Commander.* In Xenophon, *SM.*
Xenophon, *Cyn.*	Xenophon. *Cynegeticus.* In Xenohphon, *SM.*
Xenophon, *Cyr.*	Xenophon. *Cyropaedia.* Trans. Walter Miller. Loeb Classical Library. Cambridge, Mass.: Harvard University Press, 1994.
Xenophon, *Eq.*	Xenophon. *On the Art of Horsemanship.* In Xenophon, *SM.*
Xenophon, *Hell.*	Xenophon. *Hellenica.* Trans. Carleton L. Brownson. Loeb Classical Library. Cambridge, Mass.: Harvard University Press, 1961.
Xenophon, *Lac.*	Xenophon. *Constitution of the Lacedaemonians.* In Xenophon, *SM.*
Xenophon, *Oec.*	Xenophon. *Oeconomicus.* Trans. E. C. Marchant. Loeb Classical Library. Cambridge, Mass.: Harvard University Press, 1959.
Xenophon, *SM*	Xenophon, *Scripta Minora.* Trans. E. C. Marchart. Loeb Classical Library. Cambridge, Mass.: Harvard University Press, 1956.
XTS	*Xin Tangshu.* Beijing: Zhonghua shuju, 1975.
Xuanzang	Hiuen Tsiang. *Si-yu-ki: Buddhist Records of the Western World.* Trans. Samuel Beal. Reprint Delhi: Oriental Books Reprint, 1969. 2 vols.
Yang Xuanzhi	Yang Hsüan-chih. *A Record of Buddhist Monasteries in Lo-yang.* Trans. Yi-t'ung Wang. Princeton, N.J.: Princeton University Press, 1984.
Yang Yu	Yang Yü. *Beiträge zur Kulturgeschichte Chinas unter der Mongolenherrschaft: Das Shan-kü Sin-hua.* Trans. Herbert Franke. Wiesbaden: Franz Steiner, 1956.
YCS	Armstrong, Terence, ed. *Yermak's Campaign in Siberia: A Selection of Documents.* Trans. Tatiana Minorsky and David Wileman. London: Hakluyt Society, 1975.
YDZ	*Da Yuan shengzheng guochao dianzhang.* Reprint of the Yuan ed. Taibei: Guoli gugong bowu yuan, 1976.
Ye Longli	Ye Longli. *Qidan guoji.* Shanghai: Guji chubanshe, 1985.
YS	*Yuanshih.* Beijing: Zhonghua shuju, 1978.
Yūsuf	Yūsuf Khaṣṣ Ḥājib. *Wisdom of Royal Glory (Kutadgu Bilig): A Turko-Islamic Mirror for Princes.* Trans. Robert Dankoff. Chicago: University of Chicago Press, 1983.
ZA	Darmesteter, James, trans. *Zend-Avesta.* Reprint Delhi: Motilal Banarsidass, 1988. Vol. I.
ZGC	*Chan-kuo ts'e.* Rev. ed. Trans. J. I. Crump. Ann Arbor: Center for Chinese Studies, University of Michigan, 1996.

Zhao Hong	Zhao Hong. *Mengda beilu.* In *MGSL.*
Zhao Rugua	Chau Ju-kua. *His Work on the Chinese and Arab Trade in the Twelfth and Thirteenth Centuries, entitled Chu-fan-chi.* Trans. Friedrich Hirth and W. W. Rockhill. Reprint Taibei: Literature House, 1965.
Zosimus	Zosimus. *Historia Nova.* Trans. James T. Buchanan and Harold T. Davis. San Antonio: Trinity University Press, 1967.
ZT	Dondua, V. D., trans. *Zhizn tsaritsy tsarits Tamar.* Tbilisi: Izdatel'stvo "Metsniereba," 1985.
ZZ/W	Watson, Burton, trans. *The Tso Chuan: Selections from China's Oldest Narrative History.* New York: Columbia University Press, 1989.

Bibliography and Modern Scholarship

van Aarde, R. J. and Ann van Dyk

1986 "Inheritance of King Coat Colour Pattern in Cheetahs, *Acinonyx jubatus*." *Journal of Zoology: Proceedings of the Zoological Society of London* 209: 573–78.

Academy of Sciences MPR, ed.

1990 *Information Mongolia*. New York: Pergamon Press.

Adams, Daniel B.

1979 "The Cheetah: Native American." *Science* 205: 1155–58.

Adams, Douglas Q.

1999 *A Dictionary of Tocharian B*. Amsterdam: Rodopi.

Adamson, Joy

1969 *The Spotted Sphinx*. New York: Harcourt, Brace and World.

Ahsan, Muhammad Manazir

1979 *Social Life Under the Abbasids, 786–902 AD*. London: Longman.

Aigle, Denise

1997 "Le soufisme sunnite en Fārs: Shayh Amīn al-Dīn Balyānī." In Denise Aigle, ed., *L'Iran face à le domination mongole: études*. Tehran: Institut français de rechérche en Iran, pp. 231–60.

Akasoy, Anna

2000–2001 "Arabische Vorlagen der lateinischen Falknerieliteratur." *Beiruter Blätter* 8–9: 93–98.

Åkerström-Hougen, Gunilla

1981 "Falconry as a Motif in Early Swedish Art: Its Historical and Art Historical Significance." In Rudolf Zeitler, ed., *Les pays du Nord et Byzance (Scandinavie et Byzance): actes du colloque nordique et international de byzantinologie*. Uppsala: Almqvist and Wiksell, pp. 263–93.

Akhmedov, B. A.

1982 *Istoriia Balkh (XVI–pervaia polovine XVII v.)*. Tashkent: Fan.

Akurgal, Ekrem

1956 "Les fouilles de Dakyleion." *Anatolia* 1: 20–24.

Alexander, John T.

1989 *Catherine the Great, Life and Legend*. Oxford: Oxford University Press.

Allen, M. J. S. and G. R. Smith

1975 "Some Notes on Hunting Techniques and Practices in the Arabian Peninsula." *Arabian Studies* 2: 108–47.

Allen, W. E. D.

1961 "Trivia Historiae Ibericae, I. Gerfalcons for the King." *Bedi Karthlisa* 36–37: 104–10.

1971 *A History of the Georgian People*. London: Routledge.

Allsen, Thomas T.

1997 *Commodity and Exchange in the Mongol Empire: A Cultural History of Islamic Textiles.* Cambridge: Cambridge: Cambridge University Press.

Almond, Richard

2003 *Medieval Hunting.* Phoenix Mill: Sutton Publishing.

Altenmüller, Hartwig

1967 *Darstellungen der Jagd in alten Ägypten.* Hamburg and Berlin: Verlag Paul Parey.

Altherr, Thomas and John F. Reiger

1995 "Academic Historians and Hunting: A Call for More and Better Scholarship." *Environmental History Review* 19: 39–56.

Amiet, Pierre

1969 "Quelques ancêtres du chasseur royal d'Ugarit." *Ugaritica: études relatives aux découvertes de Ras Shamra*, vol. 6, Mission de Ras Shamra 17. Paris: Collège de France, Geuthner, 1–8.

Anderson, J. K.

1985 *Hunting in the Ancient World.* Berkeley: University of California Press.

Anderson, Robert T.

1971 *Traditional Europe: A Study in Anthropology and History.* Belmont, Calif.: Wadsworth.

Andreski, Stanislav

1971 *Military Organization and Society.* Berkeley: University of California Press.

Andrews, Peter Alford

1999 *Felt Tents and Pavilions: The Nomadic Tradition and Its Interaction with Princely Tentage.* 2 vols. London: Melisende.

Anson, John S.

1970 "The Hunt of Love: Gottfried von Strassburg's *Tristan* as Tragedy." *Speculum* 42: 594–607.

Anvarī, Hasan

1976 *Iṣṭilāhāt-i dīvānī dawrah-i Ghaznavī va Saljūqī.* Tehran: Kitabkhānah Ṭavūrī.

Aruz, Joan

1998 "Images of the Supernatural World: Bactria-Margiana Seals and Relations with the Near East and the Indus." *Ancient Civilizations from Scythia to Siberia* 5: 12–30.

Atkinson, Thomas

1993 "In Xanadu did Kubla Khan . . ." *Mongolia Society Newsletter* n.s. 13: 29–35.

Avery, Peter

1991 "Nādir Shāh and the Afsharid Legacy." In Peter Avery, Gavin Hambly, and Charles Melville, eds., *The Cambridge History of Iran*, vol. 7, *Nadir Shah to the Islamic Republic.* Cambridge: Cambridge University Press, pp. 3–62.

Azarpay, Guitty

1981 *Sogdian Painting: The Pictorial Epic in Oriental Art.* Berkeley: University of California Press.

Bachrach, Bernard S.

1983 "Charlemagne's Cavalry: Myth and Reality." *Military Affairs* 47: 1–20.

Back, Michael

1978 *Die Sassanidischen Staatsinschriften.* Acta Iranica 18. Leiden: E.J. Brill.

Baer, Eva

1967 The Suaire de St. Lazare." *Oriental Art* 13, 1: 36–49.

Bahari, Ebadollah

1996 *Bihzad: Master of Persian Painting.* London: I.B. Tauris.

Bailey, Harold W.

1982 *The Culture of the Sakas in Ancient Iranian Khotan.* Del Mar, Calif.: Caravan Books.

1985 *Khotanese Texts.* Vol. 7. Cambridge: Cambridge University Press.

Balter, Michael

1998 "Why Settle Down? The Mystery of Communities." *Science* 282: 1442–45.

Barber, Ian G.

1996 "Loss, Change and Monumental Landscaping: Toward a New Interpretation of the 'Classic' Maaori Emergence." *Current Anthropology* 37: 868–80.

Bardovskaya, L. V.

2002 "Hunting Pastimes at Tsarskoye Selo Menagerie." *State Historical Museum* 2002: 160–205.

Barnett, R. D.

1976 *Sculptures from the North Palace of Ashurbanipal of Assyria (688–627 B.C.).* London: British Museum Publications.

Barthold, W. (= V. V. Bartol'd)

1968 *Turkestan down to the Mongol Invasion.* 3rd ed. London: Luzac.

Bartol'd, V. V.

1963–77 *Sochineniia.* 9 vols. Moscow: Nauka.

1964 "Tseremonial pri dvore Uzbekskikh Khanov v XVIII veke." In his *Sochineniia,* vol. 2, pt. 2: 388–99.

1968 *Dvenadtsat lektsii po istorii Turetskikh narodov srednei Azii.* In his *Sochineniia,* vol. 5: 17–192.

Bates, Marston

1956 "Man as an Agent in the Spread of Organisms." In William L. Thomas, ed., *Man's Role in Changing the Face of the Earth.* Chicago: University of Chicago Press, pp. 788–804.

Bauwe, Renate

1993 "Jagdkult und seine Reflexion in der mongolischen Dichtung." In Barbara Kellner-Heinkele, ed., *The Concept of Sovereignty in the Altaic World.* Wiesbaden: Otto Harrassowitz, pp. 11–22.

Bawden, Charles R.

1968 "Mongol Notes, II. Some Shamanist Hunting Rituals from Mongolia." *Central Asiatic Journal* 12, 2: 101–43.

Bazin, Louis

1957 "Noms de la 'chèvre' en Turc et en Mongol." In *Studia Altaica: Festschrift für Nikolas Poppe zum 60. Geburtstag.* Wiesbaden: Otto Harrassowitz, pp. 28–32.

1971 "Les noms turcs de l 'aigle'." *Turcica* 3: 128–32.

Beach, Milo Cleveland

1997 *King of the World: The Padshahnama.* Washington, D.C.: Smithsonian Institution.

Beckwith, Christopher I.

1987 *The Tibetan Empire in Central Asia.* Princeton, N.J.: Princeton University Press.

Benn, Charles

2002 *China's Golden Age: Everyday Life in the Tang Dynasty.* Oxford: Oxford University Press.

Benveniste, Emile

1954 "Elements perses en araméen d'Egypte." *Journal Asiatique* 242: 297–310.

Beshevliev, Veselin

1979 *P'rvob'lgarski nadpisi.* Sofia: Izdatelstvo na B'lgarskata Akademiia na Naukite.

Beveridge, Henry

1900 "Meaning of the Word *nihilam.*" *Journal of the Royal Asiatic Society*: 137–38.

Beynen, G. Koolemans

1990 "The Symbolism of the Leopard in the *Vepkhist 'Q'aosani.*" *Annual of the Society for the Study of Caucasia* 2: 33–42.

Bielenstein, Hans

1976 "Lo-yang in Later Han Times." *Bulletin of the Museum of Far Eastern Antiquities* 48: 1–142.

1980 *The Bureaucracy of Han Times.* Cambridge: Cambridge University Press.

Bird-David, Nurit

1990 "The Giving Environment: Another Perspective on the Economic System of Gatherer-Hunters." *Current Anthropology* 31: 189–96.

1992 "Beyond the Original Affluent Society." *Current Anthropology* 33: 25–47.

Birrell, Jean

1982 "Who Poached the King's Deer? A Study in Thirteenth Century Crime." *Midland History* 7: 9–25.

Bivar, A. D. H.

1969 *Catalogue of Western Asiatic Seals in the British Museum: Stamp Seals.* Vol. 2, *The Sassanian Dynasty.* London: British Museum.

1972 "Cavalry Equipment and Tactics on the Euphrates Frontier." *Dumbarton Oaks Papers* 26: 271–91.

Blake, Stephen P.

1979 "The Patrimonial-Bureaucratic Empire of the Mughals." *Journal of Asia Studies* 29, 1: 77–94.

1983 "The Hierarchy of Central Places in North India During the Mughal Period of Indian History." *South Asia* 6, 1: 1–32.

Blüchel, Kurt G., ed.

1997 *Game and Hunting.* 2 vols. Cologne: Köneman.

Bodenheimer, F. S.

1960 *Animal and Man in Bible Lands.* Leiden: E.J. Brill.

Boodberg, Peter A.

1979 *Selected Works of Peter A. Boodberg.* Berkeley: University of California Press.

Bosworth, Clifford Edmund

1963 *The Ghaznavids: Their Empire in Afghanistan and Eastern Iran.* Edinburgh: Edinburgh University Press.

1973 The Heritage of Rulership in Early Islamic Iran and the Search for Dynastic Connection with the Past." *Iran* 11: 51–62.

Böttger, Walter
1956 "Jagdmagie im alten China: ein Beitrag zur Geschichte der Jagd in China." In Helga Steininger, Hans Steininger and Ulrich Unger, eds., *Sino-Japonica: Festschrift André Wedemeyer zum 80. Geburtstag*. Leipzig: Otto Harrasowitz, pp. 9–14.
Bower, Virginia L.
1991 "Polo in Tang China: Sport and Art." *Asian Art* 4, 1: 23–45.
Bowlus, Charles R.
1980 "Ecological Crises in Fourteenth Century Europe." In Lester J. Bilsky, ed., *Historical Ecology: Essays on Environment and Social Change*. Port Washington, Wash.: Kennikat Press, pp. 81–99.
Boyce, Mary
1982 *A History of Zoroastrianism*. Vol. 2. Leiden: E.J. Brill.
Boyer, Abel and Maurice Planiol
1948 *Traité de fauconnerie et autourserie*. Paris: Payot.
Boyle, John A.
1968 A Mongol Hunting Ritual." In *Jagd* 1968, pp. 1–9.
1969 "A Eurasian Hunting Ritual." *Folklore* 80: 12–16.
1972 "The Seasonal Residences of the Great Khan Ögedei." *Central Asiatic Journal* 16: 125–31.
1978 "The Attitude of the Thirteenth Century Mongols Toward Nature." *Central Asiatic Journal* 22: 177–85.
Bradshaw, John L.
1988 "The Evolution of Human Lateral Asymmetrics: New Evidence and Second Thoughts." *Journal of Human Evolution* 17: 615–37.
Brancaccio, Pia
1999 "Angulimāla and the Taming of the Forest." *East and West* 49: 105–18.
Braudel, Fernand
1958 "Histoire et sciences sociales: la longue durée." *Annales: économies, sociétés, civilizations* 13, no. 4: 725–53.
1985–86 *Civilization and Capitalism, 15th-18th Centuries*. 3 vols. New York: Harper and Row.
Braund, David
1994 *Georgia in Antiquity: A History of Colchis and Transcausian Iberia 550 BC–AD 562*. Oxford: Clarendon Press.
Bregel, Yuri
2000 *The Administration of Bukhara Under the Manghits and Some Tashkent Manuscripts*. Papers on Inner Asia 34. Bloomington: Indiana University, Research Institute for Inner Asian Studies.
Brentjes, Burchard
1965 *Die Haustierwerdung im Orient*. Wittenburg: A. Ziemsen.
Brewer, Douglas J., Donald B. Redford, and Susan Redford
1994 *Domestic Plants and Animals: The Egyptian Origins*. Warminister: Aris and Phillips.
Briant, Pierre
1982 "Forces productives, dépendance rurale et idéologies religieuses dans l'empire Acheménides." In his *Rois, tributs et paysans*. Paris: Belles lettres, pp. 432–73.

Brockway, Lucile
1983 "Plant Imperialism." *History Today* 33: 31–36.
Broder, Jonathan
1998 "Tangier." *Smithsonian* 9, 4: 90–100.
Browning Robert
1961 "Death of John II Comnenus." *Byzantion* 31: 229–35.
Brunhes, Jean
1920 *Human Geography*. Chicago: Rand McNally.
Brunnert, H. S. and V. V. Hagelstrom
1912 *Present Day Political Organization of China*. Shanghai: Kellog and Walsh.
Bunzel, Ruth
1938 "The Economic Organization of Primitive People." In Franz Boas, ed., *General Anthropology*. New York: D.C. Heath, pp. 327–408.
Burkert, Walther
1992 *The Orientalizing Revolution: Near Eastern Influence on Greek Culture in the Early Archaic Age*. Cambridge, Mass: Harvard University Press.
Burton, Audrey
1993 *Bukharan Trade, 1558–1718*. Papers on Inner Asia 23. Bloomington: Indiana University, Research Institute for Inner Asian Studies.
Bushell, S. W.
1873 "Notes on the Old Mongolian Capital of Shangtu." *Journal of the Royal Asiatic Society* n.s. 7: 329–38.
Campany, Robert Ford
1996 *Strange Writings: Anomaly Accounts in Early Medieval China*. Albany: State University of New York Press.
Cannadine, David
1990 *The Decline and Fall of the British Aristocracy*. New Haven, Conn.: Yale University Press.
Cannadine, David and Simon Price, eds.
1987 *Rituals of Royalty: Power and Ceremonial in Traditional Societies*. Cambridge: Cambridge University Press.
Cantor, L. M. and J. Hatherly
1979 "The Medieval Parks of England." *Geography* 64: 71–85.
Capart, Jean
1930 "Falconry in Ancient Egypt." *Isis* 14: 222.
Caras, Roger
1996 *A Perfect Harmony: The Intertwining Lives of Animals and Humans Throughout History*. New York: Simon and Schuster.
Caro, T. M.
1987 "Indirect Costs of Play: Cheetah Cubs Reduce Maternal Hunting Success." *Animal Behavior* 35: 295–97.
1994 *Cheetahs of the Serengeti Plains: Group Living in an Asocial Species*. Chicago: University of Chicago Press.
Caro, T. M. and D. A. Collins
1987a "Male Cheetah Social Organization and Territoriality." *Ethology* 74: 56–64.
1987b "Ecological Characteristics of Territories of Male Cheetahs (*Acinonyx jubatus*)." *Journal of Zoology: Proceedings of the Zoological Society of London* 211: 89–105.

Caro, T. M. and M. Karen Laurenson
1994 "Ecological and Genetic Factors in Conservation: A Cautionary Tale." *Science* 263: 485–86.
Carroll-Spillecke, Maureen
1992 "The Gardens of Greece from Homeric to Roman Times." *Journal of Garden History* 12: 84–101.
Carter, George F.
1988 "Cultural Historical Diffusion." In Peter J. Hugill and D. Bruce Dickson, eds., *The Transfer and Transformation of Ideas and Material Culture*. College Station: Texas A. & M. University Press, pp. 3–22.
Cartmill, Matt
1993 *A View to Death in the Morning: Hunting and Nature Through History*. Cambridge, Mass.: Harvard University Press.
Cassels, Richard
1984 "Faunal Extinction and Prehistoric Man in New Zealand and the Pacific Islands." In Martin and Klein, eds. 1984, pp. 741–67.
Cassin, Elena
1981 "Le roi et le lion." *Revue de l'histoire des religions* 198: 355–401.
Chan, Hok-lam
1967 "Liu Ping-chung (1216–74): A Buddhist-Taoist Statesman at the Court of Khubilai Khan." *T'oung-pao* 53: 98–146.
Chang Kwang-chih
1980 *Shang Civilization*. New Haven, Conn.: Yale University Press.
Chenciner, Robert and Magomedkhan Magomedkhanov
1992 "Persian Exports to Russia from the Sixteenth to the Nineteenth Century." *Iran* 30: 123–30.
Chia, Ning
1993 "The Lifanyuan and the Inner Asian Rituals in the Early Qing." *Late Imperial China* 14, no. 1: 60–92.
Chiodo, Elisabetta
1992 "The Horse White-as-Egg (*öndegen chaghan*): A Study of Consecrating Animals to Deities." *Ural-Altaische Jahrbücher* n.s. 11: 125–51.
Christensen, Arthur
1944 *L'Iran sous les Sassanides*. 2nd ed., rev. Copenhagen: Ijnar Munksgaard.
Christian, David
1991 "The Case for 'Big History'." *Journal of World History* 2: 223–38.
1998 *A History of Russia, Central Asia and Mongolia*. Vol. 1, *Inner Asia from Prehistory to the Mongol Empire*. Oxford: Blackwell.
2000 "Silk Roads or Steppe Roads? The Silk Roads in World History." *Journal of World History* 11: 1–26.
Chung, Saehyang P.
1998–99 "The Sui-Tang Eastern Palace in Chang'an: Toward a Reconstruction of Its Plans." *Artibus Asiae* 58: 5–31.
Ciggaar, Krijne
1986 "Byzantine Marginalia to the Norman Conquest." *Anglo-Norman Studies* 9: 43–63.

Clagett, Marshall

1992 *Ancient Egyptian Science.* Vol. 1. Philadelphia: American Philosophical Society.

Clark, Grahame

1986 *Symbols of Excellence: Precious Materials as Expressions of Status.* Cambridge: Cambridge University Press.

Clark, Stuart

1985 "The *Annales* Historians." In Quentin Skinner, ed., *The Return of Grand Theory in the Human Sciences.* Cambridge: Cambridge University Press, pp. 179–98.

Clausen, Sir Gerard

1968 "Some Old Turkic Words Connected with Hunting." In *Jagd* 1968, pp. 9–17.

1972 *An Etymological Dictionary of Pre-Thirteenth-Century Turkish.* Oxford: Clarendon Press.

Cleaves, Francis W.

1957 "The 'Fifteen Palace Poems' by K'o Chiu-ssu." *Harvard Journal of Asiatic Studies* 20: 391–479.

1978 "The Mongolian Locution *Aman Mergen* in the *Koryŏ sa.*" *Harvard Journal of Asiatic Studies* 38: 439–47.

Clermont-Ganneau, L.

1921 "Paradeisos royal Achéménide de Sidon." *Revue biblique* 30: 106–9.

Clutton-Brock, Juliet

1984 "The Master of Game: The Animals and Rituals of Medieval Venery." *Biologist* 31, 3: 167–71.

1989 *A Natural History of Domesticated Mammals.* Austin: University of Texas Press.

1995 "Origins of the Dog: Domestication and Early History." In Serpell, 1995, pp. 7–20.

Cohen, Mark Nathan

1989 *Health and the Rise of Civilization.* New Haven, Conn.: Yale University Press.

Colley, Linda

1992 *Britons: Forging the Nation, 1707–1827.* New Haven, Conn.: Yale University Press.

Collins, Randall

1992 *Sociological Insight: An Introduction to Non-Obvious Sociology.* 2nd ed. Oxford: Oxford University Press.

Conan, Michael

1986 "Nature into Art: Gardens and Landscapes in Everyday Life of Ancient Rome." *Journal of Garden History* 6: 348–56.

Coon, Carleton S.

1971 *The Hunting Peoples.* Boston: Little, Brown.

Cowen, Jill Sanchia

1989 *Kalila wa Dimna: An Animal Allegory of the Mongol Court.* Oxford: Oxford University Press.

Cummins, John

1988 *The Hound and the Hawk: The Art of Medieval Hunting.* New York: St. Martin's Press.

Dale, Stephen F.

2003 "A Safavid Poet in the Heart of Darkness: The Indian Poems of Ashraf Mazandarani." *Iranian Studies* 36, 2: 197–212.

Dandamaev, Muhammad A.
1984 "Royal Paradeisos in Babylonia." *Acta Iranica* 2nd ser. 9: 113–17.
1992 *Iranians in Achaemenid Babylonia*. Costa Mesa, Calif.: Mazda Publishers.
Dandamaev, Muhammad A. and Vladimir G. Lukonin
1989 *The Culture and Social Institutions of Ancient Iran*. Cambridge: Cambridge University Press.
Daniel, Glyn
1967 *The Origin and Growth of Archaeology*. New York: Cromwell.
Dankoff, Robert
1971 "Baraq and Burāq." *Central Asiatic Journal* 15: 102–17.
Darby, H. C.
1976a "Domesday England." In Darby 1976b, pp. 39–74.
Darby, H. C., ed.
1976b *A New Historical Geography of England Before 1600*. Cambridge: Cambridge University Press, pp. 39–74.
Davis, Simon J. M.
1987 *The Archaeology of Animals*. New Haven, Conn.: Yale University Press.
Decker, Wolfgang
1992 *Sports and Games of Ancient Egypt*. New Haven, Conn.: Yale University Press.
Dementieff, Georges
1945 "La fauconnerie en Russe: Esquisse historique." *L'oiseau et la revue française d'ornithologie* 15: 9–39.
Devèze, Michel
1966 "Forêts françaises et forêts allemandes: étude historique comparée (1re partie)." *Revue historique* 235: 347–80.
De Weese, Devin
1994 *Islamization and Native Religion in the Golden Horde: Buba Tükles and Conversion to Islam in Historical and Epic Tradition*. University Park: Pennsylvania State University Press.
Diamond, Jared
1984 "Historic Extinctions: A Rosetta Stone for Understanding Prehistoric Extinctions." In Martin and Klein, eds. 1984, pp. 824–62.
Di Cosmo, Nicola, ed.
2002 *Warfare in Inner Asian History (500–1800)*. Leiden: E.J. Brill.
Divyabhanusinh
1987 "Record of Two Unique Observations of the Indian Cheetah in the *Tuzuk-i Jahangiri*." *Journal of the Bombay Natural History Society* 84: 269–74.
Dixon, Roland B.
1928 *The Building of Cultures*. New York: Scribner's.
Doerfer, Gerhard
1963–75 *Türkische und Mongolische Elemente im Neupersischen*. 4 vols. Wiesbaden: Franz Steiner.
Dozy, R. P. A.
1991 *Supplément aux dictionnaires arabes*. 2 vols. 1881. Reprint Beirut: Librairie du Liban.

Drews, Robert

1993 *The End of the Bronze Age: Changes in Warfare and the Catastrophe ca 1200 B.C.* Princeton, N.J.: Princeton University Press.

Duby, Georges

1974 *The Early Growth of the European Economy.* Ithaca, N.Y.: Cornell University Press.

Duichev, Ivan

1985 *Kiril and Methodius: Founders of Slavonic Writing.* Boulder Colo.: East European Monographs.

Dupree, Nancy Hatch

1979 "T'ang Tombs in Chien County China." *Archaeology* 32, 4: 34–44.

Duyvendak, J. J. L.

1938 "The True Dates of the Chinese Maritime Expeditions in the Early Fifteenth Century." *T'oung-pao* 34: 341–412.

Eastmond, Antony

1998 *Royal Imagery in Medieval Georgia.* University Park: Pennsylvania State University Press.

Eaton, Randall L.

1974 *The Cheetah: The Biology, Ecology and Behavior of an Endangered Species.* New York: Van Nostrand Reinhold.

Eberhard, Wolfram

1942 *Lokalkulturen im alten China.* Vol. 1, *Die Lokalkulturen des Nordens und Westens.* Leiden: E.J. Brill.

1948 "Remarks on *Siralya.*" *Oriens* 1: 220–21.

1968 *The Local Cultures of South and East China.* Leiden: E.J. Brill.

Ebrey, Patricia

1986 "The Economic and Social History of the Later Han." In Denis Twitchett and Michael Loewe, eds., *The Cambridge History of China,* vol. 1, *The Ch'in and Han.* Cambridge: Cambridge University Press, pp. 608–48.

Ehrenreich, Barbara

1997 *Blood Rites: Origins and History of the Passions of War.* New York: Metropolitan Books.

Eisenstein, Herbert

1994 "Der *amīr šikār* unter den Mamlukensultanen." In Cornelia Munch, ed., *Deutscher Orientalistentag, Vorträge.* ZDMG, suppl. 10. Munich: Franz Steiner, pp. 129–35.

Eliade, Mircea

1974 *Shamanism: Archaic Techniques of Ecstasy.* Princeton, N.J.: Princeton University Press.

Elias, Norbert

1994 *The Civilizing Process.* Oxford: Blackwell.

Elliot, Mark C.

2001 *The Manchu Way: The Eight Banners and Ethnic Identity in Late Imperial China.* Stanford, Calif.: Stanford University Press.

Elvin, Mark

1993 "Three Thousand Years of Unsustainable Development: China's Environment from Archaic Times to the Present." *East Asian History* 6: 7–46.

Emery, F. V.
1973 "England Circa 1600." In Darby 1976b, pp. 238–301.
Epstein, Hans J.
1942–43 "The Origin and Early History of Falconry." *Isis* 34: 497–508.
1971 *The Origins of the Domesticated Animals of Africa.* Vol. 1. New York: Africana Publishing Company.
Ergert, Bernd E.
1997 "Early Treatises on Hunting." In Blüchel 1997, 1: 102–31.
Ergert, Bernd E. and Martinus Martin
1997 "Talismans and Trophies." In Blüchel 1997, 1: 238–41.
Erkes, Eduard
1943 "Vogelzucht im alten China." *T'oung-pao* 37: 15–34.
Ermolov, Leonid B.
1989 "Principal Tendencies in the Development of Hunting in Ancient and Traditional Nomadic Societies." In Seaman 1989, pp. 105–8.
Esin, E.
1968 "The Hunter Prince in Turkish Iconography." In *Jagd* 1968, pp. 18–76.
Ettinghausen, Richard
1979 "Bahram Gur's Hunting Feats or a Problem of Identification." *Iran* 17: 25–31.
Ewig, E.
1963 "Résidences et capitale pendant le haut Moyen Age." *Revue historique* 230: 25–72.
Fagan, Brian
1987 *The Great Journey: The Peopling of Ancient America.* London: Thames and Hudson.
Falk, Nancy E.
1973 "Wilderness and Kingship in Ancient South Asia." *History of Religions* 13: 1–15.
Farmer, Edward L.
1995 *Zhu Yuanzhang and Early Ming Legislation.* Leiden: E.J. Brill.
Farquhar, David
1957 "Oirat-Chinese Tribute Relations." In *Studia Altaica: Festschrift für Nikolaus Poppe zum 60. Geburtstag am 8. August 1957.* Wiesbaden: Otto Harrassowitz, pp. 60–68.
Fasmer, M.
1971 *Etimologicheskii slovar russkogo iazyka.* 4 vols. Moscow: Progress.
Fauth, Wolfgang
1979 "Der königliche Gärtner und Jäger in Paradeisos: Beobachtungen zur Rolle des Herrschers in der vorderasiatischer Hortikultur." *Persica* 8: 1–53.
Fekhner, M. V.
1956 *Torgovlia russkogo gosudarstva s stranami Vostoka v XVI veke.* Moscow: Goskul'tprosvetizdat.
Fiennes, Richard and Alice Fiennes
1970 *The Natural History of Dogs.* Garden City, N.Y.: The Natural History Press.
Finch, C., ed.
1999 *Mongolia's Wild Heritage: Biological Diversity, Protected Areas and Conservation in the Land of Chingis Khaan.* Boulder, Colo.: Avery Press.

Findley, Ellison B.

1987 "Jahāngīr's Vow of Non-Violence." *Journal of the American Oriental Society* 107: 245–56.

Fiskesjö, Magnus

2001 "Rising from Blood-Stained Fields: Royal Hunting and State Formation in Shang China." *Bulletin of the Museum of Far Eastern Antiquities* 73: 48–191.

Flint, Valerie I. J.

1991 *The Rise of Magic in Early Medieval Europe.* Princeton, N.J.: Princeton University Press.

Foote, Peter and David M. Wilson

1979 *The Viking Achievement: The Society and Culture of Early Medieval Scandinavia.* London: Sedgwick and Jackson.

Foster, Karen Polinger

1999 "The Earliest Zoos and Gardens." *Scientific American* 281, 1: 64–71.

Fox, John Gerard

1996 "Playing with Power: Ball Courts and Political Ritual in Southern Mesoamerica." *Current Anthropology* 37: 483–509 with invited commentary.

Fox, Robin Lane

1987 *Pagans and Christians.* New York: Knopf.

Franke, Herbert

1987 *Studien und Texts zur Kriegsgeschichte der südlichen Sungzeit.* Weisbaden: Otto Harrassowitz.

Friederichs, Heinz F.

1933 "Zur Kenntnis der frühgeschichtlichen Tier Welt Südestasiens." *Alte Orient* 32, 3–4: 1–45.

Friedmann, Herbert

1980 *A Bestiary for Saint Jerome: Animal Symbolism in European Religious Art.* Washington, D.C.: Smithsonian Institution Press.

Frye, Richard N.

1983 *The History of Ancient Iran.* Munich: C.H. Beck.

Gabain, A. v.

1973 *Das Leben im uigurischen Königreich von Qočo (850–1250), Tafelbund.* Wiesbaden: Otto Harrassowitz.

Gadgil, Madhav and Romila Thapar.

1990 "Human Ecology in India: Some Historical Perspectives." *Interdisciplinary Science Reviews* 15: 209–23.

Galdanova, G. P.

1981 "Le culte de la chasse chez Buriates." *Études mongoles et sibériennes* 12: 153–62.

Gamble, Clive

1993 *The Timewalkers: The Prehistory of Global Colonization.* Cambridge, Mass.: Harvard University Press.

Gardiner, E. Norman

1907 "Throwing the Javelin." *Journal of Hellenic Studies* 29: 249–73.

Garsoian, Nina G.

1981 "The Locus of the Death of Kings: Iranian Armenia-the Invented Image." In R. G. Hovanissian, ed., *The Armenian Image in History and Literature.* Malibu, Calif.: Undena, pp. 27–64.

Gaudefroy-Demombynes, Maurice
1923 *Le pèlerinage à la Mekke: étude d'histoire religieuse*. Paris: Geuthner.
Geiss, James
1987 "The Leopard Quarter During the Cheng-te Reign." *Ming Studies* 24: 1–38.
1988 "The Cheng-te Reign, 1506–1521." In Frederick W. Mote and Denis Twitchett, eds., *The Cambridge History of China*, vol. 7, pt. 1, *The Ming Dynasty*. Cambridge: Cambridge University Press, pp. 403–39.
Gelb, Ignace et al., eds.
1985 *The Assyrian Dictionary*, vol. 12. Chicago: Oriental Institute.
Gellner, Ernest
1988 *Plough, Sword, and Book: The Structure of Human History*. Chicago: University of Chicago Press.
Genito, B.
1995–97 "The Early Medieval Cemetery in Vincenne (Molise)." *Archivum Eurasiae Medii Aevi* 9: 73–98.
Gentelle, Pierre
1981 "Un 'paradis' hellénistique en Jordanie: étude de geo-archéologie." *Herodite* 1: 64–101.
Gerardi, Pamela
1988 "Epigraphs and Assyrian Palace Reliefs: The Development of Epigraphic Text." *Journal of Cuneiform Studies* 40, 1: 1–35.
Gernet, Jacques
1962 *Daily Life in China on the Eve of the Mongol Invasion*. Stanford, Calif.: Stanford University Press.
1985 *China and the Christian Impact: A Conflict of Cultures*. Cambridge: Cambridge University Press.
1995 *Buddhism in Chinese Society: An Economic History from the Fifth to the Tenth Centuries*. New York: Columbia University Press.
Gharib, B.
1995 *Sogdian Dictionary (Sogdian-Persian-English)*. Tehran: Farhangan Publications.
Ghirshman, Roman
1955 "Notes iraniennes VI: une coupe sassanide à scene de chasse." *Artibus Asiae* 18: 5–19.
1962 *Persian Art: The Parthian and Sassanian Dynasties, 249 B.C.–A.D. 651*. New York: Golden Press.
Gibb, H. A. R.
1970 *The Arab Conquests in Central Asia*. 1923. Reprint New York: AMC Press.
Gignoux, Ph.
1983 "La chasse dans l'Iran sasanide." In Gherardo Groli, ed., *Iranian Studies*. Orientalia Romana 5. Rome: Istituto Italiano per il Medio ed Estremo Oriente, pp. 101–18.
Gilbert, Lucien
1934 *Dictionnaire historique et géographique de la Mandchourie*. Hong Kong: Imprimerie de la Société des Missions-Estrangères.
Glacken, Clarence J.
1990 *Traces on the Rhodian Shore: Nature and Culture in Western Thought from Ancient Times to the End of the Eighteenth Century*. Berkeley: University of California Press.

Glasier, Phillip

1998 *Falconry and Hawking.* 3rd ed. New York: Overlook Press.

Gnoli, Gherardo

1990 "On Old Persian *Farnah.*" *Acta Iranica* 3rd ser. 30: 83–92.

Golden, Peter B.

1980 *Khazar Studies: An Historico-Philological Inquiry into the Origins of the Khazars,* vol. 1. Budapest: Akadémiai Kiadó.

1982 "Imperial Ideology and the Sources of Unity Among the Pre-Činggisid Nomads of Western Eurasia." *Archivum Eurasiae Medii Aevi* 2: 37–76.

1997 "Wolves, Dogs and Qipchaq Religion." *Acta Orientalia Academiae Scientiarum Hungaricae* 50: 87–97.

1998–99 "The Nomadic Linguistic Impact on Pre-Čінggisid Rus' and Georgia," *Archivum Eurasiae Medii Aevi* 10: 72–97.

2002 "War and Warfare in the Pre-Činggisid Western Steppe of Eurasia." In Di Cosmo 2002, pp. 105–72.

Gommans, Jos.

1998 "The Silent Frontier of South Asia, c. A.D. 1100–1800." *Journal of World History* 9: 1–24.

Goody, Jack

1993 *The Culture of Flowers.* Cambridge: Cambridge University Press.

Goudsblom, Johan

1992 "The Civilizing Process and the Domestication of Fire." *Journal of World History* 3: 1–13.

Gouraud, Jean-Louis

1990 "Les derniers aigliers: notes d'un voyage au Kazakhstan." *Études mongoles & sibériennes* 21: 123–35.

Graff, David A.

2002 "Strategy and Contingency in the Tang Defeat of the Eastern Turks, 629–630." In Di Cosmo 2002, pp. 33–71.

Grant, Christina Philip

1937 *The Syrian Desert: Caravans, Travel and Exploration.* London: A. & C. Black.

Gryaznov, Mikhail

1969 *South Siberia.* London: Cresset Press.

Gukovskii, M. H.

1963 "Soobshchenie o Rossii Moskovskogo posla v Milan (1486 g.)." In S. N. Valk, ed., *Voprosy istoriografii i istochnikovedeniia istorii SSSR: Sbornik statei.* Moscow Leningrad: Izdatel'stvo akademii nauk SSSR, pp. 648–55.

Guo, Dashun

1995 "Hongshan and Related Cultures." In Sarah M. Nelson, ed., *The Archaeology of Northeast China.* London: Routledge, pp. 21–64.

Haas, Jonathan

1982 *The Evolution of the Prehistoric State.* New York: Columbia University Press.

el-Habashi, Zaki

1992 *Tutankhamen and the Sporting Traditions.* New York: Peter Lang.

Haenisch, Erich

1935 "Die Abteilung 'Jagd' im Fünfsprachigen Wörterspiegel." *Asia Major* 10: 59–93.

1959 "Die Jagdgesetze im Mongolischen Ostreich." In Inge Lore Kluge, ed., *Ostasiatische Studien*. Berlin: Akademie Verlag, pp. 85–93.

Hamayon, Roberte N.

1994 "Shamanism in Siberia: From Partnership in Supernature to Counter Power in Society." In Nicholas Thomas and Caroline Humphrey, eds., *Shamanism, History, and the State*. Ann Arbor: University of Michigan Press, pp. 76–89.

Hamilton, James Russell

1955 *Les Ouïghours à l'époque des cinq dynasties d'après les documents chinois*. Paris: Imprimerie nationale.

Hammond, Charles E.

1991 "An Excursion in Tiger Lore." *Asia Major* 3rd ser. 4, 1: 87–100.

1996 "The Righteous Tiger and the Grateful Lion." *Monumenta Serica* 43: 191–211.

Han Baoquan, ed.

1997 *Tang Jinxiang xianzhu mu caihui taoyang*. Xi'an: Shaanxi Luyou Chubanshe.

Hanaway, William L.

1971 "The Concept of the Hunt in Persian Literature." *Boston Museum Bulletin* 69: 21–35.

Hanna, Judith Lynne

1977a "African Dance and the Warrior Tradition." *Journal of Asian and African Studies* 12: 111–33.

1977b "To Dance is Human." In John Blacking, ed., *The Anthropology of the Body*. London: Academic Press, pp. 211–32.

Hargett, James M.

1988–89 "Huizong's Magic Marchmount: The Genyue Pleasure Park of Kaifeng." *Monumenta Serica* 38: 1–48

1989 "The Pleasure Parks of Kaifeng and Lin'an During the Song (960–1279)." *Chinese Culture* 30: 61–78.

Harmatta, J.

1951 "The Golden Bow of the Huns." *Acta Archaeologica Academiae Scientiarum Hungaricae* 1: 107–49.

Harper, Prudence Oliver

1978 *The Royal Hunter: Art of the Sasanian Empire*. New York: Asia Society.

1983 "Sasanian Silver." In Yarshater 1983b, pp. 1113–29.

Harris, David R.

1996 "Domesticatory Relationships of People, Plants and Animals." In Roy Ellen and Katsuyoshi Fukui, eds., *Redefining Nature: Ecology, Culture and Domestication*. Oxford: Berg, pp. 437–63.

Haskins, Charles H.

1921 "The *De Arte Venandi cum Avibus* of the Emperor Frederick II." *English Historical Review* (July): 334–55.

1922 "Some Early Treatises on Falconry." *Romanic Review* 13: 18–27.

Haslip-Viera, Gabriel, Bernard Ortiz de Montellano, and Warren Barbour

1997 "Robbing Native American Cultures: Van Sertima's Afrocentricity and the Olmecs." *Current Anthropology* 38: 419–41, with invited commentary.

Haussig, Hans Wilhelm

1983 *Die Geschichte Zentralasiens und der Seidenstrasse in vorislamischer Zeit*. Darmstadt: Wissenschaftliche Buchgesellschaft.

1988 *Die Geschichte Zentralasiens und der Seidenstrasse in islamischer Zeit.* Darmstadt: Wissenschaftliche Buchgesellschaft.

1992 *Archäologie und Kunst der Seidenstrasse.* Darmstadt: Wissenschaftliche Buchgesellschaft.

Hawkins, R. E., ed.

1986 *Encyclopedia of Indian Natural History.* Delhi: Oxford University Press.

Hayashi, Ryōichi

1975 *The Silk Road and the Shoso-in.* New York: Weatherhill.

Hayward, Lorna

1990 "The Origin of Raw Elephant Ivory in Late Bronze Age Greece." *Antiquity* 64: 103–9.

He, Pingli

2003 *Xunshou yu fengchan: fengjian zhengchi de wenhua guiji.* Jinan: Qi Lu shushe.

Hedin, Sven

1933 *Jehol, City of Emperors.* New York: Dutton.

Heimpel, W.

1980–83 "Leopard und Gepard, A, Philologisch." In *Reallexikon der Assriologie und Vorderasiatischen Archäologie.* Berlin: de Gruyter, 6: 599–601.

Heissig, Walther

1980 *The Religions of Mongolia.* London: Routledge.

Held, Joseph

1985 *Hunyadi: Legend and Reality.* Boulder, Colo.: East European Monographs.

Hellie, Richard

1977 *Enserfment and Military Change in Moscovy.* Chicago: University of Chicago Press.

Helms, Mary W.

1988 *Ulysses' Sail: An Ethnographic Odyssey of Power, Knowledge, and Geographical Distance.* Princeton, N.J.: Princeton University Press.

1993 *Craft and the Kingly Ideal: Art, Trade, and Power.* Austin: University of Texas Press.

Hemmer, Helmut

1990 *Domestication: The Decline of Environmental Appreciation.* Cambridge: Cambridge University Press.

Hendricks, Janet Wall

1988 "Power and Knowledge: Discourse and Ideological Tranformation Among the Shuar." *American Ethnologist* 15: 218–38.

Hennebicque, Régine

1980 "Espaces sauvages et chasses royales dans le Nord de la France." *Revue du Nord* 62: 35–57.

Henning, W. B.

1939–42 "Mani's Last Journey." *Bulletin of the School of Oriental and African Studies* 10: 941–53.

Henthorn, William E.

1971 *A History of Korea.* New York: Free Press.

Herskovits, Melville J.

1951 *Man and His Works: The Science of Cultural Anthropology.* New York: Knopf.

Hervouet, Yves

1964 *Un poète de cour sous les Han: Sseu-ma Siang-jou.* Paris: Presses universitaires de France.

Herzfeld, Ernst Emil

1988 *Iran in the Ancient Near East.* 1941. Reprint New York: Hacker Art Books.

Hickerson, H.

1965 "The Virginia Deer and Intertribal Buffer Zones in the Upper Mississippi Valley." In Anthony Leeds and Andrew Peter Vayda, eds., *Man, Culture and Animals: The Role of Animals in Human Ecological Adjustments.* Washington, D.C.: American Association for the Advancement of Science, pp. 43–65.

Hicks, Carola

1993 *Animals in Early Medieval Art.* Edinburgh: Edinburgh University Press.

Higgs, Eric S., ed.

1972 *Papers in Economic Prehistory.* Cambridge: Cambridge University Press.

Hildebrand, Milton

1959 "Motions of the Running Cheetah and Horse." *Journal of Mammalogy* 40: 481–95.

1961 "Further Studies on the Locomotion of the Cheetah." *Journal of Mammalogy* 42: 84–91.

Hill, Kim

1982 "Hunting and Human Evolution." *Journal of Human Evolution* 11: 521–44.

Hillel, Daniel

1991 *Out of the Earth: Civilization and the Life of the Soil.* Berkeley: University of California Press.

Hinz, Walther

1970 "Die elamischen Buchungstäflichen der Darius Zeit." *Orientalia* n.s. 39: 421–40.

1975 *Altiranisches Sprachgut der Nebenüberlieferungen.* Wiesbaden: Otto Harrassowitz.

Hoffman, Gisela.

1957–58 "Falkenjagd und Falkenhandel in der nordischen Ländern während des Mittelalters." *Zeitschrift der deutsches Altertum und deutsche Literature* 88: 115–49.

Hofmann, H. F.

1968 "A Short Notice of Some MSS of a Few Books on Falconry, Interesting to the Altaicist." In *Jagd* 1968, pp. 77–89.

Horst, Heribert

1964 *Die Staatsverwaltung der Grosselǧūgen und Hōrazmšahs (1038–1231): Eine Untersuchung nach Urkundenformularen der Zeit.* Wiesbaden: Franz Steiner.

Hou Ching-lang and Michèle Pirazzoli

1979 "Les chasses d'automne de l'empereur Qianlong à Mulan." *T'oung-pao* 65: 13–50.

Houlihan, Patrick F.

1986 *The Birds of Ancient Egypt.* Warminster: Aris and Phillips.

1996 *The Animal World of the Pharaohs.* London: Thames and Hudson.

Hrushevsky, Michael

1941 *A History of the Ukraine.* New Haven, Conn.: Yale University Press.

Hsiao, Ch'i-ch'ing

1978 *The Military Establishment of the Yuan Dynasty.* Cambridge, Mass.: Harvard University Press.

Hsu, Cho-yun

1980 *Han Agriculture: The Formation of Early Chinese Agricultural Economy.* Seattle: University of Washington Press.

Hsu, James C. H.

1996 *The Written Word in Ancient China.* Hong Kong: Tan Hock Seng.

Hucker, Charles O.

1985 *A Dictionary of Official Titles in Imperial China.* Stanford, Calif.: Stanford University Press.

Hughes, J. Donald

1989 "Mencius' Prescription for Ancient Chinese Environmental Problems." *Environmental Review* 13, 3–4: 15-27.

Hurston, Zora Neale

1990 *Tell My Horse: Voodoo and Life in Haiti and Jamaica.* 1938. Reprint New York: Harper and Row.

Hyland, Ann

1990 *Equus: The Horse in the Roman World.* New Haven, Conn.: Yale University Press.

Ianin, V. L.

1970 *Aktovye pechati drevnei Rusi, X–XV vv.* 2 vols. Moscow: Nauka.

Iessen, A. A.

1960 "Piat chash iz Bailakana." In Struve 1960, pp. 88–97.

Impey, Lawrence

1925 "Shangtu, the Summer Capital of Kublai Khan." *Geographical Review* 15: 584–604.

Ingold, Tim

1994 "From Trust to Domination: An Alternative History of Human-Animal Relations." In Aubrey Manning and James Serpell, eds., *Animals and Human Society: Changing Perspectives.* New York: Routlege, pp. 1–19.

Ipsiroglu, M. S.

1967 *Painting and Culture of the Mongols.* London: Thames and Hudson.

Islam, Riazul

1970 *Indo-Persian Relations: A Study of the Political and Diplomatic Relations Between the Mughal Empire and Iran.* Tehran: Iranian Cultural Foundation.

Jackson, Howard M.

1985 *The Lion Becomes Man: The Gnostic Leontomorphic Creator and the Platonic Tradition.* Atlanta: Scholars Press.

Jagchid, Sechin and C. R. Bawden

1968 "Notes on Hunting of Some Nomadic Peoples." In *Jagd* 1968, pp. 90–102.

Jagchid, Sechin and Paul Hyer

1979 *Mongolia's Culture and Society.* Boulder, Colo.: Westview Press.

Jagd

1968 *Die Jagd bei den altaischen Völkern.* Wiesbaden: Otto Harrassowitz.

Jameson, E. W.

1962 *The Hawking of Japan: The History and Development of Japanese Falconry.* Davis, Calif.: Privately printed.

Jenner, W. J. F.
1981 *Memories of Loyang: Yang Hsüan-chih and the Last Capital (493–534).* Oxford: Clarendon Press.
Jarman, M. R.
1972 "European Deer Economies and the Advent of the Neolithic." In Higgs 1972, pp. 125–47.
Jéquier, M. G.
1913 "La panthère dans l'ancienne Egypte." *Revue d'ethnographie et sociologie* 4: 353-72.
Jones, E. L.
1988 *Growth Recurring: Economic Change in World History.* Oxford: Clarendon Press.
Kadyrbaev, A. Sh.
1998 *Sakskii voin-simvol dukha predkov.* Almaty: Kazak entsiklopediiasy.
Kamata, Shigeo
1989 "The Transmission of Paekche Buddhism to Japan." In Lewis R. Lancaster and C. S. Yu, eds., *Introduction of Buddhism to Korea: New Cultural Patterns.* Berkeley, Calif.: Asian Humanities Press, pp. 143–60.
Kantorowicz, Ernst
1957 *Frederick the Second, 1194–1250.* New York: Ungar.
Kara, G.
1966 "Chants de chasseurs oirates dans la recueil de Vladimirtsov." In Walther Heissig, ed., *Collectanea Mongolica: Festschrift für Professor Dr. Rintchen zum 60. Geburtstag.* Wiesbaden: Otto Harrassowitz, pp. 101–8.
Keeley, Lawrence H.
1996 *War Before Civilization.* Oxford: Oxford University Press.
Keightley, David N.
1978 *Sources of Shang History: The Oracle-Bone Inscriptions of Bronze Age China.* Berkeley: University of California Press.
1983 "The Late Shang State: When, Where, and What." In David N. Keightley, ed., *The Origins of Chinese Civilization.* Berkeley: University of California Press.
2000 *The Ancestral Landscape: Time, Space and Community in Late Shang China (ca. 1200–1045 B.C.).* Berkeley: Institute of East Asian Studies, University of California.
Keimer, Ludwig
1950 "Falconry in Ancient Egypt." *Isis* 41: 52.
Keller, Otto
1963 *Die Antike Tierwelt.* 2 vols. 1909. Reprint Hildesheim: Georg Olms.
Kent, Roland G.
1931 "The Recently Published Old Persian Inscriptions." *Journal of the American Oriental Society* 51: 228–29.
Kentucky Horse Park
2000 *Imperial China: The Art of the Horse in Chinese History.* Prospect, Ky.: Harmony House.
Khazanov, A. M.
1975 *Zoloto skifov.* Moscow: Sovetskii khudozhnik.

Kim, Ke Chung

1997 "Preserving Biodiversity in Korea's Demilitarized Zone." *Science* 278: 242–43.

Kim, Ke Chung and Edward O. Wilson

2002 "The Land That War Protected." *New York Times*, December 10: A31.

Kim, Wen-yong

1986 *Korean Art Treasures*. Seoul: Yekyong Publications.

Kitchener, Andrew

1991 *The Natural History of Wild Cats*. Ithaca, N.Y.: Comstock.

Klein, Walter

1914 *Studien zu Ammianus Marcellinius*. Klio, Beiheft XIII. Leipzig: Dietrich'sche Verlag.

Klingender, F. D.

1971 *Animals in Art and Thought to the End of the Middle Ages*. Ed. Evelyn Antal and John Harthan. Cambridge, Mass.: MIT Press.

Kliuchevskii, V. O.

1959 *Terminologiia russkoi istorii*. In his *Sochineniia*. Moscow: Izdatel'stvo sotsial'no-ekonomicheskii literatury, 6: 129–275.

Klochkov, I. S.

1996 "Two Cylinder Seals from a Sarmatian Grave near Kosikay." *Ancient Civilizations from Scythia to Siberia* 3, 1: 38–48.

Knauer, Elfriede R.

2003 "Fishing with Cormorants: A Note on Vittore Carpaccio's *Hunting on the Lagoon*." *Apollo* n.s. 158, no. 499: 32–39.

2004 "A Quest for the Origin of Persian Riding-Coats: Sleeved Garments with Underarm Openings." In Cäcilla Fluck and Gillian Vogelsang-Eastwood, eds., *Riding Costume in Egypt: Origin and Appearance*. Leiden: E.J. Brill, pp. 7–29.

Knight, John

1999 "Wildlife Trade in Asia." *International Institute for Asian Studies Newsletter* 20, (November): 8–14.

2000a "Introduction." In Knight 2000b, pp. 1–35.

2000b *Natural Enemies: People Wildlife Conflicts in Anthropological Perspective*. London: Routledge.

Koch, Ebba

1998 *Dara-Shikoh Shooting Nilgais: Hunt and Landscape in Mughal Painting*. Occasional Papers 1. Washington, D.C.: Freer Gallery of Art.

Kovalev, Roman

1999 "Zvenyhorod in Galica: An Archaeological Survey, Eleventh-Mid-Thirteenth Century." *Journal of Ukrainian Studies* 24, 2: 7–36.

Kramer, Fritz L.

1967 "Edward Hahn and the End of the 'Three stages of Man'." *Geographical Review* 57: 73–89.

Kramer, Samuel Noah

1981 *History Begins at Sumer*. 1956. Reprint Philadelphia: University of Pennsylvania Press.

Kronasser, Heinz

1953 "Die Herkunft der Falkenjagd." *Südost Forschungen* 12: 67–79.

Kuzmina, E. E.

1987 "The Motif of the Lion-Bull Combat in the Art of Iran, Scythia, and Central Asia and Its Semantics." In Gherardo Gnoli and Lionello Lanciotti, eds., *Orientalia Josephi Tucci Memoriae Dicata.* 3 vols. Rome: Istituto Italiano per il Medio ed Estremo Oriente, 2: 729–45.

Lach, Donald F.

1970 *Asia in the Making of Europe.* Vol. 2, *A Century of Wonder*, bk. 1, *The Visual Arts.* Chicago: University of Chicago Press.

Lacroix, Paul

1963 *France in the Middle Ages: Customs, Classes, Conditions.* New York: Frederich Unger.

La Fleur, William R.

1973 "Saigyō and the Buddhist Value of Nature." Parts I, II. *History of Religions* 13: 93–128; 227–48.

Lane, Edward William

1987 *Arabian Society in the Middle Ages: Studies from the Thousand and One Nights.* London: Curzon.

Lang, David Marshall

1957 *The Last Years of the Georgian Monarchy, 1658–1832.* New York: Columbia University Press.

Langer, Lawrence

1976 "Plague and the Russian Countryside: Monastic Estates in the Late Fourteenth and Fifteenth Centuries." *Canadian-American Slavic Studies* 10, 3: 351–68.

Lassner, Jacob

1970 *The Topography of Baghdad in the Early Middle Ages: Text and Studies.* Detroit: Wayne State University Press.

Latham, J. D.

1970 "The Archers of the Middle East: The Turco-Persian Background." *Iran* 8: 97–103.

Laufer, Bertold

1909 *Chinese Pottery of the Han Dynasty.* Leiden: E.J. Brill.

1913 "Arabic and Chinese Trade in Walrus and Narwhal Ivory." *T'oung-pao* 14: 315–64.

1914 "Bird Divination Among the Tibetans." *T'oung-pao* 15: 1–110.

1916 "Supplementary Notes on Walrus and Narwhal Ivory." *T'oung-pao* 17: 348–89.

1928 *The Giraffe in History and Art.* Anthropology Leaflet 27. Chicago: Field Museum of Natural History.

1967 *Sino-Iranica: Chinese Contributions to the History of Civilization in Ancient Iran.* 1919. Reprint Taibei: Ch'eng-wen.

Lavin, Irving

1963 "The Hunting Mosaics of Antioch and Their Sources." *Dumbarton Oaks Papers* 17: 179–286.

Lawergren, Bo

2003 "Oxus Trumpets, ca. 2200–1800 B.C.E.: Material Overview, Usage, Societal Role and Catalog." *Iranica Antigua* 38: 41–118.

Leclant, J.

1981 "Un parc du chasse de la Nubie pharaonique. In *Le sol, la parole et l'ecrit: 2000 ans d'histoire africaine: mélange en hommage à Raymond Manny*. Paris: Société française d'histoire d'outre-mer, pp. 727–38.

Lee, Robert H. G.

1970 *The Manchurian Frontier in Ch'ing History*. Cambridge, Mass.: Harvard University Press.

Lefeuvre, Jean

1990–91 "Rhinoceros and Wild Buffaloes North of the Yellow River at the End of the Shang Dynasty." *Monumenta Serica* 39: 131–57.

Legge, A. J.

1972 "Prehistoric Exploitation of Gazelle in Palestine." In Higgs 1972, pp. 119–24.

Legge, A. J. and P. A. Rowley-Conwy

1987 "Gazelle Killing in Stone Age Syria." *Scientific American* 257, 2: 88–95.

Legrand, Jacques

1976 *L'administration dans la domination Sino-Mandchoue en Mongolie Qalq-a*. Paris: Collège du France.

Lessing, Ferdinard D.

1973 *Mongolian-English Dictionary*. Bloomington, Ind: Mongolia Society.

Levanoni, Amalia

1995 *A Turning Point in Mamluk History*. Leiden: E.J. Brill.

Lever, Christopher

1985 *Naturalized Mammals of the World*. London: Longman.

Lewis, Mark Edward

1990 *Sanctioned Violence in Early China*. Albany: State University of New York Press.

Lewis, W. H.

1957 *The Splendid Age: Life in the France of Louis XIV*. Garden City, N.Y.: Doubleday.

Li Chi

1957 *The Beginnings of Chinese Civilization*. Seattle: University of Washington Press.

Ligeti, Louis

1965 "Le lexique mongol de Kirakos Gandzak." *Acta Orientalia Academiae Scientarum Hungaricae* 18: 241–97.

Lindberger, Elsa

2001 "The Falcon, the Raven and the Dove: Some Bird Motifs on Medieval Coins." In Björn Ambrosiani, ed., *Excavations in the Black Earth 1990–95: Eastern Connections Part One, the Falcon Motif*. Birka Studies 5. Stockholm: Birka Project for Riksantikvarieämbetet, pp. 29–86.

Lindner, Kurt

1973 *Beiträge zur Vogelfang und Falknerei im Altertum*. Berlin: de Gruyter.

Linduff, Katherine M.

1998 "The Emergence and Demise of Bronze-Producing Cultures Outside the Central Plain of China." In Mair 1998, 2: 619–43.

Linn-Kustermann, Susanne K. M.

1997 "Trophies-Antlers." In Blüchel 1997, 2: 124–25.

Linton, Ralph

1955 *The Tree of Culture*. New York: Knopf.

Littauer, Mary Aiken and Joost Crouwel

1973 "The Dating of a Chariot Ivory from Nimrud Considered Once Again." *American Schools of Oriental Research* 209: 27–33.

Litvinskii, B. A.

1972 "Das K'ang-chü-Sarmatische Farnah." *Central Asiatic Journal* 16, 4: 241–89.

Liu, James T. C.

1985 "Polo and Cultural Change: From T'ang to Sung China." *Harvard Journal of Asiatic Studies* 45: 203–24.

Livshitz, V. A.

1962 *Sogdiiskie dokumenty s gory Mug.* Vol. 2, *Iuridicheskie dokumenty i pis'ma.* Moscow: Idatel'stvo vostochnoi literatury.

Lockhart, Lawrence

1968 "The Relations Between Edward I and Edward II of England and the Mongol Il-khāns of Persia." *Iran* 6: 23–31.

Lodrick, Deryck

1981 *Sacred Cows, Sacred Places: Origins and Survivals of Animal Homes in India.* Berkeley: University of California Press.

Lombard, Denys

1974 "La vision de la forêt à Java (Indonesie)." *Études rurales* 53: 474–85.

Lowie, Robert

1937 *The History of Ethnological Theory.* New York: Farrar & Rinehart.

Lubotsky, Alexander

1998 "Tocharian Loan Words in Old Chinese." In Mair 1998, 1: 379–90.

Lukonin, Vladimir Grigor'evich

1977 *Iskusstvo drevnego Irana.* Moscow: Iskusstvo.

Machinist, Peter

1992 "Nimrod." *Anchor Bible Dictionary.* New York: Doubleday, 4: 1116–18.

MacKenzie, D. N.

1971 *A Concise Pahlavi Dictionary.* Oxford: Oxford University Press.

Mahler, Jane Gaston

1959 *The Westerners Among the Figurines of the T'ang Dynasty of China.* Rome: Istituto Italiano per il Medio ed Estremo Oriente.

Mair, Victor H.

1988 *Painting and Performance: Chinese Picture Recitation and Its Indian Genesis.* Honolulu: University of Hawaii Press.

2004 "The Horse in Late Prehistoric China: Wrestling Culture and Control from the 'Barbarians'." In Marsha Levine, Colin Renfrew, and Katie Boyle, eds. *Prehistoric Steppe Adaptation and the Horse.* Oxford: Oxbow Books, pp. 163–87.

Mair, Victor H., ed.

1998 *The Bronze Age and Early Iron Age Peoples of Eastern Central Asia.* 2 vols. Philadelphia: University of Pennsylvania Museum Publications.

Mallory, J. P. and D. Q. Adams, eds.

1997 *Encyclopedia of Indo-European Culture.* London: Fitzroy Dearborn.

Malone, Carroll Brown

1934 *History of the Peking Summer Palaces Under the Ch'ing Dynasty.* Urbana: University of Illinois.

Mansard, Valérie

1993 "Notes sur les animaux utilisés à la chasse sous Tang." *Anthropozoologica* 18: 91–98.

Markina, L. A.

2002 "Tsarinas out Hunting: Looks and Personalities." In State Historical Museum 2002: 207–51.

Marks, Robert B.

1998 *Tigers, Rice, Silk and Silt: Environment and Economy in Late Imperial China.* Cambridge: Cambridge University Press.

Martin, Janet

1980 "Trade on the Volga: The Commercial Relations of Bulghar with Central Asia and Iran in the 11th and 12th Centuries." *International Journal of Turkish Studies* 1, 2: 85–97.

1986 *Treasure of the Land of Darkness: The Fur Trade and Its Significance for Medieval Russia.* Cambridge: Cambridge University Press.

Martin, Paul S. and Richard G. Klein, eds.

1984 *Quarternary Extinctions: A Prehistoric Revolution.* Tucson: University of Arizona Press.

Martin, Paul S. and Christine R. Szuter

1999 "War Zones and Game Sinks in Lewis and Clark's West." *Conservation Biology* 13, 1: 36–45.

Martines, Lauro

1979 *Power and Imagination: City States in Renaissance Italy.* New York: Knopf.

Martynov, Anatoly I.

1991 *The Ancient Art of Northern Asia.* Urbana: University of Illinois Press.

Marzolph, Ulrich

1999 "Bahram Gūr's Spectacular Marksmanship and the Art of Illustration in Qājār Lithographed Books." In C. Hillenbrand, ed., *Studies in Honour of Clifford Edmund Bosworth,* vol. 2, *The Sultan's Turret, Studies in Persian and Turkish Culture.* Leiden: E.J. Brill, pp. 331–47.

Masson, V. M. and V. I. Sarianidi

1972 *Central Asia: Turkmenia before the Achaemenids.* London: Thames and Hudson.

McCarthy, Terry

2004 "Nowhere to Roam." *Time,* August 23, 44–53.

McChesney, R. D.

1991 *Waqf in Central Asia: Four Hundred Years in the History of a Muslim Shrine, 1480–1889.* Princeton, N.J.: Princeton University Press.

McClung, William Alexander

1983 *The Architecture of Paradise: Survivals of Eden and Jerusalem.* Berkeley: University of California Press.

McCook, Stuart

1996 "It May Be Truth But It Is Not Evidence: Paul du Chaillu and the Legitimation of Evidence in the Field Sciences." *Osiris* 2nd ser. 11: 177–97.

McCormick, Finbar

1991 "The Effect of the Anglo-Norman Settlement in Ireland's Wild and Domesticated Fauna." In Pam J. Crabtree and Kathleen Ryan, eds., *Animal Use and Culture Change.* Philadelphia: MASCA, pp. 40–52.

McDougal, Charles

1982 "The Man-Eating Tiger in Geographical and Historical Perspective." In Ronald L. Tilson and Ulysses S. Seal, eds., *Tigers of the World: The Biology, Biopolitics, Management, and Conservation of an Endangered Species.* Park Ridge, N.J.: Noyes Publications, pp. 435–48.

McEwan, Edward, Robert L. Miller and Christopher Bergman

1991 "Early Bow Design and Construction." *Scientific American* 264, 6: 76–82.

McNeill, J. R.

1994 "Of Rats and Men: A Synoptic Environmental History of the Island Pacific." *Journal of World History* 5: 299–349.

McNeill, William H.

1995 *Keeping Together in Time: Dance and Drill in Human History.* Cambridge: Cambridge University Press.

Meiggs, Russell

1982 *Trees and Timber in the Ancient Mediterranean World.* Oxford: Clarendon Press.

Meissner, Bruno

1902 "Falkenjagden bei den Babyloniern und Assyriern." *Beitrage zur Assyriologie und semitischen Sprachwissenschaft* 4: 418–22.

Melikhov, G. V.

1970 "Politika Minskoi imperii v otnoshenii Chzhurchzhenei (1402–1413 gg)." In S. L. Tikhvinskii, ed., *Kitai i sosedi v drevnosti i srednevekov'e.* Moscow: Nauka, pp. 251–74.

Melikian-Chirvani, A. S.

1984 *Le Shāh-nāme*, le gnose soufie et le pouvoir Mongol." *Journal Asiatique* 272, 3–4: 249–337.

Melnikova, O. B.

2002 "For Food and Merriment. . . ." In State Historical Museum 2002: 61–112.

Melville, Charles

1990 "The Itineraries of Sultan Öljeitü." *Iran* 28: 55–70.

Menzies, Nicholas K.

1994 *Forest and Land Management in Imperial China.* New York: St. Martin's Press.

1996 *Agro-Industries and Forestry.* Joseph Needham, ed., *Science and Civilization in China*, vol. 6, pt. 3, *Biology and Biological Technology.* Cambridge: Cambridge University Press.

Mercier, Louis

1927 *La chasse et les sports chez les Arabes.* Paris: Librairie des sciences politiques et sociales.

Mercola, Michele

1994 "A Reassessment of Homozygosity and the Case for Inbreeding Depression in the *Acinonyx jubatus*: Implications for Conservation." *Conservation Biology* 8, 4: 961–71.

Meserve, Ruth

2001a "Law and Domestic Animals in Inner Asia." In David B. Honey and David C. Wright, eds., *Altaic Affinities: Proceedings of the 40th Meeting of PIAC.* Bloomington: Indiana University, Research Institute for Inner Asian Studies, pp. 120–37.

2000b "History in Search of Precedent: Animal Judgements." *Altaica*, V, Moscow: IV RAN: 90–97.

Meuli, Karl

1954 "Ein altpersischen Kriegsbrauch." In Fritz Meier, ed., *Westöstliche Abhandlungen: Rudolph Tschudi zum siebzigsten Geburtstag*. Wiebaden: Otto Harrassowitz, pp. 63–86.

Miller, Dean A.

1998 "On the Mythology of Indo-European Heroic Hair." *Journal of Indo-European Studies* 26, 1–2: 41–60.

Mokyr, Joel

1990 *The Levers of Riches: Technological Creativity and Economic Progress*. Oxford: Oxford University Press.

Möller, Detlef

1965 *Studien zur mittelalterlichen arabischen Falkenerliteratur*. Berlin: de Gruyter.

Molnár, Ádám

1994 *Weather Magic in Inner Asia*. Indiana University Uralic and Altaic Series 158. Bloomington: Indiana University, Research Institute for Inner Asian Studies.

Morgenthau, Hans J.

1950 *Politics Among Nations: The Struggle for Power and Peace*. New York: Knopf.

Morris, Brian

2000 "Wildlife Depredations in Malawi: The Historical Dimension." In Knight 2000b, pp. 36–49.

Morrison, William J.

2000 "The Noble Beasts of Lithuania, part 2, Tauras." *Lithuanian Heritage* (January-February): 9–12.

Moscati, Sabatino

1962 *The Face of the Ancient Orient*. Garden City, N.Y.: Doubleday.

Mostaert, Antoine

1949 "A propos du mot *širolγa* de l'histoire secrète des Mongols." *Harvard Journal of Asiatic Studies* 12: 470–76.

Moynihan, Elizabeth B.

1979 *Paradise as a Garden in Persia and Mughal India*. New York: George Braziller.

Nadeliaev, V. M. et al., eds.

1969 *Drevnetiurkskii slovar*. Leningrad: Nauka.

Naumann, Rudolf and Elisabeth Naumann

1969 "Ein Kösk im Sommerpalast des Abaqa Chan auf dem Tacht-i Sulaiman und seine Dekoration." In Rudolph Naumann and Oktay Aslanapa, eds., *Forschungen zur Kunst Asiens: In Memoriam Kurt Erdman*. Istanbul: Baha Mutbaasi, pp. 36–65.

1976 *Takht-i Suleiman: Ausgrabung des Deutschen Archäologischen Instituts in Iran*. Ausstellungskataloge der prähistorischen Staatssammlung 3. Munich: Prähistorische Staatssammlung, 1976.

Naveh, Joseph and Shaul Shaked

1987 *Amulets and Magic Bowls: Aramaic Incantations of Late Antiquity*. 2nd ed. Jerusalem: Magnes Press.

Naville, Edourd

1898 *The Temple of Deir el Bahari*. Part 3. London: Offices of the Egypt Exploration Fund.

Nelson, Janet L.
1987 "The Lord's Anointed and the People's Choice: Carolingian Royal Ritual." In Cannadine and Price 1987, pp. 137–80.
Nicolai, Friedrich
1809 *Des Türkischen Gesandten Resmi Ahmet Efendi Gesandtschaftliche Berichte von Berlin im Jahre 1763.* Berlin and Stettin, n. pub.
Niesters, Horst
1997 "The Art of Falconry." In Blüchel 1997, 1: 162–93.
Noonan, Thomas S.
1995 "The Khazar Economy." *Archivum Eurasiae Medii Aevi* 9: 253–318.
Norden, Walter
1997 "Let No One Dare Steal Game from Our Forest." In Blüchel 1997, 1: 144–46.
Norman, Jerry
1978 *A Concise Manchu-English Lexicon.* Seattle: University of Washington Press.
Novgorodova, E. A.
1974 "Okhotnich'i i voennye siuzhety v drevnem izobrazitel'nom iskusstve Tsentral'noi Azii." *Central Asiatic Journal* 18, 1: 70–73.
Nylander, Carl
1970 *Ionians in Pasargadae: Studies in Old Persian Architecture.* Uppsala: Acta Universitatus Upsaliensis, 1970.
Oddy, Andrew
1991 "Arab Imagery on Early Umayyad Coins in Syria and Palestine: Evidence for Falconry." *Numismatic Chronicle* 151: 59–66.
Oded, Bustenay
1992 *War, Peace and Empire: Justifications for War in Assyrian Royal Inscriptions.* Wiesbaden: Ludwig Reichert Verlag.
Officer, Charles and Jake Page
1993 *Tales of the Earth: Paroxysms and Perturbations of the Blue Planet.* Oxford: Oxford University Press.
Okladnikov, A. P.
1964 "Notes on the Beliefs and Religion of the Ancient Mongols: The Golden Winged Eagle in Mongolian History." *Acta Ethnographica Academiae Scientiarum Hungaricae* 13: 411–14.
1981 *Petroglify Mongolii.* Leningrad: Nauka.
1990 "Inner Asia at the Dawn of History." In Denis Sinor, ed., *The Cambridge History of Early Inner Asia.* Cambridge: Cambridge University Press, pp. 41–96.
Olbricht, Peter
1954 *Das Postwesen in China unter den Mongolenherrschaft im 13. und 14. Jahrhundert.* Wiesbaden: Otto Harrassowitz.
Oppenheim, A. Leo
1965 "On the Royal Gardens in Mesopotamia." *Journal of Near Eastern Studies* 24: 328–33.
1985 "The Babylonian Evidence of Achaemenid Rule in Mesopotamia." In Ilya Gershevitch, ed., *The Cambridge History of Iran,* vol. 2, *The Median and Achaemenid Periods.* Cambridge: Cambridge University Press, pp. 529–87.
Oppenheim, A. Leo, ed.
1968 *The Assyrian Dictionary.* Chicago: Oriental Institute, vol. 1, pt. 2.

Orwell, George

1956 "Shooting an Elephant." In *The Orwell Reader.* New York, Harcourt Brace, pp. 3–9.

Osborn, Dale J. and Jana Osbornova

1998 *The Mammals of Ancient Egypt.* Warminister: Aris and Phillips.

Ostrogorsky, George

1969 *History of the Byzantine State.* New Brunswick, N.J.: Rutgers University Press.

Paltusova, I. N.

2002a "Royal Hunting." In State Historical Museum 2002: 11–27.

2002b "Hunting as a Pastime of the Imperial House." In State Historical Museum 2002: 303–45.

Pan, Yihong

1997 *Son of Heaven and Heavenly Qaghan: Sui-Tang China and Its Neighbors.* Bellingham: Western Washington University, Center for East Asian Studies.

Parker, Heidi G. et al.

2004 "Genetic Structure of the Purebred Dog." *Science* 304, 5674 (May): 1160–64.

Parrot, Andre

1961 *The Arts of Assyria.* New York: Golden Press.

Paviot, Jacques

2000 "England and the Mongols." *Journal of the Royal Asiatic Society* 3rd ser. 10: 305–18.

Pearson, M. N.

1976 *Merchants and Rulers in Gujarat: The Response to the Portuguese in the Sixteenth Century.* Berkeley: University of California Press.

Pelliot, Paul

1903 "Le Fou-nan." *Bulletin de l'école française de Extrême-Orient* 3: 248–303.

1930 "Les mots mongols dans le *Korye Să*." *Journal asiatique* 217: 253–66.

1944 "*Širolγa-siralγa*." *T'oung-pao* 37: 102–13.

1959–61 *Notes on Marco Polo.* 2 vols. Paris: Librairie Adrien-Massoneuve.

1973 *Recherches sur les chrétiens d'Asie centrale et d'extrême-Orient.* Paris: Imprimerie nationale.

Pelliot, Paul and Louis Hambis

1951 *Histoire des campagnes de Gengis Khan.* Leiden: E.J. Brill.

Perry, W. J.

1968 *The Children of the Sun: A Study in the Early History of Civilization.* 1923. Reprint London: Methuen.

Petit-Dutaillis, Charles

1915 *Studies and Notes Supplementary to Stubbs' Constitutional History.* Manchester: Manchester University Press.

Piggot, Stuart

1992 *Wagon, Chariot and Carriage: Symbol and Status in the History of Transportation.* London: Thames and Hudson.

Pittman, Susan

1983 *Lullingstone Park: The Evolution of a Medieval Deer Park.* Rainbow, Kent: Meresborough Books.

Pollard, John

1977 *Birds in Greek Life and Myth.* London: Thames and Hudson.

Polyani, Karl

1957 "Aristotle Discovers the Economy." In Karl Polyani, Conrad M. Arensberg, and Harry W. Pearson, eds., *Trade and Market in the Early Empires: Economies in History and Theory.* New York: Free Press, pp. 64–94.

Poole, Austin Lane

1958 "Recreation." In Astin Lane Poole, ed., *Medieval England.* Oxford: Clarendon Press, vol. 2, pp. 605–31.

Porada, Edith

1969 *The Art of Ancient Iran.* New York: Greystone.

Postgate, J. N.

1992 *Early Mesopotamia: Society and Economy at the Dawn of History.* London: Routledge.

Potts, Richard

1984 "Hominid Hunters? Problems of Identifying the Earliest Hunter/Gatherers." In Robert Foley, ed., *Hominid Evolution and Community Ecology: Prehistoric Human Adaptation in Biological Perspective.* London: Academic Press, pp. 129–66.

Powers, Martin J.

1991 *Art and Political Expression in Early China.* New Haven, Conn.: Yale University Press.

Price, Simon

1987 "From Noble Funerals to Divine Cults: The Consecration of Roman Emperors." In Cannadine and Price 1987, pp. 56–105.

Pulleyblank, Edwin G.

1995 "Why Tocharians?" *Journal of Indo-European Studies* 23: 415–30.

de Rachewiltz, Igor

1973 "Some Remarks on the Ideological Foundations of Chinggis Khan's Empire." *Papers on Far Eastern History* 7: 21–36.

Ramstedt, G. J.

1949 *Studies in Korean Etymology.* Helsinki: Suomalais Ugrilainen Seura.

Ratchnevsky, Paul

1937–85 *Une code des Yuan.* 4 vols. Paris: Collège de France.

1970 "Über den mongolischen Kult am Hofe der Grosskhane in China." In Louis Ligeti, ed., *Mongolian Studies.* Amsterdam: B.R. Gruner, pp. 417–43.

Rawson, Jessica

1998 "Strange Creatures." *Oriental Art* 44, 2: 24–28.

ar-Raziq, Ahmad ʿAbd

1970 "La chasse au faucon d'pres des céramiques du Musée du Caire." *Annales islamologiques* 9: 109–21.

Redfield, Robert

1956 *Peasant Society and Culture.* Chicago: University of Chicago Press.

Redford, Kent H.

1992 "The Empty Forest." *Bioscience* 42: 412–22.

Redford, Scott

2000 *Landscape and the State in Medieval Anatolia: Seljuq Gardens and Pavilions of Alanya.* BAR International Series 893. Oxford: Archaeopress.

Reed, Charles A.

1965 "Imperial Sassanian Hunting of Pig and Fallow-Deer, and Problems of the Survival of These Animals Today in Iran." *Postilla* 92: 1–23.

Reid, Anthony

1988 *Southeast Asia in the Age of Commerce.* Vol. 1, *The Lands Below the Winds.* New Haven, Conn.: Yale University Press.

1989 "Elephants and Water in the Feasting of Seventeenth Century Aceh." *Journal of the Malaysian Branch of the Royal Asiatic Society* 62, 2: 25–44.

Reinhart, A. Kevin

1991 "The Here and the Hereafter in Islamic Religious Thought." In Sheila S. Blair and Jonathan M. Bloom, eds., *Images of Paradise in Islamic Art.* Hanover, N.H.: Hood Museum of Art, Dartmouth College, pp. 15–23.

Renfrew, Colin

1986 "Introduction." In Colin Renfrew and John F. Cherry, eds., *Peer Polity Interaction and Socio-Political Change.* Cambridge: Cambridge University Press, pp. 1–18.

Rey, Maurice

1965 *Le domaine du roi et les finances extraordinaires sous Charles VI, 1388–1413.* Paris: S.E.V.P.E.N.

Riasanovsky, Valentin A.

1965a *Customary Law of the Nomadic Tribes of Siberia.* Indiana University Uralic and Altaic Series 48. Bloomington: Indiana University.

1965b *Fundamental Principles of Mongol Law.* Indiana University Uralic and Altaic Series 43. Bloomington: Indiana University.

Rice, D. S.

1954 "The Seasons and the Labors of the Months in Islamic Art." *Ars Orientalis* 1: 1–39.

Rice, David Talbot

1965 *Islamic Art.* New York: Praeger.

Ringbom, Lars-Ivar

1951 *Graltempel und Paradies: Beziehungen zwischen Iran und Europa im Mittelalter.* Stockholm: Wahlstrom & Widstrand.

Ritvo, Harriet

1987 *The Animal Estate: The English and Other Creatures in the Victorian Age.* Cambridge, Mass.: Harvard University Press.

Robinson, Charles Alexander

1953 *The History of Alexander the Great.* Vol. 1. Providence, R.I.: Brown University Press.

Rockhill, W. W.

1914 "Notes on the Relations and Trade of China with the Eastern Archipelago and Coasts of the Indian Ocean in the Fourteenth Century." *T'oung-pao* 15: 419–47.

Rogozhin, N. M.

1994 *Posol'skie knigi Rossii kontsa XV-nachala XVII vv.* Moscow: Rossiiskaia akademii nauka, Institut rossiiskoi istorii.

Rolle, Renate

1988 "Archäologische Bemerkungen zum Warägerhandel." *Bericht der Römisch-Germanischen Kommission* 69: 472–529.

Root, Margaret Cool

1979 *The King and Kingship in Achaemenid Art.* Acta Iranica 3rd ser. 9. Leiden: E.J. Brill.

Rostovtzeff, M. I. et al., eds.

1952 *The Excavations at Dura Europos, Preliminary Report of the Ninth Season of Work.* Pt. 3, *The Palace of the Dux Ripae and Dolicheneum.* New Haven, Conn.: Yale University Press.

Rozycki, William

1994 *Mongol Elements in Manchu.* Indiana University Uralic and Altaic Series 157. Bloomington: Indiana University.

Russell, Emily W. B.

1997 *People and the Land Through Time: Linking Ecology and History.* New Haven, Conn.: Yale University Press.

Ruttan, Lore M. and Monica Borgerhoff Mulder

1999 "Are East African Pastoralists Truly Conservationists?" *Current Anthropology* 40: 621–52, with invited commentary.

Saberwal, Vasant K. et al.

1994 "Lion-Human Conflict in the Gir Forest, India." *Conservation Biology* 8, 2: 501–7.

Sachs, A. J.

1953 "The Late Assyrian Royal-Seal Type, *Iraq* 15: 167–70.

Sage, Steven F.

1992 *Ancient Sichuan and the Unification of China.* Albany: State University of New York Press.

Sälzle, Karl

1997 "Riding to Hounds, German Hunting and Other Hunting Spectacles." In Blüchel 1997, 1: 132–43.

Salzman, Philip C.

1978 "Ideology and Change in Middle Eastern Tribal Societies." *Man* 13, 4: 618–37.

1980 "Introduction: Processes of Sedentarization as Adaptation and Response." In Philip C. Salzman, ed., *When Nomads Settle.* New York: Praeger, pp. 1–19.

Sansterre, Jean-Marie

1996 "La vénération des images à Ravenna dans le haut moyen âge: notes sur une forme de dévotion peu connue." *Revue Mabillion* n.s. 7: 5–21.

Sarma, I. K.

1989 "Water Reservoirs." *An Encyclopaedia of Indian Archaeology.* Delhi Munshiram Manonarlal, 302–3.

al-Sarraf, Shihab

2004 "Mamlūk *Furūsīyah* Literature and Its Antecedents." *Mamlūk Studies Review* 8, 1: 141–200.

Sarton, George

1961 *Appreciation of Ancient and Medieval Science During the Renaissance (1450–1600).* New York: A.S. Barnes.

Saunders, Nicholas J.

1994 "Tezcatlipoca: Jaguar Metaphors and the Aztec Mirror of Nature." In Roy Wills, ed., *Signifying Animals: Human Meaning in the Natural World.* London: Routledge, pp. 159–77.

Savage, Henry L.

1983 "Hunting in the Middle Ages." *Speculum* 7: 30–41.

Schafer, Edward H.

1956 "Cultural History of the Elaphure." *Sinologica* 4: 250–74.

1957 "War Elephants in Ancient and Medieval China." *Oriens* 10: 289–91.

1959 "Falconry in T'ang Times." *T'oung-pao* 46: 293–338.

1962 "The Conservation of Nature Under the T'ang Dynasty." *Journal of the Economic and Social History of the Orient* 5: 279–308.

1963 *The Golden Peaches of Samarkand: A Study in T'ang Exotics.* Berkeley: University of California Press.

1967 *The Vermilion Bird: T'ang Images of the South.* Berkeley: University of California Press.

1968 "Hunting Parks and Animal Enclosures in Ancient China." *Journal of the Economic and Social History of the Orient* 11: 318–43.

1991 "The Chinese Dhole." *Asia Major* 3rd ser. 4, 1: 1–7.

Schama, Simon

1995 *Landscape and Memory.* New York: Knopf.

Schmidt, Erick F.

1940 *Flights over Ancient Cities of Iran.* Chicago: University of Chicago Press.

1957 *Persepolis II: Contents of the Treasury and Other Discoveries.* Chicago: University of Chicago Press.

Schortman, Edward M. And Patricia A. Urban

1992 "Current Trends in Interaction Research." In Edward M. Schortman and Patricia A. Urban, eds., *Resources, Power, and Interregional Interaction.* New York: Plenum, pp. 235–55.

Schreiber, Gerhard

1949–55 "The History of the Former Yen Dynasty, Part I." *Monumenta Serica* 14: 374–480.

1956 "The History of the Former Yen Dynasty, Part II." *Monumenta Serica* 15, 1: 1–141.

Schumpeter, Joseph A.

1951 *Imperialism and Social Classes.* New York: Augustus M. Kelley.

Schwarz, Henry G.

2001 "Animal Words in Mongolian and Uyghur." *Mongolian Studies* 24: 1–7.

Scott, James C.

1976 *The Moral Economy of the Peasant.* New Haven, Conn.: Yale University Press.

Seaman, Gary, ed.

1989 *Ecology and Empire: Nomads in the Cultural Evolution of the Old World.* Los Angeles: Ethnographica.

Semenov, A. A.

1948 "Bukharskii traktat o chinakh i zvaniiakh i ob obiazannostiakh noseteli ikh v srednevekovoi Bukhare." *Sovetskoe vostokovedenie* 5: 137–53.

Serpell, James, ed.

1995 *The Domestic Dog, Its Evolution, Behaviour and Interaction with People.* Cambridge: Cambridge University Press.

Serruys, Henry

1955 *Sino-Jürched Relations During the Yung-lo Period (1403–24).* Wiesbaden: Otto Harrassowitz.

1967 *Sino-Mongol Relations During the Ming.* Vol. 2, *The Tribute System and Diplomatic Missions.* Mélanges chinois et bouddhiques 14. Brussels: Institut belge des hautes études chinois.

1974a *Kumiss Ceremonies and Horse Races: Three Mongolian Texts.* Wiesbaden: Otto Harrassowitz.

1974b "Mongol Qoriγ: Reservation." *Mongol Studies* 1: 76–91.

Shaanxi Sheng Bowuguan

1974a *Tang Li Xian mu bihua.* Beijing: Wenwu Chubanshe.

1974b *Tang Li Zhongrun mu bihua.* Beijing: Wenwu Chubanshe.

Shakanova, Nurila Z.

1989 "The System of Nourishment among the Eurasian Nomads: The Kazakh Example." In Seaman 1989, pp. 111–17.

Shaked, Shaul

1986 "From Iran to Islam: On Some Symbols of Royalty." *Jerusalm Studies in Arabic and Islam* 7: 75–91.

Sharma, R. S.

1970 "Central Asia and Early Indian Cavalry." In Amalendu Guha, ed., *Central Asia: Movements of Peoples and Ideas from Times Prehistoric to Modern.* New Delhi: Vikas Publications, pp. 174–87.

Sharp, N. C. C.

1997 "Timed Running Speed of a Cheetah (*Acinonyx jubatus*)." *Journal of Zoology* 241: 493–94.

Shaughnessy, Edward L.

1988 "Historical Perspectives on the Introduction of the Chariot into China." *Harvard Journal of Asiatic Studies* 48: 189–237.

1989 "Historical Geography and the Extent of the Earliest Chinese Kingdoms." *Asia Major* 3rd ser. 11, 2: 1–22.

Shavkunov, E. V.

1990 *Kul'tura Chzhurchzhenei-Udige XII–XIII vv. i problema proiskhozhdeniia tungusskikh narodov Dal'nego Vostoka.* Moscow: Nauka.

Shepard, Dorothy G.

1979 "Banquet and Hunt in Medieval Islamic Iconography." In Ursula E. McCracken, Lillian M. C. Randall, and Richard H. Randall, Jr., eds., *Gatherings in Honor of Dorothy E. Minor.* Baltimore: Walters Art Gallery, pp. 79–92.

1983 "Sasanian Art." In Yarshater 1983b, pp. 1055–1112.

Shepard, Paul

1996 *The Others: How Animals Made Us Human.* Washington, D.C.: Island Press.

Sherratt, Andrew

1986 "The Chase–From Subsistance to Sport." *Ashmolean* 10: 4–7.

1995 "Reviving the Grand Narrative: Archaeology and Long Term Change." *Journal of European Archaeology* 311: 1–32.

Shulman, David Dean

1985 *The King and the Clown in South Asian Myth and Poetry.* Princeton, N.J.: Princeton University Press.

Sidebotham, Steven E.

1991 "Ports on the Red Sea and the Arabia-India Trade." In Vimala Begley and Richard De Puma, eds., *Rome and India: The Ancient Sea Trade.* Madison: University of Wisconsin Press, pp. 12–38.

Silverbauer, George

1982 "Political Process in G/wi Bands." In Eleanor Leacock and Richard Lee, eds., *Politics and History in Band Societies.* Cambridge: Cambridge University Press, pp. 23–35.

Simakov, Georgii N.

1989a "Hunting with Raptors in Central Asia and Kazakhstan." In Seaman 1989, pp. 129–33.

1989b "Okhota s lovchimi ptitsami y narodov Srednei Azii i Kazakhstane." In R. F. Its, ed., *Pamiatniki traditsionnobytovoi kul'tury narodov Srednei Azii, Kazkhstana i Kavkaza.* Leningrad: Nauka, pp. 30–48.

Simmons, I. G.

1989 *Changing the Face of the Earth: Culture, Environment, History.* Oxford: Blackwell.

Simon, J. M. Davis

1987 *The Archaeology of Animals.* New Haven, Conn.: Yale University Press.

Simonian, Lane

1995 *Defending the Land of the Jaguar: A History of Conservation in Mexico.* Austin: University of Texas Press.

Sinor, Denis

1968 "Some Remarks on the Economic Role of Hunting in Central Eurasia." In *Jagd* 1968, pp. 119–28.

Sittert, Lance van

1998 "Keeping the Enemy at Bay: The Extermination of Wild Carnivora in the Cape Colony, 1889–1910." *Environmental History* 3: 333–56.

Slovar

1975– *Slovar russkogo iazyka XI–XVII vv.* Moscow: Nauka, 24 vols. to date.

Smil, Vaclav

1994 *Energy in World History.* Boulder, Colo.: Westview Press.

Smith, G. Rex

1980 "The Arabian Hound, the Salūqī: Further Considerations of the Word and Other Observations on the Breed." *Bulletin of the School of Oriental and African Studies* 43: 459–65.

Smith, Joann F. Handlin

1999 "Liberating Animals in Ming-Qing China: Buddhist Inspiration and Elite Imagination." *Journal of Asian Studies* 58: 51–84.

Smith, John Masson

1984 "Mongol Campaign Rations: Milk, Marmots and Blood?" *Journal of Turkic Studies* 8: 223–28.

Soden, Wolfram von

1959 *Akkadisches Handwörterbuch.* Wiesaden: Harrassowitz.

Soucek, Priscilla

1990 "The New York Public Library *Makhzan al-asrār* and Its Importance." *Ars Orientalis* 18: 1–37.

Speidel, Michael P.

2002 "Berserks: A History of Indo-European 'Mad Warriors.'" *Journal of World History* 13, 2: 253–90.

Speiser, E. H.

1964 *The Anchor Bible, Genesis.* Garden City, N.Y.: Doubleday.

Spuler, Bertold

1965 *Die Goldene Horde: Die Mongolen in Russland.* 2nd ed. Wiesbaden: Otto Harrassowitz.

1985 *Die Mongolen in Iran.* 4th ed. Leiden: E.J. Brill.

Sreznevskii, M. I.

1989 *Materialy dlia slovaria drevnerusskogo iazyka.* Vol. 3. Moscow: Kniga.

Stange, Mary Zeiss

1997 *Woman the Hunter.* Boston: Beacon Press.

State Historical Museum

2002 *Royal Hunting.* Moscow: Khudozhnik i kniga.

Stein, Rolf

1940 "Leao-tche." *T'oung-pao* 35: 1–154.

Steinhardt, Nancy Shatzman

1983 "The Plan of Khubilai Khan's Imperial City." *Artibus Asiae* 44, 2–3: 137–58.

1990a *Chinese Imperial City Planning.* Honolulu: University of Hawaii Press.

1990b "Imperial Architecture Along the Mongolian Road to Dadu." *Ars Orientalis* 18: 59–93.

1990–91 "Yuan Period Tombs and Their Decoration: Cases at Chifeng." *Oriental Art* (Winter): 198–221.

Sterckx, Roel

2000 "Transforming the Beasts: Animals and Music in Early China." *T'oung-pao* 86: 1–46.

Sterndale, Robert A.

1982 *Natural History of the Mammalia of India and Ceylon.* 1884. Reprint Delhi: Himalayan Books.

Stetkevych, Jaroslav

1996 "The Hunt in Arabic *Qaṣidah*: The Antecedents of the *Ṭardiyyah*." In J. R. Smart, ed., *Tradition and Modernity in Arabic Language and Literature.* Richmond: Curzon Press, pp. 102–18.

1999 "The Hunt in Classical Arabic Poetry: From Mukhadram *Qasīdah* to Umayyad *Ṭardiyyah*." *Journal of Arabic Literature* 30: 107–29.

Stiner, Mary D., Natalee D. Munro, and Todd A. Surovell

2000 "The Tortoise and the Hare: Small Game Use, the Broad Spectrum Revolution and Paleolithic Demography." *Current Anthropology* 41: 39–73.

Stoianovich, Traian

1994a *Balkan Worlds: The First and Last Europe.* Armonk, N.Y.: M.E. Sharpe.

1994b "Longue durée." In Peter A. Sterns, ed., *Encyclopedia of Social History.* New York: Garland, pp. 426–28.

Storey, William K.

1991 "Big Cats and Imperialism: Lion and Tiger Hunting in Kenya and Northen India." *Journal of World History* 2: 135–75.

Störk, L.

1972 "Gepard." *Lexikon der Ägyptologie.* Wiesbaden: Otto Harrassowitz, vol. 2, pp. 530–31.

Straus, Lawrence Guy

1986 "Hunting in Late Upper Paleolithic Western Europe." In Matthew H. Nitecki and Doris V. Nitecki, eds., *The Evolution of Human Hunting.* New York: Plenum, pp. 147–76.

Stresemann, Erwin

1975 *Ornithology from Aristotle to the Present.* Cambridge, Mass.: Harvard University Press.

Stricker, B. H.

1963–64 "*Vārəġna*, the Falcon." *Indo-Iranian Journal* 73: 310–17.

Stronach, David

1978 *Pasargadae.* Oxford: Clarendon Press.

1990 "The Garden as a Political Statement: Some Case Studies from the Near East in the First Century B.C." *Bulletin of the Asia Institute* 4: 171–80.

1994 "Parterres and Stone Watercourses at Pasargadae: Notes on the Achaemenid Contribution to Garden Design." *Journal of Garden History* 14: 3–12.

Struve, V. V., ed.

1960 *Issledovaniia po istorii kul'tury narodov vostoka: Sbornik v chest Akademika I. A. Orbeli.* Moscow-Leningrad: Izdatel'stvo akademii nauk SSSR.

Subtelny, Maria Eva

1995 "Mīrak-i Ṣayyid Ghiyas and the Timurid Tradition of Landscape Architecture." *Studia Iranica* 24: 19–59.

1997 "Agriculture and the Timurid Chahārbāgh: Evidence from a Medieval Persian Agricultural Manual." In Attilio Petruccidi, ed., *Gardens in the Time of the Great Muslim Empires.* Leiden: E.J. Brill, pp. 110–28.

Sugiyama, Jiro

1973 "Some Problems of Parthian King's Crowns." *Orient: The Reports of the Society for Near Eastern Studies in Japan* 9: 31–41.

Swadling, Pamela

1996 *Plumes from Paradise: Trade Cycles in Outer Southeast Asia and Their Impact on New Guinea and Nearby Islands Until 1920.* National Capital District: Papua New Guinea National Museum.

Taagepera, Rein

1978 "Size and Duration of Empires: The Systematics of Size." *Social Science Research* 7: 108–27.

Tan Qixiang, ed.

1982 *Zhongguo lishi ditu ji.* Vol. 7, *Yuan-Mingde qi.* Shanghai: Ditu chubanshe.

Tanabe, Katsumi

1983 "Iconography of the Royal Hunt: Bas Reliefs at Taq-i Bustan." *Orient: The Reports of the Society for Near Eastern Studies in Japan* 19: 103–16.

1998 "A Newly Located Kushano-Sasanian Silver Plate: The Origin of the Royal Hunt on Horseback for Two Male Lions on 'Sasanian' Silver Plates." In Vesta Sarkhosh Curtis, Robert Hillenbrand and J. M. Rogers, eds., *The Art and Archaeology of Ancient Iran: New Light on the Parthian and Sasanian Empires.* London: I.B. Tauris, pp. 93–102.

Tao, Jing-shen

1976 *The Jurchen in Twelfth Century China: A Study in Sinicization.* Seattle: University of Washington Press.

Taskin, V. S.

1973 "Pokhodnye lageria kidan'skikh imperatov." In G. D. Sukharchuk, ed., *Kitai: Obshchestvo i gosudarstvo.* Moscow: Nauka, pp. 101–15.

Taylor, Ian M.

1986 " 'Guan, Guan' Cries the Osprey: An Outline of Pre-Modern Chinese Ornithology." *Papers on Far Eastern History* 33: 1–22.

Teggard, Frederick J.
1941 *Theory and Processes of History.* Berkeley: University of California Press.
Thiébaux, Marcelle
1967 "The Medieval Chase." *Speculum* 42: 260–74.
Thomas, Keith
1983 *Man and the Natural World.* Oxford: Oxford University Press.
Thompson, James Westfall and Edgar Nathaniel Johnson
1965 *An Introduction to Medieval Europe, 300–1500.* New York: Norton.
Thompson, Robert and Hobart F. Landreth
1973 "Reproduction in Captive Cheetahs." In Randall L. Eaton, ed., *The World of Cats*, vol. 2, *Biology, Behavior, and Management of Reproduction.* Seattle: Feline Research Group, pp. 162–67.
Thurston, Mary Elizabeth
1996 *The Lost History of the Canine Race.* Kansas City: Andrews and McMeel.
Tibbets, G. R.
1979 *A Study of Arabic Texts Containing Material on South-East Asia.* Leiden: E.J. Brill.
Tilia, Ann Britt
1972 *Studies and Restorations at Persepolis and Other Sites of Fārs.* Rome: Istituto Italiano per il Medio ed Estremo Oriente.
Tilson, Ron
2002 "Tracking Phantom Tigers." *Minnesota: The Magazine of the University of Minnesota Alumni Association* 102, 1: 26–30.
al-Timimi, Faris A.
1987 *Falcons and Falconry in Qatar.* Doha: Ali Bin Ali Press.
Tiratsian, G. A.
1960 "Utochnenie nekotorykh detalei sasanidskogo vooruzheniia po dannym armianskogo istorika IV v. n. e. Favsta Buzanta." In Struve 1960, pp. 474–86.
Torbert, Preston M.
1977 *The Ch'ing Imperial Household Department: A Study of Its Principal Functions, 1662–1746.* Cambridge, Mass.: Harvard University Press.
Totman, Conrad
1989 *The Green Archipelago: Forestry in Pre-industrial Japan.* Berkeley: University of California Press.
Tracy, James
2001 "*Iasak* in Siberia vs. Competition Among Colonizers in Canada: A Note on Comparisons Between Fur Trades." *Russian History/Histoire Russe* 28, 1–4: 403–9.
Trigger, Bruce
1990 "Monumental Architecture: A Thermodynamic Explanation of Symbolic Behavior." *World Archaeology* 22: 119–32.
Trombley, Frank R.
1994 *Hellenic Religion and Christianization, c. 370–529.* Vol. 2. Leiden: E J. Brill.
Trümpelman, L.
1980–83 "Jagd." *Reallexikon der Assyriologie und vorderasiatischen Archäology.* Berlin: de Gruyter, pp. 234–38.
Tsintsius, V. I., ed.
1975–77 *Sravnitel'nyi slovar Tunguso-Man'chzhurskikh iazykov.* 2 vols. Leningrad: Nauka.

Tuan, Yi-fu

1968 "Discrepancies Between Environmental Attitude and Behavior: Examples from Europe and China." *Canadian Geographer* 12, no. 3: 176–91.

Tuite, Kevin

1998 "Evidence for Prehistoric Links between the Caucasus and Central Asia: The Case of the Burushos." In Mair 1998 1: 448–75.

Tuplin, Christopher

1996 *Achaemenid Studies.* Historia Einzelschriften 99. Stuttgart: Franz Steiner.

Turner, Alan

1997 *The Big Cats and Their Fossil Relatives.* New York: Columbia University Press.

Unschuld, Paul U.

1986 *Medicine in China: A History of Pharmaceutics.* Berkeley: University of California Press.

Uray-Köhalmi, Käthe

1987 "Synkretismus im Stadtkult der frühen Dschingisiden." In Walther Heissig and Hans-Joachim Klimkert, eds., *Synkretismus in den Religionen Zentralasiens.* Wiesbaden: Otto Harrassowitz, pp. 136–58.

Usmanov, Mirkasyn Abdulakhatovich

1979 *Zhalovannye akty Dzuchieva Ulusa, XIV–XVI vv.* Kazan: Izdatel'stvo Kazanskogo Universiteta.

Van Buren, E. Douglas

1939 *The Fauna of Ancient Mesopotamia as Represented in Art.* Rome: Pontificum Institutum Biblicum.

Van Milligen, Alexander

1899 *Byzantine Constantinople: The Walls of the City and Adjoining Historical Sites.* London: John Murray.

Vasilevich, T. M.

1968 "Rol okhoty v istorii tungusoiazychnykh narodov." In *Jagd* 1968, pp. 129–45.

Vermeer, Edward B.

1998 "Population and Ecology Along the Frontier in Qing China." In Mark Elvin and Liu Ts'ui-jung, eds., *Sediments of Time: Environment and Society in Chinese History.* Cambridge: Cambridge University Press, pp. 235–79.

Vilà, Charles et al.

1997 "Multiple and Ancient Origins of the Domesticated Dog." *Science* 276: 1687–89.

Viré, François

1965 "Fahd." *Encyclopedia of Islam.* 2nd ed. Leiden: E.J. Brill, vol. 2: 740–42.

1973 "A propos des chiens de chasse *ṣalūqī* et *zaġārī.*" *Revue des études islamiques* 91: 231–40.

1974 "La chasse au guépard d'après sources arabes et les oeuvres d'art musulman par Ahmad Abd ar-Raziq." *Arabica* 21: 85–88.

1977 "Essai de détermination des oiseaux-de-vol mentionnés dans les principaux manuscripts arabes médiévaux sur la fauconnerie." *Arabica* 25: 138–49.

Voeikov, Aleksandr

1901 "De l'influence de l'homme sur la terre." *Annales de géographie* 10: 97–114.

Vollmer, John, E. J. Keall, and E. Nagai-Berthrong

1983 *Silk Roads, China Ships: An Exhibition of East-West Trade.* Toronto: Royal Ontario Museum.

Voshchinina, A. I.
1953 "O sviaziakh Priural'ia s vostokum v VI–VII vv., n.e." *Sovetskaia arkheologiia* 17: 183–96.

Wagoner, Phillip B.
1995 " 'Sultan Among Hindu Kings': Dress, Titles and Islamicization of Hindu Culture at Vijayanagara." *Journal of Asian Studies* 55: 851–80.

Waida Manabu
1978 "Birds in the Mythology of Sacral Kingship." *East and West* 28: 283–89.

Walch, Karl
1997 "Hunting Dogs." In Blüchel 1997, 1: 72–103.

Waley, Arthur
1949 *The Life and Times of Po Chü-i, 772–846 A.D.* London: Allen and Unwin.
1957 "Chinese-Mongol Hybrid Songs." *Bulletin of the School of Oriental and African Studies* 20: 281–84.

Waley-Cohen, Joanna
2002 "Military Ritual and the Qing Empire." In Di Cosmo 2002, pp. 405–44.

Wallas, Graham
1923 *The Great Society.* New York: Macmillan.

Wang, Zhongshu
1982 *Han Civilization.* New Haven, Conn.: Yale University Press.

Watson, Andrew M.
1983 *Agricultural Innovation in the Early Islamic World: The Diffusion of Crops and Farming Techniques, 700–1100.* Cambridge: Cambridge University Press.

Watson, Geoff
1998 "Central Asia as Hunting Ground: Sporting Images of Central Asia." In David Christian and Craig Benjamin, eds., *Worlds of the Silk Roads, Ancient and Modern.* Silk Road Studies 2. Turnhout: Brepols, pp. 265–88.

Wechsler, Howard J.
1985 *Offerings of Jade and Silk: Ritual and Symbol in the Legitimation of the T'ang Dynasty.* New Haven, Conn.: Yale University Press.

Weidner-Weiden, Heidi
1997 "Hunting Lodges–Their Splendor and Glory." In Blüchel 1997, 1: 246–77.

Welles, C. Bradford, Robert O. Fink, and J. Frank Gilliam
1959 *The Excavations at Dura Europos.* Vol. 5, pt. 1, *The Parchments and Papyri.* New Haven, Conn.: Yale University Press.

Werth, Emil
1954 *Grabstock, Hacke und Pflug.* Ludwigsburg: Eugen Ulmer.

Wescoat, James L., Jr.
1998 "The Right of Thirst for Animals in Islamic Law: A Comparative Approach." In Jennifer Welch and Jody Emel, eds., *Animal Geographies.* London: Verso, pp. 254–79.

White, David Gordon
1991 *Myths of the Dog-Man.* Chicago: University of Chicago Press.

White, Lynn, Jr.
1966 *Medieval Technology and Social Change.* New York: Oxford University Press.

1986 *Medieval Religion and Technology*. Berkeley: University of California Press.

White, William Charles

1939 *Tomb Title Pictures of Ancient China*. Toronto: University of Toronto Press.

Whittow, Mark

1996 *The Making of Byzantium*. Berkeley: University of California Press.

Widengren, Geo

1951 "The King and the Tree of Life in Ancient Near Eastern Religion." *Uppsala Universitets Arsskrift* 51: 3–68.

1969 *Der Feudalismus im alten Iran*. Cologne: Westdeutscher Verlag.

Wilkinson, Alix

1990 "Gardens in Ancient Egypt: Their Locations and Symbolism." *Journal of Garden History* 10: 199–208.

Wilson, David Sloan

1998 "Hunting, Sharing and Multilevel Selection: The Tolerated Theft Model Revisited." *Current Anthropology* 39: 73–97.

Wilson, J. A.

1948 "Egypt." In Henri Frankfort and H. A. Groenewegen-Frankfort, eds., *The Intellectual Adventure of Ancient Man: An Essay on Speculative Thought in the Ancient Near East*. Chicago: University of Chicago Press, pp. 31–121.

1956 "The Royal Myth in Ancient Egypt." *Proceedings of the American Philosophical Society* 100: 434–47.

Wilson, Peter J.

1988 *The Domestication of the Human Species*. New Haven, Conn.: Yale University Press.

Winter, Irene J.

1981 "Royal Rhetoric and Development of Historical Narrative in Neo Assyrian Reliefs." *Studies in Visual Communications* 7: 2–38.

Winters, Robert K.

1974 *The Forest and Man*. New York: Vantage Press.

Wittfogel, Karl A.

1940 "Meteorological Records from the Divination Inscriptions of Shang." *Geographical Review* 30: 110–33.

Wittfogel, Karl A. and Feng Chia-sheng

1949 *History of Chinese Society, Liao (907–1125)*. Philadelphia: American Philosophical Society.

Witzel, Michael

1999 "Early Sources for South Asian Substrate Languages." *Mother Tongue* (October): 1–61.

Wolters, O. W.

1958 "Tāmbralinga." *Bulletin of the School of Oriental and African Studies* 21: 587–607.

Woodburn, James

1979 "Minimal Politics: The Political Organization of the Hadza of North Tanzania." In William A. Shack and Percy S. Cohen, eds., *Politics in Leadership: A Comparative Perspective*. Oxford: Clarendon Press, pp. 244–64.

Wright, Arthur F.

1979 "The Sui Dynasty." In Denis Twitchett, ed., *The Cambridge History of China*, vol. 7, pt. 1, *Sui and T'ang China*. Cambridge: Cambridge University Press, pp. 48–149.

Yarshater, Ehsan
1983a "Iranian National History." In Yarshater 1983b, pp. 343–477.
Yarshater, Ehsan, ed.
1983b *The Cambridge History of Iran.* Vol. 3, *The Seleucid, Parthian and Sasanian Periods.* 2 vols. Cambridge: Cambridge University Press.
Yule, Sir Henry and A. C. Burnell
1903 *Hobson-Jobson: A Glossary of Anglo-Indian Words and Phrases.* London: John Murray.
Zeuner, Frederick E.
1963 *A History of Domesticated Animals.* New York: Harper and Row.
Zguta, Russell
1978 *Russian Minstrels: A History of the Skomorokhi.* Philadelphia: University of Pennsylvania Press.
Zhang, Guangda
2001 "Tangdai de baolie." *Tang yanjiu* 7: 177–204.
Zhao, Ji, ed.
1990 *The Natural History of China.* New York: McGraw-Hill.
Ziiaev, Kh Z.
1983 *Ekonomicheskie sviazi Srednei Azii s Sibir'iu v. XVI–XIV.* Tashkent: Fan.
Zimansky, Paul E.
1985 *Ecology and Empire: The Structure of the Urartian State.* Chicago: Oriental Institute of the University of Chicago.
Zimmer, Heinrich
1963 *Myths and Symbols in Indian Art and Civilization.* New York: Pantheon.
Ziolkowski, Jan M.
1993 *Talking Animals: Medieval Latin Beast Poetry, 750–1150.* Philadelphia: University of Pennsylvania Press.
Zorzi, Elvira Garbero
1986 "Court Spectacle." In Sergio Betelli, ed., *Italian Renaissance Courts.* London: Sidgwick and Jackson, pp. 128–87.

Index

Acknowledgments

This volume is an outgrowth of research into the Mongols' imperial hunt and its antecedents. Over time, the search for background material took on a life of its own and I began to focus on the royal hunt as a trans-Eurasian phenomenon. Since the institution was both widespread and long-lived, the study became an exercise in "Big History," one that compelled me to cross boundaries and ignore conventional fields.

As for documentation, while I cannot claim to have exhausted any particular body of sources, I can say that I have sampled sources from diverse climes and times, some in the original and many in translation. In point of fact, the amount of material on the royal hunt is vast and well beyond the control of any individual scholar. In the end, practical considerations of time and space forced me to call a halt to my researches knowing that I had left many rich sources untapped.

In pursuing a theme that has so often led me far from my own areas of training, I have had frequent recourse to friends and colleagues who obligingly answered my questions, volunteered new data, and generously provided copies of their own and others' work. Collectively, their guidance, comments, and criticisms have greatly improved the manuscript and saved me from many errors and misunderstandings. For these kindnesses, I offer my profound thanks to Anna Akasoy, Michal Biran, Pia Brancaccio, Bruce Craig, Stephen Dale, Magnus Fiskesjö, Peter Golden, Anatoly Khazanov, Elfriede Knauer, Roman Kovalev, Xinru Liu, Stuart McCook, Charles Melville, Ruth Meserve, Judith Pfeiffer, Scott Redford, Jonathon Shepard, Andrew Sherratt, and Nancy Steinhardt. If anyone has been left out, it is a matter of inadvertence for which I offer full apologies.

I must also acknowledge the stimulus provided by the students in my course Animals in History, which I taught in the spring of 2002 at The College of New Jersey. Their thoughtful questions, opinions, and arguments helped to crystalize my own thinking on many issues addressed in this book.

Throughout the years, the Inter-Library Loan staff at the Roscoe West Library was an essential ingredient in all my research endeavors and the present volume is further testimony to their skill, professionalism, and willingness to help.

A very special thanks is due Victor Mair who from the very early stages of the project provided me with an endless stream of encouragement, advice, and bibliography, and who sponsored the manuscript for publication in the series Encounters with Asia.

I must also record my debt to Richard Eaton for his careful reading of the entire manuscript and for raising questions about its structure and argumentation that provoked and guided a final and beneficial reorganization of the book.

Once again I have to record my great gratitude to my wife Lucille Helen Allsen for her support, editorial and word processing assistance, and most of all for never appearing to tire of my most recent enthusiasm, the cultural history of animals.

Fellowships from the Guggenheim Foundation for 2002–3 and from the National Endowment for the Humanities for 2003–4 afforded me the opportunity to work full-time on this project over a period of several years. The Guggenheim also provided a publication subvention to underwrite the costs of production. For their timely and generous support, I am pleased to register my deep appreciation to both institutions.

Lastly, since these pages treat at some length felines in premodern court life, this volume is unavoidably dedicated to the felines in my life.